RAPTORS

of Eastern North America

RAPTORS
of Eastern North America

Text and Photographs by

BRIAN K. WHEELER

Range maps researched by
John M. Economidy and Brian K. Wheeler
and produced by
John M. Economidy

Foreword by
Clayton M. White

PRINCETON UNIVERSITY PRESS
PRINCETON, NEW JERSEY

Copyright © 2003 by Princeton University Press
Published by Princeton University Press, 41 William Street, Princeton, New Jersey 08540
In the United Kingdom: Princeton University Press, 3 Market Place, Woodstock,
Oxfordshire OX20 1SY

Library of Congress Cataloging-in-Publication Data

Wheeler, Brian K., 1955–
Raptors of eastern North America : the Wheeler guide / text and photographs by Brian K. Wheeler ;
foreword by Clayton M. White.
p. cm.
Includes bibliographical references and index.
ISBN 0-691-11598-2 (cl : alk. paper)
1. Birds of prey—East (U.S.)   2. Birds of prey—Canada, Eastern.   I. Title.

QL677.78 .W53   2003   598.9
598.9'0974—dc21   2002042715   *Whe*   *occ*   *4/8/08*

This book has been composed in Minion

Printed on acid-free paper. ∞

www.nathist.princeton.edu

Composition by Bytheway Publishing Services, Binghamton, New York

Printed in Italy by Eurografica

10 9 8 7 6 5 4 3 2 1

To my wife, Lisa, and my son, Garrett, with all my love

In memory of my sister,
Janet Louise Wheeler Mashue,
who enlightened the lives of all who knew her

CONTENTS

SPECIES ACCOUNTS

FOREWORD

My Australian colleague, Victor Hurley, was seated in the car beside me as we traveled to my family's ranch in the mountains of extreme northwestern Utah. It was early August 2002. We rattled along the twenty-one-mile gravel road, lined with telephone poles, and passed buteo after buteo perched on the poles; three different species of multiple colors and two age classes. Such an array can be confusing. As we passed one bird I asked Victor what species it was. "I dunno, you have too many hawks in the States. But I reckon it was not a bloody wedgie," meaning of course, not an Australian Wedge-tailed Eagle. The bird appeared, from our distance, to have nearly a completely white breast and was obviously an immature Ferruginous Hawk. At these times I have frequently referred guests to the two Clark and Wheeler raptors guides, but at that moment I thought it would be nice to have a more detailed guide I could let Victor use. Identifying raptors can be confusing, and even those whom others refer to as "experts" need help sorting them out at times.

Nearly twenty years earlier, in 1983, Bill Clark told me he had come upon a remarkable new raptor artist and photographer, a fellow by the name of Brian Wheeler, who would be illustrating Bill's forthcoming field guide. Bill asked if I would be willing to review some material for that guide. So along with Dave Mindell, my graduate student at the time, we looked at several color plates Brian had done and also some text. "Holy mackerel," I thought, "This kid is dang good, just like Bill said." Oh, the tail on the plate of the male Rough-legged Hawk needed to be revised a bit, multiple bars rather than just the subterminal band, and we could tell he was still perfecting that part of his craft. But overall a nice job and most useful for a field guide. Now, nearly two decades later, Brian K. Wheeler has produced two companion volumes, *Raptors of Eastern North America* and *Raptors of Western North America*, and in them he provides the descriptive detail I had wished I had for Victor.

Although currently a truck driver by profession, Brian has been wonderfully productive in his avocation as a raptor artist and photographer by providing material for those of us who dabble in the bird of prey world; he is an important part of that world. Traveling as a truck driver has been an excellent opportunity for him to watch for raptors to photograph. But then, his passion for raptors goes back to his childhood days in the mid-1970s in Washington State. When he moved to Connecticut in his early twenties he came under the influence of Fred Sibley, who held the master permit for Brian to band raptors. One can only guess what impact that had on Brian's drive to succeed in the bird world and in his knowledge of raptors. Brian started to take photographs in 1980, but it was not until about 1985 that he perfected his current style. He has photographed raptors throughout the country, has a keen eye for detail, and is excellent at the craft. From what I know, his prize would be photographing a white morph Gyrfalcon on the breeding grounds sitting beside its eyrie. He has participated in the trapping and research efforts of other biologists, such as along the coastal Pacific Northwest, and has a good feeling for what birds look like in the hand. *A Photographic Guide to North American Raptors* used some of his best work, but these two new volumes will outshine that guide, and I think all will agree that the work is better, more detailed. Why would these not be finer guides with 540 photos in the eastern guide and 603 in the western? You will note that he has not used computer enhancements to make things look better than they really are. What you see is what he got.

I am convinced that users of these guides will find the maps more useful than are the broad sweeping maps in most such guidebooks, Brian Wheeler sought help on range maps from Texas attorney John Economidy, who led the Coastal Bend Hawk Watch in Corpus Christi for nine years. Both agreed that the maps should be extremely detailed, show current status, enable readers to envision what range had been lost in previous decades, and serve as a standard for future researchers to gauge distributional gains or declines. You will note in the Acknowledgments that Brian has contacted literally hundreds of people across the U.S., Canada, and Mexico to get the most up-to-date status of a species, with some of it coming in as late as the date of submission to the press.

So, sit back in a comfortable chair and browse through these guides, or better, go into the field and use them. Above all, enjoy what you have in your hands because it will be a long time before something equal or better comes along.

Clayton M. White
Brigham Young University

PREFACE

R aptors have enthralled me since I was a child. I remember when I was eight and nine years old roaming the parched wheat-field and sagebrush landscape near my house in south-central Washington State looking for hawk nests. In my early teens my family moved east, and there are vivid memories while living in Iowa of seeing Bald Eagles in the winter along the Mississippi River. In my late teens, and living in central Michigan, finding my first Northern Goshawk nest was a truly exhilarating experience (and tough on jackets, as the female would often dive and hit me before I could duck behind a large enough tree!). A 12-year stint living in Connecticut put me in the midst of raptor migration heaven—all within a few minutes or a few hours drive. The 16 years I have now lived in Colorado have enabled me to easily study the vast number of raptors that summer, winter, or migrate through the Great Plains and Rocky Mountains, particularly the variably plumaged western buteos. Besides watching, studying, and photographing raptors in the various regions where I have lived in the U.S., I have traveled widely from Alaska to southern Mexico and from the Pacific to the Atlantic Coast to obtain firsthand experience with raptors. No matter where I am, whether being buffeted by a warm, stiff ocean wind in south Florida in late November with a Short-tailed Hawk kiting 50 feet overhead or being blasted by a cold front at Cape May, New Jersey, in early October and inundated with Sharp-shinned Hawks, raptors still illicit a childish exuberance.

The two raptor guides I coauthored with William S. Clark, *A Field Guide to Hawks of North America* (Clark and Wheeler, 2001) and particularly *A Photographic Guide to North American Raptors* (Wheeler and Clark 1995), were the foundations for this guide and its western counterpart. Having produced standard field guides, I wanted to develop a set of regionally formatted books that went beyond the scope of a field guide and dealt only with species breeding in North America (defined here as the continental U.S. and Canada). I developed the initial format and began working on these two guides in 1996. As data poured in, particularly on status, distribution, and range, the books quickly became even more detailed than originally planned, and they saw several evolutionary changes until the final format was decided.

I have always been keen on regional guides because they allow for more precise and applicable data that cater to a smaller geographic region. In essence, this limits the number of species one has to deal with when trying to solve identifications. It also allows for larger and more precise range maps.

The scientifically accepted demarcation of East and West in North America is the 100th meridian that invisibly slices through the eastern Great Plains. This division between East and West varies among authors, however: many adhere to the 100th, some divide along the abrupt eastern edge of the Rocky Mountains, and a few use the Mississippi River. Although the 100th is a reasonably good demarcation on the Plains for breeding Ferruginous Hawks and Prairie Falcons, it is rather meaningless for other western raptors that breed north and south of the Plains. The demarcation line that best befits raptors tends to be the Mississippi River. Only one western species, Swainson's Hawk, has a very small remnant population east of the river, and only a few true western species stray east of the river during migration and winter. Therefore, I have opted to abide by what raptors do and have divided the U.S. at the Mississippi River. Canada has been divided along the Manitoba-Ontario border and along the west coast of Hudson Bay. Hudson Bay separates the arid western Arctic of Nunavut from the damp eastern Arctic of Québec—a demarcation that also defines plumage characteristics of Gyrfalcons and Rough-legged Hawks (and which is in accordance with Gloger's Rule, which states that in many species lightly pigmented individuals occur in dry climates, darker pigmented individuals in humid climates).

The concept of the regional guides was to elaborate on the 34 species of raptors that breed in North America. For the East this includes 24 eastern-breeding species (including 2 New World Cathartidae vultures) and 2 western species (Prairie Falcon and Ferruginous Hawk) that are casual or accidental.

Accidental species for Europe and Mexico are well covered in the two books coauthored with William S. Clark. Also, there are two, great European guides, *A Field Guide to the Raptors of Europe, the Middle East, and North Africa* (Clark 1999) and *The Raptors of Europe and the Middle East* (Forsman 1999), that give additional coverage of the overseas raptors that rarely occur in the U.S. and Canada.

The photographs encompass an expansive range of plumages. Most photographs were taken after the completion of *A Photographic Guide to North American Raptors* in 1994, and the majority after 1995, when I switched over to an autofocus camera system. A few photographs that may qualify for "chance-of-a-lifetime images" date back to the 1980s. Fewer than 10 photographs have been reused from *A Photographic Guide*.

In 1985 I began to perfect, and subsequently turn into an art form of its own, the imagery of flying raptors. I have done this by using good equipment, learning what "naturally" creates a great photograph, and knowing the behavior and habitat of each species and subspecies. Being from the "old school," I am not an advocate of the new rage of computer alteration of photographs. All photographs herein are of wild raptors, and none have been tweaked by computer: what you see is what I saw and photographed. Although many photographs have less-than-aesthetic backgrounds such as wires or utility poles, these are perches that raptors often favor and where one should look for them. The few raptors that sport leg bands were not staged for photography but were captured and released by biologists for scientific study months or years before I or others photographed them. (I am an advocate of all facets of scientific raptor study, which may include banding or telemetry studies; these greatly increase our knowledge and benefit raptors.)

These two volumes are meant to be complete, self-sustaining guides. The detailed data in the species accounts are tailored to moderate- and expert-level bird enthusiasts, and people of all interest levels can enjoy the photographs and short, descriptive captions.

Raptors, like all wildlife, are experiencing severe habitat alterations in our ever-changing world. Some species are adapting and thriving. Some are not adapting and faltering. We must preserve habitat so all species can thrive. It is my hope that these books will help increase our awareness and appreciation of raptors.

Brian K. Wheeler
Longmont, Colorado

ACKNOWLEDGMENTS

I am most grateful to my wife, Lisa, who assisted me on the prospectus for these guides and who also taught me most of what I needed to know about the computer to create them. Working a full-time job, I diligently created the books in my "spare time," typically for several hours a day, months at a time. Lisa graciously and lovingly supported me during this period.

I apologize to my three-year-old son, Garrett, who had no idea what Daddy was doing. There were many days that I could not spend time with him because of work.

I thank all of my family members for their support during this long, arduous project.

This book is unquestionably better and more complete because of the assistance provided by John M. Economidy. I first queried John, after working on the books for one and a half years, for help on Bald Eagle status and range in Texas. Being the Texas regional editor for the Hawk Migration Association of North America at the time, he had access to a considerable amount of information on raptors in his home state. The rest, you could say, is history. Having a deep appreciation for raptors and seeing what I was producing, John quickly became interested in my ever-expanding project, particularly on status and distribution. He soon began assisting in research not only of Texas raptors but of virtually all raptors in North America. For the last four and a half years of the project we worked as a team, gathering the extensive data that went into the Status and Distribution section of the text and the range maps. John spent thousands of hours gathering data. With two years yet to go, he also volunteered to take on the mind-boggling task of creating the range maps on computer. I am most appreciative of his help, diligence, and expertise. Being a journalist as well as an attorney, John also proofread all species accounts for initial "clean up."

My original editor, Andrew Richford, then with Academic Press, was most supportive of my endeavor. Because of a change of publishers, however, he was unable to see my books produced under his editorship. I thank Dr. Richford for all of his help and faith in me. He gave me a chance to produce my "dream books." I also thank my new editor, Robert Kirk. He was also most supportive and, with his expertise, has made my dream come true. Ellen Foos did an incredible job directing production. Elizabeth Pierson and Sandy Sherman did a most superb job copyediting. Dimitri Karetnikov reformulated the range maps to fit the book format.

The following people and museums permitted access to their collections for plumage studies and, in many cases, shipped specimens to the Denver Museum of Nature and Science in Denver, Colorado, for me to study: Bill Alther of the Denver Museum of Nature and Science; Vicki Byre of the Oklahoma Museum of Natural History in Norman; Mary LeCroy of the American Museum of Natural History in New York City; J. V. Remsen and Steven Cardiff of the Museum of Natural History at Louisiana State University, Baton Rouge; and Robert Zinc and John Klicka of the Bell Museum of Natural History in Minneapolis, Minnesota.

Several additional people helped in numerous ways. Dudley and Nancy Edmondson, Dave Gilbertson, and Frank and Kate Nicioletti all encouraged my project and helped cut my travel costs by providing lodging on several of my photographic ventures to Duluth, Minnesota. Ned and Linda Harris were supportive throughout; Ned also joined me on several photographic ventures. Joe and Elaine Harrison encouraged all my efforts; Joe also accompanied and helped me on many trips. Jim Zipp accompanied me on photographic trips, and the use of his super-telephoto lens enhanced my photography on those occasions.

I thank the photographers who provided images that were either better than mine or were images I did not have. Their contributions most certainly enhance the books.

Many people provided data for the various biology headings in the species accounts, especially Status and Distribution. My goal was to "go to the source" to obtain firsthand information. As the books progressed, I could see each one becoming a "book of friends" because of the immense assistance from these people. Without the incredible amount of help I received, these books would not have been possible. My thanks go to all of the following people who helped so much: Bruce Anderson, Mark Bailey, Ursula Banasch, Richard Banks, Giff Beaton, Don Bennett, Frank Bennett, Mark Bennett, Vic Berardi, Daniel Berger, H. David Bohlen, Jeff Bouton, Dan Brauning, Ken Brock, Jamie Cameron, Tom Carrolan, John Castrale, John Cely, Michael Choukas, David Cimprich, William S. Clark, Dale Clinbeard, Keith Cline, Gordon Court, Normand David, Marvin Davis, Ricky Davis, William Davis, Todd Day, Eric Dean, Robert Dickerman, Vicki Dreitz, Jim Duncan, Jon Dunn, Troy Ettel, James Frank, Paul and Cecily Fritz, Marcel Gahbauer, John Gerwin, Michel Gosselin, David Grosshuesch, Mary Gustafson, Greg Hanisek, Steve Hoffman, Theo Hofmann, Geoff Holroyd, Roger Hotham, C. Stuart Houston, Pamela Hunt, Mark E. Johns, Jan Johnson, Kent Justus, Charles E. Keller, Henry Kendall, Vern Kleen, Gene Knight, Mike Lanzone, David Lee, Harry LeGrand, Tony Leukering, Jerry Liguori, Barbara Allen Loucks, Bruce Mactavish, Chris Martin, Blake Maybank, Bob McCollum, Jim McCormac, Christopher McGrath, Ken Meyer, Trish Miller, Pierre Mineau, Tom Murphy, Allen and Cathy Murrant, Kenny Nichols, Frank Nicoletti, Peter Nye, Michael O'Brien, Mark O'Donoghue, Christian Oliva, Chad Olson, Jim Ozier, Brainard Palmer-Ball, Jr., Steven Parren, Robert Paxton, Mark Peck, Rob Peeples, Wayne Petersen, Ron Pittaway, Edie Ray, J. V. Remsen, Marjorie Rines, Robert and Susan Robertson, Jim Rodgers, David Roemer, Rex Rowan, Gon Sanchez, Barbara Sargent, Mark Sasser, Judy Scherpelz, Jeff Schultz, Wayne Scott, Larry Semo, Joseph Shelnutt, Mark Shieldcastle, Chris Sloan, Tim Smart, Matt Solensky, Brian Sullivan, John Swedberg, Mark Szantyr, Dave Tetlow, Genevieve Tharp, Charlie Todd, Michael Todd, Jeff Trollinger, Kelley R. Tucker, William H. Turcotte, Peter Vickery, Shawchyi Vorisek, Brian Watts, Andrew Weik, Bill Whan, Clayton White, Becky Whittam, Myles Willard, Jeff Wilson, John and Paula Wright, Jim Zipp, and Joe Zbyrowski.

The following people provided unpublished telemetry data for "Movements" Marcel Gahbauer (Peregrine Falcon), Geoff Holroyd (Peregrine Falcon), Mark Martell (Osprey), and Ken Meyers (Short-tailed Hawk, Swallow-tailed Kite).

ABBREVIATIONS

The following abbreviations are used in the text.

AMNH	American Museum of Natural History, New York City
AOU	American Ornithologists' Union
BLM	Bureau of Land Management
Co. (Cos.)	County (Counties)
Co. Pk.	County Park
CWS	Canadian Wildlife Service
EPA	Environmental Protection Agency
HMANA	Hawk Migration Association of North America
LSU	Louisiana State University, Baton Rouge
N.F.	National Forest
N.P.	National Park
NWR	National Wildlife Refuge
Pk.	Park
Prov. Pk.	Provincial Park
RBCM	Royal British Columbia Museum, Vancouver
S.P.	State Park
USDA	U.S. Department of Agriculture
USFWS	U.S. Fish and Wildlife Service
WMA	Wildlife Management Area

I. INTRODUCTION

Identification: Solving the Puzzle

Identifying raptors is much like assembling a puzzle: you do it piece by piece. Being mainly shades of brown or black, raptors can initially be difficult to identify. If one knows what to look for and where to look, however, it may take only a few pieces of the puzzle to solve an identification. Many species have distinct traits, and it may take only one plumage marking to make an accurate identification. On some, it may take two and sometimes three markings to make a proper identification.

The major factor inhibiting easy, positive identification is that most raptors are wary and do not afford close viewing. Poor lighting, odd angles of view, and missing or broken feathers also contribute to viewer hardships.

With a good, close look, all raptors can be identified, aged, and sometimes (accipiters and falcons) sexed. Even with a close look, however, not all subspecies can be identified to race. With a distant or poor look, some raptors go unidentified because key features cannot be seen. Skilled observers can identify many distant raptors by silhouette.

PERCHING: There are three anatomical areas to consider on perching raptors: the head, wings, and tail. The body is the least important because many species share similar colors or markings. Plumage details are often readily visible because high-powered optics can provide a magnified view.

Head: The features of the head can be valuable when determining an identification. Check iris color, lore and forehead color, and bill and cere color. It is also important to know if a pale supercilium and dark eye line or malar mark are present. Most raptors have a pale region on the nape, sometimes with a dark spot inside the white region.

Wings: The markings on the greater coverts and secondaries can be important, especially on buteos. The distance from the tips of the primaries to the tail tip (the wingtip-to-tail-tip ratio) is very important on large raptors.

Tail: This is the most important area to study on a perched raptor. Study width and amount of dark barring on the dorsal surface. The pattern on the dorsal surface will often clinch an identification. The only drawback is that the dorsal surface of the tail is often partially covered by the folded wings. The ventral surface generally offers little in the way of definitive markings on a perched bird. Tail shape, however, is visible only on the ventral surface and can be of use to clinch identification. In fresh plumage, typically in the fall, many raptors have distinct white terminal bands. By mid-winter and especially spring, the white band wears off (white is a weak feather structure and wears quickly).

FLYING: There are two anatomical areas to consider on flying birds: wings and tail. Head markings are often obscured because viewing distances are typically greater than with perching birds and less powerful optics must be used on a moving subject. As on perched raptors, the body markings offer minimal help because of shared markings between species.

Wings: Every raptor species has a distinct wing shape. On some raptors, wing shape varies within a species. Juvenile buteos have narrower wings than adults, and juvenile accipiters, eagles, and falcons have wider wings than older ages. However, they all have species-distinct shapes. The only glitch is that wing shape varies with the different flight modes. Learn the wing shape of a common, easy-to-see raptor such as a Red-tailed Hawk and compare other raptors to it to visualize differences.

Wing markings are also important. Even such similar-looking species as Cooper's and Sharp-shinned hawks have subtle but visible differences on the underwing markings (and shape), particularly on juveniles. Compare the extent of barring and other markings on the dorsal and ventral surfaces of the wing, including the secondaries. The dorsal wing surface may also have such vital markings as the small crescent-shaped panel of a Red-shouldered Hawk or the large, pale, rectangular panel of a juvenile Red-tailed Hawk.

The wing attitude—how the wings are held during various flight modes—may assist identification (it is not as reliable as markings, however, because it can change drastically). Look for dihedral wing position and behavioral traits such as hovering or kiting. It is important to watch a raptor as long as possible to get a sense of its attitude and behavior. See *Hawks in Flight* (Dunne et al. 1988) for more discussions on flight attitudes.

Tail: This is the second important part of identifying flying raptors. The shape varies considerably according to flight mode and may cause confusion (*see* chapter 6). For instance, the tail tip of a Sharp-shinned Hawk can be quite square when closed while gliding but becomes quite rounded when fanned while soaring. Likewise, the short outer rectrices of a Cooper's Hawk, which greatly help in many identification situations, are often not visible on distant flying birds.

As described above in Perching, use the pattern of dark barring. Most species have distinct patterns of dark markings. In translucent lighting conditions, the dorsal pattern and color, which are the best defined, vividly show on the underside, a factor rarely seen on perching raptors. One thing to keep in mind is that on many species that have dark bars, the ventral surface of the outer one or two rectrix sets often has a different pattern than the other four or five rectrix sets. In strong light, however, the dorsal pattern often overrules the often less distinct ventral pattern.

Enjoy!

Book Concept

The species accounts present detailed information that falls into two broad categories: plumage and biology. The various headings occur in a consistent manner throughout the book.

Information on plumage is written in a formal scientific style and is organized under four main anatomical headings: Head, Body, Wings, and Tail. Much of the information is based on more than 20 years of studies in the field and museum. Information is also based, in part, on my previously published collaborations with William S. Clark. Information procured from others is cited in the text as published data (author's name and date of publication), unpublished data (author's name and "unpubl. data"), or personal communication (author's name and "pers. comm.").

Information on biology is presented in a less formal style, and in-text citations are not used. This style was adopted to ensure an easy reading format. Extensive information is organized under the headings Habitat, Habits (behavior), Feeding, Flight, Voice, Status and Distribution, Nesting, Conservation, and Similar Species.

Format for Species Accounts

AGES: Each age is described in detail under its respective plumage heading. I have followed the terminology of Humphrey and Parkes (1959), but instead of attaching the word "basic" to all non-juvenile ages as they did, I often use a combination of "basic" and the more recognizable "subadult"—thus, "basic (subadult)"—for all interim ages between juvenile and adult. I also use "adult" rather than "definitive basic" as preferred by Humphrey and Parkes *See* chapter 4.

Ages are arranged from oldest to youngest. This is because most people recognize the more distinct adult plumages before they do the mundane, often "brown" plumages of younger ages. Major plumage variations that involve two or more anatomical regions are labeled with definitive "type" names (e.g., lightly marked type, moderately marked type, streaked type, etc.). Variations of secondary features on one part of the plumage, such as a distinct tail pattern, may also be addressed as a type.

MOLT: The molt sequences on the wings and tail are described in detail for each raptor family in chapter 4, and the species accounts refer readers to this chapter. On many species, however, some information is reiterated in the species account in order to state a particular point. Interesting molt facts of an individual species are also described in this section.

SUBSPECIES: Polytypic variation has always interested me because subspecies represent unique adaptations to regional environments. Twenty-three of the 34 North American breeding species of raptors are polytypic. The consensus of the public and the scientific community in the last few decades, however, is that polytypic characters are not important issues. The American Ornithologists' Union (AOU) has not included subspecies in its *Check-list of North American Birds* since 1957 (AOU 1957).

Although I have attached colloquial names to all polytypic variations in the main plumage headings, the trinomial scientific name is adjacent to the colloquial name. On polytypic species, I use only scientific names in the body of the text.

Polytypic species that breed in North America are given as much attention in plumage and biological matters regarding their subspecies in this book as are monotypic species. Subspecies that do not breed in North America are presented in a more basic format, simply because little has changed with the stance of the AOU and because many raptor books have previously published much of this information. When dealing with the magnitude of information incorporated in this book, however, it seemed appropriate to include these references.

I present some new information available in scientific journals but otherwise not widely available. My opinion regarding subspecies plumage and status is also expressed for a few species.

Subspecies are arranged from most common to least common, or adjacent races are arranged next to each other.

COLOR MORPHS: Eight North American species, all of which breed in the West and five of which breed in the East, are polymorphic. One western species exhibits polymorphism in non-native subspecies. The East has two additional polymorphic species that are seasonal visitors from the West. Plumages are arranged from lightest to darkest and are described in detail.

SIZE: Most data on length (distance from tip of bill to tip of tail) and wingspan were obtained from published sources. Measurements on some subspecies are from both published and unpublished sources, which are cited in the text. My opinion on matters such as separating accipiter sexes by size in the field is also included.

SPECIES TRAITS: Anatomical features and markings that are shared by all ages and sexes of a species.

ADULT TRAITS: Anatomical features and markings that are shared by both adult sexes of a species.

BASIC (SUBADULT) TRAITS: In species with interim ages between juvenile and adult, anatomical features and markings that are shared by both sexes of the respective age category.

JUVENILE TRAITS: Anatomical features and markings that are shared by both juvenile sexes of a species. On some kites, this stage may only last a few months; on most raptors, it lasts about a year.

ABNORMAL PLUMAGES: Generally describes various forms of albinism but may also include the opposite aberration, melanism.

HABITAT: Often variable according to season. For migrant species this section is divided into Summer, Winter, and Migration subheadings. Even species that are resident in a particular area, however, may use different habitat after the nesting season; if so, this section is subdivided accordingly.

HABITS: Behavioral traits of a species. A species' general nature is listed first. This varies from being *tame* to *very wary*. *Tame* does not mean "tame as a household pet"; it means that a walking, unconcealed human can approach within 100 feet without a raptor exhibiting alarm. *Fairly tame* means a human cannot approach on foot but if concealed in a vehicle can approach within 100 feet without the raptor exhibiting alarm. *Moderately tame* means a raptor will become alarmed and probably fly if a vehicle approaches within 100 feet. *Wary* means a raptor will fly when approached by a vehicle that is several hundred feet away. *Very wary* means the raptor will fly when a vehicle is sighted.

Other interesting behavioral facets are also covered.

FEEDING: The first sentence in all accounts indicates if the species hunts from a perch, in flight, or by both methods. This section also describes what the species preys on and where and how it captures and eats prey.

FLIGHT: This section describes the individual variations for the three main flight modes—powered flight (flapping), gliding, and soaring—and the three secondary modes—diving, hovering, and kiting. It also elaborates on migration flight.

VOICE: Each species has distinct vocalizations. Not all species regularly vocalize, but if they do, their distinct call notes can assist identification. Nearly all species occasionally vocalize year-round, particularly when agitated. Some species, such as Red-shouldered and Red-tailed hawks, are highly vocal year-round. Most species become fairly vocal during the breeding season, when courting, or when trespassers enter their territory. Even during migration and winter, typically silent raptors such as Sharp-shinned and Cooper's hawks regularly vocalize when agitated and exhibit their distinct, separable call notes. The only species that is notoriously silent is the Golden Eagle.

Interpreting sounds phonetically is difficult, but methods such as sonograms are even more difficult to interpret. All vocalizations are shown in italics.

STATUS AND DISTRIBUTION: Below are the status designations used in this book. The numbers that accompany each designation are somewhat arbitrary because they are based on rough estimates. They reflect the most current and accurate data available, however. Some data are from published sources, and some are based on recent information from major hawkwatches (e.g., fall hawkwatch counts in Veracruz, Mexico). For polymorphic species, and for polytypic species whose subspecies are identifiable by sight and/or range, status designations are given for the species as a whole and, in a subheading, for each color morph or subspecies. Many of the status estimates for color morphs are based on my observations of the last 16 years and those of my colleagues.

Endangered. Highly threatened and extremely difficult to find; fewer than 100 individuals.

Very rare. Threatened and very difficult to find; 100–250 individuals.

Rare. Somewhat threatened and quite difficult to find; fewer than 500 individuals.

Very uncommon. Fairly low numbers and difficult to find; estimated population ranges from 500 to 10,000 individuals.

Uncommon. Moderate numbers and moderately easy to find; estimated population ranges from 10,000 to 100,000 individuals.

Common. Large numbers and easy to find. Estimated population ranges from 100,000 to 2 million individuals.

Very common. Very large numbers and easy to find. This designation is used only for Turkey Vulture, which has an estimated population of over 3 million individuals.

Local. A raptor that can have any of the above designations but is found only in a restricted location and habitat.

Accidental. Occurring far out of the normal range and not likely to be seen. Also called *vagrant.*

Casual. Occurring out of typical range but infrequently seen.

This section is usually divided into four main subheadings—Summer, Winter, Movements, and Extralimital movements—with other headings added when appropriate.

Summer and winter data correlate with the detailed range maps; if there is a plot on a map, it specifies an exact location. Summer data are mainly from published and unpublished breeding bird atlases. A great deal of information was also gathered on the Internet, by tapping local, state, and regional experts throughout the U.S., Canada, and Mexico. Winter data were primarily taken from many years of Christmas Bird Counts, previously published by the National Audubon Society and now published by the American Birding Association. Data were also obtained from several years of *North American Birds* (previously called *American Birds* and *Field Notes*). Some personal data were also used, based on many years of travel across North America.

"Movements" is further divided into Dispersal (summer or other seasons), Fall migration, and Spring migration. Migration data are based heavily on information in *Hawk Migration*

Studies, published by the Hawk Migration Association of North America (HMANA); published banding data; published and unpublished telemetry data; and personal knowledge from more than 20 years of field work. For simplicity and consistency, dates for movements are based on splitting a month into three parts: 1st–10th is "early month," 11th–20th is "mid-month," and 21st–31st is "late month."

The information in "Extralimital movements," which typically lists locations and dates, is based mainly on published data from local, state and provincial, and regional experts. However, a considerable amount of information is based on recent unpublished reports from authoritative persons. A similar method of a tripart month is used here.

NESTING: The first segment gives the start and end of the nesting season. This typically spans the period when courtship behavior begins and fledglings become independent. The start of the nesting season is more difficult to determine with raptors that are resident or remain paired year-round. This section also explains when pair formation occurs and the age of first breeding.

Courtship is consistently described, under the subheading Courtship (flight) for nearly all species and Courtship (perched) for the few species that engage in this type of behavior. Rather than describe displays time and again, courting behaviors are described in detail in chapter 5, and this chapter is referenced in the species accounts. Courting behaviors in the species accounts are in italics for easy recognition.

The remainder of this section describes nest sites, nest size, which sex builds the nest and incubates the eggs, incubation period, and fledging time.

CONSERVATION: This section elaborates on any measures that have been taken to protect a species. All raptors are covered under the Migratory Bird Treaty Act of 1918. For many years this law was rarely enforced for raptors, however, since virtually all species were considered a nuisance. Endangered and threatened species finally received additional protection under the Endangered Species Protection Act of 1970 and, since 1973, under the Endangered Species Act. Bald Eagles were protected under the Bald Eagle Act of 1940, which was amended in 1962 to include Golden Eagles. Individual states and provinces often have their own protective laws.

The Mortality subheading in this section describes survival problems that raptors encounter. Natural and human-caused mortality issues are discussed.

SIMILAR SPECIES: This section gives detailed comparisons of similar-looking raptors. Polytypic and polymorphic variations that cause confusion are also detailed. Comparisons are organized under subheadings of the various ages and/or subspecies and color morphs.

OTHER NAMES: North American colloquial names are listed. Since the ranges of some species include Mexico and Canada, Spanish and French names are also given.

REFERENCES: This is an abbreviated bibliography: full citations occur in the bibliography at the end of the book.

Plates and Captions

PLATES: The photographs depict an extensive array of plumages for all species, ages, sexes, and color morphs of North American breeding raptors. Most subspecies and plumage types are also depicted. However, it is nearly impossible to show all individual variations and types of plumages with photographs (or with illustrations).

Although I considered the aesthetic value of a photograph when making the final selection, the ultimate criterion for every photo was whether it adequately showed particular field markings. More than one photograph is often used for the same type of bird in order to suitably illustrate a field mark or plumage variation. On some, I was fortunate to have perching and flying images of the same individual, which helps in conveying total plumage features.

Individuals of obvious age classes are grouped together. Following the text layout, older ages precede younger ages. This is because adults are generally easier to identify than the often "brown-colored" younger birds. Polymorphic and polytypic species are also grouped according to age class. Polymorphic species are arranged in a light-to-dark format. Perching figures are presented before flying figures for each age class grouping.

CAPTIONS: The species name is followed by the bird's age, sex (if obvious), and color morph (where applicable). For polytypic species, all photos are of the "typical," or most widespread, subspecies unless otherwise indicated. Where a subspecies is labeled, both the colloquial and scientific name are given. The month the photograph was taken is listed last in brackets.

Information in the captions is arranged in a "bullet" format for easy, consistent reading. The bullets use the same terminology as the text and are arranged in the same anatomical order: head, body, wings, and tail. *Head* describes the bill, eyes, and important feather markings on the head. It may also include the front and sides of the neck. *Body* includes dorsal and ventral surfaces, leg feathers, tarsi, and undertail coverts. It may also include the front and sides of the neck. *Wings* includes dorsal and ventral surfaces of the remiges and coverts. *Tail* describes the rectrices and uppertail coverts. Only one or two bullets are used if a particular image does not require all four anatomical areas for identification, and to save space, body and wings may be under the same bullet, especially if there are major similarities in color or markings. The *Note* at the end of many captions presents additional information. It also gives credit on images taken by other photographers.

The location where a photograph was taken is typically not listed because it is virtually impossible to take many or most photographs for a regional book within that particular region. I thought it would appear strange to list a large number of photographs that were taken in one region and used them in the other. I photograph where the raptors are easiest to get: accipiters and falcons mainly at hawkwatches; buteos and eagles in the West, where they are much tamer than in the East. This affected the eastern guide more than the western. Case in point: the exceedingly large number of Red-tailed hawk and Swainson's hawk photographs were nearly all taken in the West, where these two species are most common and generally reasonably tame. Under optimal conditions, it would take decades to get such photographs in the East. Photographic locations may be listed if the image was taken outside of the contiguous U.S. or if it was of special interest.

Range Maps

The range maps are meant to show the most exact plotting of distribution possible. Using knowledge of a species' habitat, one can use the maps to more readily locate a particular raptor.

I was most impressed with the range maps in *A Field Guide to Warblers of North America* (Dunn and Garrett 1997). This was the first North American field guide that had thoroughly researched maps that, as much as is possible, abided by geographic regions within a species' range. Inspired by this great book, I decided something of a similar caliber needed to be done for North American raptors.

The distribution maps in this book are the result of a joint effort by my status and distribution coresearcher, John M. Economidy. John was also impressed with Dunn and Garrett's expertise, and also felt that accurate maps were much needed for raptors. We spent nearly five years of daily research tapping experts from virtually every state and province in the U.S., Canada, and Mexico for the latest in known distribution and status of many species. This was done primarily by E-mail. We also used published breeding and wintering data that dated back several years (*see* Status and Distribution, above, in Format of Species Accounts) and every state and provincial breeding bird atlas—including eight unpublished atlases.

Major obstacles that any author faces are the ever-changing habitats and ranges of birds. What might be accurate one week is not accurate the next week! Also counter in the fact that birds have wings—and thus may stray to faraway locations.

The plottings on the maps abide by geographical and topographical areas. If there is a specific location marked on the map, it *is* for a specific location. A unique quality of these maps is the city locations. Plotting cities not only gives more credence to accuracy but also helps plot a species' range. Super-accurate plotting is illustrated on maps that show county de-lineations. These finely detailed maps truly follow actual habitat zones required for a particu-lar species. Habitat alteration, either by humans or natural causes, may alter the fine detailing of these maps over time, but such detailed plotting gives a substantiated accuracy for this par-ticular period.

For polytypic species whose subspecies are identifiable by sight and/or range, a separate range map was created for each subspecies. These maps show, as do those for monotypic species, detailed, known, typical permanent, summer, and winter ranges. The data are based on published (often state ornithological journals) and unpublished (regional experts tapped by Internet) sources and personal data from hundreds of thousands of miles of travel across North America.

Only on "Krider's" form of Red-tailed Hawk does a color morph have its own map.

Several recent field guides have shown migration routes as colored zones on maps. I chose not to do this. It is fairly easy to see that migrants go from the breeding grounds (point A) to wintering grounds (point B). Also, most raptors migrate in a broad-fronted manner. Thus, all regions between point A and point B would be colored. It would not make any sense to color this region when one can logically figure it out. The captions on the maps may elaborate on heavily used routes and on where a species winters if these are not shown on the map.

Population densities are not shown. Each species' status is labeled on its map. Most rap-tors are either widespread and reasonably common throughout their typical range or they are local and uncommon to rare in their restricted range.

KEY TO MAPS

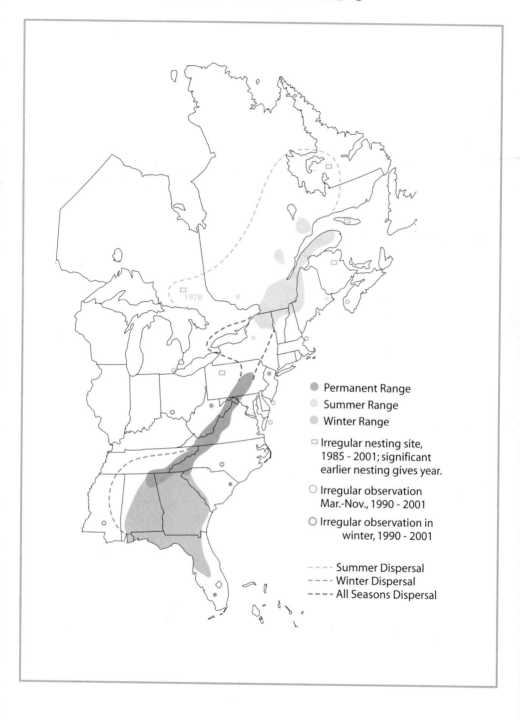

1978

Permanent Range

Summer Range

Winter Range

□ Irregular nesting site,
1985 - 2001; significant
earlier nesting gives year.

○ Irregular observation
Mar.-Nov., 1990 - 2001

○ Irregular observation in
winter, 1990 - 2001

- - - Summer Dispersal
- - - Winter Dispersal
- - - All Seasons Dispersal

II. GENERAL GLOSSARY

Accipiter. Name given to the round-winged and long-tailed woodland-dwelling "true" raptors in the genus *Accipiter*. North America has three species in this genus.

Aerial hunting. Hunting method in which the raptor is already airborne when it begins pursuit of its intended prey.

Albinism. Reduction or absence of pigment in the eyes, skin, or feathers. There are four varieties.

> **Total Albinism.** Complete absence of normal pigmentation in the eyes and skin, with both areas being pink. Feathers are pure white. This is the rarest form and rarely seen in raptors.

> **Incomplete Albinism.** Normal pigmentation is completely absent in eyes, skin, or feathers but not in all three areas. Plumage is often pure white or nearly so, but in most cases eyes and skin are normal color. However, talons are often pink colored.

> **Imperfect Albinism.** Normal pigmentation is only partially reduced in eyes, skin, or feathers but not totally in any of the three areas. Also known as "dilute plumage." Eye pigmentation is either normal or bluish. Skin areas are normal or slightly paler than normal in color. Most or all of the plumage is a tan color; any typical markings that have a rufous or tawny color are altered to a pale rusty color in this plumage.

> **Partial Albinism.** Normal pigmentation is completely lacking on portions of the body. Eye and skin areas are usually of normal coloration. Plumage is often a patchwork of normal and white feathers, or parts of several feathers may be white and other parts normal. Most common type of albinism.

Allopreening. Mutual preening between mates or between adult and sibling, but rarely between unrelated individuals.

AOU. Abbreviation for American Ornithologists' Union. Governing board of scientists that makes decisions on taxonomy and nomenclature of avian species in North America.

BLM. Abbreviation for the Bureau of Land Management. Federal agency within the Department of the Interior that oversees land use on federally owned land. Mainly associated with lands in western U.S.

Brancher. *Fledgling*-aged raptor that ventures from the confines of the nest onto nearby branches or to the ground.

Buteo. Species of raptor in the genus *Buteo*, which comprises the broad-winged, soaring hawks. There are 12 species in this genus in North America. Buteo species in the Old World are called *buzzards*.

Butte. Flat-topped, cone-shaped earth formation that is the rock skeletal remains of a hill.

Buzzard. Old World term for *buteo* species of raptors that has become a slang word for vultures in North America. As a reference to New World buteos, the term has never caught on in North America and is rarely used.

Cline. Range of variation that is gradual and continuous in scope. Used to define plumages of some species of raptors with *color morphs*, where various individuals show a continuous gradation in plumage characters between two color types.

Colloquial name. Regional name given to a *species, subspecies,* or *color morph*. It does not have scientific application but makes it easier to express the name in "everyday" language.

Conifer. Tree species with needlelike leaves that are retained all year.

Color morph. Plumage variation within some raptor species (six buteos and one falcon) that is sometimes geographically designated and occasionally is a climatic adaptation. Darker coloration of these species is the result of increased amounts of *phaleomelanin* and *melanin* (darker feather pigmentation) which results in *erythristic* (rufous morph) and *melanistic* (dark morph) birds, respectively. Many of these species also have an intermediate division between each major color morph. Also called "phase," though "morph" is the more accepted scientific term.

Continuum. See *cline*.

Contour feathers. General body plumage feathers that cover the downy, next-to-body insulating feathers.

Crepuscular. Active during twilight in the early morning and early evening.

Deciduous. Tree species that lose their leaves in autumn. Often called "hardwoods."

Dihedral. Wing attitude of a flying bird that has wings held in various V angles above the horizontal plane.

Dihedral, modified. Wing attitude in which the shoulder-to-wrist angle is held above the horizontal plane and the wrist to primary tips are on a horizontal plane.

Dihedral, low. Wing attitude held in a shallow V above the horizontal plane. Angle is less than 30 degrees above the horizontal.

Dihedral, high. Wing attitude held in a steep V above the horizontal plane. Angle is 30–60 degrees above the horizontal plane.

Dihedral, very high. Wing attitude held in a very steep V above the horizontal plane. Angle is at least 60 degrees above the horizontal plane.

Dimorphic. Showing a distinct difference in color or size. Often relates to sexual differences in raptors.

Diurnal. Active during daylight.

Double clutch. Two egg sets per year.

Erythrism. High amount of rufous (*phaeomelanin*) pigmentation in a feather structure. Produces rufous *color morph* in some buteo.

Escarpment. Hill formation in which a portion of the hill is eroded away and exposes an inner rock surface that is vertical and clifflike.

Estivation. Summer hibernation, used by many western ground squirrel species. When their nutritious food supply disappears in the hot and dry summer, they enter into a "summer sleep" which then usually continues into regular winter *hibernation*. The reproductive cycle of some raptor species is timed to the above-ground season of some ground squirrel species, which are major prey items.

Eyass. *Nestling* or *fledgling* falcon.

Eyrie. Raptor nest site; particularly used to note the nest area of a falcon. Also spelled *aerie*.

Falcon. Species of raptor in the genus *Falco;* there are seven species of falcons in North America. Also, name given to the female of a large falcon species.

Falconry. Sport hunting of game birds and animals with a captive raptor (captive reared or taken from the wild). All hunting is done within the prescribed season for the specific game species. A falconer is licensed under state and federal regulations.

Fall line. Geographic delineation in the southeastern U.S. in which there is an abrupt difference between upland and lowland elevation. Generally an arch-shaped region from Durham, N.C., to Columbia, S.C., to Columbus, Ga.

Fledgling. Young bird that has attained the power of flight but is still under care of parents.

Form. Term that defines variations within a species that has variable plumage characters.

Fratricide. Older or stronger nestling and/or fledgling that kills (and may eat) a weaker sibling; due primarily to food competition. Also known as "siblicide."

Genus. Taxonomic grouping that represents one or more closely related species. The genus name is the first part of a binomial or trinomial designation of a species' or subspecies' scientific name and is always capitalized.

Gloger's Rule. Ecological "rule" coined in C. W. L. Gloger's 1833 book *The Variation of Birds under the Influence of Climate.* The rule states that species inhabiting humid climate regions have darker pigmentation (increased amount of *melanin*) than those inhabiting drier regions. In raptors this pertains primarily to a climatic adaptation that often results in a darker colored *subspecies* and occasionally produces a higher percentage of darker *color morphs* in a more humid region.

Greenery. Green leaves or twigs with green leaves on them that are used by some nesting raptors to line or decorate the top of the nest.

Hacking. Human-assisted rearing of young raptors, using captive fledglings or relocating fledglings from areas that have a stable population to areas where the natural population has been diminished or eradicated by habitat alteration or pesticides. Hacked fledglings do not have contact with their human helpers so are not imprinted and thus retain a natural fear of humans.

Hibernation. "Winter sleep" by many rodents and other animals.

Intergrade (plumage). Occurs when an individual of one *subspecies* has plumage traits of an adjacent-breeding-area subspecies.

Intermediate (plumage). Occurs in *polymorphic* species when an individual has plumage traits intermediate in color between the two *color morphs.*

Jack. Name given to a male Merlin.

Jerkin. Name given to a male Gyrfalcon.

Kettle. Term used to describe a "flock" of raptors, usually during migration.

Melanin. Dark brown or black pigmentation in the structure of a feather.

Melanistic. Showing a high degree of *melanin* in feather structure. The added melanin produces a dark *color morph* in six buteo and one falcon species. Increased melanin also creates a darker colored subspecies in three species of raptors. Rarely, an abnormal amount of melanin produces an abnormally dark-colored individual in a species that does not typically have color morphs or subspecies.

Mixed woodland/forest. Wooded area that has a combination of *coniferous* and *deciduous* trees.

Monotypic. Species that does not have *subspecies.*

Neotropical. Referring to the region that extends from south of the central Mexican Highlands through Central America, South America, and the West Indies.

Nominate. In species with *subspecies,* the race selected as the most "typical." In the trinomial scientific name, the subspecific designation is the same as the specific designation.

Olfactory. Pertaining to the sense of smell.

Perch hunting. Detecting prey from a perch and then becoming airborne to catch it.

Pesticides. Organochlorine pesticides: Deadly and long-lived chemicals that persist for decades in the environment. DDT (dichlorodiphenyltrichloroethane) was the famous pesticide that caused the population decline of many North American raptors, most notably Osprey, Bald Eagle, and Peregrine Falcon. When metabolized, DDT becomes DDE (dichlorodiphenylethylene) and accumulates in the fat deposits of mammals and birds. In birds, DDE most commonly reduces eggshell thickness, causing eggs to break under an incubating bird. Rarely it causes direct mortality by ingestion of contaminated prey.

DDT was first used in 1946 to control insect infestations on crops and forests in Canada and the U.S. It was banned for most uses in Canada and the U.S. in 1972 and 1973, respectively. Canada and the U.S. had limited public health use of DDT, however, until 1985 and 1989, respectively. Mexico ceased its limited public health use of DDT for malaria control in 2002 and plans a total ban in 2006. Although 122 countries have banned DDT, some countries in Central and South America still use it. Other deadly organochlorine pesticides that were used in the 1950s and 1960s included dieldrin, heptachlor epoxide, and polychlorinated biphenyls (PCBs).

Organophosphate pesticides. Deadly chemicals but not as long-lived in the environment as organochlorine pesticides. Even when properly used, such chemicals are known to kill animal life. Improper and illegal use causes even greater mortality to predators and scavengers. Some organophosphate pesticides have been known to kill large numbers of Bald Eagles, Golden Eagles, Red-tailed Hawks, and other birds of prey in several cattle-ranching and dairy-farming states. Some types of organophosphate pesticides used in eastern Canada killed songbirds as well as friendly insects.

Carbamate pesticides. Less harmful to the environment than organophosphate chemicals.

Pyrethroid pesticides. Newly developed pesticides that are harmless to birds and mammals but are harmful to aquatic life.

Phaeomelanin. Rufous pigmentation in the structure of a feather. A high degree of it produces an *erythristic*, or rufous *color morph* in some species.

Phase. Alternate name for *morph*.

Plucking post. Favorite elevated perch used by a raptor to pluck feathers or other inedible portions off prey before eating or delivering it to the nest to feed a mate or youngsters.

Polygamy. Having more than one mate. There are two varieties: polygyny is one male with multiple females; polyandry is one female with multiple males.

Polymorphic. Referring to species that have *color morphs*.

Polytypic. Referring to species that have *subspecies*.

Preening. Grooming action of a bird in which individual feathers are drawn through the bill to restore their neatness and waterproofness. The bill is rubbed across the oil (uropygial) gland, which is located on the top basal region of the tail and supplies waterproofing oil for the feathers.

Race. Alternate name for *subspecies*.

Riparian. Near water.

Rousing. Cleansing action of a bird in which all *contour feathers* are elevated, wings and tail are held loosely, and the bird vigorously shakes itself. It is done either while perched or flying.

Scientific name. Two or (if referring to a subspecies) three-part name accepted worldwide that identifies each organism. The first word in the name denotes the *genus* level, the second the *species* level, and the third the *subspecies* level (if the species has one or more geographic variations). Scientific names are italicized.

Shelterbelt. Trees planted in linear formation to serve as windbreaks; planted throughout much of the West to reduce soil erosion. Shelterbelts are popular roosting and nesting areas for many raptors, especially in regions naturally void of the safe-haven elevation of trees.

Species. Population of similar individuals that are reproductively isolated.

Specimen (museum). Bird that is collected (shot or found dead) and preserved in a scientific collection. It is preserved by being "stuffed" and laid on its back in an airtight drawer in a large case. Each individual has a data tag attached to its feet that signifies the species, age, sex, collection locale, and any other pertinent details. Museum specimens are valuable tools for scientific studies. Properly cared for, they may last for centuries.

Status. Indication of how abundant a species is, how easily it is found, and how at risk it is. Estimated sizes of a species' population are given in numerical figures or in general terms. Several terms are used to define status.

Subspecies. Distinct variation within a breeding population of a *species* that is partially or totally isolated by a geographic barrier. Seventy-five percent of the population share similar plumage and/or size traits. Subspecies are adaptations to regional environments. Plumage adaptations are due mostly to climate but may also be evolutionary adaptations to selective feeding, hunting, and migratory factors. *Intergrades* occur on the periphery ranges of adjacent subspecies where individuals of the two subspecies interbreed.

Superspecies. Two or more *species* that are reproductively isolated but are otherwise very similar and probably came from similar ancestry.

Thornbush. Low to moderately high tree covered with thorns. In dense growths, areas of thornbush are virtually impenetrable.

Translucent. Allowing the passage of diffused light through a surface. Used here to describe wing and tail feathers of flying raptors when viewed from underneath with sunlight shining through. The underparts are in shadow, and diffused sunlight is transmitted through the paler areas of these feathers.

Type. Term that describes a plumage variation, often within a *species* that has *color morphs* or *subspecies*.

Urohydrosis. Cooling mechanism by which vultures (and storks) regulate body temperature by excreting onto their legs and feet. Normally pinkish and/or reddish colored legs turn chalky white.

Vermiculation. Irregular, narrow zigzag formation of markings on feathers.

Wash. In arid regions, an area between hills that during periods of heavy rain absorbs moisture and allows for more substantial vegetation growth, especially of trees. Washes are dry during nonrainy periods. Also called "dry wash."

Whitewash. White-colored excrement from raptors. Often seen as white stains below a nest or favorite perch. Especially visible on cliff-area nest locales used by falcons.

Wing chord. Distance on a folded wing from the wrist to the tip of the longest primary; it is the most accurate measurement of a bird's size.

III. ANATOMY AND FEATHER GLOSSARY

This glossary is divided into four sections: Head, Body, Wings, and Tail. This is the same order in which plumage and caption data are arranged in the species accounts.

Head

Auriculars. Short, stiff feathers that cover the ear hole. This area merges with the *cheek* to the front and is often referred to as the auricular/cheek area.

Bill. Sheath of hardened tissue over two skeletal bone sections, the upper and lower *mandibles*. The upper mandible of all raptors has a distinct, long hook.

Bill notch. On falcons, a jagged notch near the tip of the upper *mandible*, used for severing the vertebrae of prey.

Cere. Fleshy region at the base of the upper *mandible* of the bill that surrounds the *nostrils*.

Cheek. Area directly behind and under the eye. The cheek merges onto the *auriculars*, often without any separation of markings. Often referred as the auricular/cheek area.

Crown. Top of the head.

Ear. Small hole covered by the *auriculars* (except on vultures, which show the ear hole because of their bare head).

Eyeline. Dark linear mark directly behind each eye.

Facial disk. *Auricular/cheek* area that appears owl-like with distinct semi-circle formation to accentuate sound reception.

Forehead. Front, top area of head, directly behind the *cere*.

Gape. Fleshy "lip" surrounding the mouth and connecting the *mandibles*.

Hackles. Feathers on the *nape*, on the rear of the head. They are elevated or lowered in response to mood/temperature, being raised when a bird is agitated, alarmed, or cold and lowered most other times.

Hindneck. Area below the *nape* and above the *back*.

Lores. Area between the *cere* and front of the eyes. Often covered with stiff, hairlike feathers.

Malar mark. Dark mark on the lower jaw area. The mark may connect to the bottom of the eye or be isolated below the *gape*.

Mandibles. Two sections of bone that are covered with hardened tissue sheaths. The upper mandible is mostly stationary and in raptors has a long hook on the tip; the lower mandible is attached to the hinged lower jaw and is movable.

Mustache mark. Same as *malar mark*, but a name given to falcons which have a similar dark mark on the lower jaw area; on many falcons, this mark may extend up under the eye, more so than in most buteos. It lessens glare.

Nape. Rear area of the head. These feathers are erectible: See *hackles*.

Nostril. Hole on each side of the fleshy *cere* for air intake. Also called "nares" (naris, sing.).

Nostril baffle. On some raptors, especially falcons, a postlike structure in the center of each nostril to permit breathing, by slotting air into the nostrils, during high-speed aerial maneuvers. The baffles can be seen at close range.

Ocelli. Dark or light spots on the *nape* that appear as "fake" eyes, possibly to deter predators; commonly found on falcons.

Orbital ring. Fleshy eyelid surrounding the entire eye on falcons; the region in front of the eyes on the inner *lores* has a broad fleshy area. There is usually a smaller fleshy area behind the eyes.

Sclera. Membrane surrounding the eyeball. A small part is visible on the edge of the eye on some birds if it is brightly colored (e.g., red on older California Condors).

Supercilium. Pale linear area over the top of the eyes. Also called "superciliary line" or "eyebrow."

Supraorbital ridge. Bony projection over the top of the eyes on most raptors that shields and shades the eyes; covered by a thin strip of bare skin. This feature gives raptors their "fierce" look.

Throat. Area under the lower *mandible*.

Body

Back. Area covered by V-shaped feather tract that merges with the hindneck and is between the two *scapular* tracts. The back tract overlaps inner portion of each scapular tract. Also called the "mantle."

Belly. Mid-section of the *underparts*; centered over the central pectoral muscle area. Feathers that cover this region are short to moderate in length.

Belly band. Dark band on the *belly* and *flank* region.

Breast. Area below the neck and above the belly. Covered by two feather tracts running from the neck onto the *belly* and *flank* tracts.

Crop. An elastic "holding pouch" on the *breast* where food first enters the body after swallowing. In raptors that have recently eaten, the crop shows as a distended bulge. Caracaras and vultures show a large exposed fleshy area when the crop is full because the two feather tracts covering the breast separate. Also called the "craw."

Flags. Elongated, quite visible feathers that attach to the tibia region on raptors. Often called "thigh feathers."

Flanks. Elongated feathers attaching on the sides of the large pectoral muscles. They streamline the sides of the body.

Heel. Upper part of the *tarsus*.

Hindneck. Area below the *nape* and above the *back*. It is covered by a single feather tract that runs down the rear vertebrae onto the *back*.

Leg. General term for *tarsus* and *tibia*.

Leg feathers. Long, fluffy feathers that attach on the *tibia*.

Lower back. Area below the *back* and above the *rump*. Usually hidden by the *scapulars*, except in flight when this area may be visible.

Lower belly. Area covered by elongated feathers that are an extension from the *belly*; they often cover the feet when a bird is perched. There are two feather tracts which are sometimes separated on perched birds to accommodate a raised foot when resting.

Rump. Area below the *lower back*. Elongated feathers on the rump cover the *uppertail coverts* and also the oil (uropygial) gland.

Scapulars. Two distinct, large feather tracts that cover the inner area of the wings on the dorsal surface. They streamline the junction of wings and body in flight.

Talon. Long, sharply curved, needlelike toenails.

Tarsus. Visible bare flesh or scaled part of the leg: except on three species, the tarsus is mostly feathered. *Tarsi* is plural.

Tibia. Muscular "drumstick" area of the leg, above the *tarsus.*

Toes. Four in number. Toe length and exterior construction are adaptations to the type and size of prey a raptor usually feeds on.

Underparts. General term that collectively applies to *breast, belly, flanks,* and *undertail coverts.*

Upperparts. General term that collectively applies to *back, scapulars, lower back,* and *rump.* Occasionally includes the upperwing.

Wings

Alula. Stiff, knife-shaped feather group comprising three or four feathers on top of the wing, near the wrist. Controls airflow over the wing during slow flight; also allows control when wings are folded close to the body during dives.

Axillaries. Group of feathers that attach on the underside of the wing, in the "armpit" area. They streamline the junction between the wings and flanks when a bird is in flight.

Fingers. Outermost *primaries.* There are usually five to seven, and they are distinctly longer than inner primaries. Visible on many buteos and eagles.

Flight feathers. Group of long, stiff feathers comprising the *primaries* and *secondaries.* Collectively known as *remiges.*

Patagium. Elastic membrane on the front edge of the inner wing that unites the shoulder, elbow, and wrist areas. Patagial is the adjective.

Primaries. Ten stiff feathers that attach on the "hand" area of the outer wing. Part of the *flight feathers/remiges* (along with *secondaries*). They are numbered from inner to outer, with p1 being the innermost and p10 the outermost.

Primary coverts. Fairly short, stiff feathers attaching on the dorsal side of the wing at the base of each of the ten *primaries.*

Primary projection. The distance from the rear of the *tertials* to the tips of the *primaries* on a perched raptor. In the text, referred to as "short projection" (short distance between tertials and wingtips) and "long projection" (long distance between tertials and wingtips).

Primary underwing coverts. Row of short feathers attaching on the basal area of the underside of the *primaries.*

Remiges. Name given to the *flight feathers:* the *primaries* and *secondaries.* Remix is singular.

Secondaries. Several stiff feathers (the number varies somewhat) that attach on the rear of the forearm area and are part of the *flight feathers/remiges* (along with the *primaries*). They are often numbered for quick reference, especially when describing molt. Outermost is 1 or s1.

Secondary underwing coverts. Partially visible row of feathers attaching on the underside of the *secondaries.*

Tertials. Innermost three or so feathers of the *secondaries,* attaching on the elbow region. Visible mostly when perched; in flight, they are usually covered by the *scapulars.*

Trailing edge. Rear edge of all the *flight feathers* (*remiges*).

Underwing coverts. Several rows of feathers, on some species rather indistinct, that attach on the forearm and *patagial* area. Also called "wing lining."

> **Greater underwing coverts.** Attach on rear of forearm and form a visible, well-developed row overlapping the inner *secondaries*.
>
> **Median underwing coverts.** Attach on forearm and are rather long in length. They comprise a major feather row and are visible on most species.
>
> **Lesser underwing coverts.** Attach on *patagium* as an elastic group and for the most part do not have defined rows.

Upperwing coverts. Comprise several well-defined, overlapping rows of feathers.

> **Greater upperwing coverts.** Distinct row of fairly long feathers that overlap the inner *secondaries*. There is one greater upperwing covert for each secondary.
>
> **Median upperwing coverts.** Fairly distinct row of medium-length feathers attaching above the *greater coverts*. There is one median covert for every greater covert.
>
> **Lesser upperwing coverts.** Small feathers comprising several usually indistinct rows on the *patagium*. First row attaches above the median coverts. Also called "shoulder area," which technically is a misnomer.

Window. Pale underside of the *wing panel* through which light shines on pale-colored *primaries*.

Wing panel. Pale upperside surface on a portion or most of the *primaries*.

Wingtip-to-tail-tip ratio. Distance on a perched raptor from the tips of the *primaries* to the tail tip. This "measurement" is very useful in the field when separating confusing raptor species.

Tail

Deck set. Center pair of *rectrices*, which on dorsal surface overlap all others when tail is closed. Only one *rectrix* of the set is totally visible at all times. It is labeled as the r1 set.

Inner web. Portion of *rectrix* that is visible on underside of tail.

Outer web. Portion of *rectrix* that is visible on dorsal side of tail. Exception is on the top most of the *deck set*, which has both sides of the feather visible.

Rectrices. Six symmetrical sets of long, stiff feathers that form the tail. On the dorsal side, the inner feather sets overlap the outer sets. On the ventral side, the outer feather sets overlap the inner sets. The sets are numbered from innermost (*deck set*) to outermost, from r1 to r6. Rectrix is singular.

Subterminal band. Darker band just inside the tail tip.

Tail band. Horizontal band across the dorsal of the tail.

Undertail coverts. Long, often rather fluffy, contour feathers attaching on the underside of the tail bone that cover the base of the undertail. On the outer area, there is one covert for every *rectrix*.

Uppertail coverts. Short, fairly stiff feathers, one attaching at the base of each *rectrix*, overlapped on the inside by the *rump* feathers. Mistakenly called "rump" on some species.

fingers

primaries

remiges

secondaries

greater primary coverts

scapulars

lower back

back

greater upperwing coverts

rectrices (tail)

alula

uppertail coverts

rump

trailing edge

wing panel

supraorbital ridge

lores

nostril

cere

bill

bill notch

gape

cheek

auriculars

breast

orbital ring

crown

ocelli

forehead

throat

malar mark

neck

breast

eyeline

supercilium

nape

hindneck

malar mark

back

wrist

scapulars

lesser upperwing coverts

median upperwing coverts

greater upperwing coverts

tertials

secondaries

tarsi

toes

talon

primary projection

primaries

deck feathers

wingtip-to-tail tip ratio

leading edge

window

patagium

remiges (flight feathers)

lesser underwing coverts

median underwing coverts

axillaries

greater underwing coverts

breast

flanks

patagial mark

leg feathers

underwing coverts

undertail coverts

subterminal band

primary underwing coverts

belly

lower belly

secondary underwing coverts

IV. PLUMAGE, MOLT, AND AGE GLOSSARY

Plumages

Confusion abounds in labeling the various plumages and ages of raptors. The uncertainty stems from the fact that there is currently no consistently used terminology in the ornithological world. The terminology used in this book is described below and I hope will ease some of the confusion. To better understand the age progression in raptors, a basic knowledge of molt is useful (*see below*).

The descriptions here are based primarily on the widely accepted plumage and molt terminology of Humphrey and Parkes (1959). The plumage changes acquired by each age class are based on molt cycles. In most raptors, a molt cycle corresponds near the hatching date. In some cases, however, it may happen when the raptor is only a few months old (i.e., kites). The plumage descriptions for each age class below follow such molt cycles, and each plumage change that is due to molt signifies advancement into the next older age class.

The terminology used by the U.S. Department of the Interior Bird Banding Laboratory and Canadian Bird Banding Office is not used here. This terminology uses calendar age cycles rather than molt cycles. With this system, age of a bird automatically changes on January 1 of each year, not by a plumage change.

Humphrey and Parkes divided bird plumages into two categories. Basic plumage is the primary, or winter, plumage for species that have one year-round plumage. This plumage is acquired by a single annual molt that occurs during and after the breeding season; on most species and/or subspecies, it is completed prior to winter. Alternate plumage is the temporary breeding, or summer, plumage that some species, mainly songbirds, acquire by molting prior to the breeding season. They molt again after the breeding season into a basic plumage for the winter.

Diurnal raptors undergo one annual molt and for the most part have one year-round plumage. They are therefore classified as birds that have a basic plumage. On some species, the molt is not complete or is prolonged and is often temporarily suspended; however, such species still typically have only one molt per year.

Since diurnal raptors adhere to the basic plumage concept, each molt is called a prebasic molt, meaning "the molt before the basic plumage." For birds that take more than one molt to acquire adult plumage, these molts are often labeled numerically, i.e., "first prebasic molt," "second prebasic molt," and so forth. The molt into the adult plumage is sometimes called the definitive prebasic molt by some authors because it is the final molt into adult plumage. Even definitive prebasic molts are often numerically designated, i.e., "first definitive prebasic molt."

In this book, the first molt is labeled simply the "first prebasic molt." Additional numerical designation precedes the "prebasic" term if more than one plumage is needed to attain adult plumage. In adult plumages, the "definitive" numerical designation is not used (*see* Ages, below).

Molt

Molt. Replacement of old, worn body feathers (contour feathers) and wing and tail feathers with new feathers. Degree and timing of molt vary considerably. On average, some or all of the plumage is replaced on an annual basis. Age, sex, latitude, elevation, migration, and food can play a role in molt timing and duration. It usually takes several months to replace all the plumage (generally during summer and fall). In nesting adults, females begin molt prior to males. Males molt later, after their young are mostly grown or have fledged. This permits the male—the major food supplier to the female and nestlings—to have his plumage in prime condition in order to hunt effectively, and also not expend nutrients on growing his own feathers. In large raptors such as eagles, it takes 4 years to replace all remiges and rectrices.

Molt center. Beginning point on the wing and tail where molt begins. Molt progresses in a particular direction, generally symmetrically, on each wing and the tail from the molt center.

Molt unit. Group of feathers on the wings that molt as a unit. Molt units can advance in variable directions from the *molt center.*

Molt wave. Partial or complete molt of a *molt unit.* If a partial molt of the molt unit occurs, then molt begins during the next molt at the location where it ceased (see *suspended molt*). Also called "molt front."

Serially descendant molt. Simultaneous molt at more than one *molt center* and *molt unit.*

Suspended molt. Temporary suspension of molt. This normally occurs during winter and migration in order to save energy growing feathers when food is in short supply or when energy is needed for migration. Molt resumes from the location of the stopping point at a later date.

MOLT PATTERNS ACCORDING TO FAMILY CLASSIFICATION

Accipitridae Wing and Tail Molt Pattern—Accipiters, Buteos, and Harriers. (Data based in part on Edelstam 1984 and Forsman 1999.)

Wing (Remiges). Primaries comprise 10 feathers with a molt center on the innermost primary (p1). Molt advances outwardly to the outermost (p10) in a single, complete molt unit. On larger species, however, molt may be partial and may not extend all the way to p10 in one molt season. In a partial molt, p8–10 are often retained old feathers. Primary greater coverts molt in unison with the remiges.

Secondaries and tertials comprise 13 feathers with 4 molt centers and molt units. The outermost secondary is s1, the innermost s13. There is a molt center at s1 and molt advances inwardly to s4 (molted in order of s1, 2, 3, 4). On the mid-wing there is a molt center at s5 that advances inwardly to s8 (molted in order of s5, 6, 7, 8). On the inner secondaries (tertials), a molt center is at s13 and molt advances outwardly to s11 (molted in order of s13, 12, 11). From s10, molt advances to s9.

On most hawks, this is a complete molt each year. On some large species, however, the outer two to four primaries and mid-wing secondaries may not be replaced during the first molt, and subsequent molts may not be complete either. In general, s4 and 8 are the last to molt and are the remiges most likely to be retained in a partial molt. Secondary greater coverts molt in unison with the remiges. Tertial molt is completed prior to the rest of secondary molt.

Tail (rectrices). The tail has 12 rectrices with 2 molt units. Molt begins on the deck set (r1) and goes to the outermost set (r6). Molt on r6 may begin before r1 is fully grown. The typical sequence is for r3 and 2, and r4 and 5, to molt after r1 and 6 are grown. Rectix molt may be serially descendant, with r3 and 5, and 4 and 2, molting simultaneously.

Accipitridae Wing and Tail Molt Pattern—Eagles. (Data based on Edelstam 1984 and Forsman 1999.)

Wing (Remiges). Primaries molt as a single molt unit; however, it takes up to 4 years, with annual molt waves, to replace the entire 10 feathers. Advancement of the annual molt waves depends on latitude, health, and diet. Molt begins with a molt center at p1 and advances outwardly to p10. Inner primaries may molt two or three times prior to the replacement of the outer primaries (p9 and 10). Primary greater coverts molt in unison with the remiges.

Secondaries and tertials comprise 17 feathers with 4 molt centers and molt units. Molt is serially descendant. On the outer secondaries, there is a molt center at s1 and it advances inwardly as a molt unit to s4 (molted in order of s1, 2, 3, 4). On the mid-secondaries, there is a molt center at s5 and it advances inwardly as a molt unit to s9 (molted in order of s5, 6, 7, 8, 9). On the inner secondaries, a molt center is at s14 and advances outwardly as a molt unit to s10 (molted in order of s14, 13, 12, 11, 10). On the tertials, a molt center is at s17 and advances outwardly as a molt unit to s15 (molted in order of s17, 16, 15). Secondary greater coverts usually molt in unison with the remiges. See individual eagle accounts for variables in molt of the remiges.

Tail (rectrices). There are 12 rectrices, and molt sequence is similar to that of smaller Accipitridae, but molt timing varies with the two eagle species. See individual species accounts for species variation.

Pandioninae Wing and Tail Molt Pattern. (Data based on Edelstam 1984 and Palmer 1988.)

Wing (Remiges). Ten primaries, molted in a similar pattern as in other Accipitridae (p1–10). However, only part of the primaries are molted before a new wave begins on the inner primaries. Most inner primaries may have molted twice before p10 is molted for the first time (p10 is the last to be replaced). Therefore, the primaries will have three ages of remiges once molt has progressed far enough along.

Secondary molt is similar to that of eagles, with 17 feathers.

Tail (rectrices). There are 12 rectrices. Molt begins after wings have started their molt. It begins from the deck feathers (r1) and proceeds outward (with some variation).

Cathartidae Wing and Tail Molt Pattern.

Wing (Remiges). Molt is similar to that of eagles (Accipitridae; *see above*), with 10 primaries and 17 secondaries. California Condors molt their remiges in annual waves and may take 4 years to complete all feather replacement.

Tail (rectrices). There are 12 rectrices. Molt is symmetrical and begins on the deck set (r1), then the outermost set (r6), then r2–5. Rectrix molt may be serially descendant as noted in Acciptridae.

Falconidae Wing and Tail Molt Pattern. (Data based on Edelstam 1984, Forsman 1999, and Palmer 1988.)

Wing (Remiges). Primaries comprise 10 feathers, and molt begins on the mid-region (p4), then usually proceeds to p5; it sometimes begins on p5, however. From p4 (or 5), it advances both inwardly and outwardly in an irregular sequence that varies with each species. Regardless, p10 is the last primary to molt. Primary greater coverts molt in unison with the remiges.

Secondaries and tertials comprise 13 feathers with 2 molt centers and 3 molt units. Molt advances outwardly and inwardly from the mid-secondaries (s5). From s5, it extends outwardly in the order of s4, 3, 2, 1. Also from s5, it extends inwardly in the order of s6, 7, 8, 9, 10. The outermost secondary, s1, is the last to molt. Tertial molt begins on s13, goes to s12, and ends at s11. Tertial molt is finished prior to completion of molt of the outer secondaries. Secondary greater coverts molt in unison with the remiges.

Tail (rectrices). Molt is identical to that of Accipitridae, with 12 rectrices.

Ages (from Youngest to Oldest)

Nestling. Young raptor confined to the nest. Early stage: adorned in a downy feather coat (usually with two downy stages). Mid-stage: contour feather coat is acquired. Late stage: contour feather coat is quite grown but downy feathers retained on head; wings and tail not fully grown.

Fledgling. Young raptor that has left the nest but is still fed by the parents. Adorned in the early stage in a contour feather coat that still is not fully grown, especially remiges and rectrices. Often labeled as a brancher at this stage. Birds are not capable of flight. In mid-stage, plumage is mostly grown but wings and tail are still not fully developed. Capable of reckless flights. In late stage, the contour plumage has been aquired for a while and wings and tail are fully grown. Capable of controlled, sustained flights.

Juvenile. Young raptor that is fully grown and totally self-sufficient. Juvenile plumage may be retained for only a few months on a few species, but usually for 1 year on most species. Some large raptors may retain portions of this first plumage for several years. "Juvenal" also designates any less-than-adult age. A prebasic molt precedes any change into another plumage and/or age class. See *immature*. *Note:* Some authors use "juvenal" as an adjectivial term to describe plumage features of this age class.

Immature. General term for any plumage and/or age that is less than adult.

Subadult. General term for any plumage and/or age that is older than juvenile but not yet adult. *Note:* In this book, "subadult" is used synonymously with "basic" plumage and/or age. On species with one interim subadult plumage and/or age, it is labeled "basic I (subadult I)." On species with more than one subadult plumage and/or age, additional designations have a numerical labeling, i.e., basic I (subadult I), basic II (subadult II), etc.

First adult. Adult plumage with some immature traits. Under field conditions, however, these characteristics may not always be visible and the bird may look like a typical adult.

Young adult. Full adult plumage and/or age that has one or possibly more minor traits that are considered to be adult, but differs somewhat from older-aged adults. Often pertains only to eye color.

Adult. Final stage of plumage development. Minor plumage changes may continue to occur with advancing age—mainly of the plumage becoming less marked and paler. Technically known as "definitive basic plumage," or the final stage of basic plumage and/or age development.

V. FLYING AND PERCHING DISPLAYS GLOSSARY

Flying Displays

This section describes many of the aerial displays used by raptors. Most are used for courting, though some may be used at any time of year for social interaction. Most species engage in at least some type of aerial antics in order to entice a mate, establish or defend territories, or warn of danger. Most raptor species perform one or more of these displays, although a few do not engage in any type of aerial display. Aerial displays are italicized in the species accounts for easy recognition. Courtship displays are listed in the Nesting section of each account; other aerial displays may be listed in Habits or Flight.

Aerial food transfer. Male gives prey item to female, either by talons or bill, or prey may be dropped by male and caught by lower-flying female. Moderate- or high-altitude display.

Aerial-kissing. Closely flying pair of birds touch bills while airborne. Moderate- or high-altitude display.

Begging-flight. Level flight by female with wingbeats kept below the horizontal plane and tail fanned. Accompanied by whining calls. Also called "cuckoo-flight." Performed at any altitude.

Cartwheeling. Closely flying birds grasp and lock talons, then engage in a free-fall tumble. They often come very close to ground level before separating. Display may be performed at any time of year by some species. It begins at a high altitude and ends at a low altitude.

Diving swoop. One sex of a pair or prospective pair swoops down from a higher altitude in a moderate-angled dive toward lower bird, then overshoots lower bird at same altitude and glides past.

Drop-and-catch. Playful antics of a bird dropping and catching objects in mid-air. Moderate- or high-altitude display.

Escort flight. Territorial flight in which individual of an occupied area flies alongside an intruding conspecific to boundaries of territory. See also *leg-lowering.*

Exaggerated-flapping. Wings are raised very high on upstroke and lowered very low on downstroke. Flight is on a level course or slightly undulating. Moderate- or high-altitude display. This is a more accentuated version of *slow-flapping.*

Eyrie fly-by. Purposeful level flight in front of prospective nest site. Moderate- or high-altitude display.

Figure eight. Performed usually by males of larger falcons in which they loop around in a figure-eight pattern.

Flash roll. Male of a large falcon rolls 90 degrees to one side and then the other side in level flight. See also *roll* and *undulating roll.*

Flight-play. One individual dives toward another, often engaging in brief sideways rollover maneuvers and, when passing each other, often extending talons. Moderate- to high-altitude dislay.

Flutter-flight. Level flight in which wings are flapped in very shallow strokes. Generally performed by females of all falcons. Also called "flutter-glide."

Flutter-flying. Level flight in circles or in figure-eight loops with rapid, shallow wingbeats. Performed at any altitude.

Fly-around. Seen mainly in Bald Eagles, where male intensely flies around its presumed territory.

Follow-flight. Generally in mated pairs of Turkey Vultures. A bird follows closely behind lead bird, twisting and turning, often for extended periods. A gentle variation of *Tail-chasing*.

High-circling. High-altitude soaring over territorial area by an individual of a prospective or mated pair. Often called "mutual high-circling" when two birds engage in this display. If performed by a pair, they may be in the same thermal but not necessarily near each other. High-altitude display.

Hover-flight. Courtship flight performed by male Osprey in which bird angles its body upward with slow, labored, nearly stalled flight. A fish is carried in talons during the display.

Leg-dangling (leg-hanging). Legs are lowered downward while one or both birds engage in *high-circling, flutter-flight,* or *V-flutter*. High-altitude display.

Leg-lowering. Territorial interaction in which two individuals fly close together along territorial borders and repeatedly glide downward and land with stiffly held, lowered legs. Moderate- and low-altitude display. Often accompanies *escort flight*.

Mutual floating display. In large falcons, male is positioned slightly above female while soaring, then both slowly descend with wings partially closed and held a bit above horizontal, tail spread, and legs lowered. Both birds maintain same distance as they descend.

Pair-flight. Both sexes glide and soar close together in synchronized formation. High-altitude display.

Parachuting. Male (usually) glides down to female with his wings held high above body and fluttering and his legs lowered. Female rolls over and presents her extended talons to male when he approaches her. Moderate- or high-altitude display.

Passing-and-leading display. Male of a large falcon flies past a female, then begins to weave back and forth in front of her. Moderate- or high-altitude display.

Pothooks. Series of short, steep vertical dives interspersed with short upswings. High-altitude display.

Power-diving. High-speed vertical dive accompanied by sideways twists. High-altitude display.

Power-flight. High-speed direct flapping interspersed with rollover maneuvers. Performed at any altitude.

Pursuit-flight. Male closely chasing a female.

Rocking-glide. Sideways rollover maneuvers while gliding. Performed at any altitude.

Roll. Male of a large falcon rolls back and forth while in a steep dive.

Sky-dancing. Succession of shallow or moderately deep undulations consisting of closed-winged dives. Dives can be fairly long and end with moderate upswings. Undulations may be interspersed with short distances of gliding or flapping. Often performed at high altitudes.

Sky-dancing (high intensity). Succession of deep undulations consisting of closed-winged dives ending with sharp upswings that may include an upside-down rollover. Moderate- or high-altitude display, occasional at lower altitudes.

Slow-flapping. Accentuated, slow, and deliberate wing flapping with wings raised high above body on upstroke in a very accentuated manner on a level flight course. Moderate- or high-altitude display. See also *exaggerated-flapping*.

Slow-landing. Wings are held high, with slow flaps from wrist area. Legs are extended forward with tail fanned and lowered as raptor approaches a perch. Moderate- or low-altitude display.

Tail-chasing. Typically a male pursuing a female, often in gentle swooping downward maneuvers. Performed at any altitude.

Talon-grappling. Upper individual dives toward or is flying above a lower individual while lower bird rolls upside-down and both birds grasp each other's talons. High-altitude display.

Undulating roll. Male of a large falcon rolls sideways while in level flight, then begins a steep dive, then swoops up and repeats maneuver. A roll variation of *sky-dancing*.

V-flight. Long, steep, angled dive that ends with a sharp upswing. High-altitude display.

V-flutter. Level flight with wings held in a pronounced dihedral high over body and fluttered just enough to remain airborne; legs extended downward. Low- to moderate-altitude display.

Z-flight. Series of long, steep dives interspersed with short-distance level flight. Display begins at a high altitude and ends at a low altitude.

Perching Displays

Except for falcons, most raptors do not engage in displays while perched. Many falcons, however, have quite elaborate sexual courtship displays while perched. Most of the displays below correspond to falcons unless otherwise noted. Other types of raptors may engage in one or two perching displays. Perching displays are shown in italics in the species accounts. Displays associated with courtship are in the Nesting section; others are in Habits and sometimes Voice.

Allopreening. Mutual preening within a pair. Also seen among related individuals and occasionally among unrelated individuals.

Billing. Pair members nibble at each other's bill; seen in large falcons.

Circle display. Performed by vultures. Male struts around female, his neck bowed and arched forward and his wings partially or fully spread, and circles female. Male usually faces female, but sometimes his back is toward her. Male may inflate throat and neck air pouches and emit hissing noises.

Copulation-solicitation. Female assumes a horizontal stance with wings held loosely and tail lowered (*Accipiter*), or wings drooped and tail raised (*Falco*).

Curved-neck display. Prior to copulation, males of large falcons stand erect and arch neck forward with bill pointing downward. No vocalization is made.

Female ledge display. Female of a large falcon walks to nest scrape with exaggerated high stepping motion with body in a horizontal posture. She utters call notes but does not look at male. See also *male ledge display*.

Food-begging. Female vocalizes in a continuous whine, usually with her plumage fluffed out, or sometimes perched in a squatted position.

Food transfer. Bill-to-bill transfer of prey item from male to female. Performed by virtually all raptor species.

Head-bow posture. Head is pointed downward, often accompainied by vocalization and up-and-down head bowing. Can be performed by both sexes.

Head-throwback display. Performed only by Crested Caracara. Performed when there is agonistic confrontation with conspecifics, particularly in social feeding situations. Head is quickly snapped onto back and bill is pointed skyward; usually accompanied by vocalization.

High-perching. Solitary individual or a pair perching on a high exposed perch to advertise territory. If a pair, both birds may perch near each other.

Hitched-wing display. After landing in a *slow-landing* display, male raises wrists of folded wings, lowers his head, and compresses body plumage.

Horizontal head-low bow. Either sex of a large falcon has its body at a horizontal posture with all feathers compressed and head bowed 90 degrees from body angle.

Male ledge display. Male of a large falcon walks toward nest scrape with exaggerated high steps, with head bowed low and body at a horizontal position, and looks at female. He utters call notes. See also *female ledge display.*

Mutual ledge display. Both sexes of a large falcon walk to nest scrape performing high stepping actions with bodies in a horizontal posture. See also *male/female ledge displays.*

Mutual plumage stroking. Bald Eagle pairs gently stroke each other's plumage.

Nest displays. Concerns Merlins: both birds are at potential nest site and make *tic* calls. Male lies on nest, arches back, droops and shakes wings, and fans tail.

Perch-and-fly. One or both individuals of a large falcon pair land at prospective nest site or other nearby perch, sit or walk around momentarily, then quickly take off.

Tiptoe-walk. Male approaches nest site in an exaggerated high stepping motion.

Vertical head-low bow. Either sex of a large falcon perches in an upright posture with body feathers compressed and head lowered, often pointing away from mate.

Wail-pluck display. Male of a large falcon emits a "wail" call as he plucks prey.

VI. PERCHING AND FLYING ATTITUDES

aptors exhibit numerous behavioral attitudes when perching and flying. The position of a perching bird indicates if the individual is relaxed, reconditioning feathers, alarmed, feeding, or ready to take flight. The position of the wings and tail on a flying bird indicates if the bird is soaring, flying fast or slow, hunting, or feeding. Major body positions that a viewer will encounter are shown and described below.

Perching

A. Relaxed or in light wind. Body is postured at a vertical angle. A bird may stand on two feet, but when it is very relaxed, one of the legs and feet are raised and tucked up, often hidden underneath the belly feathers. Or one foot may be clenched and its knuckles rested on top of the perch. Feathers are fluffed and a bird appears larger in cool or cold temperatures (fluffed feathers allow the downy feathers next to the body to trap more air and thus provide more insulation). *Note:* Juvenile "Eastern" Red-tailed Hawk.

B. Forward leg-extension. A very relaxed posture in which one leg is extended forward and rests on the top or forward portion of the perch. The rear of the tarsus rests on the perch, or the entire leg is extended forward so the tibia rests on the front of the perch and the tarsus and foot are in a straightened, stiff-legged position. *Note:* Juvenile Mississippi Kite.

C. Preening. Body is postured at any angle but is in a vertical angle in light winds. Raptors only preen when they feel safe and relaxed. Feathers are slipped through the bill, which is typically oiled by the uropygial gland: Birds typically close their eyelids when preening to avoid injury to their eyes. *Note:* Adult Rough-legged Hawk.

D. Rousing. Between preening sessions and often prior to taking flight, birds fluff all their feathers and vigorously shake their bodies to rid themselves of dirt and loose feathers. *Note:* Juvenile White-tailed Hawk.

E. Sunning. Kites and vultures are especially inclined to sun themselves. The dorsal area is situated to face the sun, the wings may be partially or fully extended, and the tail is typically spread. All raptors spread their wings and tail to dry out after getting wet. *Note:* Juvenile Mississippi Kite.

F. Mantling. Wings are partially or fully spread and the tail is spread: This posture is used in three behavioral attitudes: (1) when a raptor that has prey on the ground attempts to shield it from the view of other raptors that may pirate the food; (2) as a threat posture to ward off approaching or nearby raptors from taking captured or pirated prey; and (3) as a threat posture if the raptor is injured and is being approached by a human or predator. In the last two cases, the nape feathers (hackles) are erected to exhibit defiance and to make the bird appear larger and more dominant. *Note:* Adult Red-tailed Hawk.

G. Feeding. Raptors typically stand on prey to hold it in place. If perched on a branch, falcons and kites hold prey with a lowered leg that braces the rear of the tarsus (heel) on the perch. Avian prey is plucked of feathers in the region that will be eaten, mainly the breast. Mammalian prey is plucked of its fur in areas that will be eaten, mainly the inner, thick leg muscles. Small bones, and sometimes larger leg bones, are devoured. Ospreys eat the forward part of the fish first. *Note:* Adult Osprey eating a fish.

H. Wing-leg stretch. Prior to taking flight, raptors typically stand on one leg, then simultaneously raise and stretch the other leg and same-side wing; first one side, then the other. The tail is often simultaneously spread with each wing-leg stretch. *Note:* Adult Swainson's Hawk.

I. Wing flex. Prior to taking flight, and usually after *defecating* and performing the *wing-leg stretch*, raptors lean over at a horizontal angle and raise both partially opened wings above their body. The head and neck are bowed downward and extended outward. *Note:* Basic II (subadult II) Bald Eagle.

J. Defecating. Prior to taking flight, all raptors lean over at a horizontal angle, lower their lower belly feathers, raise their tail, then shoot out a stream of white excrement. They may defecate and then assume a regular perching position; however, flight is usually imminent within seconds or minutes after defecating. *Note:* Juvenile Sharp-shinned Hawk.

K. Alarmed or in strong wind. Alarmed birds that are ready to take flight lean over in a more horizontal position. In strong winds, even relaxed raptors lean over and face into the wind to be more aerodynamic and to reduce feather ruffling caused by wind. Feathers are compressed and birds appear thin and sleek in warm and hot temperatures (feather compression reduces the insulating factor of the downy feathers next to the body). *Note:* Juvenile "Eastern" Red-tailed Hawk.

Flying

L. Powered flight. Wings are flapped. Tail is usually closed but is sometimes opened for stability. Flight mode is used to gain speed quickly or maintain a fast speed. *Note:* Adult "Harlan's" Red-tailed Hawk.

M. Soaring. An energy-efficient flight mode in which a bird maximizes a rising air mass. The rising air provides excellent conditions in which a bird rotates in a circular motion with wings fully extended and tail typically fanned. Falcons have a slight backward bend at the wrist, even when the wing is fully extended; all other raptors have a straight or forward thrusting leading edge of the wing. There are two types of soaring: (1) **thermal soaring**, when a bird rises on a warm, rising air column created by a warm ground surface, and (2) **dynamic soaring**, when a bird rises on strong winds deflecting off a land form. *Note:* Juvenile Sharp-shinned Hawk.

N. Slow glide. Wings are slightly closed and all raptors show a slight bend at the wrist. Wingtips are partially closed and become somewhat pointed. Tail is closed to reduce drag. Some raptors may also use this position when *soaring*, particularly when *dynamic soaring*. *Note:* Juvenile Sharp-shinned Hawk.

O. Moderate glide. Wings are nearly half closed and all raptors show a definitive bend at the wrist. Wingtips are fairly pointed. Tail is closed to reduce drag. *Note:* Juvenile Sharp-shinned Hawk.

P. Fast glide. Wings are more than half closed and all raptors show a definitive bend at the wrist. Wingtips become pointed. Tail is closed to reduce drag. Some raptors may also use this position when *kiting*. *Note:* Juvenile Sharp-shinned Hawk.

Q. Banking. Wings are fully extended and even falcons may exhibit a straight leading edge of the wings as they push against the air. Alula are extended for stabilization. Tail is widely fanned to act as a brake and rudder. *Note:* Juvenile Sharp-shinned Hawk.

R. Diving. Wings are partially opened in most dives but are nearly closed during the highest-speed dives. Tail is partially open for stability but can be closed. *Note:* Adult Peregrine Falcon.

S. Hovering. A stationary altitude maintained by flapping the wings, typically when hunting. Head points downward searching for prey. Tail is widely fanned to maintain or gain altitude. Legs are sometimes lowered to assist balance. *Note:* Juvenile light morph Rough-legged Hawk.

T. Kiting. A stationary altitude is maintained by gliding on a brisk wind current. Wings are partially closed and tail is closed. *Note:* Adult dark morph Short-tailed Hawk.

U. Aerial feeding. Falcons, kites, and a few buteos may feed on small prey while in flight. Feeding typically occurs when *soaring* or in a *slow glide.* The foot holding the prey is extended forward and the head is lowered to reach the prey. *Note:* Adult Mississippi Kite.

V. Distended crop. Raptors typically gorge themselves when a large amount of food is available. After an extensive feeding session, they often exhibit an enlarged breast because of an overly stuffed crop. On many raptors, the distended breast notably affects the bird's appearance. Also, the added weight of food in the crop may affect how a bird flies. Particularly on smaller raptors, wingbeats become labored and slower than normal, and the alteration may well make identification more difficult at moderate and long distances. *Note:* Juvenile Golden Eagle.

A.

B.

C.

D.

E.

F.

G.

H.

I.

J.

K.

L.

M.

N.

O.

P.

Q.

R.

S.

T.

U.

V.

VII. PHOTOGRAPHY

I was a painter of gallery-type renditions of life-sized birds and an illustrator of raptor books long before I began to pursue raptor photography. I began to dabble with photography in the early 1970s, but mainly as a reference tool for my paintings. During this time, I used photography to catalog images of fresh foliage and captive birds. Throughout the 1970s and into the early 1980s, I was not keen on using photography for anything but obtaining reference material. I did not like the limitations imposed with wildlife photography and could not afford better, more expensive equipment that can help overcome some of the limitations.

I began intense research and illustration on the original *A Field Guide to Hawks of North America* in 1983. My photography, now mainly of wild and captive raptors, began to be more intense, but it was still relegated to reference use. This slowly began to change, however. A few quality images began to emerge from my large stock of mostly poor-quality reference images.

By 1984, the "bug" was beginning to infect me; I desperately wanted to obtain higher quality photographs of raptors, particularly flying raptors. By this time, I realized there are three criteria for obtaining great raptor photos, particularly of the difficult-to-get underside flight images. First, one needs to have a quality lens that lets in a maximum amount of light, to help "overexpose" the typically shadowed, dark underside of flying raptors. Second, one has to photograph flying shadow-side raptors over a pale-colored ground surface, in order to assist the overexposure by reflecting light up underneath raptors. And third, a blue or dark gray sky is advantageous in creating an aesthetically pleasing background that also contrasts with the pale feather edgings of the wings and tail.

August 1985 was the turning point in my photography. After trading and selling my photographic equipment over a period of years in order to gradually get better optics, I finally scraped together enough money to purchase my dream lens: a Nikkor 400 mm f/3.5. This is the lens I used for the next 10 years. The large aperture let in a maximum amount of light to help in my overexposure method of flight photography. Although the lens was heavy, I was still able to hand-hold it for easy maneuverability (I have never used gunstock mounts and rarely use tripods). From this point on, I tried to coordinate the benefits of this extraodinary lens and situating myself near photographically conducive backgrounds. The images in *A Photographic Guide to North American Raptors* (including the images by W. S. Clark) were photographed exclusively with this lens. For additional magnification on skittish perched raptors, I attached a Nikon 1.4X extender, which created a respectable 560-mm telephoto lens (at the time, all brands of 2X extenders were of poor quality). During my 10-year use of the Nikkor 400 mm, I first used Nikon FM2 bodies, then graduated to workhorse F3s, and finally to superb F4s. I used all camera bodies with motor-drive units, either attached or integral (F4).

The photographic world, however, was coming of age: autofocus equipment was entering mainstream professional use. I was a disbeliever until famed bird artist Arthur Morris, who had joined me on a photography stint in Duluth, Minnesota in October 1995, showed me the astounding results of autofocus. I was quickly converted! By November of that year, I made the switch and sold my beloved Nikkor 400 mm (and Nikon F4 bodies) and bought Canon autofocus equipment, which at the time was the leader in high-speed, silent-focusing autofocus technology.

The exquisitely sharp Canon 300 mm f/2.8 autofocus lens has been my primary lens ever since. For additional magnification of more distant flying raptors, I use the incredibly sharp Canon 1.4X extender; for perched birds, I used a Canon 2X extender. At first, I used Canon 1N bodies with motor drives and a superquiet Canon A2 body for close-perching birds (raptors are very sensitive to the sound of a camera shutter, even when 100 feet away). I now use the EOS 3 body and still use an A2 for perching birds (Canon has since discontinued making the A2).

I rely on my knowledge of raptor behavior to get close to the birds and have rarely used the large supertelephoto lenses. The Canon 600-mm autofocus lens (now with the amazing IS [Image

Stabilizer] system), especially with a 1.4X or 2X extender attached, produces a coveted 840- or 1,200-mm focal length of impecable sharpness.

Autofocus is not infallible, however, and it still takes skill and some luck to obtain superb results. Regardless, one is still able to garner more sharp, in-focus images than with manual focus equipment.

My film usage has also varied over time. I used Kodachrome 64 until 1992. This fine-grained, sharp film is slow and does not reproduce warm colors very well. I tried the old Fujichrome 100 but was not impressed. In 1993 and 1994, I used Fujichrome Velvia (ISO 50) pushed one stop (100 ISO). I obtained many great images with this finely grained film, but the reds were often too overbearing. I began using Fujichrome Sensia in 1995 and Sensia II (both ISO 100) when it came out a few years later. These are superbly color-balanced, natural-looking films. For the last two years I have been using the professional-grade Sensia II, Provia F (100 ISO), and in the last year I have been pushing Provia F one stop (200 ISO) with superb results.

Digital camera bodies are now being used by many professionals. Although they have some advantages over film cameras (e.g., no film, quiet), I do not see myself jumping into the digital game just yet.

Raptor Music

Feathered batons slicing the air,

Composing the stirring notes of flight.

Twisting, tumbling through thermal melodies,

Wind played like a drum.

Wings pounding, rolling,

Now lilting skyward harp-like,

Then sliding down-scale,

Gliding over medleys of unseen currents,

Exposing chords of ruffled delight.

A symphonic aerial ballet

Rendered with instruments of perfection.

Encore!

by Steve Millard

Species Accounts

TAXONOMY OF VULTURES

Black Vulture, Turkey Vulture, and California Condor are no longer considered true diurnal raptors in the order Falconiformes. These three species are part of the New World vulture family, Cathartidae. These vultures have many of their own unique traits; however, they also share several anatomical and behavioral traits (e.g., inability to grasp objects with their feet, urohydrosis, voicelessness, courtship displays, and lying down on the ground or perch) with the New World stork family, Ciconiidae.

The taxonomic niche for Cathartidae, however, is still in question. DNA research verifies that these vultures are not related to true raptors, but recent studies are inconclusive as to whether they are taxonomically closer to storks or raptors (Seibold and Helbig 1995). Recent morphology (syringeal) research still places these vultures in Falconiformes (Griffiths 1994).

Despite the ongoing taxonomic dilemma, the AOU (1998) has reassigned the New World vultures from Falconiformes to Ciconiiformes, the storklike birds. The vultures still remain in their own family, Cathartidae, but are now placed immediately after Ciconiidae and are separated from Falconiformes by Phoenicopteriformes (flamingos, ibises, and spoonbills) and Anseriformes (geese and ducks).

Regardless of taxonomy, these vultures are unquestionably very raptorlike, particularly in flight. Considering their historical taxonomic association with true raptors, and the fact that they pose identification problems with raptors, they are therefore treated here.

BLACK VULTURE
(Coragyps atratus)

AGES: Adult and juvenile, with a transitional subadult stage with development of head and upper neck features and molt. Adult plumage and head and neck characters are acquired during the second year when 1 year old. Juvenile plumage is worn the first year, but head features and bill color gradually change to more adultlike towards the end of this period. Adults and juveniles have minor plumage differences and different head features. Sexes are identical.

MOLT: Cathartidae wing and tail molt pattern (*see* chapter 4). First prebasic molt from juvenile to adult begins when about 1 year of age in the spring or early summer and extends until fall. Bare skin region of the upper neck and bill features of juveniles, however, begin to gradually change to partial adultlike characters when about 6–8 months old. Little is known of subsequent prebasic body molts.

SUBSPECIES: Polytypic with two races in North America. However, only one subspecies, nominate *C. a. atratus*, is found in the East. *C. a brasiliensis*, which is smaller, inhabits s. Arizona and tropical portions of Mexico and south into

South America. *C. a. foetens* is a large subspecies inhabiting parts of South America. Subspecies are based primarily on subtle size differences; *atratus* and *brasiliensis* are not separable in the field.

COLOR MORPHS: None.

SIZE: Large raptorlike bird. Length: 23–28 in. (58–71 cm); wingspan: 55–63 in. (140–160 cm).

SPECIES TRAITS: HEAD.—**Gray or black featherless head and upper neck.** Neck skin is highly adjustable and can be retracted or distended at will. Skin adjustment of the neck can make the bare skin portion of upper neck appear long or short. The feathered part of lower neck (ruff) covers all of the upper neck and nape when raised. **Very narrow bill.** BODY.—**Black. Long tarsi and toes are gray, but urohydrosis turns them white by the chalky accumulation of excrement.** WINGS.—**When perched, the primaries extend a short distance beyond the tertials. In flight, outer six primaries (p5–10) have white quills and a whitish area on each feather that forms a large white panel. Whitish panel is visible on both upper and lower surfaces but is most pronounced on underside of the wings.** TAIL.—**Black, short, and square-tipped.**

Note: Dorsal plumage is often splattered with white excrement. Since Black Vultures often roost communally (*see* Habits), higher perched birds often excrete onto lower perched individuals.

ADULT TRAITS: HEAD.—**Pale yellowish brown on the upper and lower mandibles on the bill tip. Pale or medium gray skin on head and upper half of neck is covered with wrinkles and tubercles.** Lower neck feathers are glossy iridescent greenish black. BODY.—**Glossy iridescent greenish black.**

BASIC (SUBADULT) TRAITS (FIRST PREBASIC MOLT STAGE): This is a transitional stage from juvenile to adult head, neck, and plumage features and occurs during the second year when birds are 1 year old. It begins in late spring in Florida and from late spring to early summer farther north and extends into the fall. HEAD.—Essentially like late-stage juvenile in the early part of this period. Bill tip may also be dusky on the central part of the upper mandible as in late-stage juvenile, but many subadults quickly acquire the all-yellow adultlike bill tip. The lower part of the bare neck skin gradually acquires more adultlike, enlarged, pale gray wrinkles. In the later stages, adultlike wrinkles finally appear on the nape, crown, and face. BODY.—First prebasic molt replaces rather faded brownish black juvenile feathering with darker, glossy iridescent greenish black adult feathering. WINGS.—Replacement of the three tertials with darker adult feathers is one of the first noticeable adult plumage acquisitions. Glossy, greenish black newly acquired adult feathering is very apparent among the faded, old brownish black juvenile feathers.

JUVENILE TRAITS (LATE STAGE): HEAD.—**Bill tip partially changes to pale yellowish brown on portions of both mandibles. Small grayish wrinkles form on the lower front region of the bare neck.** BODY.—Except for fading, plumage features do not alter from early/mid-stages until the first prebasic molt. Blackish plumage turns more brownish because of fading and wear.

JUVENILE TRAITS (EARLY/MID-STAGES): HEAD.—**Black tip on the upper and lower mandibles of the bill. Smooth black skin on head and upper half of neck.** Neck feathers are brownish black and when ruff is not elevated,

extend up the hindneck a bit farther than on adults, but similar to adults when feathered neck is retracted. *Note:* For a few weeks following fledging, remnant buff-colored, wispy downy feathers are still attached to the very upper part of the lower, feathered portion of the neck and on the bare skin of the nape and crown. There is often a large wispy downy patch on the nape and crown. BODY.—**Black with little iridescent quality.**

ABNORMAL PLUMAGES: Total/incomplete albino.—Several records of mainly white individuals (Palmer 1988; H. Kendall pers. comm.). **Imperfect albino.**—Several records of pale whitish brown individuals (Palmer 1988). *Note:* Both aberrant plumages are rare and not depicted.

HABITAT: Forested and semi-open humid regions. All regions may have hollow dead trees, fallen logs, rock outcrops, caves, abandoned buildings, or abandoned rock quarries for nest sites. Black Vultures primarily inhabit subtropical latitudes but have recently expanded into mid-latitude, temperate humid regions. Found mainly in lowlands. In moderate montane elevations of the n. Appalachian Mts. in Pennsylvania but absent from high montane elevations of the s. Appalachians in southern states.

HABITS: Tame in southern areas but wary in northern parts of range. Gregarious. May gather in flocks of hundreds and sometimes thousands of individuals, especially in the nonbreeding season. Exposed, elevated objects, both natural and human-made, are used for perch sites. This species is also very terrestrial. Black Vultures are fond of clean, fresh water and regularly drink and bathe. Large congregations form at favorite watering areas.

Allopreening occurs between pairs and between parents and recently fledged offspring; also occasionally between Black Vultures and juvenile and subadult Crested Caracaras. Caracaras are the recipient of the preening action. Caracaras bow their heads to have their napes preened or straighten heads to have their chin preened by vultures. Caracaras initiate the preening behavior by moving closer and making head gestures to a nearby vulture.

Bare portion of neck skin is retracted in cool temperatures and the feathered part of neck conceals all the bare skin, including the nape. Tail is cocked upwards and a horizontal posture assumed when walking or galloping. Black Vultures regularly "sun" themselves. Body temperature is regulated by urohydrosis. Black Vultures regularly sit upright on their haunches (heels) or lie down when on a perch or ground.

FEEDING: An aerial scavenger. Feeds primarily on any type and size of dead creature. Prefers fresh carrion but also eats decaying meat. Occasionally eats vegetable matter such as sweet potatoes. On rare occasions, kills newborn animals such as piglets and calves by pecking out their eyes. Also preys on eggs and live nestlings of colonial nesting herons and cormorants and is known to kill opossums and skunks. Regularly forages in open-pit garbage dumps. In Mexico has been seen feeding on human excrement. Aggressive when feeding, Black Vultures constantly squabble among themselves and drive off other scavengers, including Turkey Vultures. Black Vultures cannot smell and must rely on visual acuity to locate food sources. Food is located while flying at high altitudes and observing the behavior of other predators or scavengers.

FLIGHT: Powered flight consists of short bursts of snappy, stiff-winged flaps interspersed with variable-length glide sequences. Wings are held in a low dihedral when soaring and on a flat plane when gliding. Black Vultures often hop several times on the ground to gain momentum for flight but if necessary are capable of launching into direct flight. When landing, they may also hop or bounce several times before coming to a complete stop. Black Vultures do not hover or kite. They "dip" wings frequently to maintain speed and stability.

VOICE: Technically voiceless. Grunts and hisses when food-begging and agitated. An airy, low-toned *wuff* is a commonly heard sound when alarmed.

STATUS AND DISTRIBUTION: Permanent resident.—*Common* in typical range. Estimated population is unknown. Numbers appear healthy and stable. Black Vultures have been rapidly expanding into the northern part of the e. U.S., particularly in New England, in recent years. However, it is not known if numbers are actually increasing. Overall population is probably much reduced from historical times when refuse disposal and farming and ranching practices were less regulated, allowing

vast numbers to thrive. Suitable safe-haven breeding sites have also been greatly reduced with changes in land management. Northward range extension may be due to the increased population of White-tailed Deer. Natural deer mortality, road-killed deer, or deer that are killed and not retrieved by hunters provide a substantial food source for vultures.

Connecticut: Recently established resident. First state breeding confirmed in early Apr. 2002 near Kent in w.-cen. Fairfield Co. Range encompasses the southern half of Litchfield Co. and n. Fairfield Co. Western edge of range is New York State line. Northern portion of range extends from Kent eastward to Litchfield, south along the Naugatuck River to confluence of the Housatonic River at Derby, then westward to Bethel and Ridgefield. Individuals have also been seen in the east-central part of state near Windham, Windham Co. Vultures frequent open-pit dumps in some areas. *Massachusetts:* Established as a first-state-record breeder in 1998 with a pair near Milton, Norwalk Co. Annually seen in various counties. Since the 1950s, sightings have been documented in every county. *New Jersey:* Resident in many areas of the state. *New York:* Resident in small numbers in Orange and Ulster. First state breeding record in 1997 near New Paltz, Ulster Co. *Ohio:* Approximately 100–150 pairs locally breeding in isolated pockets in the state. Listed as a Species of Special Interest. Expanding range in southern counties and northward into central and eastern counties in the last decade. Major breeding population centers are in cen. Adams Co. (Ohio Brush Creek Valley), nw. Hocking Co. and s.-cen. Fairfield Co. (Clear Creek Valley), and w.-cen. Holmes Co. and ne. Knox Co. Smaller breeding populations are in s. Richland, w.-cen. Tuscarawas, w.-cen. Licking, and s.-cen. Warren Cos. Counties with poorly established populations and sporadic breeding: sw. Preble, cen. Hamilton, e. Highland, w.-cen. Ross, e. Brown, w. Adams, se. Scioto, e. Washington, and s.-cen. Belmont. *Indiana:* Nesting is documented in the following counties: Lawrence, s. Monroe (Monroe Lake area), Ripley, Crawford, Harrison, Jefferson, e. Clark, and Switzerland. Range is expanding in the southeastern part of state with sightings in Ripley, Jackson, Dearborn, Union, and Franklin Cos. There are recent, irregular sightings in Wayne Co. Formerly nested in the west-central part of the state in Parke, Putnam, Clay, and Owens Cos.; with the loss of many floodplain forests, however, breeding habitat has been lost. *Pennsylvania:* Year-round resident in most of mapped range but withdraws from higher elevations in winter.

Winter.—Large groups often form. Some remain in expanded northern breeding range, even in the very northern portion of range in w. Connecticut. Also recorded in e.-cen. of Connecticut in Windam Co. No. Pennsylvania birds may withdraw from montane elevation summer range and move to valley areas. There may be a considerable localized wandering during this season in quest of ample food. Rarely found on Florida Keys.

Extralimital wintering.—Regular in small numbers in sw. Massachusetts; irregular along coastal Maine; one Nov. record (collected) Prince Edward Island; Dec.–Jan. records from n. New Brunswick although none apparently surviving through winter; two Dec. records (collected, sighting) in Nova Scotia.

Movements.—Northern populations disperse and migrate. This is seen by increasingly large numbers in recent years at hawkwatch sites in New Jersey and Pennsylvania. Southern populations may engage in some localized dispersal. Black Vultures are not tallied at many southern hawkwatch sites because of the difficulty in separating large local populations from actual migrants. Lengths of seasonal movements are unknown. Many southern populations and some northern individuals are sedentary.

Fall migration/dispersal: Sep.–Nov. with a peak from mid-Oct. to early Nov.

Spring migration/dispersal: Not well known but appears to be Mar.–Apr.

Extralimital movements.—Wide-ranging northward dispersal has been an annual occurrence in various parts of the East since the 1980s but was irregular previous to this. Dispersal occurs Apr.–Oct. but may extend into Nov. and even Dec. and Jan.

Regular, annual dispersal (purple dashed line on map) along coastal Maine; coastal New Brunswick, including the very northern part of province; n. Gaspé Peninsula to Sainte-Madeleine-de-la-Riviere-Madeleine and rarely along St. Lawrence River to Saint-Andre-de-Kamouraska, Qué.; occasionally Prince Edward Island; rarely n. and e. Nova Scotia. Regularly disperses in Ohio north of mapped areas to south shore of Lake Erie.

Fairly regular dispersal is noted to south shores of e. Great Lakes; irregular to north shores of Lakes Erie and Ontario and to cen. and w. Great Lakes. *Indiana:* Casual in spring and summer in northern two-thirds of state; there are records for Marshall Co. *New York:* Nearly annual along south shore of Lake Ontario in spring, especially in Monroe Co. Sightings have occurred for the St. Lawrence River valley, Jefferson Co., with the most recent record in early Sep. 2000. *Ontario:* (1) First recorded in late Jul. 1947 north of Niagara Falls; (2) Cayuga, Haldimand-Norfolk Co., in late Aug. 1974; (3) Kingsville, Essex Co., in mid-Sep. 1979; (4) Point Pelee N.P. in mid-Aug. 1981; (5) Lambton Co. in late Jul. 1982; (6) Long Point Prov. Pk. for 2 days in mid-Feb. 1984; (7) Point Pelee N.P. in late Mar. 1984; (8) Walsingham, Haldimand-Norfolk Co., for two days in early Jul. 1986; (9) Aldershot, Halton Co., for 9 days from late Dec. to early Jan. 1987–1988; (10) Port Hope, Northumberland Co., in mid-Feb. 1991; (11) Point Pelee N.P. for 2 days in late Apr. 1991; (12) Holiday Beach Conservation Area, Essex Co. in late Oct. 1991; (13) Long Point Prov. Pk. in mid-Apr. 1992; (14) Grimsby, Niagara Co., in early Apr. 1992; (15) Long Point Prov. Pk. in early Oct. 1993; (16) Fifty Point Conservation Area, Hamilton-Wentworth Co., in late May 1994; (17) Pierre Lake Camp 34, Cochrane Co., from mid-Aug. to early Sep. 1994; (18) Prince Edward Point, Prince Edward Co., for 2 days in late May 1997; (19) Harrow, Essex Co., in early Apr. 1998; (20) Willowdale, Toronto Co., in mid-Apr. 1998; (21) Richmond Hill, York Co., in mid-Sep. 1998; (22) Caledonia, Haldimand-Norfolk Co., for 3 days in early Nov. 1998; (23) Kendal, Durham Co., and Wesleyville, Northumberland Co., in late Apr. and early May 1999 (considered one bird); (24) Point Pelee N.P. for 2 days in late Apr. 1999; (25) Long Point Prov. Pk. for 2 days in mid- to late May 1999; (26) Ancaster, Hamilton-Wentworth Co., in early Nov. 1999. Additionally, there are at least four recent probable records: (1) Long Point Prov. Pk. in early Jun. 2000, (2) Bruce Peninsula in the Lake Huron-Georgian Bay area in early Jul. 2000, (3) Point Pelee N.P. in late Jul. 2000; and (4) Rondeau Prov. Pk. in mid-May 2001. *Michigan:* (1) Berrien Co. in early Apr. 1972; (2) Leelanau Co. in late May 1974; (3) Chippewa Co. in early Jul. 1984; (4) Barry Co. in late Apr. 1995; (5) Emmet Co. in early Apr. 1997; (6) Keweenaw Co. in early Sep. 1999; (7) Chippewa Co. in late Oct. 1999; (8) Grand Traverse Co. in early Dec. 1999; (9) Wayne Co. in early Mar. 2000. *Wisconsin:* Five records, the first in Rock Co. in 1925. Most recent record is from Sheboygan Co. for 10 days in mid- to late Nov. 1996. *Vermont:* Rare inland at this latitude. A single bird was seen in Chittenden Co. in early Sep. 2000.

NESTING: Jan.–Aug.

Courtship (flight).—*Pair-flight* and *tail-chasing* (*see* chapter 5).

Courtship (perched).—*Circle display* and *allopreening* (*see* chapter 5). Neck sacs may be inflated when courting. Pair formation may last until a mate dies.

No nest is built. Nest sites are in dark protected areas, usually on the ground under dense thickets, or in hollow logs or caves. Cavities in standing trees or abandoned buildings on lower floor levels and attics are also used. Egg-laying begins in mid-Jan. in Florida, early Feb. along the Gulf Coast, early Apr. in mid-latitudes, and late Apr. in northeastern part of range. Two eggs, rarely 1–3, incubated by both sexes for 37–41 days. Nestlings have buff-colored downy feather coat. Nestlings and fledglings are fed regurgitated food by both parents. Fledge in 75–80 days. Fledglings are first seen accompanying parents in mid- to late May in s. Florida (before Turkey Vultures are fledged).

Fledglings depend on parents an additional 56–84 days.

CONSERVATION: No measures are taken. Northward expansion is on the species' own accord.

Mortality.—Illegal shooting, ingestion of poisons at carcasses, and occasional collisions with vehicles. Natural mortality occurs at nest sites since this species is a ground nester and nests are accessible to terrestrial predators.

SIMILAR SPECIES: (1) Turkey Vulture.— PERCHED (only juveniles are confused with Black Vultures).—Grayish head is pinkish around nares. Brownish black plumage. Long primary projection beyond tertials. FLIGHT.— Remiges are uniformly pale gray on underside. Wingbeats are slow and labored. Long tail extends far beyond feet. As Black Vulture, also "dips" wings. **(2) Bald and Golden eagles immatures.**—FLIGHT.—Similar dark color, but any white in wings is on inner primaries, not tip. Very slow wingbeats.

OTHER NAMES: BV. *Spanish:* Zopilote Negro. *French:* Urubu noir.

REFERENCES: AOU 1997, 1998; Bohlen 1989; Brauning 1992; Bylan 1998, 1999; Castrale et al. 1998; Clark and Wheeler 2001; Dodge 1988–1997; Ellison and Martin 2000; Godfrey 1986; Griffiths 1994; Howell and Webb 1995; Kale et al. 1992; Kaufman 1996; Kirk and Mossman 1998; Levine 1998; McWilliams and Brauning 2000; Morrison 1996; Nicholson 1997; Palmer 1988; Palmer-Ball 1996; Peterjohn and Rice 1991; Ridout 1998; Robbins 1991; Seibold and Helbig 1995; Sullivan 1996; Veit and Petersen 1993; Walsh et al. 1999.

BLACK VULTURE, *Coragyps atratus:* Common. Expanding range north to se. NY, CT, and MA. Annual dispersal to Canadian maritime provinces. Regular along Lake Huron. Irregular to Lakes Michigan and Superior.

Plate 1. Black Vulture, adult [May] ▪ Yellow bill tip. Pale gray wrinkled skin on head and upper neck. ▪ Black plumage. White tarsi and feet. ▪ *Note:* In bright light, plumage is iridescent greenish black.

Plate 2. Black Vulture, subadult (1st prebasic molt stage) [May] ▪ Yellow bill tip. Juvenile-like black skin on head and upper neck with some adultlike pale gray wrinkles. ▪ Black plumage with a few old brownish black juvenile feathers. ▪ *Note:* Head and body changing from juvenile to adult features. Worn juvenile feathers among new black adult feathers.

Plate 3. Black Vulture, juvenile (late stage) [Nov.] ▪ Mostly yellow bill tip. Smooth black skin on head and upper neck with fuzzy brown feathers. Adultlike pale gray wrinkles on front neck. ▪ Black plumage. White tarsi and feet. ▪ *Note:* Adultlike features appear on bill and lower part of bare neck when 6–8 months old. Plumage fades to brownish black.

Plate 4. Black Vulture, juvenile (early/mid-stages) [May] ▪ Black bill tip. Smooth black skin on head and upper neck with fuzzy brown feathers. ▪ Black plumage. White tarsi and feet. ▪ *Note:* Recently fledged birds have wispy, buff-colored feathers on top of neck feathers and head. Downy neck feathers are lost soon after fledging.

Plate 5. Black Vulture, adult [Feb.] ▪ Gray head. ▪ Large white panel on tip of broad, black underwings. ▪ Short black tail. ▪ *Note:* White panel is on outer 6 primaries. Soaring and banking birds fan tails widely.

Plate 6. Black Vulture, juvenile [Nov.] ▪ Black head. ▪ Large white panel on tip of broad, black underwings. ▪ Short black tail. ▪ *Note:* Juveniles similar to adults but have darker heads, neater plumages. Gliding birds close tails.

Plate 7. Black Vulture, adult [Feb.] ▪ Gray head with yellow bill tip. ▪ Large white panel on tip of upper wings.

TURKEY VULTURE
(Cathartes aura)

AGES: Adult, subadult, and juvenile. Adult characters are probably attained by the end of the second year. Subadult is a transitional stage that occurs during the second year. It acquires full adult plumage and gradually loses juvenile traits on the head and bill. Juvenile plumage is worn the first year. However, there is a gradual but noticeable change to more adultlike head and bill coloration that begins when about 6–8 months old.

MOLT: Cathartidae wing and tail molt pattern, which is identical to large raptors of accipitridae; see chapter 4 (molt data based in part on Palmer 1988). First prebasic molt begins on the innermost primary, lower neck feathers, and back. Much of the neck molts prior to molt on other body regions. Molt can be detected on some southern-latitude-hatched juveniles in Nov. (s. Florida) and on mid- and northern-latitude birds in early spring (head and bill color also slowly changes to more adultlike character at this time; see Juvenile Traits). Several primaries are replaced prior to the start of molt on the secondaries. By May, southern birds may have molted over half their primaries. Rectrix molt begins after remix molt is well under way.

Subsequent prebasic molts on remiges and rectrices may occur during any month of the year, but only a minimal amount of molt occurs in winter months (Kirk and Mossman 1998). Remix molt is often serially descendent, with two or three molt centers molting at the same time along various molt waves. This molt strategy is typical of large birds that cannot replace all flight feathers in 1 year. Up to the inner five primaries (p1–5) may be new and molted by May on mid- and northern-latitude adults. Body molt is complete in the first prebasic molt and probably fairly complete in subsequent molts.

SUBSPECIES: Polytypic with three races inhabiting North America, but only one is found in the East. C. a. septentrionalis is found throughout much of the e. U.S. (except interior Maine), in s. Ontario and Québec, and in portions of coastal New Brunswick and Nova Scotia. In the West, it extends its range to Minnesota, Iowa, e. Nebraska, Kansas, Oklahoma, and e. Texas. Nominate C. a. aura breeds in Arizona, s. Nevada, N. Mexico, s. Texas, south to Costa Rica, and on the Greater Antilles. It winters from Mexico south to Panama. C. a. meridionalis breeds in areas north of aura and west of septentrionalis in the West. It winters from the southern portion of its breeding range south to s. Brazil and Paraguay.

Meridionalis averages larger than aura but smaller than septentrionalis; however, there is considerable overlap. Some taxonomists consider meridionalis as part of aura. The distinction between the races is minor at best and is complicated by intergrading where their ranges meet. The two subspecies are inseparable in the field. Often, the only difference between meridionalis and aura is the length of in-hand-measured wing bones (Rea 1998).

Three additional subspecies reside from Central America to s. South America: (1) C. a. ruficollis inhabits the lowlands from s. Costa Rica to n. Argentina, including areas east of the Andes in South America; (2) C. a. jota is in the highlands of cen. and s. Colombia and south to s. Argentina; and (3) C. a. falklandica is found in the Pacific Coast region from Ecuador south to s. Chile, including the Falkland Islands.

COLOR MORPHS: None.

SIZE: A large raptorlike bird. Males average slightly larger than females, but sexes are not distinguishable in the field. The resident s. Florida population averages smaller than northern birds. Length: 24–28 in. (61–71 cm); wingspan: 63–71 in. (160–180 cm).

SPECIES TRAITS: HEAD.—Bare skin on the head and upper neck. Neck skin can be distended or retracted depending on temperature and mood. Bare skin area of upper neck is long when distended but concealed by the lower neck (ruff) feathers when retracted. Nape skin is smooth when the upper neck skin is distended but is wrinkled when retracted. BODY.—Blackish plumage. **Tarsi are reddish but often variably pinkish or whitish from urohydrosis: (1) only the upper front portion of the tarsi is reddish and rest of tarsi and feet are white, (2) all of tarsi are reddish and only feet are white, or (3) all of tarsi and feet are**

clean and reddish (mainly after being cleansed by walking in moist areas). Bare-skinned crop becomes distended after extensive feeding. In flight, the toes extend to the rear border of the undertail coverts. WINGS.—**In flight, wings are long with nearly parallel front and trailing edges. There are six distinct "fingers" on the outer primaries. Underside of remiges is uniformly pale gray and contrasts sharply with the dark gray greater coverts and blackish brown underwing coverts.** Upperwing coverts have broad, pale brownish edges. The primaries have yellowish white quills on both the ventral and dorsal surfaces. Long primary projection beyond the tertials when perched. TAIL.—**Fairly long and wedge-shaped. The outer rectrices are sequentially shorter than the deck set. Ventral surface is uniformly gray and darker than the remiges.** *Note:* Turkey Vultures regularly have white excrement splattered on dorsal areas of the body. Since this species often roosts communally (*see* Habits), higher perched birds often excrete onto lower perched birds.

ADULT TRAITS: HEAD.—**Yellowish white (ivory) bill. Medium or bright red head with a purplish hindneck.** There is minimal variation on the amount of white tubercles on the lores and under the eyes in *septentrionalis*. Crown, nape, and hindneck are variably covered with black hairlike feathers: some birds are sparsely covered, others quite fuzzy. **Lower neck is covered with glossy greenish, bluish, and purplish iridescent black feathers.** *Note on tubercles.*—(1) *Very extensive tubercles:* White bumps on the lores and below the eyes, extending above the eyes as a white patch on the crown. There may be some small black hairlike feather tufts among the lore tubercles. Uncommon type in the East. (2) *Extensive tubercles:* Large cluster of white bumps on the lores and under the eyes. A few black hairlike tufts may grow between the white bumps. Virtually all *septentrionalis* have this type of tubercle growth. (3) *Moderate tubercles:* Small linear group of small white bumps on the lores and under the eyes. A moderate amount of black hairlike feathers on the lores surrounding the tubercles. A few *septentrionalis* have this lesser amount of tubercles. (4) *No tubercles:* Lores have a large black hairlike feather patch and lack white tubercle bumps; no tubercles under the eyes.

Septentrionalis rarely lacks tubercles. BODY.—**Blackish brown and highly iridescent on freshly molted feathers on the back and scapulars.** Scapular feathers are broadly edged with pale brown and appear more brownish than the back, particularly on the black lower neck region. Non-iridescent, blackish brown breast, belly, flanks, leg feathers, and undertail coverts. Brownish breast and belly contrast sharply with the black iridescent lower neck. Crop skin is dark pink. WINGS (dorsal).—Wing coverts are blackish and highly iridescent when newly molted and broadly edged with pale brown; become less iridescent and more brownish with wearing and fading. Secondaries and tertials are narrowly edged with pale brown. In fresh plumage, new secondaries are also partially iridescent. WINGS (ventral).—Remiges are uniformly pale gray. TAIL.—Brownish black on the dorsal surface and medium gray on the ventral surface.

BASIC (SUBADULT) TRAITS (LATE STAGE): HEAD.—**Small dusky area on tip of white (ivory) bill on the upper mandible; the lower mandible is white.** The dusky bill tip probably gradually disappears during the second year; it is the remnant dark area of the largely dark bill of the juvenile age class (*see* Juvenile Traits). **Head gradually acquires the bright red as on adults.** White tubercles are partially or fully formed on individuals that posses them when adults. Lower neck feathers are glossy iridescent black as on adults. BODY, WINGS, and TAIL.—As on adults. *Note:* This age class constitutes birds that are 1.5 to 2 years old that have lost most juvenile bill markings and gained full or nearly full adult head features and full adult plumage.

BASIC (SUBADULT) TRAITS (EARLY STAGE): This is basically a late-stage juvenile that has begun to show adult feathering on the neck and exhibits some wing molt. As bill and head color continues to change and molt continues, it gradually turns into a late-stage subadult. HEAD.—**Dark tip on the distal area of the bill is reduced to less than one-half or one-third of the upper mandible; the lower mandible is white. Medium or dark pink head gradually turns more reddish but still retains a varying amount of fuzzy juvenile feathering on the nape and hindneck.** Lower neck molts into iridescent black feathering as on adults. BODY.—

Faded brownish body contrasts with the new dark black lower neck feathers. Additional molt produces the darker adult plumage, with broad pale brown edges on all feathers (but still retains the darker black neck). The crop is pale grayish or grayish pink. *Note:* This is the transitional molt stage and change in head features from juvenile to subadult that occurs late in the first year and into the early part of the second year.

JUVENILE TRAITS (LATE STAGE): HEAD.—**Bill is blackish or dark brownish on the distal half and whitish on the basal half of both mandibles. Head is uniformly medium pink with the retained early-stage thick growth of a grayish brown downy feather coat on the crown, nape, and hindneck.** *Note:* There is a gradual transition from early-stage head coloration to late stage (*see below*). Lower neck feathers are blackish brown with little or no iridescent quality. BODY.—Much of the iridescence on the back and scapulars wears off and the plumage appears more brownish and not as blackish as in early stage. All of the body, including lower neck, is uniformly blackish brown. The crop is pale grayish. WINGS.—The narrow white edgings on the greater, median, and first row of lesser upperwing coverts of early stage have worn off, but the neat, same-age, pale brown edged appearance on the upperwing coverts is retained. Underside of the remiges fades to pale gray and is similar to the color of adults. TAIL.—Underside fades to medium gray. *Note:* This age distinction pertains to birds generally older than 6–8 months, when noticeable color change of head and bill is occurring.

JUVENILE TRAITS (EARLY STAGE): HEAD.—**Bill is blackish on the distal two-thirds and whitish on the basal third on both mandibles. Naris opening and distal half of lower mandible are pale pink or pale pinkish gray and gradually turn medium pink with increasing age. The rest of head is smooth-skinned and medium gray. Crown, nape, and hindneck are covered with thick, fuzzy, grayish brown downy feathers. The lores have a blackish hairlike feather patch. A pinkish color gradually develops around the eyes and ear with increasing age. Lower neck feathers are brownish black, with only a minimal or moderate amount of iridescent quality.** *Note:*

Recently fledged birds exhibit remnant, wispy white downy feathers on the top area of the lower neck feathers, nape, and crown. BODY.—Uniformly brownish black, including the lower neck, with neat, pale brown edges on all back and scapular feathers. Feathers have only a minimal or moderate amount of greenish, bluish, or purplish iridescent quality. The ventral areas of body are non-iridescent brownish black. WINGS (dorsal).—All coverts are neatly edged with pale brown. Greater, median, and first row of lesser coverts have thin white edges. WINGS (ventral).—**Remiges are medium pale gray but, being same age and new, are slightly darker than irregular-aged adult remiges.** TAIL.—Medium dark gray on ventral surface and also slightly darker than on adults. *Note:* This age distinction is from fledging to about 6–8 months. *Additional Note:* In southern wintering areas, particularly Florida, classic examples of both early- and late-stage juvenile head and plumage features can be seen, often in the same communal group. This is because early-nesting southern populations are more advanced in head-color transition and feather wear than late-nesting northern populations wintering in southern latitudes.

ABNORMAL PLUMAGES: Although rare, various degrees of albinism are more common in Turkey Vultures than in any other raptorlike species except Red-tailed Hawks (Clark and Wheeler 2001; Kirk and Mossman 1998; BKW pers. obs.). Numerous records exist of all-white birds. Incomplete or partial albinos, with scattered white feathers, are reported regularly. Imperfect albinos are also fairly regular: head can be the normal red, but irises may be whitish or bluish; body feathers may be a moderate dark brownish with very pale edgings; remiges and rectrices are often tan or whitish. *Note:* An imperfect albino is depicted on plate 23; other types are not shown.

HABITAT: Summer.—Inhabits a vast array of geographic and topographic regions. Range varies from subtropical to northern temperate zones. All regions in the East encompass moderately humid or humid climates. Inhabited areas vary from remote, densely wooded or semi-open regions, to rural and agricultural locales. Topography can be flat, hilly, or mountainous. All areas may have dense undergrowth, rocky outcrops, or cliffs for suitable nest sites.

Winter.—Habitat can be similar to summer areas, but there is no requirement for dense vegetation, rock slides, or cliffs. Turkey Vultures are found in rural and agricultural regions more than during the breeding season; also on islands and mainland seashores. Geographic regions are lower temperate to subtropical and generally at elevations and latitudes south of regular snowfall.

Migration.—Similar to summer and winter habitat.

HABITS: Tame to fairly tame in the South, especially in Florida, but quite wary at northern latitudes. Very wary when feeding. Solitary in breeding season. Solitary or gregarious in other seasons. Night roosts may number in the hundreds or, at southern latitudes, in the thousands. Where ranges overlap, roosts with Black Vultures. Exposed branches, buildings, utility poles (but not wires), towers, and other elevated structures are used for perches. Also quite a terrestrial species.

In cool or cold temperatures, the feathered part of lower neck can be raised to cover the bare neck skin of the upper neck and nape. Sunning occurs regularly, especially in mornings prior to the first flight and after rain. Body temperature is regulated by urohydrosis. Vultures commonly sit upright on their haunches (heels) or lie down when perched on a thick branch or on the ground.

FEEDING: An aerial scavenger. Carrion is detected by sight or smell. Has a highly developed olfactory system and is the only North American vulture species that can smell. Fresh carrion is preferred, but if a fresh source is not available decaying meat is eaten. Vegetable matter is rarely eaten, but will eat decaying pumpkins. Feeds on a variety of carrion, from small to large mammals, birds, reptiles, amphibians, and stranded fish. Turkey Vultures are more likely to feed on smaller carrion than Black Vultures. Carrion is approached warily. Vultures land far away from it, then timidly walk up to feed, but are always poised to fly if danger arises. Small prey objects may be carried for short distances in the bill. Open-pit garbage dumps are common feeding areas. Turkey Vultures are submissive to the smaller, more aggressive, and dominant Black Vulture. Turkey Vultures rarely kill small prey.

FLIGHT: A highly aerial species. Wings are held in a high dihedral when soaring and in a high or modified dihedral when gliding. In moderate or strong winds, the energy-efficient back-and-forth rocking motion is the most common flight mode. Flight is steady in calm winds. Powered flight is used to gain altitude quickly in inclement weather or to launch into flight. Flight may be at low altitudes, barely skimming the ground or treetops, or, particularly when migrating, at very high altitudes. Turkey Vultures do not hover or kite. Wings are frequently "dipped" when flying to maintain speed and stability. On windy days, migrants may begin daily flights before dawn.

VOICE: Technically voiceless, but grunts and hisses when agitated.

STATUS AND DISTRIBUTION: *Very common.* Probably the most common raptor-type bird. Fall counts at hawkwatch sites in Veracruz, Mexico, tally extraordinary numbers: 1.7 million in 1998, 1.5 million in 1999, 1.8 million in 2000, 2 million in 2001, and 2.6 million in 2002. Most of these migrants are from the West, but some are from western populations of the East. Estimated total population for North America probably exceeds 3 million birds. A few migration locations tally large numbers. Over 30,000 vultures, all coming from e. Ontario and w. Québec, are counted annually in the fall at Lake Erie Metro Park in Wayne Co., Mich.

Summer.—Since the 1970s, Turkey Vultures have rapidly expanded their range into s. Canada. Expansion is possibly due to increased numbers of White-tailed Deer. Natural mortality, road kills, and hunting produce increased deer carrion for vultures. The increase in vulture numbers may also be attributed to reduced mortality from shooting, trapping, and poisoning. *Ontario:* Extensive range expansion in all areas as seen by the large number of fall migrants that pass from s. Ontario into se. Michigan. Range is extending northward, particularly in the western part of province. *Québec:* Regular summer sightings north of Rimouski, but breeding is not yet confirmed along this area of the St. Lawrence River Valley. *New Brunswick:* First breeding occurred in 1998 at St. John. Regular in summer along the southern coast and occasionally as far north as the Lavillette region. *Nova Scotia:* A common year-round resident in a few western areas. However, nesting has not been confirmed. Found primarily from Wolfville south to Digby and southward along Digby Neck to Brier Island. Also found in summer eastward to the Annapolis Valley. Irregular in summer on the eastern side of province to Bridgewater and occasionally elsewhere.

Common in the e. U.S. in summer. Prior to range extending into Canada, northernmost breeding range in the East extended to Camden, Maine, where breeding first occurred in 1982.

C. a. aura is typically found in the sw. U.S. and southward to Central America, but also inhabits various Caribbean islands. It is a permanent resident on the Bahama Islands (Grand Bahama, Great Abaco, Andros), Cuba, Jamaica, Isla de la Juventud, Hispaniola, and sw. Puerto Rico. *C. a. aura* was introduced on some of these islands.

Winter.—Turkey Vultures withdraw from the northern half of breeding range. In order to locate food, most winter south of major snow regions. Most eastern birds winter in the s. U.S. Birds from western regions of the East may winter as far south as Central America (a juvenile banded in Wisconsin migrated to Belize). Large roosts form in southern states, particularly Florida. The highest Christmas Bird Counts of Turkey Vultures in the U.S. are tallied in Florida.

A few regularly winter on Brier Island, N.S. An occasional bird winters at Yarmouth, N.S., and rarely to Glace Bay, N.S. (adult in Jan.). Extralimital birds were in Washtenaw Co., Mich., in the winters of 1999–2000 and 2000–2001.

Movements.—Northern populations are quite migratory. Birds in the s. U.S. migrate short distances or are sedentary. Northern populations leapfrog southern populations.

Fall migration: In the Lake Erie region, movement begins in mid- to late Aug. and abruptly ends in mid-Nov. Stragglers continue moving until late Nov. Peak migration period is in mid-Oct. In the Mid-Atlantic region, migration begins in late Aug. with fairly large numbers moving until late Dec. and with a peak in early to mid-Nov. All ages migrate simultaneously. Thousands of birds are still migrating into s. Florida in early to mid-Dec. Large numbers move up and down the Keys throughout fall and winter.

Spring migration: In the Mid-Atlantic region, extends from early Feb. to mid-Jun. with a peak in mid-Mar. In the Lake Ontario region, extends from early Mar. to late May and peaks from late Mar. to early Apr., with stragglers continuing into Jun. Breeding adults precede juveniles and probably nonbreeding adults. Late season migrants are mainly 1-year-olds.

Extralimital movements.—Reported as far north as Fort Severn and Moose Factory in n. Ontario. In Québec, occurs annually and possibly breeds along the St. Lawrence River. Range extends along the river just north of Rimouski. Fairly regular in e. Nova Scotia, from e. Cape Breton Island in the north to Cape Sable in the south. Single birds have occurred in Glace Bay, N. S., in Jan., May, Aug., Sep., and Oct.

NESTING: Begins in Feb. in southern latitudes and Apr.–May in northern regions. Nesting activities are completed May–Sep., depending on latitude. Pairs remain mated as long as a mate survives. Age of first breeding is unknown but probably not until a few years old.

Courtship (flight).—*Follow-flight*, which may include stints of *tail-chasing*, may last as long as 3 hours.

Courtship (perched).—*Circle display* with inflated throat and neck sacs. Birds may utter low-pitched groaning sounds.

No nest is built. Eggs are laid on the ground with no preparation of the ground surface at the nest site. Dark protected areas away from human disturbance are sought for nest sites. Primary sites are in rocky outcrops with caves or crevices, under rock ledges or fallen stumps, in hollow stumps, under thick brush piles or dense undergrowths, on the floor of abandoned buildings, and rarely in elevated nests of other large birds. Nest sites are often in dense woodlands. Sites may be used annually for several years. Two eggs, rarely 1–3, are incubated by both sexes for 38–40 days. Youngsters fledge in about 77 days but depend on parents for several more weeks. Nestlings are fed regurgitated, digested foods by both parents. Nestlings are covered with white downy feathers.

CONSERVATION: No measures taken. A stable, adaptive, and thriving species.

Mortality.—Illegal shooting, lead poisoning from ingested bullet fragments and shot pellets in carcasses of game mammals and birds not retrieved by hunters, ingested poisons slated

TURKEY VULTURE, *Cathartes aura:* Very common. Expanding breeding range northward in Canada. Regular in summer in QC along St. Lawrence River and coastal NB and NS. Breeding confirmed at Saint John, NB.

for varmints, collisions with power lines and vehicles, and electrocution on utility poles.

SIMILAR SPECIES: (1) Black Vulture.— PERCHED (confused only with juvenile Turkey Vultures).—Adults have pale or medium gray and very wrinkled, fleshy heads. Juveniles have smooth black head and upper neck. Tarsi may be a similar whitish but are never pinkish. Primary projection is short. FLIGHT.—White panels on the outer primaries. White toes extend to the tail tip. Short, square black tail. **(2) Rough-legged Hawk, dark morph juveniles.**—FLIGHT.—Undersides of remiges and rectrices can appear uniformly pale with a two-toned effect; however, the trailing edge has a dusky band. **(3) Golden Eagle.**—PERCHED.—Yellow cere. Pale tawny nape. FLIGHT (ages/individuals with all-dark underwings).—Adults and subadults have a fairly distinct dark trailing edge on the underside of the remiges. Underwings of juveniles are a similar uniform medium gray and also two-toned. Both species have six "fingers" on the outer primaries and a wedge-shaped tail. Head and bill are moderately large on eagles. Eagles may rock back and forth in strong winds but are not as tipsy as most vultures. Trailing edge of wing bows discernibly outward. Dihedral of wing attitude is not as pronounced.

OTHER NAMES: TV. *Spanish:* Aura Cabecirroja, Zopilote Aura. *French:* Urubu à Tête Rouge.

REFERENCES: AOU 1997; Baicich and Harrison 1997; Bohlen 1989; Brauning 1992; Brewer et al. 1991; Bylan 1998, 1999; Cadman et al. 1987; Clark and Wheeler 2001; Dodge 1988–1997; Erskine 1992; Granlund 2001; Griffiths 1994; Howell and Webb 1995; Kale et al. 1992; Kellogg 2000; Kirk and Mossman 1998; Nicholson 1997; Palmer 1988; Palmer-Ball 1996; Peterjohn and Rice 1991; Rea 1998; Seibold and Helbig 1995; Veit and Petersen 1993; Walsh et al. 1999; Wheeler and Clark 1995.

Plate 8. Turkey Vulture, adult (very extensive tubercle type) [May] ▪ White bill. Bare red head and upper neck; white tubercles around eyes and on crown. ▪ Glossy black neck feathers. ▪ Distinct pale edges on brownish black wings. ▪ *Note:* Most extensive amount of white tubercles that may adorn adults.

Plate 9. Turkey Vulture, adult (extensive tubercle type) [Feb.] ▪ White bill. Bare red head and upper neck; large cluster of white tubercles in front of and below eyes. ▪ Glossy black neck feathers. ▪ Distinct pale edges on brownish black wings. ▪ Reddish tarsi. ▪ *Note:* Average amount of white tubercles.

Plate 11. Turkey Vulture, adult [Dec.] ▪ Sunning posture: wings spread with back facing sun. Common posture in morning and after rain.

Plate 10. Turkey Vulture, adult (moderate tubercle type) [Jun.] ▪ White bill. Bare red head and upper neck; small cluster of white tubercles in front of and below eyes. ▪ Glossy black neck feathers. ▪ Distinct pale edges on brownish black wings. ▪ Mostly white tarsi. ▪ *Note:* Excrement splattered on back.

Plate 12. Turkey Vulture, adult [Dec.] ▪ White bill. Bare red head. ▪ Uniformly pale gray remiges contrast with black underwing coverts and body. ▪ Uniformly medium gray tail.

Plate 13. Turkey Vulture, adult [Dec.] ▪ White bill. Bare red head. ▪ Brownish upperwing coverts.

Plate 14. Turkey Vulture, adult [Dec.] ▪ Wings held in high dihedral when gliding and soaring.

Plate 15. Turkey Vulture, subadult (late stage) [Dec.] ▪ White bill with dark tip. Bare red head and neck. ▪ Glossy black neck feathers. ▪ Distinct pale edges on brownish black wings. ▪ *Note:* Identical to adult except bill tip darker.

Plate 16. Turkey Vulture, subadult (early stage) [Dec.] ▪ White bill with dark tip. Bare pink head. ▪ Black adult feathers growing on neck and back. Brownish plumage. ▪ Molting (missing) inner two primaries (p1 and 2). ▪ *Note:* As on late-stage juvenile except molting adult feathers. Much of body and wings molts before head color changes to more adultlike character.

Plate 17. Turkey Vulture, subadult (early stage) [Dec.] ▪ White bill with dark tip. Bare pink head. ▪ Brownish black plumage with new black adult feathers on neck. ▪ Uniformly pale gray remiges. Molting (missing) inner two primaries (p1 and 2).

Plate 18. Turkey Vulture, subadult (early stage)
[**Dec.**] ▪ Engaging in "wing dip" motion. ▪ *Note:* Wings are often dipped in downward motion when gliding to maintain speed and stability.

Plate 19. Turkey Vulture, juvenile (late stage)
[**Dec.**] ▪ Outer half of bill dark, inner half white. Medium pink head and neck; crown and hindneck covered with fuzzy brown downy feathers. ▪ Uniformly brownish black plumage. ▪ *Note:* 6–8 months old with pinkish head; plumage is full juvenile, but white tips on upperwing coverts have worn off.

Plate 20. Turkey Vulture, juvenile (early stage)
[**Dec.**] ▪ Outer 2/3 of bill dark, inner 1/3 white. Pale pinkish gray head with fuzzy brown downy feathers. ▪ Uniformly brownish black plumage with narrow white tips on wing coverts. ▪ *Note:* This bird is younger than bird on plate 19 but older than bird on plate 21.

Plate 21. Turkey Vulture, juvenile (early stage)
[**Aug.**] ▪ Outer 2/3 of bill dark, inner 1/3 white. Gray fuzzy downy feathers on head with pale pink around nares and outer half of lower mandible. ▪ Uniformly brownish black plumage with narrow white tips on wing coverts. ▪ *Note:* Recently fledged and about 4 months old.

Plate 22. Turkey Vulture, juvenile (early stage) [Oct.] ▪ Dark bill and gray head. ▪ Brownish black plumage. ▪ Uniformly medium gray remiges contrast with dark underwing coverts. ▪ *Note:* Underside of remiges darker than on older birds.

Plate 23. Turkey Vulture, adult (imperfect albino) [Aug.] ▪ White bill, reddish head, pale iris. ▪ Blackish neck feathers. Washed out color on rest of body. ▪ *Note:* Turkey Vultures rarely exhibit albinism.

OSPREY
(Pandion haliaetus)

AGES: Adult and juvenile. Sexes of both ages are somewhat dimorphic in the amount of breast markings, but there is overlap. Those breeding in northern latitudes tend to be more extensively marked on the head and breast than southern birds (Palmer 1988). Except for minor variation on breast markings, there are virtually no other plumage variations in either age group.

Substantial feather wear occurs on the dorsal feathers of juveniles by mid-fall. By late Oct., the white scalloped dorsal feather edgings may be virtually worn off on some individuals. Juvenile iris color gradually changes to more adultlike color by autumn.

MOLT: Pandioninae wing and tail molt pattern. The first prebasic molt on the primaries begins in the winter when juveniles are about 6 months old (Forsman 1999). Outermost primary (p10), which becomes excessively worn, is retained for nearly 2 years (Edelstam 1984). Serially descendant molt waves replace inner primaries at least two times before p10 is replaced for the first time. Molt on the secondaries begins 1–3 months after primaries have begun molting (Forsman 1999). Rectrix molt also begins after primaries have been molting for some time. There are no data on body molt.

Subsequent prebasic remix molt of adults is fairly continuous except during periods of migration and, for males, during the breeding season, when molt generally ceases. Remiges may have two to four molt waves in progress at the same time (Forsman 1999). Body feathers may be replaced annually since the plumage of many adults can be nearly uniformly worn and faded.

SUBSPECIES: Polytypic. One primary race, *P. h. carolinensis*, is in the U.S. and Canada. This race inhabits the contiguous U.S. south to the Florida Keys; portions of coastal Baja California and coastal Sonora, Mexico; and the boreal forest of Alaska and Canada.

"Ridgway's" race, *P. h. ridgwayi*, is resident mainly in the Caribbean region. *P. h. Ridgwayi* or intergrades with *carolinensis* can also be found in very small numbers among the more numerous *carolinensis* in s. Florida, particularly on the Keys (Palmer 1988; BKW pers. obs. and photographs on Big Pine Key).

Plumage data on *ridgwayi* are based on specimens (*n* = 3) from the Bahamas and Belize, loaned by the Museum of Natural Science, LSU, and del Hoyo et al. (1994).

Subspecies elsewhere in the world: (1) Nominate *P. h. haliaetus*, which is fairly similar in plumage to *carolinensis*, but is more consistently darker and more heavily marked. It breeds across Eurasia, Japan, Taiwan, and the Canary and Cape Verde Islands. *Haliaetus* winters to s. Africa, India, w. Indonesia, and the Philippines. (2) *P. h. cristatus* is resident in Australia, east to New Caledonia, north to New Guinea and the Philippines, and west to Sumatra. This small race lacks dark crown and nape markings and the dark auricular mark is small and does not connect to the hindneck. Breast markings may be present on both sexes, but are often more prevalent on females. Plumage data are based on photographs in Olsen (1998) and Debus (1998).

COLOR MORPHS: None.

SIZE: A large raptor. Males average somewhat smaller than females. *Ridgwayi* is a bit smaller than *carolinensis*. Length: 20–25 in. (51–64 cm); wingspan: 59–67 in. (150–170 cm).

SPECIES TRAITS: HEAD.—Black bill except the basal part of the lower mandible, which is pale blue. Pale blue cere. Black lores with a black crescent above the eyes. **Black auricular stripe extends onto the side of the head and connects to the brown hindneck.** Long, bushy nape feathers (hackles) can be compressed or erected at will. Small black spot on the central crown may connect with the black crescent over the eyes. Small black triangular-shaped mark on the top rear area of the hackles. BODY.—Dark brown upperparts. White underparts. Variably marked breast: (1) unmarked (most males, very few females), (2) moderately marked (some males, many females), (3) heavily marked (very few males, most females). Legs are long and the tarsi are pale bluish gray. Rear area of the tarsi and toes are covered with short, sharp spicules for grasping slippery fish. WINGS.—Long, fairly narrow with parallel front and trailing edges. Wingtips are rounded. **A large black rectangular patch is on the carpal region of the under-**

wing. The black carpal patch merges with the black secondary greater underwing coverts, which form a diagonal to the body. Inner primaries are whitish, barred, and form a whitish panel against the darker gray secondaries. Perched birds exhibit a white linear stripe from the wrist and shoulder area to the elbow along the inner edge of the patagial region. Wingtips of perched birds extend far beyond the tail tip. TAIL.—Brown on the dorsal surface and white on the ventral surface and banded with black.

ADULT TRAITS (P. h. carolinensis): HEAD.—Top of the head is white except for the black crown and top-of-nape spot. Iris color is medium yellow, but varies in being either a cool yellow or slightly warmer and orangish. BODY.—All dorsal areas are uniformly dark brown. However, worn-plumaged birds can be medium or even pale brown, in patches or on extensive areas. WINGS (dorsal).—Uniformly dark brown upperwing. WINGS (ventral).—Underwing coverts are white. **Carpal patch on the underwing is generally solid black.** Secondaries are dark gray with narrow, pale barring on the outer feathers and solid dark gray on the inner feathers. TAIL.—White terminal band is irregularly worn and fairly narrow.

ADULTS OF "RIDGWAY'S" (P. h. ridgwayi): Data based on adult male specimens (*n* = 2) from Calabash Cay, Belize, and Grand Turk Island, Bahamas. HEAD.—White except for the small black crescent on the lores and a small projection above the front of the eyes. The crown may be all white or have a few dark streaks. The dark top-of-nape spot is present. The dark auricular patch does not connect with the dark brown hindneck as it does on *carolinensis*. BODY, WINGS, and TAIL.—Similar to *carolinensis* but paler on the underside. The male specimens lacked breast markings; females may also lack markings or have a minimal amount of markings.

JUVENILE TRAITS (P. h. carolinensis): HEAD.—Iris color is orange as nestlings, fledglings, and younger juveniles. Some retain the orangish iris color until late fall. Iris color gradually changes to more adultlike yellow. By mid-Oct., some may possess near adultlike yellow iris color. Crown is extensively streaked with black and the nape region is washed with tawny. BODY.—**Dark brown upperparts have broad white tipped feathers on all back, scapular,**

and uppertail covert feathers on old nestlings, fledglings, and younger juveniles. WINGS (dorsal).—**Dark brown with broad white tips on all covert feathers through fall as described in Body.** By Oct., white feather tips on older juveniles may show signs of wear and become narrower. By late fall or winter, much of the white tips on much older juveniles wears off and upperparts become more uniformly brown. WINGS (ventral).—**Black carpal patch is often mottled with tawny.** Dark gray secondaries have distinct whitish bands on the outer feathers and gray or indistinct pale bands on the inner feathers. Underside of the secondaries appears paler and more banded than on adults. White underwing coverts and axillaries are washed with tawny. TAIL.—Neatly formed broad white terminal band.

JUVENILES OF "RIDGWAY'S" (P. h. ridgwayi): Data based on one female specimen from Great Inagua Island, Bahamas, from early Dec. HEAD.—Similar to *ridgwayi* adults in having minimal dark head markings with very sparse dark streaking on the crown, a dark top-of-nape spot, and only an isolated dark auricular mark that does not connect to the dark hindneck. *Note:* Head is much paler than any juvenile *carolinensis*. BODY.—Upperparts as in juveniles of other subspecies in having broad, white-edged feathers on the dorsal regions in fresh plumage and narrow white edges when plumage is worn. Underparts are also similar to juveniles of other races in being washed with tawny on the underwing coverts and axillaries. The breast was immaculate white on the female specimen (nearly always marked on juvenile female *carolinensis*).

ABNORMAL PLUMAGES: A melanistic adult was in Monroe Co., Fla., from the mid- to late 1990s (Clark 1998). This bird was dark brown throughout, including the head. Undersides of the remiges were uniformly gray, but the undertail was similar to typical birds in being pale and banded.

HABITAT: Summer.—Found along fresh, brackish, or salt water areas in temperate and subtropical regions. Water areas vary from artificial impoundments, natural lakes and streams, and seashores. Readily accesses human-used waterways.

Winter.—In the U.S., mainly found in subtropical areas, but some occupy the southern temperate zone. Most winter in subtropical and tropical areas south of the U.S.

Migration.—The majority stay near waterways; however, inland migrants are often found far from water for portions of the journey. *P. h. ridgwayi* is found on saltwater islands and coastal tropical areas in all seasons.

HABITS: Individuals vary from being wary to tame. Those around human-accessed areas can be quite tame. Ospreys perch on any type of elevated structure. Basically solitary, but they may nest in loose colonies in some locations. Outer front toe can be rotated to face the rear in order to grasp fish more firmly. Bushy nape feathers are compressed in hot weather and erected in cool weather and when alarmed. Ospreys often swoop down and skim their clenched feet in water.

FEEDING: An aerial hunter. Feeds almost exclusively on live fish. Dead fish are rarely taken. Ospreys also rarely feed on other types of prey: birds (mainly small water fowl) and small amphibians and reptiles. Ospreys dive in a head-first plunge from as high as 100 ft. (30 m). Feet are lowered during the dive and extended forward of the head just upon impact with the water and fish. The Osprey may snatch the fish by skimming the water's surface in a shallow-angled dive, if the fish is very near the surface, or, more typically, dive steeply into the water and be momentarily partially submerged, then fly out of the water, grasping the fish and shaking vigorously to rid itself of water. Captured fish are immediately manipulated to point head first and belly down when being transported. Most fish are clutched with both feet when being taken to a perch. Partially eaten, small-size fish remnants and small intact fish may be transported in flight with one foot. Prey is eaten while standing on a perch.

FLIGHT: Wings held in an arched position when soaring or gliding. Wings are folded at a sharp angle at the wrist when gliding. Gliding birds create an "M"-shaped appearance with their sharply angled wings. Wings are extended in a nearly straight, perpendicular angle from the body when soaring. Powered flight is with slow, deep wingbeats with irregular gliding and flapping sequences. Ospreys regularly hover when hunting. In certain areas and wind conditions, they may momentarily kite.

VOICE: A vocal species in all seasons. Vocalizations occur between pairs, unrelated conspecifics, and towards intruders of any kind crossing into nesting territories. The most common call is a loud, sharp, high-pitched whistled *cheeurp*, either as a single note or as a long, rapid series of notes. When agitated, the *cheeurp* may be quite harsh and uttered for extended periods. A drawn-out, loud, equally high-pitched *eeeep* is emitted at various times. Highly vocal during courting activities.

STATUS AND DISTRIBUTION *(P. h. carolinensis):*
Summer.—*P. h. carolinensis* is locally *fairly common*. Estimated population in the U.S. in 1981 was 8,000 pairs; estimated population in 1994 was nearly 14,000 nesting pairs. Current status is undoubtedly considerably greater since their population is steadily growing (*see below*). Published figures do not represent the substantial number of Ospreys that nest in e. Canada (or in w. Canada and Alaska). The Osprey is still listed as a Threatened Species in several states, but is not a Federally listed species. Pennsylvania recently downlisted the Osprey from Endangered to Threatened status. In Canada, the Osprey was on the Blue List from 1972 to 1981; however, it was delisted due to a positive population recovery.

Osprey populations were greatly affected by the organochlorine era. In some states with formerly low nesting numbers, pesticide poisoning extirpated the breeding population. Populations in many eastern states, however, have mushroomed since the late 1970s due to the ban of DDT in Canada and the U.S. and the implementation of human-assisted programs to boost breeding potential. Midwestern states, which historically had low breeding populations, have naturally had a slower recovery from the very low or nonexistent breeding populations of the organochlorine era. However, Osprey reproductive complications currently exist in some areas. For reasons that are unclear, New Jersey's Atlantic coastal nesting pairs had poor reproductive success in the late 1990s. Elsewhere in bay areas along the mid-Atlantic Coast, nesting success was high during this period. Overall, pairs are expanding into formerly inhabited and newly colonized-regions.

Number of pairs per state listed below is from 1994 data from Houghton and Rymon (1997). As noted previously, the status in several states has grown; if known, approximate number of current pairs are noted in parentheses.—Alabama: 23, Connecticut: 95, Delaware: 75–85, Florida: 2,500–3,000, Georgia: 225–275, Illinois: 0 (1), Indiana: 1 (2 in 2001, but a third pair was at a nest site but not breeding), Kentucky: 16, Maine: 1,300–1,800, Maryland: 1,000–1,400, Massachusetts: 260 (283 in 1995, 350 pairs in 1999), Michigan: 223, Mississippi: 55–65 (mainly coastal, 2 pairs in north), New Hampshire: 29 (over 40), New Jersey: 200, New York: 315, North Carolina: 800–1,200 (mainly coastal), Ohio: 1 (12 in 2001), Pennsylvania: 20 (39 in 2000), Rhode Island: 44, South Carolina: 800–1,000 (mainly coastal), Tennessee: 66, Vermont: 12, Virginia: 1,300–1,500, West Virginia: 3 (at least 8 as of 1998), and Wisconsin: 391.

Two-year-olds return from wintering areas to the U.S. and Canada, but only one-quarter to one-half return to locales near their natal areas; however, they do not breed. Nearly all 3-year-olds return to areas near their original natal areas to breed. Nonbreeding individuals are sometimes recorded during the summer months in interior regions not mapped as being regular breeding range.

Winter.—*Adults:* Regular in winter along the Gulf Coast, all of Florida, and north along the Atlantic Coast to n. North Carolina. Irregular wintering occurs northward from n. North Carolina along the Atlantic Coast to Delaware. Ospreys are very irregular along the New Jersey coast in winter; there are numerous Dec. records, but only a handful of Jan. records. There are also very rare records farther north along the Atlantic Coast to Nova Scotia. Osprey also sparingly winter in inland locations across the southern half of Louisiana, Mississippi, and Alabama Northern adult breeding populations winter from the s. U.S. southward to s. Brazil, Bolivia, and Peru.

Juveniles: Winter from Cuba and Belize southward to areas in South America as described for adults, and remain on the winter grounds until the spring of their second year.

Movements.—Highly migratory except some s. Florida birds. Ospreys breeding along the East Coast and wintering on the Caribbean islands and South America take extensive over-water, island-hopping routes across the Caribbean Sea. Those breeding in the western areas of the East may (1) make a long over-water trans-

Gulf of Mexico flight, (2) adhere to a coastal route along the w. Gulf of Mexico, or (3) take a diagonal path across the U.S. to Florida and cross to the Caribbean islands and continue to South America. Recent telemetry studies have revealed numerous interesting facets concerning Osprey migration. Large numbers migrate along the Atlantic Coast; however, substantial numbers also cross inland areas in the U.S. and Canada.

The migration data described below are from preliminary telemetry studies by The Raptor Center of the University of Minnesota.

Fall migration: Adults.—Adult migration begins quite early, but is a protracted event that spans about 5 months for all the population to migrate south. Females tend to migrate before males, but some males are also early migrants. Once nesting duties are complete, some adults may disperse short distances in any direction prior to embarking on an actual southward course. Once migration has started, movement to the winter grounds is often accomplished in 1–2 months. Juveniles, some adult males, and a few adult females make up the large numbers seen at coastal autumn hawkwatch sites.

Those nesting in southern latitudes begin their migration at an earlier date than later-nesting northern birds. From Florida north to Long Island, N.Y., migration for breeding adults, particularly females, may begin as early as mid- to late Jul., especially for Florida birds, but usually does not begin until sometime in Aug. for more northern breeding adults. Migration may begin as late as early Oct. for some males. Adults may arrive on winter grounds as far south as Bolivia, South America, as early as mid-Aug. More typically, adults arrive on the winter grounds from late Aug. through Sep., and extending through Nov. Many adults, particularly females, arrive on the winter grounds in South America 2–6 weeks before peak of autumn migration occurs in the U.S.

All ages.—As noted above, fall migration is an extended affair. Hawkwatches begin counting in mid-Aug. or early Sep. and migrant Ospreys are already being seen. Large numbers of adults have already migrated prior to the start of official counting at hawkwatches. Florida juveniles appear to also migrate south by midsummer since they are not seen in early Aug. Along the w. Great Lakes, peak movements oc-

cur in mid-Sep. with migration ending by mid-Oct. Along the e. Great Lakes, peak numbers also occur in mid-Sep. and tapers off in mid-Oct., but stragglers are seen until mid-Nov. On the Mid-Atlantic Coast, large numbers are tallied in a steady, all-season passage. The peak mid-Atlantic movement is from late Sep. to early Oct., but near-peak numbers are often tallied in mid-Sep.; stragglers occur through Nov. In Veracruz, Mexico, migrants occur from late Aug. to late Nov. and peak in early Oct.

Spring migration: All ages.—Breeding adults leave the winter grounds south of the U.S. around mid-Feb. Spring hawkwatches in the U.S. begin counting in late Feb. or early Mar., and the first northward returning adults are seen along the Mid-Atlantic Coast at this time. Migration extends to at least mid-Jun. Peak of adult movement is in mid-Apr., but can be in early Apr. Nonbreeders, which are likely returning 2-year-olds, probably make up the May and Jun. contingent of migrants. Adults first return along the e. Great Lakes in late Mar. and peak in late Apr. or early May. Nonbreeders continue moving into Jun. Along the w. Great Lakes, the first arrivals are seen in mid-Apr. (rarely in early Apr.), peak in late Apr. or early May, and with stragglers occurring into Jun.

P. h. ridgwayi race is a permanent resident in the Caribbean and part of the Gulf of Mexico. Its status is unknown. Its range is limited to the Bahamas; Cuba; small islands (cays) surrounding Cuba; east to the Virgin Islands, including St. Croix I., George Dog I., and Anegada I.; and along the eastern coast of the Yucatán Peninsula in Mexico, and Belize and adjacent islands. *Rare* or very *uncommon* on the Florida Keys and possibly other s. Florida locations. Some s. Florida birds may be intergrades with *carolinensis*. This race has been documented breeding on Big Pine Key, Fla.
NESTING: Begins in late Nov. and early Dec. on the Florida Keys and as late as early Jun. in northern latitudes. Depending on latitude, fledging stage spans from Apr. on the Keys to late Aug. in northern latitudes. Ospreys do not attempt to breed until at least 3 years old. Pairs often reunite to breed each year until one dies; however, unlike eagles, most pairs do not remain together year-round. (Telemetry data

show that pairs may take far different migration routes and occupying different wintering areas.) Instances of polygyny may occur in areas of high population density.

Courtship (flight).—*High-circling* by both members of the pair and *sky-dancing* and *hover-flight* by males (*see* chapter 5). A great deal of vocalization occurs among courting birds.

Both sexes bring nesting materials. Females do most of the actual nest construction. New nests may be only a shallow layer of sticks. Nests are regularly reused, and refurbished old nests may be up to 6 ft. (2 m) deep. Nests may be placed on the ground on islands lacking terrestrial predators and human disturbance or up to 80 ft. (24 m) high in trees and on rocks. Tree nests are typically in the top-most section of trees and often in dead trees. Nests in live trees are placed in exposed upper sections. Artificial structures include buoys, metal towers, buildings, barrels, and other unusual human-made implements. Ospreys also readily accept human-made platforms erected on poles that have metal bases to prevent access by ground predators. Nests are usually placed near or over the water, but can be up to 6 miles (10 km) from water.

Both sexes incubate, although females perform the majority of the 38-day task. Males mainly provide food. Typical clutch consists of 3 eggs. Clutches sometimes have 2 eggs, but rarely have 4. A single clutch is laid per season. Nestlings fledge in 44–59 days. Fledglings are cared for by their parents until they are 93–103 days old.

CONSERVATION: Reintroduction programs.— Hacking programs to assist the Osprey's comeback were created in the following states: Alabama, Kentucky, Michigan, New Hampshire, New Jersey, New York, Ohio, Pennsylvania, Tennessee, Wisconsin, and West Virginia.

Alabama: 66 Ospreys were hacked in the northern and central part of the state from 1983 to 1988. *Kentucky:* 96 birds were hacked from 1981 to 1989. *Michigan:* The hacking program began in the late 1990s at Maple River State Game Area, Clinton Co., and at Kensington Metro Park, Livingston Co., to boost the population in the lower part of the Lower Peninsula. Hacking was still in progress in 2001. *New York:* 37 Ospreys were hacked at the

Allegheny Reservoir, Cattaraugus Co., and 31 were released at Oak Orchard Wildlife Management Area, Genesee Co., from 1980 to 1987. These released birds were taken from healthy populations on Long Island. Additionally, New York supplied young Ospreys for hacking programs in Kentucky and Ohio. *Ohio:* Hacking began in 1996 and is still in progress as of the summer of 2001. *Pennsylvania:* 265 birds were released in several areas in an intense hacking effort from 1980 to 1996. *Tennessee:* Hacked Ospreys from 1979 to the early 1980s. *Indiana:* Hacking has not been done, however, the state is contemplating a program in the future. *Wisconsin:* Hacking occurred in Muskego, Waukesha Co., in the late 1990s. *West Virginia:* The state released 41 young Osprey in a hacking program from 1984 to 1989 on the South Branch of the Potomac River, Hampshire Co.; Tygart Lake, Taylor Co.; and Blennerhasset Island, Wood Co.

Artificial nest construction programs.— Numerous states also boosted naturally existing and hacked populations by erecting artificial nesting platforms on moderate-height poles. These artificial structures not only increase nest site availability but also produce sturdy and safe nest sites. Slippery-surfaced shields are attached to the poles of the nest platforms to prevent terrestrial predators from climbing up to the platform and raiding eggs and nestlings. A substantial number of Osprey pairs in numerous states and provinces utilize artificial nest structures.

Utility poles are being retrofitted in some areas of the East to prevent both electrical problems caused by Ospreys building nests on poles and mortality of this species.

Pesticide bans.—The ban on organochlorine pesticide use, particularly DDT, greatly assisted Osprey populations to recover in the last three decades. This lethal pesticide was first used in 1946 in Canada and the U.S.

Canada took a series of steps to discontinue the sale and use of DDT that began in 1968 with a ban on spraying forests in national parks. The major Canadian ban came on Jan. 1, 1970 (announced Nov. 3, 1969), when DDT use was permitted for insecticide use on only 12 of the 62 previously sprayed food crops. However, all registration for insecticide use on food crops was stopped by 1978. Canada, however, permitted DDT use for bat control and medicinal purposes until 1985. Canadian users and distributors were also allowed to use existing supplies of DDT until Dec. 31, 1990.

The U.S. also had a series of steps to ban DDT, but halted the overall sale and use more quickly. In 1969, the USDA stopped the spraying on shade trees, tobacco crops, aquatic locations, and in-home use. The USDA placed further bans on its use on crops, commercial plants, and for building purposes in 1970. The Environmental Protection Agency banned all DDT sale and use on Dec. 31, 1972; however, limited use for military and medicinal purposes was permitted until Oct. 1989. In 1974, the U.S. banned the use of Aldrin and Dieldrin, both deadly chemicals that may have affected wildlife as much as did DDT.

Mexico was expected to discontinue government-sponsored DDT use for malaria control in 2002 and has planned a total ban of DDT by 2006.

As of 2000, possibly five other Latin American countries still used DDT and other organochlorine chemicals without restrictions. These include countries where older Osprey winter and where younger Osprey may spend their first year.

There are 122 countries, including the U.S. and Canada, that have signed a United Nations-sponsored treaty banning eight deadly organochlorine pesticides: Aldrin, Chlordane, DDT, Dieldrin, Endrin, Heptachlor, Mirex, and Toxaphene. There are also two industrial chemicals, Hexachlorobenzene (also a pesticide) and PCBs, and two by-products of industrial processes, dioxins and furans, that have been banned.

Organophosphate pesticides, although not as persistent in the environment as organochlorine pesticides, can be deadly to some aquatic life that fish eat and therefore affect Osprey.

Carbamate pesticides were less harmful to the environment than organophosphate chemicals, and were used to control insect infestations in e. Canadian forests.

Pyrethroid pesticides are harmless to birds

and mammals and are currently used to control insect infestations in e. Canadian forests. However, some of these may be deadly to aquatic life and affect the food that fish eat, thereby affecting Osprey.

Mortality.—Acid rain affects fish populations and reduces Osprey food supply in some areas. Illegal shooting occurs on both the breeding and wintering grounds. Excessive human disturbance of nest sites may cause nest abandonment. Avian and mammalian predators abound. Gulls and Raccoons, in particular, cause mortality on unattended eggs and small nestlings. Coyotes kill youngsters on the ground. Electrocution from utility poles is prevalent. As described above, pesticides may still affect Osprey in certain locations.

SIMILAR SPECIES: (1) **Bald Eagle, lightly marked type and moderately marked type 1- to 3-year-olds.**—PERCHED.—All have a dark auricular and side of head stripe, which is very Osprey-like. One-year-olds are similar in that bill and cere are black or gray; 2- and 3-year-olds have brownish or yellowish bills and ceres. All have a small dark breast patch contrasting to a white belly, and dark leg feathers. Wingtips are shorter than tail tip. FLIGHT.—All ages exhibit considerable white on the underside, but do not have a black carpal patch. Tails are often whitish but unbanded. (2) **Great Black-backed Gull.**—FLIGHT.—Size is similar, and arched wing position also similar. Wingtips are black on ventral surface and, on juveniles and subadults, dark wingtips on the dorsal surface.

OTHER NAMES: Fish Hawk. *Spanish:* Gavilan Pescador. *French:* Balbuzard Pecheur.

REFERENCES: Brauning 1992, Brewer et al. 1991, Buckelew and Hall 1994, Bylan 1998, Cadman et al. 1987, Clark 1998, Debus 1998, del Hoyo et al. 1994, Dodge 1988–1997, Edelstam 1984, Environment Canada 2001, Erskine 1992, Ewins 1995, Forsman 1999, Godfrey 1986, Houghton and Rymon 1997, Howell and Webb 1995, Kale et al. 1992, Kellogg 2000, McWilliams and Brauning 2000, Mumford and Keller 1984, Nicholson 1997, Olsen 1998, Palmer 1988, Palmer-Ball 1996, The Raptor Center 1999a, Walsh et al. 1999, Wheeler and Clark 1995.

OSPREY, *Pandion haliaetus carolinensis:* Fairly common. Very local near waterways. Population is rapidly increasing from ban of DDT. Very irregular north of NC in winter. Winters to cen. South America. *P. h. ridgwayi* on Caribbean islands, and small numbers in s. Fla., especially Keys.

Plate 24. Osprey, adult [Feb.] ▪ Yellow iris. Black eyeline connects to hindneck. ▪ Type with unmarked breast. Uniformly dark brown upperparts. ▪ *Note:* Holding a fish.

Plate 25. Osprey, adult [Dec.] ▪ Yellow iris. Black eyeline connects to hindneck. Bushy nape. ▪ Type with heavily marked breast. Uniformly dark brown upperparts.

Plate 26. Osprey, adult "Ridgway's" *(P. h. ridgwayi)* [Dec.] ▪ Black eyeline does not connect to hindneck. ▪ Unmarked breast. ▪ Uniformly dark brown upperparts. ▪ *Note:* Paler head and ventral areas than North American race, *P. h. carolinensis.* Photographed on Big Pine Key, Fla.

Plate 27. Osprey, adult [Mar.] ▪ Black eyeline. ▪ Type with moderately marked breast. ▪ Large, solid black carpal patch on wrist of wing. Dark secondaries and pale primaries. Wings held in "M" shape when gliding.

Plate 28. Osprey, adult [May] ▪ Head-on view with wings held in an arch when gliding.

Plate 29. Osprey, adult [Dec.] ▪ Engaged in a shallow angle dive with lowered legs.

Plate 30. Osprey, adult [Mar.] ▪ Black eyeline.
▪ Large, solid black carpal patch on wrist of wing.
▪ *Note:* Fish carried with head pointing forward, usually with both feet (fish is partially eaten).

Plate 31. Osprey, juvenile (older) [Oct.] ▪ Black eyeline. ▪ Dark brown upperparts with very narrow white feather tips. ▪ *Note:* White tips on dorsal feathers often wear off by mid- to late fall.

Plate 32. Osprey, juvenile (fledgling) [May] ▪ Orange iris. Crown of head is heavily marked; Black eyeline connects to hindneck. ▪ Dark brown upperparts are tipped with white. ▪ *Note:* This bird could fly well but returned to nest to feed and rest.

Plate 33. Osprey, juvenile (fledgling) [May] ▪ Black eyeline. ▪ Dark brown upperparts are tipped with white.

Plate 34. Osprey, juvenile (younger) [Oct.] ▪ Black eyeline. ▪ Type with moderately marked breast. ▪ Large, black carpal patch is mottled with tawny. Tawny wash on underwing coverts. Very dark secondaries and pale primaries. Wings held in an "M" shape when gliding.

SWALLOW-TAILED KITE
(*Elanoides forficatus*)

AGES: Adult and juvenile. Sexes are similar. Ages are superficially alike, but are separable by tail length and, to a lesser degree, by dorsal color. Juvenile age class is held for nearly 1 year.

MOLT: Accipitridae wing molt pattern (*see* chapter 5). Primaries molt a few remiges prior to beginning molt on the secondaries. Based on close in-field photography (BKW pers. obs.), rectrix molt appears to begin, as on most raptors, on the central deck set (r1). Based on in-field observations, Meyer (1995; K. Meyer pers. comm.) suggests that some may begin rectrix molt on the outermost set (r6).

Prebasic molt begins on juveniles and non-breeding adults in mid- to late Apr. with the innermost primary. By May, 1-year-olds may exhibit several white blotches on the dorsal surface of the upperwing coverts caused by missing feathers. Because of the missing upperwing coverts, small translucent "windows" may be visible on the ventral surface of the white underwing coverts when seen in shadowed overhead flight. Rectrix molt begins in May or Jun. after remix molt is under way. Body, remix, and rectrix molt is complete each year.

Note: One-year-olds photographed in Florida in late May had replaced p1 and 2, dropped p3 and 4, had replaced the innermost rectrix set, but had not yet molted the outermost rectrix set.

Adult molt data are based on Meyer (1995). On breeding adults, and typical of most nesting raptors, remix molt begins in late May to early Jun. on females and late Jun. to mid-Jul. on males. All remiges, rectrices, and contour feathers are completely molted annually. Remix molt is rapid and is mainly complete by mid-Aug. to early Sep.

SUBSPECIES: Polytypic with two races. *E. f. forficatus* inhabits the s. U.S. and *E. f. yetapa* is found from s. Mexico through the northern two-thirds of South America.

Adults of *yetapa* are similar to the dorsal color of adult *forficatus*, but have more of a greenish cast on the inner portion of each feather. Juveniles of *yetapa* are overall more greenish on the dorsal areas than *forficatus*.

COLOR MORPHS: None.

SIZE: A medium-sized raptor. Length: 20–25 in. (51–64 cm). Tails of adults are a minimum of 2 in. (5 cm) longer than those of juveniles and generally fairly distinct from the shorter-tailed juveniles. Recently fledged birds will appear very short tailed since it takes an additional few weeks after fledging to complete the growth of the long feathers of the outer rectrix set. Wingspan: 47–54 in. (119–137 cm).

SPECIES TRAITS: HEAD.—Small black bill and pale bluish cere. Iris color is dark brown. Lacks a supraorbital ridge (presence of the supraorbital ridge give raptors the "stern" look). White head. BODY.—**White underparts. Glossy iridescent, medium purplish blue upperparts with a noniridescent black area on the back and forward one-third of the scapulars.** Feet are small and pale gray or bluish gray; occasionally flesh colored on portions of their feet. WINGS.—**Long and narrow with pointed wingtips. White underwing coverts and black undersides of the remiges. Dorsal surface of the remiges and distal upperwing coverts are an iridescent medium purplish blue. The forward part of the lesser coverts is noniridescent black and forms a distinct dark black band across the upperwing coverts. This black band blends with the black region on the forward scapulars and back. Inner tertials and inner greater secondary coverts are mainly white. When kites are perched, this region shows as a large white patch behind the scapulars. All of the white area on the tertials and inner coverts is concealed by the scapulars when in flight.** TAIL.—**Black and deeply forked. Innermost rectrix set (r1) is very short. Each sequential outer rectrix set gets progressively longer and creates the forked shape.**

ADULT TRAITS: HEAD.—All white. BODY.—Ventral areas are immaculate white. Iridescence on upperparts is a medium purplish blue. WINGS.—Iridescence on upperwing is also a medium purplish blue. TAIL.—Very long and very deeply forked. The outer rectrix set (r6) is much longer than the preceding set (r5).

JUVENILE TRAITS: HEAD.—At close range, nestlings and fledglings have a tawny wash and tawny shaft streaking on the head and neck.

The tawny areas typically fade quickly and appear adultlike white soon after fledging. BODY.—Breast may also have a tawny wash or slight tawny shaft streaking through the fledgling period; however, this also wears and fades off and is rarely seen on fledged birds. Iridescent gloss on the upperparts is a medium purplish blue with a greenish cast. Dorsal color is subtly different than that of adults. The iridescent greenish dorsal cast is sometimes difficult to detect in the field. As in adults, the iridescent lower scapulars contrast with the noniridescent darker black band on the back and forward scapulars. WINGS.—Iridescence on the greater upperwing coverts is also the same color as the rear scapulars and contrasts with the darker black back, forward scapulars, and lesser upperwing coverts. In very fresh plumage, greater upperwing coverts, including primary coverts and tips of the primaries, have very narrow white tips. The white tips are not readily visible at long distances on recently fledged birds. The white tips quickly wear off by late summer. TAIL.—Long and deeply forked. Outermost rectrix set (r6) is moderately longer than the preceding set (r5). The r6 set of juveniles is noticeably shorter than the r6 set on adults. When recently fledged with still-growing feathers on the r6 rectrix set, the tail is fairly short and only moderately forked. In fresh plumage, a very narrow white edge adorns each rectrix tip; however, this feature is practically invisible under field conditions. On the dorsal surface, the rectrices may exhibit a slight greenish cast.

ABNORMAL PLUMAGES: None reported.

HABITAT: Summer.—Semi-open areas with small or extensive tracts of second growth and mature, tall coniferous (mainly pine) or deciduous (mainly cypress) trees. Species of pine include primarily Slash Pine in Florida and Loblolly Pine in South Carolina (and possibly elsewhere). Open savannahs with scattered small patches of pines or cypress strands are also inhabited. Kites are generally found in riparian locales in wet prairies, marshes, bayous, rivers, lakes, deciduous or coniferous swamps, or mangrove swamps. However, Swallow-tailed Kites are also found in semi-open, dry upland areas with tracts of pine and hardwood in the central highland counties of Florida, including regions adjacent to citrus groves and cattle pastures. Suburban nesting locales with tall trees are also inhabited in several areas in Florida. Climate in all currently occupied geographic areas is hot and humid; however, formerly inhabited temperate, moderately humid latitudes.

Migration.—Found in above described habitats, but forages a considerable amount over agricultural zones, including citrus groves and sugar cane fields.

Winter.—Similar to summer habitat but in tropical latitudes in South America.

HABITS: Tame. Gregarious. Swallow-tailed Kites often nest, forage, roost, and migrate in small groups. They exhibit little fear of humans. A highly aerial species and is one of the most aerial North American raptors. Perching occurs mostly for night roosting, during inclement weather, and for certain nesting activities. Sunning behavior occurs in the morning prior to flight and also after periods of rain in order to dry feathers.

Often found in the company of Mississippi Kites during breeding season in all areas except in cen. and s. Florida. Out-of-range individuals are also sometimes seen with Mississippi Kites.

FEEDING: Strictly an aerial hunter. Small and large insects, frogs, lizards, nestling birds, and small snakes are primary prey items. Kites regularly bring wasp nests, including stinging species, back to nests sites and feed on the larvae. Insects are mainly captured in flight, and Swallow-tailed Kites rarely engage in anything more than very short, but often acrobatic pursuits. Insects and other types of prey are masterfully snatched from outer branches and foliage of trees and bushes and from other types of short or tall vegetation. Captures prey with feet. Prey is eaten while soaring or gliding except when feeding young or transferring prey to another parent to feed young. Aerial feeding is accomplished by extending the foot clutching the prey forward and bowing the head down to the extended foot. Low-level aerial hunting occurs most often in the morning and late afternoon when insect prey is also at low altitudes. Foraging altitudes may increase substantially during midday; however, low altitude hunting may also occur at this time. Swallow-tailed Kites primarily feed on insects except during breeding season, when vertebrates form an extensive dietary component. Carrion is not eaten.

FLIGHT: Supremely buoyant and elegant aerial maneuvers. Most aerial activities involve energy efficient soaring and gliding, with the long forked tail used as a constantly adjusting rudder. Powered flight is used in short pursuits of prey, when chasing intruders at nest sites, and for stabilization during low altitude foraging. Wingbeats are slow and methodical. Wings are held on a flat plane with wingtips gently bending upwards when soaring. Wings are held on a similar flat-winged fashion or bowed slightly downward when gliding. When pursuing prey, very acrobatic maneuvers are often made with exquisite tail fluctuations. When soaring, the tail is widely spread, exhibiting the deeply forked shape. When gliding, tail character may be widely fanned, moderately fanned, or nearly closed.

Long over-water flights occur during migration. Migrating birds may travel at very high altitudes. Drink and bathe by skimming the surface of the water. Swallow-tailed Kites do not hover or kite.

VOICE: Three main call notes: (1) A clear, sweet, whistled *klee, klee, klee,* repeated two to four times, is the common call when agitated, by males after copulating, and during food transfers. Emitted by solitary birds, pairs, or by individuals of a group flying overhead. (2) *Tew-whee* is similar to *klee* call, but slurs upwards at the end of the note and repeated two to six times. Emitted during courtship flights, by females after copulating, and by individuals on nests when mates are approaching. *Eeep* is uttered by both sexes and given as a single note or in a short series of notes. Call is given by males and females when passing food (while perched), by females soliciting copulation or food, and by nestlings and fledglings as a food-begging call. (3) *Chitter* is a very soft call at roost sites when birds take off and land before settling down or before morning flight.

STATUS AND DISTRIBUTION: Summer.—*Very uncommon* **summer resident.** Estimated population is 800–1,150 pairs or approximately 3,200–4,600 birds in the U.S. at the end of the breeding season. Population is low, but appears stable at the present time. Sixty to 65 percent of the breeding population is in Florida. With about 110 pairs, South Carolina lists them as an Endangered Species. Georgia, Alabama, and Mississippi have no more than 100 pairs in each state. Kites do not have a status designation by state agencies in Florida, Georgia, Alabama, or Mississippi.

Florida: In peninsular Florida, breeding range is quite contiguous except from Martin Co. south to s. Broward Co. Kites are absent, however, in Hillsborough, w. Polk, and n. Lake Cos. Density is fairly high in the eastern panhandle and sporadic in the western panhandle. *Georgia:* Mainly found on the coastal plain region along major rivers. *South Carolina:* S. Allendale Co. south to s. Jasper Co., mainly along the Savannah River and drainages; cen. Dorchester Co., e. Charleston Co., and extreme e. Colleton Co., eastern half of Berkeley Co., southern one-third of Williamsburg Co., and to n. Georgetown Co. Northernmost nesting for the species (documented in 1999) is along the Great Pee Dee River in Horry Co. *Alabama:* Isolated breeding mainly along lower portions of Tombigbee, Alabama, and Tensaw Rivers; also along the lower Conecuh River in Escambia and Covington Cos.; Geneva Co.; and Eufala NWR, Barbour Co. *Mississippi:* Primarily found along the Pearl, Pascagoula, and lower Chickasawhay Rivers.

Historical: Breeding range formerly extended to n.-cen. Minnesota, where they last bred in 1907. In the East, formerly nested along the Mississippi River from n. Illinois, but also bred in Cook Co., Ill., in the early to mid-1800s. Kites were often found in the northern and central part of the state from spring through fall. Breeding also occurred along the Ohio River from s. Illinois to extreme sw. Ohio, in w. Tennessee, and southward throughout much of Mississippi and the southern half of Alabama. Swallow-tailed Kites disappeared as a breeding species in Ohio in the mid-1800s and thereafter were accidental in occurrence. In Ohio, Swallow-tailed Kites probably bred in Crawford, Fayette, Hamilton, Marion, Pickaway, Portage, Ross, Stark, and Warren Cos. Historical range along the Atlantic Seaboard has not changed as Swallow-tailed Kites have never bred north of South Carolina.

Drastic population decline ensued from the late 1800s to mid-1900s. By 1910, the Swallow-tailed Kite's breeding range had shrunk substantially to states it currently inhabits due to massive habitat alteration of mature woodlands in riparian areas and human persecution. Populations stabilized within their reduced range since 1940.

Winter.—It appears that much of the North American population winters in a fairly small region in w.-cen. and sw. Brazil. Large roosts have been found in Nov. Gregarious foraging probably occurs, and large communal roosts have been found. *E. f. forficatus* winters within the breeding range of Brazil's population of *yetapa*.

Movements.—Kites migrate in small flocks or singly.

Fall migration: An early-season migrant. After nesting, birds may disperse in any direction prior to actually migrating. Large premigratory roosts form in cen. and s. Florida from mid-Jun. through Aug. with peak numbers occurring in late Jul. In Florida, large roosts form in Brevard, Collier, Glades, Lake, and Volusia Cos. In Mississippi, fairly large premigration roosts occur on the Pascagoula River from mid- to late Jul. Actual migration may begin in mid-Jul. and extend into Sep. The majority of individuals move from late Jul. through Aug. in the U.S. Stragglers occur into Oct. in the s. U.S. Migration may last until late Oct., when they arrive on winter grounds. Adults precede most juveniles. Movements may last 3 months.

Based on ongoing telemetry data by K. Meyer (unpubl.) on Florida-tracked kites, the major migration route in the fall between Florida and the winter grounds in South America is an over-water route from s. Florida to the Yucatán Peninsula of Mexico. Migrants may stop in or fly over w. Cuba en route between Florida and the Yucatán. From the Yucatán, migrants wend their way on a mainly land-based course through e. Central America. They enter South America at Colombia and cross the Cordilleras, then angle southeast to their wintering area in Brazil.

Two other migration routes that may be taken from breeding areas farther west, from w. Florida to Mississippi: (1) A trans-Gulf of Mexico crossing to the Yucatán Peninsula or s. Mexico, as seen by observers on off-shore oil rigs; or (2) angle east along the coast to Texas, then continue south into e. Mexico, as seen by hawkwatch observers in e. and s. Texas and Veracruz, Mexico. In all cases, a considerably larger number of migrants are seen at a hawkwatch in Costa Rica than in any U.S. or Veracruz hawkwatch site. This may correlate with the telemetry data that the majority reach this latitude by bypassing most land-based routes in the U.S. and Mexico.

In Veracruz, 286 were counted in the late summer and fall of 2001 with a peak of 112 in one day in late Aug. At the new Talamanca, Costa Rica, Hawkwatch, 1,319 were seen in the fall of 2001.

Spring migration: The first adults return to s. Florida in late Feb. Adults breeding in Georgia and South Carolina may not arrive at nesting areas until mid-Mar. One-year-olds and nonbreeding adults arrive later than breeding adults, mainly in Apr. and May. A considerable amount of wandering occurs with some spring arrivals.

Although data is not available, birds may retrace their fall routes to Florida. Migrants have been observed leaving the Yucatán Peninsula in Feb. at very high altitudes heading north over water. The trans-Gulf of Mexico crossing is used by an unknown number of migrants. The land-based e. Mexico and e. Texas route is used by a small to moderate number of kites.

Extralimital movements.—Regular northward dispersal spring through fall along the Mid-Atlantic Coast. *North Carolina:* Nearly annual in the spring at Cape Hatteras. *New Jersey:* There are at least 45 records for the state. The most recent sighting was in Cape May Co. in mid-Jun. 2000. More than half of the records are from May, many from Apr. and Jun., and four records from Sep. *Delaware:* Irregular along coastal Delaware, especially at Cape Henlopen.

Accidental north of typical breeding areas in interior eastern states. *Tennessee:* Most recent record was in late Jul. 2000 consisting of three individuals in Sequatchie Co. *Indiana:* Historical sightings in Allen, Clark, Clinton, Decatur, Franklin, Greene, Knox, Monroe, Porter, and Vigo Cos. Sightings since 1982: (1) Near Lafayette, Tippecanoe Co., in late May 1982; (2) Muscatatuck NWR at the Jackson-Jennings Co. line in late Aug. 1983; (3) Lawrenceburg, Dearborn Co., in mid-Aug. 1997 (also crossed over Ohio River into Kentucky); (4) Lincoln S.P., Spencer Co., in late Aug. 1997; (5) near Indianapolis, Shelby Co., in early Sep. 2001. *Ohio:* Three recent-era records of single birds. Seen along Lake Erie and the Ohio River: (1) Sandusky Co. in late May 1975, (2) Ashtabula Co. in mid-Jun. 1989, and (3) Holmes Co. from early to mid-Sep. 1997. *Kentucky:* (1) Sighting in Alamo, Sherwood Co., in mid-Aug. 1996 (unpubl.); (2) Boone Co. in mid-Aug. to early Sep. 1997 (same individual as #3 sighting in Indiana); (3) Central Kentucky WMA, Madison Co., in late Jul. 2001 (unpubl.). *Michigan:* One record from Leelanau Co. in late Aug. 2000. *Wisconsin:* Twelve records, with the first in 1848 in Racine Co. Since 1990, three records: (1) Marquette Co. in mid-May 1992, (2) Green Lake Co. in late Aug. 1997, and (3) Dane Co. in late May 1999. *Maryland:* Cumberland, Allegany Co., in the fall of 1974. *Virginia:* Montgomery Co. in mid-May 1998. *West Virginia:* Mill Hill, Greenbrier Co., in early Sep. 1908. *Pennsylvania:* Several records from the 1800s from the southern part of the state; a 1952 record from Chestnut Hill, Philadelphia Co., in mid-May. Recent-era sightings of mainly single birds: (1) Armstrong Co. in early Sep. 1976; (2) near Shippensburg, Cumberland-Franklin Cos., in mid-Jun. 1981; (3) Media, Delaware Co., in mid-Jun. 1982; (4) Jonas, Monroe Co., in late May 1991; (5) Birchrunville, Chester Co., from early to mid-Jun. 1991; (6) Latrobe Reservoir in Westmoreland Co. in late Jun. 1991; (7) up to three birds between Bowmansville and Knauers on Berks-Lancaster Co. line from late May to early Jun. 1995; (8) York Co. in late Sep. 1996; and (9) Carbon Co. in mid-Jul. 1998. *New York:* Fairly regular with 27 records, with 17 sightings after 1978. Eighteen are spring records, with 13 along Long Island and five along Lakes Erie and Ontario at hawkwatch sites. Seven records are from the summer and two from Long Island in the fall, with the latest in early Oct. All records are of single birds. Records since 1990: (1) Jamaica Bay NWR, N.Y., in mid-Apr. 1993; (2) Albany Co. in mid-May 1993; (3) New York City in early May 2000; and (4) Chautauqua Co. (Ripley Hawkwatch) in early May 2000. *Connecticut:* (1) Hamden, New Haven Co., in early Jun. 1987; (2) Mansfield Center, Tolland Co., from early to late Jun. 1989 involving two individuals; and (3) Stamford, Fairfield Co., in early May 2000. *Massachusetts:* Over 35 records with most on coastal areas and islands. First recorded in Cohasset in mid-May 1940. Most records are from Cape Cod. Sightings have occurred from early Mar. to late Sep. All sightings involve single birds, and most were one-day-only sightings. Records from 1990 to 2001: (1) Martha's Vineyard in late Apr. 1990, (2) Nantucket I. in late Apr. 1990, (3) West Yarmouth in early Mar. 1991, (4) Assonet in early Jun. 1992, (4) Truro in mid-Apr. 1993, (5) Martha's Vineyard (Oak Bluffs) in late May 1996. (6) Hyannis in mid-May 1996, (7) Nantucket I. in mid-Jun. 1997, (8) Tuckernuck I. in late Jul. 1997, (9) Nantucket I. in late Jul. 1997, (10) N. Truro in early Jun. 1999, (11) Marshfield in early Jun. 1999, (12) Hyannis in late Mar. 2000, (13) Truro in early May 2000, (14) Cambridge in mid-May 2000, Martha's Vineyard in early May 2000, (15) Chatham in early May 2000, (16) Harvard in mid-May 2000, (17) N. Truro in early Jun. 2000. *Vermont:* (1) Waitsfield, Washington Co., in late Apr. 1913; (2) Middlebury, Addison Co., in mid-Sep. 1983; and (3) Washington, Orange Co., in mid-Sep. 1986. *New Hampshire:* (1) A historical record from 1875 for Franklin, Merrimack Co.; (2) New Hampton, Belknap Co., for 11 days from mid- to late May 1965 (photograph); and (3) Danville, Rockingham Co., for 1 day in early May 1979. *Maine:* (1) Monhegan Island for 7 days in late May 1986, (2) Bremen in Jun./Jul. 1986, and (3) at Lubec in early Jul. 1989. *Ontario:* All sightings are of single birds. Records are for one day unless noted otherwise: (1) historical specimen record before 1907 for Toronto; (2) Sturgeon Creek in mid-May and Point Pelee N.P., Essex Co., in late May 1978 (same bird); (3) Buckhorn for 11 days from mid- to late Jun. 1982; (4) Wakami Lake Provincial Park, Sudbury District, in mid-Jul. (adult); (5) Point Pelee N.P. in early May 1987; (6) Walsingham, Long Point Provincial Park, and Port Rowan, Haldimand-Norfolk Co., for 2 days in mid-May 1987; (7) Sturgeon Creek, Holiday Beach Conservation Area, and Point Pelee N.P., Essex Co., for 20 days from mid-Aug. to early Sep. 1988 (juvenile); (8) Grimsby, Niagara Co., in mid-Apr. 1994; (9) Walsingham, Haldimand-Norfolk Co., for 4 days in late May and Long Point Provincial Park for 1 day in early Jun. 1995 (same bird); (10) Pelee Island, Essex Co., in late Aug. 1995; and (11) Kirkwall, Hamilton-Wentworth Co., in late Apr. 1996. *Nova Scotia:* (1) Lower East Pubnico (specimen) in Aug. 1905, (2) a single individual between Louisbourg and Sydney in late Apr. 1997, (3) an adult in Glace Bay in late Mar. 2001, (4) a single bird on Cape Sable Island in early Aug. 2001.

NESTING: Begins in late Feb. in s. Florida and Mar. in all other areas, and is completed in all regions in Jul. Nests singly or in small, loosely formed colonies. One or two nonbreeding birds often accompany breeding pairs but rarely assist in nesting duties.

Courtship (flight).—*Diving-swoop* (*see* chapter 5). Any pair member may swoop down on the other lower-gliding individual, then glide past; often two or more pairs are involved. Courtship flights are accompanied by considerable amount of vocalization (mainly *tew-whee* but also *klee* notes).

Kites do not breed until they are at least 2 years old. One-year-olds may return to natal areas but apparently do not breed. Both members build nests. New nests may be built or may reuse old nests. Nests are built in live trees and are placed near the top of one of the tallest trees in the tract for easy aerial access. Nests often range to at least 100 ft. (30 m) high; however, in such trees as mangroves, may be as low as 35 ft. (11 m), although still placed in the top section of trees. Nests may be somewhat oblong in shape and average 20 in. (52 cm) long and 17 in. (42 cm) wide. Nest structure comprises small sticks, which are broken off from branches with their feet while in flight, lichens and Spanish Moss. Material is continually added to nests during the course of use. Both sexes incubate, but females average longer stints of incubation.

Two eggs are typical, but may only have 1 and occasionally 3. The eggs are incubated for about 28 days. Youngsters fledge in 36–42 days. Kites lay only one clutch per season.

CONSERVATION: Only South Carolina, which has listed the Swallow-tailed Kite as an endangered species, has implemented guidelines for habitat protection. Forestry practices in national forests have been altered to benefit the kite.

Environmentalists are concerned with preservation of ample, suitable habitat in the other inhabited states, particularly in Florida where increased agriculture and urbanization occurs. Protection of premigration roost area habitat is essential.

Telemetry studies have been ongoing and assist knowledge of migration routes, roosting areas, and wintering areas.

Mortality.—Historically, shooting was a factor in population decline. Illegal shooting still occurs but is a minor threat.

Natural mortality occurs with loss of eggs and nestlings due to inclement weather, especially being blown out of treetop nests. S. Florida nesting pairs that use the frail, imported Australian Pine suffer high nest losses due to high winds. Avian predators, including depredation from Bald Eagles, causes some mortality. Only minor depredation occurs from mammalian species. Parasites cause nestling mortality.

SIMILAR SPECIES: None concerning raptors. At a distance might be confused with the Magnificent Frigatebird, particularly juveniles, which have white heads and underparts.

OTHER NAMES: Swallowtail. *Spanish:* Milan Tijereta. *French:* Milan á Queue Fourchue.

REFERENCES: Baicich and Harrison 1997; Bohlen 1989; Burgiel et al. 2000; Davis 1999; Eberly 1999; Godfrey 1986; Hall 1983; Iliff 1998; Kale et al. 1992; Levine 1998, Maybank 1997; McWilliams and Brauning 2000; Meyer 1994, 1995, 1996; Meyer and Collopy 1995, 1996; Meyer et al. 1997; Mumford and Keller 1984; Palmer 1988; Paxton et al. 1998; Ripple 2000; Robbins 1991; Stevenson and Anderson 1994; Tufts 1986; Veit and Petersen 1993; Walsh et al. 1999.

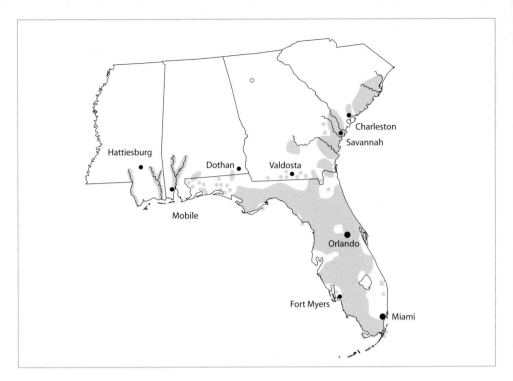

SWALLOW-TAILED KITE, *Elanoides forficatus:* Very uncommon. 850–1,150 pairs. Winters in w.-cen. and sw. Brazil.

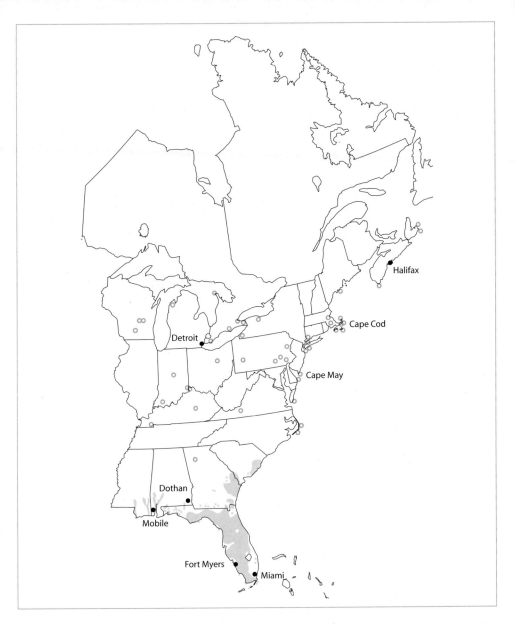

Halifax

Cape Cod

Detroit

Cape May

Dothan

Mobile

Fort Myers

Miami

SWALLOW-TAILED KITE, *Elanoides forficatus:* Regularly disperses Mar. to Sep. to the Great Lakes and along the Atlantic Coast.

Plate 35. Swallow-tailed Kite, adult [May] ▪ White head. ▪ White ventral body. ▪ Very long, deeply forked black tail.

Plate 36. Swallow-tailed Kite, adult [May] ▪ White head. ▪ Black iridescent dorsal body. ▪ Large white patch on base of tertials and inner greater upperwing coverts. ▪ Very long, deeply forked black tail.

Plate 37. Swallow-tailed Kite, adult [May] ▪ White ventral body. ▪ White underwing coverts and black remiges. ▪ Very long, deeply forked black tail. ▪ *Note:* Inner 2 primaries (p1 and 2) are molting and missing.

Plate 38. Swallow-tailed Kite, adult [May] ▪ White ventral body. ▪ White underwing coverts and black remiges. ▪ Very long, deeply forked black tail. ▪ *Note:* This kite is eating a small insect. Small prey eaten while flying.

Plate 39. Swallow-tailed Kite, adult [May] ▪ Iridescent purplish blue upperparts have a non-iridescent black band across back and upperwing coverts. ▪ Very long, deeply forked black tail.

Plate 40. Swallow-tailed Kite, juvenile (1-year-old) [May] ▪ White ventral body. ▪ White underwing coverts and black remiges. ▪ Long, deeply forked black tail. ▪ *Note:* Molting inner 4 primaries (p1–4), upperwing coverts, and 2 central rectrices (r1 set). Molting upperwing coverts create translucent spots on underwing coverts.

Plate 41. Swallow-tailed Kite, juvenile (1-year-old) [May] ▪ Purplish blue upperparts may show a greenish cast. Non iridescent black band on back and upperwing coverts. White spots on upperparts are molting, missing feathers. ▪ *Note:* Same kite as Plate 40. Fresh-plumaged juveniles in summer and fall are not in molt.

WHITE-TAILED KITE
(Elanus leucurus)

AGES: Adult, subadult (basic I), and juvenile. Adult plumage is acquired when 1-year-old. Subadult plumage is a transitional molt stage from juvenile to adult; however, there is often a short period with minimal molt or lack of molt. Juvenile plumage is retained for only a few months.

MOLT: Accipitridae wing and tail molt pattern (*see* chapter 4). First prebasic molt from juvenile to subadult begins when juveniles have been fledged for about two months and are about 3.5–4 months old (Palmer 1988, Dunk 1995). Contour body molt is completed when about 6 months old, but may take longer. Molt begins on the crown of the head, then appears on the back, scapulars, and breast. Rectrices begin molting when kites are about 7–8 months old, after contour body molt is nearly complete or is complete. Wing covert molt begins prior to remix molt, but is completed during the span of the remix molt. Remiges do not molt until approximately 1 year of age. At this time, body molt has been completed for several months, and at least some or most rectrices have also been molted.. There is a short time span of about 1–2 months when contour feather molt is basically complete and rectrix molt has not started. When the first prebasic molt is finally completed on the wings, full adult plumage is attained.

First prebasic body molt mainly occurs in summer through fall. Juveniles of later-hatched broods may be in body molt in fall and winter.

Subsequent prebasic molts are annual and complete. Molt is primarily spring through fall. Contour feathers, rectrices, and remiges molt in unison.

SUBSPECIES: Polytypic with two races. *E. l. majusculus* inhabits the U.S. and Central America and *E. l. leucurus* inhabits South America. *E. l. leucurus* is smaller and has a shorter tail but is otherwise identical in plumage to *majusculus*.

The White-tailed Kite was considered a subspecies of the Black-shouldered Kite (*Elanus caeruleus*) of Africa, s. Europe, and Asia; however, studies on plumage, proportion, and behavioral differences illustrated that they were separate species (Clark and Banks 1992). In 1994, the AOU formally split them.

COLOR MORPHS: None.

SIZE: A medium-sized raptor. Males average smaller than females but there is considerable overlap. Length: 14–16 in. (36–41 cm); wingspan: 37–40 in. (94–102 cm).

SPECIES TRAITS: HEAD.—**Narrow black bill. Yellow cere and gape.** Black inner lores. Large eyes. BODY.—**Short yellow or orangish tarsi and feet.** WINGS.—**In flight, wings are long and narrow with parallel front and trailing edges. Wingtips are moderately pointed.** When perched, wingtips are just short of the tail tip. WINGS (ventral).—**Large black spot or rectangle shape on the carpal region. Primaries are dark gray, but graduate to a paler gray on the inner primaries.** WINGS (dorsal).—**Large black shoulder patch on the median coverts and all lesser upperwing coverts.** TAIL.—**Moderately long. The deck rectrix set is a bit shorter than all other rectrices and creates a notched or somewhat forked shape when closed. Deck rectrix set is pale gray and all other sets are white.**

ADULT TRAITS: HEAD.—Iris color varies from reddish orange to red. **Crown and nape are pale gray, rest of head is white.** BODY.—Immaculate white ventral surface. **Back and scapulars are uniformly pale gray. Yellowish-orange tarsi and feet.** WINGS.—**Ventral surface of the secondaries is very pale gray. Uniformly black shoulder patch on the upperwing coverts.** TAIL.—**The gray deck rectrix set and white outer rectrix sets are unmarked.**

BASIC I/SUBADULT I (LATE STAGE): HEAD.— As on adults, but iris color is typically more orangish. Dark streaking behind the eyes of "early stage" is absent. BODY.—As on adults on dorsal and ventral surfaces. WINGS.—All remiges are retained juvenile feathers. White tips of the juvenile plumage on the tertials, secondaries, and primary greater coverts are completely worn off; however, narrow white tips may be retained on the inner primaries. Upperwing coverts may be retained juvenile feathers with all white edgings worn off or possess some nonwhite-tipped adult feathering. TAIL.—Retained juvenile rectrices with the dusky subterminal band or may have molted in a few unmarked adult rectrices. Molting rectrices are often partially grown.

Note: There may be a span of 2 or more months in which birds may be in a nonmolting plumage.

BASIC (SUBADULT I; EARLY STAGE): HEAD.— Newly molted gray crown is similar to an adult's; however, the crown and the area immediately behind the eyes may retain some sparse dark brown juvenile streaking. BODY.—A moderate amount of new, pale gray adult feathers are among juvenile feathers on all areas of the back and scapulars. Retained juvenile feathers are a faded pale brownish gray with worn, narrow white tips. At a distance, the dorsal area can appear rather uniformly grayish. Tarsi and feet are yellow. WINGS.—Retained juvenile remiges. White tips of the tertials, secondaries, and greater upperwing coverts are either worn and very narrow or are completely worn off. The white tips of median upperwing coverts are worn off and all brownish-tipped lesser upperwing coverts are also worn off. TAIL.—Retained juvenile rectrices with the dusky subterminal band.

Note: A continual change into adult plumage occurs with ongoing molt.

BASIC I/SUBADULT I (VERY EARLY STAGE): HEAD.—Crown is mainly adultlike pale gray, but may have some retained juvenile dark streaking. The area behind the eyes also has retained juvenile dark streaking. Iris color is pale orangish brown, but can be quite reddish. BODY.—Like on juveniles, but the rufous-tawny "necklace" wash on the breast is often reduced by molt and sun bleaching. Back and scapulars are medium brownish gray with somewhat worn, moderately wide white tips. Tarsi and feet are yellow. WINGS and TAIL.— As on juveniles.

Note: This stage is the earliest prebasic molt stage in the molt sequence beyond the juvenile plumage. It essentially appears like a juvenile with the exception of the grayish crown and narrower, worn white tips on dorsal feathers.

JUVENILE TRAITS: HEAD.—Crown is white or washed with pale tawny and narrowly streaked with dark brown. The area immediately behind the eyes is also streaked with dark brown. Iris color is pale or medium brown, but may be orangish brown. BODY.—Back and scapulars

are medium brownish gray with a broad white tip on each feather. Breast is washed with a variable-sized, rich tawny "necklace." Short tawny streaks may extend below the necklace onto the belly and forward flanks. Tarsi and feet are yellow. WINGS.—All remiges are broadly tipped with white. Greater upperwing coverts are broadly tipped with white. The feathers of the median covert tract on the black shoulder patch have narrow white tips; many lesser coverts are narrowly tipped with pale brown. Gray upper surface of the remiges and greater upperwing coverts is slightly darker than an adults. Ventral surface of the secondaries is pale gray (and slightly darker than on adults). TAIL.—Narrow dusky subterminal band.

Note: This plumage is retained for about 3.5 months.

ABNORMAL PLUMAGES: None.

HABITAT: Florida (year-round).—Open and semi-open wet or dry undisturbed or human-altered prairies, grasslands, pastures, overgrown fields, and freshwater marshes. Widely scattered bushes or trees dot the open areas. Scattered single bushes or trees or moderately spaced groups of bushes and trees are found in semi-open regions. Majority of the nesting territories in Florida are in human-altered plant communities. Climate is hot and humid.

HABITS: White-tailed Kites vary from being a tame to wary species. Exposed branches, posts, and wires are favored perches. They do not perch on utility poles. The highest perch on a tree is typically used. In very windy conditions, kites may seek shelter in protected, heavily foliaged, lower portions of a tree.

The tail is bobbed repeatedly: It is cocked upward from the angle of the body, then slowly lowered. The tail-bobbing action is a display against conspecific intruders into territory. *Talon-grappling* (see chapter 5) occurs as an agonistic confrontation between conspecifics.

White-tailed Kites can be gregarious and may form large communal night roosts in late fall and winter. However, since the Florida population is small, night roosts are small. The largest Florida gathering was 14 birds in w. Dade Co. in 1990.

FEEDING: An aerial hunter. Hunting takes place at altitudes of 15–80 ft. (5–25 m). White-tailed Kites prey almost exclusively on small rodents. Kites infrequently prey on small birds, lizards, and insects that are on the ground.

FLIGHT: Wings are held in high dihedral when soaring and gliding. Powered flight is with moderately fast wingbeats. Kites hover with shallow-beating wings when hunting. Legs are sometimes lowered when hovering. If legs are lowered, they are often fully extended, with toes widely spread. In strong winds, hunting White-tailed Kites may kite for short stints. Prey is captured by an awkward-looking dive, with the bird angled headfirst and wings fully extended high above the body. Landing birds daintily glide to or gently drop onto a perch, with feet fully extended downward, often with quivering wingbeats.

VOICE: A fairly vocal species, particularly if disturbed. A soft *cherp* is emitted when mildly agitated. A grating, raspy *kree-aak* is emitted when very agitated, when bringing prey to a nest, and when nestlings and fledglings are food-begging (sounds like a Barn Owl's call). A guttural, grating *grrkkk* when chasing intruders.

STATUS AND DISTRIBUTION: *Very uncommon* to *rare* and local in cen. and s. Florida. Only a few breeding pairs reside in the state. The population is increasing. White-tailed Kites were first seen in Florida in the early 1880s. Considered rare, local, and on the verge of extirpation by the early 1930s. Last historical nesting in the state was in 1930. There were a few sightings in n. Florida and the Florida Panhandle from the late 1940s through the 1990s.

In 1986, White-tailed Kites re-emerged as a breeding species with a nest in Broward Co. From 1986 to 1993, 17 kite nests were found. From 1996 to 2000, seven new nest sites were found. A new nesting pair was located in sw. Broward Co. in 2001. A pair was seen in the summer of 2001 in nw. Palm Beach Co. White-tailed Kites nest in the following counties: w. Broward, cen. and s. Dade, and s. Highlands. Probable nesting occurs in cen. and s. Brevard Co. White-tailed Kites are possibly more prevalent than is currently known since much of their habitat in cen. Florida, is on large, private, inaccessible ranches.

In the 1990s, sightings of one or two birds occurred in nw. De Soto, Glades, w.-cen. and s. Okaloosa, w.-cen. Okeechobee, w. Osceola, se.

Polk, e.-cen. Sarasota, n. Suwannee, and se. Wakulla Cos.

Extralimital breeding.—In the East, regular sightings are rare north of Florida. Mississippi is the only eastern state north of Florida that has had regular sightings and the only confirmed nesting. The first sight record for Mississippi was in late Oct. 1982 in Hancock Co., and nesting confirmed in 1983. Through late Oct. 1992, sightings of different individuals occurred in various parts of the county *in all months* except Jul. Sightings were also recorded for Jackson Co., Miss. in 1988. White-tailed Kites first nested in Hancock Co., Miss., in 1988.

Movements.—Primarily sedentary. Pairs often remain on territory year-round. This species is very prone, however, to engage in very irregular northward dispersal and nomadic movements.

Extralimital movements.—An accidental species north of Florida. *Alabama:* At least 10 records for coastal Mobile and Baldwin Cos. in fall and winter. *Kentucky:* Hickman Co. in early May 1991. *Illinois:* Williamsfield, Knox Co., for two days in early May 1987. *Indiana:* (1) Near Lake Monroe, Monroe Co., in mid-Apr. 1981; and (2) Warrick Co. in mid-May 1994. *Virginia:* Northhampton Co. in late Apr. 1998 for the state's only record. *New Jersey:* Cape May Co. in early Jun. 1998 for the state's only record. *South Carolina:* (1) Bull's Island in early May 1929; (2) Charleston Co. in early May 1929; (3) Clemson, Oconee Co., in early Jun. 1952; (4) Clemson, Oconee Co., in mid-May 1953; and (5) Greenwood, Greenwood Co., in early Jul. 1978. There were two additional records from the 1800s (collected by J. J. Audubon). *North Carolina:* Three of the four modern-era sightings were on coastal areas. All were single birds: (1) New Hanover Co. in early Jan. 1957, (2) Hanover Co. in early Apr. 1989, (3) Haywood Co. in late Jul. 1993 (inland area), and (4) Currituck Co. in mid-May 2001 (under review by the records committee). *New York:* Dutchess Co. in 1983 for the state's only record. *Massachusetts:* Martha's Vineyard in late May 1910 for the state's only record. *Tennessee:* Lake Co. in mid-Apr. 2001 (adult). *Wisconsin:* (1) Portage Co. for 21 days from early to late Jun. 1964, (2) Wood Co. for 3 days in mid-May 1987, and (3) Burnett Co. in early Sep. 1989.

NESTING: In Florida, Feb.—Jul. (and possibly later). Pairs may remain intact year-round. New pairs are formed in late winter or early spring. Although double clutches are typical in Texas and California (where they may attempt three clutches), only single clutches are currently known for Florida pairs.

Courtship (flight).—*Flutter-flight* and *V-flutter flight*, with *leg-dangling* (*see* chapter 5), are performed by males. In *leg-dangling*, legs are fully extended downwards and toes widely spread. In *V-flutter flight*, the quivering wings may be held at such a high angle that they nearly touch each other.

Nests are built by females and placed in the upper portion of bushes or small trees that are 10–32 ft. (3–10 m) high (Florida data). Nest structures are 20 in. (51 cm) in diameter and 8 in. (21 cm) deep, very compact, and made of twigs and lined with grasses. If the first nest fails or a pair begins a second brood, a new nest is built in another location within the territory. Clutches range from 3 to 6 eggs, with 4 eggs being most typical. Clutches of 6 eggs are rare. The eggs are incubated only by the female for 30–32 days. Only females feed the nestlings. Males hunt and guard territories. Fratricide

(siblicide) does not occur. Fledging occurs when 28–35 days old. Fledglings are fed by aerial prey transfer, while on nests, or on perches. Pairs may start a second nest while still feeding fledglings from the first brood. Parents cease caring for the first brood once the second brood hatches.

CONSERVATION: No measures are practiced in Florida. Many pairs nest in the Everglades N.P. in Dade Co., and are fully protected. In Highlands Co., nesting pairs are on inaccessible private lands. Habitat alteration affects nesting success. In some areas, prescribed water level control and fires may affect local breeding.

Mortality.—Little is known other than natural depredation by larger diurnal raptors and owls. There is also nest depredation by grackles, crows, mammals, and snakes. As with any raptor, they are susceptible to being shot.

SIMILAR SPECIES: (1) **Mississippi Kite.**—No range overlap during breeding season. (**1A**) **Adults.**—PERCHED.—Uniformly dark gray dorsum, including upperwing coverts. Black tail. FLIGHT.—Gray ventral surface of wings. Black tail. Does not hover. (**1B**) **Juveniles.**—PERCHED.—Lightly streaked individuals are similar to recently fledged White-tailed Kites

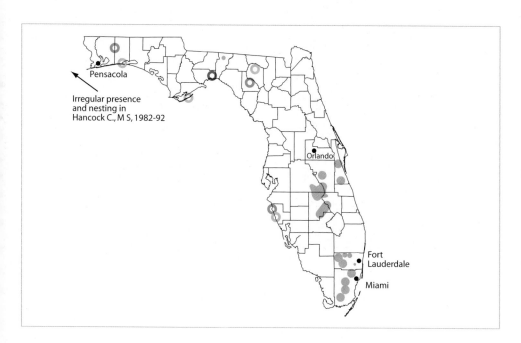

WHITE-TAILED KITE, *Elanus leucurus:* Uncommon. Local. Irregular dispersal northward to WI and MA.

that are heavily marked with rufous-tawny on ventral region. Uniformly dark brown upperwing coverts. Tail is blackish (and may not be banded). FLIGHT.—Uniformly mottled rufous-brown underwing coverts. Dark tail. **(2) Northern Harrier.**—Range overlap Sep.–Apr. **(2A) Adult males.**—PERCHED.—Pale lores. Long legs. Wingtips are shorter than the tail tip. FLIGHT.—Head and neck are gray and appear hooded. Black area on outer half of the primaries; black bar on trailing edge of secondaries. White patch on the uppertail coverts. **(2B) Northern Harrier, adult females.**—PERCHED.—Same as on adult males. FLIGHT.—Hooded look with brown head and neck. Barred underside of remiges; dark bar on trailing edge of underwing. In dorsal view, exhibits white uppertail covert patch. **(3) Non-**

raptors (gulls).—Several small and medium-sized gulls may superficially appear similar and cause a double-take; however, wings are held in an arch when gliding or soaring; all may hover like a kite. Laughing Gull (all nonbreeding plumages), year-round; Bonaparte's Gull in winter; Ring-billed Gull in winter.

OTHER NAMES: None used. *Spanish:* Milano Cola Blanca, Milan Coliblanco. *French:* Élanion à Queue Blanche.

REFERENCES: Baicich and Harrison 1997, Bohlen 1989, Clark and Banks 1992, Dunk 1995, Iliff 1998, Kale et al. 1992, McMillian and Pranty 1997, Palmer 1988, Post and Gauthreaux 1989, Pranty and McMillian 1997, Stevenson and Anderson 1994, Tennessee Ornithological Society 2001, Veit and Petersen 1993, Walsh et al. 1999.

Plate 42. White-tailed Kite, adult [Oct.] ▪ Red iris, yellow cere, and black bill. ▪ Gray back and scapulars. ▪ Large black shoulder patch.

Plate 43. White-tailed Kite, adult [Oct.] ▪ Red iris, yellow cere, and black bill. ▪ Mainly white head and white underparts. ▪ Large black shoulder patch. ▪ Underside of tail is plain white.

Plate 44. White-tailed Kite, adult [Feb.] ▪ White underparts. ▪ Small black carpal spot and dark gray primaries; very pale gray secondaries. ▪ Underside of tail is plain white.

Plate 45. White-tailed Kite, adult [Dec.] ▪ Gray remiges with large black shoulder patch. ▪ Upperside of tail is white with 2 gray mid-rectrices.

Plate 46. White-tailed Kite, adult [May] ▪ When hunting, kites hover, often with lowered legs.

Plate 47. White-tailed Kite, adult [Sep.] ▪ When prey is sighted, kites dive head-first to the ground with wings raised above their bodies and legs lowered.

Plate 48. White-tailed Kite, subadult (late stage)
[Feb.] ▪ Mainly white head. ▪ White underparts
and gray upperparts are adult feathers. ▪ Large
black shoulder patch. Retained juvenile remiges
have narrow white tips on primaries. ▪ Retained
juvenile tail with dusky subterminal band. ▪ *Note:*
Adult body plumage, but retains very worn juvenile remiges and rectrices. Tail in cocked posture.

Plate 49. White-tailed Kite, subadult (late stage)
[Dec.] ▪ Gray upperparts. ▪ Large black shoulder
patch; gray upper wing. ▪ Retained juvenile tail
with dusky subterminal band; gray mid-rectrices.
▪ *Note:* Retained juvenile remiges and rectrices.
White tips on primary coverts.

Plate 50. White-tailed Kite, subadult (early stage)
[Jan.] ▪ Orangish iris. Most brownish colored juvenile crown feathers have molted. ▪ Faded juvenile upperparts with a few gray adult feathers. White
underparts. ▪ Large black shoulder patch. Narrow
white tips on greater coverts and primaries. ▪
Note: Worn juvenile feathers with new adult feathers on head, underparts, and some scapulars.

**Plate 51. White-tailed Kite, subadult (very early
stage) [Feb.]** ▪ Orangish iris. Most juvenile
brownish colored crown feathers have molted. ▪
Brown scapulars with white tips; orangish breast. ▪
Large black shoulder patch. Greater coverts and
remiges are tipped with white. ▪ Dusky subterminal tail band. ▪ *Note:* Mainly juvenile plumage
with adultlike head.

Plate 52. White-tailed Kite, juvenile [May] ▪ Brownish iris. Brown streaking on crown. ▪ Grayish brown upperparts with broad white tips. ▪ Large black shoulder patch. Broad white tips on greater coverts and remiges. ▪ *Note:* Recently fledged.

Plate 53. White-tailed Kite, juvenile [May] ▪ White underparts have tawny breast markings. ▪ Small black carpal patch. Dark gray primaries; pale gray secondaries. ▪ Underside of tail is white with dusky subterminal band. ▪ *Note:* Recently fledged. Hovering flight.

SNAIL KITE
(Rostrhamus sociabilis)

AGES: Adult, several interim basic (subadult), and juvenile stages.

Males have about three interim subadult plumages and/or years to attain the classic adult body plumage. However, it takes several additional years and molts to assume absolute full adult plumage on the underwing pattern. It is unknown how long it actually takes males to attain full adult features on the underwing. Based on limited data, it may take at least 8 years and perhaps longer for some individuals to attain full adult underwing characters.

Females also have a very gradual progression of plumage changes as their age advances and may take at least 10 years to achieve the "final," darkest type of adult female plumage. Because of plumage similarities between subadult females and midaged adult females, only one interim female subadult stage can be distinctly labeled.

Adult and older subadult sexes have fairly consistent sexually dimorphic iris color. Iris color does not alter with age once the respec-

tive sexual color is attained during the second year. Iris color is brighter and more visible under most lighting conditions on males than on females.

Juveniles have slightly narrower wings than older ages.

Snail Kites have been the subject of intense demographic studies for decades, with hundreds of banded, known-aged individuals, but little information has ever been published on the plumages of the various ages. The exact length of time each respective age class is held beyond the juvenile stage is unknown. However, it appears molt sequences may be completed annually after the first prebasic molt. Molt is particularly noticeable on females and subadults because of their feather patterns. Birds in brown plumages are worn and faded in the spring and summer and new and fresh in fall and winter. Extreme variables that span the extended breeding season and often the very early age of first breeding (*see* Nesting), food availability and individual variation may reflect molt timing and plumage characters in advancing age classes. Snail Kites also appear to be a rather long-lived species, with substantial numbers surviving beyond 10 years of age. Longevity of kites may affect gradual plumage transition and individual variation (*see below*).

Several banded, known-age wild kites were photographed and studied at close range on Lake Kissimmee, Osceola Co.; in the Everglades of n. Dade Co.; and on Lake Tohopekaliga, Osceola Co. Numerous museum specimens were also examined. Although specimens are not of known-aged birds, they allow close inspection of molt and plumage sequence and comparison against actual known-aged birds in the wild. Plumage data herein are based on the compilation of the small sample of photographed known-aged birds and numerous other individuals that were either photographed or were museum specimens.

Known-aged photographed Snail Kites: (1) Six-month-old juvenile entering the first prebasic molt (black band on right leg, "D over Y") was hatched in early Jun. 1996 and photographed in late Nov. 1996. (2) Ten-month-old juvenile in first prebasic molt (black band on right leg with "Z over V") was hatched in late Mar. 1997 and photographed in mid-Feb. 1998 (by J. Zipp in the Everglades). (3) Two-year-old female (yellow band over a red band with "1 over U" on the red band on right leg) was hatched in May 1999 and photographed in May 2001. (4) Four-year-old female ("26" on a black band on right leg) was hatched in the spring of 1987 and photographed in the summer of 1991. (5) Five-year-old female ("5 over Y" on red band on right leg) was hatched in the spring of 1992 and photographed in late winter of 1997 (by K. T. Karlson at Tohopekaliga Lake). (6) Nine-year-old female (same bird as #5) was photographed again in the spring of 2001 (on Lake Kissimmee). (7) Adult female ("58" on a black band on right leg) was a minimum of 3 years old when banded as an adult in the spring of 1992 and was photographed in the spring of 1996. The head and ventral features, however, probably make her at least 10 years old (*see below*). (8) Seven-year-old adult male ("7 over O" on a red band on right leg) was hatched in the spring of 1994 and photographed in the spring of 2001. (9) Fourteen-year-old adult male ("30" on a yellow band on right leg) was photographed in the spring of 1996 (on Lake Kissimmee). (10) Nineteen-year-old adult male (same bird as #9)

was photographed again in the spring of 2001 (also on Lake Kissimmee).

Male plumages.: Adult male.—Full adult body plumage is acquired in the fourth prebasic molt when about 4 years old. The only previously published documentation of males attaining adult plumage in a prescribed time frame are captive adult males from Argentina that entered their adult plumage in their fourth year (Sykes et al. 1995). However, the definition of "adult" plumage can be quite vague. Based on limited data on known-aged birds, it may take several additional molts and/or years before achieving full adult stature in having the completely dark underside of the remiges. There are a substantial number of "adult" males in full adult body plumage that exhibit a variable amount of pale barring on the underside of the remiges, characters that are mainly found on younger adult males. Adult male #8, at 7 years of age, still had younger-age traces of pale barring on the underside on a couple of remiges and greater primary coverts on both wings. *Note:* Plumage account of adult male is divided into "older" and "younger" categories.

Subadult (basic) III male.—Plumage is acquired in the third prebasic molt when about 3 years old. Body plumage is essentially adultlike but with variable traces of retained immature feathers and immature-like feathers. The underside of the remiges are completely barred. There are no banded, known-aged birds that were available in this age class for absolute verification; however, molt and plumage data from adjacent ages were used to substantiate this age group.

Subadult (basic) II male.—Plumage is acquired in the second prebasic molt when about 2 years old. This stage has never been previously described in the age chronology and adds an additional time span before males achieve the full adult body plumage. There were also no banded, known-aged birds located for absolute age verification. Data are based on museum specimens that clearly illustrate birds that were molting out of the subadult (basic) stage. These individuals were molting into a similar pale-edged dorsal feather pattern that they had as a subadult (basic) I. The birds were also in the process of replacing a worn adultlike tail pattern, which was first obtained in the subadult I (basic I) stage. Also, information is based on photographed birds with very adult malelike iris color in moderately heavily marked brown-colored plumages. Head and ventral markings are more heavily marked than in the subadult I (basic I) class. Tarsi and foot color can be similar to adult male's, and at times, possibly cere and lore color. *Note:* Separable from similar-aged female at close range by the brighter red iris and usually by a more reddish orange tarsus and foot color.

Subadult (basic) I male.—Plumage is fully acquired in the first prebasic molt when barely over 1 year old, and is worn for most of the second year of life. The first plumage characters signifying this age class appear when birds are 4–5 months old, but may not be readily apparent until rectrix molt begins at nearly 6 months of age, and with the beginning of remige molt somewhat later. This plumage is very similar and often identical to the juvenile plumage except for the newly acquired adult-like tail pattern. Nearly full body feathering is acquired at 10–12 months of age. This age class is easily identifiable in the early stage by the retained brown juvenile iris color. In the latter part of the second year, iris color gradually changes to the red color of the respective adult sex. Retained, worn juvenile feathering is apparent on dorsal regions of the body and on the outer remiges until around the 1-year-old mark. Kite #1, at 6 months of age, had just begun its transition into subadult I age class. Kite #2, at 10 months of age, had replaced several head and scapular feathers, a few upperwing coverts, and about one-half of the primaries. Much of the tail has been molted into feathers with an adultlike pattern (with r6 set partially grown).

Juvenile male.—Plumage features are retained for only 4–5 months. This short time span is typical of many kite species. *Note:* Not separable from juvenile females.

Female plumages.: Adult female.—Acquisition of the "adult" plumage can be acquired when 2 years old (subadult/basic II), but may take until 3 (subadult/basic III) or possibly 4 years old (subadult/basic IV) to gain darker head and ventral markings. There are no determined criteria of plumage features that are assigned to "full" adult females other than being darker on the head and more heavily marked on the ventral areas than juveniles and

subadult (basic) I birds. In females, however, there is a very gradual darkening of plumage features on many if not most individuals with increasing age. Sykes and Bennetts in Sykes et al. (1995) say that females attain the "final" dark type plumage, with the dark head and ventral areas, beginning at about age 10. Kite #3, at 2 years of age was moderately marked on the ventral regions. Kite #4, at 4 years of age, was fairly heavily marked and probably an "average" adult female. Kite #5, for instance, was typically paler on the head and ventral regions in 1997 at 5 years of age than she was in 2001 at 9 years of age. However, when 5 years old, kite #5 was only moderately marked and paler than kite #4 was at 4 years of age. Considerable plumage variation exists. Kite #5, at 9 years of age, was not as dark on the head and ventral areas as numerous other very dark headed and dark bodied but unaged females that, based on Sykes et al. (1995), are presumably at least 10 years old.

Subadult (basic) I females are identical to the respective age in males except midway in the age class the darker red iris color typical of females may become noticeable. *See above* "subadult/basic" description of kites #1 and #2.

Juvenile female.—Not separable from juvenile males. As in males, plumage is retained for only 4–5 months.

MOLT: Accipitridae wing and tail molt pattern (see chapter 4). The first prebasic molt begins at 4–5 months of age when the juvenile plumage begins to molt into the identical or nearly identical-looking subadult (basic) I age. This is documented with two birds (kites #1 and 2), but substantiated by numerous other individuals in the field and museums from spring, summer, and fall that are nearly 1 year old or just over 1 year old and have achieved various amounts of new feathering among old, worn juvenile feathers. Molt begins on the head and forward ventral areas, expands onto the middle upperwing coverts, then continues onto the scapulars and back. Rectrices begin molting when about 6 month old, and is a very rapid molt. Remiges begin to molt later, probably when 7–9 months old. Remix and body molt is in progress and rectrix molt is mainly complete when birds reach 1 year of age. When about 10 months to 1 year old, primary molt is about half complete (p1–3 or p1–5) and secondary and tertial molt is just beginning (on s1, 5, and s12–14). On the upperwing coverts, all middle, greater, and patagial area coverts will molt prior to an isolated block of old, retained juvenile feathers on the distal lesser coverts. Greater wing coverts may precede the molt of the respective secondaries, but seem to molt in unison with the primaries.

The second prebasic molt is based on only one known-aged bird (kite #3). Molt appeared to have begun on this bird before attaining the 2-year-old mark. Rectrix molt was nearly complete for the second time at the 2-year-old mark. Timing of the rectrix molt seems logical since the rectrices begin molting quite early in the molt time table in the first prebasic molt. Also, at 2 years of age, the primaries may acquire seven new inner feathers by the second birthday. Amount of body molt appears to be moderate. *Note:* Body and wing covert molt is easy to detect on younger subadults as the new feathers are broadly edged with tawny and contrast sharply with the older, worn feathers, which lack pale edges.

Additional older prebasic molts generally occur from spring through fall; however, this may have some variation. A sizable number of subadults and adults are in a fairly harmonious molt sequence on their remiges and bodies in May. Kites may molt several inner primaries (often p1–5) and begin secondary molt by this time (s1 and s5, and the tertials). Kites occasionally appear to have serially descendant molt on the primaries with two sets of feathers molting simultaneously (e.g., p1 and 2 and p8 and 9). Body, remix, and rectrix molt appear to be nearly synchronous on older ages.

SUBSPECIES: Polymorphic with three subspecies. *R. s. plumbeus* is found only in cen. and s. Florida. *R. s. plumbeus* also inhabits certain areas on Cuba. See Sykes et al. (1995) for detailed occupied areas in Florida and Cuba.

Two additional races in the American Tropics (Howell and Webb 1995, Sykes et al. 1995): (1) *R. s. major* is fairly common to common along the Gulf Plain of Mexico from cen. Veracruz to Chiapas, with a narrow range extension to the Pacific Coast at Guerrero; has been seen in Nayarit. *R. s. major* seasonally inhabits the Yucatán Peninsula, Mexico, and is also found in n. Guatemala and nw. Honduras. This is the largest race with the largest bill. (2) *R. s.*

sociabilis is very widespread but locally distributed from Nicaragua south into South America, east of the Andes Mts., to Brazil, e. Bolivia, e. Paraguay, n. Argentina, and Uruguay. *R. s. sociabilis* is the smallest subspecies.

COLOR MORPHS: None.

SIZE: Medium-sized raptor. Females average slightly larger than males but there is a considerable amount of overlap (Sykes et al. 1995). Length: 16–19 in. (41–48 cm); wingspan: 41–44 in. (104–112 cm).

SPECIES TRAITS: HEAD.—**Narrow bill with a long, sharply decurved upper mandible. Bare skin on the lores and basal area of the lower mandible.** A supraorbital ridge is lacking, which produces the "stern" look of most raptors. BODY.—**Long, thin talons are quite straight.** WINGS.—**Long and fairly broad with very rounded wingtips.** When perched, wingtips project beyond the tail tip. TAIL.—**Moderately long and square-tipped. White uppertail and undertail coverts. White basal region of the outer rectrices on both the dorsal and ventral surfaces.**

ADULT TRAITS: HEAD.—Red iris, but color is somewhat sexually dimorphic. Iris color of males is always vivid red; iris color of females may not appear red unless seen in intense, low-angled light. TAIL.—**Blackish, crisply edged band across the tail. Subterminal band is wide and pale brown with a narrow white tip.**

ADULT MALE (OLDER): HEAD.—Iris color is a bright red and higly visible under any lighting condition. **Cere, gape, basal area of the lower mandible, and lore skin varies from yellow or pale orangish when not breeding to a bright orange, reddish orange, or orangish red when breeding.** Cere is often somewhat paler and more yellowish than the lores, base of lower mandible, and gape in any season. **Medium bluish gray head and neck.** BODY.—**Underparts are medium bluish gray, but may have a brownish cast on worn feathers. Upperparts are bluish gray but also become a bit brownish on the scapulars when plumage is worn and faded. Legs and feet vary in being orange, reddish orange, or orangish red; however there is minimal color change between breeding and nonbreeding birds. Tarsi and feet are somewhat more reddish than the cere, but similar to the color of the lores on breeding birds.** WINGS.—**Underside of remiges, including**

the greater primary coverts, are uniformly dark gray. All lesser underwing coverts are bluish gray. Upperwing coverts are brownish gray, but may be as bluish as the rest of the upperparts. Upperwing coverts contrast with the much darker remiges and primary greater coverts and create a two-toned effect.

Note: Age of attaining this age class is unknown. It may take adult males several years to assume the uniformly dark underwing once full adult male body plumage has been acquired at 4–5 years of age. Once adult body plumage is acquired, there appears to be no further variations. There was no difference in the plumage of the kite that was photographed at 14 years old and again at 19 years old. His plumage was more faded due to exposure to the elements when photographed in late May than in early Mar.

ADULT MALE (YOUNGER): HEAD and BODY as on older male. WINGS.—Underside of the remiges are variably barred with whitish and pale gray. Primary greater underwing coverts also have pale grayish barring. Bases of the outer one or two primaries may be barred or mottled with white or are all-white. The pale barred remiges are slowly replaced through subsequent molts with feathers having a lesser amount of barring and eventually enter in the above older age class. Younger adult males have the identical two-toned effect on the upper surface of the wings as older males.

Note: Based on limited data of known-aged birds, this age class may constitute adult males that are 4–7 years old. A 7-year-old male (kite #8) still had faint pale gray barring on two secondaries and many greater primary underwing coverts on each wing. However, there may be considerable individual variation, and younger or older birds may also possess or lack barring.

ADULT MALE (BLACK TYPE): HEAD and BODY.—Much darker than typical adult males, especially on the head and back. Plumage is sometimes quite bluish black or brownish black. Scapulars and belly can become somewhat brownish with wear. WINGS.—Upperwing coverts often have a brownish tone and two-toned when contrasting against the darker remiges.

Note: Age of these birds is unknown; however, seen on several "older" type males. A fairly common plumage variation.

ADULT FEMALE (OLDER): HEAD.—Iris color is a dark red, but may appear very dark red under low light conditions. Cere, gape, basal area of lower mandible, and lores are yellow or orangish yellow; very rarely are these areas as orange or reddish as on breeding males. Head, nape, and hindneck are dark brown, but can become quite grayish on some birds in worn plumage. Forehead may be dark or have a small whitish patch. Generally lacks a pale supercilium, but may have a small, partial supercilium above the auriculars. A white "chin strap" extends from the throat up onto the jaw and under the eyes. BODY and WINGS (fresh plumage).—Underparts are dark brown with a few tawny blotches on the breast, belly, and lower belly; flanks are solid dark. Leg feathers are dark brown. Tarsi and feet are yellowish orange or orange, even on most breeding birds, and generally a bit brighter and more orangish than the cere and lores. Tarsi and feet are rarely reddish orange during breeding season. Upperparts, including all upperwing coverts, are scalloped with fairly broad tawny-edged feathers. BODY and WINGS (worn plumage).—Underparts are dark brown with some whitish blotches on the breast, belly, and lower belly; flanks are solid dark. Upperparts are uniformly medium brown because the feathers have faded and all pale tawny feather edgings have worn off. With molt from spring through fall, new, dark brown tawny-edged feathers sprout amongst the faded plumage. WINGS.—Pale gray or somewhat pale tawny undersides of the remiges are marked with narrow or moderately wide dark barring. Wide dark trailing edge on the underside of the secondaries have a dusky area inside of the trailing edge that creates a very broad dark rear border of the underwing. Basal area on the underside of the outer four or five primaries may be white and either have a lesser amount of dark barring or lack barring. Underwing coverts are dark brown and mottled with tawny-rufous. Upperwing area is uniformly brown and not two-toned as in adult males.

Note: This age class consists of birds that are approximately 10 years old or older (based on Sykes and Bennetts in Sykes et al. 1995).

ADULT FEMALE (YOUNGER): HEAD.—Iris color is dark red. Cere, gape, basal area of the lower mandible, and lores as on "older" females. Forehead is whitish. On younger birds, the supercilium is fairly broad and connects with the pale forehead. On older birds, a small pale patch on forehead may be retained, but the supercilium becomes very narrow or is lacking over the eyes but broadens into a moderate sized pale patch above the auriculars. In fresh plumage, pale head areas are tawny. In worn plumage, pale areas become white. Nape and hindneck are dark brown, but can become very gray on some individuals when plumage is worn. **Broad dark line behind the eyes connects to the dark patch on the rear one-third of the auriculars; the forward auriculars, cheeks, and throat are white or pale tawny.** As a rule, as birds get older, they gradually get darker on the head. With the reduced pale supercilium above the auriculars, the dark eyeline broadens and eventually is not apparent as it expands and merges with the large dark auricular area and dark crown. BODY and WINGS.—Same fade and wear variables as described above for "older" females. The back and forward scapulars can also become quite grayish in worn plumage. Ventral areas are moderately blotched, broadly streaked, or a mixture of blotching and streaking with dark brown; flanks are more extensively marked than the breast and belly and may be solid brown. Generally do not have streaking on the ventral areas. As a rule, ventral areas gradually darken with increasing age. Pale areas are tawny when fresh and new, but fade to white when worn and faded. Leg feathers are dark brown, but may be tawny or whitish and mottled with dark on younger birds.

Note: This description covers a span from 2-year-olds (subadult II/basic II; kite # 3) up to nearly 10-year-old birds (kite #4, 5, and 6).

BASIC (SUBADULT) TRAITS: Tail pattern identical to adults. Shared plumage traits between sexes in the first and second plumages; however, older subadult females (basic/subadult II and III) are generally not separable from mid-aged adult females. Subadult traits are more definable in males.

BASIC III (SUBADULT III) MALE: HEAD.—Iris is bright red as on adult males. Head is medium or dark grayish as on adult males or quite brownish on the head and neck. Throat may either have a large white patch or white streaking (but does not extend up onto the jaw

and under the eyes as a "chin strap" as on older, dark females). Some may have a partial whitish supercilium behind the eye. Cere, gape, and lore color as on older males; intensity of color is dependent on breeding status. BODY.—Medium grayish or dark grayish underparts and upperparts often have a distinct brownish tone. Underparts are either grayish brown or brown and have some tawny or rufous edged or mottled feathers. Juvenile-like brown streaking and/or mottling is often retained on the lower belly. Leg feathers are tipped or mottled with tawny or rufous. WINGS.—Whitish or pale gray underside of the remiges are marked with broad black barring. The greater primary coverts are black with narrow white bars.

BASIC II (SUBADULT II) MALE: HEAD.—Iris color is adultlike bright red. Cere, gape, basal area of the lower mandible, and lores can be either orangish yellow or orange; at height of breeding, may possibly be orangish red as in older males. White and/or pale tawny on the forehead, supercilium is narrow or lacking over the eye, but broadens over the auricular area. Narrow dark eyeline connects to a moderately large dark brown auricular patch. Sides of the neck and nape are dark brown; but, as in females, can become quite grayish with wearing and fading. BODY.—Upperparts are dark brown and scalloped with tawny-edged feathers in fresh plumage, but pale edgings wear off and plumage fades and becomes uniformly brown. Ventral areas are moderately blotched with brown. Pale areas are tawny in fresh plumage, but become white when worn and faded. Leg feathers are dark with some pale markings. Tarsi and feet are orange, reddish orange, or orangish red. WINGS.—Upperwing coverts are scalloped in fresh plumage and uniformly medium brown when faded and worn. Undersides of remiges are barred as in adult females. TAIL.—As in adults.

Note: Separable from similar-age and/or younger adult females only by brighter red iris color and possibly more reddish color on the tarsi and feet.

BASIC I (SUBADULT I) MALE/FEMALE: HEAD.—Iris is dark brown but gradually changes to respective sexual red color during the latter part of the age class. Cere, gape, basal area of the lower mandible, and lores are pale yellow or yellow. Pale forehead and broad supercilium. Supercilium may end over the auriculars or extend onto and encircle the nape, as it does on many juveniles. Supercilium is tawny when in fresh plumage, but fades to white. A narrow or moderately wide dark eyeline connects to small brown patch on the rear of the auriculars. *Note:* Head can be nearly identical to a juvenile's. BODY.—Upperparts molt into the pale tawny, broadly edged pattern as they had when they were juveniles. A few retained, worn, non-edged juvenile scapular feathers are situated amongst new feathers for a few months. The ventral body is either narrowly streaked like a juvenile or lightly covered with brown blotches. A large dark patch is on the sides of the neck. Many individuals molt directly into the identical ventral markings they had as juveniles. Leg feathers are pale tawny and spotted with some dark markings. Tarsi and feet are slightly orangish yellow. WINGS.—Upperwing coverts are tawny-edged. However, a large patch of faded old juvenile feathers remain on the middle upperwing coverts until most other feathers have molted. Undersides of the remiges are pale grayish or tawny and barred throughout with narrow bars, but the trailing edge of the secondaries is composed of a wide dark band and a dusky area in front of the dark band, as on all older ages. Remiges take several months to molt out of the old, faded and worn juvenile feathering. New, darker remiges are noticeable on the inner few primaries, s1 and s5 secondaries, and on the tertials (most visible feathers on perched birds). Individuals at or just beyond 1 year of age may still have several outer juvenile primaries. TAIL.—Molts into the crisply edged, black banded pattern. This pattern is fully achieved before reaching 1 year of age.

Note: Plumage begins to be acquired at about 4–5 months of age and completed just after attaining 1 year of age. Data based on kites #1 and #2. Plumage is held for much of the second year, but rectrices and remiges are molted for the second time before ending the second year.

JUVENILE TRAITS (BOTH SEXES): Dark brown iris. Pale yellow cere, gape, and basal area of the lower mandible. Lores are whitish or grayish. Broad, pale supercilium connects from the pale forehead and often wraps around the nape.

Narrow dark eyeline connects to a small brown patch on the rear of the auriculars. Sides of the head are often pale and unmarked. A dark patch is on the sides of the neck. BODY.—Dorsal body is broadly scalloped with pale tawny, but is a rich tawny when recently fledged. Breast, belly, and lower belly are narrowly streaked with dark brown. Flanks have broader dark markings than rest of the underparts. Tarsi are pale yellow. Leg feathers are pale and may have some dark spotting. WINGS.—Undersides of the remiges are pale grayish and become white on the basal area of the outer primaries. Remiges are patterned with narrow dark barring except on the outer few primaries. Trailing edge of the secondaries has a moderately wide dark band, but not the wide dusky inner area ahead of the dark band, as on older birds. TAIL.—**Brown with whitish narrow terminal band. The brown band is fairly crisply defined on the inner three rectrix sets but is diffused and poorly defined on the outer three sets (not the crisp, black delineation of all older ages).**

Note: Plumage is retained for only 4–5 months.

ABNORMAL PLUMAGES: None reported.

HABITAT: Warm, clear, calm, freshwater marshes and shallow lakes with marshy areas made up of submerged vegetation, low floating and standing vegetation, and expanses of open water. Breeding areas have partially submerged taller growths of woody vegetation or cattails along portions of the shoreline for nesting. Roosting sites may be in bushes or small trees growing on land or in water. Foraging areas and territories have various types of low over-water perch structures for perching and feeding.

Nonbreeding and nomadic birds range widely to various freshwater canals, rivers, swamps, and small impoundments with low, open vegetation.

HABITS: A rather confiding, tame raptor. Gregarious in all seasons.

Perches on mainly exposed vegetation at moderate or low elevation. Also perches on water-level, floating vegetation. In some areas, kites may perch on utility wires and various types of posts, but not on utility poles. Prey is brought back to a favorite perch and eaten.

FEEDING: Mainly an aerial hunter, but also a

perch hunter. Feeds almost exclusively on the Apple Snail. Snail Kites rarely prey on other species of snails, small turtles, crayfish, and snakes.

Intake of prey other than Apple Snails occurs mainly during periods of drought and in cold weather, when Apple Snails are inactive or stay farther beneath the surface of the water and are more difficult to capture at greater submerged depths. Hunting forays for Apple Snails extend for longer periods and with less success during cold weather.

Snails Kites capture snails with their feet and transport their prey to a favorite perch or nest site either in their feet or in their bills. Most of the time, Apple Snails are deftly plucked from the water's surface or just under the surface; however, kites will submerge their legs and bellies in water to reach a snail.

Once a kite has returned to a perch, the snail is snipped from the attachment point of the shell and extracted from its shell, then is either swallowed whole or is eaten in pieces. The snail's shell is dropped beneath the kite's perch.

FLIGHT: The head points downwards with irregular sequence of flapping and gliding when hunting. Flapping consists of slow, labored wingbeats. Wings are held in an arch when gliding. Wings also held in an arched position when soaring. Kites may soar to very high altitudes. Hovers frequently when hunting. Snail Kites do not kite.

Kites hunt mainly at altitudes of 5–30 ft. (1.5–10 m) high by taking a direct path, an erratic path, or tacking into the wind. When foraging along edges of vegetation or shorelines, kites regularly hold a straight flight path. Flights are more erratic over open water or over large expanses of partially submerged or floating vegetation. When a snail is sighted, a kite will bank sharply or gently glide down and snatch the snail out of the water. On several occasions Snail Kites have been seen making gentle-angled dive descents from well over 100 ft. (30 m) over open water and capture snails.

VOICE: One single main vocalization with several variations. A monotone nasal buzzing *qua-a-a-a-a-a-a-a* of varying duration, but sometimes a more emphatic, stacatto *qua-ack-ack-ack-ack-ack-ack*. Call may be shorten at times to a nasal buzzing *quack*. (Human imitation is done by constricting the

throat muscles and inhaling air.) Male's call is higher pitched than that of female's. Quite vocal, especially during social interactions and courtship.

STATUS AND DISTRIBUTION: Found only in the U.S. in cen. and s. Florida. Listed as a Federally Endangered Species since 1967 under the Endangered Species Conservation Act of 1967, then under the Endangered Species Act of 1973. Estimated population as of the late 1990s are 1,500 individuals (V. Dreitz, unpubl.). Current population is considered overall fairly stable and possibly increasing. However, populations fluctuate with widespread drought conditions that periodically affect cen. and s. Florida.

Snail Kite populations were annually monitored from 1969 to 1994, with numbers varying from 65 to 1,000 birds. Low counts usually coincided with periods of widespread drought. More recent estimates are based on additional knowledge of expanded, isolated range areas and more extensive, comprehensive surveying and monitoring. Status data is also assisted by telemetry. In the 1940s and 1950s, in the low point of the kite's status, less than 40 birds were tallied.

Historically, one-fourth of the Florida Peninsula was freshwater marsh; now, only one-half of the original wetlands area exists.

Current distribution mirrors that of the 1980s and includes several isolated small and large lakes, marshes, and impoundments in Collier, Glades (Lake Okeechobee), Hendry, Highlands, Indian River, Lee, Martin, Orange, Osceola (mainly Tohopekaliga Lake, East Tohopekaliga Lake, and Lake Kissimmee), and St. Luci Cos. A contiguous series of large-acreage managed wetlands (Water Conservation Areas 1, 2A, 2B, 3A, and 3B), which are remnants of the original Everglades, are found from ne. Monroe, se. Collier, and n. Dade Cos. north through portions of Broward and e. Palm Beach Cos. These contiguous areas of the Everglades still harbor the majority of the population, particularly Water Conservation Area 3A.

Movements.—Generally sedentary but highly nomadic within regional areas. Most nomadic excursions take them within typical areas of known range and habitat. Nomadic wanderings occur during any year and at any time of the year, regardless of water level. All ages have a tendency to engage in nomadic excursions or dispersal to other portions of their range. Nomadism and dispersal may be somewhat more apparent during extensive drought conditions with birds extending into atypical areas.

Southward movement out of northern counties may occur during cold weather periods of the winter months. This is undoubtedly due to the fact that the kites are not able to procure a sufficient supply of Apple Snails during periods of cold temperatures (see Feeding).

NESTING: Mainly Jan.–Aug. Nesting, however, has been documented in all months. Either sex may first breed when 9 months old (and molting from juvenile to subadult/basic I age). Nests in loosely formed colonies or at solo sites. Colonial nesting areas may be reused for several years. Some colonial nesting may be on the periphery of colonial sites of Anhingas and wading birds (e.g., various heron and ibis species). Males build nests and may construct a nest prior to obtaining a mate. Females assist in the upkeep of nest once constructed. Double broods are common.

During seasons of optimal water depth and supply of Apple Snails, either member of a pair will desert its mate and family prior to fledging and remate and renest. The deserted parent then raises the nestlings and fledglings by itself.

Water-level conditions, particularly severe drought, may dictate breeding potential within local and regional areas. Snail Kites may not breed on a large scale or may experience high rate of nest failure during years of low water levels. Depending on the reproductive stage, the nesting success of a pair may not be impeded by a change in local water level.

Nests are placed over water in various types of vegetation that grow from the water. Nest sites vary from being placed just above water level on matted vegetation or up to 15 ft. (5 m) high in cattails, bushes, and small trees. Occasionally, nests may be up to 33 ft. (10 m) high. During periods of high water levels, nests are more likely to be placed in partially submerged, strong woody vegetation along shorelines. In low-water-level periods, the receded water leaves most woody plant species on dry ground and thus forces kites to nest in soft, weak, nonwoody vegetation such as cattails that are still partially submerged.

Nests are highly variable in size and structure and may be comprised of woody sticks or soft stems of reeds. Nests placed in cattails are built atop bent-over clusters of cattail stalks. Nest sites are either hidden or exposed in live or dead structures, but are readily accessed by flight from above the nest. Nests are generally fairly large, rather flat, and often loosely constructed. Size: 10–23 in. (25–58 cm) in diameter and 3–17 in. (8–44 cm) deep. Inner bowl of the nest is lined with fine pieces of material and may include some greenery.

Courtship (flight).—Displays are performed by males for potential mates: *Sky-dancing* and *slow-flapping* are the most common, and the male often carries either a small or large stick in his bill. *Mutual soaring, tumbling,* and *talon-grappling* occur much less frequently. See chapter 5 for courtship descriptions.

Courtship (perched).—Once a male has attracted a female, he may offer her snails or sticks.

One to 5 eggs, but average 3 eggs. Eggs are incubated by both sexes for 26–28 days. Youngsters are capable of sustained flight when 42–56 days old, but "branch" about one week before attaining flight. Fledglings are dependent on their parents and nest site for feeding and roosting until 9–11 weeks old.

CONSERVATION: An intensely managed species due to its endangered status and water control programs in Florida. As an endangered species, Snail Kites also benefit from the protection afforded by the Endangered Species Act. Within logical means, water levels are controlled for optimum breeding and foraging. Many lakes are periodically drained or sprayed to control vegetation overgrowth that inhibits kite foraging. Nutrient-rich water entering many lakes and marshes from urban and agricultural areas promotes rapid growth of undesirable aquatic plants that reduce foraging habitat. The State of Florida is implementing large-scale ecosystem-restoration plans for water control; these plans will benefit the Snail Kite, as well as other aquatic-dependent species.

In the past, artificial nest platforms made of wire baskets have been installed in some areas where nests are built on frail cattail and are very susceptible to collapse.

Mortality.—Illegal shooting occurs on a limited basis during the fall and winter waterfowl season. Nests are occasionally destroyed by airboats. Natural mortality occurs, with frail nests collapsing and predators killing nestlings and fledglings.

SIMILAR SPECIES: Northern Harrier, both sexes and ages.—Range overlap Sep.–Apr. PERCHED.—Only juvenile females, with dark brown iris color, can be confused with Snail Kite when head is visible. Streaking on older females is similar to the Snail Kite's. Wingtips fall short of the tail tip when perched. FLIGHT.—Shares white uppertail coverts with the kite, but lacks white on outer basal region of tail. Wings are narrow and held in a dihedral when gliding and soaring.

OTHER NAMES: Formerly called the Everglade Kite. No other names used. *Spanish:* Gavilan Caracolero, Milano Caracolero. *French:* Milan des Marais.

REFERENCES: Baicich and Harrison 1997, Dreitz 2000, Howell and Webb 1995, Johnsgard 1990, Kale et al. 1992, Palmer 1988, Rodgers et al. 1988, Sykes et al. 1995, Wheeler and Clark 1995.

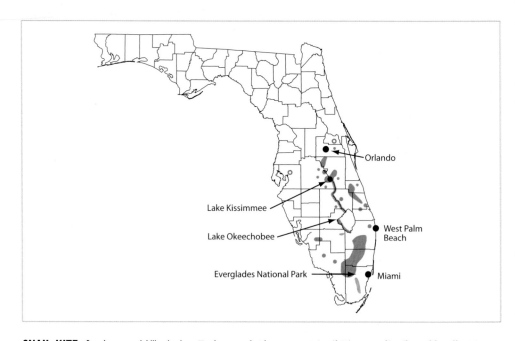

SNAIL KITE, *Rostrhamus sociabilis plumbeus:* Endangered. About 1,500 Snail Kites are distributed locally. Movements occur between all areas in all seasons.

Plate 54. Snail Kite, adult male [May] ▪ Thin, sharply hooked bill. Bright red iris. Orange cere and lores. Bluish-gray head. ▪ Bluish-gray body. ▪ Bluish-gray wing coverts; black remiges. ▪ *Note:* This is a banded bird that is 19 years old.

Plate 55. Snail Kite, adult male (dark type) [May] ▪ Thin, sharply hooked bill. Bright red iris. Yellow cere and lores. Blackish head. ▪ Grayish-black body. ▪ *Note:* Adult males of any age can be quite blackish. Nonbreeding males have pale ceres and lores.

Plate 56. Snail Kite, adult male (dark type) [Mar.] ▪ Thin, sharply hooked bill. Bright red iris. Orange cere and reddish orange lores. Blackish head. ▪ Blackish-gray body. ▪ Remiges are black and darker than coverts. ▪ *Note:* Adult males of any age can be quite blackish. Breeding males have vividly colored fleshy areas.

Plate 57. Snail Kite, adult male (older) [May] ▪ Gray head. ▪ Gray body; white undertail coverts. ▪ Uniformly gray remiges and underwing coverts. ▪ Black tail with crisp edges on white terminal band and basal bands. ▪ *Note:* It may take adult males several years to attain all-dark underside of remiges.

Plate 58. Snail Kite, adult male (younger) [May] ▪ Gray head. ▪ Gray body; white undertail coverts. ▪ Moderately barred remiges and greater coverts. ▪ Black tail with crisp edges on white terminal and basal bands. ▪ *Note:* Body as on older adult males, but has a variable amount of gray barring on remiges.

Plate 59. Snail Kite, adult male (younger/older) [May] ▪ Gray upperparts. ▪ Gray upperwing coverts contrast with black remiges. ▪ Black tail with crisp edges on the white basal band; white up-pertail coverts. P10 and s1 are partially grown; p1–5 are new feathers.

Plate 60. Snail Kite, adult male [Mar.] ▪ Foraging kites look down and flap and glide on arched wings.

Plate 61. Snail Kite, subadult (basic) III male [May] ▪ Bright red iris. ▪ Whitish throat. ▪ Whitish or tawny mottling on bluish gray-blackish underparts. ▪ *Note:* Similar to old, worn-plumaged females except white is only on throat and iris is a brighter red. A mated, nesting bird.

Plate 62. Snail Kite, subadult (basic) III male
[**May**] ▪ Bluish-gray body with pale mottling on underparts and leg feathers. ▪ Pale gray barring on all remiges and primary greater coverts. ▪ Black tail with crisp edges on white terminal and basal bands; white undertail coverts. ▪ *Note:* Similar to old, worn-plumaged females except white is only on throat. Nesting bird.

Plate 63. Snail Kite, adult female (older) [Mar.] ▪ Thin, sharply hooked bill; yellow cere and lores. Dark red iris. Dark brown head with white "chin strap" that extends under eyes. ▪ Dark brown underparts with some tawny and white mottling. Yellow tarsi and feet. ▪ *Note:* Females take about 10 years to get the dark head with white only on "chin strap."

Plate 64. Snail Kite, adult female (older) [May] ▪ Thin, sharply hooked bill; yellow cere and lores. Dark red iris. Dark brown head with a white "chin strap" extending to eyes. Very small supercilium patch. ▪ Old, worn brown plumage with new, tawny-edged feathers. ▪ *Note:* Tawny edges wear off by mid-winter. Holding an Apple Snail.

Plate 65. Snail Kite, adult female (older) [May] ▪ Thin, sharply hooked bill; yellow cere and lores. Dark red iris. Dark brown head with a white "chin strap" extending to eyes. Mid-aged and older females may have gray heads. Small white supercilium. ▪ Mid-aged and older females may have gray backs and forward scapulars.

Plate 66. Snail Kite, adult female (older) [May] ▪ Gray head with white "chin strap." Small white supercilium. ▪ Dark brown underparts with some pale mottling. White undertail coverts. ▪ Whitish remiges with distinct black barring; broad black terminal band. ▪ Black tail with crisp edges on white terminal and grayish basal bands. ▪ *Note:* Snails are carried in feet or bill.

Plate 67. Snail Kite, adult female (older) [May] ▪ Gray head with a white "chin strap." Small white supercilium. ▪ Grayish back and forward scapulars. ▪ White upper tail coverts and base of black tail. ▪ *Note:* Snails are carried in bill or feet.

Plate 68. Snail Kite, adult/subadult female (younger) [May] ▪ Thin, sharply hooked bill; yellow cere and lores. Dark red iris. White forehead, short supercilium, throat, and cheeks; dark eyeline. ▪ Dark brown underparts have a moderate amount of pale mottling/streaking.

Plate 69. Snail Kite, subadult (basic)I [Mar.] ▪ Brown iris. Yellow cere and lores. Whitish forehead, long supercilium, throat, and cheeks. ▪ Fresh, pale edged feathers; some remiges are old brown juvenile. ▪ Crisply edged black band on underside of tail. ▪ *Note:* 1 year old. Molts back into a juvenile-like plumage except on tail, which is adultlike. Molt begins when 4 or 5 months old.

Plate 70. Snail Kite, subadult (basic) I [May] ▪ Yellow cere and lores. Brown iris. Whitish forehead, long supercilium, throat, and cheeks. ▪ New pale-edged feathers growing on scapulars. ▪ New greater coverts; old juvenile lesser coverts and secondaries. ▪ *Note:* Younger than kite on plate 69. Molting back into a juvenile-like plumage. Molt begins when 4 or 5 months old.

Plate 71. Snail Kite, subadult (basic) I [May] ▪ Pale head with dark eyeline. ▪ Dark blotches/streaks on whitish underparts. ▪ Wide black band on rear of wing. ▪ Crisply edged adultlike black tail band; white basal tail band and undertail coverts.

Plate 72. Snail Kite, juvenile [Nov.] ▪ Pale head with thin dark eyeline. ▪ Narrowly streaked underparts; dark neck patch. ▪ Narrow dark rear edge of underwing. ▪ Nondescript dusky tail band.

Plate 73. Snail Kite, juvenile [Aug.] ▪ Dark brown iris. Yellow cere and gray lores. Rich tawny head with a thin dark eyeline. ▪ Narrowly streaked rich tawny underparts. Broad tawny edgings on upperparts. ▪ *Note:* Recently fledged. Tawny color fades to whitish within 1–2 months.

Snail Kite 99

MISSISSIPPI KITE
(Ictinia mississippiensis)

AGES: Adult, basic I (subadult), and juvenile.

Adults have sexually dimorphic plumages that are fairly diagnostic at field distances.

Basic I (Subadult) also have sexually dimorphic plumages and adhere to the same sexual traits as seen in the respective adult sex. Subadult age is not a separate plumage, but is a transitional molt stage consisting of adult and juvenile features. Subadults also have individual variation because of variable stages of molt progression.

Juveniles have a considerable amount of individual variation on body, wing, and tail markings, but do not have sexually dimorphic differences. Plumage is retained only a few months.

MOLT: Accipitridae wing and tail molt pattern (*see* chapter 4).

Adult.—Acquired when 1.5 years old. Females begin molt in Jun. or Jul. and males begin in Jul. or Aug. Molt begins with loss of the innermost primary (p1). Some females molt several inner remiges, but males generally molt only one or two remiges while in the U.S. Some females may also molt the innermost (r1) and outermost (r6) rectrices. However, many females—but no males—begin rectrix molt while in the U.S. Most molt, including body molt, occurs on the winter grounds. Any wing and tail molt that began in Jun. through Aug. is probably suspended during fall migration, then resumed once on the winter grounds. An adult specimen from the winter grounds in n. Argentina in mid-Jan. (AMNH) was just completing its annual wing molt with the replacement of the outermost primary set (p10).

Basic I (Subadult I).—This transitional stage consists of a very prolonged, continuously molting, first prebasic molt from juvenile to adult. The metamorphic plumage change begins when juveniles are on the winter grounds. Exact timing is unknown, but probably begins when about 4–6 months old, which is similar to most kite species. *Note:* Juveniles in early and mid-Oct. do not show signs of prebasic molt and are up to 4.5 months old at this time (*n* = 2 from Honduras; LSU). Molt continues

when the kites return to the U.S. and is completed when once again on the winter grounds. Molt is not completed until the birds are 1.5 years old. Head and breast are molted prior to other feather regions. *Note:* All new plumage acquired by molt is adult feathers.

Eye, cere, and foot colors change to adult colors prior to returning to the U.S. in spring. A considerable amount of body molt generally takes place on the winter grounds, but only a moderate amount occurs in summer. Body plumage is fairly adultlike when the kites return to the U.S. Further body molt progression into adult plumage is usually, but not always, completed by the end of summer.

Wings and tail molt on a partial basis during summer. Wing molt begins within a span from mid-May to mid-Jun. on the innermost primary (p1), then advances outwardly throughout the summer and fall, but rarely past p7 while in the U.S. As in most raptors, one or two old primaries are sequentially dropped ahead of incoming new adult replacements, so only a small gap of missing feathers is obvious. In mid-Jun., however, some individuals drop up to four inner primaries in quick succession before new adult replacements come in, thus creating a huge gap in the midwing area. Only the outermost secondary (s1) and the three tertials are molted while in the U.S. Molt on primaries and secondaries is completed on the winter grounds.

Most greater upperwing coverts are gradually replaced during the summer. Underwing coverts are also gradually replaced during the summer, except the greater underwing covert tract, which is not molted until on the winter grounds. Axillaries molt prior to the underwing coverts.

Tail molt begins from Jul. to Sep. Rectrix molt begins on deck rectrix set (r1), then proceeds to the outermost set (r6). However, odd birds may have other sequences (r4 sometimes is the first set to molt). Molt into adult rectrices rarely surpasses the innermost and outermost sets while in the U.S., and is completed on the winter grounds. Rarely, tail molt may begin as early as May.

Plumage transition is divided into three

headings: very early stage, early stage, and late stage. Advanced or delayed molt of various anatomical areas makes it difficult to accurately label plumage stages on some individuals. Very early and early stages correspond to a span from spring to early summer and late stage aligns with mid-summer to early fall periods.

SUBSPECIES: Monotypic. Closely related to and forms a superspecies with Plumbeous Kite of Central America (*see* Adult Female Traits: Band-tailed Type).

COLOR MORPHS: None.

SIZE: A medium-sized raptor. Males average somewhat smaller than females, and size is often visibly apparent in the field. Length: 12–15 in. (30–38 cm); wingspan: 29–33 in. (74–84 cm).

SPECIES TRAITS: HEAD.—Large black lore spot in front of the eyes. BODY.—Short, thick tarsi and toes. WINGS.—**When perched, wingtips extend somewhat beyond the tail tip. In flight, wings are very long and narrow, with parallel front and trailing edges on the secondaries, and taper to pointed wingtips. In soaring flight, outermost primary (p10) is distinctly shorter than longest primaries (p8 and 9).** However, when gliding, p10 is usually concealed by the overlapping longer primaries. When perched, secondaries are sometimes nearly covered by the greater coverts. TAIL.—**Square-tipped. When closed, tail is notched, and on males, it is often forked. Outer rectrix set flares slightly outward on the outer feather edge.**

ADULT TRAITS: HEAD.—**Pale grayish or whitish; throat is white. Dark gray bill and cere. The cere can be pale gray.** Red irises. BODY.—**Tarsi and toes are typically gray on the upperside and yellowish orange or orange on the underside, except on the upper tarsi, which may be bright orange.** Toes and tarsi are occasionally orangish on the upperside. **Medium gray underparts and dark bluish-gray upperparts.** WINGS.—**Upper surface of secondaries are very pale gray, but appear white at a distance. A white bar on the trailing edge of secondaries is apparent on the underwing when in flight.** Pale upper surface of secondaries is most visible from above in flight. **Secondaries appear as a narrow pale gray bar when perched; however, they are often covered by the greater coverts and barely visible.** Primaries are black on the upper surface and

dark gray on the undersides, and may have a variable amount of rufous on both the inner and outer webs. TAIL.—**All black on upper surface.**

ADULT MALE: HEAD.—**Pale gray or very pale gray and often appears white at a distance; palest on crown.** BODY.—**Uniformly pale gray underparts.** Lower belly and undertail coverts are the same color as the breast, belly, and flanks. **Upperparts are uniformly dark bluish gray.** Scapulars occasionally have a small white spot on the basal region of some feathers. WINGS.—Pale gray dorsal surface of the secondaries remains unchanged throughout the year. Underwing coverts are uniformly gray. TAIL.—**Uniformly black on the undersides.** Quills on the outermost set of rectrices (r6) are either black or white only on the very basal region.

ADULT FEMALE: HEAD.—**Medium gray, but sometimes pale gray. Medium gray-headed individuals often have a discernibly pale, whitish forehead, supercilium, and throat.** BODY.—**Medium gray or sometimes pale gray underparts.** Lower belly is either (1) the same gray color as the rest of the underparts or (2) white and appears as a fairly large white patch, which is most visible in flight as a white patch ahead of the tarsi and feet. Underparts may have small white spots on basal region of many feathers on the belly and flanks (and appear much like a subadult). **Upperparts are very dark bluish gray with a brownish cast.** Scapulars often have white spots on basal region of some feathers. Undertail coverts (1) are white with a gray mark on the tip of each feather and appear spotted, blotched, or barred; (2) may be all white; or (3) are solid gray like the rest of the underparts. WINGS.—The pale grayish sheen may wear off on the dorsal surface of the secondaries and become medium grayish or brownish gray. Underwing coverts often have pale speckling. TAIL.—Quills of the outermost rectrix set (r6) are white their entire length. There are two main variations of undertail patterns: (1) *Pale type*: **Pale gray on the inner three-fourths or four-fifths of each feather of the outer rectrix set with dusky or black tips on the distal one-fourth or one-fifth; all other rectrices are solid black. Tail appears to be pale gray with a moderately wide darker terminal band when**

closed. *Note:* Common pattern. (2) *Black type:* **Undertail is uniformly black (the quills of outermost rectrix set are still all white).** *Note:* Fairly common pattern.

ADULT FEMALE (BAND-TAILED TYPE): Two adult females with partial narrow white tail bands and one with a fully banded tail (with extensive rufous in the primaries) were photographed in Lamar, Colo., in 1999 and 2000; a fully banded type was also seen in Jun. 2001 and photographed in Aug. 2002, at the same location. Plumages of these birds were otherwise like typical adult females. It is unknown if this unusual pattern exists throughout the entire population. *Note:* A rare plumage and easily confused with subadults, and easily overlooked as an adult plumage variation.

BASIC I (SUBADULT I) TRAITS: Bill, cere, eyes, and feet are like adult's. Back and scapulars are primarily adultlike. Head, body, and undertail coverts are also like the respective adult sex. During typical residence in the U.S. (May–Sep.), transformation to adultlike plumage occurs in replacing most retained old rufous or brown juvenile feathering on the breast, belly, flanks, and upperwing coverts. Transition to adult plumage is partial on underwing coverts, primaries, and tail while in the U.S. Transition of scapulars and upperwing coverts to adult plumage is mainly complete. Secondaries are primarily retained, worn brown juvenile feathers. Old, tattered juvenile secondaries are uniformly brown at all times because the grayish sheen on the upper surface and white trailing edge of fresh juvenile plumage are worn off. Subadults have the same four underwing and three undertail patterns described in Juvenile Traits until partially altered by molt.

BASIC (SUBADULT; LATE STAGE): HEAD.—As on respective sex of adult. BODY.—Underparts acquire the adultlike gray color; however, some retain a few remnant juvenile rufous or brown markings on the underparts. Some females exhibit white spotting on underparts and both sexes can have scattered white spots on the scapulars. WINGS.—Upperwing coverts are primarily adultlike dark bluish gray. Greater secondary coverts are new adult feathers and, like adults, are often a slightly paler gray than the median and lesser coverts. Underwing coverts are predominantly or totally adultlike

gray, except the greater coverts, which are retained mottled or spotted brown or rufous juvenile feathers. New adult inner primaries are steadily acquired during this stage. New dark grayish or blackish primaries have crisply delineated, thin white tips and contrast sharply to the faded, worn, brown outer juvenile primaries. Since newly molted feathers are adult feathers, and many adults exhibit rufous markings on several primaries, many subadults have a rufous tinge on the several newly acquired primaries. Several new primaries project beyond the tertials when perched and are quite visible when perched and in flight. Secondaries are retained brown-colored juvenile, except the outermost (s1), as well as the three tertials, which molt into adult pale gray feathers. TAIL.— Deck rectrix set (r1) and outermost rectrix set (r6) often molt to adult blackish feathers while in the U.S. A few acquire only adult rectrices on the deck set (r1) while in the U.S. *Note:* When perched and viewed from the front, late stage females with partially banded or unbanded types look similar to adult females.

BASIC (SUBADULT; EARLY STAGE): HEAD.—As on respective sex of adult. BODY.—(1) Underparts regularly retain up to 50 percent rufous or brown streaked and barred, pale-edged, remnant juvenile ventral feathers. Many have white streaks and blotches on the breast, belly, and flanks. These white areas are caused by pale edges of the retained juvenile feathers, gaps of missing feathers, and, on some females, by white basal areas of new adult feathers. Mottled juvenile-mixed underparts may be retained into the fall. (2) Underparts may also be solid, adultlike gray on some individuals, even in May. WINGS.—(1) Upperwing coverts may be nearly full adult; (2) most upperwing coverts are adultlike with a few retained brown juvenile feathers intermixed; or (3) upperwing coverts may be mainly retained brown juvenile feathers with a few grayish adult feathers intermixed. Greater upper covert tract is primarily brown juvenile feathering; however, the inner half of the tract can be replaced with adult gray in the early part of this stage. Large white blotches are often present on the innermost greater coverts and tertials because previously overlapping feathers are temporarily lost due to molt. Underwing coverts are retained rufous or brown juvenile feathers; however, they are sometimes mixed with adult gray feathering. Axillaries obtain the adultlike gray before the rest of the underwing coverts. Newly acquired inner primaries are dark grayish or blackish adult feathers with crisply edged white tips. New adult primaries are not readily visible when perched, as there are only a few of them and they are covered by the long tertials; however, the new dark feathers are highly visible in flight. A variable-sized gap often occurs on the inner primaries with dropped, but not quickly replaced, new primaries from mid-Jun. to mid-Jul. Up to four primaries may be dropped before new adult replacements come in. Since newly molted feathers are adult feathers, and many adults exhibit rufous markings on several primaries, many subadults have a rufous tinge on the few newly acquired primaries. TAIL.—Fully retained juvenile.

BASIC (SUBADULT; VERY EARLY STAGE):
HEAD.—As on respective sex of adult. BODY.—Underparts are mainly adultlike gray on the breast, but the belly and flanks can be 50–100 percent retained juvenile streaking. The grayish head (especially on females) and breast, contrasting with the pale belly and flank area on birds that were paler type juveniles, may create a hooded appearance. Upperparts are primarily retained, worn and faded brown juvenile feathers on the scapulars; the back region is partially adultlike gray. WINGS.—Upperwing coverts are mostly retained brown-colored juvenile with few, if any, gray adult feathers. Underwing coverts are fully retained juvenile feathers, including the axillaries. There is some molt on the inner primaries, but with few adult replacements. TAIL.—Retained juvenile of any of the three variations.

Note: Only small number of birds are in this barely molted first prebasic molt stage in May and Jun.

JUVENILE TRAITS: HEAD.—**Grayish-streaked head (lacking a dark malar mark); short, broad, white supercilium.** Black lore area. Iris color is medium brown. Yellow cere. BODY (ventral).—Variable-width rufous or brown streaking on white or tawny breast and belly; flanks are typically barred. There are three variations of underpart markings on the breast, belly, and flanks. (1) *Narrowly streaked type:* Narrow streaking with dark areas being less than 50 percent of feather width. *Note:* Com-

mon pattern. (2) *Moderately streaked type:* Moderately wide dark streaking being 50 percent of feather width. *Note:* Common pattern. (3) *Broadly streaked type:* Each feather is mainly dark with a very narrow pale outer edge. At a distance, underparts may appear nearly uniformly rufous or brown. *Note:* Uncommon pattern. BODY (dorsal).—Dark brown upperparts have very narrow white or tawny edgings on the scapulars. Scapulars also have large white area on the basal region of most feathers, creating a spotted or blotched appearance when fluffed. Tarsi and toes are yellow throughout, but may be brownish or grayish on upperside of the toes (as in older ages). WINGS.—**Prominent white bar on the trailing edge of the secondaries. Dorsal surface of secondaries has a pale grayish sheen.** Underwing coverts vary from being solid rufous or brown to mottled rufous or brown. White markings on undersides of the remiges are highly variable; there are four major variations. (1) *All-dark type:* All remiges are solid dark gray. *Note:* Common pattern. (2) *Moderate white type:* Some white on inner primaries (p1–3) and basal area of the outermost primary (p10). *Note:* Common pattern. (3) *Extensive white type:* **Basal region of all primaries is white and forms a large white panel.** *Note:* Common pattern. (4) *Very extensive white type:* **Basal region of all primaries and a narrow band of basal region of all secondaries are white.** The extensive amount of white forms a very large white panel on the primaries and a broad white linear area on the basal region of the secondaries. *Note:* Uncommon pattern. TAIL.—White terminal band is very narrow or absent. Tail is mostly solid brownish black on dorsal surface; when fanned, partial white banding, if present, may show on inner webs of rectrices. Ventral surface of tail is dark gray with a moderately wide darker terminal band. Undertail pattern has three major variations: (1) *Banded type:* Three or four complete, narrow white bands on all rectrices. White bands are visible at all times. Darker terminal band is sometimes distinct. *Note:* Common pattern. (2) *Partially banded type:* One or two narrow white bands on the basal area of inner rectrices. Outer one or two rectrix sets are often unbanded. Since inner rectrices are overlapped and hidden by outer rectrices when the tail is closed, undertail appears unbanded on a closed tail (*see below*). White bands are typically visible only when tail is fanned. However, sometimes a faint, narrow white band may be present on the inner web of the basal region of outer rectrix set, and visible when tail is closed. Wide dark terminal band is very distinct. *Note:* Fairly common pattern. (3) *Unbanded type:* Undertail lacks any definition of white bands, and the wide dark terminal band is distinct. *Note:* Uncommon to rare pattern.

JUVENILE (HEAVILY MARKED TYPE): HEAD.— As on "typical." BODY.—Upperparts as on typical juveniles Underparts are the broadly streaked type. WINGS.—Undersides of remiges are consistently the all-dark type. TAIL.—Undertail patterns are either the partially banded type or unbanded type.

Note: Uncommon plumage.

ABNORMAL PLUMAGES: None. However, band-tailed type adult females are very unusual occurrence (BKW pers. obs.).

HABITAT: Summer.—Low elevation river floodplains, lakes, and swamps that are adjacent to densely wooded or semi-open wooded tracts of tall, old-growth deciduous trees. Conifers are prevalent in many areas, however, kites rarely associate with pure coniferous tracts (other than flying over them). Mixed deciduous trees and Loblolly Pine, which grows in moist lowland regions, most often used in the Southeast. Kites are locally adapting to urban locales with deciduous and mixed deciduous-coniferous trees. In urban settings, areas with tall trees are inhabited, even locations with extensive human activity such as residential areas, golf courses, cemeteries, parks, and campuses. Hot and humid climate.

HABITS: Tame. A tolerant species that is highly adaptable to human activity. Where acclimated to humans, Kites can be approached closely while on foot. Nesting birds are sometimes very aggressive towards human intruders. Gregarious species; retains such feeding and roosting habits in winter. Sunning is a regular activity, especially during the morning. Exposed branches, wires, and poles are favored perches. Leisure perching occurs periodically throughout the day, often for extended periods. All ages, but especially fledglings, may perch within concealed branches or shaded, exposed branches for long periods to escape the hot sun. Kites regularly communally bathe and drink along river and creek edges and pools and puddles. Mississippi Kites are quite playful and intently chase each other. They also engage in harmless but intense, playful pursuits of larger songbirds too large and agile to kill (e.g., Common Grackles and European Starlings). An awkward stance is assumed upon landing— tipping forward—almost as if losing balance.

FEEDING: Aerial and perch hunter. Mainly feeds on large flying insects and specializes in cicadas. Mississippi Kites occasionally feed on small bats and small birds, particularly nestlings and inexperienced fledglings. They have been seen preying on species as large as recently fledged Blue Jays and Purple Martins. Kites may also prey on small terrestrial mammals, amphibians, and reptiles. When feeding on insects, they discard inedible parts such as legs and wings prior to eating. Fresh carrion is rarely eaten. Virtually all aerial species of prey are captured while airborne. Aerial hunting takes place at moderate to high altitudes. Perch hunting is at low to very low altitudes, often just above ground level. Perch hunting occurs mainly in the morning and late afternoon when insects are also at low altitude or when thermal conditions are minimal and prevent high-altitude flight.

Kites capture all prey with their feet. When engaged in aerial feeding, prey is held by one foot, which is extended forward, and the head lowered to pick the insect from the extended foot. If prey is taken to nests or fledglings, it is carried in the bill.

FLIGHT: Considerable amount of time is spent lithely gliding and soaring at various altitudes. *Wings are held on a flat plane and primary tips flex slightly upward or in a low dihedral when soaring.* Wings are held on a flat plane when gliding. Powered flight is accessed a moderate amount of the time. Kites may flap for extended periods when lift conditions are poor, when rising from the ground, or when in pursuit of prey. Wingbeats are fairly deep, loose, and moderately fast. Uses very acrobatic aerial dives and twists when pursuing prey or in playful antics. Kites regularly dive from high altitudes to a chosen perch or, with adults, to feed nestlings and fledglings. Mississippi Kites do not hover.

VOICE: A loud, high-pitched, whistled *phee-*

toooooo; the last syllable is drawn out and often a decrescendo. A piercing, monotone staccato whistled *phee-too-too-too-too* is a greeting call. Sometimes an abrupt, high-pitched, short whistled *phee-too* is emitted, which may be repeated several times; it also is a greeting call. During courting encounters and when whining for food, adult females and fledglings, respectively, emit a very soft whistled *pheer*. Quite vocal during nesting season, especially fledglings, which call incessantly. *Note:* Calls are imitated exceptionally well by Northern Mockingbirds and European Starlings.

STATUS AND DISTRIBUTION: Summer.—*Common* but locally distributed. Population is generally stable in all states, and increasing in some areas. Estimated overall population in the U.S. is based on full-season fall migration counts in Veracruz, Mexico, where all the U.S. population passes each year during migration. Totals for recent fall season tallies at Veracruz: 186,000 in 1998, 127,000 in 1999, 101,800 in 2000, 214,000 in 2001, and an amazing 308,500 in 2002. Full-season counts are currently too few to detect a definitive trend; however, the most recent Veracruz fall count appears promising that substantial numbers of kites exist. Counts in prior years did not begin early enough in the season to accommodate this early-season migrant.

Listed as an Endangered Species in Illinois (at least 60 pairs) and Tennessee, and a Species of Special Concern in Kentucky. There are no status designations for other eastern states, and this species appears stable and expanding in all inhabited states.

In northern areas along the Mississippi River, populations exist mainly adjacent to the floodplain. *Illinois:* Confirmed, probable, or possible breeding occurs in Adams, Pike, Jackson, Union, Alexander, and Calhoun (near Hardin) Cos. *Kentucky:* Largely absent from the state from the 1920s to mid-1960s. Kites began to reoccupy former range thereafter. Breeding is confirmed only for w. Fulton and Union Cos. However, they probably or possibly breed in the Mississippi River floodplain in Hickman, Carlisle, and Ballard Cos. Listed as a Species of Special Concern. *Tennessee:* Confirmed or possible breeding in Lake, Dyer, Lauderdale, Tipton, Shelby, Weakley, Carroll, Madison, and Haywood Cos. There are three additional counties that have possible breeding or somewhat extralimital sightings: Robertson, Henderson, and Hardeman.

Kites are densely populated within core breeding areas along the Mississippi River floodplain in Mississippi. Distribution is local but fairly dense within the Gulf Coastal Plain regions in Mississippi, Alabama, Georgia, and South Carolina.

Recent breeding expansion has occurred north of previously known range in the east-central part of the East and along the Mid-Atlantic Seaboard. *Indiana:* Has nested in Lincoln SP, Spencer Co., and in Pike S.F., Pike Co., for a few years. Breeding was documented in June 2000 in Warrick Co. Kites may possibly breed in other areas in the southern part of the state. *North Carolina:* Summering and suspected breeding has occurred in select locales since the early 1970s. Kites breed in the following areas: Laurinburg, Scotland Co. (20–35 birds seen for several years); Pee Dee River in Anson and Richmond Cos.; Roanoke Rapids, Halifax Co.; scattered areas in Halifax Co.; portions of the Roanoke River; Goldsboro, Wayne Co.; Johnston Co. along the Neuse River; Newport, Carteret Co.; recently found nesting in New Bern, Craven Co. Summering and possible breeding may occur for upper portions of the Northeast Cape Fear River and Cape Fear River. Breeding on the Cape Fear River now extends as far north as Lillington and in Harnett Co. *Virginia:* A pair has been nesting in Woodbridge, Prince William Co., since 1996. Regular summer sightings also occur in adjacent counties. A summer resident for several years along the Meherrin River in the southern part of the state. *Florida:* Possible expansion is occurring in Jacksonville; however, breeding is not confirmed.

Increasingly common in urban areas in the East, but is not as common an "urban raptor" as in many parts of the West.

Winter.—South America, east of the Andes Mts. from n. Colombia south to Paraguay and n. Argentina. As seen with the number of migrants counted in Bolivia (*see below*), much of the population winters in the southern portion of the winter range. Extremely rare wintering, or, more probably, early or late migrants are noted on occasion in the se. U.S. during early and late winter months.

Movements.—Long-distance migrant. Commonly migrates in small to fairly large flocks, but may also migrate singly. Flocks sometimes comprise hundreds of individuals. Large night roosts are often formed. Virtually all passage to and from the East is via an over-land route through Louisiana to e. Texas, south along the Coastal Bend region of Texas, through e. Mexico (east of the Sierra Madre Oriental) and Central America, and to and from South America via w. Colombia. A few individuals island hop from s. Florida to and from n. South America.

Fall migration: Punctual, very early-season migrant. Movements extend from early Aug. to Sep., peak in late Aug., and with stragglers occurring into Oct. All ages move simultaneously; however, late-nesting adults and late-fledged juveniles probably make up the late Sep. and Oct. contingent of stragglers. Those nesting at the northern periphery of their range in Illinois may not leave nesting areas until early Sep.

A few are seen in a span from early to late Oct. on the middle Florida Keys at Curry Hammocks S.P. on Little Crawl Key. Five were seen in 1996, eight in 1997, 22 in 1999, 13 in 2000. All birds were going south, with none returning northward (as many Keys migrants do). There are also several spring and fall sight records in the southern part of Florida south of typical breeding range. Mississippi Kites are not known to embark on trans-Gulf of Mexico flights.

In the State of Veracruz, Mexico, at Cardél and Chichicaxtle, the migration season spans from mid-Aug. to mid-Oct. (largest numbers are seen at Chichicaxtle). There is a major first peak from late Aug. to early Sep. (for all ages), which lasts several days, and a secondary peak in mid-Sep. with a short, but abrupt upswing in numbers (probably juveniles and late-nesting adults). In 1999, peak day on Aug. 31 brought over 15,000 kites at Chichicaxtle; the secondary peak day on Sep. 15 brought nearly 11,000 kites. In 2000, the Sep. 5 peak day had over 15,500 kites; the secondary peak occurred on September 18th with nearly over 13,500 Kites. The peak day in 2002 occurred on Sep. 1 with 96,000 kites; Aug. 30 had over 25,500 and Aug. 31 had 51,800, then another 26,000 on Sep. 2nd. Most migrants have passed by late Sep., with only a trickle of movement in Oct.

Large numbers are counted in cen. Bolivia. In the fall of 2000, nearly 38,000 were seen during partial-season coverage. In the fall of 2001, with extended full-season coverage, over 118,000 were tallied: 6,600 in Sep. (begining in mid-Sep.), nearly 71,000 in Oct., and nearly 41,000 in Nov. Peak numbers are seen in mid-Oct. This substantial number shows that many or most winter in the southern part of their winter range.

Spring migration: Late Mar. to early May for adults. Adults peak in s. Texas in early to mid-Apr. Adults rarely arrive in eastern breeding areas in n. Florida as early as late Mar. Typically, they arrive in Florida in early Apr. and in Illinois in late Apr. Subadults primarily migrate in a span from May to mid-Jun.

Extralimital movements.—Subadults and sometimes adults overshoot typical breeding range from mid-Apr. to early Oct. A few juveniles also wander from Aug. to early Oct. and venture far north of their natal haunts. Kites are fairly regular as far north as n. Great Lakes and n. New England coast. *Kentucky:* Sightings occur east of the Mississippi River in spring and summer. Counties in which recent sightings have occurred: Warren in 1978, Bullit in 1983, Meade in 1985, Grayson in 1988, Jefferson in 1999, two birds in Ohio in 1998, one or two birds in Muhlenberg and Ohio in 1999. *Tennessee:* Occasionally found away from typical haunts along the Mississippi River. There is a recent record from the southeastern area in Bradley Co. *Illinois:* Records from the Chicago area, Jefferson Co., and McLean Co. *Indiana:* (1) Bloomington, Monroe Co., in early May 1959; (2) Geist Reservoir in Marion-Hamilton Cos. in early May 1970; (3) Gibson Co. in late April 1976; (4) Two birds near Columbia City, Whitely Co., in late May 1984; (5) Wayne Co. in late May to early Jun. 1987; (6) Salaomie Reservoir, Wabash Co., in early Jun. 1987; (7) Laporte Co. in late Jun. 1991; (8) Indiana Dunes National Lakeshore, Porter Co., in late Apr. 1992; (9) Indiana Dunes Nat'l. Lakeshore, Porter Co. in mid-May 1999; (10) two subadults in Lebanon, Boone Co., in early Jun. 1999; and (11) a subadult in Bloomington, Monroe Co., in early Jul. 1999. *Wisconsin:* Eighteen records, with the first record in Sep.

1970 in Oneida Co. Records from 1990 to 2001: (1) Portage Co. in late Apr. 1990, (2) Ozaukee Co. in mid-May 1998, (3) Waukesha Co. in mid-May 1999, (4) Door Co. in early May 2000. *Ohio:* First recorded in the state in mid-May 1978 in Franklin Co. There are nine additional records of single birds: (1) Lucas Co. in mid-May 1982, (2) Lucas Co. in mid-May 1985, (3) Shelby Co. in early Jun. 1987, (4) Delaware Co. for 2 days in late Jun. 1987, (5) Ashtabula Co. in early Jun. 1992, (6) Lucas Co. in mid-May 1996, (7) Ottawa Co. in mid-May 1997, (8) Summit Co. in early Jul. 1999, and (9) Clermont Co. for 2 days in early Jul. *Pennsylvania:* Over 17 records since 1974 with most from the eastern areas of the state. Most are single birds and 1-day-only sightings. Recent sightings in the following counties: Beaver in late Jun. 1988, Luzerne in mid-Oct. 1989, Berks and Lancaster from late May to early Jun. 1995 (four records for Berks Co.), Lancaster in mid-Jun. 1998, mid-Jun. in Lackawanna, and Northampton in early Jul. 2000, Lancaster-Lebanon in late May 2001. Rare west of the Appalachian Mts. *New Jersey:* Annual in small numbers in s. Cape May Co. in the spring. Most are seen from late May through mid-Jun., but can be as early as late Apr. and as late as mid-Jul. It is estimated that an average of nine birds, with several often occurring simultaneously, is seen each spring in Cape May Co. From 1991 to 1998, only three records existed for the fall. Irregular, but widespread elsewhere in the state. Virtually all sightings are of subadults. *Delaware:* Irregular, mainly in spring along the coast at Cape Henlopen. *Michigan:* Fourteen records, primarily in the spring, with two records in the fall. Seen in the following counties: Chippewa (several records), Allegan, Kent, Monroe, and Wayne. *New York:* First record was from late May to early Jun. 1979 on Staten Island. Since then, 23 additional records have been compiled. Many of sightings have occurred in the spring, and most at hawkwatch locations, especially in Monroe Co. The majority of sightings are along the south shore of Lakes Erie and Ontario and the Atlantic Coastal region. It is possible that they are annual along the Great Lakes in spring and early summer. Sightings from 1990 to 2001: (1) Oswego Co. (Derby Hill Hawkwatch) in early May 1990; (2) Schuyler Co. in early Jul. 1993;

(3) Central Park, New York City; (4) Monroe Co. (Braddock Bay Hawkwatch) in early Jun. 1999; (5) Great Gull Island, Suffolk Co., in late Jul. 1999; (6) Monroe Co. in early Jul. 2001. *Wisconsin:* Eighteen accepted records spanning 1970 to 2000. First recorded in Sep. 1970 in Oneida Co. Records from 1990 to 2001: (1) Portage Co. in late Apr. 1990, (2) Ozaukee Co. in mid-May 1998, (3) Waukesha Co. in mid-May 1999, (4) Door Co. in early May 2000. *Maryland:* Fairly regular in spring at Fort Smallwood Co. Park, Ann Arundel Co., and in St. Mary's Co. *Connecticut:* (1) Stamford, Fairfield Co., in mid-Jun. 1995; (2) South Windsor, Hartford Co., in early May 1997; (3) Redding, Fairfield Co., in mid-May 1999; and (4) Oxford, New Haven Co., in late Jun. 2001. All records are of single birds seen in one locale for one day only. *Rhode Island:* (1) Ninegret NWR, near Charlestown in late May 1997 and (2) Block Island in late May 1997. There may be a few additional older records for this state. *Massachusetts:* First recorded in Middlesex Co. in early Jul. 1962. Reports became regular in the late 1970s. There are currently over 40 records for the state as of 2000. Numerous records are in spring and summer in the eastern part of the state, particularly on Cape Cod where they are nearly an annual occurrence. There are often multiple annual sightings. Rarely recorded in the fall. Records from 1990 to 2000: (1) Plymouth in early May 1990, (2) N. Truro in mid-May 1990, (3) Chatham in late Apr. 1991, (4) E. Brookfield in mid-May 1991, (5) Chatham in late May 1993, (6) Pembroke in late May 1993, (7) Marshfield in late Sep. 1994, (8) W. Newbury in mid-May 1995 (subadult), (9) Truro in mid-Jun. 1995, (10) S. Wellfleet in mid-Jun. 1995, (11) Eastham in mid-Jun. 1995 (two birds), (12) Lakeville in mid-Jun. 1996 (subadult), (13) Cuttyhunk Island in late May 1996, (14) Lakeville in mid-May 1996 (adult), (15) Rowley in early May 1997, (16) Orleans for two days in late May 1997, (17) Orleans for 4 days in early Jun. 1997, (18) Provincetown, Cape Cod, in late May 1998, (19) N. Truro in early Jun. 1999 (two subadults), (20) Eastham in late Mar. 2000 (subadult), (21) N. Truro in late May 2000 (subadult), (22) Truro in early May 2000. On Jun. 6, 2002, an amazing nine birds were seen in 1 day at Provincetown. *Vermont:* No of-

ficial records for the state. *New Hampshire:* (1) Bristol, Grafton Co., in mid-Apr. 1982; and (2) Durham, Strafford Co., in early May 1982 (also seen later in the month in the same town). *Maine:* Two records for Lubec in late May 1991 and late Jun. 1997. *Ontario:* (1) Toronto in mid-Sept. 1951; (2) Bradley's Marsh, Kent Co., in mid-May 1964; (3) Point Pelee N.P. (PPNP) in mid-May 1971 (adult); (4) Grimsby, Niagara Co., in mid-May 1975; (5) Long Beach, Niagara Co., in late May 1977 (adult); (6) PPNP for 5 days in May 1979; (7) PPNP for 2 days in mid-May 1982; (8) PPNP for 8 days in mid- and late May 1984; (9) Strabane, Hamilton-Wentworth Co. in late May 1984; (10) PPNP in late May 1987; (11) Long Point Prov. Pk. in late May 1987; (12) PPNP in mid May 1989; (13) PPNP for 4 days in mid-May 1991 (adult); (14) PPNP and Wheatley Prov. Pk. for 4 days in mid-May 1992; (14) PPNP in mid-May 1993; (15) PPNP for 2 days in mid-May 1996; (16) Grimsby, Niagara Co., in mid-May 1997; PPNP in mid May 1997; (17) PPNP in mid-May 1998; St. Williams Forestry Station, Haldimand-Norfolk Co. in early Jun. 1998; (18) PPNP in mid-May 1999 (subadult); (19) PPNP in mid-May 1999 (adult; same day as #18); (20) PPNP in early Jun. 1999; and (21) PPNP in mid-Jun. 1999. There are additional, not-yet-published records through the spring of 2001. *Québec:* First provincial record of a single subadult bird at Amos in early Jun. 2001. It was seen for the rest of the month at the same location. This represents the northernmost dispersal documentation in the East.

NESTING: May to mid-Sep. Leisurely paced and completed in a span from mid-Jul. to mid-Sep. Nests singly or in small or large, loosely formed colonies of up to 20 pairs. In colonies, nesting pairs are widely spaced and occupy separate trees. In urban settings, nesting pairs may cluster in various portions of a town or city. Territorial aggression sometimes occurs between Kites.

Courtship (flight).—Sky-dancing (*see* chapter 5) has occasionally been seen; otherwise, aerial displays are not exhibited.

Courtship (perched).—Males offer prey to females. Males, which are perched, entice females, which are often flying, by emitting the *phee-too-too-too-too* call. Males may offer prey to females prior to copulation. Most do not breed until 2 years old.

Nests are small, often oval-shaped, and about 11 x 14 in. (28 x 36 cm) in diameter and 5 in. (13 cm) deep. However, some new nests are much smaller and may only be 6 in. (15 cm) by 8 in. (20 cm) in diameter. In these small nests, the tails of the incubating or brooding adults extend fully beyond the edge of the nests. The nest structures may be either poorly constructed or compactly made of small, thin twigs and branches. Nests are decorated through the entire period with a considerable amount of greenery. Nests are well concealed in the very upper part of secondary branch clusters in densely foliaged deciduous trees. Kites rarely nest in pine trees. If a pine species is chosen, then primarily uses Loblolly Pine. Nest materials are broken off with their bills and carried in bills, but large pieces are sometimes carried with their feet. When breaking off nest twigs, Kites often engage in rather awkward antics and regularly hang upside down and flap their wings for balance while vigorously trying to snap off twigs. Nests are up to 135 ft. (40 m) high. Old nests are often reused. Both sexes build the nest and share nest duties, including feeding the young. The 2 eggs are incubated for 30 days. Youngsters fledge in about 34 days. Fledging occurs from mid-Jul. to late Aug., but can be as late as early Sep. in northern latitudes, especially if it is a renest attempt. Fledglings are fed primarily by males for another 21–28 days. Fledglings become independent in a span from late Jul. to mid-Sep. Recently fledged youngsters may gather in groups and are often still food-begging and being fed by their parents. Parents feed only their offspring.

Subadults usually form groups within colonies. Some assist in nest-building and regularly carrying nest materials during the nest-building period, although not always to actual nest sites. A few may assist adults in feeding nestlings. Very rarely, subadults will mate with adults.

CONSERVATION: No measures taken in most states. A hack program from 1983 to 1990 released 117 individuals in w. Tennessee at Hatchie NWR and Paris Landing S.P., with young birds taken from healthily populated areas in Kansas.

Mortality.—Historical decline in much of the East due to shooting and destruction of mature wooded riparian habitat. Agriculture conversion along fertile river bottoms, particularly along the Mississippi River, has caused a substantial decline in Kite numbers. Illegal shooting still occurs on a limited basis in the U.S. Many are probably shot during migration or while on winter grounds south of the U.S. Destruction of prime nesting habitat in lowland, old-growth forests continues. Being rather poorly constructed and placed in the very tops of trees, the flimsy nests, eggs, and nestlings often get blown out of trees during severe summer storms.

SIMILAR SPECIES: (1) **White-tailed Kite.**—PERCHED.—Identical black lores. Large black shoulder area on the upperwing coverts. Whitish tail in all plumages. FLIGHT.—Large black spot on carpal region of underwings. Upperwings as in "Perched." Frequently hovers. (**1A**) **Adults.**—Identical red irises. White underparts, pale gray upperparts. Bright yellow feet. (**1B**) **Juveniles.**—Similar when perched. Irises are orangish brown. Similar orangish rufous markings on underparts, but more restricted to breast region. (2) **Sharp-shinned Hawk.**—PERCHED.—Yellow irises; pale in front of eyes. Rufous streaking on breast similar. Similar dark brown upperparts, including white spotting. Long, thin tarsi. Wingtips much shorter than tail tip. Tail is distinctly banded on dorsal side. (3) **Merlin, adult females/juveniles of** *F. c. columbarius.*—PERCHED.—Yellow fleshy orbital area. Similar dark irises. Similar brown upperparts. Thin tarsi. Tail pattern similar, but often have pale bands on dorsal side. FLIGHT.—Similar shape. Outermost primary almost same length as longest, but caution in autumn: Adult females are still molting p10,

and it may be much shorter than longest (p8 and 9) and similar to a Kite's proportion. Underwings distinctly spotted on remiges. Wingbeats very rapid. Tail pattern as in Perched. (4) **Peregrine Falcon.**—PERCHED.—Dark "mustache." Pale flesh orbital area. Wingtip-to-tail tip ratio similar. FLIGHT.–Similar shape; use caution. Outermost primary almost as long as tip of wing. Powerful wingbeats, flaps for considerable distances. (**4A**) **Adults.**—Black cap and "mustache." Yellow orbital region. Fine barring on flanks. Upperparts similar bluish to adult kite. Underwing very barred/spotted. (**4B**) **Juveniles.**—Dark eyeline connects with dark "mustache." Pale blue orbital region. Underparts similar to juvenile Mississippi Kite, but streaking always dark brown. Upperparts similar, but lack white spotting. Underwing similar to the all-dark type underwing pattern of juvenile kite, but always have tawny spotting on remiges. Wide white terminal band on tail.

OTHER NAMES: None regularly used. *Spanish:* Milano Migratorio, Milano de Mississippi. *French:* Milan du Mississippi.

REFERENCES: Baicich and Harrison 1997; Bent 1961; Bohlen 1989; Bolen and Flores 1993; Brockman 1968; Castrale et al. 1998; del Hoyo et al. 1994; Godfrey 1986; Howell and Webb 1995; Justus 1997; Kale et al. 1992; Kalla and Alsop 1983; Kellogg 2000; Levine 1998; Lott 1999; McWilliams and Brauning 2000; Nicholson 1997; Olivo 2001, 2002; Palmer 1998; Palmer-Ball 1996; Parker 1999; Paxton et al. 2000; Perkins 1997; Pettingill 1977; Ridout 1998; Robbins 1991; Snyder and Snyder 1991; Stevenson and Anderson 1994; Veit and Petersen 1993; Walsh et al. 1999.

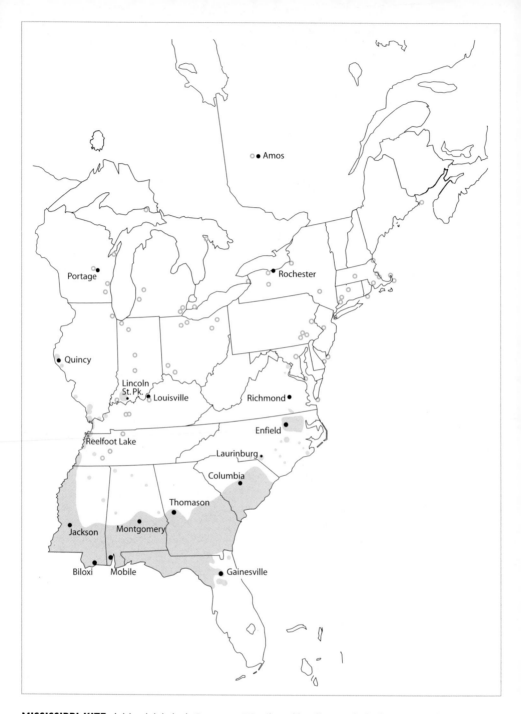

MISSISSIPPI KITE, *Ictinia mississippiensis:* Common. Distributed locally. Regularly disperses to the Great Lakes and s. New England from mid-Apr. to early Oct. Most dispersal occurs in May and Jun.

Plate 74. Mississippi Kite, adult male [Jun.] ▪
Very pale gray head. Black bill, gray cere. Red iris. ▪
Dark bluish gray upperparts. ▪ Whitish secondaries form a narrow whitish bar. ▪ Black dorsal surface of tail. Tail notched when closed.

Plate 75. Mississippi Kite, adult male [Aug.] ▪
Pale or very pale gray head. Black bill, gray cere.
Red iris. ▪ Medium gray underparts. ▪ Wingtips extend beyond tail tip. ▪ Black tail; quills are black.

Plate 76. Mississippi Kite, adult male [Aug.] ▪
Pale or very pale gray head. Black bill, gray cere.
Red iris. ▪ Dark gray upperparts. ▪ Whitish secondaries; black primaries, often with rufous markings. ▪ Black tail. ▪ *Note:* Sunning posture: wings may be fully extended. Males begin annual molt in Aug.–Sep., starting with the inner primaries: 2 inner primaries are new (grayish) on this bird.

Plate 77. Mississippi Kite, adult male [Sep.] ▪
Pale or very pale gray head. ▪ Uniformly medium gray underparts. ▪ Long, pointed wings with outermost primary (p10) much shorter than wingtips.
▪ Black, squared-edged tail; quills are black. ▪
Note: Holding a cicada in left foot.

Plate 78. Mississippi Kite, adult male [Sep.] ▪ Pale or very pale gray head. ▪ Uniformly medium gray underparts. ▪ Long, pointed wings with outermost primary (p10) much shorter than wingtips. ▪ Black, squared-edged tail; quills are black. ▪ *Note:* Aerial feeding posture when gliding and soaring. Feeding on a cicada held in its left foot.

Plate 79. Mississippi Kite, adult male [Aug.] ▪ Pale or very pale gray head. ▪ Uniformly medium gray underparts. ▪ Long, pointed wings with outermost primary (p10) much shorter than wingtips. Inner 3 primaries (p1–3) are lost due to molt, creating a gap in wings. ▪ Black, squared-edged tail; quills are black. ▪ *Note:* Males begin annual molt starting with inner primaries in Aug.–Sep. Maximum molt stage while in U.S.

Plate 80. Mississippi Kite, adult female [Jun.] ▪ Pale to medium gray head. Black bill, gray cere. Red iris. ▪ Very dark gray upperparts. ▪ Gray secondaries. ▪ *Note:* Most females are slightly darker, brownish than males. Dorsal surface of secondaries are typically darker than on males.

Plate 81. Mississippi Kite, adult female [Aug.] ▪ Pale to medium gray head. Black bill, gray cere. Red iris. ▪ Medium gray underparts. Some have white on undertail coverts. ▪ Gray secondaries. ▪ Pale type tail has a dark band on pale gray outer rectrix set; quills are white. All other rectrices are black.

Plate 82. Mississippi Kite, adult female [Aug.] ▪
Pale to medium gray head. Black bill, gray cere. Red
iris. ▪ Medium gray underparts. Some have gray
undertail coverts. ▪ Gray secondaries. ▪ Black
type tail has uniformly black rectrices; quills are
white.

Plate 83. Mississippi Kite, adult female [Jun.] ▪
Pale or medium gray head. ▪ Medium gray underparts with whitish lower belly. ▪ Long, pointed
wings with outermost primary (p10) much shorter
than wingtips. ▪ Pale type tail has a dark band on
outer rectrix set; quills are white on outer rectrix
set. ▪ *Note:* Amount of rufous on primaries is not
a sexual trait.

**Plate 84. Mississippi Kite, adult female (band-
tailed type) [Aug.]** ▪ Medium gray underparts
with whitish lower belly and undertail coverts. ▪
Outermost primary (p10) much shorter than
wingtips. Rufous wash on some primaries. Inner 3
primaries are new; p4 is dropped (typical molt
stage for females in late summer). ▪ Pale type tail
has partial white or gray bands; quills are white. ▪
Note: Rare tail pattern found only on females. Photographed in Prowers Co., Colo.

Plate 85. Mississippi Kite, adult female [Jun.] ▪
Pale or medium gray head. ▪ Very dark gray upperparts. ▪ Whitish secondaries contrast with rest
of the upperparts. ▪ *Note:* Females may not show
extensive white on secondaries; males nearly always
have distinct white secondaries.

Plate 86. Mississippi Kite, subdult female (late stage) [Aug.] ▪ Pale or medium gray head. Black bill, gray cere. Red iris. ▪ Very dark gray upperparts. ▪ Very dark gray upperwing coverts except new, paler gray greater coverts. New pale gray tertials. Brownish, retained juvenile secondaries. New (gray) inner primaries. ▪ Black central rectrix is partially grown on tail.

Plate 87. Mississippi Kite, subadult female (early stage) [Jun.] ▪ Pale or medium gray head. Black bill, gray cere. Red iris. ▪ Very dark gray upperparts; some white spotting. ▪ Wing coverts are mainly brown juvenile with incoming new, gray feathers. Old brown juvenile remiges. Often white blotches on inner wing. ▪ *Note:* Less-advanced molt than on many subadults by early Jun.

Plate 88. Mississippi Kite, subadult female (early stage) [Jun.] ▪ Pale or medium gray head. Black bill, gray cere. Red iris. ▪ Medium gray underparts are often speckled with white and have a few retained, brownish juvenile feathers. ▪ Banded type retained juvenile tail has thin white bands.

Plate 89. Mississippi Kite, subadult male (early stage) [Jun.] ▪ Very pale or pale gray head. Black bill, gray cere. Red iris. ▪ Medium gray underparts may be fully adult on some birds, even in late spring. ▪ Mix of old, brown juvenile and new gray adult wing coverts. Brown juvenile secondaries. ▪ Banded type retained juvenile tail has thin white bands.

Plate 90. Mississippi Kite, subadult female (late stage) [Aug.] ▪ Medium gray underparts with whitish lower belly and undertail coverts. ▪ Mainly gray underwing coverts. ▪ Tail is banded type, has thin white bands; r1 is new adult feather (not shown), r6 set is partially grown black adult feathers. ▪ *Note:* Kites regularly dive to a chosen perch.

Plate 91. Mississippi Kite, subadult female (late stage) [Aug.] ▪ Medium gray underparts with whitish lower belly and undertail coverts. ▪ Mainly gray underwing coverts. Extensive-white type wing has white juvenile primaries. P1–5 are new, dark feathers. ▪ Banded type juvenile tail has thin white bands; new black adult middle rectrix (r1) set.

Plate 92. Mississippi Kite, subadult female (late stage) [Jul.] ▪ Uniformly medium gray under-parts. ▪ All-dark type wing. P1–3 are new/growing dark feathers, p4 is missing. ▪ Partially banded/all-dark type juvenile tail is all dark when closed. Partially banded type shows partial, thin white bands when widely fanned.

Plate 93. Mississippi Kite, subadult female (early stage) [Jun.] ▪ Pale or medium gray head. ▪ Gray underparts are mix of juvenile streaking and white speckling. White lower belly. ▪ Moderate-white type wing with white on outer primaries. P1–3 new/growing dark feathers. ▪ Banded type juvenile tail has thin white bands.

Plate 94. Mississippi Kite, subadult female (early stage) [Jun.] ▪ Gray underparts have some white areas; white lower belly. White, spotted undertail coverts. ▪ Extensive-white type wing with large white patch on primaries. Missing p1–4, creating large gap in wings. Outermost primary (p10) is much shorter than wingtip. ▪ Banded type juvenile tail has thin white bands.

Plate 95. Mississippi Kite, subadult female (early stage) [Jun.] ▪ Gray underparts with moderate amount of white speckling and retained juvenile streaking. Whitish lower belly. ▪ Very extensive type of wing with white patch on primaries and base of all secondaries. Missing p1 and 2. ▪ Banded type juvenile tail has thin white bands. ▪ *Note:* Entering into the first stage of remix molt.

Plate 96. Mississippi Kite, subadult male (early stage) [Jun.] ▪ Gray underparts with only a few white specks. ▪ Moderate type wing with whitish areas on inner primaries and outer 2 primaries. Coverts are mainly juvenile with some gray; axillaries have molted into gray feathers. No remix molt. ▪ Banded type juvenile tail has thin white bands.

Plate 97. Mississippi Kite, juvenile (either sex) [Sep.] ▪ Black bill, yellow cere. Dark brown iris. Gray head with a short, white supercilium and white throat; black lore spot. ▪ Moderately wide rufous or brown streaking. ▪ Wingtips reach or extend beyond tail tip. ▪ Banded type tail has 3 or 4 thin white bands. ▪ *Note:* Some are more narrowly streaked on the underparts.

Plate 98. Mississippi Kite, juvenile (either sex) [Aug.] ▪ Black bill, yellow cere. Dark brown iris. Gray head with a short, white supercilium and white throat; black lore spot. ▪ Moderately wide rufous or brown streaking. ▪ Wingtips extend beyond tail tip. ▪ Partially banded type tail is all dark when closed. ▪ *Note:* Recently fledged youngsters are highly vocal.

Plate 99. Mississippi Kite, juvenile (heavily marked type; either sex) [Sep.] ▪ Black bill, yellow cere. Dark brown iris. Gray head with a short, white supercilium and white throat; black lore spot. ▪ Broadly streaked underparts appear solid rufous or brown. ▪ Wingtips extend beyond tail. ▪ Partially banded type tail is all dark when closed.

Plate 100. Mississippi Kite, juvenile (either sex) [Sep.] ▪ Black bill, yellow cere. Dark brown iris. Gray head with a short, white supercilium and white throat; black lore spot. ▪ Dark brown upperparts often have large white spots on scapulars. ▪ Wingtips extend beyond tail. ▪ Tail is uniformly black on dorsal side.

Plate 101. Mississippi Kite, juvenile (either sex) [Sep.] ▪ Tawny or white underparts are moderately streaked with rufous or brown. ▪ Extensive-white type wing with large white patch on base of primaries. Rufous brown markings on coverts. ▪ Banded type tail has thin white bands. ▪ *Note:* Juveniles have somewhat broader secondaries than older birds.

Plate 102. Mississippi Kite, juvenile (either sex) [Sep.] ▪ Tawny or white underparts are streaked with rufous or brown. ▪ Moderate-white type wing with small white areas on inner and outer primaries. Rufous-brown markings on coverts. ▪ Banded type tail has thin white bands. ▪ *Note:* Juveniles have somewhat broader secondaries than older birds.

Plate 103. Mississippi Kite, juvenile (heavily marked type; either sex) [Aug.] ▪ Broadly streaked underparts appear solid rufous or brown at a distance. ▪ All-dark type wing lacks white markings. Coverts are heavily marked. ▪ Partially banded type tail shows a few thin white bands when widely fanned. All-dark type lacks pale bands. ▪ *Note:* Juveniles have somewhat broader secondaries than older birds.

BALD EAGLE
(Haliaeetus leucocephalus)

AGES: Adult (basic V and older; sometimes basic IV), four interim basic/subadult ages (basic/subadult I–IV) that correspond to 1- to 4-year-old birds in their second to fifth years of life, and juvenile during the first year of life. There is a minimal amount of variation in adults, a considerable amount of variation in subadults, and a moderate amount of variation in juveniles. Sexes are similar.

Adult plumage is typically acquired as a 5-year-old when a basic/subadult V in its sixth year of life, but it can be attained as a 4-year-old when a basic/subadult IV in its fifth year of life (McCollough 1989; *see* Figure 2 in Clark 2001). Some adults may retain traces of younger-age characters on the head until at least eight years old (McCollough 1989).

Basic ages/subadults slowly change from juvenile to adult plumage through partial annual molts. Each age class is held for 1 year. Basic ages/subadults best exhibit their respective age characters when in flight and when viewed at a dorsal angle when perched. With a considerable amount of individual variation, the three older subadult ages can often be difficult and sometimes impossible to separate from adjacent ages. Basic/subadult IV and basic/subadult V and older ages can be identical in all aspects. Basic/subadult IV and III can share similar bill, head, body, and tail markings. Basic/subadult III and II can also share similar markings as previously described. Basic/subadult I is distinct and is easily separable from older subadults. Juvenile feathering is retained in the first two subadult plumages and sometimes in the third plumage.

Juvenile plumage is held for the first year. Juveniles are easily separable from older birds. Juveniles have longer, more pointed secondaries and rectrices than older ages. This creates a broader wing and a longer tail.

MOLT: Accipitridae wing and tail molt pattern (*see* chapter 4). Wing and tail molts are complex and variable and it is important to understand the various molt centers and molt waves in order to age subadult birds. Latitude, diet, and other factors affect timing and intensity of molt. Birds that are born in Florida begin molting in November; birds from the n. U.S. and Canada begin molting in Mar. or Apr. Eagles from interim latitudes begin molting at interim times.

Note: Eagles have the typical 10 primaries as most raptors, but have 17 secondaries, four more than smaller raptors; the secondary molt is an important segment in the sequence of aging.

The annual molt is an incomplete feather replacement on most anatomical areas. A large portion of body and wing covert feathers are replaced, a small portion of remiges are replaced, and all or virtually all rectrices are replaced. Younger subadults may have one or two molt waves in progress at the same time, and older subadults and adults may have two or three molt waves in progress. Birds from southern latitudes have a longer period in which to molt than birds from northern latitudes; thus they typically replace more feathers during the annual molt.

Molt is a similar sequence to that of White-tailed Eagles; however, in most cases, molt and the progression of molt waves is slightly more accelerated for the respective age of Bald Eagles.

Data on molt are based on Edelstam (1984) and Forsman (1999) on White-tailed Eagles, Clark and Wheeler (2001), Wheeler and Clark (1999), W. S. Clark pers. comm., and BKW pers. obs. of wild birds and museum specimens. McCollough (1989) had exceptional plumage study data on 135 known-age birds but did not correlate it with molt sequences, particularly on the remiges.

On the remiges and upperwing coverts, retained juvenile feathers are longer and more pointed than new, older-age subadult feathers. The longer the juvenile feathers are retained, the more they become faded brown, frayed, or broken. Subadult remiges can also be aged by the amount of fading and fraying: new feathers are dark and neat, older feathers are more brownish and ragged on the their rounded tips. Molt is serially descendent, with two or three molt waves in progress at the same time.

First prebasic molt: Molt out of juvenile into subadult I (1-year-old) plumage. Molt is com-plete on the head and tail. Typically, molt is fairly complete on the contour feathers of the dorsal and ventral body; however, only a partial molt is undertaken by some eagles, and they may retain a large amount of old juvenile feathering. Molt is always incomplete on the upper- and underwing coverts, which retain some juvenile feathering. The greater upperwing coverts molt with the respective remiges; all other upperwing coverts molt in an irregular order. Remix molt is incomplete: *Slow molt.*—On the primaries, p1–4 are replaced (in that order); p5–10 are retained juvenile. On the secondaries, s1 is replaced and the three tertials, s17–15, are replaced (in that order); all other 13 secondaries are retained juvenile. Molt may occur on s5. *Moderate molt.*—On the primaries, p1–5 are replaced; p6–10 are retained juvenile; however, p6 may molt on southern-breeding birds. On the secondaries, s1 and 2, s5 and 6, s14–12 (in that order), and the tertials, s17–15 (in that order), are replaced. The other seven secondaries, s3 and 4 and s7–11, on the middle section of the wing are retained juvenile. *Fast molt.*—Mainly seen on birds born at southern latitudes. On the secondaries, s7 and 11 may also be replaced.

Note: Key factor on perched and flying birds are the large number of retained faded, long, and pointed juvenile secondaries; on perched birds, the tertials (s15–17) are new and dark colored subadult I and contrast sharply with the retained juvenile secondaries.

Second prebasic molt: Molt out of subadult I into subadult II (2-year-old) plumage. Molt is fairly complete on the head and complete on the tail. Molt is incomplete on the body and retains a small amount of subadult I feathering. Remix molt is incomplete: *Slow molt.*—On the primaries, p1 is replaced for the second time; p5–8 or, less commonly, p5–9 are replaced for the first time. P2–4 are retained subadult I feathers. P9 and10 or p10 are retained juvenile. On the secondaries, s4 and 9 are retained juvenile, s1 is an old subadult I, s2 and 3 are new subadult II, s5–8 are new subadult II or s5 is an older subadult I, s10–14 are new subadult II, and s15–17 are replaced for the second time and are new subadult II. *Moderate molt.*—On the primaries, p1 and sometimes p2 are replaced for the second time, p6–9 are replaced for the first time, p10 and sometimes p9 are retained old juvenile feathers, and p2–5 or 3–5 are retained subadult I feathers. On the secondaries, s4 is a retained old juvenile (and is the last juvenile secondary to be lost), s1 and 2 are old subadult I, s3 is replaced for the first time and is a new subadult II, s5 and 6 are old subadult I, s7–9 are replaced for the first time and are new subadult II, s10 and 11 are replaced for the first time and are new subadult II, s12–14 are old subadult I feathers, and s15–17 are replaced for the second time and are new subadult II feathers. *Fast molt.*—On the primaries, p1 and 2 are replaced for the second time, p6–9 are replaced for the first time and are new subadult II, p10 is a very old juvenile, and p2–5 or p3–5 are retained subadult I feathers. On the secondaries, all juvenile feathers have been replaced. S1 and 2 are old subadult I feathers, s3 and 4 are new subadult II, s5 and 6 are old subadult I feathers, s7–9 are new subadult II feathers, s10 and 11 are replaced for the first time and are new subadult II, s12–14 are old subadult I, and s15–17 are replaced for the second time and are new subadult II feathers.

Note: Key factor mainly on perched birds viewed from the rear is the new, dark tertials (s15–17) that contrast with the older subadult I s12–14 and new, dark subadult II s10 and 11.

Third prebasic molt: Molt out of subadult II into subadult III (3-year-old) plumage. Molt is fairly complete on the head and complete on the tail. Body molt is incomplete but retains only some feathering from the previous year or two. Wing covert molt is incomplete. Remix molt is incomplete: *Slow molt.*—On the primaries, p1 is usually a retained subadult II (replaced annually in the first two molts; rarely replaced in this molt), p2–4 are replaced for the second time, p5–9 are retained subadult II feathers, and p10 is a retained juvenile. On the secondaries, s4 and 9 may be the newest and darkest feathers. S14 and 13 (molted in that order) are also new and dark; s11 and 10 were molted in the second prebasic molt and are older than the adjacent outer secondaries; and s12, which is a very old subadult I feather and a "key" feather for aging this subadult class, is one of the oldest subadult-type feathers of the secondaries (sometimes along with s1 and 2 and s5 and 6). S15–17 are not molted (but were molted in each of the prior two molts)

and somewhat faded. Secondaries that were molted in the first prebasic molt, such as s1 and 2 and s5 and 6, may also molt for the second time. *Fast molt.*—On the primaries, p1 and 2 have been replaced twice and are retained subadult II; p3–5 are also replaced for the second time, but during the subadult III period; p6–9 are old subadult II feathers; and p10 is replaced for the first time as a new subadult III feather. On the secondaries, the molt pattern is similar as described for slow molt; however, some birds molt the inner secondaries more rapidly and, rather than molting only s14 and 13 (in that order), they may extend molt into s12 and sometimes s11—which leaves s10 as an old subadult II feather and the oldest of that portion of the wing.

Note: Key factor of this age class is the very old, faded, and frayed retained subadult I s12. This very old feather is visible in flight and at a dorsal angle when perched. Also, the fairly old retained subadult II tertials (s15–17) are important feathers to see for proper aging.

Fourth prebasic molt: Molt out of subadult III into subadult IV (4-year-old) plumage; adult plumage is sometimes attained. Molt on the head is incomplete. Tail molt may be incomplete, if so, retains only one or two rectrices from the third prebasic molt. Body molt is incomplete and may retain a small amount of feathering from the previous one or two ages. Remix molt is incomplete and becomes even more irregular than in the previous three molts: On the primaries, p1–5 or p1–6 are newer; p1, or p1 and 2, and p4–6 are the last to molt and the newest feathers. Birds that were in slow molt in the previous prebasic molt may have a new p10; otherwise, p10 is moderate in age and fade character. On the secondaries, replacement of several feathers occurs in the approximate sequence of earlier molts; however, sequence may become irregular.

Subsequent prebasic molts: These are molts within the adult age class. Subsequent molts may gradually lessen any retained subadult traits on the head and sometimes tail. Molt is incomplete on virtually all parts of the body, wing, and tail. Remix molt is often an irregular sequence of feather replacement.

SUBSPECIES: Considered to have two subspecies that are based solely on size that spans from large to small birds. The demarcation between sizes is extremely arbitrary since they vary on a clinal north-south trend. *H. l. alascanus* breeds north of 40°N, and *H. l. leucocephalus* breeds south of this latitude. *See* Size. for more information.

Note: As with Harris's Hawk and Northern Goshawk, the author does not consider subspecies that are based only on size, particularly if there is a clinal trend.

COLOR MORPHS: None.

SIZE: A large raptor. Within regional populations, there is no overlap between sexes: Males are smaller than females. There is a clinal trend in size, with southern-latitude birds being the smallest and northern-latitude birds, particularly from Alaska, being the largest. Southern females average slightly smaller than northern males; southern birds can be up to 7 in. (18 cm) shorter than northern birds of the same sex (Stalmaster 1987). Juveniles, with their longer tails, are 1.25–1.5 in. (3–4 cm) longer than adults of the same sex and similar latitude (Stalmaster 1987). The measurements are for the range of sizes of southern and northern birds. Length: 27–37 in. (69–94 cm); wingspan: 71–96 in. (180–244 cm).

Note: Due to restoration programs that released hundreds of nestling eagles from various origins, the "size and subspecies" factor is distorted (*see* Conservation). Large-sized eagles from Alaska and small-sized eagles from Florida were released into areas of the U.S. that had either smaller or larger "natural" sizes. However, all states tried to keep larger eagles in northern latitudes and smaller eagles in southern latitudes to conform with trend of larger birds in the north and smaller birds in the south.

SPECIES TRAITS: HEAD.—**Large, deep bill.** Forehead, nape, and hindneck feathers are regularly elevated in cool temperatures and during certain moods. BODY.—The yellow to orangish yellow tarsi are unfeathered on the very lower part. WINGS.—**There are six "fingers" on the outer primaries.**

ADULT TRAITS: HEAD.—**Uniformly medium yellow or orangish yellow bill, cere, and gape; gape and sometimes cere are paler than the bill. Iris is pale lemon yellow. Head and neck are white with a sharp demarcation line between the white lower neck and the brown back and breast.** Some full adults, even birds

that are at least 8 years old, may have a small amount of dark speckling on the auriculars, nape, and hindneck (McCollough 1989). BODY (dorsal).—**Dark brown with thin pale tawny edges on most feathers. Upper half of the lower back is dark brown and the lower half of the back and rump are white.** BODY (ventral).—**Dark brown with thin pale tawny tips on most feathers, creating a scalloped appearance. The undertail coverts are white.** WINGS (dorsal and ventral).—**Dark brown coverts are edged with pale tawny and appear scalloped.** *Note:* Molting birds may show patches of white on the underwing coverts due to missing feathers. **Remiges are blackish. On the ventral surface, the basal region on the outer three or four primaries is pale gray.** TAIL (dorsal and ventral).—**Rectrices and uppertail coverts are white and form a white unit with the white lower back and undertail coverts.** Occasionally, older adults still retain some black speckling on the tips of some rectrices.

Note: This definitive basic plumage may be found on a few basic/subadult IV (4-year-olds), but is most typical of birds that are basic V (5-year-olds) or older. *Additional note:* Basic/subadult IV that appear totally adultlike on the bill, head, and body when perched may still exhibit subadult characters on the underwing (*see below*).

BASIC IV (SUBADULT IV) TRAITS: There are two main variations. Eagles that are more advanced in molt are similar to full adults and those that retain one or more younger subadult traits are fairly similar to adults. HEAD.—Both types have a sharp demarcation line between the white head and the brown back and breast. WINGS.—All remiges have been replaced for at least the first time, which includes the outermost primary (p10) on slow-molting birds; some remiges have been replaced two or three times. Five or six inner primaries (p1–5 or 6) will be newer, darker, and less frayed then the outer primaries (p6 or 7–10). The three tertials (s15–17) may be new feathers since they were not molted the previous year.

Note: Since subadult III and IV both may have new p10, the larger number of newer, darker inner primaries helps separate the two ages in flight.

BASIC IV (SUBADULT IV; ADVANCED/ADULT

TYPE): HEAD.—**Uniformly medium yellow or orangish yellow bill and cere.** Gape is pale yellow. **Iris is pale lemon yellow.** Head and neck have immaculate white feathers as on most adults. BODY (dorsal).—Dark brown with adultlike feathering, including the white lower half of the back and rump. BODY (ventral).—Dark brown and adultlike on the belly and flanks. The undertail coverts are all white. WINGS (dorsal).—Adultlike dark brown with thin pale edges on all coverts. WINGS (ventral).—A few very advanced birds may have all-dark underwing coverts and remiges and are identical to full adults. However, as described in Adult Traits, even birds with very adultlike heads and bodies can have a considerable amount of white on the underwing region. TAIL.—Immaculate white uppertail coverts and rectrices.

BASIC IV (SUBADULT IV; TYPICAL TYPE): HEAD.—**Medium yellow or orangish yellow bill with a brownish or grayish smudge on the lower mid-part of the upper mandible. Cere is often gray or brown with a yellow fringe around the nares and on the front edge. Iris is either pale lemon yellow or pale gray.** Head has a very narrow brown line or patch on the top of the auriculars that often extends down the sides of the neck. Some may also have brown feathering on the white forehead and sometimes on the crown. BODY (dorsal).—As in adult type, but often have a few white specks on the back and dark blotches on the white portion of the lower back and rump. BODY (ventral).—Some are all-dark as adult type, but many also retain some white blotching on the belly and flanks. The white undertail coverts my be all white or have a few dark blotches. WINGS (dorsal).—Adultlike dark brown with pale edges on all coverts. WINGS (ventral).—Most have a small to moderate amount of white subadult markings on the axillaries, underwing coverts, and secondaries. TAIL.—Most have white rectrices with irregular dark tips on a few or most feathers, which may form a partial or complete dark terminal band. Sometimes there is a dark strip on the outer web of the outermost rectrices and scattered black mottling on the inner portion of some or many feathers. The uppertail coverts are white, but may have dark blotches.

BASIC III (SUBADULT III) TRAITS: This is the first age class with fairly adultlike characters, but all birds still retain a fair amount of younger subadult traits. There are two main plumage types, which reflect the amount of retained younger subadult characters. Advanced types have acquired more adultlike characters with a darker plumage and paler head, and those with younger subadult traits have more white blotches on the body and wings. HEAD.—Bill and cere color is variable and does not correlate with the plumage stage; gape is always pale yellow: (1) Advanced birds have mostly medium yellow or orangish yellow bills, including the cere. (2) Less-advanced birds may have yellowish brown or grayish bills with a more yellowish region on the lower basal part of the upper mandible. The central part of the bill is streaked with dark brownish or grayish that extends from the cere to the tip of the bill. The lower mandible is yellowish but still has some brownish or grayish areas. The cere is also brownish or grayish with yellow fringing the front edge, as well as the nares. The head and neck are whitish, but the demarcation line between the brown back and breast is only moderately defined. Dark brown feathers form streaks that create an ill-defined border between the lower neck and back and breast. This is especially apparent on the front and rear of the neck. The whitish nape and hindneck, in particular, are often extensively streaked with dark brown. Iris color varies: pale brown, pale gray, or pale yellow. BODY.—*See* types. WINGS.—Slow-molting individuals may retain a very old juvenile outermost primary (p10), which by this time, is very faded brown and frayed. Many have replaced p10, which would then be a neat, dark colored feather. All other primaries have been replaced one or two times and are new or fairly new, and are dark and neatly formed feathers. Of note are the newer, darker p1–4, which are more new feathers than on a subadult II and fewer than on a subadult IV. All secondaries have been replaced one or two times by annual molts, and the ventral surface may still exhibit white patterns as seen on younger birds. Virtually all have an old subadult I feather on the inner region of the secondaries at the s12 position, which is older and more faded brown than any nearby feather. S13 and 14 are newly grown subadult III, dark, and neatly formed. Adjacent secondaries, s10 and 11, are moderately old and moderately faded subadult II feathers. The tertials, s15–17, are also older subadult II feathers and are more faded and brown than s13 and 14, but are not as pale as the subadult I feather, s12. On rapidly molting individuals, s10 may be the oldest feather of the inner secondaries. On the upperwing coverts, most eagles retain a very small number of old subadult II median and lesser coverts on the inner part of the wing; some may still have one or more very old subadult I coverts. TAIL.—Highly variable in the amount of black-and-white pattern. Dorsal surface varies from being (1) all black with some white mottling, (2) mainly white on the central rectrices with an irregular black terminal band and black on the outer feathers, or (3) very white on most rectrices with an irregular black terminal band. The ventral surface is mainly white with a black strip on the outer web on the outer rectrix set and an irregular black terminal band. Some have irregular black edges on several rectrices; a few lack the black outer edge. The uppertail coverts are often white.

BASIC III (SUBADULT III; ADVANCED/HEAVILY MARKED TYPE): HEAD.—Head is fairly white with a narrow dark patch on the upper half of the auriculars that does not attach to the gape. Forehead, crown, nape, and hindneck have a moderate amount of dark brown streaking on the white feathers. BODY (dorsal).—Adultlike, but there are usually blotches on the white part of the lower back and rump. The back may have a few white specks. BODY (ventral).— Adultlike, but the white undertail coverts have some dark blotching and mottling. WINGS (dorsal).—Adultlike. WINGS (ventral).— There is a small amount of white speckling on the underwing coverts; axillaries may be all-dark brown or have a very small amount of white speckling. The secondaries may be all dark and adultlike or have only a small amount of white on a couple of feathers. TAIL.—Any of the three patterns described in Basic III (Subadult III) Traits, but more likely to have a more whitish dorsal surface.

BASIC III (SUBADULT III; MODERATELY MARKED TYPE): HEAD.—Head is moderately white with a moderately wide dark patch on all of the auriculars that extends from the gape on the lower edge of the dark mark (dark patch is

as wide as on most subadult II eagles). Forehead, crown, nape, and hindneck have an extensive amount of dark streaking on pale tawny or white feathers. A fairly distinct whitish supercilium is formed by the dark auricular patch and the dark forehead and crown. The front of the neck and hindneck are quite dark and form an ill-defined border from the back and breast. BODY (dorsal).—The back has a moderate or extensive amount of white speckling that forms an inverted white triangle. *Note:* The white triangle can be paler and more distinct than on heavily marked types of subadult I and II. The lower back and rump are dark with some white mottling. BODY (ventral).—A moderate amount of white speckling on the dark brown flanks and belly. The white undertail coverts have a considerable amount of dark markings. WINGS (dorsal).— Adultlike, but most birds have remnant subadult II feathering that may have distinct white edges on one or more greater and median upperwing coverts on the inner part of the wing. WINGS (ventral).—There is a moderate or sometimes an extensive amount of white markings on the underwing coverts, axillaries, and some secondaries. Any secondaries with white markings have the white contained inside a broad black terminal band. TAIL.— Any of the three variations described in Basic III, (Subadult III) Traits; however, they are more likely to have darker tail variations.

Note: Not separable from heavily marked type of subadult II unless wing molt sequence is well observed.

BASIC II (SUBADULT II) TRAITS: There are two main plumage types that have a variable amount of white on the different anatomical areas. As a rule, they are darker with a lesser amount of white than all types of subadult I eagles, except lightly marked type. HEAD.— Bill and cere color is highly variable and does not correlate with the different plumage types. Gape is always yellow, but there are three main variations: (1) Brownish or grayish with a yellowish area on the lower basal region of the upper mandible; lower mandible is mostly yellowish. Cere is also a similar grayish with yellow surrounding the nares. *Note:* Common type. (2) Medium yellow with a wide brownish or grayish strip from the mid-cere to the tip of the bill; lower mandible is yellow. Cere is brownish or grayish with yellow fringing on the nares. *Note:* Fairly common type. (3) All-yellow upper and lower mandibles and similar to color of adults. *Note:* Uncommon to very uncommon type. Iris color is usually pale brown or pale gray, but is occasionally pale yellow. BODY (dorsal and ventral).—Highly variable. *See* Types. WINGS (dorsal and ventral).—*See* Types. Key features of this age class, which are most visible in flight: (1) The faded, retained subadult I secondaries in the s12–14 position; (2) birds in slow and moderate stages of remix molt will show long, pointed, and faded retained juvenile secondaries in the s4, or s4 and 9 positions; (3) the outer one or two primaries, p9 and 10, will also be worn and frayed retained juvenile feathers; and (4) p1 and 2 are new, dark feathers. On perched birds, the freshly molted tertials (s15–17) are darker and less worn than the adjacent s12–14 feathers. White markings on the upperwing coverts are less obvious than on subadult I eagles. A few scattered, very bleached tan-colored juvenile feathers are retained on the lesser upperwing coverts, particularly on the inner part of the wing. TAIL.—Two main types: (1) Dorsal surface, which is on the outer web of each feather, is primarily black with some white mottling, and (2) dorsal surface is white on the central one or two sets of rectrices and all other sets have black outer webs; tips of all rectrices have a wide black terminal band. In both types, the inner feather web is white or white sprinkled with black; when the tail is widely spread, it will appear very white with narrow dark edges and a black terminal band. Since the inner webs are white, the ventral surface is white with a variable amount of black mottling. The outer edge of the tail is black, and there is a moderately wide black terminal band.

BASIC II (SUBADULT II; MODERATELY MARKED TYPE): HEAD.—The demarcation line on the base of the whitish neck and the dark brown back and breast is moderately defined. Two types of head patterns: (1) *Moderately white type.*—Moderately wide dark brown auricular patch extends from the gape and connects with the moderately dark streaking on the nape and hindneck. The forehead and crown are brownish and often created a broad supercilium. The white areas of the head often have narrow dark streaking. *Note:* Common type. (2) *White*

type.—A narrow brown patch on the upper half of the auriculars that is similar to subadult III and connects under the eyes but does not extend to the gape. The patch connects with the lightly streaked nape and hindneck. The white areas of the head are often unmarked or very lightly streaked. *Note:* Uncommon type. BODY (dorsal).—Whitish hindneck merges with the white inverted triangle-shaped area on the back. The white back has a small to moderate amount of dark blotches. The lower back and rump are dark brown and mottled with white. BODY (ventral).—Dark brown breast forms a large, distinct bib that contrasts with the white belly, and flanks. The dark bib is sometimes mottled with white but is still distinct. The white belly and flanks are lightly to moderately spotted with dark brown (but never unmarked as in some eagles of subadult I age). Leg feathers are dark brown; in flight, they form a dark "V" against the white belly and flanks. The undertail coverts are a mix of white and dark brown markings. WINGS (dorsal).—Moderately broad white edges on most median and first row of lesser upperwing coverts. WINGS (ventral).—There is an extensive amount of white on the underwing coverts and axillaries. There is often a distinct white bar on the median underwing coverts. The inner one to three primaries may show some white, and several middle and inner secondaries will also exhibit white patches that are bordered by a wide black terminal band on the trailing edge.

BASIC II (SUBADULT II; HEAVILY MARKED TYPE): HEAD.—Rarely has the white type and regularly has the moderately white type. A large number of eagles of this plumage type, however, have a darker head pattern. *Heavily marked type.*—Head is tawny with a moderately wide dark brown auricular patch that extends from the gape and connects with the dark brown nape and hindneck; crown is a darker tawny and is often darker on the forehead. Demarcation of the neck to the back and breast is very ill-defined. The throat is whitish. BODY (dorsal).—Dark brown and adultlike with only a few white specks on the back; some may lack white speckling. *Note:* Dorsal region is as dark as many subadult III and some subadult IV birds. Lower back and rump are dark brown with some white speckling. BODY (ventral).—Dark brown with a very small amount of white speckling on the belly and flanks; sometimes lacks speckling. Undertail coverts can be dark with some light areas or moderately white with some dark areas. WINGS (dorsal).—Mainly dark brown with little if any white edges on the coverts. WINGS (ventral).—Mainly dark brown coverts with a small amount of white mottling on the axillaries, lesser underwing coverts, and median coverts (lacks a white bar on median coverts). Underside of the remiges is dark or has only a small amount of white markings.

Note: This plumage variation is very similar and often inseparable from moderately marked type of subadult III. It is necessary to see wing molt in order to categorize this age as iris and bill colors overlap with subadult III.

BASIC I (SUBADULT I) TRAITS: There are three main plumage types that are labeled according to the amount of white feathering. Unlike older subadults, variations do not appear to be correlated to a more rapid advancement towards adult plumage. HEAD.—Unlike older subadults, there is little variation on bill and cere color: (1) Bill is dark gray with a paler grayish or yellowish area on the lower basal region of the upper mandible and a yellow fringe on front of the cere and around the nares, or (2) uniformly gray on bill and cere. The lower mandible is often yellowish on the basal region. The cere is dark gray and may have a yellow fringe around the nares. Gape is pale yellow. Iris color is pale brown, pale gray, or rarely pale yellow. BODY (dorsal and ventral): Variable in the amount of white markings; *see* Types. WINGS (dorsal and ventral).—Variable in the amount of white markings; *see* types. The stage of remix molt easily identifies this age class. Even though there are minor variations, they are always separable from older subadults and juveniles. On birds viewed from behind, the three new tertials (s15–17) contrast sharply to the more faded, worn, and longer brownish juvenile feathers on most of the rest of the secondaries. In flight, the jagged trailing edge created by the large number of retained juvenile secondaries contrasts with the shorter, more rounded subadult I feathers. White markings on retained juvenile feathers often extend to the tip of each feather. White markings on new subadult I feathers are bordered

on the trailing edge of each feather by a wide black band. The outer half of the wing has worn and frayed juvenile primaries. TAIL.— Two main variations that can be found on any plumage type: (1) *All-black type.*—All black or lightly sprinkled with white on the dorsal surface. (2) *White type.*—White on the central one or two rectrix sets and black on all other sets. On both types, the inner feather web of each rectrix is white or sprinkled with black. When widely fanned, the tail can appear fairly white on the black type and very white on the white type. On the ventral surface, the tail is mainly white and lightly or moderately sprinkled with black, with a moderately defined black terminal band.

BASIC I (SUBADULT I; LIGHTLY MARKED TYPE): A very lightly marked plumage type that can appear to be albinistic. However, all-white feather markings are simply more extensive than in the two darker types and are not irregular white areas, as found on albinistic birds. HEAD.—*White type.*—Moderately wide, isolated dark brown patch that extends from the gape onto the auriculars (same width of auricular patch as on most subadult II eagles). The rest of the head and neck, including the crown, nape, and hindneck, are white. BODY (dorsal).—The back is white with a very small amount of dark spotting and merges with the white hindneck. The white back forms a distinct inverted white triangle that blends with the white hindneck. Many of the scapulars have white edges. The lower back is white with some dark spotting. BODY (ventral).—The breast has a small to moderate-sized dark brown bib. On some, the breast is lightly mottled with dark brown and the bib is poorly defined. The white lower neck contrasts sharply with the top of the brown bib. The belly and flanks, are either white with small dark spots or unmarked and pure white. The leg feathers are dark brown with some white mottling and form a dark "V" against the rest of the white underparts when in flight. The undertail coverts are dark with some white areas. WINGS (dorsal).—The median and first rows of lesser upperwing coverts are white with narrow dark center streaks. The tips of many greater upperwing coverts are broadly edged with white. The rest of the coverts are dark brown. WINGS (ventral).—All of the underwing coverts and axillaries form an extensive white area. The retained juvenile secondaries are largely white. The new subadult I secondaries, typically s1 and 2, s5 and 6, and s12–14, may be covered with extensive white markings but they are bordered on the trailing edge by the wide black terminal band. TAIL.—Mainly the white type.

BASIC I (SUBADULT I; MODERATELY MARKED TYPE): HEAD.—Two variations of head patterns: *Moderate type.*—Moderately wide dark patch extends from the gape and onto the auriculars. The head and neck, including the crown, nape, and hindneck, are tawny-brown and streaked with dark brown. *Dark type.*—A wide dark patch extends from the lower mandible and onto and below the auriculars as a large dark side-of-head patch. The head and neck are tawny-brown or dark tawny brown and streaked with dark brown and is only slightly paler than the breast. The throat is whitish. BODY (dorsal).—The back is white with moderate to large dark spots and forms a distinct inverted white triangle. Scapulars have narrow white or tawny edges on many feathers. The lower back has some white spotting. BODY (ventral).—The breast is dark brown and forms a distinct bib. The dark bib is often mottled with white, but is still very distinct. The belly and flanks are white and covered with small to moderate-sized dark spots; occasionally nearly unmarked. The leg feathers are dark brown and, in flight, contrast against the white belly and flanks. The undertail coverts are dark brown. WINGS (dorsal).—The median and first rows of lesser upperwing coverts may have moderate or wide white edges; sometimes rather white with narrow dark center streaks on each feather. The inner greater upperwing coverts may have white or tawny mottling or edging on most feathers. WINGS (ventral).—The axillaries are white, the lesser underwing coverts are mottled brown and white, and the median coverts are often white and form a distinct white bar along the midwing. The remiges may have a moderate or extensive amount of white markings. TAIL.—Either of the two types described in Subadult Traits.

BASIC I (SUBADULT I; HEAVILY MARKED TYPE): HEAD.—Either the moderate type or dark type, but more likely to be the latter. The throat is whitish. BODY (dorsal).—The back is dark brown on the upper two-thirds and speckled with white on the distal one-third (a white triangle is not apparent, as on the other types). The back is sometimes all dark. Scapulars lack pale edges on the feathers. Lower back is dark brown. BODY (ventral).—Large dark brown bib on the breast. The belly and flanks are white and covered with moderate to large dark brown spots. The leg feathers are dark brown and form a dark "V" when the birds are flying. The undertail coverts are dark brown. WINGS (dorsal).—The upperwing coverts are either uniformly dark brown or the inner median and greater coverts may have narrow pale tips or edges. WINGS (ventral). Axillaries are mainly white, the lesser coverts are darker and mottled with brown and white, and a fairly distinct white bar is on the median covert tract. Remiges have a moderate amount of white on each feather. TAIL.—Mainly the dark type.

JUVENILE TRAITS: HEAD.—Uniformly dark brown with a whitish throat. On some birds, small tawny tips form on the nape and hindneck feathers. Most have a few white streaks on the sides of the neck. **Bill and cere are black; gape is pale yellow.** Iris is dark brown. BODY (dorsal).—A paler brown than the head. BODY (ventral).—**Breast is darker brown than the tawny flanks and lower belly and forms a bib.** Many eagles exhibit a small amount of white streaking the lower part of the bib, and many have few dark brown blotches on the flanks and belly. **Leg feathers are dark brown and contrast with the paler belly and flanks.** The undertail coverts vary from being dark brown to white with dark streaks down the center of each feather. WINGS (dorsal).—Upperwing coverts are the same brown color as the back and scapulars and are paler than the head and remiges. The inner one-third of the greater- and first rows of lesser coverts are pale tawny and forms a pale brown patch on the inner wing that is visible while perching or flying. The tips and outer edges of the inner six secondaries (s12–17 are pale tawny or pale brown and much paler than the rest of the remiges. The greater upperwing coverts are medium brown and paler than the rest of the upperwing coverts. **In flight, the black remiges contrast with the paler brown upperwing coverts and form a two-toned ef-**

fect. WINGS (ventral).—There are two types of underwing patterns: (1) *White type.*—Underwing coverts and axillaries are nearly all white, including all of the patagial region. There is a narrow dark bar along much of the first row of lesser coverts and on part of the inner portion of greater covert feathers. The greater coverts have an extensive amount of white on a large part of each feather. The remiges have an extensive amount of white on the inner two or three primaries, on the outermost secondary, and on the inner 12 secondaries. Only three or four secondaries are dark (s2–4), and they divide the white regions on the inner primaries and secondaries. On the inner secondaries, the white extends to the tips of the feathers; on the middle secondaries the white usually ends before reaching the tips. *Dark type.*—The axillaries are white, there is some white mottling on patagial coverts, a white bar extends out on the median coverts, and the secondary greater coverts have white tips. The remiges have a minimum to moderate amount of white on the outer one to three primaries and inner few secondaries. TAIL.—Three variations on dorsal and ventral surfaces: (1) *All-black type.*—Dorsal and ventral surfaces are completely black. (2) *Moderately white type.*—The dorsal surface is black with a sprinkling of white, particularly on the central one or two rectrix sets. On the ventral surface, the tail is also a mix of black and white with a moderately wide or wide black terminal band and a narrow black band on the outer edge. The ventral surface can be mainly white with the black terminal band and narrow black outer edge. (3) *White type.*—Tail is white except the outer web of each feather is black, and the moderately wide or wide terminal band is black on both surfaces.

JUVENILE (WORN PLUMAGE): BODY (dorsal and ventral).—A few months after fledging, and especially towards the end of the age cycle, the body plumage fades considerably due to exposure to the sun. The back, scapulars, and upperwing coverts bleach to pale brown. The belly and flanks bleach to pale tawny or very pale tawny and contrast sharply with the dark brown breast, neck, head, and leg feathers.

JUVENILE (FRESH PLUMAGE): BODY (dorsal and ventral).—When recently fledged and lacking extensive exposure to the sun, the plumage is darker than on older juveniles. The back, scapulars, and upperwing coverts are medium brown, but still a bit paler than the dark brown head. The belly and flanks are medium to dark tawny, but still contrast a bit against the dark brown breast, neck, head, and leg feathers.

JUVENILE (STREAKED TYPE): As typical juvenile in either fresh or worn plumage except for the flanks and portions of the belly. BODY.—The flanks may be white instead of tawny and streaked with dark brown. The belly is mostly tawny but may be somewhat whitish on the upper area near the flanks. The belly is variably streaked and spotted with dark brown. The leg feathers are dark brown as on typical birds.

ABNORMAL PLUMAGES: There are numerous records of imperfect albino (dilute plumage) juveniles and adults (Clark and Wheeler 2001, BKW pers. obs.). See photograph of an imperfect albino adult in Clark and Wheeler (2001). Imperfect albino juveniles have similar color patterns as normal juveniles but have nearly white bellies and flanks and light brown head, neck, breast, and upperparts. There is an extensive amount of white on the underwing and undertail (BKW pers. obs. and photos). There are records of partial albino juveniles in the West (Clark and Wheeler 2001).

HABITAT: Summer: Breeds and summers in riparian areas: bays, lakes, marshes, rivers, sea coasts, and swamps. Typically found in isolated regions, but some southern pairs nest near human-inhabited areas. All areas have tall trees. Climate varies from hot and humid in the south to cool humid in the north.

Winter: Similar riparian habitats as in summer where there is open water, but also found in areas away from water if there is sufficient food. Large numbers gather at dams, where there is often an abundant supply of dead or stunned fish. Absent from most high elevation areas.

Migration: Found in any type of habitat, including montane areas, but the largest numbers are seen near lowland riparian locations.

HABITS: Typically a wary species; however, some individuals are fairly tame, particularly in southern regions. Nesting pairs are quite wary and become highly agitated by humans intruding into nesting territories.

Bald Eagles may perch in one location for

several hours, especially during winter, to conserve energy or wait for a feeding opportunity. Large, exposed branches are preferred perches. Eagles also readily perch on the ground, ice, and many artificial objects. Except in Florida, Bald Eagles in the East rarely perch on utility poles. During the hot summer months, southern birds will perch in sheltered, shaded areas of trees and become inconspicuous.

They are solitary during the breeding season, but become gregarious in the nonbreeding season, and large numbers often congregate to feed and roost. Prime winter feeding and roosting locations may host hundreds of eagles. Pairs remain together year-round, even if they migrate. Pairs often perch side-by-side.

When perched, two animated body positions exhibit social and sexual behavior and are accompanied by vocalization: (1) *Straight-necked.*—Neck is fully extended in a straight line ahead of the body with the head and bill also held in the same line. (2) *Head-toss.*—Head and neck are tossed upwards in a vertical angle with the neck fully extended.

FEEDING: Perch and aerial hunter. Bald Eagles are opportunistic feeders; however, they are adept hunters and mainly feed on live prey during the breeding season. During the nonbreeding season, eagles become even more opportunistic and lazy, pirate food from conspecifics and other raptors, and scavenge for carrion of all types and sizes. Pairs will cooperatively hunt.

Aerial hunters make random, low to high altitude forays over potential feeding areas. Prey may be captured on the ground or water and occasionally in the air (*see* Flight).

Eagles capture most prey by grabbing it with their talons, but when standing or walking in shallow water or along shorelines, they may also use their bills.

Diet varies regionally and seasonally, but fish are a primary prey in most regions and seasons. Live fish are caught in most areas year-round, but mainly in the breeding season. Dead, dying, or stunned fish form a major part of their diet in many areas in the nonbreeding season. In spring feed on winter-kill fish from thawing lakes, ponds, and streams.

Live and dead ducks, geese, and other water-type birds, especially American Coots, are preyed upon in all seasons. Maritime-area eagles may feed on Common- and Thick-billed murres, Razorbills, Black Guillemots, and Atlantic Puffins.

Large rodents form a small part of the diet in much of the eagle's range, especially Muskrats. Woodchucks are also preyed upon in parts of the East, especially in inland areas of Ohio.

Turtles also make up a portion of the diet.

In winter, White-tailed Deer that are killed by hunters and vehicles or die of natural causes form an integral part of the diet of scavenging eagles that do not associate with water. Domestic cattle that have died and afterbirth are scavenged. Eagles also scavenge at open-pit garbage dumps and in local areas where dead chickens and other animals are discarded.

FLIGHT: Soars and glides with wings held on a flat plane. May soar with the wings held in a very low dihedral. Powered flight consists of unique wingbeats that separate them from other raptors and large birds, even when observed at great distances. The upstroke is high and the downstroke is low, which creates an exaggerated upwards motion on the upstroke. Bald Eagles nearly always end a wingbeat on a downstroke before entering a glide or soar (F. Nicoletti, unpubl. data). Powered flight is an irregular series of flapping and gliding.

Also unique to Bald Eagles is the "flare-up" display. Eagles of all ages will flare up to signal danger to nearby flying eagles by banking sharply upwards at a vertical angle with their wings flapping and legs either tucked up or lowered.

VOICE: A highly vocal raptor during all seasons. The calls of males are higher-pitched than females. Call notes are high-pitched, crisp, and metallic-sounding. (1) *Ca-ack* or *kah* call is emitted during alarm, especially around nest sites, and may be repeated numerous times. (2) *Whee-he-he-he* is a staccato-sounding call given in a decrescendo and slows towards the end. It is uttered when eagles are annoyed by conspecifics or other bird species (crows, gulls, ravens), during pair formation (accompanied by *head-toss*), when a female begs for food from a male, and when copulating. (3) *Yaap* is a wailing, gull-like call that is repeated numerous times and is often intermixed with the #2 call. The call is given at the nest by displaying adults and hungry chicks, and also away from the nest by fledged, food-begging young. (4)

Chatter or *chitter* is a series of rapidly uttered short *ca-ack* notes given by adults at nest sites and with eagles engaging in conflicts with conspecifics at feeding and roosting sites.

STATUS AND DISTRIBUTION: Currently listed as a Threatened Species in the lower 48 states. Alaska and Canada have always had healthy breeding populations, and the Bald Eagle was never listed as endangered or threatened.

Laws prohibiting killing Bald Eagle's, organochlorine pesticide bans in Canada and the U.S., state programs that assisted population growth, and retention of critical habitat have helped Bald Eagles in the lower 48 states gain a new foothold and re-establish themselves. With this assistance and the species' resilience, eagle populations have been steadily growing, often significantly, in many areas.

Summer: CANADA: Approximate current number of nesting pairs for each province are listed below. *Labrador:* 13 pairs. *New Brunswick:* 40 pairs. *Newfoundland:* 1,000 pairs. *Nova Scotia:* 200 pairs. *Ontario* (northwest region): 1,000 pairs with the greatest density in the Lake of the Woods area and other lakes in the southwestern portion of this region. Density declines northeast of Red Lake. Common in the Thunder Bay region and around Lake Nipigon. *Ontario* (southern region): 25 pairs. Most are concentrated south of Windsor and the Long Point region. Recent breeding has occurred at Navy Island in the Niagara River. *Quebec:* 25 pairs. Mainly breed in the western part of the province north of Ottawa and especially on Anticosti Island in the Gulf of the St. Lawrence.

UNITED STATES: Populations in some states were originally boosted with release programs. In 1999, there were an estimated 5,748 pairs of eagles in the lower 48 states (compared to 100,000 pairs estimated in 1782, when it became our national symbol). Known breeding or territorial pairs are listed for 1982/1998 for comparison in their comeback; more recent data, if known, are in parentheses. *Alabama:* 0/23 pairs (43 pairs in 2002). A reintroduction program helped population growth. In 1998, nests were found in the following counties: Baldwin, Barbour, Cherokee, Chilton, Choctaw, Coosa, Dallas, Hale, Henry, Jackson, Lee, Madison, Marshall, Perry, and Pickens. *Connecticut:* 0/2 pairs (4 pairs in 2001). Breeds along the Connecticut River in East Windsor, Essex, Middleton, Rocky Hill, and Suffield; also at Lake Zoar and Barkhamsted Reservoir. *Delaware:* 4/13 pairs (14 pairs in 2001). Resident on Blackbird Creek south of Odessa, Drawyers Creek north of Odessa, at Bombay Hook and Prime Hook NWRs. on the St. Jones River south of Dover, at Churchman's Marsh south of Wilmington, near McDonough, and at Burnt Swamp at the headwaters of the Pokomoke River in Sussex Co. *District of Columbia:* 0/0 pairs (4 pairs in 2001). A nest on National Park Service land near Bolling Air Force Base in 2000 was the first successful nest in the district in 50 years. Three other nests are near and downstream from the Woodrow Wilson Bridge. *Florida:* 340/980 pairs (1,102 pairs in 2001). This state has the largest number of breeding pairs of any eastern state. Total population estimated at 2,931–4,242 birds. Some are urban nesting pairs. Three-fourths of the nests are on private land. Pairs are concentrated in coastal counties in the lower peninsula and inland from Lake Okeechobee north to Gainesville and Jacksonville. In the panhandle, nests are mainly north and south of Tallahassee and at St. Vincent NWR. *Georgia:* 0/37 pairs (49 pairs in 1999). Eagles were absent as breeders in the state in 1971–1977. A hacking program helped boost the population. Nesting occurs in the following counties: Baker, Bibb, Brooks, Bryan, Camden, Chatham, Chattahoochee, Cherokee, Coffee, Columbia, Decatur, Dougherty, Early, Glynn, Greene, Hancock, Harris, Hart, Heard, Jefferson, Lanier, Lee, Liberty, Lincoln, Long, Lowndes, McDuffie, McIntosh, Monroe, Murray, Quitman, Thomas, Troup, and Twiggs. *Illinois:* 5/43 pairs. A reintroduction program boosted the population. Nests in the following counties: Alexander, Calhoun, Carroll, Fayette, Greene, Jackson, Jo Daviess, Johnson, Mason, Pope, Pulaski, Union, Whiteside, Williamson, and Winnebago. *Indiana:* 0/15 pairs (36 pairs in 2002). Breeding population was assisted by an introduction program. Pairs are in the following counties: Bartholomew, Brown, Carroll, Cass, Crawford, Daviess, Gibson, Greene, Harrison, Jackson, Knox, Martin, Monroe, Morgan, Owen, Parke, Posey, Tippecanoe, and Vermillion. *Kentucky:* 0/13 pairs (26 pairs in 2002). Nests in e. Kentucky only on the Rich Creek branch of the

Yatesville Lake in Lawrence Co. *Maine:* 72/202 pairs. Maine had a 12 percent decline in its nesting population in 1997. However, in the same year, a record 179 eaglets fledged. *Maryland:* 58/232 pairs (315 pairs in 2001). Breeds in 18 counties, but concentrated near the shoreline of the Chesapeake Bay and the following tidal rivers: Chester, Choptank, Patuxent, Potomac, and Sassafras. Counties with the most nesting pairs: Dorchester (56), Charles (35), Kent (21), Harford (13), Saint Mary's (16), Queen Anne's (14), Talbot (13), and Somerset (10). *Massachusetts:* 0/9 pairs. A reintroduction program helped population growth. Nests at the Quabbin Reservoir (5 pairs); on the Connecticut River at Gill, Hadley, Sunderland, and West Springfield. Also present at Middleboro and Sandisfield. *Michigan:* 98/291 pairs (343 pairs in 1999). Nests at Isle Royale N.P. in Lake Superior and in all counties in the Upper Peninsula. In the Lower Peninsula, found in the following counties: Allegan, Bay, Ionia, Midland, Monroe, Ottawa, Saginaw, and Tuscola. *Mississippi:* 0/22 pairs. Nests at American Legion Lake, Bay Spring Reservoir, Grenada Lake, Okatibbee Lake, Old River Lake, Ross Barnett Reservoir, Sardis Lake, and the three coastal counties. *New Hampshire:* 0/2 pairs (6 pairs in 2001). Breeds at Umbagog, Lake Coos Co.; near Nubanusit Lake, Hillsborough Co.; along the Connecticut River, Cheshire Co.; and the Second Connecticut Lake, Coos Co. *New Jersey:* 1/16 pairs (23 in 1999). A hacking program helped population growth. Resident at Merrill Creek Reservoir and Round Valley Reservoir in the northwestern part of the state, near Rancocas Creek near Willingboro. Also found on the intercoastal plain near the Wading River north of New Gretna and on the southern coastal plain on Cohansey, Mill, Nantuxent, and Stowe Creeks; near Belleplain; near the Great Egg Harbor River in the MacNamara Wildlife Management Area; and in Gloucester Co. *New York:* 2/40 pairs (67 in 2001). There was only one remaining pair in 1965. Population was greatly boosted by a reintroduction program. In 2001, pairs were located in the southern region in the following counties, with total number of pairs in parentheses. Albany (1), Columbia (3), Delaware (11), Dutchess (3), Greene (1), Otsego (1), Schoharie (2), Sullivan (14), and Ul-

ster (92). In the northeastern region, found in the following counties: Franklin (8), Hamilton (1), and St. Lawrence (3). Near Lake Ontario. Along Lake Ontario, found in the following counties: Jefferson (2), Orleans (2), and Oswego (2). In the Finger Lakes region, breeds in the following counties: Cayuga (2), Livingston (2), and Seneca (1). Near Lake Erie breeds in the following counties: Cattaraugus (4), Erie (1), and Wayne. *North Carolina:* 0/17 pairs. Inland counties with nests in 1998 include Chatham, Granville, Guilford, and Stanly. Coastal areas with nesting pairs in 1998 were in Beaufort, Chowan, Hyde, Pamlico, Pasquotank, Pitt, Tyrrell, and Washington Cos. *Ohio:* 7/47 pairs (63 pairs in 2001, 79 pairs in 2002). This state has a few urban nesting eagles. Stronghold for breeding is in the marshes of w. Lake Erie. Counties with at least one pair in 2001: Coshocton, Delaware, Erie (7), Geauga (2), Guernsey, Harrison, Henry, Huron, Knox (2), Lorain (2), Lucas (5), Mahoning, Marion, Mercer, Noble, Ottawa (10), Portage (4), Ross, Sandusky (10), Seneca (4), Trumbull (5), Wayne, Wood, and Wyandot (5). *Pennsylvania:* 4/29 pairs (53 in 2001). A reintroduction program assisted population growth. Nesting pairs are concentrated in the northwestern part of the state at the Allegheny Reservoir in McKean and Warren Cos., Union City Reservoir in Erie Co., and in the following other northwestern counties: Butler (2), Crawford (9), Forest, Mercer, and Venango. In the northeastern part of the state, pairs are in Pike and Wayne Cos. Pairs are also along the lower Susquehanna River. Scattered nest sites are at Cameron Co., Harrisburg International Airport, Cowanesque Reservoir and Pine Creek in Tioga Co., and Raystown Lake in Huntingdon Co. *Rhode Island:* 0/0 pairs. Along with Vermont, this state does not have breeding pairs. *South Carolina:* 21/129 pairs (168 pairs in 2001). Common along rivers and bays in the southernmost counties. Also nests at Lake Marion, Lake Moultrie, Wateree Lake, and along the Savannah River. *Tennessee:* 0/38 pairs (43 pairs in 2000). A large number of eagles were released in the 1980s and 1990s. *Vermont:* 0/0 pairs. Along with Rhode Island, this state does not have breeding pairs. *Virginia:* 45/250 pairs (312 pairs in 2001). Inland nests are at Lake Manassas, near Warrenton, Mason Neck S.P. in Fairfax Co.,

Culpepper Co., Fauquier Co., and the John Kerr Reservoir (Buggs Island Lake) in Halifax and Mecklenburg Cos. Nesting territories in 1997 were along the following major rivers and their tributaries: Rappahannock and Plankatank (69); Potomac and Great Wicomico (51); James and Chickahominy, and Lower Tidewater (5); York, Pamunkey, and Mattaponi, plus Mobjack Bay (25). There are 16 pairs on the eastern shore in Accomack and Northampton Cos. *West Virginia:* 1/6 pairs (7 pairs in 2001). Nests in Grant, Hardy, Mineral, and Pendleton Cos. and on Blennerhassett Island on the upper Ohio River in Wood Co. *Wisconsin:* 207/689 pairs. Common in the many lakes of n. Wisconsin. Nests in Crawford and Sauk Cos. in sw. Wisconsin.

Winter: Found throughout breeding range except in n. Ontario, Québec north of the St. Lawrence River, and Labrador. Highest concentrations are along the Atlantic coastal area and Mississippi River. About 2,500–4,000 Bald Eagles winter along the Mississippi River from Minneapolis, Minn., to south of St. Louis, Mo. The drawing card on the Mississippi River are the locks and dams that provide open water and abundant prey in the form of dead and stunned fish and waterfowl. Fairly large numbers winter along the Ohio River and on larger lakes from Mississippi east to s. Georgia and especially Florida.

Eagles wintering in e. New York breed or summer in Labrador, Maine, New Brunswick, w. and e. Ontario, and Québec.

Eagles winter as far north as open water or ample food permits. Frigid winter weather is not a deterrent if there is adequate food.

Movements: Resident or short- to moderate-distance migrant. Pairs in Canada and the n. U.S. migrate only because of a lack of food during winter. Pairs in central and southern regions are typically resident. Most eastern hawkwatches record low to moderate numbers of Bald Eagles during the fall and spring migration. Hawkwatches that see moderate numbers see them mainly in the early part of the fall. In the East, Eagle Valley Hawkwatch in Grant Co., Wisc. sees the largest numbers in the late fall.

Northward spring and summer dispersal.— Juveniles born at southern and middle latitudes (at least to the latitude of New York) disperse north from natal areas after becoming independent. Subadults and some adults from similar latitudes also disperse north from former natal or soon-to-be breeding areas for the spring and summer. Northward dispersal begins in Apr. and escalates throughout May and Jun. Northward movement may continue through Aug. as birds wander up to northern latitudes. More northern breeders do not fledge early enough to disperse.

Florida-raised birds may disperse as far north as Nova Scotia, west through s. Québec and s. Ontario to Manitoba; in the U.S., as far west as Arkansas. New York-raised birds may disperse east to Massachusetts, north to Nova Scotia and New Brunswick, or west across s. Québec to Wisconsin.

Once the summer wandering has ended, a southward migration ensues, as the eagles return to original natal latitudes.

Fall migration: Southern and middle-latitude birds begin their southward sojourn as early as late Jul. Most do not begin until Aug. and Sep. Peak numbers are mainly seen from mid- to late Sep. from Ontario to New Jersey, but may occur as late as early October. Adults also make up a fair percentage of these early migrants, which lends credence to some older birds, possibly nonbreeders, also engaging in northward summer excursions.

There is overlap between the late southward movement of southern birds and early movement of northern birds. After the distinct mid-Sep. to early Oct. peak of many returning southern birds, there appears to be a lull in movements before the minor peak of northern birds occur in late fall. Fall migration is an unpredictable event for northern birds which is based on weather patterns. If the autumn is mild, migration may occur late and be protracted. If winterlike weather comes early, a mass exodus from the northland occurs early and quickly. Peak movements may occur from late Oct. to mid-Nov. in Ontario, but do not occur until late Nov. or Dec. in more southern regions. Southward migrants are still seen at Hawk Mountain near Kempton, PA, into Jan.

Spring migration: The first migrants, mainly of adults, are seen at hawkwatches in late Feb. or early Mar. There is also typically an increase of eagles staging at prime feeding areas at this time. In New York and Michigan, early peak movements of primarily adults occur in late

Mar. Based on telemetry data, all ages of eagles wintering in s. New York may leave wintering grounds from mid-Feb. to late Mar.; younger birds may leave as late as mid-Apr. Migration of northern birds continues throughout Apr. and May and overlaps with early northward dispersing southern birds. Breeding or summering grounds may be reached in as little as 9 days to as long as 39 days.

NESTING: Florida birds may begin in Oct., and n. Canadian birds may begin in May. Pairs at interim latitudes begin in mid-winter or early spring.

Breeding may occur when 3 years old, but it usually does not occur until birds are at least 4–5 years old. Breeding occurs at younger age in areas where the population is growing, which has been the case in the last 2 decades with the population boom. Where the population is established and saturated, only older birds may breed.

Pairs typically remain together until one dies. Polyandry and polygyny infrequently occurs. Males tend to return closer to natal/hack sites to breed than do females, a trait seen in many raptor species.

Courtship (flight).—Both sexes perform *mutual soaring, pursuit-flight,* and *talon-grappling* that turns into *cartwheeling.* Males perform *fly-around* and *sky-dancing.*

Courtship (perched).—*Billing* and *mutual plumage-stroking.* The *head-toss* is used at times. Pairs often perch side-by-side.

Nest locations are typically near water. Nests are often used for many years and gradually become larger with repeated use. Alternate nests are often in a territory. Nests are mainly in large, live trees, and placed below the canopy. Large pines are favored nesting trees in many regions. Nests are also placed on rock out-crops. In the East, nests are rarely placed on the ground on islands. In 2002, a most unusual ground nest in Michigan was located in a cornfield.

New nests may be 1–3 ft. (0.3–1 m) deep and 3–6 ft. (1–2 m) in diameter. Old nests can be up to 12 ft. (4 m) deep and 8.5 ft. (3 m) in diameter. The nest is comprised of large sticks, and the nest bowl is regularly lined with greenery consisting of grasses, stems, and often pine needles. Both sexes build or refurbish nests.

Eggs are laid at several day intervals. Both sexes incubate the typical clutch of 2 eggs for 34–36 days. Three eggs are sometimes laid, and 1-egg clutches are rare. Fratricide (siblicide) is common, with the larger, stronger nestling overpowering the smaller, weaker nestling. Youngsters fledge in 70–77 days, but occasionally take up to 88 days to fly. Fledglings stay with their parent for up to 2 additional months.

CONSERVATION: The Bald Eagle, along with the Osprey and Peregrine Falcon, suffered from the widespread use of organochlorine chemicals from the late 1940s to the mid-1970s. The eagle population in some states was either decimated or greatly reduced during this period. The bans on deadly pesticide use allowed eagles in most areas to rebound. As with all raptors, Bald Eagles have suffered tremendously from shooting until public awareness turned the tide to produce legal protection. Several states and one province assisted population recovery with reintroduction programs.

Pesticide bans: The first step that was taken to not only help Bald Eagles, but to benefit all wildlife and humankind, was to ban organochlorine pesticides, particularly DDT. This lethal pesticide was first used in 1946 in Canada and the U.S. This ban, however, was nearly too late to help the decimated population of Bald Eagles in the East.

Canada took a series of steps to discontinue the sale and use of DDT that began in 1968 with a ban on spraying forests in national parks. The major Canadian ban came on Jan. 1, 1970 (announced Nov. 3, 1969), when DDT use was permitted for insecticide use on only 12 of the 62 previously sprayed food crops. However, all registration for insecticide use on food crops was stopped by 1978. Canada, however, permitted DDT use for bat control and medicinal purposes until 1985. Canadian users and distributors were also allowed to use existing supplies of DDT until Dec. 31, 1990.

The U.S. also had a series of steps to ban DDT, but halted the overall sale and use more quickly. In 1969, the USDA stopped the spraying on shade trees, tobacco crops, aquatic locations, and in-home use. The USDA placed further bans on its use on crops, commercial plants, and for building purposes in 1970. The Environmental Protection Agency banned all DDT sale and use on Dec. 31, 1972; however, limited use for military and medicinal purposes was permitted until Oct. 1989. In 1974, the U.S. banned the use of Aldrin and Dieldrin, both deadly chemicals that may have affected wildlife as much as DDT.

Mexico was expected to discontinue government-sponsored DDT use for malaria control in 2002, and has planned a total ban of DDT by 2006.

As of 2000, possibly five other Latin American countries still use DDT and other organochlorine chemicals without restrictions.

The U.S. and Canada, along with 120 other countries, have signed a United Nations-sponsored treaty banning eight deadly organochlorine pesticides: Aldrin, Chlordane, DDT, Dieldrin, Endrin, Heptachlor, Mirex, and Toxaphene. There are also two industrial chemicals, Hexachlorobenzene (also a pesticide) PCBs, and two by-products of industrial processes, dioxins and furans, that have also been banned.

Organophosphate pesticides, although not as persistent in the environment as organochlorine pesticides, can be deadly to some aquatic life that fish eat and therefore affect eagles.

Carbamate pesticides were less harmful to the environment than organophosphate chemicals and were used to control insect infestations in e. Canadian forests.

Pyrethroid pesticides are harmless to birds and mammals and are currently used to control insect infestations in e. Canadian forests. However, some of these may be deadly to aquatic life and affect the food that fish eat, therefore affecting eagles.

Protective laws: Even though the Bald Eagle has been the national symbol of the U.S. for over 2 centuries, wanton killing still occurred throughout the 1930s. Bounties were paid for dead eagles until legal protection was enacted in 1940, when the Bald Eagle Protection Act was passed (it was amended in 1962 to include the Golden Eagle). The 1940 act prohibited killing, taking, or selling body parts and feathers. To counteract the decimating effects of organochlorine pesticides on the Bald Eagle population in the contiguous 48 states, the USFWS on Mar. 11, 1967, listed the Bald Eagle as endangered south of the 40th parallel under the Endangered Species Preservation Act of 1966. With the enactment of the more powerful Endangered Species Act in 1973, the

USFWS listed the Bald Eagle as an Endangered Species on Feb. 14, 1978 in the lower 48 states except in Michigan, Minnesota, Oregon, Washington, and Wisconsin, where the eagle was listed as a Threatened Species. With the Bald Eagle's surprisingly strong comeback from near-decimation from pesticides, on Jul. 12, 1995, the USFWS reclassified it from an Endangered Species to a Threatened Species in all lower 48 states. On Jul. 6, 1999, the USFWS proposed delisting the eagle. Many states still classify the Bald Eagle as endangered.

In 1986, the U.S. Supreme Court held that Native Americans must abide by mandated protective laws. Since the 1970s, the USFWS has collected eagle body parts and feathers from eagles that have found dead in the wild, illegally killed and confiscated eagles, and eagles in rehabilitation facilities and zoos; the parts have been stored at its National Eagle Repository in Commerce City, Colo. The USFWS distributes the parts and feathers to Native American tribes for ceremonial use. The repository annually receives about 900 Bald and Golden eagle carcasses for distribution.

Restoration programs: Ontario and 12 eastern states implemented reintroduction programs in the 1970–1990s, but mainly in the 1970s and 1980s. Due to organochlorine pesticide contamination of the 1940s to early 1970s and encroaching civilization, the breeding population in many states had been either totally eliminated or had only remnant pairs.

Three methods were used to rebuild populations: (1) *Egg transplant.*—Putting healthy eggs taken from wild nests and putting them into nests of remnant pairs that were experiencing thin-shelled eggs due to pesticides. In 1970, Maine was the first state to use this method. (2) *Fostering.*—Released birds were obtained by three methods: (A) Importing wild nestlings from other states and provinces with healthy populations; (B) eggs taken from wild nests from other states and provinces with healthy populations were hatched and raised in captivity until release; (C) nestlings from captive origins, including captive breeding facilities at the USFWS Patuxent Research Laboratory in Laurel, Md.; zoos; and rehabilitators. The nestlings were put in nests and fostered by extant wild pairs. (3) *Hacking/releasing.*— Young eagles were obtained by the same three methods as described for Fostering. Once old enough, they were put into large, sheltered elevated wooden structures (usually tall towers) in suitable natural environments. The fledglings were fed by concealed caretakers until they could fend for themselves.

Alaska supplied most of the eaglets that were released in various states. Manitoba, Minnesota, Nova Scotia, Saskatchewan, and Wisconsin supplied large numbers; California, Ontario, and Washington supplied moderate numbers; Florida, Maryland, Michigan, Missouri, and Virginia supplied a few eaglets.

From 1984 to 1992, Florida supplied 393 eggs to restoration programs. The eggs were artificially incubated and the nestlings raised and distributed to foster nests and hack sites in Alabama, Georgia, Mississippi, North Carolina, and Oklahoma. The Sutton Avian Research Center in Oklahoma raised and distributed 275 eagles for release to Alabama, Georgia, Mississippi, and North Carolina from 1985 to 1992.

CANADA.—*Ontario:* To bolster the reduced population in s. Ontario, the Canadian Wildlife Service released 16 fledglings on Long Point, Haldimand-Norfolk Co., from 1983 to 1985.

UNITED STATES.—For the most part, "small-sized" eagles were released in southern latitudes and large-sized eagles in northern latitudes. *Alabama:* 91 eagles were hacked 1985–1991. *Georgia:* 89 eagles were hacked 1979–1995. *Indiana:* 73 eagles were released at Monroe Reservoir 1985–1989. *Maine:* The first state to engage in a restoration program. Egg transplants and chick fostering were done in the mid- to late 1970s. *Massachusetts:* 42 eagles imported from Manitoba and Nova Scotia were released 1982–1988. *Mississippi:* 98 eagles released 1986–1992. *New Jersey:* Began hacking in 1983 with 27 released as of 1985. *New York:* 198 eagles were released 1976–1988 in four counties: Albany, Franklin, Genesee, and Seneca. Young wild eagles were obtained mainly from Alaska (88%), Michigan, Minnesota, and Wisconsin and from the USFWS at Patuxent. The first breeding of a hacked pair occurred in 1980. *North Carolina:* Releases occurred 1983–1988. *Ohio:* Eaglets were fostered into nests of active pairs that suffered chick losses 1980–1987. Researchers tried to keep two similar-aged youngsters in most nests. Eaglets were obtained mainly from the USFWS Patuxent facility, Ohio zoos, and from nests that had been blown out of trees and young had survived. *Pennsylvania:* 70 eagles were released 1983–1988. Fledglings were also fostered once a viable breeding population was established. *Tennessee:* 248 eagles from Alaska and Wisconsin were released 1980–1996.

Mortality: The Bald Eagle has few natural enemies once it has attained fledging age. Nestlings may be killed by Bobcats, Great Horned Owls, and Raccoons while in the nest. Fledglings that are on the ground may fall prey to Coyotes and, in northern regions, Timber Wolves. Severe weather, especially hurricanes on coastal areas, can blow nestlings out of nests or destroy nests and occupants.

Human-induced mortality takes its toll on the eagle. Illegal shooting still occurs, even with the passage of the Bald Eagle Act of 1940. Pesticide contamination is now minimal but still occurs with organophosphate and carbamate pesticides. Eagles are also victims of electrocution, collisions with vehicles, entanglement in fishing lines, lead poisoning, and leg-hold traps.

Bald Eagles have recently succumbed to a new disease, avian vacuolar myelinopathy. It was first called the Coot and Eagle Brain Lesion Syndrome since eagles first contracted it from eating American Coots, a major prey in some winter areas; however, the disease has now been discovered in other species of waterfowl. The disease creates lesions on the myelin sheath that insulates nerve fibers in the brain and causes disorientation, motor problems, and death. Dead Bald Eagles were first discovered with the disease in 1994 on DeGray Lake in Clark Co., Ark. Since then, diseased eagles also have been found in Georgia, North Carolina, and South Carolina. The exact cause of the disease is unknown.

SIMILAR SPECIES: COMPARED TO JUVENILE AND SUBADULT.—(1) **Golden Eagle, adult.**—PERCHED.—Bill is blackish on outer half and bluish on inner half; cere is yellow. Distinct pale tawny nape and hindneck. Feathered legs are often not visible. FLIGHT.—All-dark underwing generally separates from all younger Bald Eagles. However, in extensive molt, white blotches, even on the axillaries, caused by missing feathers on the underwing coverts and may appear very Bald Eaglelike.

Typically glides and soars with wings in dihedral. (2) **Golden Eagle, juvenile and subadult.**—PERCHED.—As in adult. FLIGHT.—Individuals with a small amount of white on the underside of the remiges are similar but typically lack white on the axillaries. Use caution on summer and fall molting birds as they will have varying amounts of white blotching on the underwing coverts and even axillaries. On juveniles, the outer web of the outer tail feather is white; on subadults, it may be dark and similar to that of Bald Eagles. (3) **Osprey.**—Subadults I–III can have a very distinct dark patch or line on the auriculars and appear Ospreylike. Lightly marked type subadult I and moderately marked type subadult II Bald Eagles have an extensive amount of white and can appear as pale on the ventral areas as an Osprey. COMPARED TO NON-RAPTORS.—(4) **Great Blue Heron.**—FLIGHT.—At moderate to long distances with the neck retracted, and nearly invisible long legs, the heron can be ea-gle-like. Wingbeats, however, are steady, shallow, with an even up-and-down stroke.

OTHER NAMES: American Eagle, White-headed Eagle. *Spanish:* Áquila Cabeza Blanca, Áquila Cabeciblanca. *French:* Pygargue à tête blanche.

REFERENCES: Baicich and Harrison 1997; Brewer et al. 1991; Buckelew and Hall 1994; Bylan 1998, 1999; Cadman et al. 1987; Castrale et al. 1998; Castrale and Ferchak 2000; Castrale and Parker 1999a, 1999b; Clark and Wheeler 2001; Commission for Environmental Cooperation 1997; Dodge 1988–1997; Edelstam 1984; Environment Canada 2001; Erskine 1992; Forsman 1999; Godfrey 1986; Howell and Webb 1995; Jeffers 2000; Johnsgard 1990; Kale et al. 1992; McCollough 1989; Kellogg 2000; McWilliams and Brauning 2000; Millar 2002; Nicholson 1997; Nye 1982, 1988, 1990, 1992, 1997; Palmer 1988; Palmer-Ball 1996; Robbins 1996; Stalmaster 1987; Stevenson and Anderson 1994; USFWS 1995, 1999a; Walsh et al. 1999.

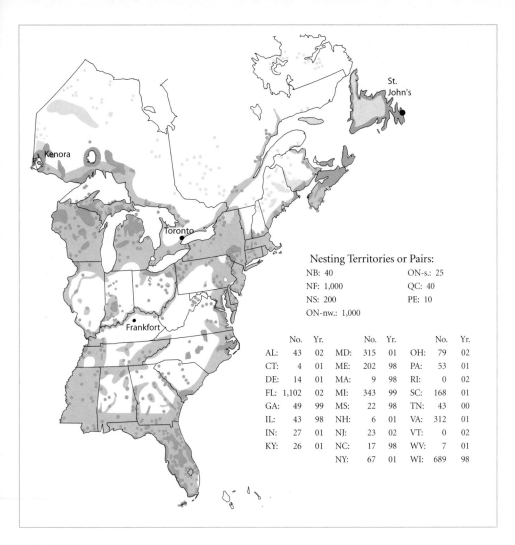

Nesting Territories or Pairs:

NB:	40	ON-s.:	25
NF:	1,000	QC:	40
NS:	200	PE:	10
ON-nw.:	1,000		

	No.	Yr.		No.	Yr.		No.	Yr.
AL:	43	02	MD:	315	01	OH:	79	02
CT:	4	01	ME:	202	98	PA:	53	01
DE:	14	01	MA:	9	98	RI:	0	02
FL:	1,102	02	MI:	343	99	SC:	168	01
GA:	49	99	MS:	22	98	TN:	43	00
IL:	43	98	NH:	6	01	VA:	312	01
IN:	27	01	NJ:	23	02	VT:	0	02
KY:	26	01	NC:	17	98	WV:	7	01
			NY:	67	01	WI:	689	98

BALD EAGLE, *Haliaeetus leucocephalus:* Common in Canada. Listed as endangered in e. U.S. except for MI and WI, 1967–95. Then, redesignated as threatened. Delisting is proposed. Southern immatures and some adults spend spring and summer in n. U.S. and s. Canada. Subspecies not delineated. Number of nesting pairs are increasing annually in most states beyond displayed data.

Plate 104. Bald Eagle, adult [Dec.] ▪ Yellow bill and cere. Pale yellow iris. White head and neck. ▪ Brown body and white undertail coverts. ▪ White tail.

Plate 105. Bald Eagle, adult [May] ▪ White head and neck. ▪ Brown body. ▪ Dark underside of wings. ▪ White tail.

Plate 106. Bald Eagle, adult [May] ▪ White head and neck. ▪ White lower back. ▪ White uppertail coverts and tail.

Plate 107. Bald Eagle, basic/subadult IV [Mar.] ▪ Yellow bill. Pale yellow iris. White head often has dark markings on auriculars and crown. ▪ Brown body. ▪ Brown upperwings. ▪ White tail may retain dark markings on portions of rectrices (retained dark subadult III rectrix). ▪ *Note:* May attain full adult body plumage at this age.

Plate 108. Bald Eagle, basic/subadult IV [Feb.] ▪ Brownish areas on yellow bill. White head and neck often have dark markings on auriculars and crown. ▪ Brown body. ▪ Most have white areas on coverts, sometimes on secondaries. ▪ White tail may have dark areas on tips of most rectrices. White undertail coverts. ▪ *Note:* Photograph by Ned Harris.

Plate 109. Bald Eagle, basic/subadult III (moderately marked type) [Mar.] ▪ Yellowish brown bill, yellow cere. Pale brown iris. Whitish head and neck; dark auricular patch. ▪ Many have white speckling on back. ▪ Old tan-colored subadult I secondary (s12) and respective greater covert identifies this age. ▪ *Note:* Told from heavily marked type subadult II by wing molt.

Plate 110. Bald Eagle, basic/subadult III (moderately marked type) [Jan.] ▪ Yellowish brown bill and cere. Pale yellow iris. Whitish head and neck; dark auricular patch; ill-defined junction of whitish neck and brown body. ▪ White markings on coverts and secondaries. Very old, faded brown juvenile primary (p10); 4 new inner primaries. ▪ White tail with dark border.

Plate 111. Bald Eagle, basic/subadult II (moderately marked type) [Feb.] ▪ Yellowish brown bill and cere. Pale brown iris. Whitish head; dark auricular patch. ▪ Dark spotting on white back and belly. Dark bib. ▪ A few worn, remnant white-edged subadult I wing coverts. ▪ *Note:* Photograph by Ned Harris.

Plate 112. Bald Eagle, basic/subadult II (heavily marked type) [Jan.] ▪ Yellowish brown bill, yellow cere. Pale brown iris. Dark auricular patch; tawny head and neck. ▪ Mainly dark brown underparts. ▪ Whitish tail with dark border. ▪ *Note:* Similar to subadult III; separable by remiges. This eagle retains old juvenile remiges (p9 and 10; s4) [not shown].

Plate 113. Bald Eagle, basic/subadult II (moderately marked type) [Feb.] ▪ Yellowish brown bill and cere. ▪ Dark bib and white-spotted belly; dark leg feathers. ▪ Whitish axillaries and some wing coverts. Retains frayed juvenile outermost primaries (p9 and 10). Neatly edged trailing edge of wings. ▪ *Note:* Some subadult II birds will retain only p10. Photograph by Ned Harris.

Plate 114. Bald Eagle, basic/subadult II (heavily marked type) [Sep.] ▪ Dark auricular patch; tawny head and neck. ▪ Dark body with a few white specks. ▪ Whitish axillaries. Outermost primaries are retained, frayed juvenile (p9 and 10); retained, long juvenile secondary (s4). ▪ *Note:* Similar to subadult III, but separable by retained juvenile remiges.

Plate 115. Bald Eagle, basic/subadult II (moderately marked type) [Dec.] ▪ Pale head, dark auricular patch. ▪ Dark bib, white-speckled belly. ▪ Mainly whitish axillaries and wing coverts. ▪ Retains juvenile outermost primaries (p9 and 10), 2 retained, long, faded brown juvenile secondaries (s4 and 9). ▪ *Note:* Slow molt type for age class.

Plate 116. Bald Eagle, basic/subadult II (moderately marked type) [Feb.] ▪ Yellow bill and cere. Dark auricular patch; tawny head and neck; ▪ White inverted triangle on back; mottled white on lower back. ▪ Outer primaries retain frayed juvenile feathers (p9 and 10). ▪ Upper surface of tail varies from blackish to whitish. ▪ *Note:* Photograph by Ned Harris.

Plate 117. Bald Eagle, basic/subadult I (lightly marked type) [Feb.] ▪ Gray or black bill, often with a pale spot on base of upper mandible. Pale gray iris. Wide dark auricular patch; whitish head and neck. ▪ Small, mottled brown bib. Very white belly. ▪ Extensive white on some upperwing coverts; white tips on greater coverts. A few bleached, tan-colored, retained juvenile upperwing coverts. ▪ *Note:* Photograph by Ned Harris.

Plate 118. Bald Eagle, basic/subadult I (moderately marked type) [Nov.] ▪ Black bill with a pale spot on base of upper mandible; yellow fringe on cere. Pale yellow iris. Wide dark auricular patch; tawny head and neck. ▪ Large, brown bib. White belly with brown spotting. ▪ White band on some upperwing coverts.

Plate 119. Bald Eagle, basic/subadult I (moderately marked type) [Mar.] ▪ Gray bill with a pale spot on base of upper mandible. Pale gray iris. Wide dark auricular patch; tawny head and neck. ▪ White inverted triangle on back. ▪ Retained, bleached, tan-colored juvenile feathers on inner part of upperwing coverts.

Plate 120. **Bald Eagle, basic/subadult I (heavily marked type) [Dec.]** ▪ Black bill with a pale spot on base of upper mandible; yellow fringe on cere. Pale brown iris. Very wide dark auricular patch extends from the lower mandible on the tawny-brown head. ▪ Dark back. ▪ Dark upperwing coverts. Most secondaries are faded brown juvenile feathers; new dark tertials and inner secondaries.

Plate 121. **Bald Eagle, basic/subadult I (moderately marked type) [Dec.]** ▪ Dark bib, white-spotted belly; dark leg feathers. ▪ White axillaries and white-mottled coverts. Jagged rear edge of secondaries have two groups of long, pointed juvenile feathers. Juvenile outer primaries (p6–10).

Plate 122. **Bald Eagle, basic/subadult I (lightly marked type) [Dec.]** ▪ Very wide dark auricular patch; white head and neck. ▪ Small, brown bib; white belly; dark leg feathers. ▪ White axillaries and coverts. Extensive white on secondaries and inner primaries. Jagged rear edge of secondaries have two groups of long, pointed juvenile feathers. Juvenile outer primaries (p5–10).

Plate 123. **Bald Eagle, basic/subadult I (moderately marked type) [Mar.]** ▪ Tawny head and neck. ▪ Dark bib; white belly is heavily spotted; dark leg feathers. ▪ White axillaries; white mottled coverts. Slow molt with only outermost and a few inner secondaries replaced, all others are retained juvenile. Outer 6 primaries (p5–10) are juvenile feathers.

Plate124. Bald Eagle, basic/subadult I (moderately marked type) [Feb.] ▪ White back and belly are spotted with brown. ▪ A few faded tan-colored juvenile feathers on the inner coverts. Jagged rear edge of secondaries retains two groups of long, pointed, juvenile feathers (s2–4, s7–11). ▪ Tails are whitish on some birds. ▪ *Note:* Photograph by Ned Harris.

Plate 125. Bald Eagle, juvenile (worn plumage) [Mar.] ▪ Black bill and cere. Dark brown iris. Dark brown head and neck; crown sometimes paler. ▪ Dark brown bib; faded, pale tawny belly. ▪ Moderately white type tail with some white mottling.

Plate 126. Bald Eagle, juvenile (worn plumage) [Mar.] ▪ Black bill and cere. Dark brown iris. Dark brown head and neck; white streaking on neck. ▪ Faded pale brown upperparts. ▪ Faded pale brown wing coverts; palest on inner greater coverts. Blackish secondaries contrast with rest of dorsal wing. Tertials have pale tips.

Plate 127. Bald Eagle, juvenile (fresh plumage) [Jul.] ▪ Dark brown head with tawny tips on nape feathers. ▪ Medium dark brown upperparts. ▪ Medium dark brown wing coverts; outer greater coverts are often dark; secondaries are blackish. ▪ White type tail with extensive white on inner rectrix sets. Black terminal band and outer rectrix sets.

Plate 128. Bald Eagle, juvenile (fresh plumage; fledgling) [Jul.] ▪ Black bill and cere. Dark brown iris. Very dark brown head and neck. ▪ Very dark brown bib; dark tawny belly is slightly paler than breast.

Plate 129. Bald Eagle, juvenile (fresh plumage; fledgling) [Jul.] ▪ Black bill and cere. Dark brown iris. Very dark brown head and neck. ▪ Dark brown upperparts. ▪ Dark brown wing coverts; blackish secondaries. ▪ All-black type tail.

Plate 130. Bald Eagle, juvenile (worn plumage) [Mar.] ▪ Dark brown head and neck; pale throat. ▪ Dark brown bib; pale tawny belly; dark brown leg feathers. ▪ White type underwing with nearly all-white axillaries and coverts. Extensive amount of white on inner secondaries and inner primaries. Neat, serrated rear edge of secondaries.

Plate 131. Bald Eagle, juvenile (fresh plumage) [Sep.] ▪ Dark brown head and neck; pale throat. ▪ Dark brown bib; dark tawny belly; dark brown leg feathers. ▪ Dark type underwing with white axillaries and mottled white coverts; white bar on median coverts. Small amount of white on inner secondaries and inner primaries. Neat, serrated rear edge of secondaries.

Plate 132. Bald Eagle, juvenile (streaked type; worn plumage) [Dec.] ▪ Dark brown head and neck; pale throat. ▪ Dark brown bib. Pale tawny or whitish belly is spotted and streaked with dark brown. Dark brown leg feathers. ▪ White type underwing. Axillaries and coverts are white. Extensive amount of white on inner secondaries and inner primaries.

Plate 133. Bald Eagle, juvenile (fresh plumage) [Sep.] ▪ Dark brown head and neck. ▪ Medium brown upperparts. ▪ Wing coverts are medium brown with a pale brown area on the inner greater and median coverts. Remiges are blackish and contrast with rest of wings and body. ▪ All-black type of dorsal tail.

Plate 134. Bald Eagle, juvenile (worn plumage) [Feb.] ▪ Dark brown head and neck. ▪ Pale brown upperparts. ▪ Pale brown wing coverts. Remiges and most greater coverts are blackish and contrast with rest of wings and body. ▪ White type tail with white on middle rectrix set and dark outer webs on all other sets. *Note:* Photograph by Ned Harris.

NORTHERN HARRIER
(Circus cyaneus)

AGES: Adult, basic I/subadult (first-adult), and juvenile. Adults and subadults have sexually dimorphic plumages; however, age distinction within each sex class is not readily apparent at field distances. Some adults may alter subadult plumage features gradually over a few molts (Macwhirter and Bildstein 1996). Subadult age is a separate plumage, but may retain a very small amount of juvenile feathering. Juvenile sexes are separable at close range by iris color and size (*see* Size). Juvenile plumage held for 1 year, but iris color gradually alters during the course of this time.

MOLT: Accipitridae wing and tail molt pattern (*see* chapter 4). First prebasic molt begins in a span from late Apr. to May and completed by late Oct. or Nov. This is a complete molt except some birds retain one or more juvenile greater underwing coverts (J. Liguori unpubl. data). This plumage feature is very difficult to see under field conditions and, if present, is more obvious on males. Birds are quite advanced in molt by late Sep.

Subsequent prebasic molts are complete. Molt may begin in early to mid-May on females and about 2 weeks later on males (Macwhirter and Bildstein 1996). However, a substantial number of birds in adult-to-adult prebasic molts are still in exceedingly heavy molt during Sep. By early Sep., some have molted a majority of the primaries, but only a few secondaries have molted (s1 and s5), and body molt is less than 50 percent complete. Molt is completed within a span from late Oct. to late Nov.

SUBSPECIES: Two races. *C. c. hudsonius* occupies North America in breeding season. Nominate race, *C. c. cyaneus* (the Hen Harrier), breeds in Europe and Asia and winters south to n. Africa and tropical regions of Asia.

Note: The two races are considered by some authors to be separate species. Adult males are quite different from each other. The Hen Harrier is uniformly solid pale gray on head, breast, back, scapulars, upperwing, upper tail, and has more extensive black on ventral surface of outer primaries than does the North American race. Adult females are similar to one another. Juveniles are also similar, but Hen Harriers tend to be much more heavily streaked on the underparts and paler orangish.

COLOR MORPHS: None regularly occurring (*see* Abnormal Plumages).

SIZE: Sexually dimorphic with little or no overlap. Males are smaller. With practice, size is often visibly apparent in the field. MALE.—Length: 16–18 in. (41–46 cm); wingspan: 38–43 in. (97–109 cm). FEMALE.—Length: 18–20 in. (41–51 cm); wingspan 43–48 in. (109–122 cm).

SPECIES TRAITS: HEAD.—Greenish yellow or yellow cere. **Defined auricular disks. Whitish, short supercilium and slash mark under each eye forms a pale spectacle that surrounds the eye.** Supraorbital ridge is present, but lacks bare skin area on the ridge. Small, flat-topped head. **Head and neck are darker than ventral areas and appear hooded.** BODY.—Slim body. Long yellow tarsi. **White uppertail coverts, sometimes with narrow dark streak on some feathers.** WINGS.—**Long and moderately narrow wings with moderately rounded wingtips. Five very distinct "fingers" on the outer primaries.** Wingtips can appear rather pointed when gliding. Wide black band on trailing edge of underside of the secondaries. TAIL.—Long and moderately rounded.

ADULT AND SUBADULT TRAITS: HEAD.— Adults have yellow irises that are generally somewhat brighter on males. There are no other shared traits between the adult sexes or between subadults.

ADULT MALE (FRESH PLUMAGE): HEAD.—Pale or bright orangish yellow irises. **Some individuals exhibit a distinct whitish "spectacle" area of the supercilium and slash mark under the eye and others have a uniformly medium gray head. Rear edge of auriculars lacks outline of pale fringed feathers. Front of neck and upper breast are medium gray, and along with the gray head, contribute to the hooded appearance.** BODY (ventral).—Lower breast, belly, flanks, leg feathers, and undertail coverts are white with variable amount of mainly rufous but sometimes gray markings. Lower breast and belly are lightly or moderately spotted or are sometimes thinly streaked on the breast area. Some have a rufous wash on the lower breast. Flanks are also lightly or moderately marked and are likely to be somewhat barred. Leg feathers are generally unmarked, but may be lightly spotted. Undertail coverts are marked with a dark arrowhead-shaped design on each feather and often have a tawny or rufous wash on a portion of each feather. BODY (dorsal).—Neck, back, and scapulars are a medium gray, dark brownish gray, or grayish brown. Some harriers can be quite dark-backed and brownish in fresh autumn plumage. WINGS (ventral).—**White with an extensive black patch on the outer five primaries ("fingers"), a grayish trailing edge of inner five primaries, and a broad black band on the trailing edge of all secondaries.** Inner portion of all remiges is either unmarked or partially marked with irregular, fine barring. Axillaries are always finely spotted or barred with rufous or gray. Underwing coverts, including greater primary coverts, are either unmarked or partially spotted or barred with fine rufous or gray markings. WINGS (dorsal).—Medium brownish gray lesser upperwing coverts have a whitish or sometimes tawny mottled area on the first row of coverts; greater coverts have a pale gray band on the inner portion of the tract. **A large black area covers the outer five primaries, with the wide black band on the trailing edge of secondaries. The inner primaries and inner portion of secondaries are pale gray and generally much paler than the more brownish wing coverts, scapulars, and back.** TAIL.—Pale gray on the dorsal surface with a moderately wide black subterminal band and four or five narrow dark bands on the inner tail. Deck rectrix sets and sometimes other inner rectrix sets may be unmarked. Outer dark bands on the basal region of tail are often rufous, but can only be distinguished at close range.

Note: Plumage spans from mid-summer to early winter when adorned in freshly molted feathers. Older males may gradually become paler with subsequent molts on dorsal areas and may have fewer ventral markings. There undoubtedly is also individual variation, with some birds being paler and less heavily marked and others being darker and more heavily marked.

ADULT MALE (WORN PLUMAGE): BODY and WINGS (dorsal).—Back, scapulars, and upper-

wing coverts fade to a medium brownish gray or a pale brownish gray; however, most have a discernibly brownish cast. A few individuals can appear almost uniformly gray on dorsal areas; however, head and very pale gray dorsal surface of the remiges are still slightly paler than rest of the upperparts.

Note: Plumage span is from late winter to early summer, when it has faded due to sun bleaching and wear.

BASIC I (SUBADULT I) MALE (FRESH PLUMAGE): HEAD.—Iris color is lemon yellow, but occasionally orangish yellow, as on adult males. **Head color is variable: (1) Crown and auriculars are often brown or rufous brown and contrast rather sharply with the brownish gray nape and neck; (2) uniformly brownish gray on the crown and auriculars and forms a uniform color unit with head, nape, and neck; or (3) uniformly grayish and similar to older males, and paler than the rest of the upperparts. Auriculars lack a pale border fringe and are not distinct. Front of neck is brownish gray or whitish and often has a rufous wash on the lower part and, along with the head, forms a dark hood. Whitish spectacle of the supercilium and patch area below each eye is very distinct on all birds.** BODY (ventral).— Breast is washed with tawny or rufous and often streaked with dark rufous or brown; it is occasionally white with rufous or brown streaking. Belly and lower belly are variably marked with rufous spots or arrowhead shapes and vary from being rather heavily marked to lightly marked. Leg feathers are generally lightly spotted with rufous. BODY (dorsal).— Dark grayish brown or dark brown but without a grayish tinge on the back and scapulars. WINGS (ventral).—**As on adult males and exhibit the identical broad black area on outer primaries and the wide black band on trailing edge of secondaries.** Axillaries are marked with rufous and are either narrowly barred or thickly barred. Highly variable in the amount of markings on the white underwing coverts: (1) All underwing coverts are extensively marked with rufous spots on the lesser coverts (patagial area) and rufous-brown or brown barring on median coverts. The greater primary coverts are barred. (2) Underwing coverts are lightly marked or unmarked. If marked, they are concentrated on the median coverts and greater primary coverts. Remiges vary from being unbarred to moderately barred, mainly at the base of the primaries and some secondaries. WINGS (dorsal).—All coverts are dark grayish brown or dark brown with a pale tawny or whitish mottled area on inner lesser coverts. **Except for the black outer primaries and wide bar on the trailing edge of secondaries, remiges are pale brownish gray. TAIL.—Pale gray on the dorsal surface with a moderately wide, dark subterminal band and about five narrower dark inner bands. The outermost dark bands are often rufous.** Undertail is pale, with similar pattern as on dorsal surface.

Note: Plumage spans from fall to early winter.

BASIC I (SUBADULT I) MALE (WORN PLUMAGE): BODY and WINGS (dorsal).—Upperparts fade to medium grayish brown or medium brown. All other features as in fresh plumage.

Note: Plumage span is from late winter to early summer, when extreme fading from sun bleaching and wearing occurs.

ADULT FEMALE (FRESH PLUMAGE): HEAD.—Crown and auriculars are either solid dark brown or brown with tawny streaking. **Neck and hindneck are brown with distinct pale tawny streaking and are darker than rest of the ventral region and, along with the fairly dark head, form a hood. Pale tawny spectacles surround the eyes. Facial disk is well defined with a pale white or tawny fringe surrounding outer edge of the auriculars.** Iris color varies with age but takes a minimum of 3 years to attain the all-yellow color of older birds (Hamerstrom 1968). Iris color varies from (1) pale brownish yellow, (2) lemon yellow, or (3) pale orangish yellow. BODY (ventral).—Base color of underparts is rich tawny or rufous-tawny in fresh autumn plumage, but fades within a span of late fall through winter (*see below*). Underparts are variably streaked on the belly and lower belly: (1) occasionally heavily streaked, (2) moderately marked, or (3) have only sparse streaking or dash markings on the belly and lower belly and may appear virtually unmarked at field distances. Flanks are streaked on the forward half and have a broad, arrowhead-shaped dark brown mark on the rear half. Some feathers on the rear flank area may have a dark brown cross bar on basal portion of the arrowhead-shaped marked feathers.

Note: The arrowhead-shaped and cross bar markings on rear flank feathers are not always readily visible at many distances or angles, particularly if overhead. Undertail coverts have a short, dark streak on each feather. Leg feathers are lightly covered with small, brown diamond-shaped or arrowhead-shaped markings. BODY (dorsal).—Upperparts are dark brown. Scapulars may have some tawny edgings and a few tawny blotches. WINGS (ventral).—**Overall appearance of underwing covert region is pale with a broad dark band on the axillaries and median coverts. At close range, the dark brown median coverts have a narrow tawny fringe on each feather and some pale spotting; all other coverts are tawny with narrow dark markings. Dark brown axillaries have a minimal amount of pale spotting and edging, thus appear very dark. The remiges are uniformly pale grayish, but are sometimes a slightly darker gray on the secondaries. There is a broad dark band on the trailing edge on the secondaries, two narrow dark bands on the inner secondaries, and narrow barring on all primaries.** WINGS (dorsal).—Secondaries and primaries are medium brownish gray or sometimes pale grayish with distinct dark bands (Macwhirter and Bildstein 1996). *Note:* Pale, barred dorsal surface of the remiges separates adult ages of females from juveniles, which have dark, unbarred secondaries. Those with pale grayish remiges are typically separable from most subadult females. Dark brown median coverts have a pale gray bar on the basal area of each feather. All coverts have pale tawny feather edgings, and tawny blotches occur on the distal rows of lesser coverts. TAIL (ventral).—**Pale with two, broad, nearly equal-width dark bands. The outer rectrix set is pale and unmarked except for the dark subterminal band or faint bands on the basal region.** TAIL (dorsal).–**Deck rectrix set and adjacent inner one to three sets (r1–4 sets) are medium gray with four or five nearly equal-width dark bands. The subterminal band is usually somewhat wider, and the outer rectrix sets are a rich tawny with three or four dark bands.**

Note: Overall plumage fades by late winter through early summer.

ADULT FEMALE (WORN PLUMAGE): BODY (ventral).—Base color of ventral areas fades to pale tawny or white. BODY and WINGS (dorsal).—Back, scapulars, and upperwing coverts fade to medium brown. Remiges fade to grayish with very discernible dark bands.

Note: Plumage span occurs from late winter to early summer.

BASIC I (SUBADULT I) FEMALE (FRESH PLUMAGE): HEAD.—**Medium brown crown and auriculars with little if any tawny streaking. A moderate amount of tawny streaking is on the brown neck and hindneck and forms a hood along with the head. A well-defined whitish or tawny rim surrounds the auriculars. Sharply defined pale tawny or whitish spectacles around the eyes.** Iris color is variable, but lightens and turns more yellowish with age. Iris color based on Hamerstrom (1968). Iris colors: (1) medium brown, (2) pale brown, or (3) pale brownish yellow. On some younger birds, the medium brown iris color may not change from the springtime color of most juvenile females. BODY (ventral).—Base color of ventral areas is a rich tawny or rufous-tawny. At times, freshly molted ventral color can be nearly as intense as on some juveniles. A variable amount of adult female like streaking is on the belly, lower belly, and forward flanks; broad arrowhead-shaped markings are on the distal flanks. As with older females, ventral markings range from heavily marked to very sparsely marked individuals. *Note:* Age does not seem to be a factor in the amount of ventral markings. Data are based on in-hand live birds and close field photographs correlating eye color and molt. Leg feathers are lightly marked with small, brown diamond shapes, arrowhead shapes, or spots. BODY (dorsal).—Dark brown with minimal pale edgings or blotches. WINGS (ventral).—As in adult females, including all remiges being either uniformly pale or secondaries being slightly darker gray. WINGS (dorsal).—Remiges are either a medium brownish gray or pale brownish gray and are distinctly barred with black and similar to many adult females (dorsal color of the remiges of some adult females are quite gray). Median and lesser coverts are often not as pale tawny-edged as on older females. Basal area of greater coverts has a pale gray bar. At least through Oct., faded, retained juvenile secondaries may be apparent (mainly s4 and s7 and 8). *Note:* The paler grayish and barred dorsal

surface of the secondaries usually separates subadult and adult females from juveniles at field distances. TAIL.—As on adult females.

BASIC I (SUBADULT I) FEMALE (WORN PLUMAGE): BODY and WINGS (ventral).—As adult females in worn plumage. BODY (dorsal).—As adult females in worn plumage.

JUVENILE TRAITS (FRESH PLUMAGE): HEAD.—**Dark brown crown and auriculars with a distinct pale outer rim on the auricular disks; pale spectacles are also very distinct. Dark brown neck and hindneck have a minimal or moderate amount of rich rufous-tawny streaking and forms a hood along with the head.** BODY (ventral).—**Bright, rich, rufous-tawny (orange) belly, lower belly, and flanks.** Breast and flanks are narrowly streaked with dark brown, the belly and lower belly are unmarked. Leg feathers are unmarked. Undertail coverts are unmarked. BODY (dorsal).—Solid dark brown back and scapulars. WINGS (ventral).—Rufous-tawny (orange) wing coverts, but the carpal region is often paler and more whitish. **Median coverts and axillaries are dark brown with narrow tawny edges and appear as a broad dark band. Pale gray primaries are fully barred; secondaries are medium gray and discernibly darker than the primaries, with the innermost secondaries being even darker. Secondaries have the wide black band on the trailing edge and two narrower dark inner bands that may be obscured by the fairly dark gray inner secondaries.** WINGS (dorsal).—Uniformly dark brown on the secondaries. *Note:* The uniformly dark brown dorsal surface of secondaries separates juveniles from subadult and adult females–which have paler remiges and exhibit noticeable barring. Primaries may be somewhat paler than the secondaries and exhibit faint barring. A broad, pale tawny bar on the lesser coverts. TAIL (dorsal).—**Deck rectrix set is medium gray and the outer five sets are pale tawny. A wide dark subterminal band with four or five moderately wide, dark inner bands.** TAIL (ventral).—Two wide dark bands are visible; the outer rectrix set often does not show dark banding, if it does, dark bands are faint.

Note: Plumage color and markings are similar for both sexes.

JUVENILE TRAITS (WORN PLUMAGE): BODY

(ventral).—Underparts fade to a pale tawny and often nearly white by late spring. Fading may be noticeable as early as late November and is usually quite obvious by Feb. Extreme fading occurs in Apr. and May. However, there are a few individuals that are still a fairly rich tawny color even in May. BODY and WINGS (dorsal).—Brown upperparts typically fade and wear to medium brown; however, less faded individuals may still retain a fairly dark brown color in spring.

JUVENILE MALE: Iris color from summer to early fall and sometimes until mid-winter, is pale gray or pale brown. Iris color gradually changes to pale lemon yellow midway through juvenile plummage. On early-changing birds, iris color may become quite yellowish by late Sep., but color generally does not change substantially until Oct. or Nov. By Dec., many have attained lemon-colored irises. By Feb., most have changed to the lemon coloration. However, slow-changing individuals may still have pale grayish or brownish irises even in mid-winter. Virtually all springtime birds have attained the lemon-colored irises. Iris color may undergo little additional change and remain a pale lemon into subadult age. *Note:* Very rarely, fall juvenile males will have dark brown irises (B. Sullivan pers. comm.).

JUVENILE FEMALE: Iris color from summer to early winter is dark brown. By mid- to late winter, iris color gradually changes to medium brown and may have little if any additional change as they enter into the subadult age class.

ABNORMAL PLUMAGES: None recorded in the East. Two records in the w. U.S. of melanistic individuals: (1) an adult male from Glenn Co., Calif., in Jan. 1991 (Howell et al. 1992); (2) an adult female seen in Oct. 1998, in the Mission Valley area in Lake Co., Mont. (C. Olson pers. comm.). Both birds lacked white uppertail coverts.

HABITAT: Summer: Predominantly open areas, especially freshwater, saltwater, and brackish marshes; also, meadows, lightly used pastures, abandoned fields, bogs, and moorlands. Harriers are regularly found in upland regions of dry meadows and abandoned fields.

Winter: Similar areas as used in summer, but they commonly use drier habitats: abandoned fields, lightly or heavily grazed pastures, and harvested agricultural fields. Northern Harriers are regularly found in rural areas with ample habitat.

Migration: Similar to summer and winter habitat areas. Also, seen along high mountain ridges but seeks lower, open areas for roosting and foraging each day.

HABITS: A wary species. Harriers rarely remain perched around humans, even when being viewed from the shelter of a distant vehicle. Gregarious in all seasons, but especially in the nonbreeding season. It is common to see up to four individuals, mainly juveniles, migrating together; however, birds of mixed ages may also occur in these small groups. Large communal night roosts often form in winter on the ground. Winter territories may be defended or shared by several individuals. Northern Harriers commonly stand on the ground; however, they seem to prefer to perch on slightly elevated clumps of earth or low vegetation, fence posts, or, to a lesser extent, tops of low bushes. Harriers rarely perch in trees; if so, perching height rarely exceeds 20 ft. (6 m) and is on outer, exposed branches of mainly small trees. In very windy conditions, they may stand behind tall vegetation or clumps of earth for protection.

The Northern Harrier has a highly developed sense of hearing, enhanced by the distinct owl-like auricular disks.

FEEDING: An aerial hunter. Harriers forage at low altitudes and rely on their acute hearing and sight.

Prey is captured on the ground or, with avian prey, sometimes while they are airborne up to about 20 ft. (6 m) in altitude. Harriers mainly feed on small prey: rodents, rabbits, hares, birds, reptiles, amphibians, and insects. Harriers are dependent on *Microtus* voles in many regions. Males feed more on small avian prey than do females. Females often capture avian prey that are somewhat heavier than themselves by grabbing them and holding them down. Females may drown small ducks on the water in this manner. Unusual prey of females include Ring-billed Gulls that are captured in flight. Prey is typically devoured at the point of capture or is taken to a slightly elevated perch or to a safer location a short distance away. Drowned prey is dragged to shore and eaten. Hunting is done during all daylight hours but is often suspended during hot periods of day. A crepuscular species, and hunting often takes place early and late in the day. Carrion is often consumed, particularly species that are too large to kill.

FLIGHT: Wings are held in a high dihedral, low dihedral, or modified dihedral when gliding. Wings are held in a low dihedral soaring. At low-altitude flight, the glide mode is often in a side-to-side tilting manner, especially in windy conditions; in light winds, glides are level and steady. Powered flight is with mechanical, shallow wingbeats. Being smaller, males have quicker beats than females. Three main flight mannerisms: hunting, migrating, and courtship.

Hunting: Slow, methodical coursing at low altitudes over the ground or low vegetation with head pointing downward and looking and listening. Flight is at low altitudes and is either at a stable level or in an undulating style, skimming the ground or vegetation tops, then swinging upward in a low arch, then back down to ground-skimming height. A zigzag, erratic path may be taken over large habitat areas or may follow a straight course down leading lines of tall vegetation along fence lines, canals, and ditches. Hunting birds may intermittently flap, glide, or hover. Northern Harriers may occasionally kite for very short stints in strong winds. When prey is detected, harriers quickly bank—flipping sideways, tail fanned, then drop to the ground with fully extended legs. Harriers may dive repeatedly from low altitudes in vole-infested areas, especially at vole nest sites.

Migrating: Flight is at high altitudes in light or moderate winds and at low altitudes in strong winds. Flight is a combination of glides interspersed with a series of methodical wingbeats. Glides are stable and birds do not tilt side-to-side. Sometimes Harriers flap their wings for considerable distances before gliding. Northern Harriers occasionally migrate nocturnally, including at least 15-mile (25 km) over-water crossings. *Note:* Appears falconlike in high-altitude flight.

Courtship: See Nesting.

VOICE: When agitated, a variable-length series of a rapid, chatterlike, moderately pitched, squeaky notes: *cheh-cheh-cheh-cheh*. When mildly agitated or curious, a squeeze-toy-like,

high-pitched *squee-aah*; may be a single note or repeated numerous times.

STATUS AND DISTRIBUTION: *Fairly common.* Population fluctuates each year depending on summer prey availability and breeding success. **Summer.**–*Canada:* Breeds extensively throughout all of Ontario, s. Québec, Newfoundland, and the Maritime Provinces. Isolated summering and/or breeding occurs in Labrador north of typical range. Breeds at Churchill Falls and Red Bay area and possibly breeds near Goose Bay. Isolated, sparse breeding occurs in two main regions in cen. Labrador. *United States:* Breeds extensively in Wisconsin, Michigan, New York, and Pennsylvania. Northern Harriers breed sparsely in Illinois, Indiana, Ohio, New Jersey; also, coastal Delaware, Maryland, and Virginia. Very sparse nesting occurs in w. and n. Vermont, n. New Hampshire, and the Outer Banks region and sometimes adjacent mainland areas of North Carolina. Summer sightings were documented in 2000 in Lake and Dyer Cos., Tenn. Very isolated and sporadic nesting in recent years in Muhlenberg, Ohio, Logan, and Hart Cos. in Kentucky. Mississippi has verified nesting in Quitman Co. One nesting location is known in Stratford, Fairfield Co., Conn., and on The Nature Conservancy land in Washington Co., R.I. There are probably at least two nesting locations in West Virginia. In Massachusetts, Northern Harriers nest on islands (e.g., Nantucket, Martha's Vineyard, and surrounding small islands). The last mainland nesting record was in Worcester Co. in 1990.

Winter: In northern regions, found from cen. Wisconsin and Michigan, s. Ontario, then extends along the St. Lawrence River to Québec City, w. and s. New York, s. New England, coastal Maine, and s. Nova Scotia. Winters throughout all of the central and southern latitude states. Also winters on the Bahamas, Cuba, and Dominican Republic. Winter range of the western population extends to s. Central America.

Movements: Protracted migration in both fall and spring.

Fall migration: Mid-Aug. to late Dec. Large numbers begin to move in late Aug., with movements tapering off by late Nov. In the northern areas, most movement drops off substantially by late Nov., with only a few birds still moving in Dec. There are no definitive peaks. There is a fairly steady movement throughout the entire period. Juveniles predominate in the early portion of the season and adults in the latter part, especially males, but all ages move throughout the course of the migration period.

Spring migration: Adults begin migrating in early Mar. along the cen. Atlantic Coast, in mid-March in the e. Great Lakes, and in late Mar. in the n. Great Lakes region. Adults peak in late Mar. to early Apr. in southern and central latitudes and in mid-Apr. in northern latitudes. Males precede females. Juveniles are the latest to move; however, some juveniles are seen throughout the adult migration period. A secondary adult peak (subadults?), which may also contain a fair number of juveniles, occurs in mid-Apr. along the south shore of the e. Great Lakes. Movement of juveniles continues until late May, with a peak occurring in mid-May; a trickle of juveniles, however, often continues into early to mid-Jun. along the e. Great Lakes.

NESTING: Begins in mid-Mar. in southern areas and as late as mid-May in northern regions. Nesting activities end in Jul. or Aug. Pairs may be monogamous or males may practice polygyny and have up to five females in a harem. Nesting birds often form loose colonies. A few 1-year-olds, in juvenile plumage, may breed. This is more likely to occur with females than with males. Most do not breed until 2 years old.

Courtship (flight).—*Sky-dancing* (high intensity) with very elaborate maneuvers by males and to a lesser extent by a few females. Males may also perform sky-dancing during spring migration at various nonbreeding locales. *High-circling* and *aerial food transfers* are performed by mated pairs. Once territories are established, males exhibit *leg-lowering* to other males. Females perform *leg-lowering, escort-flight,* and *talon-grappling* to conspecific intruders (mainly females). The *cheh-cheh-cheh* chatter call accompanies many types of displays. (*See* chapter 5 for courtship descriptions.)

Nests are built on the ground and usually surrounded by protective vegetation; also nests in clumps of tall vegetation over water. Nests are 15–25 in. (39–63 cm) in diameter. Generally 1–7 eggs, but up to 10 are known. Large clutches may be a sign of two females laying in the same nest. Eggs are incubated 30–32 days by females. Youngsters fledge in 30–35 days, with the larger females taking longest. Females feed the young. Males hunt and deliver prey to females. If females are not present at the nest, prey is dropped by the males, but they do not feed the nestlings.

CONSERVATION: Listed as state Endangered Species in Illinois, Indiana, New Jersey, Connecticut, and Rhode Island. Listed as a Threatened Species in Tennessee, New Hampshire, Massachusetts, and New York. Listed as a Species of Special Concern in Wisconsin, Michigan, and Vermont. In Canada, listed as a Secure Species, except in Labrador, where its status is undetermined and the species is at its northernmost breeding range, and the Yukon, where listed as a Sensitive Species.

Mortality: Breeding is undoubtedly affected in many areas by agricultural practices and declining marshes and grasslands. Harriers suffered during organochlorine era of late 1940s to early 1970s, but rebounded quickly after the ban on DDT in the 1970s. Organophosphate poisoning for rodent control is a possible current threat. Illegal shooting occurs in certain areas. Harriers are susceptible to illegal shooting by errant waterfowl hunters. Lead poisoning obtained from eating dead or wounded waterfowl was a mortality factor until the nationwide ban in 1991 on lead shot.

SIMILAR SPECIES: (1) Northern Goshawk, juveniles.—PERCHED.—Similar to subadult and adult females in many aspects in color and markings. Pale supercilium, but lacks pale area under irises; auricular disk often well defined; use caution. Pale tawny bar on greater upperwing coverts. Short tarsi. Primaries much shorter than tail tip. FLIGHT.—Six "fingers" on outer primaries. Uniformly pale underwing coverts. Dark uppertail coverts. Wings held on a flat plane when gliding and soaring. **(2) Swainson's Hawk, light morphs.**—PERCHED.—Confusion possible between juvenile Swainson's and subadult and adult female harriers. Wingtips equal to tail tip. Pale mottling on scapulars. FLIGHT.—Wings held in similar dihedral at all times; use caution. Narrow white "U" on uppertail coverts; narrowly banded tail. Narrow dark bars on underside of remiges; solid dark outermost primaries. **(3) Rough-legged Hawk.**—FLIGHT.—Very

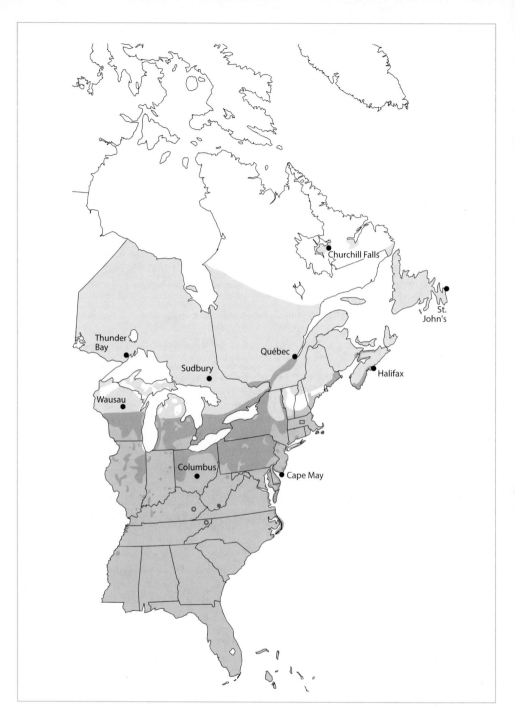

NORTHERN HARRIER, *Circus cyaneus hudsonius:* Fairly common. Found in wet or dry habitat. Absent from many areas in New England. High densities of migrants are found locally along coastlines. Winters to s. Central America and Caribbean islands.

similar flight attitude (jizz) and easily confused at long and moderate distances, especially compared to heavier, bulkier female harriers. Harriers share white uppertail coverts of light morph; look for dark carpal area on underwing of Rough-legged. **(4) Peregrine Falcon.**—FLIGHT.—Deceptively similar in high-altitude silhouette view. Falcon's body-to-wrist distance is very short (long, angular on harrier); tail is shorter. Wingbeats steady and powerful; soars and glides with wings on a flat plane.

OTHER NAMES: Harrier, Gray Ghost (adult male); formerly called Marsh Hawk. *Spanish:* Gavilan Pantanero, Gavilan Rastrero. *French:* Busard Saint-Martin.

REFERENCES: Bildstein and Collopy 1985; Brauning 1992; Buckelew and Hall 1994; Bylan 1998, 1999; Cadman et al. 1987; Castrale et al. 1998; Clark and Wheeler 2001; Craig et al. 1982; Dodge 1988–1997; Environment Canada 2001; Erskine 1992; Forsman 1999; Godfrey 1986; Howell et al. 1992; Laughlin and Kibbe 1985; Leberman 2000; Lee and Irvin 1988; Macwhirter and Bildstein 1996; Nature Conservancy 2001; Palmer 1988; Palmer-Ball 1996; Peterjohn and Rice 1991; Robbins 1996; Russell 1991; Veit and Petersen 1993; Walsh et al. 1999.

Plate 135. Northern Harrier, adult male (fresh plumage) [Nov.] ▪ Defined auricular disk; all-gray head and neck; slight whitish spectacles around eyes. Orangish yellow iris. Flat-topped head. ▪ Dark grayish brown back and scapulars. ▪ Grayish upperwing coverts. ▪ *Note:* Harriers regularly stand on the ground.

Plate 136. Northern Harrier, adult male (fresh plumage) [Nov.] ▪ Defined white spectacles around eyes. ▪ Dark grayish brown back and scapulars. ▪ Dark grayish brown upperwing coverts; whitish bar on lesser coverts. Pale gray remiges with a wide black bar on rear edge of secondaries; large black patch on outer primaries. ▪ White uppertail coverts. Gray tail with black bands.

Plate 137. Northern Harrier, adult male (worn plumage) [Apr.] ▪ Gray head and neck; white spectacles around eyes. ▪ Medium grayish brown back and scapulars. ▪ Medium grayish brown upperwing coverts. Pale gray remiges with a wide black bar on rear edge of secondaries; large black patch on outer primaries. ▪ White uppertail coverts. Gray tail with black bands. ▪ *Note:* Dorsal color fades considerably by spring.

Plate 138. Northern Harrier, adult male (worn plumage) [Apr.] ▪ Uniformly gray head and neck. ▪ Medium pale brownish gray back and scapulars. ▪ Medium pale brownish gray upperwing coverts. Pale gray remiges with a wide black bar on rear edge of secondaries; large black patch on outer primaries. ▪ White uppertail coverts. Partially banded gray tail. ▪ *Note:* Palest type of male plumage; possibly an old bird.

Plate 139. Northern Harrier, adult male (fresh plumage) [Nov.] ▪ Gray head and neck form a hood; slight spectacle definition around eyes. ▪ White underparts are spotted with gray or rufous. ▪ White underwing has a wide black bar on rear edge of secondaries; large black patch on outer primaries.

Plate 140. Northern Harrier, subadult male (fresh plumage) [Jan.] ▪ Rufous-brown auriculars and crown with distinct auriculars; gray nape. Pale yellow iris. ▪ White underparts with rufous markings. ▪ *Note:* Harriers often perch on low, open objects.

Plate 141. Northern Harrier, subadult male (fresh plumage) [Dec.] ▪ Rufous-brown auriculars. Grayish brown neck. Tawny wash on breast; white belly and flanks are heavily marked with rufous. White underwing coverts are heavily marked with rufous. ▪ Moderate dark barring on white remiges; wide black bar on rear edge of secondaries; large black patch on outer primaries. ▪ *Note:* Some are more lightly marked.

Plate 142. Northern Harrier, adult female (fresh plumage) [Nov.] ▪ Streaked tawny head and neck with distinct pale spectacles around eyes and pale rim on auricular disks. Yellow iris. ▪ Whitish underparts are narrowly streaked. ▪ Wing coverts are edged with tawny and have white blotches on median coverts. Pale gray primaries are distinctly barred.

Plate 143. Northern Harrier, adult female (worn plumage) [Apr.] ▪ Distinct spectacles around eyes and pale rim on auricular disk. ▪ Medium brown upperwing coverts with pale tawny feather edges. ▪ Pale gray remiges with very distinct barring, including a wide black bar on rear edge of secondaries. ▪ White uppertail coverts.

Plate 144. Northern Harrier, adult female (fresh plumage) [Jan.] ▪ Brownish head and neck form a hood. Defined auricular disk. Yellow iris. ▪ Rear flanks are barred. ▪ Barred, pale gray remiges, including a wide dark bar on rear edge of secondaries. Secondaries sometimes slightly darker than primaries. Dark axillaries and greater coverts.

Plate 145. Northern Harrier, subadult female (fresh plumage) [Jan.] ▪ Dark auricular disk with pale rim. Dark tawny head and neck form a hood. Brown iris. ▪ Pale tawny underparts are barred on rear flanks and moderately streaked on forward flanks and belly. ▪ *Note:* Iris color changes from medium or pale brown to yellow in about 3 years.

Plate 146. Northern Harrier, subadult female (fresh plumage) [Sep.] ▪ Brown head; brown iris. ▪ Dark brown back and scapulars. ▪ Medium gray remiges with distinct black barring, including wide bar on rear edge of secondaries. Retains a few pale brown juvenile secondaries, which will be replaced in a few weeks. ▪ White uppertail coverts. Banded tail with gray center and tawny outer rectrices.

Plate 147. Northern Harrier, subadult female (worn plumage) [Feb.] ▪ Brownish head and neck creates a hood. ▪ Lightly streaked/spotted underparts; rear flanks have brown arrowhead-shaped markings. ▪ Pale remiges; sometimes secondaries slightly darker; wide black bar on secondaries. ▪ *Note:* Adult and subadult females may either be lightly or heavily marked on underparts.

Plate 148. Northern Harrier, juvenile female (fresh plumage) [Dec.] ▪ Dark brown iris. Dark brown head and neck. Pale spectacles around eyes and pale auricular disk rim. ▪ Dark brown back and scapulars. ▪ Dark brown wing coverts with a tawny patch. Solid brown remiges. ▪ *Note:* Dark brown irises lighten to medium brown by spring.

Plate 149. Northern Harrier, juvenile male (fresh plumage) [Jan.] ▪ Pale yellow iris. Dark brown head and neck. Pale spectacles around eyes and pale auricular disk rim. ▪ Dark brown back and scapulars. Medium tawny-orange underparts have brown streaking on the breast and flanks. ▪ *Note:* Iris color changes from pale brown or pale gray to pale yellow by late fall to mid-winter.

Plate 150. Northern Harrier, juvenile male/female (fresh plumage) [Jan.] ▪ Dark brown head and neck. ▪ Tawny-orange underparts. ▪ Wings held in a high dihedral. Dark secondaries. ▪ White uppertail coverts. ▪ *Note:* Classic hunting strategy by coursing low over the ground with head pointing down.

Plate 151. Northern Harrier, juvenile male (worn plumage) [Mar.] ▪ White spectacles around eyes; pale yellow iris. ▪ Medium brown back and scapulars. ▪ Remiges have a minimal amount of dark barring (less than in subadult and adult females). ▪ White uppertail coverts. Banded tail with gray center and pale tawny outer rectrices. ▪ *Note:* Dorsal color of both sexes fades by spring.

Plate 152. Northern Harrier, juvenile female (fresh plumage) [Sep.] ▪ Dark brown head and neck form a hood. Pale spectacles around eyes, pale rim on auricular disk. Dark brown iris. ▪ Bright tawny-orange underparts. ▪ Dark brown axillaries and median coverts. Secondaries darker than primaries. Barred remiges with a wide black bar on rear edge of secondaries.

Plate 153. Northern Harrier, juvenile male (fresh plumage) [Oct.] ▪ Dark brown head and neck. White spectacles around eyes and pale rim on auricular disk. Pale gray iris. ▪ Tawny-orange underparts have brown streaking on the flanks. ▪ Dark brown axillaries and median coverts. Secondaries darker than primaries.

Plate 154. Northern Harrier, juvenile female (worn plumage) [Apr.] ▪ Brown head and neck form a distinct hood. ▪ Underparts have faded from the bright tawny-orange of autumn birds to very pale tawny or whitish on spring birds. ▪ Dark brown axillaries and median coverts. Dark secondaries and pale primaries. ▪ *Note:* This is the palest extreme, which occurs from sun bleaching.

SHARP-SHINNED HAWK
(*Accipiter striatus*)

AGES: Adult, basic I (subadult I), and juvenile. Adult plumage is usually attained when 2 years old, but some males may acquire full adult plumage when 1 year old. Adult dorsal color is sexually dimorphic, rarely overlaps, and is visible at field distances. If there are similarities in dorsal color, it is generally females assuming malelike color.

Basic I (subadult I) plumage is acquired when 1 year old. Plumage is identical to respective adult sex but may retain a small amount of juvenile feathering. Juvenile feathering, however, is not always visible in the field. As previously described, some males may molt entirely out of juvenile feathering and appear as adults. Iris color of subadults (orange) overlaps with the color of some adults.

Juvenile plumage is worn the first year. Sexes are basically identical but there is considerable individual variation, especially on the underparts. Iris color brightens and plumage color fades from mid-winter through spring.

MOLT: Accipitridae wing and tail molt pattern (*see* chapter 4). First prebasic molt from juvenile to subadult or adult occurs from mid-May to Nov. Molt begins on the innermost primaries, then proceeds to the tertials, back, and scapulars. By mid-Jun., only the three innermost primaries and tertials may be molted and only a few new dorsal feathers may have grown in. The first prebasic molt may be incomplete and retain a few juvenile feathers on the upperwing coverts and rump. Retained rump feathers are not readily visible under field conditions. First prebasic molt may be complete on some males. During fall migration, subadults may be molting the outermost primaries, secondaries (s4 and 8), and rectrices (r2 and 5, which are possibly the last to molt). All remiges and rectrices are fully replaced by the end of the molt cycle each fall.

Subadult to adult and subsequent adult annual prebasic molts are fairly complete and extend from late May through Nov. Males begin molt later than females. Adults occasionally retain a few old adult feathers on the upperwing coverts, secondaries, rump, uppertail coverts, and tail (r2 and 5). All primaries are replaced by the end of the molt in Oct. or Nov. During autumn migration, adults are molting the outer primaries, secondaries, and rectrices (r2 and 5, but often r6 are the last to molt).

SUBSPECIES: Polytypic, but only one race, *A. s. velox*, is the East. All plumage data here pertain to this subspecies. It is widespread and occurs throughout much of North America. The "Queen Charlotte" race, *A. s. perobscurus*, is an example of Gloger's Rule. This dark-colored subspecies inhabits the Queen Charlotte Islands and adjacent island and coastal areas of British Columbia and se. Alaska. "Sutton's" race, *A. s. suttoni*, is a Mexican subspecies that extends the northern periphery of its range into extreme se. Arizona and possibly sw. New Mexico and s. Texas. Four additional races: (1) *A. s. madrensis* is in s. Mexico; (2) *A. s. fringilloides*, which is very rare, is on Cuba; (3) nominate *A. s. striatus* is on Hispaniola; and (4) *A. s. venator* is on Puerto Rico and has been on the U.S. Endangered Species List since 1994.

Three species are considered subspecies of *A. striatus* by some taxonomists. del Hoyo et al. (1994) treat them as separate species that form a superspecies with *A. striatus*: (1) White-breasted Hawk (*A. chionogaster*) in the highland areas from s. Mexico to n.-cen. Nicaragua; (2) Plain-breasted Hawk (*A. ventralis*) in the mountains of n. and se. Venezuela, Colombia, Ecuador, Peru, and w. Bolivia; and (3) Rufous-thighed Hawk (*A. erythronemius*) of s. Brazil, Uruguay, and se. Bolivia to n. Argentina.

COLOR MORPHS: None.

SIZE: A small raptor and smallest of the three accipiters. Very sexually dimorphic with no overlap. Proportionately, the most dimorphic of any North American raptor. With practice, sexes are separable in the field. Males are considerably smaller than females. MALE.—Length: 9–11 in. (23–28 cm); wingspan: 20–22 in. (51–56 cm). FEMALE.—Length: 11–13 in. (28–33 cm); wingspan: 23–26 in. (58–66 cm).

SPECIES TRAITS: HEAD.—Petite bill. Small, round-shaped head, even when nape feathers are erected. **Yellow skin on supraorbital ridge, if exposed, is visible only at close range.** In flight, appears short-necked and small-headed. BODY.—**Very long, thin tarsi and toes are thinner than a pencil. Tarsi are yellowish orange or yellow on males and yellow on females.** WINGS.—When perched, wingtips are considerably shorter than the tail tip. **In flight, moderately short and broad with very rounded wingtips.** Undersides of all remiges are distinctly barred. Accipiters have six "fingers" on the outer primaries. TAIL.—Long. Three or four equal-width dark bands on the dorsal side. On the ventral side, the outer rectrix set has narrow dark bands that do not align with the wide dark inner bands. Four distinct tail-tip shapes are visible only on the ventral surface of a closed tail. (1) *Notched type* (males only): **Outer rectrix sets are longer than the central set and form a notch on the center of the tail.** *Note:* Some females exhibit notched tails, mainly because of irregular feather overlap. (2) *Squared type* (both sexes but mainly males): **All rectrices are the same length.** (3) *Rounded type* (both sexes): **Outer rectrix sets are somewhat shorter than the inner sets.** (4) *Very rounded type* (females only): A few have very rounded or wedge-shaped rectrices. Central set (r1) is longest, and each outer set is sequentially shorter. *Note:* All tail patterns appear more rounded on fanned tails, particularly when soaring. In soaring flight, widely fanned tail seen in certain angles of intense light can also make the paler gray area behind the dark subterminal band appear as a fairly wide white terminal band.

ADULT TRAITS: HEAD.—Iris color varies from orange to dark red. Iris color of males attains a deeper red and darkens more quickly than on females. The change in iris color does not occur at a rate that can be used as an exact aging criteria. Birds with red irises are older than 1 year. **A black mask may surround under and behind the eyes, and may extend as a black eyeline. Pale rufous auriculars often fade to pale grayish by spring. Crown and nape are medium bluish or grayish and are typically the same color as the upperparts. The crown and sometimes nape may be a somewhat darker gray.** Some birds have a partial or full narrow white supercilium. BODY.—**Uniformly medium bluish or grayish upperparts.** Breast, belly, flanks, and leg feathers have sharply delineated rufous and white barring. Undertail coverts are white and unmarked. WINGS.— **Upperwing coverts medium bluish or grayish and are same color as rest of the upperparts. Underwing coverts are mainly tawny but sometimes whitish.** Underwing coverts may have a combination of dark brown or rufous streaking, spotting, or barring. The axillaries are rufous barred. TAIL.—Bluish or grayish pale uppertail bands with equal-width, wide dark bands. *Note:* In late summer through late fall (mainly Sep.–Oct.), adults are in extensive tail molt and many rectrices are still growing. Irregular feather lengths may alter shape of tail tip.

Adult male: HEAD.—**Medium grayish blue crown and nape.** Rarely has a pale supercilium. BODY.—**Medium grayish blue upperparts.** Rarely has bluish gray upperparts. Leg feathers are sometimes nearly solid rufous with narrow white tips. WINGS.—**Medium grayish blue upperwing coverts.** TAIL.—Grayish blue pale bands on uppertail. **In fresh plumage in fall and winter, regularly has a distinct, fairly wide white terminal band.**

Adult female: HEAD.—**Medium gray crown and nape.** Many have a pale supercilium. BODY.—**Medium gray upperparts but may be grayish brown on some individuals. Upperparts may fade to grayish brown on virtually all birds by spring.** Leg feathers are rufous-white barred; they are rarely mostly rufous with narrow white tips. WINGS.—**Medium gray upperwing coverts.** TAIL.—**Medium gray pale uppertail bands. Terminal band is narrow pale gray or white but may have a fairly wide white band in fall and winter.**

Adult female (blue-backed type): (1) A few females are malelike grayish blue on the head, nape, back, and forward part of scapulars during all seasons. The lower part of scapulars, rump, and upperwing coverts are usually the typical gray. (2) Some are uniform bluish gray and only slightly more grayish than males. On both types, the pale gray dorsal bands are as on typical adult females.

BASIC I (SUBADULT I) TRAITS: As previously described, plumage is basically identical to respective adult sex and often not separable from adults under field conditions. Irises are always orange. (Little if any color change occurs from springtime juveniles.) Many birds have a partial or full thin whitish supercilium. Subadults may retain worn, pale brown juvenile feathering on the upperwing coverts and rump until the next molt in late spring and summer. Retained juvenile feathers on the upperwing coverts are uniformly brown; those on the rump have narrow tawny-rufous tips on each brown feather but are not visible under field conditions. *Note:* In the fall, old, worn upperwing coverts on adults may also be very brownish and similar to old, worn juvenile feathers of subadults.

JUVENILE TRAITS: HEAD.—**Crown, nape, and hindneck are dark brown or tawny brown with pale tawny streaking, especially on the nape. Auriculars are tawny-rufous. Long, thin, white supercilium. Supercilium, however, may be partial or lacking. Iris color is medium orangish yellow or yellow ochre from fledging until mid-winter; rarely pale lemon yellow.** BODY (ventral).—White or tawny underparts are variably streaked with rufous or brown on the breast, belly, and lower belly. The flanks are distinctly barred with rufous or brown. There are three variations of ventral markings. (1) *Narrowly streaked type* (many males; a few females).—Breast, belly, and lower belly are narrowly streaked. The lower belly generally has less streaking or occasionally is unmarked. Flanks may be partially barred. Both rufous and brown markings are common on this variation, but females are more likely to have rufous markings. (2) *Moderately streaked type* (both sexes).—**Fairly broad uniform streaking on breast, belly, and lower belly. The lower belly often has less streaking. Streaking often broadens into partial "lobes" on the breast and belly feathers and forms a partially barred effect. Flanks are broadly barred.** Rufous coloration predominates with this variation. (3) *Broadly streaked type* (some males; many females).—**Breast, belly, and lower belly are uniformly marked with broad, dense streaking. Streaking typically broadens into "lobes" or partial bars on the breast and belly and makes the underparts appear quite barred (and adultlike). Distinct, broad barring on the flanks.** Virtually all markings are rufous in this variation. Leg feathers are either streaked or variably barred with rufous or dark brown. BODY (dorsal).—Dark brown upperparts have narrow rufous or tawny edges, most pronounced on the upperwing coverts. Males are more likely to have pronounced pale feather edges on scapulars and back, but there is considerable variation. Many females also exhibit distinct pale feather edges, and some males have only a minimal amount of pale edging. Basal region of each scapular has a large white area, making the scapulars appear very "blotched" when fluffed in cold temperatures or when rousing. White, unmarked undertail coverts. WINGS (dorsal).—Upperwing coverts have pale tawny-rufous edges. WINGS (ventral).—*Male:* (1) **Trailing edge of the inner primaries and secondaries may have a narrow or moderately wide, sharply defined dark band** or (2) **a nondescript gray band.** *Female:* (1) **Trailing edge of inner primaries and secondaries has a nondescript gray band** or (2) **rarely, a well-defined dark grayish or black band, which is most prevalent on heavily marked type females. Axillaries are barred with rufous; some males may be barred with dark brown.** Underwing coverts are tawny, rarely whitish. TAIL.—Upper surface is pale grayish brown with three or four equal-width, wide dark bands. Tail tip typically has a narrow pale gray band but may have a narrow white band.

JUVENILE (LIGHTLY MARKED TYPE): HEAD.—Crown, nape, and hindneck are brown and streaked with tawny. Supercilium is white and very wide. Cheeks and most of the auriculars are white except for a small brownish area on the rear part of the auriculars. BODY.—White underparts are narrowly streaked as in narrowly streaked type. Flanks may have partial barring or narrow streaking. Very narrow brown or rufous streaking on leg feathers. Overall appearance of the underparts is very pale. Upperparts have pronounced tawny edges on all back and scapular feathers. WINGS.—Upperwing coverts are distinctly edged with pale tawny. White underwing coverts are finely marked with rufous or brown; axillaries are generally partially barred with rufous. TAIL.—As on typical *velox. Note:* Plumage type is on some males and a few females.

JUVENILE (HEAVILY MARKED TYPE): HEAD.—Crown, auriculars, nape, and hindneck are dark brown and lack tawny streaking. Pale supercilium is absent. BODY.—Dark brown upperparts generally lack paler tawny-rufous feather edgings. Underpart streaking varies as described in the three variations described in Juvenile traits. Females typically have broadly

streaked type underparts, but males often have narrowly or moderately streaked type underparts. WINGS.—Upperwing coverts are dark brown and lack pale feather edgings. Tawny underwing coverts are heavily marked with dark brown. TAIL.—As on typical *velox.*

JUVENILE (LATE WINTER/SPRING, ALL TYPES): HEAD.—Iris color changes to orange (and remains this color into subadult age class). BODY and WINGS (dorsal).—Pale feather edgings wear off and upperparts fade and wear to a uniform medium brown.

ABNORMAL PLUMAGES: Imperfect albinism.—Occurs primarily in juvenile females (sightings and specimens have been females). Bill, irises, cere, and legs can be normally colored, or some or all anatomical regions may be paler, including pale bluish irises. Most of plumage is white, including upperparts. As is typical in this type of albinism, rufous-pigmented anatomical regions found on normal individuals are also exhibited in this plumage. Head and neck are pale rufous-brown. Pale rufous streaking is present on the breast, belly, and flanks. Scapulars and upperwing coverts have pale rufous edges on most feathers. Remiges and rectrices are white and lack barring. Data based on Clark and Wheeler 2001; F. Nicoletti pers. comm.; museum specimen. *Note:* Very rare plumage type and not depicted.

HABITAT: Summer.—Breeds in dense stands of thickly foliaged young and mid-aged, succession-stage, coniferous, mixed coniferous-deciduous, and rarely pure deciduous wooded areas with dense understories. Wooded areas may be shelterbelts, small woodlots, or extensive forests. Artificial conifer plantations of moderate-aged trees may also be occupied. Virtually all inhabited areas have a water source; if it is a stream or river, it is quiet-running water.

Densely foliaged conifers trees are the main component of suitable nesting territories, and most nests are placed in conifers. Conifers may be in the following settings: (1) same-age, contiguous coniferous forests; in Wisconsin, mainly inhabits Black Spruce bogs; (2) a small group of conifers surrounded by shorter deciduous trees or bushes; (3) a small group of conifers surrounded by taller deciduous trees; (4) occasionally a single conifer that is shorter than the surrounding densely growing deciduous trees. Very dense pure deciduous areas are occasionally used for nesting territories. Nest sites are in wooded areas with small or moderate-sized trees that are covered with dense branches and foliage or have abnormally dense, diseased growths of branches and dense foliage.

Winter.—Can be identical to breeding habitat, but also found in semi-open areas without regard to tree species or size. Regularly inhabits rural and urban areas with moderate tree growth and sometimes regions with minimal tree size and density.

Migration.—Similar to summer and winter habitat but also found along seashores with short, brushy vegetation and along mountain ridges.

HABITS: Relatively tame to tame. Possesses an extremely hyper and antagonistic temperament. Constantly harasses large passerines that are too large to kill and larger raptor. Perches mainly on concealed branches but sometimes on exposed branches. Occasionally on wires and posts. *Sharp-shinned Hawks do not perch on telephone poles.* A very reclusive species, especially in the breeding season.

FEEDING: Perch and aerial hunter. Perches for short periods when perch hunting. Aerial hunting consists of random flights. Small avian species form bulk of diet. Males generally feed on sparrow- and warbler-size prey; females up to American Robin and even jay- or quail-sized prey. Downy Woodpeckers and Black-capped Chickadees form major part of diet in n. Wisconsin. Sharp-shinned Hawks rarely feed on small prey such as rodents, bats, reptiles, and insects (mainly large moths). Hunting is done in upper canopy of tall trees, in or beneath canopy in small trees, and along edges of wooded and brushy areas. May also occur at high altitude above trees or at low altitude in open areas. Prey is captured while it is airborne or perched. In the breeding season, plucking posts are used. In all other seasons, prey is usually devoured near point of capture. Sharp-shinned Hawks often perch on the ground where prey is plucked and then eaten. Prey may also be taken to a more concealed location, on the ground under dense, low-hanging foliage or higher among densely foliaged branches. Prey is captured with lightning-fast grasps of the long, spindly toes. Sharp-shinned Hawks do not feed on carrion.

FLIGHT: Powered flight consists of a regular cadence of several rapid wingbeats interspersed with short glides. Soars often. Rarely completes a full revolution without resorting to a stint of flapping. When soaring, wings are held on a flat plane front edge of wings is forward of a perpendicular angle to the body. Wings are held either on a flat plane or bowed slightly downward when gliding. With their short, broad wings and long tail, Sharp-shinned Hawks fly through densely wooded tangles with incredible agility. Flight is at very high altitudes when migrating in light winds but at treetop or near ground level in strong winds. Impressive short or moderate-length vertical dives are often performed to pursue airborne prey or to perch in tree canopies. When hunting in open areas, Sharp-shinned Hawks often skim the ground or low vegetation and sometimes use an undulating, songbirdlike flight mode. The songbirdlike flight consists of a few quick flaps interspersed with a slide in which the wings are closed next to the body. Sharp-shinned Hawks do not hover or kite.

VOICE: Generally silent except during courtship, when agitated in nesting territory, and when harassing other predators. Emits a soft, single-note, songbirdlike *chirp* when mildly agitated or curious. When highly agitated, a high-pitched, rapid *kee-kee-kee* or a soft, high-pitched *kyew, kyew, kyew:* usually a three-note call, but can be four or more notes in a series. Nestlings and fledglings emit an equally high-pitched *kree:* single notes or a series of notes. During and after food transfers with males, females emit a soft, clear *kek.* Voice is easily separable from nasal call of Cooper's Hawk.

STATUS AND DISTRIBUTION: Summer.—*Common.* One of the most common North American raptors. Estimated population is unknown. Population is probably stable. Very elusive in summer and difficult to census. Most common in the contiguous boreal forest of the n. U.S. and Canada. This remote region has an incredible density and array of small songbird prey species, particularly warblers.

Locally an uncommon or rare breeding species in most areas of e. U.S., except at higher elevations of the Appalachian Mts. *Note:* Mapped summer areas in Illinois, Indiana, and Ohio are more extensive than shown in respective breeding bird atlases. Summer locations in these states were based on habitat as well as actual nesting documentation.

There are a few recent documented breeding and summer records in the s. U.S. *Tennessee:* A pair was found in Memphis in late Jun. 2000 for the first nesting in the western part of the state. *Mississippi:* Jones (2 nests in 1998), Perry, Claiborne, and Jackson Co. *Alabama:* No data. *Georgia:* 13 records, with the southernmost documented breeding in Jones Co.; a mid-Aug. juvenile female sighting in Tift Co. (possibly a very early migrant?). Sharp-shinned numbers far surpass those of Cooper's Hawks at eastern hawkwatch sites.

Winter.—Generally winters farther south than breeding and natal areas. Juvenile females winter farther south than other ages and sexes. The se. U.S. has a high wintering density. Some regularly winter as far north as Nova Scotia and n. New Brunswick. A few winter on Cuba. Solitary and quite nomadic. Territories may be established where prey is ample and stable. Common in rural and urban locales with birdfeeders.

Movements.—Short- or long-distance migrant. Large concentrations occur along geographic barriers. Large numbers pass along mountain ridges and shores of the Great Lakes in fall and spring. Extremely large numbers migrate along the Atlantic Coast, particularly in fall and to a lesser extent in spring. Inland mountain ridges and Great Lakes are used by all ages. The Atlantic Coast is a primary juvenile corridor in fall; however, a small number of subadults and adults are found here in the latter part of the season. Although Sharp-shinned Hawks travel in a solitary manner, on optimal migrating days large numbers get congested along geographic barriers and appear as if they are traveling in small flocks. More likely than Cooper's Hawks and Northern Goshawks to make long-distance overwater crossings. This is seen with birds wintering on Cuba and regularly seen with migrants on the Dry Tortugas off Florida.

Fall migration: Mid-Aug. to Nov. with stragglers into Nov. Movement is age and sex coordinated. Juveniles migrate first. Juvenile females peak in mid-Sep., males in mid- to late Sep. Adults and subadults migrate later. In adults, females precede males. Subadults precede respective sex of adult. Adult females peak in late Sep., adult males in early to mid-Oct. A few juvenile females are late stragglers and migrate with adult males.

Spring migration: Mar.–Jun. Adults precede juveniles. Adults peak from late Apr. to early May, with males preceding females. Juveniles peak in early to mid-May, with stragglers into Jun.

NESTING: May to mid-Aug. Males arrive on the breeding grounds before females and establish territories. One-year-olds sometimes breed while in juvenile plumage. These are primarily juvenile females mated to adult males, but sometimes 2 juvenile-aged birds mate. Most do not breed until 2 years old.

Courtship (flight).—*High-circling, slow-flapping,* and *sky-dancing* (*see* chapter 5). Undertail coverts are flared and retracted outwards beyond the closed tail during most aerial courting activities. Vocalization may accompany high-circling.

Sharp-shinned Hawks may return to the same territory but rarely reuse the same nest. Old nests may occasionally be used for 2 consecutive years, very rarely for 3 years. They typically build a new nest each year, often on top of old American Crow nests, leafy squirrel nests, or mistletoe growths. Both sexes bring nest material, but females build the structure. Nests are lined with bark chips but not greenery. They are constructed of thin sticks and are 24 in. (60 cm) in diameter and about 6 in. (15.2 cm) deep. They are placed 16–70 ft. (5–21 m) high and are typically hidden next to the trunks of densely foliaged conifer, rarely in densely foliaged or branched deciduous trees. Females assume all nest duties, and males hunt. Males are not known to incubate. Clutches vary from 2 to 6 eggs but are typically 4 or 5. The eggs are white or bluish and speckled with brown and are incubated 34–35 days. Youngsters branch in 21–24 days, fledge in 24–27 days, are fully developed at 38–40 days, and become independent in about 49 days. Nesting pairs are highly secretive but may become agitated and vociferous with human presence at nest sites, but are rarely aggressive.

CONSERVATION: Sharp-shinned Hawks suffered, as did all avian-feeding raptors (which are near the top of the food chain), during the organochlorine era. Numbers currently appear healthy and stable. The ban on organochlorine pesticides, particularly DDT, no doubt helped populations recover in the last three decades.

Mortality.—Sharp-shinned Hawks may still be

affected by pesticides. Carbamate pesticides may have contributed to some mortality. Newer generation pyrethroid pesticides are harmless to birds and mammals (but affect aquatic life). Large numbers of Sharp-shinned Hawks are injured or killed when they collide with windows and vehicles. Illegal shooting occurs in the U.S. and south of the U.S. in winter. In Mexico, juvenile females have suffered most because they are more common at that latitude in winter than juvenile males and adults. Shooting has possibly lessened in Mexico in recent years, as seen by fewer band recoveries from shot birds.

SIMILAR SPECIES: (1) Cooper's Hawk, males.— An age-old problematic species for both adult and juvenile as concerns female Sharp-shinned Hawks. Cooper's Hawks are always *longer in length*, on average 3 in. (8 cm), and *longer in wingspan*, on average 4 in. (10 cm). With practice, both species can be separated on proportional differences without ever seeing plumage marks. Vocalizations of the two species very different: nasal *kek* of a Cooper's Hawk is separable from the high-pitched *kee* of Sharp-shinned Hawk. PERCHED.—Hackle may be raised, which makes the head appear very large; however, in warm temperatures head feathers may be tightly compressed and head may appear quite small. Gray supraorbital ridge skin, if exposed, is visible at only close range. Tarsi and toes are moderately thick (near pencil thickness). On underside of tail, outer rectrices are sequentially shorter than inner ones: use caution when comparing very rounded type tail of female Sharp-shinned Hawks as they can be very like Cooper's Hawk. White terminal band on tail is wide in fall but may be mostly worn off by spring. FLIGHT.—When soaring, front edge of wings is perpendicular to body angle. Head often projects quite a distance beyond front of wings. Often soars with wings in a low dihedral. Longer tailed; shape as for Perched. **(1A) Adult males.**—Crown always darker than upperparts. Upperparts more bluish and rarely overlap with gray color of female Sharp-shinned Hawks. Auriculars and nape are pale gray or rufous (nape is always medium bluish gray on Sharp-shinned Hawks). Underside of inner primaries and secondaries often has minimal amount of dark barring (Sharp-shinned Hawks always have prominent barring). **(1B) Subadult males.**—Similar rufous auriculars, but nape is either pale grayish or pale rufous (nape is always medium bluish gray on Sharp-shinned Hawks). Bluish gray upperparts (gray on adult female/subadult Sharp-shinned Hawks). **(1C) Juveniles males.**—Iris color is generally duller at all seasons: pale gray or lemon yellow in fall and medium orangish yellow in spring. Underparts are similar, especially compared to lightly marked type Sharp-shinned Hawks: use caution on thickness and extent of streaking. Streaking on a Cooper's Hawk is almost always dark brown, rarely rufous. Crisp, dark band on trailing edge of underwing. Upperparts usually have more tawny feather edges. Axillaries are barred with dark brown (rufous on most Sharp-shinned Hawks). **(2) Merlin, all races.**—PERCHED.—Dark brown irises. Throat feathers often puffed. Wingtips nearly reach tail tip. Tail has narrow whitish or tan bands; wide white terminal band. FLIGHT.—Pointed wingtips. Uniformly dark underwing. Constant, rapid wingbeats. Tail as described in Perched. **(3) Kestrel.**—PERCHED.—Dark irises. Dark facial stripes. Bobs tail down and up. Wingtips near tail tip. FLIGHT.—Pointed wingtips. Erratic flapping and gliding sequences. Rufous tail. **(4) Mississippi Kite, juveniles.**—PERCHED.—Dark irises. Dark lores in front of eyes. Underpart streaking similar. Short, thick tarsi and toes. Wingtips equal or extend beyond tail tip. Dark tail has narrow white bands on underside or lacks bands.

OTHER NAMES: Sharp-shin, Sharpie, Shin. *Spanish:* Gavilán Estriado, Gavilán Pajarero. *French:* Épervier Brun.

REFERENCES: Baicich and Harrison 1997; Bent 1961; Brewer et al. 1991; Buckelew and Hall 1994; Bylan 1998, 1999; Cadman et al. 1987; Castrale et al. 1998; del Hoyo et al. 1994; Clark and Wheeler 2001; DelOrme Publishers 1991a, 1991b; Evans and Rosenfield 1985; Environment Canada 2001; Hoffman and Darrow 1992; Howell and Webb 1995; Johnsgard 1990; Laughlin and Kibbe 1985; Meehan et al. 1997; Moore and Henny 1983; Nicholson 1997; Palmer 1988; Palmer-Ball 1996; Peterjohn and Rice 1991; Purrington 2000; Quinn 1991; Reynolds 1983; Reynolds and Meslow 1984; Reynolds and Wight 1978; Robbins 1996; Rosenfield and Evans 1980; Shackelford et al. 1996; Todd 1963; USFWS 1994; Veit and Petersen 1993; Walsh et al. 1999.

SHARP-SHINNED HAWK, *Accipiter striatus velox:* Common. Secretive in summer but conspicuous in migration and in winter. Very local in summer in southern states.

Plate 155. Sharp-shinned Hawk, adult male [Sep.]
▪ Medium grayish blue crown and nape. Black area encircling eyes. Rufous auriculars. Red iris. ▪ Medium grayish blue upperparts. Rufous-barred white underparts. Long, spindly tarsi and toes. ▪ *Note:* Older males tend to have dark red irises.

Plate 156. Sharp-shinned Hawk, adult male [Sep.]
▪ Medium grayish blue crown and nape. Black area encircling eyes. Reddish orange iris. ▪ Medium grayish blue upperparts. Long, spindly tarsi and toes. ▪ Long, grayish blue tail has 3 or 4 equal-width black bands; distinct white terminal band. ▪ *Note:* Iris gets more reddish with age.

Plate 157. Sharp-shinned Hawk, adult/subadult male [Sep.] ▪ Medium grayish blue crown and nape. Black area encircling eyes. Rufous auriculars. Orange iris. ▪ Medium grayish blue upperparts. Long, spindly tarsi and toes. ▪ Long, grayish blue tail has 3 or 4 equal-width black bands; distinct white terminal band. ▪ *Note:* Subadults and some younger adults have orange irises.

Plate 158. Sharp-shinned Hawk, adult male [Sep.]
▪ Grayish blue crown and nape; rufous auriculars. ▪ Grayish blue upperparts. ▪ Long, grayish blue tail has 3 or 4 equal-width black bands; square-tipped tail; distinct white terminal band.

Plate 159. Sharp-shinned Hawk, adult female
[**Sep.**] ▪ Medium gray crown and nape, often with
a thin whitish supercilium; black encircling eyes;
rufous auriculars. Reddish orange iris. ▪ Medium
gray upperparts. Rufous-barred white underparts,
including leg feathers. Long, spindly tarsi and toes.

**Plate 160. Sharp-shinned Hawk, adult female
(blue-backed type)** [**Sep.**] ▪ Medium bluish gray
crown and nape, often with thin whitish supercilium; black encircling eyes; rufous auriculars.
Orangish red iris. ▪ Medium bluish gray upperparts. Long, spindly tarsi and toes. ▪ *Note:* Dorsal
color on some females nearly as bluish as on males.

Plate 161. Sharp-shinned Hawk, subadult female
[**Sep.**] ▪ Medium gray crown and nape. Black encircling eyes; rufous auriculars. Orange iris. ▪
Medium gray back and scapulars. ▪ Medium gray
wing coverts; a few retained brown juvenile feathers on upperwing coverts. ▪ *Note:* Females often
retain some brown juvenile feathers on dorsal areas.

**Plate 162. Sharp-shinned Hawk, adult female
(blue-backed type)** [**Sep.**] ▪ Medium bluish gray
crown and nape; rufous auriculars. ▪ Medium
bluish gray upperparts. ▪ Very rounded type tail
tip on some females has outer rectrices much
shorter than inner feathers. Distinct white terminal
band. ▪ *Note:* Tail tip as rounded as on Cooper's
Hawk.

Plate 163. Sharp-shinned Hawk, adult female
[**Sep.**] ▪ Rufous-barred white underparts. ▪ Distinctly barred remiges. Tawny underwing coverts spotted and barred with brown or black. Six "fingers" on outer primaries. ▪ Square-type tail tip on some females (and many males) has rectrices that are same length.

Plate 164. Sharp-shinned Hawk, adult female
[**Sep.**] ▪ Rufous-barred white underparts. ▪ Distinctly barred remiges. Tawny underwing coverts spotted and barred with brown or black. Six "fingers" on outer primaries. ▪ Square-type tail tip on some females (and many males) has rectrices that are same length. Tail slightly rounded when fanned.

Plate 165. Sharp-shinned Hawk, juvenile female
[**Sep.**] ▪ Medium yellow iris. Brown head and auriculars with narrow whitish supercilium. ▪ Dark brown upperparts often uniformly colored. Long, thin, spindly tarsi. ▪ Coverts often uniformly brown. ▪ Long, gray tail has 3 or 4 equal-width black bands; thin pale terminal band.

Plate 166. Sharp-shinned Hawk, juvenile male
[**Sep.**] ▪ Medium yellow iris. Brown head and auriculars with narrow white supercilium. ▪ Dark brown upperparts often narrowly edged with tawny-rufous. Long, thin, spindly tarsi. ▪ Coverts often edged with tawny-rufous. ▪ Long, gray tail has 3 or 4 equal-width black bands; thin pale terminal band.

Plate 167. Sharp-shinned Hawk, juvenile female [Sep.] ▪ Medium yellow iris. Brown head and auriculars with narrow white supercilium. ▪ Dark brown upperparts often narrowly edged with tawny-rufous. Moderately streaked type underparts have moderately wide rufous-brown streaks. Long, thin, spindly tarsi. ▪ Rounded-type tail tip on both sexes with outer rectrices somewhat shorter than inner rectrices.

Plate 168. Sharp-shinned Hawk, juvenile female (lightly marked type) [Oct.] ▪ Medium yellow iris. Pale head with distinct white supercilium. ▪ Narrowly streaked type white underparts have thin rufous-brown or dark brown streaks; often less streaked on lower belly. ▪ Rounded-type tail tip with outer rectrices somewhat shorter than inner rectrices. ▪ *Note:* Palest extreme for both sexes. Female similar to a juvenile Cooper's Hawk. Photographed Cape May, N.J.

Plate 169. Sharp-shinned Hawk, juvenile male (heavily marked type) [Oct.] ▪ Medium yellow iris. Uniformly dark brown head. ▪ Uniformly dark brown upperparts. ▪ Narrow grayish terminal band. ▪ *Note:* Darkest extreme for both sexes. Photographed Cape May, N.J.

Plate 170. Sharp-shinned Hawk, juvenile female (springtime) [May] ▪ Iris changes from medium yellow to orange by spring. ▪ Dorsal color fades to medium brown.

Plate 171. Sharp-shinned Hawk, juvenile male
[Oct.] ▪ Moderately streaked type underparts uniformly marked with moderately wide brown/rufous-brown streaks. ▪ Barred remiges; males have wide black or gray band on rear edge of wings. Six "fingers" on outer primaries. Rufous-barred axillaries. ▪ Square-type tail tip has rectrices that are same length. Long tail.

Plate 172. Sharp-shinned Hawk, juvenile female
[Oct.] Moderately streaked type underparts uniformly marked with moderately wide rufous-brown streaks. ▪ Barred remiges; females typically have wide gray band on rear edge of wings. Six "fingers" on outer primaries. Rufous-barred axillaries. ▪ Round-type tail tip with outer rectrices somewhat shorter than inner rectrices. Long tail.

Plate 173. Sharp-shinned Hawk, juvenile female
[Oct.] ▪ Broadly streaked type underparts uniformly marked with wide rufous-brown streaks. ▪ Barred remiges; females typically have wide gray band on rear edge of wings. Six "fingers" on outer primaries. Rufous-barred axillaries. ▪ Very rounded type tail tip with outer rectices much shorter than inner rectices. Long tail.

Plate 174. Sharp-shinned Hawk, juvenile female
[Oct.] ▪ Moderately streaked type underparts uniformly marked with moderately wide rufous-brown streaks. ▪ Barred remiges; females typically have wide gray band on rear edge of wings. ▪ Square-type tail tip has all rectrices same length. Long tail. ▪ *Note:* Classic glide postion with wrists equal to eyes.

Plate 175. Sharp-shinned Hawk, juvenile male
[Oct.] ▪ Narrowly streaked type underparts are
narrowly streaked with brown/rufous-brown; often
less marked on lower belly. ▪ Wings angled forward of perpendicular line to body when soaring.
Barred remiges; males have wide black or gray
band on rear edge of wings. ▪ Square-type tail tip
has all rectrices same length.

COOPER'S HAWK
(Accipiter cooperii)

AGES: Adult, basic I (subadult I), and juvenile.
Adult plumage is acquired when 2 years old.
Adults are sexually dimorphic on head and
dorsal color and separable in the field.

Basic I (subadult I) plumage is acquired
when 1 year old. It is similar to the respective
adult sex but has visible color differences on
the auriculars and nape. Subadults may retain
some juvenile feathering on the upperwing
coverts and rump. The rump is not readily visible under field conditions. *Note:* Head and
nape characters of adult and subadult sexes are
based primarily on studies by J. Liguori (unpubl. data).

Juvenile plumage is retained the first year
with minor individual but no sexual variation.
By spring, plumage fades and eye color brightens. Juveniles have somewhat longer tails than
adults and subadults.

MOLT: Accipitridae wing and tail molt pattern

(*see* chapter 4). First prebasic molt from juvenile to subadult is generally an incomplete
molt and occurs from mid-Apr. through Nov.
Juvenile feathers are often retained on the upperwing coverts and rump until the next molt.
Outermost primary (p10), usually a secondary
(s4), and some rectrices (mainly r2 and 5) are
the last feathers to molt in a typical annual cycle. All remiges and rectrices are molted completely by end of the molt cycle.

Molt from subadult to adult plumage and
subsequent annual adult prebasic molts are
fairly complete or are complete and extend
May–Nov. Males begin molt later than females.
Some adults may retain a few old, worn adult
feathers that are not annually molted on the
upperwing coverts, rump, outer primaries (p9
and 10), secondaries (s4 and 8), and often tail
(r2 and 5).

SUBSPECIES: Monotypic.
COLOR MORPHS: None.
SIZE: Medium-sized raptor and mid-sized of
the three accipiters. Sexually dimorphic with

little or no overlap in eastern birds and generally separable in the field. Males are smaller than females. MALE.—Length: 14–16 in. (36–41 cm); wingspan: 28–30 in. (71–76 cm). FEMALE.—Length: 16–19 in. (41–48 cm); wingspan: 31–34 in. (79–86 cm.). Over the range of the species, Cooper's Hawks of the East are large individuals (Whaley and White 1994).

SPECIES TRAITS: HEAD.—**Long hackles can be elevated to produce a large, square-headed appearance. Gray supraorbital ridge skin, if exposed, is visible only at close range.** BODY.—**Moderately thick and long tarsi and toes are about pencil thickness.** WINGS.—**In flight, short and broad, with very rounded wingtips.** Wings are proportionately the shortest and most round-tipped of the accipiters. Accipiters have six "fingers" on the outermost primaries. Wingtips extend halfway down the tail on perched birds. TAIL.—**Very long and proportionately longest of the accipiters. Central rectrix set is longest with each outer set sequentially shorter than the previous set. Rectrix formation is visible only on the underside of closed tail. Tail can appear square-shaped when closed and quite rounded when fanned. Each rectrix tip is very rounded with a broad white terminal band.** White terminal band on the deck set (r1) may wear off by spring. Three or four neatly formed, equal-width black bands on the uppertail. On the ventral side, outermost rectrix set has narrow black bands that do not align with the equal-width bands.

ADULT TRAITS: HEAD.—Iris color varies from orange to red and generally darkens with age. Rate of color change varies individually and sexually and cannot be used as an exact aging criteria. Color change advances more quickly and gets darker on males. Iris color data from Rosenfield and Bielefeldt (1997). **Dark gray or black crown forms a cap that is either slightly darker or much darker than rest of the upperparts. Auriculars and nape are always paler than cap and rest of dorsum. The pale nape is only visible on perched birds.** BODY.— Medium grayish or bluish on the back, scapulars, rump, and uppertail coverts. White breast, belly, leg feathers, and flanks are barred with rufous. WINGS.—Grayish or bluish upperwing coverts. Undersides of remiges are promi-

nently barred on the outer primaries and variably barred on the inner primaries and secondaries. White axillaries are barred with rufous. White underwing coverts are spotted and barred with rufous.

Adult male: HEAD.—Iris color varies from orange to dark red and may take 4–7 years to attain the deepest red coloration. **Uniformly pale gray nape and auriculars, but sometimes a slight pale rufous tinge on auriculars and sides of nape (but not as rufous as on subadult males). Very dark gray or black cap is typically much darker than dorsum.** BODY.—**Back, scapulars, rump, and uppertail coverts are medium grayish blue and remain this color in all seasons.** WINGS.—**Medium grayish blue upperwing coverts. Undersides of the outer six or so primaries are distinctly barred, but the inner primaries and secondaries are pale gray with a minimal amount of dark barring** (F. Nicoletti unpubl. data).

Adult female: HEAD.—Iris color varies from orange to orangish red or medium red. **Rear of nape is always pale gray; however, auriculars and sides of nape are variable: (1) pale rufous, (2) pale rufous with grayish tinge, or (3) pale gray (uncommon variation).** Cap may be dark gray and only marginally darker than upperparts or much darker blackish. Some have a pale grayish forehead and supercilium; if present, reduce prominence of the darker cap. BODY.—**Back, scapulars, rump, and uppertail coverts are medium gray. Dorsal areas may retain this color in all seasons, but it fades by spring.** WINGS.—**Medium gray upperwing coverts.** Undersides of all remiges are prominently barred.

Adult female (brown-backed type): HEAD.— **As on typical adult females except cap is dark brown.** BODY and WINGS.—**Upperparts fade and wear to medium brown during a span from mid-winter to mid-summer.** Underparts, including upper surface of wings, as on typical adult females. Grayish dorsal plumage is attained with the next molt in summer and fall; however, it still may be more brownish than typical adult female. TAIL.— Pale dorsal bands are pale brown. *Note:* Uncommon fade and wear pattern.

BASIC I (SUBADULT I) TRAITS: Identical in most plumage aspects to respective adult sex. Separable from respective adult only at fairly close range. HEAD.—**As on adults, pale auriculars and nape are distinct. Cap is either dark gray and marginally darker than upperparts or much darker black.** *Separable from respective sex of adult by auricular and nape color.* Both sexes often have a pale rufous forehead and short supercilium; if present, reduces the prominence of darker cap. Iris color is medium yellow or orange. Iris color generally changes more quickly on males. BODY.—Retains either a large patch or scatter of brown juvenile feathers on the rump. Any retained feathering is visible only at close range when viewed from above. WINGS.—May retain scattered brown juvenile feathers on the upperwing coverts. Undersides of all remiges are distinctly barred on both sexes. TAIL.—Same as on adults.

Subadult male: HEAD.–Iris color is typically orange but may be yellowish orange. **Auriculars are always pale rufous, but nape color varies: (1) pale gray on all of nape, (2) pale rufous on sides of nape and gray on rear of nape, or (3) all-rufous nape (and auriculars; like subadult female). BODY.—Medium grayish blue back, scapulars, and uppertail coverts during all seasons. WINGS.—Medium grayish blue upperwing coverts, except for the small amount of any retained brown juvenile feathers.**

Subadult female: HEAD.—Iris color is orangish yellow in the fall and turns orange by spring. **Auriculars and all of the nape are uniformly pale rufous (with no variation).** BODY.—**Medium gray back, scapulars, and uppertail coverts, and may retain this color in all seasons. WINGS.—Medium gray upperwing coverts except any retained brown juvenile feathers.**

Subadult female (brown-backed type): HEAD.—As on typical subadult females except cap is dark brown. BODY, WINGS, and TAIL.—As on brown-backed adult females (*see above*).

JUVENILE TRAITS: HEAD.—Iris color is (1) **pale gray, (2) pale grayish green, or (3) pale lemon yellow from fledging to early winter. Rarely, iris color is medium orangish yellow in fall.** Tawny or brown head and neck often appear hooded. Some birds may have a short, pale tawny or white supercilium. BODY (ventral).—Variably streaked underparts are either (1) all white or (2) breast is washed with tawny

and rest of the underparts are white. Ventral markings: (1) breast is covered with narrow streaking, with less narrow streaking on the belly, and the lower belly has extremely narrow streaking or is unmarked; (2) on the palest individuals, breast is narrowly streaked but belly and lower belly are unmarked. Flanks are (1) narrowly streaked, (2) have a small diamond-shaped mark, or (3) have a partial dark brown bar on the inner portion of the longest streaked or diamond-shaped feathers. Overall effect is a very pale-bellied appearance. Dark brown markings on leg feathers are (1) narrowly streaked, (2) diamond-shaped, or (3) partially barred on the inner portion of each feather. White and unmarked undertail coverts. BODY (dorsal).—Dark brown with a tawny edge on each feather. Most scapular have a large white area on the basal region, making them appear very blotched, especially when fluffed in cold temperatures or when rousing. WINGS.—Dark brown upperwing coverts, including greater coverts, with each feather edged with tawny. *Crisp, dark gray or black band on trailing edge of remiges on the underwing.* Axillaries are barred with dark brown. TAIL.—Medium brown with three or four equal-width dark brown bands; rarely, has narrow white linear borders next to some dark bands.

JUVENILE (HEAVILY STREAKED TYPE): HEAD.—As on typical juveniles. BODY.—Breast and belly are heavily streaked; however, belly may have less streaking. Lower belly is fairly heavily streaked or covered with diamond-shaped markings. Dorsal body as on typical juveniles. Leg feathers are quite heavily marked with diamond-shaped markings, and often barred on the inner part of each feather. Overall appearance is dark bellied and dark legged. Undertail coverts are white and unmarked as on typical juveniles. *Note:* Not depicted.

JUVENILE (LATE WINTER/SPRING, ALL TYPES): HEAD.—Iris color changes to orangish yellow. This color may be retained into subadult age class in some females. BODY and WINGS (dorsal).—Pale feather edgings wear off and plumage fades and wears to a uniform medium brown.

ABNORMAL PLUMAGES: Atypically barred subadult.—Upper breast is streaked with rufous, lower breast and belly are covered with rufous arrowhead-shaped markings; flanks are broadly barred with rufous. All other plumage are normal. *Note:* Uncommon ventral pattern and noted on both sexes (BKW pers. obs.). Not depicted. **Unbarred adult.**—White unmarked belly, lower belly, flanks, and leg feathers have a hint of faint rufous markings on upper breast. WINGS.—White underwing coverts. Head and dorsal features are normal (BKW pers. obs.). *Note:* documented on a female specimen from New York. **Imperfect albino.**—Found primarily in juveniles. Iris, bill, and foot may be normally colored, or some or all of these areas may be paler. The iris may be pale bluish. Head and neck are pale rufous or whitish. Upperparts are white and may have faint rufous edges on many feathers. Remiges and rectrices are white and lack dark barring. White underparts are unmarked or have faintly rufous streaked (Clark and Wheeler 2001). *Note:* Very rare plumage and not depicted.

HABITAT: Summer.—Dry and moist upland and moist lowland areas with moderately old deciduous, coniferous, or mixed trees. Large contiguous woodlands, small woodlots, small conifer shelterbelts, and coniferous plantations are inhabited. Nesting pairs are found in undisturbed areas as well as in rural, suburban, and occasionally urban settings adjacent to semi-open or open areas. In suburban and urban centers, becoming fairly common breeders in city parks, campuses, cemeteries, and residential areas–including those with actively used yards (providing the birds are not bothered). Most nesting areas have densely foliaged canopies and understories; however, many suburban and urban areas have rather open understories. In the East, Cooper's Hawks inhabit humid to moderately humid climates from sea level to montane elevations.

Winter.—As in summer habitat, but birds typically inhabit lower elevations and more southern latitudes. Regularly inhabit semi-open and open areas with minimal tree growth. Commonly found in rural and urban locales with moderate tree growth.

Migration.—Often in semi-open and open marsh and dune areas of beaches and along mountain ridges.

HABITS: Moderately tame; those nesting in suburban and urban settings can be tame. Fairly hyper temperament. Long hackles are of-ten elevated, especially when threatened or in cool temperatures, giving the large, square-headed look. Concealed or exposed elevated perches are used. Fairly reclusive, but the most likely accipiter to use exposed perches. Fence posts and wires are regularly used for perches. *Cooper's Hawk is the only accipiter to perch on telephone poles.* Solitary except when breeding.

FEEDING: A perch and aerial hunter. Perch hunting consists of short or moderate-length perching stints. Regularly perches at low heights in dense branches or foliage of trees or bushes in order to surprise potential prey. Aerial forays are random excursions. A variety of small to medium-sized songbirds and game birds and small to medium-sized rodents form diet. Hunting is done in open sections of forest understories, along edges of woodlands and clearings, and in open areas. Readily pursues prey on foot into dense vegetation. Nesting pairs have plucking posts on branches, logs, or stumps in breeding territories. Prey is typically eaten near the point of capture in all other seasons and is regularly consumed on the ground. Avian prey is plucked prior to being eaten.

FLIGHT: Powered flight is a regular cadence of several fast wingbeats interspersed with short glides. Glides with wings held on flat plane or bowed slightly downward. Soars with wings held on flat plane or in a low dihedral, with front edges held rigidly perpendicular to the body. Several soaring revolutions are completed without resorting to powered flight. Head appears to project far beyond front of wings when gliding or soaring–an optical illusion created by the perpendicularly held wings. With their short, broad, rounded wings and long tail, Cooper's Hawks can navigate through densely wooded vegetation with incredible agility. Hunting occurs at low to moderate altitudes. In open areas, hunting birds may skim the ground or low vegetation at very low altitudes or may dive from high altitudes. Migratory flights are at high altitudes in light winds and at tree top or ground level in strong winds. Cooper's Hawks occasionally hover and kite for short periods in strong winds when exhibiting antagonistic behavior or waiting for hidden prey.

VOICE: Very nasal *kek-kek-kek* of varying duration when alarmed or agitated. A single, nasal *kek* by males when delivering food to females or when approaching nests. When curious or mildly agitated, a soft, single, nasal *kyew*. The nasal quality of call notes is readily separable from those of Sharp-shinned Hawks and Northern Goshawks.

STATUS AND DISTRIBUTION: Overall *uncommon* in the East. Estimated population is unknown but is probably stable and may be increasing. Numbers appear to be rebounding after the organochlorine pesticide era in North America.

Summer.—Quite adaptable to human-altered habitat providing ample, moderate-aged wooded tracts are retained. Becoming an increasingly common rural, suburban, and urban raptor in some regions of the East, particularly where Mourning Doves and other dove species have proliferated. Generally reclusive in the breeding season, and even urban nesting birds can go undetected. Expanding range northward in e. Canada: breeds to Québec City, Qué., and Hampstead, N.B.

Winter.—Southern-latitude birds are generally sedentary. Northern birds may be sedentary or winter farther south and at lower elevations than breeding or natal areas. Northern birds are often nomadic. Some may establish territories in areas with abundant and stable food supply. Many haunt birdfeeders in rural and urban areas. Juveniles, especially females, winter farther south than other ages. Cooper's Hawks are fairly conspicuous in winter. Some winter at the northern periphery of the breeding range in Québec City, Qué., and St. John, N.B. Large numbers winter in Mexico. They commonly winter to s. Florida, including the Keys. Some winter to Costa Rica and, rarely, to Colombia. Extralimital wintering in Nova Scotia has occurred near Halifax and the southern tip of the province.

Unlike Sharp-shinned Hawks, Cooper's Hawks are reluctant to make extensive over water crossings. They are common on short over water crossings such as in the Florida Keys but rarely winter on the Caribbean islands. There are only two records of Cooper's Hawks for Cuba (Sharp-shinned regularly winter on Cuba). Cooper's Hawks are rarely seen on the Dry Tortugas during migration.

Movements.—Short- and moderate-distance migrant. Some populations are fairly sedentary. Cooper's Hawks become very conspicuous during migration, especially along geographic barriers such as mountain ridges and coastal regions of the Great Lakes and Atlantic Coast. Cooper's Hawks of all ages often concentrate along the Great Lakes and Appalachian Mt. ridges in fall and spring.

Fall migration: Late Aug. to Dec. Juveniles precede adults, and females precede males of both ages. Juveniles peak from late Sept. to early Oct., adults in mid-Oct. Mid-Atlantic coast migrating subadults and adults are most prevalent after mid-Oct. Juveniles predominate along the Mid-Atlantic coast in fall, but only small numbers of subadults and adults use coastal areas in the fall.

Spring migration: Late Feb. to early Jun. Adults precede juveniles and peak from late Mar. to early Apr. Adult movements taper off after mid-Apr. Adult males precede adult females in order to establish breeding territories. Juveniles peak from mid- to late Apr., with stragglers into Jun.

NESTING: Mar.–Jun. in southern regions and Apr.–Jul. in northern latitudes. One-year-old females in juvenile plumage often mate with adult males. Rarely, two juvenile-aged birds pair and nest. Subadults regularly breed.

Courtship (flight).—*Sky-dancing, slow-flapping,* and *high-circling* (*see* chapter 5). Undertail coverts are flared outwardly and then retracted, with the tail being closed in the last two courting flights.

Most nest sites have densely foliaged canopies and understories with a nearby clearing and quiet water source. Some suburban and urban nest sites, however, often have little or no understory or ground foliage. For added secrecy, many pairs nest in conifers, especially pines. A new nest is usually built each year in a different tree in a territory, but pairs may reuse an old nest for up to 3 years. Nests are built by both sexes, but males often do bulk of the work. Nests are 24–28 in. (61–71 cm) in diameter and may become quite deep and bulky with repeated use. Nests are lined with bark chips and some greenery. Leafy squirrel nests are often used as platforms. Nests are well hidden and are typically placed in the upper portion of a tree. In deciduous trees, nests are placed in main crotches, minor outer crotches, or sometimes on lower-canopy horizontal branches. In conifers, nests are placed next to trunks. Nests are 20–60 ft. (6–18 m) high.

Normally 4 (white) eggs, but may have up to 7. The eggs are incubated for 34–36 days. Youngsters fledge in 30–34 days and are independent in about 56 days. Female tends to nesting duties; male hunts, but incubates while female feeds. Male rarely delivers prey to nest: he transfers it to female at a point away from nest for female to deliver and feed nestlings. Extra food is cached on branches of nearby trees for later use. Nesting adults are sometimes moderately aggressive and occasionally very aggressive toward humans.

CONSERVATION: This highly adaptable species, though uncommon, seems to be thriving in our constantly changing, human-altered environment. Being a predator mainly of birds, it has benefitted from the ban on organochlorine pesticide use, particularly DDT. Populations rebounded on their own once DDT use stopped. **Mortality.**—Carbamate pesticides may have contributed to some mortality. Newer generation pyrethroid pesticides are harmless to birds and mammals (but affect aquatic life). Illegal shooting in North America, especially south of U.S. in winter. Many birds fly into large windows. Pesticide contamination of prey species that winter in South America may still contribute to mortality.

SIMILAR SPECIES: (1) Sharp-shinned Hawk, females.—A long-standing identification dilemma for adults and juveniles when compared to male Cooper's Hawks. There is no overlap in size between the two species. Large female Sharp-shinned Hawks are considerably shorter in length and wingspan than male Cooper's Hawks. Numerous differences separate the two species. Proportional differences can separate them even when actual markings are not seen. PERCHED.—Small, round-shaped head at all times; however, Cooper's Hawks often compress their head feathers in warm temperatures so head also appears quite small. Yellow supraorbital ridge skin, if exposed, is apparent only at close range (often concealed by fluffed head feathers). Long, thin tarsi. Rectrix length on underside of tail is helpful, but use caution: females very round-tipped type tail with identical to Cooper's Hawks. Voice is very different from Cooper's Hawks, with soft chirping and high-pitched *kee*

or *kyew* notes. FLIGHT.—When soaring, front edge of wings is held forward of the perpendicular angle to the body. Head appears small (often an illusion with the forward-angled wings). Tail shape as in Perched. **(1A) Adult females.**—Crown of head and nape same bluish/gray color as dorsal areas and always darker than rufous auriculars. Females are grayish on dorsal areas, not bluish of male Cooper's Hawks. Underside of flying female is difficult to separate from underside view of male Cooper's Hawk using plumage markings: use proportions and wing attitude. Dusky color and dark brownish markings on underwing coverts helpful. *Note:* Only significant confusion will be with subadult male Cooper's Hawks, but their nape is always a paler gray or rufous. **(1B) Juvenile females.**—Irises are medium orangish yellow in fall and orange by late winter, but respectively brighter in all seasons than on Cooper's Hawks. Females generally have rufous streaked underparts; a few have narrow dark brown streaking. Beware of lightly marked types; they rival the lightly streaked underparts of most male Cooper's Hawks. Underwing in flight usually has grayish band on trailing edge on remiges, not crisp, dark band of Cooper' Hawks. Axillaries are barred with rufous (dark brown on Cooper's Hawk). COMPARED TO JUVENILE.—**(2) Northern Goshawk, juveniles.**—PERCHED.—Irises are a brighter yellowish orange, except in recently fledged birds, in which they are pale grayish: use caution in mid- to late summer. Short, thick tarsi. Greater upperwing coverts have pale tawny bar. Tail shape can be similar with sequentially shorter outer rectrices, but each rectrix is more pointed on goshawk. Tail of both species has broad white terminal band in fall. FLIGHT.—Dark band on trailing edge of underwing similar. Use caution with lightly marked type: underparts of these pale individuals can be as narrowly streaked as on Cooper's Hawk. May lack dark streaking on undertail coverts. Tail as in Perched. **(3) Red-shouldered Hawk, juveniles.**—PERCHED.—Medium brown irises. Dark malar mark. Throat is often dark. Wingtips extend to near tail tip. Long tarsi. FLIGHT.—Panel or window on upper and lower wing surfaces is tawny or white. Some *alleni* and *extimus* have distinct barring on underside of all remiges: use caution. Very

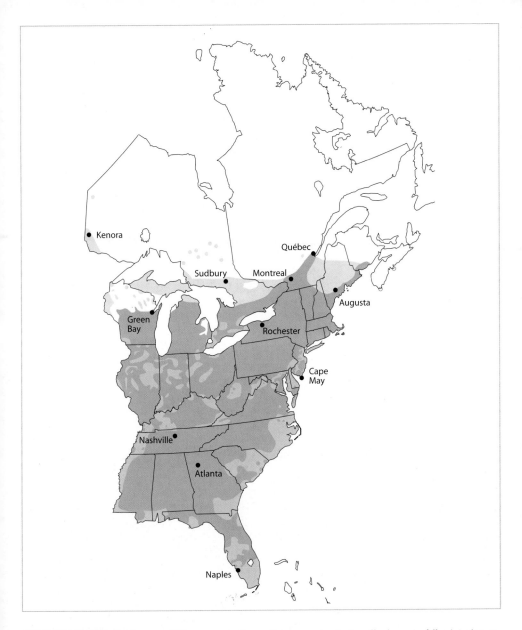

COOPER'S HAWK, *Accipiter cooperii:* Uncommon. Expanding range north. Locally dense in fall migration at mountain ridges and especially coastlines.

narrow gray or white tail bands. **(4) Broad-winged Hawk, juveniles.**—PERCHED.—Medium brown irises. Dark malar stripe. Wingtips extend to near tip of tail. Short, thick tarsi and toes. FLIGHT.—Very pointed primaries. Undersides of remiges have little if any barring. All rectrices are the same length on underside of tail. Caution on wide-banded type tail: it can be very accipiter-like with three nearly equal-width dark bands, including the non-aligning outer set.

OTHER NAMES: Cooper's, Coop. *Spanish:* Gavilán Pollero, Gavilán de Cooper. *French:* Épervier de Cooper.

REFERENCES: Brewer et al. 1991; Buckelew and Hall 1994; Bylan 1998, 1999; Cadman et al. 1987; Castrale et al. 1998; Clark and Wheeler 2001; del Hoyo et al. 1994; DeLorme Publishers 1991a, 1991b; Dodge 1988–1997; Erskine 1992; Hoffman and Darrow 1992; Howell and Webb 1995; Johnsgard 1990; Kale et al. 1992; Kaufman 1996; Kellogg 2000; Laughlin and Kibbe 1985; Lott 1999; Nicholson 1997; Palmer-Ball 1996; Peterjohn and Rice 1991; Robbins 1996; Rosenfield and Bielefeldt 1993, 1997; Stevenson and Anderson 1994; Walsh et al. 1999; Whaley and White 1994.

Plate 176. Cooper's Hawk, adult male [Apr.] ▪ Black crown (cap); pale gray auriculars and nape. Red iris. ▪ Grayish blue dorsal areas. White underparts finely barred with rufous. ▪ Very long tail with much shorter outer rectrix sets.

Plate 177. Cooper's Hawk, adult male [Apr.] ▪ Black crown (cap); pale gray auriculars and nape. Red iris. ▪ Grayish blue dorsal areas.

Plate 178. Cooper's Hawk, adult male [Sep.] ▪ Black crown (cap); pale gray auriculars and nape. Red iris. ▪ Grayish blue dorsal areas. ▪ Very long tail has 3 or 4 equal-width black bands; broad white tail tip; much shorter outer rectrix sets. ▪ *Note:* Still molting new secondaries: dark feathers are new adult feathers. Photograph by Jerry Liguori.

Plate 179. Cooper's Hawk, adult male [Sep.] ▪ Gray auriculars and nape. ▪ White underparts finely barred with rufous. ▪ Primaries distinctly barred, secondaries finely barred and often nearly lack barring. Coverts spotted and barred with rufous. ▪ Very long tail with much shorter outer rectrix sets; broad white tail tip.

Plate 180. Cooper's Hawk, adult female [Apr.] ▪ Black crown (cap), pale rufous auriculars, pale gray nape. Red iris. ▪ White underparts finely barred with rufous. ▪ Gray upperwing coverts and back. ▪ Very long tail with much shorter outer rectrix sets ▪ *Note:* Upperparts distinctly more grayish than on adult or subadult males.

Plate 181. Cooper's Hawk, adult female (brown-backed type) [Apr.] ▪ Dark brown crown (cap), pale rufous auriculars, pale gray nape. Reddish orange iris. ▪ White underparts finely barred with rufous. Back and scapulars medium brown. ▪ Upperwing coverts medium brown. ▪ *Note:* Common variant for adult and subadult females.

Plate 182. Cooper's Hawk, adult female [Sep.] ▪ Black crown (cap), pale rufous auriculars, gray nape. ▪ Gray upperparts. ▪ Very long, pale gray tail has 3 or 4 equal-width black bands. Broad white tail tip; much shorter outer rectrix sets. ▪ *Note:* Photograph by Jerry Liguori.

Plate 183. Cooper's Hawk, adult female [Oct.] ▪ Black crown (cap), rufous auriculars, and pale gray nape. ▪ White underparts are finely barred with rufous. ▪ Remiges are fully barred. May have dark gray band on rear edge of remiges. Rufous markings on underwing coverts. ▪ Very long tail with much shorter outer rectrix sets.

Plate 184. Cooper's Hawk, adult female (left), subadult male (right) [Apr.] Female: Dark gray crown (cap), pale supercilium, gray auriculars and nape. Gray upperparts. ▪ Male: Black crown (cap), pale rufous supercilium, rufous auriculars and nape. Grayish blue upperparts. ▪ *Note:* Mated pair. Typical size difference between sexes.

Plate 185. Cooper's Hawk, subadult male [Oct.] ▪ Wings held at perpendicular angle to body when soaring and banking. Rufous markings on coverts. All remiges fully barred. May have dark gray band on rear edge of remiges. ▪ White underparts finely barred with rufous. ▪ Very long tail with much shorter outer rectrix sets.

Plate 186. Cooper's Hawk, juvenile male [Oct.] ▪ Pale gray iris. Tawny-brown head, sometimes with short, pale supercilium. ▪ Long, moderately thick tarsi and toes. ▪ Very long, pale gray tail with 3 or 4 equal-width black bands and broad white tip. ▪ *Note:* Sexes similar.

Plate 187. Cooper's Hawk, juvenile male [Oct.] ▪ Pale gray iris. Tawny-brown head, sometimes with short, pale supercilium. ▪ White underparts narrowly streaked with dark brown; often less heavily streaked on lower belly. Distal flank feathers may be partially barred. Long, moderately thick tarsi and toes. ▪ Very long tail with much shorter outer rectrix sets. ▪ *Note:* Sexes similar.

Plate 188. Cooper's Hawk, juvenile male [Oct.] ▪ Pale gray iris. Pale tawny-brown head, often with short supercilium. ▪ White underparts narrowly streaked on breast, belly, and flanks and unmarked on lower belly. ▪ Very long tail with much shorter outer rectrix sets. ▪ *Note:* Sexes similar. Palest variant.

Plate 189. Cooper's Hawk, juvenile female (springtime) [Apr.] ▪ Orangish yellow iris. ▪ Upperparts fade to medium brown. ▪ White tail tip often wears off. ▪ *Note:* Iris color much more yellowish than in juvenile Sharp-shinned Hawk or Northern Goshawk, which have orangish irises in spring. Prey is Great-tailed Grackle (photographed in s. Texas).

Plate 190. Cooper's Hawk, juvenile female [Oct.]
▪ Tawny-brown head. ▪ Dark brown upperparts with pale tips on some upperwing coverts. ▪ Very long, gray tail with 3 or 4 equal-width black bands; broad white tail tip. Tail rounded when fanned. ▪ *Note:* Sexes similar.

Plate 191. Cooper's Hawk, juvenile male [Oct.] ▪ Long neck. ▪ White underparts narrowly streaked, often less heavily streaked on lower belly. ▪ Broadly barred remiges with crisp black rear edge (darker, more defined than on juvenile female Sharp-shinned Hawk). Brown-barred axillaries (rufous on Sharp-shinned Hawk). ▪ Very long tail with much shorter outer rectrix sets. Broad white tail tip. ▪ *Note:* Sexes similar.

Plate 192. Cooper's Hawk, juvenile male [Oct.] ▪ White underparts narrowly streaked, often less heavily streaked on lower belly. ▪ Broadly barred remiges with crisp black rear edge (darker, more defined than on juvenile female Sharp-shinned Hawk). Wings held at perpendicular angle to body when soaring. Brown-barred axillaries (rufous on Sharp-shinned Hawk). ▪ Very long rounded tail with shorter outer rectrix sets. White tail tip not always distinct. ▪ *Note:* Sexes similar.

NORTHERN GOSHAWK
(*Accipiter gentilis*)

AGES: Adult, basic I (subadult I), and juvenile. Adult and subadult I have moderately sexually dimorphic plumages. Adult plumage is acquired when 2 years old. Subadult plumage is acquired when 1 year old. Juvenile plumage is worn the first year. Juveniles have longer secondaries, which create a broader wing, and have longer tails than older ages.

MOLT: Accipitridae wing and tail molt pattern (*see* chapter 4). First prebasic molt from juvenile to subadult occurs mid-Apr. through Nov. This is often an incomplete molt and may retain a variable amount of juvenile feathering. The secondaries often retain old, worn juvenile feathers on s4, s4 and 8, or s7 and 8 and 9. Some males molt fully into new subadult feathering on all the remiges. Almost all subadults have scattered juvenile feathering on the upperwing coverts. The rump tract is partially or totally retained juvenile feathers. The majority of the tail (r2–5) may be retained juvenile rectrices, or some males molt fully into new subadult rectrices.

Subadult to adult molt and subsequent annual adult prebasic molts begin May–Jul., with males beginning later than females, and are finished in Nov. Annual molts are not complete and retain some old adult feathering on the body, secondaries, and tail. Some adults retain a few old juvenile feathers into the second prebasic molt.

SUBSPECIES: Polytypic. *A. g. atricapillus* is the only race found in the East. It is also found in much of the West and probably extends south, at high elevations and in very small numbers, to s. Jalisco and e. Guerrero, Mexico. *Note:* All data pertain to *atricapillus*.

The darker and smaller "Queen Charlotte" race, *A. g. laingi*, is an example of Gloger's Rule. Its range includes the Queen Charlotte Islands, B.C., and adjacent island areas of se. Alaska southward to Vancouver Island, B.C.

Northern Goshawks of montane regions of se. Arizona and n. Mexico, labeled as *A. g. apache* by some authors, are not recognized as a distinct race by the AOU. These southwestern birds average only slightly larger than individuals from other mainland populations, and plumages do not appear to be separable from *atricapillus*.

There are six additional subspecies: (1) nominate *A. g. gentilis* of Europe and extreme nw. Africa, (2) *A. g. arrigonii* of Corsica and Sardinia, (3) *A. g. buteoides* of n. Eurasia, (4) *A. g. albidus* of ne. Siberia and Kamchatka, (5) *A. g. schvedowi* of Asia to s. and cen. China, and (6) *A. g. fujiyamae* of Japan.

COLOR MORPHS: None.

SIZE: A large raptor and largest of the three accipiters. Sexually dimorphic but not always separable in the field. Proportionately the least dimorphic of the accipiters. Males are smaller than females. MALES.—Length: 18–20 in. (46–51 cm); wingspan: 38–41 in. (97–104 cm). FEMALES.—Length: 21–24 in. (53–61 cm); wingspan: 41–45 in. (104–114 cm).

SPECIES TRAITS: BODY.—**Fairly short, thick tarsi and toes. Long undertail coverts can be fluffed and extended outwards beyond the edge of the tail.** WINGS.—**In flight, moderately short with broad secondaries that taper to narrower, rounded wingtips.** Wingtips can become quite pointed when gliding. Accipiters have six "fingers" on the outermost primaries. When perched, wingtips extend halfway down the tail. TAIL.—Long and wedge-shaped. On the underside, each outer rectrix set is sequentially shorter, with outermost set (r6) being much shorter than the deck set (r1).

ADULT TRAITS: HEAD.—**Dark gray or black crown, black nape, white supercilium, and black auricular patch. From many angles, the black auriculars, situated between the white supercilium and whitish cheek, are the most distinctive feature on the head.** White supercilium often extends as a white mottled area onto the black nape. The supercilium is often lightly streaked with black. Iris color varies from orange to red and typically darkens with age, especially on males. BODY.—**Grayish vermiculated or barred underparts.** Immaculate, long white undertail coverts. Bluish gray upperparts, including the hindneck. *Note:* There is some overlap between the sexes in dorsal coloration and ventral markings, with females more likely than males to assume traits of the opposite sex. WINGS.—**Dark upperside of**

remiges contrasts sharply with paler grayish upperwing coverts, back, and scapulars. Underwing appears uniformly pale gray with distinct, wide dark barring on the outer primaries and little if any barring on the grayish secondaries. TAIL.—Bluish gray uppertail is variably barred with a fairly broad white terminal band.

Adult male: HEAD.—Iris color varies from reddish orange to bright red and typically achieves a more vivid red than in females. BODY.—Breast, belly, flanks, and leg feathers are patterned with fine vermiculation and lack black shaft streaking. Underparts appear uniformly pale gray at field distances. Males are sometimes more adult-female-like, with partial barring and coarser vermiculation. Pale bluish gray upperparts. TAIL.—**Uppertail may be (1) solid bluish gray, (2) have two or three partial dark bands on the central rectrices,** or (3) **have partial dark bands on all rectrices.** Undertail is (1) solid gray, (2) solid gray with a dark subterminal band, or (3) has two or three equal-width dark bands, except the outer rectrix set, which may have narrow, non-aligning dark bands. Uppertail coverts are typically uniformly bluish gray.

Adult female: HEAD.—Iris color varies from orangish to dark red. Irises are occasionally dark reddish brown, very rarely dark brown. BODY.—**Breast, belly, flanks, and leg feathers are variably marked with dark gray vermiculation or barring, and most have a distinct black shaft streak on each feather: (1) moderately barred, (2) covered with either a finely or coarsely patterned vermiculation and no prominent shaft streaking (and adult-male-like), or (3) have a combination of vermiculation and barring.** Medium bluish gray or medium gray upperparts typically have a slight brownish tone; however, some birds are more bluish and look adult-male-like. TAIL.—**Three or four distinct, wide, equal-width dark bands on the uppertail.** Undertail also has distinct equal-width dark bands except the outer rectrix set, which has narrow, non-aligning dark bands. Uppertail coverts may be tipped with white.

BASIC I (SUBADULT I) TRAITS: Superficially resembles the respective-sex adult plumage; however, generally more distinctly marked and darker on the dorsal areas than the respective

adult. HEAD.—**As on adult except the white supercilium is typically very streaked with black. The distinct black auricular patch is bordered by the whitish supercilium and pale gray cheeks.** Iris color varies from yellowish orange to pale red and averages brighter on males. BODY.—Lower back and rump often retain scattered, worn brown juvenile feathers, or an extensive amount of juvenile feathering may be retained as a large brown patch. Males may molt almost entirely out of any juvenile feathering on the rump. Some birds retain a few old brown juvenile feathers on some scapulars and uppertail covert feathers. WINGS.—Scattered brown juvenile feathers may be on some upperwing coverts, but some males may molt almost entirely out of any retained feathering. Secondaries often retain some juvenile feathers (s4, s7 and 8, sometimes s9) or molt fully into new subadult feathering. Primaries generally molt into new feathers, but a few may retain juvenile outer primaries (p8–10). All new subadult remiges are distinctly barred on the underside. **As on adults, paler blue-gray upperwing coverts, scapulars, and back contrast with the darker remiges.** TAIL.—May retain old juvenile feathering; if so, old rectrices are very worn and the white terminal band is worn off. Variations of rectrix molt: (1) deck and outermost rectrix sets (r1 and 6) are always new subadult, but the middle sets (r2–5) may be retained, old juvenile feathers; and (2) all rectrices may molt into new subadult blue-gray feathers. New subadult rectrices have a fairly broad white terminal band. The uppertail coverts may be tipped with white.

Basic I (subadult I) male: HEAD.—Iris color varies from yellowish orange to pale red. White supercilium is generally streaked with black. BODY.—Medium bluish gray or medium gray upperparts are typically the same color as on most adult females, rarely paler and more bluish and adult-male-like. **Underparts are also similar in pattern to most adult females; rarely, more finely vermiculated and adult-male-like. Unique to subadult males; some have a variably distinct "bib" on the breast, consisting of large, dark, arrowhead-shaped marks and thick bars. TAIL.—Dorsal surface is crossed by three or four distinct, equal-width, wide dark bands. A few birds lack dark banding on the dorsal surface and ap-**

pear much like an adult male. Undertail has equal-width dark bands, except the outer set which has narrow, non-aligning dark bands. *Note:* At field distances, may not be separable from adult males.

Basic I (subadult I) female: HEAD.—Iris color varies from orangish yellow to orange but may change to orangish brown by spring. There is considerable dark streaking in the white supercilium. BODY.—Dark gray upperparts have brownish cast and are darker than on adults and subadult males. **Breast, belly, flanks, and leg feathers are distinctly marked with wide, coarse, dark gray or black barring. Each ventral feather has a prominent wide, black shaft streak.** TAIL.—**Uppertail is distinctly crossed with three or four equal-width, wide dark bands.** Undertail has wide, equal-width dark bands, except the outer rectrix set which has narrow, non-aligning dark bands.

JUVENILE TRAITS: HEAD.—**Most have a long, broad white supercilium; however, some have a short supercilium, and a few lack this mark. Most exhibit a facial disk pattern around the rear of the auriculars with a brown patch on the auriculars. Most show a partial, dark malar mark. Iris color is orangish yellow; by spring, it changes to orange.** Iris color is rarely medium brown. *Note:* Nestlings and recently fledged birds have pale gray irises Jun.–Aug., but most change to orangish yellow soon after fledging. BODY.—Whitish or tawny underparts are covered with wide or moderately wide, uniform dark brown streaking from the breast to lower belly. Dark brown markings on leg feathers consists of (1) heavy streaking, (2) diamond-shaped marks, or (3) partial barring. **Undertail coverts are variably marked: (1) a large or moderately large diamond- or arrowhead-shaped dark brown mark on all feathers,** (2) a thin dark brown streak on the shaft area of each feather, (3) a thin dark streak on only the distal coverts, or (4) unmarked feathers. Medium to dark brown upperparts, including rump and uppertail coverts, are mottled with tawny and appear pale and blotchy. Feathers on the nape and all of the neck are distinctly streaked with tawny. WINGS.—**Greater coverts and sometimes median upperwing coverts of most individuals have a prominent, broad tawny or white bar; a few**

lack this pale bar. In flight, broad secondaries are much wider than the primaries. Underside of all remiges is prominently barred, and often wavy, especially on the outer primaries and secondaries. A crisp, moderately wide dark band is on the trailing edge of the wings. TAIL.—**Long and wedge-shaped when seen from the underside. Tip of each rectrix is pointed. On the upperside, each rectrix has three to four wide, often off-set, equal-width dark bands bordered by thin white lines. On fanned tail, dark bands may appear somewhat irregular and wavy.** Tail has a broad white terminal band that extends to the distal edge of the dark subterminal band. White tips of central pair of rectrices generally wear off by spring. *Note:* Recently fledged, springtime, and brown-eyed types are not depicted.

JUVENILE (LIGHTLY MARKED TYPE): HEAD.—As on typical juvenile, but white supercilium is always prominent and neck is extensively streaked with tawny. BODY.—Upperparts are medium brown and extensively mottled with tawny; birds appear very pale-backed. Underparts are pale tawny or whitish and are either (1) uniformly streaked from the breast to lower belly with narrow dark brown streaking or (2) may have less dark streaking on the lower belly. Leg feathers are (1) lightly streaked, (2) have small diamond-shaped markings, or (3) are white and unmarked. Undertail coverts often have (1) thin dark shaft streaks on only the most distal feathers or (2) may be unmarked and pure white. TAIL.—As on typical juveniles. *Note:* Classic specimens are in the Bell Museum of Natural History, University of Minnesota, Minneapolis, Minn. ($n = 2$ from autumn in Minnesota [feature the palest individuals]) and the AMNH, ($n = 2$ from autumn in New Jersey and New York).

ABNORMAL PLUMAGES: Partial albino adult.—Record of a bird with some white feathers scattered throughout the body (Clark and Wheeler 2001).

HABITAT: Summer.—Moderate-sized to extensive tracts of old-growth and older second-growth coniferous, deciduous, or mixed woodlands with moderately dense or dense canopies. Deciduous trees in northern areas are mainly Quaking Aspen and Paper Birch; in southern regions, mainly various species of oak, maple, and American Beech. Conifer species include Eastern Hemlock and Eastern White Pine in southern latitudes and White Spruce in northern latitudes. Second-growth tracts and open expanses may be adjacent to old-growth tracts. Dry woodlands are interspersed with small clearings of power-line clear-cuts, logging roads, hiking trails, or meadows. A quiet water source, consisting of a lake, creek, or small ground seepage, is typically located in a territory. Montane elevations are inhabited in New York, Pennsylvania, and West Virginia. In New Jersey, found primarily at higher elevations, but isolated breeding has occurred in lowland, mature cedar swamps. In northern-latitude states and provinces, inhabits low and high elevations. Foraging habitats may be similar to nesting habitats, beneath understories of mature forests, but also include second-growth woodlands and open meadows.

Winter.—Same as summer habitat for all ages. Juveniles, but also some subadults and adults, often range into very low-elevation areas: wooded tracts of any age, wooded rural and urban locales, and occasionally regions with minimal tree growth.

Migration.—Heavily wooded areas to semi-open coastal scrub habitat.

HABITS: Moderately wary species but sometimes fairly tame. Northern Goshawks have a fairly high-strung temperament. They are reclusive and have minimal contact with humans. Breeding birds can be very aggressive towards humans intruding into nesting territories. Concealed branches are preferred perches. *Goshawks do not perch on posts and utility poles along well-traveled roadways.* Solitary away from breeding grounds. Highly tolerant of cold weather if sufficient food is available. Undertail coverts are fluffed outward when agitated and during some courting displays (*see* Nesting).

FEEDING: Perch and aerial hunter. Perches for moderate lengths of time when perch hunting. Aerial hunting consists of random excursion flights. Goshawks are extremely aggressive and relentless when pursuing prey. Prey may be pursued on foot into thick brush. Hunting occurs mainly under the canopy, near forest floors, in small woodland openings, along edges of open-wooded areas, and sometimes over open expanses. Squirrels, rabbits, hares, large songbirds, and small to medium-sized game birds comprise diet. Avian prey is captured while it is on the ground or, rarely, when airborne at low altitudes and is plucked prior to being eaten. Adults have plucking posts in nesting territories. Northern Goshawks are fairly dependent on Red Squirrel, Eastern Chipmunk, Eastern Gray Squirrel, American Robin, Blue Jay, Northern Flicker, and Willow Ptarmigan. In northern regions, they are highly dependent on, and subsequently quite affected by, the cyclic populations of Snowshoe Hare and, in part, Ruffed Grouse.

FLIGHT: Powered by regular cadence of moderately fast wingbeats interspersed with short to medium-distance glides. Wings are held on a flat plane when gliding and soaring. When soaring, front edge of the wings is held at a slight angle forward of a perpendicular line to body. Hunting flights are at low to very low altitudes. Flight is at high altitudes at other times, especially during migration and courtship. Quite an agile raptor considering its large size. Rarely hovers or kites.

VOICE: Generally silent except around nest and when courting. A repetitive, harsh, loud, emphatic *cack, cack, cack* is the typical agitated call. A drawn-out, high-pitched, wailing *kree* is common courtship and food-begging call. Males have a higher-pitched call. Food delivery call of males is a soft, throaty, staccato *kuk* (C. Flatten data). Fledglings are extremely vocal.

STATUS AND DISTRIBUTION: Summer.—Estimated population is unknown. *Very uncommon* and distributed in very low density. Historical changes affecting Northern Goshawks have occurred across much of e. U.S. and to a lesser extent s. Canada since the 1800s with extensive deforestation, demise of the Passenger Pigeon, and increased urbanization. However, the species is reoccupying former portions of its southern range where second-growth woodlands have been protected and matured. Overall population in the e. U.S. is probably stable. Listed as a Sensitive Species in Wisconsin, Endangered in New Jersey, and has Undetermined status in Pennsylvania (with proposal for Vulnerable). In Canada, listed as a Sensitive Species in Nova Scotia and a Secure Species in all other eastern provinces except Newfoundland and Labrador where status is Undetermined.

Connecticut: Southward range extension in isolated, protected mature woodlands into New

Haven Co. Regularly found throughout the rugged, wooded western and northeastern portions of the state. *Massachusetts:* This state has seen quite a range expansion in recent decades, and goshawks are now found in most counties except on Cape Cod. *Michigan:* As in Wisconsin, breeding regularly occurs in northern counties and Upper Peninsula. Isolated breeding occurs in the following central and southern counties: cen. Newaygo, n. Mecosta, se. Midland, sw. Muskegon, se. Ottawa, and se. Tuscola. *New Jersey:* Breeders are mainly in the highlands of the northwestern part of the state, but isolated and possibly irregular nesting has been documented in the low-elevation areas in cen. Hunterdon and w.-cen. Ocean Co. *Pennsylvania:* This state has a sizable population in montane areas. *West Virginia:* Breeding documented for Tucker and Pocahantas Co. *Wisconsin:* Breeds throughout northern counties with isolated breeding in the following central and southern counties: Sheboygan, Washara, Juneau, and Monroe. Southern expansion into former range has occurred. Goshawks are now found in counties that were not previously known to have nesting.

In the low-diversity spruce-aspen boreal forest of n. Ontario, s. and cen. Québec, n. Wisconsin, and n. Michigan, Northern Goshawks undergo natural periodic status fluctuations that are due mainly to the cyclic trends of Snowshoe Hare and, in part, Ruffed Grouse. Snowshoe Hare populations fluctuate dramatically and trigger declines and movements of several predator species. Hare numbers increase—then often plunge—on approximately 10-year cycles. Ruffed Grouse in the above states and provinces also undergo approximate 10-year population changes. Low numbers of Snowshoe Hare and Ruffed Grouse temporarily affect goshawk winter survival and reproductive success and force a migratory "irruption" of adults to occur (*see* Movements). This is accentuated when year-round secondary prey species in the boreal forest cannot supply an adequate food supply for goshawks, particularly in winter when migratory or hibernating prey species are not available.

Note on Snowshoe Hare and Ruffed Grouse: Snowshoe Hare.—The Snowshoe Hare is found throughout all of the Northern Goshawk range in the East but extends a bit farther south than

the hawk in the Appalachian Mts., to se. Tennessee and w. North Carolina. The greatest population volatility, with tremendous highs and devastating lows, occurs in w. Canada, particularly in the Yukon. A notable degree of fluctuation occurs in n. Michigan, n. Wisconsin, and n. Ontario.

Cycles of Snowshoe Hare numbers and the southward influx of adult goshawks in fall and winter have been seen in the e. U.S. since the late 1800s. The most recent severe population crash of Snowshoe Hares occurred throughout much of the boreal forest in Alaska and Canada in the early 1970s. It caused a massive goshawk irruption into the U.S., including all of the East, in the fall and winter of 1972–1973. Since then, Snowshoe Hare populations in boreal forest of e. Canada appear to have had irregular, partial population cycles that vary from 8 to 11 years and have produced only minimal status changes and irruptive patterns of adult Northern Goshawks in the East. W. Canada has experienced quite regular and sharp cyclic fluctuations of Snowshoe Hares and, likewise, regular irruptions of adult goshawks.

Hare population cycles, where they occur, are attributed primarily to a rapid population increase and subsequent severe food shortage, disease, and tremendous depredation by a booming predator base. Some biologists believe there is also a possible link to cyclic solar sunspots that temporarily affect the boreal ecosystem and produce the cycle activity in Snowshoe Hares. Because of a much more diverse ecosystem, little or no cyclic patterns for Snowshoe Hares are detected in the e. U.S., except as previously described for n. Wisconsin and Michigan.

Ruffed Grouse.—Grouse cycles (first triggered by the decline of Snowshoe Hare) appear to be a secondary but still important factor in adult goshawk irruptive movements. Ruffed Grouse are found throughout much of the goshawk range in the East, but their range extends farther south than the range of the goshawk, to s. Tennessee and w. North Carolina, and farther east, to e. New Jersey, e. Connecticut, Rhode Island, and e. Massachusetts. However, Ruffed Grouse do not extend as far north as goshawks (or Snowshoe Hares) in Québec and Labrador.

The last major downward cycle was about 1993 in Wisconsin, Michigan, and probably e. Canada, and it may have assisted in producing the moderate adult goshawk irruption that fall in the e. U.S. This cycle was undoubtedly prompted by the major Snowshoe Hare downcycle in the early 1990s in the Canadian boreal forest as well as in n. Wisconsin and Michigan. Grouse population crashes, where they occur, appear to be due to intense depredation from several boreal forest predators (e.g., Lynx, Coyote, Northern Goshawk, and Great Horned Owl) switching over to a primarily Ruffed Grouse diet following the rapid decline of Snowshoe Hare. Also, Ruffed Grouse reach their greatest density in aspen habitat, and aspen trees have cyclic production of male catkins, which are a major food source for grouse in winter.

Cyclic factors for Ruffed Grouse do not exist for the e. U.S. east of Wisconsin and Michigan or for New Brunswick, Canada. In this region, the ecosystem is much more diverse, and numerous non-cyclic, year-round prey species exist. Goshawks, having a varied and ample prey supply in this region, do not exert unusually high depredation on grouse and therefore do not contribute to forcing grouse into cyclic trends.

Winter.—Adults may remain on or near breeding territories unless forced to vacate because of a food shortage, mainly of Snowshoe Hare and Ruffed Grouse. Juveniles typically depart natal regions. Individuals moving out of breeding and natal territories remain solitary and are highly nomadic. During severe prey shortages, as seen in winter 1972–1973, even adults may extend their range far south of typical wintering areas. Florida records: three specimen and four sight records to 1992. Sightings are from the northeastern part of the state in 1972 and 1979 in Leon, Duval, and St. Johns Co. There is an old skeleton record for St. Petersburg. Recent Bermuda records: one (adult) in 1972.

Movements.—Depending on age, sex, and location, Northern Goshawks can be (1) sedentary, (2) engage in short dispersal or shifting movements in any direction, or (3) perform short-distance southward migrations. In the East, most juveniles and some subadults and adults migrate each year. Moderate numbers of adults inhabiting the boreal forest vacate, as an irruption, regional food-void breeding areas when Snowshoe Hare and Ruffed Grouse populations crash. Numbers of migrating juveniles outnumber adults even during most irruption years in the East. Concentrations occur along geographic barriers such as mountain ridges, the Great Lakes, and n. and cen. Atlantic Coast areas.

Adult irruptions are less punctual and less dramatic in the East than in the West, especially since 1982. Recent adult irruptions appear to have occurred in the fall and winter of 1972, 1981–1983, and 1993. High numbers of northward-returning adults were detected the subsequent spring of each respective irruption (e.g., 1973, 1982–1984, and 1994). The w. and cen. Great Lakes regions align with the punctual 10-year cyclic increments that the West has had (e.g., 1972, 1982, and 1992). The 1972 invasion was dramatic and included all areas of the East: large numbers of adults pushed far south of normal winter range. Large numbers of juveniles tallied at hawkwatch sites, as seen in 1995 and 1997, produce overall numbers that may rival or exceed adult irruption tallies.

Fall migration (all years the same): Mid-Sep. to Jan. Juveniles peak from late Oct. to early Nov., adults in mid- to late Nov., with small numbers trickling through into Dec. Subadults are possibly more prevalent in the earlier part of the "adult" period.

Spring migration (all years the same): Feb.–May. Adults peak in mid-Mar. along the e. Great Lakes and in mid-Apr. along the w. Great Lakes. Juveniles peak in mid- to late Apr., with stragglers occurring until Jun. High counts in East seasonally may tally 100–200 goshawks at prime hawkwatch sites.

NESTING: Apr. to early Sep., depending on latitude.

Courtship (flight).—*High-circling, slow-flapping*, and *sky-dancing* (see chapter 5). Undertail coverts are flared and retracted regularly with tail partially spread, especially in high-circling.

Nests are up to 36 in. (91 cm) in diameter, composed of large sticks, and decorated with greenery. They are 15–75 ft. (5–23 m) high in primary or secondary forks in deciduous trees or next to the trunks in conifers. In conifers, may occasionally be placed quite a distance from trunks. Up to five alternate nests can be found in a territory, with the occupied nest being rotated every 1–5 years. Goshawks may occupy abandoned nests of other large birds such as Common Ravens. Nests typically are in live trees with a dense canopy cover. Dead trees are occasionally used, and canopy cover is often obtained from nearby live trees. Nest trees are in a stand of tall old-growth or older second-growth trees. Younger second-growth stands and semi-open expanses may be adjacent to the nest tract. Nest sites are near small clearings of meadows, fallen trees, lightly used roads, power-line cuts, and quiet water sources.

Females assume all nest duties, and males hunt. Males rarely come to the nest. Males transfer prey to females at points away from the nest. One to 4 eggs are incubated 34–35 days by female. Youngsters fledge in 36–42 days and are independent in 84–94 days. Nesting success may be poor or nesting may not occur in local northern regions during low food-cycles surrounding Snowshoe Hare and Ruffed Grouse irruption years. Because of ample prey abundance, nesting occurs and success is high between irruption years. One-year-old females may successfully nest while in juvenile plumage. These younger-aged females mate with adult males, often in areas that have hare and grouse irruptions, and often after irruptions. Most birds do not breed until at least 2 years old.

CONSERVATION: No measures are taken. There are no forestry practices that ensure protection from tree harvest in nest territories in the East. **Mortality.**—Primarily habitat destruction and illegal shooting. Great Horned Owls prey on all ages.

SIMILAR SPECIES: COMPARED TO JUVENILE.—(1) **Northern Harrier, adult females.**—PERCHED.—Facial disk, yellow irises, streaked underparts, mottled brown upperparts, tail length and pattern similar to goshawk: use caution. Long, thin tarsi. FLIGHT.—Dark axillaries, median underwing coverts. Wings held in a dihedral. Five "fingers" on outer primaries. White uppertail coverts. (2) **Cooper's Hawk, juveniles.**—PERCHED.— May have a short pale supercilium but rarely have a partial dark malar stripe or brown auricular patch. Iris color pale grayish to pale lemon yellow in fall, medium orangish yellow

in spring, but always paler and not as orangish as in respective-season goshawk. Use caution with nestling or recently fledged goshawks which have pale gray eyes (Jun.–Aug.). Moderately long tarsi. Upperwing coverts uniformly brown with pale tawny only on feather edges. Very rarely has thin white borders along dark bands on dorsal surface of tail. Cooper's Hawks commonly perch on posts and poles along roadways. FLIGHT.—Very rounded wingtips; wings held perpendicular to body when soaring. Both species have a distinct, dark band on trailing edge of underwings. Upperwing coverts are uniformly dark. Rectrices have rounded tips (both species have broad white terminal band in fall). Use caution on underpart markings: a heavily marked Cooper's Hawk is as heavily streaked as a lightly marked type goshawk. Voice is a nasal *kek, kek* or a soft, nasal *kyew*. (3) **Red-shouldered Hawk, juveniles.**—PERCHED.—Pale supercilium; wide dark malar mark; throat is often dark. Iris color is medium grayish brown: use caution with "brown-eyed" goshawks. Long, thin tarsi. FLIGHT.—Distinct tawny or white crescent-shaped panel on lower and upper surface of outer wing. Outer primaries have five "fingers." *B. l. lineatus* has little if any barring and a gray trailing edge on underside of remiges. Numerous narrow pale tail bands. Voice: *keyair*. (4) **Broad-winged Hawk, light morph juveniles.**—PERCHED.—Pale supercilium and wide dark malar mark. Iris color is medium gray or brown: use caution on "brown-eyed" goshawks. Uniformly dark upperwing coverts. Wingtips almost reach tail tip. Short, thick tarsi and toes. Perch along roadways on poles and wires. FLIGHT.—Underside of remiges has little if any barring; gray trailing edge; three to four "fingers" on the outer primaries. Wingtips are very pointed at all times. Voice: high-pitched *pee-heeeee*. (5) **Gyrfalcon.**— PERCHED.—Dark irises; bare orbital skin in front of eyes. FLIGHT.—Lacks "finger" definition on outer primaries. Wrist is bent at an angle rather than being held in a straight edge when soaring. (5A) **Gray morph juveniles.**— Moderate dark malar distinction. Underparts similarly streaked: use caution. Underside of wing in flight shows faint, narrow dark barring; often darker axillaries, medium coverts. Bluish tarsi and toes.

NORTHERN GOSHAWK, *Accipiter gentilis atricapillus:* Very uncommon. Juveniles, some subadults, and a few adults winter in winter-only range. All ages extend to dashed line during some cyclic irruptions.

COMPARED TO ADULT.—(5B) **Gray morph adults.**—Dark irises. Minimal to moderate dark malar distinct; auricular patch is ill-defined and gray (not black). White underparts have short streaks and spots; barred flanks and leg feathers. Underside of primaries has numerous narrow, faint bars; primaries are paler than secondaries. Undertail coverts have some barring. Numerous narrow, dark and light tail bands.

OTHER NAMES: Goshawk, Gos, Golden Gos. *Spanish*: Gavilán Azor. *French*: Autour des Palombes.

REFERENCES: Andrle and Carroll 1988; Bent 1961; Block et al. 1994; Bohlen 1989;Brauning 1992; Brewer et al. 1991; Brockman 1968; Buckelew and Hall 1994; Burt and Grossenheider 1976; Bylan 1998, 1999; Cadman et al. 1987; Clark and Wheeler 2001; del Hoyo et al. 1994; Dodge 1988–1997; Godfrey 1986; Hall 1993; Howell and Webb 1995; Ingle 1999; Laughlin and Kibbe 1985; Palmer 1988; Reynolds and Wight 1978; Shefferly 1996; Stevenson and Anderson 1994; Veit and Petersen 1993; Walsh al. 1999; Yukon Dept. Renewable Resources 1990.

Plate 193. Northern Goshawk, adult female [Oct.] ▪ Black auricular patch contrasts with supercilium and white cheeks. Orangish red iris. ▪ Bluish gray upperparts. Underparts finely barred with gray; dark, vertical shaft streaks on most feathers. White, often fluffy, undertail coverts. Long, bluish gray tail. ▪ *Note:* Adult males similar but may have more finely marked underparts.

Plate 194. Northern Goshawk, adult male [Oct.] ▪ Black auricular patch contrasts with white supercilium and cheeks. Red iris. ▪ Pale bluish gray upperparts. ▪ Dark brownish black remiges contrast with bluish wing coverts. ▪ Long grayish tail typically unbanded.

Plate 195. Northern Goshawk, adult female
[Oct.] ▪ Black auricular patch contrasts with white supercilium and cheeks. Orangish red iris. ▪ Bluish gray or gray upperparts. ▪ Remiges darker than grayish wing coverts. ▪ Black tail bands; often has white tips on uppertail coverts. ▪ *Note:* Upperparts of adult females often more grayish than on adult males.

Plate 196. Northern Goshawk, adult female
[Oct.] ▪ Black auricular patch contrasts with white supercilium and cheeks. Reddish iris. ▪ Underparts finely barred with gray. ▪ Gray remiges barred (males often barred only on primaries). ▪ Broad black tail bands. ▪ *Note:* Sexes often inseparable when seen from below in flight. Males often appear solid gray on underparts.

Plate 197. Northern Goshawk, subadult male
[Oct.] ▪ Black auricular patch contrasts with white supercilium and gray cheeks. Orange iris. ▪ Bluish gray back and scapulars. Finely barred gray underparts. ▪ Retained brownish juvenile feathers on bluish gray upperwing coverts. Retained juvenile secondaries (s4 and 8). ▪ Grayish tail typically banded.

Plate 198. Northern Goshawk, subadult female
[Oct.] ▪ Black auricular patch contrasts with white supercilium and gray cheeks. Yellowish orange iris. ▪ White underparts coarsely barred with black; each feather has distinct black shaft streak. Upperparts (not shown) dark grayish brown and much darker than in other ages and sexes.

Plate 199. Northern Goshawk, subadult male [Oct.] ▪ White supercilium, black auricular patch. ▪ Bluish gray upperparts with retained brown juvenile feathers on rump. ▪ Retained brown juvenile feathers on wing coverts and secondaries (s4 and 8). ▪ Gray banded tail fully molted into subadult age class.

Plate 200. Northern Goshawk, subadult male [Oct.] ▪ Black auriculars contrast with white supercilium and grayish cheeks. Orangish red iris. ▪ Underparts barred with gray. Some subadult males have extensive black markings on breast. ▪ Barred, gray remiges are fully subadult feathers. ▪ Wedge-shaped tail.

Plate 201. Northern Goshawk, juvenile [Oct.] ▪ Tawny head and hindneck; brown auricular patch; white supercilium; orangish yellow iris. ▪ Medium brown upperparts edged with tawny or white and blotched with white. ▪ White or tawny bar on greater and sometimes median upperwing coverts. ▪ Thin white lines border irregular black tail bands. Pointed rectrix tips.

Plate 202. Northern Goshawk, juvenile [Sep.] ▪ Tawny head and neck; brown auricular patch; partial, dark malar mark; orangish yellow iris. Supercilium sometimes indistinct. ▪ Moderately streaked tawny underparts. Large, brown, diamond-shaped marks on undertail coverts. ▪ Wedge-shaped tail. Pointed rectrix tips.

Plate 203. Northern Goshawk, juvenile [Oct.] ▪
White supercilium; brown auricular patch; partial,
dark malar mark. ▪ White bar on greater and
some median upperwing coverts.

Plate 204. Northern Goshawk, juvenile [Oct.] ▪
Partial, dark malar mark. ▪ Heavily streaked underparts. Arrowhead-shaped dark marks on all
undertail coverts. ▪ Dark wavy bands on outer
primaries and secondaries. Wide dusky band on
trailing edge of remiges. ▪ Pointed rectrix tips. ▪
Note: Heavily marked type plumage.

Plate 205. Northern Goshawk, juvenile [Oct.] ▪
Dark malar mark. ▪ Moderately streaked underparts. Dark marks on undertail coverts. ▪ Wavy
bands on outer primaries and secondaries. Wide
black band on trailing edge of remiges. ▪ Wedge-
shaped tail with pointed rectrix tips. ▪ *Note:* Moderately marked type plumage.

**Plate 206. Northern Goshawk, juvenile (lightly
marked type) [Oct.]** ▪ White supercilium and
partial, dark malar mark. ▪ White underparts narrowly streaked on flanks, breast, and belly; unmarked lower belly and leg feathers. Unmarked,
white undertail coverts. ▪ Irregular dark tail
bands. Pointed rectrices. ▪ *Note:* Palest plumage.
Ventral markings, including pale underwing
coverts, rival pale-marked juvenile Cooper's
Hawks. Sexed as female by size.

RED-SHOULDERED HAWK
(Buteo lineatus)

AGES: Adult and juvenile. Sexes are similar in both age classes, but in adults females are often more distinctly marked. Adult plumage attained during the second year. Juvenile plumage is held for much of the first year. Juveniles have longer tails than adults.

MOLT: Accipitridae wing and tail molt pattern (*see* chapter 4). The first prebasic molt begins on the breast, then is noticeable on the back and scapulars. Molt proceeds to the remiges beginning on the innermost primary (p1). Molt on secondaries and rectrices begins somewhat later. Unlike in other similar-sized raptors, the first prebasic molt is generally a complete molt.

Resident southern birds from s. and cen. Florida may begin the first prebasic molt in mid-Nov. as seen with incoming new breast feathers. Northern birds do not begin the molt until mid- or late Apr. On southern birds, molt into adult plumage reaches the halfway point by late May and ends by Sep. or Oct. On northern birds, molt ends by Oct. or Nov.

Subsequent adult prebasic molts begin later than the first prebasic molt for the respective latitude. Adults from southern latitudes do not begin until May or Jun., are in extensive molt in early Aug., and complete molt in Sep. or Oct. Adults in middle and northern latitudes are in extensive molt in mid-Sep. and complete their molt by late Oct. or Nov. Much of the body molts prior to the start of head molt. This is clearly seen on *B. l. extimus*, which may have a totally worn, white head, but darker, fresh body plumage in early Aug.

SUBSPECIES: Polytypic with four races in North America. Three races inhabit the e. U.S. and se. Canada. Adjacent subspecies have a broad zone of overlap. Specific demarcation of each subspecies' breeding range is somewhat unclear, particularly in the western part of the East. Nominate "Eastern" race, *B. l. lineatus*, is widespread in the East in the cen. and n. U.S. and se. Canada. "Southern" race, *B. l. alleni*, is found south of *lineatus*. "South Florida" race, *B. l. extimus*, is found south of *alleni* in the southern half of the Florida peninsula.

In the West, *B. l. lineatus* breeds in e. Iowa, se. Kansas, e. and cen. Minnesota, and e. and s. Missouri. *B. l. alleni* breeds in Arkansas, Louisiana, Oklahoma, and Texas. The range demarcation between *lineatus* and *alleni* is unclear in the West. *B. l. alleni* breeding range herein follows, in part, the AOU 5th check-list (1957) and extends north and west of previously published range data in Johnsgard 1990 and Crocoll 1994. I consider *B. l. texanus* as part of *alleni*. The brilliance of adult plumage varies throughout *texanus* and *alleni* breeding ranges, including *alleni* range in the East, and juveniles of the two types are identical (data from Clark and Wheeler 2001; museum specimens and photos; photos by J. M. Economidy). According to the *Texas Breeding Bird Atlas* (Benson and Arnold 2001), Red-shouldered Hawk does not breed in much of the previously published *texanus* range in s. Texas. It also does not breed in e. Mexico (Howell and Webb 1995). *B. l. elegans* is found from cen. Baja California, Mexico, throughout California and to sw. Oregon. *Elegans* is expanding north and east of historical range. *Note:* Based on anatomical and genetic similarities with Gray Hawk (formerly *Buteo nitidus*), Palmer (1988) assigned Red-shoulder Hawk to the genus *Asturina*. Gray Hawk was assigned to the genus *Asturina*, as *Asturina nitidus* (AOU 1997), but Red-shouldered Hawk was retained in *Buteo*.

COLOR MORPHS: None.

SIZE: Medium-sized raptor. Size decreases clinically from north to south: *B. l. lineatus* is the largest, *B. l. alleni* is mid-size, and *B. l. extimus* is the smallest of the Northern American races. Sizes of adjacent races are difficult to detect in the field and overlap. Sexes overlap in size, with females averaging larger. Wing-chord length in millimeters for each race according to Palmer (1988): lineatus.—male 309–346, female 315–353; alleni.—male 284–330, female 281–340; extimus.—male 278–291, female 299–305. Total length and wingspan measurements, however, are not available for each race. Length: 15–19 in. (38–48 cm); wingspan: 37–42 in. (94–119 cm).

SPECIES TRAITS: HEAD.—**Distal three-fourths of the bill is black and the basal one-fourth is pale blue.** Bright yellow cere.

BODY.—Long yellow tarsi. WINGS.—Pale crescent-shaped panel on the dorsal surface and a pale crescent-shaped window on the ventral surface of the basal region of the outer primaries. Wingtips are fairly rounded, with p6–9 being nearly the same length. **ADULT TRAITS:** HEAD.—Dark brown irises. The crown and nape feathers are long and can be raised to create a large-headed appearance. **The hackles are long and spikelike when raised.** BODY.—Narrow rufous barring is equal in width to the white or tawny portion on each feather. Breast often has wider rufous barring and may be solid rufous and form a variably distinct "bib" compared to the barred belly and flanks. WINGS (dorsal).—**Large, dark rufous shoulder patch on the lesser upperwing coverts. White barring on the black greater upperwing coverts and secondaries. The white panel on the basal region of the black outer primaries is composed of white barring.** WINGS (ventral).—**The white remiges have a wide black band on the trailing edge and are totally barred on the inner area.** When backlit in translucent light, the white panel of the dorsal surface shows as a white crescent-shaped window on the ventral surface. The underwing coverts and axillaries are tawny with rufous streaking and barring and appear two-toned compared to the white and barred remiges. TAIL.—**Black on the dorsal surface and dark gray on the ventral surface with a white terminal band and narrow white inner bands. All races have three narrow white bands on dorsal surface on the deck rectrices.** On the ventral surface, only one white band shows when the tail is closed; four or five show when the tail is fanned.

ADULTS OF "EASTERN" (*B. l. lineatus*): HEAD.—Dark brown crown and nape with a paler tawny supercilium and auricular region. Distinct dark malar mark on the lower jaw. Throat is all white, white and streaked with dark brown, or dark brown. BODY (dorsal).—Dark brown with a small amount of medium grayish and rufous on the outer edge and inner pale bar on the back and scapular feathers. BODY (ventral).—**Dark shaft streaks on the breast and dark shaft streaks or blobs on the belly and flank feathers are the classic feature of this subspecies. Females exhibit this feature more than males. Some males lack the**

dark markings (and appear similar to *alleni*). In autumn, the ventral feathers are new and fresh and are medium or dark rufous. By spring, the ventral barring bleaches and fades to pale rufous or tawny (if present in the autumn, dark markings are still visible). Leg feathers are white or pale tawny and marked with thin rufous barring. The undertail coverts are white or pale tawny and are typically unmarked but may have some rufous bars. *Note:* Generally separable from other races by the dark ventral markings. If these are not present, as on many males, *lineatus* cannot be safely separated from *alleni*.

Adult female (atypically barred type): HEAD, BODY (dorsal), WINGS, and TAIL as on typical adults. BODY (ventral).—Breast and belly are white with broad rufous streaks and blotches with some partial rufous bars. Often has fairly wide dark shaft streaks and blotches as on typical adults. Flanks may have widely spaced rufous bars. At a distance, this type looks more streaked and spotted and not barred as a typical adult. *Note:* Uncommon to very uncommon type.

ADULTS OF "SOUTHERN" (*B. l. alleni*): HEAD.—The crown and nape can be dark brown and identical to *lineatus* or medium gray and slightly paler, particularly on birds from n. Florida. Some may have medium brown crown and nape and slightly or much paler tawny, grayish, or whitish supercilium and auricular region and appear very pale headed. Dark malar mark is obvious on dark-headed types, less obvious on pale-headed types. Throat is like the three variations described for *lineatus*. *Note:* Females tend to have darker heads. Pale-headed birds may nearly rival the head color of *extimus*. BODY (dorsal).—Dark brown with a moderate amount of medium grayish and rufous on the outer edge and inner pale bar on the back and scapular feathers. BODY (ventral).—**The rufous-barred underparts lack dark streaks or blobs.** At most, the breast, belly, and flanks have very thin dark shaft streaks on some feathers. The rufous-barred underparts may be medium or dark rufous in fresh late-summer and autumn plumage but fade to pale or medium rufous or tawny by winter or spring. Leg feathers and undertail coverts are marked as on *lineatus*. *Note:* Separable from *lineatus* that have dark ventral markings but not separable from those that lack dark markings. Pale-headed birds are similar to some *extimus*.

ADULTS OF "SOUTH FLORIDA" (*B. l. extimus*):
HEAD.—Pale to very pale-headed. Females tend to have darker, more brownish heads. Crown is typically pale gray with narrow dark brown streaking but may be pale brown with dark brown streaking. The nape may be somewhat tawny or brownish on all birds. Supercilium and auricular regions are whitish and often paler than the crown and nape. Males, in particular, may have very pale gray heads. On very pale gray-headed birds, the supercilium and auricular regions and crown and nape blend as a uniformly pale gray unit. Dark malar mark is absent or is very faint. Throat is white and unmarked. In summer, the head becomes exceptionally worn and faded and appears nearly white; however, body plumage is much darker. BODY (dorsal).—Dark or medium brown with extensive pale grayish and rufous on the outer edge and inner pale bar on the back and scapular feathers. The inner feather bar on the distal scapulars may be white. *Note:* Upperparts bleach and fade to a paler tone from the fresh late-summer and fall plumage. BODY (ventral).—When freshly molted, ventral barring is pale or medium rufous (and as dark as on many *alleni* and *lineatus*). Because of extreme bleaching and fading, the pale or medium rufous barring fades to pale or very pale tawny by winter and spring. The breasts on some birds may almost turn grayish from extreme bleaching and fading. Dark ventral streaking is absent or there are only thin dark shaft streaks on some feathers. Leg feathers are white with thin rufous barring. Undertail coverts are white and unmarked. WINGS (dorsal).—Even though the body plumage often undergoes extreme bleaching and fading, the rufous upperwing coverts, which are protected from the elements by the overlapping scapulars when a bird is perched, remain fairly dark rufous. WINGS (ventral).—The tawny-rufous underwing coverts also remain fairly dark since they are not subject to bleaching and fading by the sun.

JUVENILE TRAITS: HEAD.—Dark brown crown and nape with a pale tawny or whitish supercilium. Dark brown malar mark on the lower jaw. Irises are medium brown. BODY (dorsal).—

Dark brown with a few irregular tawny or white blotches on the basal area of some scapular feathers. WINGS (dorsal).—**Pale crescent-shaped panel on the basal region of the outer primaries. Pale gray or white barring on the dark brown secondaries.** Rufous patch on the lesser upperwing coverts is typically ill-defined and rarely shows in the field, particularly when perched. WINGS (ventral).—**Pale panel of the dorsal surface shows as a pale window on the underwing in translucent light.**

JUVENILES OF "EASTERN" (*B. l. lineatus*):
HEAD.—**Throat is (1) white with a broad mid-throat streak, (2) white and streaked, or (3) all dark with a narrow white edge on each side. Birds with a dark throat appear hooded.** BODY (ventral).—Pale tawny or white underparts. The breast, belly, and flanks are marked with large dark brown blobs or short streaks. The lower belly has fewer dark markings or is unmarked. Leg feathers are typically unmarked, but a few birds have very small dark spots or small partial bars, particularly birds inhabiting the southern edge of range (and picking up *alleni* traits). Undertail coverts are unmarked. WINGS (dorsal).—**Crescent-shaped panel is pale tawny. The secondaries typically have pale gray barring, but this may be absent on a few birds.** WINGS (ventral).—White remiges have a moderately wide dusky trailing edge and narrow dark barring on most of the rest of the inner remiges. **The crescent-shaped panel shows as a pale tawny area in translucent light.** The panel may have some dark barring on it. The outer primaries may be uniformly dark or superimposed with darker partial barring. TAIL (dorsal).—**Dark brown with a wide dark subterminal band and five or six narrow pale bands. The distal three or four pale bands are pale gray, the basal one to three pale bands typically rufous. The distal pale band is slightly darker gray than the other pale gray bands.** TAIL (ventral).—Medium gray with narrow pale gray inner bands. The basal rufous bands show when the tail is fanned and viewed in translucent light. *Note:* Separable from *alleni* and *extimus* by absence of leg and flank barring and unbarred, dark blob pattern on ventral areas.

JUVENILES OF "SOUTHERN" (*B. l. alleni*):
HEAD.—As on *lineatus,* with the same three variations of throat markings. BODY (ven-

tral).—Pale tawny or white underparts. Breast and belly have dark brown heart- or arrowhead-shaped markings that may be barred on the inner part of the feather. These markings may elongate into streaks. The lower belly has fewer similar-shaped but smaller dark markings. The flanks have broad, widely spaced dark brown barring. The leg feathers are lightly or moderately barred with dark brown. Undertail coverts are pale tawny or white and either unmarked or partially barred. WINGS.—Dorsal and ventral surfaces are marked as on *lineatus*, but pale barring on the secondaries is consistently more pronounced and is often white. Rarely has a whitish panel on the dorsal surface of the primaries. Dark barring may be more pronounced than on *lineatus*, especially on the tawny panel and outer primaries. Nearly always has pale gray or white barring on the dorsal surface of the secondaries. TAIL.—As on *lineatus*; however, the basal rufous bands are absent on many birds and pale bands are pale gray. *Note:* Separable from *lineatus* by presence of leg barring and flank barring. Not readily separable from *extimus* but usually more heavily marked on ventral areas and tawny wing panel. **JUVENILES OF "SOUTH FLORIDA" (*B. l. extimus*):** HEAD.—As on *lineatus* and *alleni*, but the throat is more likely to be white with a dark mid-throat streak. BODY (ventral).—Pale tawny or white underparts. **The breast is typically heavily streaked with dark brown, and the belly is much more lightly marked with short streaks, small dark spots, or arrowhead shapes. The more heavily marked breast often appears as a bib. The flanks may be sparsely barred or marked as the belly but are still more lightly marked than the breast.** Leg feathers are lightly barred with brown. WINGS.—**Most have a white panel on the dorsal surface of the primaries; a few may have a tawny panel. Has the identical pale gray or white barring on the secondaries as** *lineatus* and *alleni*. TAIL.—**Narrow pale tail bands are typically gray; rarely has rufous basal bands.** *Note:* Separable from *lineatus* and most *alleni* by white wing panels; otherwise very similar to *alleni* but usually less heavily marked on ventral areas.
ABNORMAL PLUMAGES: Albino and partial albino birds have been documented in the East.
HABITAT: *B. l. lineatus*. Summer.—Lowland

wooded floodplains with mature deciduous trees and swamps and marshes adjacent to mature deciduous or mixed deciduous-coniferous woodlands. Higher elevation upland, mature deciduous or mixed deciduous-coniferous woodlands with areas of water are also inhabited. This race is becoming fairly common in suburban locales adjacent to or in ample-sized, moist woodlots. Suburban pairs have been regular in the southern half of the range, particularly in the Mid-Atlantic coastal region, but are now a regular occurrence in the northern half of the range.
***B. l. lineatus*. Winter.**—May remain in summer habitat or occasionally move to semi-open areas in wet or sometimes dry locations. These include forest or woodlot edges and along clear-cut shoulder areas of highways. Backyards of rural and suburban areas that have birdfeeders are occasionally haunted.
***B. l. lineatus*. Migration.**—Similar to summer and winter habitats, but also includes mountain ridges, large lakes, and seashores.
***B. l. alleni*. All seasons.**—Similar to habitat of *lineatus*. This is a common raptor in suburban areas that have proper habitat, particularly in the southern part of its range. In winter, commonly found in semi-open wet or dry areas. Water-filled irrigation and drainage ditches and flooded weedy fields and rice fields are regularly used.
***B. l. extimus*. All seasons.**—Found in wet lowland areas. Inhabits forested and semi-open areas in the breeding season and often forages in open areas in the nonbreeding season. Suburban areas are regularly used in all seasons.
HABITS: *B. l. lineatus* is wary but occasionally fairly tame, *alleni* is fairly tame or tame, and *extimus* is tame. Head feathers, including the pointed hackles, are raised in cool temperatures. Any elevated perch is used, including utility-pole wires. During breeding season, high, open perches may be selected. When foraging, low, open perches are used. *B. l. alleni* and *extimus*, in particular, seek sheltered perches during hot periods of the day.
FEEDING: Mainly a perch hunter but an occasional aerial hunter. Perch hunting primarily occurs from a low or moderate-height perch in which bird drops down in a low, direct flight; also done by walking on the ground. Aerial hunting takes place when the bird is flying and

a prey species happens to be in its path. Red-shouldered Hawks are generalist feeders, and diet varies with geographic region and season. Small mammals, amphibians, reptiles, and invertebrates (especially crayfish) form the bulk of the diet. Small birds, fish, and insects are occasionally preyed on. Carrion is occasionally eaten.

FLIGHT: Powered flight consists of a fairly regular series of moderately fast wingbeats interspersed with short glides. Soaring flight occurs regularly, particularly when courting or migrating. Wings are held on a flat plane when soaring and arched downwards when gliding. Long, impressive dives are made in courtship flights. Red-shouldered Hawks rarely hover or kite.

VOICE: A highly vocal raptor. Vocalizes regularly at any time of year. The most commonly heard call is a drawn-out, loud, sharp *kee-yair* or *kee-aah*. It may be repeated numerous times and is used to establish territories or give alarm. A sharp *kip* note is emitted when excited or alarmed and may be a single or repeated note. *Keeyip* is a variation of the *kip* note. Courting birds emit a loud, drawn-out, three-syllable *kee-ann-err*; a short, squeaky *kee-aah*; or a high-pitched *scree*. This vocalization may also be repeated many times and may be altered to a *kee-yerr* or *kendrick* sound. A soft, repeated *kee* may be given by brooding or incubating females.

STATUS AND DISTRIBUTION: Estimated population is unknown. Population is probably stable. However, all three eastern subspecies have experienced population declines from historical times. Wetland drainage, deforestation, and urbanization are responsible for most habitat loss. Wetlands are now more carefully managed, and forests in many regions are growing to maturity height. The altered habitat also increases competition with larger and dominant Red-tailed Hawks and Great Horned Owls.

B. l. lineatus. **Summer.**—*Uncommon.* Densest population is probably in the eastern half of its range. Extensive areas of Illinois, Indiana, Kentucky, Michigan, New Jersey, Ohio, and Wisconsin are agricultural lands and lack suitable nesting habitat. Isolated breeding occurs near Halifax, N.S. Listed as Endangered in Illinois and New Jersey; Threatened in Michigan, New York, and Wisconsin; of Special Concern in Connecticut and Indiana; and is on a watch list in Maine and Massachusetts. Ontario considers it rare; population declines occurred there in the early 1900s and numbers had declined considerably by the 1930s because of habitat loss.

B. l. lineatus. **Winter.**—The northern third of breeding range is typically vacated. A few regularly winter in s. Nova Scotia. Irregular extralimital wintering has occurred in ne. New Brunswick and nw. Nova Scotia. Rarely winters south of cen. Florida. At least to s. New England, adults may remain on or near breeding territories.

B. l. lineatus. **Movements.**—Northern populations are migratory and move short or moderate distances. Southern populations may remain sedentary or move short distances. Concentrations occur in spring and fall along Lakes Erie and Ontario. Concentrations occur in the fall along the Mid-Atlantic region and n. Appalachian Mts:

Fall migration: Juveniles move before adults. Along the north shore of Lake Erie, Mid-Atlantic Coast, and n. Appalachian Mts., juveniles may be seen in early Sep., but numbers do not increase until early Oct. Peak numbers of juveniles occur in mid- to late Oct. and taper off by early Nov. In the same regions, adults first appear in mid-Oct. and peak along Lake Erie in early Nov. and along the Mid-Atlantic and Appalachian regions in mid-Nov. Adults straggle past Lake Erie through Nov. and into Dec. A few adults keep moving along the Appalachians until Dec., but decent numbers keep moving along the coast well into Dec.

Spring migration: Adults move before juveniles. Very small numbers occur along the south shore of Lake Superior, small numbers along the Mid-Atlantic region, and sizable numbers along the south shore of Lake Ontario. Adults are first seen in the Mid-Atlantic region in mid-Feb. and peak in early to mid-Mar. Adults appear along Lake Ontario in early Mar. and may peak as early as mid-Mar., but usually not until late Mar. Along the south shore of Lake Superior, the first adults appear in late Mar., but numbers are so low that peaks rarely occur. A few juveniles accompany the adult movement, but most juveniles do not appear in numbers until Apr. Peak movement in all areas is in mid-Apr. with stragglers occurring until early May along the Mid-Atlantic and mid-May along Lakes Ontario and Superior.

B. l. alleni. **Summer.**—*Common.* Listed as a Special Concern species in Mississippi. On its northern boundary intergrades with *lineatus*; on its southern boundary, with *extimus.*

B. l. alleni. **Winter.**—Adults are mainly resident, but some may winter farther south. Juveniles may winter south of natal areas and commonly reach s. Florida.

B. l. alleni. **Movements.**—Probably sedentary or a short-distance migrant. Juveniles disperse out of natal territories. Individuals embarking on short migrations probably move a bit later than *lineatus* in the fall and earlier in the spring.

B. l. extimus. **All seasons.**—*Common.* Sedentary. Intergrades with *alleni* in cen. Florida between Orlando and Lake Okeechobee. Juveniles disperse out of natal territories, and adults may shift to new breeding territories.

NESTING: *B. l. lineatus* begin nesting in Feb. in the southern latitudes and in Mar. or Apr. in northern latitudes and end in Jun. or Jul. *B. l. alleni* begin nesting in Jan. or Feb. and end in May or Jun. *B. l. extimus* begin nesting as early as Nov. but usually in Dec. or Jan. and end in May or Jun. The southern races, *extimus* and *alleni*, begin nesting while *lineatus* is still on the winter grounds.

One-year-old females adorned in juvenile plumage may pair with adult males. Most do not breed until at least 2 years old when in full adult plumage.

Courtship (flight).—*High-circling* and *leg-dangling* by both sexes and *sky-dancing* by males. Pairs are highly vocal in courtship flights.

Both sexes build or refurbish nests. Nests may be used for several years; and a few unused nests may be in territories. Old leafy squirrel nests or nests of other birds may be used as platforms for new nests. Heights of nests vary from 20 to 62 ft. (6–19 m). *B. l. extimus* nests are often on the lower end of the height spectrum. Nests are placed in a main crotch of mainly deciduous trees. If coniferous trees are used, nests are placed next to the trunk. *B. l. alleni* and *extimus* nests may be in Palmetto Palms. Live trees are always used for nest sites.

Both sexes build the compact and sturdy nests, which are 18–24 in. (46–61 cm) wide and 8–12 in. (20–30 cm) deep. Greenery lines the nests. The 2–3 eggs are incubated primarily by the female for about 33 days. Male performs some incubation duty but mainly provides food to female. Youngsters fledge when about 35–45 days old. Fledglings stay with parents for a few more weeks, then leave natal areas. A single brood is raised each year.

CONSERVATION: No direct measures are taken. Saving moist, mature woodlands and woodlots is essential to maintaining and increasing the current population. Creation of wooded wetlands creates new habitat. Maturing moist woodlands and woodlots in natural, rural, and suburban areas also create new habitat.

Mortality.—Mainly suffers from natural causes, especially predation by Great Horned Owls. Illegal shooting occurs, and a few are hit by vehicles.

SIMILAR SPECIES: COMPARED TO ADULTS.—**(1) Broad-winged Hawk, adults.**—PERCHED.—Iris is orangish brown. Rufous ventral barring is typically more brownish and coarsely patterned. Dorsal surface of wing is uniformly brown. Has single broad white or pale gray dorsal tail band or additional narrower pale band. FLIGHT.—Underside of basal region of outer primaries white and unmarked; narrow black barring on secondaries. Tail as in Perched. Voice is a high-pitched whistle, *pee-hee.* **(2) Northern Harrier, juveniles.**—FLIGHT.—At a long distance the uniformly colored tawny-rufous belly and flanks can appear similar to the rufous barring of a Red-shouldered Hawk. The dark brown median coverts and axillaries on the Northern Harrier easily separate from a Red-shouldered Hawk. COMPARED TO JUVENILES.—**(3) Northern Goshawk, juveniles.**—PERCHED.—Pale gray iris of recently fledged birds is similar; in the fall iris is yellowish orange. Dark malar mark is absent or ill defined. Undertail coverts may have large dark marks but are never barred as on some *B. l. alleni.* Tail has three to four equal-width dark bands. FLIGHT.—Pale throat with a single dark mid-throat streak. Dark barring on the underside of the outer primaries is broad and prominent; sometimes exhibits similar pale window in translucent light on the basal areas of the outer primaries. Tail as described in Perched. **(4) Broad-winged Hawk, juveniles.**—PERCHED.—Throat is white with a single

"EASTERN" RED-SHOULDERED HAWK, *Buteo lineatus lineatus:* Uncommon. Expanding range north into Maritimes. Very uncommon in s. FL in winter. Adults mainly resident at least to CT.

dark mid-throat streak. Leg feathers are unmarked as on *B. l. lineatus,* or spotted or thickly barred and not thinly barred with brown as on *alleni* and *extimus.* Dorsal surface of secondaries is uniformly dark brown. Dorsal tail is medium brown with narrow dark bars. FLIGHT.—Throat as described in Perched. Large rectangular window on primaries and

upperside is uniformly brown. When soaring, tail is pale with several narrow dark bars. (**5**) **Red-tailed Hawk, juveniles.**—PERCHED.—*B. j. borealis* and light morph *B. j. calurus* have pale gray or yellow irises, white unmarked breasts, dark barred dorsal surface of secondaries, and numerous narrow dark tail bands. Intermediate morph *calurus* has similar streaked

"SOUTHERN" RED-SHOULDERED HAWK, *Buteo lineatus alleni:* Common. Mainly resident, but some winter in s. FL. The subspecies border with "Eastern" race is not fully understood.

breast but dark belly. FLIGHT.—Large rectangular window on underside of primaries and upperside is pale brown and contrasts with the darker secondaries and inner half of the wing. Tail is pale brown with numerous, narrow dark bands.

OTHER NAMES: Redshoulder, Shoulder. *Spanish:* Aguililla Pechirrojo, Aguililla Pecho Rojo, Gavilán Ranero. *French:* Buse à Épaulettes.

REFERENCES: Andrle and Carroll 1988; AOU 1957, 1997; Arnold 2001; Baicich and Harrison 1997; Benson and Arnold 2001; Bohlen 1989; Brauning 1992; Brewer et al. 1991; Buckelew and Hall 1994; Bylan 1998, 1999; Cadman et al. 1987; Castrale et al. 1998; Clark and Wheeler 2001; Crocoll 1994; DeLorme Publishers 1991a, 1991b, 1995; Dodge 1988–1997; Erskine 1992; Godfrey 1986; Howell and Webb 1995; Johnsgard 1990; Kale et al. 1992; Kellogg 2000; Laughlin and Kibbe 1985; Mumford and Keller 1984; Nicholson 1997; Palmer 1988; Palmer-Ball 1996; Peterjohn and Rice 1991; Robbins 1996; Walsh et al. 1999; Wheeler and Clark 1995.

"SOUTH FLORIDA" RED-SHOULDERED HAWK, *Buteo lineatus extimus:* Common throughout s. FL. Intergrades with "Southern" race at northern edge of range. Resident.

Plate 207. Red-shouldered Hawk, adult "Eastern" (*B. l. lineatus*) [Dec.] ▪ Dark brown iris. Brown head; tawny supercilium and auriculars. ▪ Medium to dark rufous, thinly barred underparts; breast may be solid rufous bib. Dark shaft streaks or blobs on many ventral feathers are unique to *lineatus* but lacking on many males. Underparts fade by spring.

Plate 208. Red-shouldered Hawk, adult "Southern" (*B. l. alleni*) [Feb.] ▪ Dark brown iris. Tawny-brown head. ▪ Medium to dark rufous, thinly barred underparts; breast may be solid rufous bib. Ventral areas lack dark markings; inseparable from many *lineatus* males. ▪ White checkering on black wings. ▪ Single white band shows on closed tail. ▪ *Note:* Female of mated pair.

Plate 209. Red-shouldered Hawk, adult "Southern" (*B. l. alleni*) [Nov.] ▪ Dark brown iris. Brown head with pale supercilium and auriculars. ▪ Medium to dark rufous, thinly barred underparts; breast more heavily barred. ▪ Black wings checkered with white. ▪ Single white band shows on closed tail.

Plate 210. Red-shouldered Hawk, adult "South Florida" (*B. l. extimus*) [Nov.] ▪ Dark brown iris. Pale grayish head; brownish on nape. ▪ Medium to pale, thinly barred rufous underparts lack dark shaft markings. ▪ Rufous shoulder patch usually hidden. White checkering on black wings. ▪ Black tail has 3 white bands. ▪ *Note:* Female of mated pair.

Plate 211. Red-shouldered Hawk, adult "South Florida" (*B. l. extimus*) [May] ▪ Dark brown iris. Pale grayish or whitish head. ▪ Pale, thinly barred rufous underparts. Long tarsi. ▪ Rufous shoulder shows if not hidden by scapulars. White checkering on black wings. ▪ Black tail has 3 white bands. ▪ *Note:* Head and underparts quite pale by late winter and spring because of fading.

Plate 212. Red-shouldered Hawk, adult "Eastern" (*B. l. lineatus*) [Jan.] ▪ Black-and-white checkered wing with distinct, white-checkered, crescent-shaped panels near tips of primaries. Rufous shoulders. ▪ Black tail has 3 narrow white bands.

Plate 213. Red-shouldered Hawk, adult "Eastern" (*B. l. lineatus*) [Mar.] ▪ Brown head. ▪ Uniformly rufous-barred underparts with large black streaks or blobs unique to this race. ▪ Barred remiges with black-and-white-barred, crescent-shaped panel near tips of primaries. ▪ Single white tail band. ▪ *Note:* Photo by Jerry Liguori.

Plate 214. Red-shouldered Hawk, adult "Southern" (*B. l. alleni*) [Feb.] ▪ Solid dark rufous bib, rufous-barred belly, flanks, and leg feathers. ▪ Black-and-white-barred remiges; barred, white panel shows on left wing. Panels do not show if light is not at correct angle. ▪ Black tail with 1 full band, 1 partial band. ▪ *Note:* Same bird as on plate 208. Some adult male *lineatus* are similar.

Plate 215. Red-shouldered Hawk, adult "South Florida" (*B. l. extimus*) [Nov.] ▪ Pale head. ▪ Solid medium-rufous bib, rufous-barred belly, flanks, and leg feathers. ▪ Black-and-white-barred remiges; barred, white panel shows on left wing. ▪ Up to 3 narrow white tail bands show when tail is fanned.

Plate 216. Red-shouldered Hawk, adult "Southern" (*B. l. alleni*) [Feb.] ▪ Wings held in a bowed position when gliding. ▪ *Note:* Carrying crayfish in bill.

Plate 217. Red-shouldered Hawk, juvenile "Southern" (*B. l. alleni*) [Jan.] ▪ Medium brown iris. Throat often dark. ▪ Flanks barred with brown. ▪ Pale gray barring on secondaries. Rufous shoulder barely shows on juveniles. ▪ Narrow pale tail bands: basal pale bands may be rufous. ▪ *Note: B. l. lineatus* (not shown perched) similar but streaked or spotted on flanks.

Plate 218. Red-shouldered Hawk, juvenile "Southern" (*B. l. alleni*) [Jan.] ▪ Brown head with paler supercilium and auriculars. Medium brown iris. Throat often dark. ▪ Streaked or partially barred breast, spotted belly, and barred flanks. Leg feathers (not shown) finely barred. ▪ *Note:* Same bird as on pale 217.

Plate 219. Red-shouldered Hawk, juvenile "South Florida" (*B. l. extimus*) [Nov.] ▪ Brown head with paler supercilium and auriculars. Medium brown iris. Throat often dark. ▪ Brown upperparts. ▪ Pale gray barring on secondaries. ▪ Long, brown tail has narrow, pale gray bands (rarely rufous bands on basal area).

Plate 220. Red-shouldered Hawk, juvenile "South Florida" (*B. l. extimus*) [Nov.] ▪ Brown head with paler supercilium and auriculars. Medium brown iris. Throat often dark. ▪ Streaked to partially barred breast often forms bib with lightly marked spotted belly and spotted/barred flanks. Leg feathers (not shown) finely barred with brown. ▪ Pale grayish barring on secondaries.

Plate 221. Red-shouldered Hawk, juvenile "Southern" (*B. l. alleni*) [**Nov.**] ▪ Medium brown iris. Throat often dark. ▪ Brown-barred underparts. Finely barred leg feathers. ▪ Tawny crescent-shape panel on outer 6 primaries. Pale gray barring on secondaries. Rufous shoulder barely shows. ▪ Pale gray bands on tail. ▪ *Note: B. l. lineatus* has identical tawny panel on wings.

Plate 222. Red-shouldered Hawk, juvenile "Eastern" (*B. l. lineatus*) [**Oct.**] ▪ Brown head and throat ▪ Brown streaks or blobs on underparts; leg feathers nearly always unmarked. ▪ Tawny, crescent-shaped window on base of outer 6 primaries. Inner primaries and all secondaries barred. ▪ Numerous narrow, pale gray tail bands; often rufous bands on basal area.

Plate 223. Red-shouldered Hawk, juvenile "South Florida" (*B. l. extimus*) [**Nov.**] ▪ Thick dark midthroat stripe. ▪ Heavily marked breast creates bib; flanks and belly less heavily spotted and partially barred. Finely barred leg feathers. ▪ Most *extimus* and very few *alleni* or *lineatus* have white-barred, crescent-shaped panels (top)/windows (bottom). ▪ Numerous narrow, pale tail bands.

BROAD-WINGED HAWK
(Buteo platypterus)

AGES: Adult, subadult, and juvenile. Many individuals retain a few juvenile feathers and are considered a basic I (subadult I) age. Juvenile plumage is retained the first year. Juveniles have distinctly longer tails than adults and subadults, but the width of their wings is similar to older ages.

MOLT: Accipitridae wing and tail molt pattern (*see* chapter 4). Rapid, fairly complete first prebasic molt from juvenile to subadult and/or adult occurs May–Oct. Molt is first visible early to mid-May with a gap at the primary-secondary junction caused by the dropped innermost primary (p1). Primary molt may be complete, or may be incomplete and retain the outer one to three juvenile feathers (p8–10). The deck rectrices (r1) begin molt shortly after primaries start to molt. Tail molt is mainly complete by late Sep. and rarely retains a juvenile rectrix set. Secondaries begin molt soon after inner primaries and central rectrices have begun molt. A few juvenile secondaries may be retained (s4 and 8; occasionally s3, 4, 8, and 9). A few juvenile upperwing coverts also may be retained. Rump molt may be incomplete and retain old, faded brown juvenile feathers into the subadult age. Any retained juvenile feathering is retained until the next prebasic molt the following early summer. *Note:* It is unknown if all 1-year-olds retain remnant juvenile feathering. A substantial number of individuals show retained juvenile feathering during fall and spring migration periods.

Subsequent prebasic molts from subadult to adult and within adults are also rapid and fairly complete. Molt begins in Jun. and ends Sep.–Oct. During fall migration, retained old feathers are often visible on the upperwing coverts and sometimes outer three primaries (p8–10, sometimes p7–10) and a secondary (s4, possibly more).

There is massive feather replacement in Jun. and Jul. in all prebasic molts. Birds appear exceptionally ratty, particularly in the first prebasic molt.

SUBSPECIES: Polytypic with six races. *B. p. platypterus* is the only race in North America.

Five additional subspecies that originated from *platypterus* are on islands in the Caribbean: (1) *B. p. cubanensis* in Cuba; (2) *B. p. brunnescens* in Puerto Rico; (3) *B. p. insulicola* in Antigua and Barbados; (4) *B. p. rivieri* in Dominica, St. Lucia, and Martinique; and (5) *B. p. antillarum* in Grenada, the Grenadines, St. Vincent, and Trinidad and Tobago.

COLOR MORPHS: Polymorphic with two color morphs: light and dark. There are no intermediate morphs. *B. p. platypterus* is the only race with color morphs. *Tail patterns of both color morphs are identical for the respective age classes.* Adult light morph has considerable variation on ventral markings. Juveniles exhibit variable markings on the ventral surface of the body and on the tail.

SIZE: A medium-sized raptor and a small buteo. Males average smaller than females, but there is considerable overlap and sexes are not separable in the field. Measurements are for all ages; juveniles are longer than adults because of their longer tail length. Length: 13–17 in. (33–43 cm); wingspan: 32–36 in. (81–91 cm).

SPECIES TRAITS: HEAD.—**Bill is all black except for a small pale bluish spot on the lower part of the upper mandible.** BODY.—Short tarsi. WINGS.—**In flight, wings are moderate in length, somewhat broad, with rather pointed wingtips (p7 and 8 longest and equal in length). Trailing edge is slightly bowed when soaring and straight-edged when gliding.** When perched, wingtips are moderately shorter than tail tip. *Note:* "Broad-winged" is a misnomer for this species. Wings are proportionately the same width as on several other buteo species.

ADULT TRAITS: HEAD.—**Pale orangish brown irises.** WINGS.—**Undersides of remiges are uniformly white and have a moderate amount of narrow dark barring on the secondaries and inner primaries.** Sometimes a pale rectangular window is exhibited on the primaries when the underwing is backlit. Typical of adult buteos, a broad black band is on the underside trailing edge of the remiges. Underside of primary tips has broad black tips. TAIL (dorsal).—**Black with one wide pale gray band on the mid-section of the dorsal side, sometimes an additional narrow white or pale gray band on**

the base. TAIL (ventral).—**Black with one broad white band that is always visible on the mid-section. When fanned, an additional one or two narrow white inner bands may also show.** All the white bands may align neatly, or on some individuals, the outermost rectrix set may have narrow, irregular dark bands that do not align with the wide black and white bands on the ventral side (adult, not juvenile feathers).

ADULT LIGHT MORPH (HEAVILY BARRED TYPE): HEAD.—Rufous-brown with a discernibly darker malar stripe and white lores. BODY (ventral).—**White underparts are variably marked with wide barring or broad arrowhead-shaped markings on the breast and belly; flanks are always thickly barred. Markings are rufous-brown, rarely bright rufous.** (1) All underparts may be uniformly marked with wide barring or arrowhead-shaped markings or (2) breast may be somewhat more densely marked, either solid or mottled, but darker than the barring or arrowhead-shaped markings on the belly and barring on the flanks to create somewhat of a "bib." White flanks and leg feathers are barred with brownish rufous. BODY (dorsal).—Dark brown upperparts. Uppertail coverts are white-tipped (and often appear as a narrow tail band). WINGS.—**Dorsal surface is uniformly brown.** Pale underwing coverts are white or pale tawny with a small amount of brownish rufous markings; however, some are a rich tawny with fairly heavy markings. Axillaries are barred. *Note:* Common plumage type.

ADULT LIGHT MORPH (PALE-BELLIED TYPE): HEAD and TAIL.—As on heavily barred type. BODY.—Breast is virtually solid rufous brown and creates a bib that contrasts sharply with the sparsely marked white belly and flanks. Belly is (1) sparsely covered with rufous-brown arrowhead-shaped markings or (2) virtually lacks dark markings. Flanks are always covered with widely spaced, narrow or moderately wide rufous-brown bars. WINGS.—Pale tawny or white, lightly marked underwing coverts. *Note:* Common plumage type.

ADULT LIGHT MORPH (LIGHTLY BARRED TYPE): HEAD and TAIL.—As on heavily barred type. BODY.—All of the underparts are uniformly patterned with sparse markings. Breast is (1) covered with moderately wide or narrow rufous-brown arrowhead-shaped markings or (2)

has sparse streaking. Belly is also lightly marked with small arrowhead-shaped marks or narrow bars. Flanks have widely spaced, narrow bars. Leg feathers are narrowly barred. WINGS.—Pale tawny or white, very lightly marked underwing coverts. *Note:* Uncommon plumage type.

ADULT DARK MORPH: HEAD.—Whitish lores; rest of head, including forehead, is dark brown. BODY.—Uniformly dark brown, including the undertail coverts. WINGS.—Dark brown underwing coverts.

BASIC (SUBADULT) TRAITS: HEAD.—Iris color as on adults. BODY and TAIL.—As on respective color morph and plumage type of adults, except rump may have retained juvenile feathers. WINGS.—Variable amount of juvenile feathers retained on remiges and upperwing coverts, until the next molt the following summer (*see* Molt, above). *Note:* Separable from adults only at close range.

JUVENILE TRAITS: HEAD.—Bright yellow cere; medium brown irises. WINGS.—Undersides of remiges are uniformly white with narrow dark barring on the secondaries and inner primaries. Narrow grayish band on trailing edge of the underwing. Underside of the primary tips is either solid gray or has narrow dark barring. When backlit, undersides of primaries often exhibit a translucent rectangular window, especially when wings are held in a glide position. *Note:* On perched birds, the wingtips are somewhat shorter than the tail tip and cover three-fourths of the tail. TAIL.—Medium brown on the dorsal surface and whitish on the ventral surface with two major patterns of black banding. (1) *Narrow-banded type:* **Three to five neatly formed, moderately narrow or narrow bands with a wide dark subterminal band.** Rarely, the dark bands on deck rectrices may be somewhat chevron-shaped. Patterns with three dark bands have moderately wide bands, patterns with four or five dark bands have narrow bands. *Note:* Common pattern. (2) *Broad-banded type:* **Two wide dark inner bands that are nearly as thick as the wide dark subterminal band—and may appear as three equal-width dark bands. On the underside, dark bands on the outermost rectrix set are much narrower and do not align with the wider dark bands.** *Note:* Fairly common pattern; can appear quite adultlike.

JUVENILE LIGHT MORPH (LIGHTLY STREAKED TYPE): HEAD.—Pale tawny or whitish supercilium and slightly darker tawny auricular area; dark malar stripe. Lacks a dark eyeline, and throat has a thin dark center stripe. BODY.—Breast, belly, flanks, and leg feathers are pale tawny or white and generally unmarked. Some birds are sparsely streaked on the sides of the breast and flanks. Unmarked white undertail coverts. WINGS (dorsal).—**Secondaries and greater coverts are uniformly dark brown with little or no dark barring. Primaries are the same color as the secondaries or show a slightly paler panel (compared to juvenile Red-shouldered and Red-tailed hawks).** WINGS (ventral).—Unmarked whitish underwing coverts and axillaries, or axillaries may be lightly streaked. *Note:* Fairly common plumage type. This looks like a juvenile light morph Short-tailed Hawk, particularly in flight.

JUVENILE LIGHT MORPH (MODERATELY STREAKED TYPE): HEAD.—As on lightly streaked type. BODY.—Pale tawny or white underparts are moderately streaked on breast and belly and partially barred on rear portion of flanks. Belly is generally more heavily streaked than the breast, which may be unmarked or lightly streaked, and shows a belly band. Leg feathers vary considerably in pattern of dark brown markings: (1) heart shaped, (2) V shaped, or (3) spotted. Unmarked white or tawny undertail coverts. Uppertail coverts have narrow white tips on each feather. WINGS.—**Upper surface as in lightly streaked type.** Underwing coverts are lightly or moderately marked, especially on the patagial area. Axillaries have dark brown, moderate-sized diamond-shaped markings or are partially barred. *Note:* Common plumage type.

JUVENILE LIGHT MORPH (HEAVILY STREAKED TYPE): HEAD.—As on lightly streaked type. BODY.—Breast and belly are covered with dense streaking or broad arrowhead-shaped markings (and may appear somewhat adult-like), and flanks are broadly barred. Leg feathers as on moderately streaked type or thickly and neatly barred. Unmarked white undertail coverts. WINGS.—**Upper surface as in lightly streaked type.** Underwing coverts are moderately or densely covered with dark markings, particularly on the patagial region. Axillaries are covered with large diamond-shaped brown markings or have partial barring. *Note:* Fairly common plumage type.

JUVENILE LIGHT MORPH (WORN PLUMAGE, ALL TYPES): By spring, many exhibit very faded head with a pronounced white supercilium. Auricular region also fades and may be white. Dark malar stripe is still apparent.

JUVENILE DARK MORPH (ALL-DARK TYPE): HEAD.—Whitish lores; rest of head, including forehead, is dark brown. BODY.—All of body, including upperparts, underparts, and undertail coverts, is uniformly dark brown. At close range, narrow tawny edgings on underparts may be visible on breast of some individuals. Undertail coverts have a pale tawny tip on each feather. WINGS.—Underwing coverts are either solid dark brown or covered with small, pale speckling. *Note:* Common plumage type.

JUVENILE DARK MORPH (STREAKED TYPE): HEAD.—All dark as on all-dark type or may have fairly distinct pale tawny supercilium and auriculars. BODY.—Upperparts as on all-dark type. Underparts have distinct pale tawny-rufous streaking on breast, belly, and flanks. WINGS.—Underwing coverts are tawny-rufous with a dark streak on central area of each feather and may appear more rufous than dark brown. *Note:* Uncommon to common plumage type.

ABNORMAL PLUMAGES: Total and/or incomplete albino adult: sight record of a white adult (Clark and Wheeler 1987); albino adult at Duluth, Minn. (F. Nicoletti pers. comm.). Partial albino juvenile: sight record of juvenile with scattered white feathers (Clark and Wheeler 2001). *Note:* Rare plumage types not depicted.

HABITAT: Summer.—Found in large tracts of mid-aged and mature deciduous or mixed woodlands interspersed with small openings and water sources. Generally found in woodlands of at least 100 acres (40 ha). Primarily inhabits remote regions but may also occupy areas with moderate human settlement in large wooded tracts. In Canada, found in lowland spruce-aspen regions of the southern boreal forest. In the U.S. inhabits lowland and low montane elevations.

Winter.—In the U.S., found in semi-open, variable-aged semi-tropical deciduous tracts, often near human-occupied areas. In major wintering areas south of the U.S., tropical dry and wet woodlands and semi-open regions and rain forests from sea level up to montane elevations are inhabited. Wooded areas vary from small tracts to forests with openings. Regularly found in human altered areas.

Migration.—Roosts are in areas with trees, including orchards and suburban locales.

HABITS: A tame raptor. Solitary except during migration. Migrating birds become gregarious and form variable-sized flocks (kettles). Exposed or concealed branches, including telephone poles and utility wires, are used for perches. Migrating birds only roost in trees. Very secretive species during the breeding season.

FEEDING: A perch hunter; rarely an aerial hunter. Diet consists of small rodents, amphibians, reptiles, birds, crustaceans, and large insects. Prey is captured on the ground and occasionally on outer tree branches. When perch hunting, low to moderate-height perches are used. In live trees, Broad-winged Hawks perch below canopy level. Carrion is not eaten. During migration, Broad-winged Hawks are opportunistic and may feed below night roosts in mornings, evenings, and during periods of inclement weather. Some may spend a day or more at one locale, foraging even in prime migrating weather. May also fast for extended periods during migration.

FLIGHT: Powered by regular cadence of several moderately fast wingbeats interspersed with short to long-distance glides. Glides and soars with wings held on a flat plane. Vast distances are traveled in an energy-efficient method during migration by soaring to extremely high altitudes and then gliding for several miles. During migration, flights begin in mid-morning and end in late afternoon; rarely extend until dusk in the East. Migration flights may occur at altitudes exceeding human sight when thermal conditions are optimal. Migrating birds seeking night roosts may dive into selected wooded tracts from fairly high altitudes. Broad-winged Hawks do not hover or kite.

VOICE: Primary call is a loud, high-pitched, and ear-piercing *pee-heeeeee*. The last syllable is very drawn out. Females and fledglings emit a high-pitched whine when food-begging. Quite vocal in breeding season. Vocalizes when agitated by intruders trespassing into nesting territories and in aerial courtship. Moderately vocal in the nonbreeding season.

STATUS AND DISTRIBUTION: Overall one of the most *common* breeding raptors in the U.S. and Canada. Population is probably stable. Virtually the entire North American population migrates in a narrow corridor and a compressed time span through Veracruz, Mexico, where birds can be counted with reasonable accuracy in the fall. Estimated North American population has varied between 1.5 million in 2000 and 2.4 million in 2002. Information throughout this section refers to light morph birds unless otherwise indicated.

Summer.—*Common* resident in the U.S. and Canada. Density is very high in the spruce-aspen boreal forest of Canada and in much of the eastern deciduous forests of the U.S. Large portions of s. Wisconsin, s. Michigan, Illinois, Indiana, w. Ohio, and w. Kentucky, lack suitable habitat, and Broad-winged Hawks are absent from these regions. They are largely absent from the Coastal Plain region of North Carolina, South Carolina, and Georgia.

Winter.—Primarily found from Colima to Chiapas, Mexico, southward through Central America and South America, in n. and e. Peru, Colombia, Venezuela, Bolivia, and s. Brazil. Broad-winged Hawks arrive on winter grounds south of the U.S. from late Oct. to late Nov.; those wintering in Mexico may arrive from early to mid-Oct. In the U.S., fairly large numbers of all ages, but the majority being juveniles, typically winter in s. Florida. Most winter from Lake Okeechobee and southward, and especially on the Keys. Some s. Florida wintering birds are "wayward" individuals that missed the navigational course to major winter grounds in Central and South America. Banding data confirm, however, that some adults return annually to s. Florida. Casual along the Gulf Coast of Alabama and Mississippi. Accidental extralimital wintering of juveniles occurs along the Atlantic seaboard to Connecticut; Moncton, N.B.; and Chester and Halifax, N.S.

Movements.—Migrants form small to large flocks, but for portions of the long journey may also migrate singly. Large flocks may comprise thousands of individuals. Migration lasts 4–8 weeks. Movements may cease during periods of inclement weather and to feed.

Fall migration: Highly punctual for all ages, with all birds moving simultaneously from mid-Aug. to mid-Oct. There is a distinct peak across the e. U.S. in the mid- to third week of Sep. Some juveniles trickle down before the main event, but they also comprise most of the late stragglers. Juveniles are seen annually in the Mid-Atlantic region until mid- to late Nov. *Note:* Largest number of migrants in the East have occurred at Lake Erie Metro Park, Wayne Co., Mich. On Sep. 17, 1999, an astounding 555,371 were recorded (the U.S. 1-day record). However, the average annual total for 1995–2000 was 228,200 birds.

Migration from the East is via a broad-fronted path in a westerly and southwesterly direction towards the w. Gulf of Mexico, into e. Texas, south around the Coastal Bend of Texas, and then into e. coastal Mexico (east of the Sierra Madre Oriental), through Central America, and finally into South America.

A secondary southward path is into the Florida peninsula and onto the Florida Keys. Several thousand birds are seen annually heading south through the Keys. Once in the Keys, however, many reverse their migration and head back north to mainland areas of s. Florida. *Note:* At Curry Hammock S.P., Little Crawl Key, 3,286 were documented heading south and 1,923 heading back north in fall of 2000.

Spring migration: Adults precede most juveniles by 2–4 weeks; however, a few early juveniles accompany the adult flight. Very punctual movements of adults span late Mar. to early Apr. in s. Texas. Peak numbers in the cen. Atlantic Coast occur in mid-Apr. The first migrants along the e. Great Lakes are typically seen in mid-Apr. However, migrants may be seen along the e. Great Lakes in early Apr. Adults peak along the e. Great Lakes in late Apr., along the n. Great Lakes in early May. Juvenile migration is protracted and extends from late Apr. to mid-Jun. Along s. Lake Ontario, there is a trickle of movement into early Jul. Peak migration along the cen. Atlantic Coast is in mid- to late May, in late May to early Jun. along the cen. and e. Great Lakes. *Note:* Juveniles are in first prebasic molt from mid-May and later and appear quite ratty.

Migration path is northward out of South America, into Central America, along e. coastal Mexico, north along the Coastal Bend region of Texas, and then spreads out in a broad-fronted easterly and northeasterly manner to nesting and natal areas. Since Broad-winged Hawks are reluctant to cross large bodies of water because of the lack of thermal lift, concentrations often occur along the Great Lakes, Gulf of Mexico, and Atlantic Coast. Short over-water crossings, however, occur over the Florida Keys.

Dark morph in the East.—*Rare* to *accidental* migrant. Sightings in the East have only been at hawkwatch sites. *Michigan:* Whitefish Point, Paradise. Rare migrant. Somewhat regular although not seen every year. There are a few records for late Apr. through mid-May. Lake Erie Metro Park, Wayne Co. Rare migrant. Possibly a rare annual fall migrant in extremely small numbers. There were two records from 1983 to 1998; one seen each fall in 1999, 2000, and 2001. All records are from mid-Sep. to early Oct. *Note:* It is often difficult to locate dark morphs within the massive, often high-altitude migrant flocks of light morphs at this migration site. *New York:* Accidental migrant and mainly seen in late Apr. with the bulk of adults. Braddock Bay S.P., Greece, has at least six records spanning several years in late Apr. and one unusual record in late Jun. 2001. *Ontario:* There are single records for the following areas: (1) Niagara Peninsula Hawkwatch near Grimsby, Niagara Co., in late Apr. 1977; (2) Thunder Bay, Thunder Bay Co., in early May 1985; (3) Woodstock, Oxford Co., in mid-Aug. 1992 (adult). *New Jersey:* Cape May Point S.P. Possible sight records, but none verified with photographs. *Florida:* Possible records in fall and winter, but none published or documented with photographs. *Other states:* Accidental migrant in spring and fall. *Note:* Light morphs are sometimes misidentified as dark morphs when seen at high altitudes and in poor light conditions.

Dark morphs are rare in the West. Known breeding range is the narrow band of spruce-aspen woodlands of the boreal forest in Alberta, e. British Columbia, and sw. Northwest Territories. They have been seen during summer in Manitoba in Turtle Mountain Prov. Pk. and near Brandon.

NESTING: Begins in late Apr. in southern latitudes and early to mid-May in northern regions. Pair formation occurs after arrival on the breeding grounds. One-year-old females, still in juvenile plumage, sometimes mate with adult males. Nesting is completed by late Jul.

Courtship (flight).—*High-circling* and *sky-dancing* (*see* chapter 5). Often vocalizes during high-circling.

Nest trees are in tracts of similar-sized trees near woodland openings. Generally nests in deciduous trees, rarely in conifers. Nests are placed in the first major crotch of deciduous trees or next to the trunks of conifers 20–40 ft. (7–12 m) high. Nest is a poorly constructed mass of sticks 15–17 in. (38–43 cm) in diameter, 5–12 in. (13–30 cm) deep, and lined with greenery. A new nest is constructed or an old nest may be reused. New nests are sometimes built on top of old American Crow nests, nests of other raptor species, or (leafy) squirrel nests. Two or 3 eggs, incubated 28–31 days, mainly by female, but male takes over when female feeds. Nestlings branch in 29–31 days, fledge in 35–42 days, and become independent in about 70 days.

CONSERVATION: No measures are taken. Loss of ample-sized woodlands for nesting is a possible concern in the U.S. with increased urbanization and forest fragmentation. Habitat destruction on winter grounds in Mexico and Central and South America is a possible concern.

Mortality.—Illegal shooting occurs in North America in the summer and particularly south of the U.S. in fall and winter. Because of a general diet, pesticide contamination has been minimal. There is minimal risk with future pesticide contamination.

SIMILAR SPECIES: COMPARED TO ADULT LIGHT MORPH.—**(1) Red-shouldered Hawk, adults.**—*B. l. lineatus* range overlaps spring to fall; *alleni* all year in Florida; *extimus* Sep.–Mar. in Florida PERCHED.—Dark brown irises. *B. l. lineatus* and *alleni* have narrower, finer, brighter rufous-barred underparts. *B. l. extimus* is pale headed with dull rufous-barred underparts. All races have long tarsi, black and white checkering on wings, three narrow white bands on dorsal side of tail. FLIGHT (all races).—Black and white barring on outer primaries; white panel/window on basal area of outer primaries. *Note:* Some *lineatus* and *alleni* have dark bibs that are similar to a pale-bellied type Broad-winged Hawk. COMPARED TO LIGHT MORPH JUVENILE.—**(2) Cooper's Hawk, juveniles.**—PERCHED.—Pale yellowish or gray irises. Uniformly colored head; no dark malar stripe. Wingtips much shorter than tail tip. Use caution with broad-banded type tail: equal-width bands are similar (use wingtip-to-tail-tip ratio). FLIGHT.—Remiges heavily barred on underside. **(3) Northern Goshawk, juveniles.**—PERCHED.—Gray irises of recent fledglings similar; older juveniles have yellowish orange irises. Dark malar stripe, if present, very narrow and not well defined. Shares prominent pale supercilium. Pale bar on greater coverts. Tail can be similar to broad-banded type; thin white borders along dark bands on dorsal side. FLIGHT.—Undersides of remiges heavily barred. **(4) Red-shouldered Hawk, juveniles.**—PERCHED.—Head can be identical in all races, including dark mid-throat stripe. Some *B. l. lineatus* have all-dark throats and defined dark eyeline. *B. l. alleni* and *extimus* have thin bars on leg feathers and heart-shaped or barred underparts, especially on the breast. All races have long tarsi, pale barring on dorsal surface of secondaries, and pale tail bands that are narrower than dark bands. **(5) Short-tailed Hawk, light morph juveniles.**—PERCHED.—Pale throat is unmarked. Thick dark eyeline. Wingtips equal to tail tip. FLIGHT.—Pale gray secondaries. Kites and parachutes. Wingtips bend upwards when kiting and soaring.

OTHER NAMES: Broadwing, Wing, Broadie. *Spanish:* Aguililla Alas Anchas, Aguililla Aluda. *French:* Petit Buse.

REFERENCES: Andrle and Carroll 1988; Brauning 1992; Brewer et al. 1991; Buckelew and Hall 1994; Bylan 1998, 1999; Cadman et al. 1987; Castrale et al. 1998; Center for Conservation, Research, and Technology 2000; Clark and Wheeler 2001; del Hoyo et al. 1994; DeLorme Publishers 1991a, 1991b; Dodge 1988–1997; Erskine 1992; Goodrich et al. 1996; Hoffman and Darrow 1992; Howell and Webb 1995; Johnsgard 1990; Kale et al. 1992; Kerlinger and Gauthereaux 1985; Laughlin and Kibbe 1985; Lott 1999; Nicholson 1997; Palmer 1988; Palmer-Ball 1996; Peterjohn and Rice 1991; Robbins 1996; Stevenson and Anderson 1994; Tufts 1986; Veit and Petersen 1993.

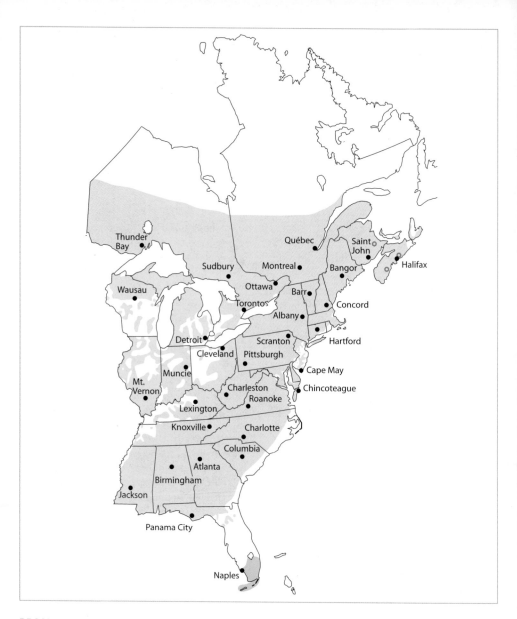

BROAD-WINGED HAWK, *Buteo platypterus:* Common. Migrates in huge flocks to and from winter grounds in s. Mexico and Central and South America each fall and spring. Fairly large numbers winter in s. FL. Rare in winter to Maritimes.

Plate 224. Broad-winged Hawk, adult (heavily barred type) [Sep.] ▪ Brown head. Pale orangish brown iris. ▪ Underparts marked with dark brown. Densely barred breast forms partial bib; belly and flanks thickly barred; leg feathers narrowly barred. Plain brown upperparts. ▪ Single broad white band shows when tail is closed.

Plate 225. Broad-winged Hawk, adult (pale-bellied type) [Oct.] ▪ Rufous-brown head. Pale orangish brown iris. ▪ Nearly solid rufous-brown breast forms bib; flanks barred, breast and belly sparsely covered with arrowhead-shaped marks. ▪ Single broad white band shows when tail is closed.

Plate 226. Broad-winged Hawk, adult/subadult (lightly barred type) [Nov.] ▪ Brown head. Pale orangish brown iris. ▪ Breast marked with broad arrowhead-shaped marks, belly lightly marked, flanks sparsely barred. ▪ Single broad white band shows when tail is closed. ▪ *Note:* Palest type of ventral markings for adults and subadults. Adults and subadults are not separable when perched.

Plate 227. Broad-winged Hawk, adult (heavily barred type) [Sep.] ▪ Nearly uniformly barred underparts. ▪ Underside of remiges thinly barred; wide black band on rear edge; coverts can be tawny and moderately marked. Fairly pointed wingtips when soaring or banking. ▪ Many birds show 2 broad white bands when tail is fanned.

Plate 228. Broad-winged Hawk, adult (heavily barred type) [Sep.] ▪ Uniformly barred underparts, including breast. ▪ Underside of remiges thinly barred; wide black band on rear edge; coverts can be tawny and moderately marked. Pointed wingtips when gliding. ▪ Single broad white band shows when tail is closed.

Plate 229. Broad-winged Hawk, subadult (lightly barred type) [May] ▪ Breast sparsely streaked, belly covered with arrowhead-shaped marks, flanks sparsely barred. ▪ White underwing coverts unmarked. Outer 3 primaries are old, faded brown juvenile feathers. ▪ Single broad white band shows when tail is closed. ▪ *Note:* Adults similar. Photo by Dudley Edmondson.

Plate 230. Broad-winged Hawk, subadult (heavily barred type) [May] ▪ Underparts uniformly barred with rufous. ▪ Retains juvenile remiges; pale areas on wingtip and rear edge (p10 and s4, 8, 9). Some birds show up to 3 broad white bands; bands on outer rectrix set often do not align with inner bands. ▪ *Note:* Separable from adults at close range.

Plate 231. Broad-winged Hawk, adult [Sep.] ▪ Uniformly brown upperparts, including remiges and coverts. ▪ Black tail has 2–3 white or gray bands: mid-tail band is widest. White tips on uppertail coverts (sometimes appears as white band).

Plate 232. Broad-winged Hawk, adult dark morph [Sep.] ▪ All of head and body uniformly dark brown. ▪ Uniformly whitish remiges thinly barred; wide black band on rear edge; coverts dark brown. ▪ Single broad white tail band shows when tail is closed. ▪ *Note:* Photographed at Duluth, Minn.

Plate 233. Broad-winged Hawk, juvenile (lightly streaked type) [Nov.] ▪ Brown head with tawny supercilium and auricular areas, black malar mark. ▪ White underparts narrowly streaked on sides of neck and flanks. Unmarked leg feathers. ▪ Wingtips shorter than tail tip.

Plate 234. Broad-winged Hawk, juvenile (moderately streaked type) [Sep.] ▪ White supercilium, tawny auricular areas, black malar mark. ▪ Underparts streaked on sides of neck, spotted or streaked belly, barred flanks. ▪ Secondaries and greater coverts solid brown. ▪ Narrow-banded type tail with wide, dark subterminal band, narrow dark inner bands.

Plate 235. Broad-winged Hawk, juvenile (heavily streaked type) [Nov.] ▪ Brown head with white supercilium, tawny auricular areas, black malar mark, medium brown iris. ▪ Underparts densely covered with wide brown streaking on breast and belly, barring on flanks. Short tarsi.

Plate 236. Broad-winged Hawk, juvenile [Sep.] ▪ Brown head with white supercilium, black malar mark, medium brown iris. ▪ Solid brown secondaries and greater coverts. Wingtips distinctly shorter than tail tip. ▪ Narrow-banded type tail has wide black subterminal band, 3 or 4 narrow inner bands. ▪ *Note:* Same bird as on plate 234.

Plate 237. Broad-winged Hawk, juvenile [Nov.] ▪ Brown head with white supercilium, tawny auricular areas, black malar mark, medium brown iris. ▪ Solid brown secondaries and greater coverts. Wingtips distinctly shorter than tail tip. ▪ Broad-banded type tail has 3 nearly equal-width dark bands; subterminal band often a bit wider. *Note:* Same bird as on plate 235.

Plate 238. Broad-winged Hawk, juvenile dark morph (streaked type) [Sep.] ▪ Dark brown head, including throat and forehead; pale lores. ▪ Dark brown underparts streaked with tawny. ▪ Narrow-banded type tail has dark subterminal tail band, narrow inner bands. ▪ *Note:* Also has all-dark type plumage with uniformly dark brown underparts. Photographed in Prowers Co., Colo.

Plate 239. Broad-winged Hawk, juvenile (moderately streaked type) [Sep.] ▪ Thin center stripe on throat. ▪ Moderately streaked underparts. Flanks barred, breast unmarked. ▪ Rectangular window may show on primaries. Pointed wingtips when gliding. ▪ Narrow-banded type tail has wide subterminal band, several inner bands.

Plate 240. Broad-winged Hawk, juvenile (lightly streaked type) [Sep.] ▪ Thin center stripe on throat. ▪ Underparts thinly streaked on sides of neck and flanks. ▪ Remiges thinly barred; moderately wide dark rear edge. Unmarked coverts. Wingtips often barred. ▪ Broad-banded type tail has 3 wide dark bands (2 visible on closed tail); outer rectrix set has narrow, non-aligning bands.

Plate 241. Broad-winged Hawk, juvenile [Sep.] ▪ Brown upperparts. ▪ Solid brown secondaries. ▪ Narrow-banded type tail has wide dark subterminal band, 3 or 4 narrow dark inner bands.

Plate 242. Broad-winged Hawk, juvenile [Sep.] ▪ Brown upperparts. ▪ Faint, dark barring on secondaries (typically solid brown). ▪ Broad-banded type tail has 3 equal-width dark bands, 2 or 3 pale bands (somewhat adultlike). White markings on uppertail coverts.

Plate 243. Broad-winged Hawk, migrant flock (kettle) [Oct.] ▪ Migrants gather in flocks that comprise a few hawks or hundreds or thousands.

SHORT-TAILED HAWK
(Buteo brachyurus)

AGES: Adult and juvenile. Adult plumage is acquired when 1 year old. Juvenile plumage is worn the first year. Some juveniles have slightly longer tails than adults.

MOLT: Accipitridae wing and tail molt pattern (*see* chapter 4). Based on photographed individuals in Florida, the first prebasic molt probably begins in Apr. Molt is first apparent with loss of innermost primary (p1) and central rectrices. The first prebasic molt appears to be a complete molt and is finished by mid-Nov. No data on subsequent prebasic adult molts except they appear to be completed by mid-Nov.

SUBSPECIES: Polytypic with two races. *B. b. fuliginosus* inhabits Florida. It is also resident from Mexico south to Panama. One additional race, nominate *B. b. brachyurus*, inhabits Colombia, w. Ecuador, east to the Guianas, Brazil, southward through e. Peru, e. Bolivia to Paraguay and n. Argentina.

White-throated Hawk (*B. albigula*) of the Andean highlands in South America is considered to be a subspecies of *brachyurus* by some authors; however, hybrids do not occur in overlap zones, and it is probably a separate species (del Hoyo et al. 1994).

COLOR MORPHS: Polymorphic with light and dark morphs. Intermediate morphs do not exist. Adults have minimal plumage variation in either morph. Minor plumage variations exist in juvenile light morphs. Juvenile dark morphs show considerable amount of plumage variation.

SIZE: A medium-sized raptor and a small buteo. Males average slightly smaller than females but sexes are not separable in the field. Length: 15–17 in. (38–43 cm); wingspan: 32–41 in. (81–104 cm).

SPECIES TRAITS: BODY.—**Dark brown uppertail coverts.** WINGS.—When perched, wingtips of the long primaries extend to the tail tip. **In flight, long wings are fairly broad and the trailing edge of the secondaries bows outward from the body and then tapers to the moderately pointed wingtips.** Wingtips become very pointed when gliding. *Note:* "Short-tailed" is a misnomer: tail length is not any

shorter in proportion to overall size than it is in many buteo species.

ADULT TRAITS: HEAD.—**Most have a narrow white mask around the forehead and outer lores next to cere; inner lores are dark.** Dark brown irises, are visible only at close range. WINGS.—**Undersides of remiges are medium gray with a small white area on the basal region on the outer four primaries.** Typical of adult buteos, there is a wide black band on the trailing edge of the wing; however, this band is wider than on most other adult buteos. TAIL.—**Two patterns, which are most visible on the ventral surface. Undertail is whitish, uppertail is medium brown.** (1) *Banded type:* **Moderately wide dark subterminal band and three or four complete, narrow dark inner bands. Uppertail has narrow dark bands.** (2) *Partially banded type:* **Moderately wide dark subterminal band with two to four incomplete, narrow dark inner bands, or lacks inner dark bands and exhibits only the dark subterminal band. Uppertail has a moderately wide dark subterminal band. The inner tail may have faint, partial dark bands or be unbanded.**

ADULT LIGHT MORPH: HEAD.—**Uniformly dark brown, including the malar region, and appears hooded.** Throat is white and merges with the white underparts. BODY.—**Immaculate white underparts.** At close range, a small rufous patch may be visible on the sides of the neck. Uniformly dark brown upperparts, including the uppertail coverts. WINGS (ventral).—White underwing coverts contrast sharply with medium gray remiges. WINGS (dorsal).—Dark brown upperwing coverts are the same color as the back and scapulars and contrast with the darker greater coverts and remiges, creating a two-toned effect. An additional two-toned effect is often created with the even darker primaries and primary coverts contrasting with the slightly paler secondaries and inner half of the wing.

ADULT DARK MORPH: HEAD.—**Uniformly blackish brown except for narrow white mask.** BODY and WINGS.—**Uniformly blackish brown, including undertail coverts and underwing coverts.**

JUVENILE TRAITS: HEAD.—**Medium brown irises are visible only at close range. Some birds**

have a white forehead and outer lores; however, all of lore area may be white. WINGS.—**Undersides of the secondaries and outer half of the primaries are pale gray and inner half of the primaries are white; forms a large white panel on the primaries (panel is much larger than adult's).** Typical of most juvenile buteos, there is a narrow gray band on the trailing edge of the remiges. TAIL.—Base color on the ventral surface is whitish, medium brown on the dorsal surface. *Note:* Two main tail patterns, but with considerable variation. Tail patterns are most diagnostic on the ventral surface. (1) *Banded type:* **Four to seven complete, narrow, dark inner bands with the subterminal band being the same width, somewhat wider, or much wider than the inner bands. The equal-width pattern averages fewer dark bands on the ventral surface (4–6).** Uppertail pattern of banding is also distinct, with four or five dark bands inside the subterminal band. *Note:* Pattern is mainly on dark morphs in Florida. (2) *Partially banded type:* **Undertail has a moderately wide dusky subterminal band, or the subterminal band may be diffused and nearly absent. Undertail has either (1) partial, narrow, dark inner banding on mainly the outer rectrix sets with the inner rectrix sets being unmarked, or (2) no markings except for the possibly darker, dusky subterminal band. Uppertail is mainly unmarked except for the dark subterminal band; however, it may have small dark spots on the deck rectrices or faint, incomplete dark bands.** *Note:* Pattern is on most and possibly all Florida light morphs and many Florida dark morphs. Patterns are often similar to those of adults; however, adults do not have equal-width banding or a dusky subterminal band.

JUVENILE LIGHT MORPH: HEAD.—**Bold face pattern: narrow, pale supercilium; short, broad, dark eyeline that extends under and behind the eye; broad dark malar mark; a narrow pale stripe on the cheek between the dark eyeline and malar. Head pattern is visible at moderate distances.** On some, head is darker with less pronounced pale supercilium and pale cheeks, but the broad dark line behind the eyes is still apparent. *Note:* **Throat is unmarked.** BODY.—(1) *Unmarked type.*—Cream-colored underparts with sparse dark streaking on sides of the neck, but the rest of

the underparts are unmarked. *Note:* Common type. (2) *Streaked type.*—Sides of the neck, flanks, and mid-belly are narrowly streaked with dark brown. *Note:* Uncommon type. Underparts of both types fade and become whitish by spring. Back, scapulars, rump, and uppertail coverts are uniformly brown. WINGS (dorsal).—Upperwing coverts are the same color brown as the back and scapulars, but greater coverts and all remiges are slightly darker and form a two-toned effect with upperwing surface. An additional two-toned effect is often created by the even darker primaries and primary coverts that contrast with the slightly paler inner half of the wing. WINGS (ventral).—Unmarked, cream-colored underwing coverts contrast somewhat with slightly darker, pale gray secondaries.

JUVENILE DARK MORPH (MOTTLED TYPE): HEAD.—Blackish brown, but auriculars often paler. BODY.—Uniformly blackish brown breast forms a bib which contrasts with paler, white-mottled and/or-spotted belly, flanks, and undertail coverts. WINGS.—Underwing coverts are blackish brown and mottled with white; they are much darker than the secondaries. *Note:* Common plumage type.

JUVENILE DARK MORPH (STREAKED TYPE): HEAD.—Blackish brown with a large whitish patch on the auriculars and throat, and often with partial, pale supercilium. BODY.—Blackish brown breast has some white streaking but still forms a distinct bib with the sharply contrasting white underparts which are narrowly streaked with dark brown. WINGS.—White underwing coverts are narrowly streaked with dark brown. Underwing coverts and secondaries appear uniformly pale grayish at a distance; whitish primaries are paler than rest of the underwing. *Note:* Fairly common plumage type.

JUVENILE DARK MORPH (ALL-DARK TYPE): HEAD.—Blackish brown. BODY.—Uniformly blackish brown. WINGS.—Uniformly blackish brown underwing coverts are much darker than the remiges. At close range, faint, light speckling may be visible on the axillaries and some underwing coverts. *Note:* Very uncommon to rare plumage type.

ABNORMAL PLUMAGES: None noted.

HABITAT: Summer.—Breeds in mature, remote, densely wooded tracts in or adjacent to semi-open meadows, savannahs, swamps, or bays. Wooded tracts are composed of pines, oaks, cypress, Sabal Palms, mangroves, or mixed woodlands.

Winter.—Can be identical to breeding habitat. Also regularly found in semi-open woodlands and near developed areas with ample semi-open or open areas for foraging and groves of tall trees for roosting. Regularly inhabits suburban and business park areas with this habitat.

Migration.—Similar to summer and winter habitats.

HABITS: Tame. Most exhibit little fear of humans during the nonbreeding season when at low-altitude flight or perching. Perching occurs only for night roosting, during inclement weather, when feeding, and occasionally for very short periods after missed capture attempts. *Short-tailed Hawks do not perch in trees along highways or on utility poles, wires, or posts.*

FEEDING: Exclusively an aerial hunter. Preys almost entirely on small birds perched on or near the ground and on outer branches of bushes and trees. Red-winged Blackbirds, Eastern Meadowlarks, Palm Warblers (major prey on Big Pine Key, Fla., in winter), Boat-tailed Grackles, Mourning and White-winged doves, and Eurasian Collared-Doves are major prey species. Small rodents and reptiles comprise a small fraction of diet. Warbler-sized birds are decapitated and the body swallowed whole. Captured prey is (1) immediately taken to a branch in the canopy of a nearby tree, partially plucked, then eaten or (2) may be decapitated and swallowed whole while the hawk is soaring or gliding. Unlike in most raptors, a relaxation period of perching does not occur after feeding. If feeding is done on a perch, aerial activities are immediately resumed once the prey is eaten.

Hawks capturing prey on the outer branches of trees may plunge from heights of a few hundred meters, hit the prey, and cling onto the branches, often hanging sideways or upside down until the prey is secured, then fly off with the prey. *Note:* In the state of Nayarit, Mexico, an adult was observed making a 500-ft. (150-m) vertical dive to capture a small passerine on the outer branches of a large tree. The hawk crashed into the branches, clung sideways and upside down for several seconds—flapping its wings for balance—then

flew off with the prey. The hawk proceeded to decapitate and partially pluck the prey, then eat it in one gulp.

FLIGHT: An incredibly aerial raptor. Along with Swallow-tailed Kite, one of the most aerial raptor and the most aerial buteo. Primary flight modes are soaring, gliding, parachuting, and kiting. In all modes, wings are held on a flat plane with the primary tips flexing somewhat upwards. Powered flight is used sparingly to gain altitude quickly after prey capture, attempted capture, or in inclement weather when aerial lift conditions are poor. Typically, Short-tailed Hawks soar to high altitudes and then glide into or tack the wind when hunting. If wind velocity is sufficient, kiting is used for considerable lengths of time at moderate and high altitudes in areas with abrupt wall-like wooded edges. Gliding and kiting occur at low altitudes in high winds, often just above treetop or rooftop level. When prey is detected, the hawks engage in (1) a long, impressive angled or vertical dive; (2) a series of short vertical or angled dives that are periodically interrupted with stints of parachuting; or (3) slowly parachute vertically downward and then make a short dive at the end. This flight process is repeated constantly throughout the day. Short-tailed Hawks do not hover.

VOICE: Vocalizes primarily near nest sites when disturbed by intruders and during courtship and food transfers. Call is a high-pitched, drawn-out *keeee* with a slight decrescendo slur at the end (making a somewhat two-syllable sound). On rare occasions, vocalization occurs in the nonbreeding season when two individuals of any age or sex are near each other in flight. Call is a high-pitched *kree, kree, kree.*

STATUS AND DISTRIBUTION: *Very uncommon* Florida resident. Estimated population is unknown but is very small. Population is probably considerably fewer than 500 birds. Status is poorly known due to the difficulty in getting an accurate census because of aerial habits and remote, often inaccessible habitat. There is growing concern about status, especially with the rapidly changing Florida landscape. Biologists are tracking a few individuals with telemetry to learn more about this species' habits. Christmas Bird Counts tally only small numbers. In the e. U.S., Short-tailed Hawk has not been documented north of Florida. Dark morphs comprise about 75% of the Florida population.

B. b. fuliginosus is locally fairly common to common in other portions of its range in Mexico and Central America; however, considerable habitat alteration is also occurring in these regions.

Summer.—Breeds in very low density throughout the Florida peninsula where suitable habitat exists. Possible and/or probable nesting occurs inland north to Putnam Co. and, on the western coast, to Dixie Co. In the spring of 2000, a possible pair was seen in nw. Alachua Co. Other probable sightings in Alachua Co. occurred in late Feb. 1994, early Mar. 1998, and late Feb. 1926 (a collected individual). Short-tailed Hawks do not breed in the west-central, east-coastal, and southeastern portions of the state. Possible breeding may occur on Big Pine Key as adults have been present in mid-Mar. and have recently been seen in summer. Summering has occurred on Key West but not breeding. In the late 1800s, formerly nested north to Wakulla Co. Adults may remain on or near breeding grounds until the southward migration.

Winter.—Population becomes compacted in the southern third of the state. Most winter from Lake Okeechobee southward onto the larger Keys to Key West. Irregular wintering occurs north to Orange and Levy Cos. In prime locales, a few individuals will share foraging territory without agonistic interaction. Everglades N.P., s. Dade Co., tallies the highest numbers during the winter.

Movements.—Very short-distance migrant within the Florida peninsula and Keys. Those breeding south of Lake Okeechobee may be sedentary or move even shorter distances.

Late summer dispersal: Based on telemetry data (K. Meyer unpubl. data), prior to actually migrating, juveniles may wander short distances in any direction from natal areas after fledging.

Fall migration: Oct.–Dec. Migrants show up on the middle Keys, at the hawkwatch at Curry Hammock S.P. on Little Crawl Key, beginning in mid-Oct. Movements are still occurring in mid-Nov. when the hawkwatch ends. Migration peak is unknown but has varied from late Oct. to mid-Nov. on the Keys. Once on the lower Keys, several individuals often head back north, or work their way up and down the Keys during the late fall and winter. On the middle Keys in 1996 and 1997, 11 and 27 Short-taileds were counted, respectively, including north- and south-bound birds (counts ended in late Oct.). On Little Crawl Key, 19 were counted in 1999 and 40 in 2000. There was a longer count season in 2000, and this may reflect a higher number of migrants. Many Short-tailed Hawks join flocks of the several thousand Broad-winged Hawks and Turkey Vultures also moving back and forth on the Keys.

Spring migration: Jan.–Mar. Considerable movement seems to occur from late Jan. to mid-Feb. Adults may arrive at n. Florida breeding territories by mid-Feb. Most adults are on territories by mid-Mar.

Note: Data on movements are limited at the present time; however, increased length of autumn counts on the Keys and telemetry studies will provide more data in the future.

NESTING: Feb.–Jul.

Courtship (flight).—*High-circling* and *sky-dancing* (*see* chapter 5). Prey or nest materials are sometimes carried in courtship flights.

Nests are built mainly by females, but males supply most material. Nests are bulky stick masses lined with greenery and are about 2 ft. (61 cm) in diameter and 1 ft. (30 cm) deep. They are placed near the main trunks or on bromeliads 15–95 ft. (5–29 m) high in pines, cypress, mangroves, oaks, or Sabal Palms. Nest trees are often in dense, inaccessible wooded tracts. The 2 eggs, rarely 3, are laid mid-Mar. through Apr. and are incubated about 34 days. Fledging period is currently unknown but is probably like in other similar-sized raptors (35–45 days). If two nestlings hatch, only one usually survives. Mixed-color-morph pairs are more common than same-colored pairs.

CONSERVATION: No measures are taken at the present time. Since the population is low, future mandated protection is possible to preserve vital nesting habitat in Florida.

Mortality.—Logging and urbanization are possibly affecting breeding habitat, especially in central and northern parts of the Florida peninsula. Illegal shooting has been documented but does not appear to be a major mortality factor. Being an avian feeder, this species may have been affected during the organochlorine pesticide era of the 1940s–1970s.

SIMILAR SPECIES: (1) **Red-shouldered Hawk, *B. l. extimus/alleni* juveniles.**—Most common raptor in Florida. Range overlap all year. PERCHED.—Streaked underparts, especially breast. Wingtips are distinctly shorter than the tail tip. FLIGHT.—Tawny or white wing panel/window on base of outer primaries. Use caution: they often make long, spectacular dives during courtship, sometimes when hunting. Highly vocal: *keyair.* (2) **Broad-winged Hawk.**—Range overlap mid-Sep. to Apr. Vocalizes on winter grounds. Often seen flying with Short-tailed. PERCHED.—Regularly perches along highways on branches, poles, and wires. Wingtips are distinctly shorter than the tail tip. FLIGHT.—Undersides of remiges are uniformly white. Similar pointed wing shape but shorter winged; wings held on a flat plane; trailing edge straighter; dorsal wing surface is uniformly dark. Soars and glides with wings on a flat plane. Does not kite or parachute, and rarely dives. (2A) **Adult dark morphs.**—Accidental in s. Florida. Uniformly whitish remiges; wide white tail band on black tail. Use Flight data. (2B) **Juvenile light morphs, lightly streaked types.**—When perched or flying at close range, a narrow dark mid-throat stripe. Similar grayish trailing edge of underwing; underwings have large translucent rectangular window on primaries. Tail pattern important: dark bands are complete (partial or lacking on Short-tailed Hawk). Underparts are a virtual look-alike with juvenile light morph Short-tail. *Lacks dark eyeline.* Uppertail coverts appear somewhat pale tipped when seen from above. Use Flight data for other aerial separation. (2C) **Juvenile dark morphs.**—Accidental in s. Florida. Uniformly whitish remiges. Tail pattern can be identical to dark morph Short-tailed Hawk: use extreme caution. Use Flight data. (3) **Swainson's Hawk.**—Range overlap Oct.–Apr. May be seen flying with Short-tailed. PERCHED.—Shares similar wingtip-to-tail-tip ratio. Quite tame. Perches on very open, elevated objects and on the ground. FLIGHT.—Wing shape similar, trailing edge more straight edged, and wingtips usually more pointed. Wings held in dihedral. Hovers but rarely parachutes. Kites, dives, and flaps wings regularly.

Uppertail coverts on all but dark morph adults have white U shape when seen from above (mainly dark on all light morph Short-tailed Hawks). (3A) **Adult (all morphs).**—Dark gray undersides of remiges. (3B) **Adult light morphs.**—Can be very similar to adult light morph Short-tailed Hawks. Similar head with white mask and throat and no dark malar: use caution. Generally has bib on breast; a few have "split bib" or lack bib and are identical to adult light morph Short-tailed Hawks. Undersides of dark gray remiges more uniform, contrast more sharply with pale coverts. Use uppertail covert data in Flight. Dorsal surface of wing is similar in pattern, with darker flight feathers and paler coverts. (3C) **Adult dark morphs.**—Rufous underwing coverts. White or tawny undertail coverts. Head may be identical, with white mask. (3D) **Basic I (subadult I) (all morphs).**—Pronounced white spot on undersides of wing on basal region of outer two to four primaries (fall to early winter). Wide dark band on trailing edge of remiges. Use uppertail covert data in Flight. Dark morph has pale undertail coverts. (3E) **Juvenile (all morphs).**—Undersides of remiges are pale gray; dark gray trailing edge; small white spot on base of outer primaries; dark "comma" mark on the primary covert tips on underwing. Numerous narrow, equal-width dark tail bands. Use uppertail covert data in Flight. (3F) **Juvenile light morphs.**—Dark mid-throat stripe visible when perched or in low-altitude flight. Similar when perched except pale edging on dorsal feathers. Use uppertail covert data in Flight. (3G) **Juvenile dark morphs.**—Pale throat with dark mid-throat stripe. Underparts heavily streaked. Pale undertail coverts. Use uppertail covert data in Flight. (4) **Red-tailed Hawk.**—PERCHED.—Perches along roadways on trees, poles, posts, and wires. FLIGHT.—Wingtips flex upwards a bit when soaring: use caution. Kites, parachutes, dives; regularly flaps wings and hovers. (4A) *B. j. harlani* **adults.**—Range overlap Nov.–Mar. Casual or accidental in s. Florida. Dark morph similar to adult dark morph Short-tailed Hawk. Tail patterns can be identical at field distances, especially on dark gray tail type since mottling may not be visible in the field and some do not have mottling. Wingtips are generally shorter than tail tip when perched. Use Flight data. (**4B**) **Juvenile (all races and morphs**).—Greenish cere. Pale irises. Wingtips much shorter than tail tip. Pale brown panel on uppersides of primaries and primary greater coverts; white translucent window on undersides. (**4C**) **Juveniles (*B. j. borealis/umbrinus*).**—Range overlap all year. Lacks dark eyeline. White patch on scapulars. Dark patagial mark on underwing. White U on uppertail coverts when seen from above. (**4D**) **Juvenile (dark morphs, *B. j. calurus/harlani*).—**

Range overlap late Oct.–Mar. Casual in s. Florida. Use Flight data.

OTHER NAMES: None regularly used. *Spanish:* Aguililla Cola Corta. *French:* Unknown.

REFERENCES: del Hoyo et al. 1994; Hoffman and Darrow 1992; Howell and Webb 1995; Johnsgard 1990; Kale et al. 1992; Kellogg 2000; Lott 1999; Palmer 1988; Snyder and Snyder 1991; Stevenson and Anderson 1994.

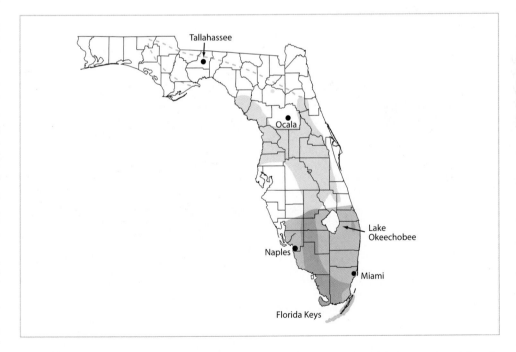

SHORT-TAILED HAWK, *Buteo brachyurus:* Very uncommon and local in summer. Disperses and rarely breeds within dashed line. Winters irregularly in all of breeding range but concentrates in s. FL.

Plate 244. Short-tailed Hawk, adult light morph
[**Aug.**] ▪ Dark head and white throat. ▪ White body. ▪ Medium gray remiges have white area on base of outer 4–5 primaries. Remiges contrast with white wing coverts. Wide black band on rear edge of remiges. ▪ Partially banded type tail with wide black subterminal band, partial dark inner bands.

Plate 245. Short-tailed Hawk, adult dark morph
[**Feb.**] ▪ Dark brown or black head and body. ▪ Medium gray remiges have white area on base of outer 4–5 primaries. Wide black band on rear edge of remiges. ▪ Banded type tail with wide black subterminal band, several narrow dark inner bands.

Plate 246. Short-tailed Hawk, adult dark morph
[**Jan.**] ▪ Dark brown or black head and body. Typically has dark inner lores (white on this bird). ▪ Medium gray remiges have white area on base of outer 4–5 primaries. Wide black band on rear edge of remiges. ▪ Partially banded type tail with wide black subterminal band, partial dark inner bands.

Plate 247. Short-tailed Hawk, juvenile light morph (unmarked type) [**Nov.**] ▪ White mask and outer lores; dark inner lores. Narrow white supercilium; short, thick, dark eyeline; white auriculars; wide dark malar mark; unmarked throat. ▪ Unmarked cream-colored underparts. ▪ Partially banded type tail with few if any dark markings. ▪ *Note:* Just ate a Palm Warbler, Big Pine Key, Fla.

Plate 248. Short-tailed Hawk, juvenile dark morph, (mottled type) [Nov.] ▪ White mask and outer lores; dark inner lores. Tawny streaking on auriculars. ▪ Dark breast forms bib; dark belly and flanks mottled with white. ▪ Banded type tail with equal-width pattern of banding. ▪ *Note:* Just ate a Palm Warbler, Big Pine Key, Fla.

Plate 249. Short-tailed Hawk, juvenile light morph, (unmarked type) [Nov.] ▪ White auriculars; wide, dark malar mark; white unmarked throat. ▪ Cream-colored underparts. ▪ Pale gray secondaries and inner primaries contrast with large white region of primaries and coverts. ▪ Partially banded type tail with dusky subterminal band.

Plate 250. Short-tailed Hawk, juvenile dark morph (mottled type) [Nov.] ▪ Dark brown head. ▪ Dark brown breast forms bib; white mottled belly and flanks. ▪ Pale gray secondaries and distal half of inner primaries contrasts with large white basal region of primaries. Coverts mottled with white. ▪ Partially banded type tail with dusky subterminal band.

Plate 251. Short-tailed Hawk, juvenile dark morph (streaked type) [Nov.] ▪ Pale auriculars. ▪ Dark, streaked breast forms bib; streaked, white belly. ▪ Pale gray secondaries and distal half of inner primaries contrasts with large white basal region of primaries. ▪ Partially banded type tail with dusky subterminal band, partial inner dark bands.

Plate 252. Short-tailed Hawk, juvenile dark morph (all-dark type) [Nov.] ▪ Head, body, and wing coverts dark brown; small amount of white spotting only on axillaries. ▪ Pale gray secondaries and distal half of inner primaries contrast with large white basal region of primaries. ▪ Banded type tail with equal-width dark banding. ▪ *Note:* Rare plumage type.

SWAINSON'S HAWK
(*Buteo swainsoni*)

AGES: Adult, basic I (subadult I), and juvenile. Adult plumage is acquired when 2 years old in the third year of life. Subadult plumage is acquired when 1 year old and retained the second year. This plumage is either quite similar to that of juveniles or is a combination of juvenile and adult traits. In either case, the tail and underwing patterns are adultlike. Tail length and wing width are also adultlike. Sexual differences are not apparent. Juvenile plumage is held for much of the first year. Juveniles have somewhat shorter secondaries and longer rectrices, which create a narrower wing and slightly longer tail than on older ages. There are no sexual variations in this age class.

MOLT: Accipitridae wing and tail molt pattern (*see* chapter 4). The first prebasic molt begins when juveniles are 10.5 to 11 months old. Based on museum specimens and live birds, molt begins in late Apr. when birds are still migrating north. By early May, molt is obvious on the inner primaries and central and sometimes outer rectrices. In early May, p1–3 may be replaced, new back and scapular feathers are sprouting among old faded feathers, and there are new leg feathers. On the tail, the deck rectrices (r1) and, a bit later, the outermost set (r6), begin growing new feathers. The tertials begin to molt at this time, but the rest of the secondaries do not molt until later in spring. Molt on the head, belly, and flanks begins in late May and Jun. Head molt may not be apparent even in early Jul. At this time, some birds have very pale and worn head feathers that have not yet been replaced with new subadult feathers. Body molt, including head, is completed in Sep. or Oct. Tail molt occurs during fall migration and is completed in Oct. or Nov. Remix molt is still occurring in Sep. and Oct. during migration. At this time, the outer two to four primaries (p7–10) are retained worn and frayed juvenile feathers, whereas the newly acquired feathers are dark with pale tips. However, remix molt may cease for a short period while on the winter grounds.

A few (s4 and 8) or several juvenile secondaries are retained in Sep. and Oct., but fewer as the fall season advances.

Molt on secondaries may be continuous throughout the fall and winter until all subadult feathers are fully replaced. By early spring, subadults exhibit full adultlike secondaries by time they arrive in the U.S. Replacement of the outer two to four primaries also occurs during the winter or early spring. In spring, some subadults have fully molted into new outer primaries, but others in late May and early Jun. are often just finishing their molt on the outermost primary (p10), which is the last primary to molt (spring molt based on BKW pers. obs.; B. Sullivan and J. Liguori data on in-hand birds). *Note:* Pattern of completing all remix molt during winter and early spring is atypical for a large buteo. Most species cease their molt during the winter months and do not resume until spring.

The second prebasic molt into adult plumage appears to be a continuation of the subadult remix molt that extends from winter while on the wintering grounds or begins in early spring. Body molt begins in late spring (late May or Jun.). All areas molt during the summer and fall, and adult plumage is gained by late summer. Some individuals in the first adult plumage may still have partial head features that resemble younger birds (e.g., pale supercilium and auricular areas).

Subsequent adult prebasic molts begin during or after the nesting season. As in most species, males do not start their molt until nesting is nearly over or is over. Remix molt may be serially descendant, with two molt waves growing at the same time. Outer primaries that were not molted the previous year may start to replace feathers at the point where they left off last fall, and inner primaries may begin molting again. Also, it appears that birds may replace remiges in an irregular sequence and have two or three molt waves in a serially descendent pattern. Body molt is well under way during the Sep. and Oct. migration period in the U.S. Rectrices may also still be molting at this time. As is typical in larger raptors, body, remix, and possibly rectrix molt is not complete each year.

SUBSPECIES: None.

COLOR MORPHS: Polymorphic. For a species that does not have subspecies, Swainson's Hawk exhibits the most diverse and easily visible array of plumages of any North American raptor (rivaled only by Red-tailed Hawk; however, this species is polymorphic). There is a continuum of plumage variations between light and dark morphs. There are three major color morphs: light, intermediate (rufous), and dark. To fully illustrate the clinal trend between the three major morphs, intermediate morphs are shown: light intermediate morph forms a clinal link between light and intermediate morphs, and dark intermediate morph forms a clinal link between intermediate and dark morphs. Because Swainson's Hawks have a continuum of plumage characters and numerous subtitles, it is often difficult to affix a categorical morph designation to a particular bird. This problem is compounded by the fact that subtle color variations look different when viewed at various angles and distances. Also, some plumage traits vary with the sex; this is most apparent from light to intermediate morph birds. *See* Color morph distribution in Status and Distribution for discussion of geographic range of morphs.

SIZE: A large raptor. Males average smaller than females but there is considerable overlap. Length: 17–21 in. (43–53 cm); wingspan: 47–54 in. (119–137 cm). Juveniles appear slightly longer than subadults and adults because they have longer rectrices.

SPECIES TRAITS: Bill is all black except for small bluish area on the lower basal region of the upper mandible and basal area of the lower mandible. WINGS.—In flight, the front and trailing edges of the long wings are parallel from the body to the wrist area, then taper to pointed wingtips (p9 or p8 and 9 are the longest primaries). Ventral surface of the remiges is gray.

ADULT TRAITS: HEAD.—Dark brown irises. Yellow cere. WINGS.—**Ventral surface of the remiges is dark gray with a wide black band on the trailing edge. When perched, the wingtips extend just beyond the tail tip.** TAIL.—**Medium gray or brown, more brownish when worn. Wide black subterminal band and crossed with numerous narrow inner dark bands.** Pale gray on the ventral surface with the banded pattern highly visible.

ADULT LIGHT MORPH TRAITS: Sexes can be separated 95% of the time by head and breast color (*see below* Male and Female light morph). HEAD.—**White forehead and outer lores form a white mask. Inner lores are dark.** Occasionally, the forehead is dark. Some birds of either sex may have a partial, pale supercilium and auricular regions. BODY (ventral).—Neck and breast are variable brownish and form a distinct bib. Either sex can have a "split bib" with the central portion being white and forming an incomplete bib. These may be younger adults or individual variations on older adults. All the underparts are either white or pale tawny. The amount of markings on the underparts varies: (1) On the palest individuals, the underparts are unmarked. *Note:* Common variation in males, uncommon in females. (2) Typically, the upper belly has a few small brown or rufous specks and the flanks have partial, thin barring. *Note:* Common variation for both sexes. (3) On the heaviest marked individuals, the upper belly may be lightly marked with spots, arrowheads, or diamonds. The flanks are narrowly barred with rufous or brown. *Note:* Common variation for both sexes. Leg feathers and undertail coverts are always unmarked. BODY (dorsal).—Dark brown with a variable amount of pale tawny or rufous-tawny edges on the scapular feathers. The rump is dark brown. WINGS (ventral).— **As with the belly, the underwing coverts and axillaries are either white or uniformly tawny and contrast sharply with the dark gray remiges.** Coverts may be unmarked or have a small amount of brown or rufous spotting, particularly on the axillaries. WINGS (dorsal).—Marked as the rest of the upperparts. TAIL.—Uppertail coverts have a moderately wide white area on each feather and can appear as a white U-shaped band.

Adult male light morph: HEAD.—Crown and auriculars are medium gray or, rarely, brown. Nape and hindneck are rufous. BODY (ventral).—The bib is the rufous type (may appear orangish rufous or orangish brown) or rufous-brown/medium brown type. Any markings on the belly and flanks are rufous. Body (dorsal).—Pale feather edgings are often broad and distinct.

Adult female light morph: HEAD.—Except for the white mask, the head, nape, and hind-

neck are uniformly dark brown. The auriculars occasionally have a slight grayish cast. BODY (ventral).—Bib is either rufous-brown/medium brown or dark brown type. BODY (dorsal).—Moderately distinct or ill-defined pale edges on scapulars and upperparts often appear darker and more uniformly colored than on males.

ADULT LIGHT INTERMEDIATE MORPH TRAITS: Sexes can be separated 95% of the time by head and breast color (*see below* Male and Female light intermediate morph). HEAD.—White mask is similar to light morph's. Essentially as on light morph, but ventral areas become more extensively marked. BODY (ventral).—*Barred type:* White or tawny underparts are fully covered with moderately wide rufous or dark brown barring on the belly, lower belly, and flanks. Barring may be wide and dense on the most heavily marked birds. The flanks may have a large arrowhead-shaped mark on each feather and are more heavily marked than the belly. Leg feathers are finely barred. *Note:* Common plumage type. *Unbarred type:* Underparts may be (1) uniformly pale or medium rufous or tawny and often darker on the flanks or (2) dark tawny on the belly and flanks, with a wide dark brown streak on each feather. The lower belly, leg feathers, and undertail coverts are pale or medium tawny and usually unmarked. *Note:* Uncommon to very uncommon plumage type. BODY (dorsal).—As on light morph but with minimal amount of pale edging on the scapular feathers. WINGS (ventral).—Pale underwing coverts are white or tawny. On the barred type, axillaries are generally barred, with some barring possible on the rest of the coverts. Sometimes coverts are heavily barred. On the unbarred type, axillaries may either be pale or darker brownish. **The dark gray remiges contrast sharply with the paler coverts.** WINGS (dorsal).—As on rest of the upperparts. TAIL.—Uppertail coverts are a white U shape as in light morph.

Adult male light intermediate morph: HEAD.—As on light morph males with gray crown and auriculars. Nape and hindneck, however, vary but are the same color as bib color (*see below*). The gray crown and auriculars may be more difficult to detect on birds with darker brown nape and hindneck. BODY (ventral).—Bib can be rufous, rufous-brown, or dark brown type. On the barred type of underparts, individuals with rufous type bibs typically have similarly colored barring on the belly, flanks, and leg feathers. Those with rufous-brown and dark brown types of bibs can either have rufous or dark brown barring.

Adult female light intermediate morph: HEAD.—As on light morph female with uniformly dark brown crown, auriculars, nape, and hindneck. BODY (ventral).—Same as the two bib colors described for light morph female. On the barred type of underparts, color of the barring is typically dark brown but can be rufous-brown.

ADULT INTERMEDIATE (RUFOUS) MORPH TRAITS: Sexes can be separated 95% of the time by head and breast color (*see below* Male and Female intermediate morph). HEAD.—As on respective sex of the previous two morphs. **White mask and throat are still well defined.** BODY (ventral).—Underparts are somewhat sexually dimorphic (*see below*). Bib is variably colored but belly, flanks, and leg feathers are always rufous (*see below*). The rufous color is the result of having solid rufous feathers, but may have dark brown barring or vertical streaking superimposed over the rufous feather, or have a broad rufous barred pattern. *Note:* The dark brown barring or central feather streaking can be exceptionally broad on some birds. **Undertail coverts are contrastingly white and occasionally have small dark spots on each feather.** BODY (dorsal).—Dark brown with a minimal amount of pale edging on the feathers. WINGS (ventral).—White, tawny, or rufous underwing coverts. Axillaries are generally a bit more heavily marked and deeper colored than the coverts, and are usually the same color as the belly. **The dark gray remiges contrast sharply with the paler coverts.** WINGS (dorsal).—As on the rest of the upperparts with a minimal amount of pale edging. TAIL.—Uppertail coverts have a narrow white U shape to them, but this is somewhat less defined than on the two previous morphs.

Adult male intermediate morph (all-rufous type): HEAD.—Typically has gray crown and auriculars and rufous nape and hindneck as on light morph. BODY (ventral).—Front of the neck, breast, belly, flanks, and leg feathers is uniformly rufous. This type does not have a dark brown bar superimposed on the rufous feather. There may be some rufous barring on

the lower belly. *Note:* Common plumage type for males.

Adult male intermediate morph (bib type): HEAD.—Crown and auriculars are grayish, but nape and hindneck are brown. BODY (ventral).—Some individuals have a rufous-brown or dark brown type bib that contrasts with the rufous belly, flanks, and leg feathers. *Note:* Fairly common to very uncommon plumage type for males.

Adult female intermediate morph: HEAD.—Dark brown throughout. BODY (ventral).—Virtually all have rufous-brown or dark brown bib that contrasts at least somewhat with the paler rufous belly, flanks, and leg feathers. Individuals with rufous-brown bib, however, may have marginal contrast between bib and breast.

ADULT DARK INTERMEDIATE (DARK RUFOUS) MORPH TRAITS: Sexes can be separated some of the time by head color (*see below* Male and Female dark intermediate morph). HEAD.—White mask on the forehead may be similar to the previous morphs or reduced in size. Throat is typically dark with white streaking; rarely, it can be quite white. BODY (ventral).—Three main variations in this morph: (1) *Dark type:* Front of the neck, breast, belly, and flanks is dark brown and has no bib delineation. Lower belly and leg feathers are deep tawny or, more typically, rufous and may be barred with dark brown. (2) *Dark-bellied type:* Rufous-brown breast and subtly darker or much darker brown belly and flanks form a belly band. Leg feathers are rufous or rufous-brown as on the breast. *Note:* Seen on either sex. (3) *Dark rufous type:* All of the underparts are dark brown with rufous edgings on most feathers, creating a dark rufous appearance. **On all types, the undertail coverts are either white or tawny and may be unmarked or partially barred but contrast with the darker underparts.** BODY (dorsal).—All-dark upperparts. Uppertail coverts are either all dark or have narrow tawny edging. WINGS (ventral).—Wing coverts are typically rufous or deep tawny. Axillaries are solid dark brown or heavily barred with rufous. **The dark gray remiges contrast sharply with the paler underwing coverts.** WINGS (dorsal).—Uniformly dark brown like rest of the upperparts.

Adult male dark intermediate morph: HEAD.—Grayish crown and auriculars may be visible only at close range. *Note:* Not readily separable from adult female dark intermediate morph.

Adult female dark intermediate morph: HEAD.—Uniformly dark brown except for the pale mask and whitish throat.

ADULT DARK MORPH TRAITS: Sexes are difficult to separate by head color. HEAD.—Generally dark brown for both sexes, but males may have a grayish tinge on the auriculars. There generally is no white mask in this morph. **The forehead is dark brown, the outer lores white, and the inner lores dark. The throat is dark brown.** Rarely may have all-white lores. Also, rarely has whitish on the forehead and throat. (Types with remnant white on the forehead and throat are probably dark intermediate morphs.) BODY (ventral and dorsal).—Uniformly dark brown. Some birds have a rufous tinge on the leg feathers and lower belly. **Undertail coverts are either white or tawny and vary from unmarked to heavily barred but contrast sharply with the dark underparts.** WINGS (ventral).—Rufous with dark brown axillaries and a dark brown diagonal line on the first row of lesser coverts. **There is still some contrast with the rufous underwing coverts and the dark gray remiges.** Rarely, underwing coverts are dark brown with some rufous mottling. Very rarely, underwing coverts are uniformly dark brown. TAIL.—Uppertail coverts are dark brown.

BASIC I (SUBADULT I) TRAITS: HEAD.—Yellow cere. Medium brown irises. **All morphs have a medium brown or dark brown crown, pale supercilium, narrow dark eyeline, pale auriculars, and dark malar mark that extends onto the sides of the neck and breast.** In darker morphs, the pale areas are more tawny than on lighter birds. *Note:* All have a dark stripe down the middle of the throat. BODY.—Ventral and dorsal areas resemble those of the respective juvenile-plumage morphs. However, all subadult morphs have a variation that has more adultlike barring on ventral areas and less pale edging on the dorsum and resembles adults. WINGS.—**Wide black subterminal band on the trailing edge. Dark gray remiges are also similar to those of adults. The outer two to four primaries are retained juvenile feathers in autumn. They are bleached white**

on the basal region and contrast sharply against the new and darker subadult remiges. The secondaries may retain several or a few juvenile feathers (at least s4 and 8, often many more). The retained juvenile secondaries are shorter than the new subadult feathers and have a pale, worn dusky trailing edge that contrasts against the wide black band of the new subadult feathers. When perched, wingtips are either equal to the tail tip or barely longer. TAIL.—As adult's, with a wide black subterminal band. *Note:* In Sep. and Oct., subadults are in extensive remix and rectrix molt and have a mix of retained juvenile and new adultlike feathers. By spring, all such feathers have molted into adultlike character.

BASIC I (SUBADULT I) LIGHT MORPH TRAITS: BODY (ventral).—**Distinct dark malar and dark patch on the side of the neck and breast, which may encircle the front of the breast as a mottled, partial bib.** White or tawny underparts possibly with a few dark spots, arrowhead shapes, or diamond shapes on the flanks and sometimes a few dark markings on the midbelly area. Leg feathers and undertail coverts are unmarked. BODY (dorsal).—*Juvenilelike.*—Dark brown with broad pale edging as on a juvenile and pale, mottled scapular patch. *Adultlike.*—All dorsal areas may be nearly uniformly dark or with narrow, pale feather edging. WINGS (ventral).—White or tawny and unmarked; axillaries may also be unmarked or have a few dark spots. WINGS (dorsal).—*Juvenilelike.*—Distinct pale edging and spotting and a large pale patch on the mid-scapulars. *Adultlike.*—Coverts are practically uniformly dark with faint pale edgings. TAIL.—Uppertail coverts are pale tawny or white and barred.

BASIC I (SUBADULT I) LIGHT INTERMEDIATE MORPH TRAITS: BODY (ventral).—Dark patch on malar, side of neck, and breast as in light morph. *Juvenilelike.*—As on light morph, but all of breast and belly are lightly spotted or streaked. Flanks have larger arrowhead- or diamond-shaped markings, often with thick barring on the inner portion of the feathers. *Adultlike.*—Flanks are thinly barred. Leg feathers may have some spots or partial barring. Undertail coverts are unmarked. BODY (dorsal).—As on light morph, with the same juvenilelike and adultlike patterns. WINGS (ventral).—Underwing coverts are white or tawny and lightly covered with dark spotting, including the axillaries.

BASIC I (SUBADULT I) INTERMEDIATE MORPH

TRAITS: BODY.—As on light morph. *Juvenilelike.*—Base color of underparts is tawny but fades to white by spring. Breast and belly are covered with a moderate amount of dark brown streaking. Markings on the flanks often have larger, broad arrowhead-shaped markings and thick barring on the inner portion of each feather. *Adultlike.*—Flanks and belly are distinctly barred with dark brown and have a dark arrowhead- or diamond-shaped mark on the center of each feather. Leg feathers are moderately barred. Undertail coverts are white or tawny and have some dark arrowhead markings. BODY (dorsal).—As on light morph for both juvenilelike and adultlike patterns. WINGS (ventral).—Underwing coverts are tawny and moderately covered with dark spotting; axillaries are barred. TAIL.—Uppertail coverts are marked but still appear quite pale tawny.

BASIC I (SUBADULT I) DARK INTERMEDIATE

MORPH TRAITS: BODY (ventral).—Base color is usually rich tawny. There are two types of underpart patterns: (1) *Streaked type: juvenilelike.*—Moderately heavily marked with uniform streaking on the breast and belly. Flanks have large dark arrowhead- or diamond-shaped markings with thick inner-feather barring. Leg feathers are distinctly barred. *Adultlike.*—Flanks and belly are heavily barred and have a large dark streak or diamond-shaped mark on each feather. (2) *Dark-bellied type (juvenilelike only).*—Tawny breast is moderately streaked with dark brown; belly, flanks, and leg feathers are heavily or very heavily streaked and present a belly-band appearance. Lower belly is less heavily marked than flanks and belly and further accentuates the belly-band look. Undertail coverts are pale tawny or tawny and barred. WINGS (ventral).—Rich tawny base color and either moderately or fairly heavily marked, especially with a barred pattern. TAIL.—Uppertail coverts are slightly pale.

BASIC I (SUBADULT I) DARK MORPH TRAITS:

HEAD.—As on paler morphs but supercilium, auriculars, and throat are rich tawny. BODY (ventral).—Three main variations in this

morph: (1) *Streaked type (juvenilelike only):* Identical to juvenile dark morph, with thick, dark brown uniform streaking on the breast and belly and large dark arrowhead- or diamond-shaped markings on the flanks. Flanks are nearly solid dark. Leg feathers are dark with narrow pale edging or heavily barred. (2) *Dark bellied type (juvenilelike only):* Similar to dark-bellied type of dark intermediate morph except breast is darker and somewhat streaked or mottled with narrow tawny edges on some belly and flank feathers. Leg feathers are virtually solid dark brown but may have narrow tawny edging. (3) *All-dark type:* Nearly uniformly dark brown with only a few pale tawny specks scattered on the underparts. Leg feathers are dark brown. On all types, undertail coverts are tawny and somewhat barred. BODY (dorsal).—Streaked type has some pale tawny edgings, but the other two types are all dark. WINGS (ventral).—Streaked type is a rich tawny with heavily marked pattern of spotting and barring; the other two types are dark with some tawny mottling. *Note:* **In the fall, the pale, bleached outer two to four retained juvenile primaries are very obvious as they contrast against the dark underside of the wing.** TAIL.—Streaked type may have some pale tawny tips on the coverts; the other two types have all-dark coverts.

JUVENILE TRAITS (WORN PLUMAGE): In spring

and early summer, at least until mid-Jul. when about 1 year old, juveniles that were fairly pale headed in fresh plumage may exhibit extreme wearing and fading on the head feathers and become bleach-headed. This is most noticeable on the crown, which may be virtually white instead of brown, but the dark eyeline and neck patch are still apparent. May occur in any morph, but is less common in dark morphs.

JUVENILE TRAITS (FRESH PLUMAGE): HEAD.—

Typically has yellow cere but sometimes pale greenish. Medium brown irises. Medium brown or dark brown crown, pale supercilium that connects to the pale forehead, narrow dark eyeline, pale auriculars, and a dark malar mark that extends onto the sides of the neck and breast. *Note:* **All have a pale throat with a dark center streak. In fresh late-summer and autumn plumage, pale areas on the head are tawny but gradually become white**

with wearing and fading. Any morph can have a paler or darker crown; those with pale crowns tend to become very bleached and pale by spring. WINGS (ventral).—**Underside of remiges is nearly uniformly pale or medium gray (paler than on older ages) and covered with narrow dark barring. Basal region of the outer one to three primaries is paler and whitish. Trailing edge of the underwing has a narrow dusky band. When perched, wingtips are barely shorter than the tail tip or equal to it.** WINGS (dorsal).—Remiges are uniformly dark brownish black with somewhat paler coverts. TAIL.—**Uppertail is medium grayish or brownish and crossed by numerous narrow bands. The subterminal band is the same width as the inner bands or marginally wider.** JUVENILE LIGHT MORPH TRAITS: BODY (ventral).—**Dark malar, side of neck, and breast patch are distinct. Dark patch sometimes continues onto the mid-breast area as a partial bib.** Underparts are either unmarked or the flanks may have small or moderate-sized arrowhead- or diamond-shaped markings and the belly may be sprinkled with short streaks or spots. Leg feathers are unmarked. Undertail coverts are unmarked. BODY (dorsal).—Dark brown with distinct tawny edge on all feathers. A large white or tawny patch on the middle of each scapular tract. WINGS (ventral).—Wing coverts are unmarked. WINGS (dorsal).—Pale edging on all coverts. TAIL.—Uppertail coverts are pale.

JUVENILE LIGHT INTERMEDIATE MORPH TRAITS: BODY (ventral).—**Dark malar, side of neck, and breast patch are distinct. The dark patch often continues as a partial bib across the front of the breast.** All of the belly and forward flanks are lightly spotted or streaked with dark brown; rear of the flanks may have larger arrowhead- or diamond-shaped dark markings. Leg feathers may be lightly spotted or barred. Undertail coverts are unmarked or have small arrowhead-shaped marks. BODY (dorsal).—As on light morph. WINGS (ventral).—Wing coverts are often lightly marked with dark brown, including the axillaries. WINGS (dorsal).—As on light morph. TAIL.—As on light morph.

JUVENILE INTERMEDIATE MORPH TRAITS: BODY (ventral).—**Dark malar, side of neck, and breast patch are distinct. Patch regularly wraps around the front of the breast as a partial bib.** All of the belly and forward portion of the flanks are moderately streaked with dark brown; rear of flanks is covered with large arrowhead-shaped markings and wide barring on the inner portion of the longest feathers. Leg feathers are moderately barred with brown. Undertail coverts are partially barred. BODY (dorsal).—As on light morph but often with fewer pale areas; however, still shows pale scapular patches. WINGS (ventral).—Underwing coverts are moderately marked with dark spots, and the axillaries are barred or streaked. WINGS (dorsal).—As on on light morph. TAIL.—Uppertail coverts are marked but still pale.

JUVENILE DARK INTERMEDIATE MORPH TRAITS: BODY (ventral).—**Dark malar, side of neck, and breast patch are large and dark. Patch often wraps around the front of the breast as a mottled bib.** Two main types of markings: (1) *Streaked type*: Belly and forward flanks are heavily streaked and rear flanks are densely covered with large dark arrowhead- or diamond-shaped markings and wide barring on the inner portion of the longer rear feathers. (2) *Dark-bellied type*: Breast is moderately streaked, but belly and flanks are densely streaked and mottled and appear as a dark belly band. Lower belly is not as heavily streaked as belly and promotes an even more obvious belly-band look. Leg feathers of both types are heavily barred. Undertail coverts are barred. BODY (dorsal).—Similar to markings on light morph but with narrower pale edging. WINGS (ventral).—Wing coverts are rather heavily marked, and axillaries are barred with dark brown. TAIL.—Uppertail coverts are somewhat pale.

JUVENILE DARK MORPH TRAITS: BODY (ventral).—Uniformly streaked on breast and belly or breast is somewhat paler with narrower streaking (but not as obvious a difference as in dark-bellied type of dark intermediate morph). Flanks are covered with broad, dark arrowhead- and diamond-shaped markings and appear virtually solid dark. Leg feathers are heavily barred. Undertail coverts are barred but distinctly paler than the rest of the underparts. BODY (dorsal).—Moderate amount of tawny pale edging on the scapulars. WINGS (ventral).—Coverts are heavily marked with dark brown, and axillaries are barred. WINGS (dorsal). Moderate amount of pale edging on the coverts. TAIL.—Uppertail coverts may have narrow tawny tips but do not stand out as a large pale area.

ABNORMAL PLUMAGES: Partial albinism has been documented. Light morph adults, even very gray-headed males, occasionally have white supercilium and auricular areas and only partial bibs (BKW pers. obs.).

HABITAT: Summer.—In Illinois, the only breeding location in the East, Swainson's Hawks are found in very restricted areas, primarily in semi-open cattle pastures and hay fields adjacent to dairy farms. Peripheral habitat often consists of corn and soybean fields. Nesting pairs have been located near farmhouses adjacent to dairy farms. Some birds may be in small tracts of non-native grassy fields. Isolated mature trees, small wooded patches, or larger woodlots may be interspersed among the fields, and pastures and are used for nesting sites. Terrain is mainly low, gently rolling hills. Climate is warm and humid.

Winter.—Semi-open and open regions with relatively flat terrain. Light agricultural zones, pastures, grasslands, and prairies are favored haunts in the typical wintering area in Argentina. In s. Florida, found mainly in agricultural zones, pastures, and grasslands.

Migration.—Found in a variety of habitats. Foraging birds are mainly in some type of semi-open or open grassy or moderately agricultural habitat. Migrants are seen along mountain ridges, lake shores, and sea shores.

HABITS: Generally a tame raptor and becomes well acclimated to humans in certain areas. Nesting pairs are solitary. Nesting pairs and their siblings remain as a family clan until fall migration. When breeding duties are completed, however, all ages become gregarious and join in small to large flocks for migration and winter. Nonbreeding birds in the summer are generally found in small groups or as singles.

Swainson's Hawks perch on the ground or any elevated object, including utility wires. Migrants seem to prefer elevated perches, if available, for roosting. When roosting in trees, several hawks often perch in a single tree. If elevated perches are not available, the hawks, often hundreds, will readily roost on the ground. Ground-roosting birds seek open, fallow (dirt) fields or fields with very short vegetation for optimal visibility of potential predators. Hawks perching on the ground like to sit on top of slightly elevated clumps of earth. Migrants are also fond of water and will sit around shorelines of ponds and in the shallow water of ponds and irrigation runoff pools. During inclement weather, shelter is often sought by perching on the ground on the lee side of clumps of dirt or dense vegetation.

FEEDING: Perch and aerial hunter. When perch hunting, may drop down or fly from an elevated perch to capture prey or may run on the ground like a chicken adeptly pursuing large insects. Aerial hunting is a commonly used foraging method.

Insects are captured on the ground with the hawk's feet or bill or in the air with their feet. Swainson's Hawks often capture flying insects in impressive acrobatic aerial maneuvers. Flying insects are also eaten while the hawks are soaring or gliding. Vertebrate prey are captured with the hawk's feet and are eaten on the ground at the point of capture, transported to another ground or elevated location, or taken to the nest site to be devoured. Swainson's Hawks regularly feed in fields that have been or are being harvested, plowed, or burned.

Little is known of the prey species of the few breeding pairs in Illinois. As in the West, breeding pairs no doubt feed on vertebrates to provide ample protein to nestlings. Ground squirrels (probably Thirteen-lined and possibly Franklin's), other rodents, and Eastern Cottontail Rabbits probably form the bulk of the summer diet. Breeding birds occasionally feed on small birds, reptiles, and large insects. Nonbreeding summering birds feed extensively on large insects, especially grasshoppers. During migration and in winter (in South America), all ages of Swainson's Hawks feed almost exclusively on grasshoppers.

Feeding occurs regularly during migration. Western migrants in the fall in e. Colorado may spend part of a day, a whole day, or a few days in one location aerial and perch hunting grasshoppers. Migrants in s. Texas feed extensively in fields infested with grasshoppers and caterpillars. They also are found in burned or plowed fields (accompanied by White-tailed Hawks and Crested Caracaras). Aerial feeding has been observed in e. Mexico in the autumn.

Based on telemetry data, California migrants may stop for a week or more in various locations along the southward migration path in s. California, w. Mexico, and Central America.

FLIGHT: Wings are held in a high or low dihedral when soaring and a modified or low dihedral when gliding. Powered flight is regularly used. Wingbeats are moderately slow but snappy. Very high altitudes are attained when migrating. Exceptionally long glides, often extending for several miles, are used when migrating in order to be energy efficient. Hovering and kiting occur frequently when hunting. Rather impressive acrobatic dives and twists accompany pursuits of insects and chasing of intruders.

VOICE: Vocalizes primarily when disturbed at nest sites and rarely heard elsewhere. Adults emit a loud, somewhat raspy *keeyaah, keeyaah* or *keeair, keeair.* Also may have short *kee, kee, kee* notes. Nestlings and fledglings have the typical raptor begging call of a high-pitched whining *skree, skree, skree.*

STATUS AND DISTRIBUTION: Overall in North America, a common raptor. Estimated population is 450,000 to 1 million individuals, based on fall counts of migrants at Veracruz, Mexico (*see* Movements). Fall tallies at Veracruz have varied over the years from 273,000 to 541,000. An amazing 1,062,500 Swainson's Hawks were counted in the fall of 2001 (much of the count verified with digital photos). This substantial increase does not reflect a population growth but is tied to count location and viewer capabilities. Numbers passing Veracruz are still thought to be undercounted, even with the 1 million birds seen in 2001. Thousands of Swainson's Hawks are often seen in late afternoon migrating in the foothills of the mountains far inland of the two official hawkwatch sites and are not tallied. *Note:* One million Swainson's Hawks were also tallied in fall 2002. *Additional Note:* The breeding population in the East is an easterly remnant of a population that mainly ends in e. North and South Dakota, south to cen. Oklahoma and e. Texas. Small fragmented populations exist in eastern, remnant prairie regions of the West in w. and s. Minnesota, n. Iowa, and w. Missouri.

Color morph status distribution (overall in North America).—Only light morphs breed east of the Great Plains. Darker morphs breed only in the West, primarily west of an imaginary line from cen. Saskatchewan south to e. New Mexico. Thus, breeding birds in Illinois are light morphs. All morphs can be found in the East during migration and in winter in Florida, however, light morphs predominate.

Summer.—In the East, Swainson's Hawk breeds only in n. Kane and s. McHenry Cos. in Illinois. It is listed as a state Endangered Species. There have never been more than five pairs nesting in any given year in the state (there were five pairs in Kane Co. in 1973). In 1996–2000, up to four pairs nested. In 2001, only two pairs were known to have nested, with one pair in each county. Possible nesting may occur in cen. Fayette Co. Only a moderate effort is made to locate possible pairs in the state. The current nesting pairs are potentially threatened by urbanization. Swainson's Hawks formerly nested in Illinois, Boone and Winnebago and possibly in DeKalb and Ogle Cos. The species was first found nesting in Illinois in 1875 in Richland Co.

One-year-olds and subadults molting into their first adult plumage spend the summer moving about singly or in small flocks in a nomadic fashion wherever prey is most abundant. Most do not return to natal areas.

Winter.—Virtually all Swainson's Hawks winter in n. and cen. Argentina with smaller numbers in Uruguay and s. Paraguay. The hawks arrive on the breeding grounds from early Nov. to early Dec. Once there, they may shift around to forage in different areas. Swainson's Hawks are gregarious and feed and roost in flocks containing thousands of birds.

There are no banding or telemetry data that confirm the wintering area of the few Illinois breeding pairs. Individuals from s. Minnesota, however, have been telemetry-tracked to Argentina, and Illinois birds probably also winter there.

Florida has an annual contingent of wintering birds, nearly all juveniles and subadults. Numbers vary considerably each year. The most ever recorded were 300 in s. Dade Co. in 1952. A few move down onto the cen. Keys but rarely spend the winter there. Most that travel down the Keys eventually head northeast back up to the Florida mainland. Some, undoubtedly confused, birds move up and down the Keys for a while with the large flocks of Turkey

Vultures. Big Pine Key has had as many as 60 Swainson's Hawks in Nov., but there are very few by Dec.

Movements.—A highly migratory raptor. Canadian birds may travel 7,000 miles (11,500 km) each spring and fall to wintering areas in Argentina. Among raptors, Swainson's Hawks are surpassed in migratory distance only by "Arctic" Peregrine Falcons (*Falco peregrinus tundrius*). Migration is very punctual. Considerable information regarding migration routes and timing has appeared since the mid- to late 1990s from telemetry.

Fall migration: Southward movements may begin in late Aug. Illinois birds may leave by early Sep. From Illinois, the theoretical path would be a southwesterly course towards e. or n.-cen. Texas, and from Texas, south into e. Mexico and staying east of the Sierra Madre Oriental. The hawks wend their way through Central America and enter South America at the Panama-Colombia border and cross the Cordillera Mts. of e. Colombia, then stay near the eastern edge of the Andes through w. Peru and Bolivia and drop into nw. Argentina. Based on telemetry, some birds angle farther east and cross w. Brazil and cen. Bolivia, then enter n.-cen. Argentina and proceed to the winter quarters a bit farther south in Argentina. Typical migrants may stop and feed for short periods as described in Feeding. As on individuals telemetry-tracked from Alberta to Argentina, the long migration is completed in about 50 days.

Huge numbers of migrants funnel down into cen. Texas and into e. Mexico. Some far western birds may take other pathways. On the cen. Great Plains, peak movement is in late Sep.; peak in s. Texas is in mid-Oct. (about 1 week after the peak for Broad-winged Hawks). The migration period in Veracruz, Mexico, spans from late Sep. to early Nov. The majority of migrants are clustered between early and mid-Oct. and peak in mid-Oct. Stragglers occur through Nov. In Texas, Swainson's Hawks flocks are often mixed with large numbers of Turkey Vultures and a few Broad-winged Hawks. In s. Mexico, Swainson's Hawk flocks may comprise thousands of birds and may also include thousands of Turkey Vultures and Broad-winged Hawks. (Migration timing of Turkey Vulture is similar to Swainson's Hawk,

with similar peak period; however, the vulture's migration extends somewhat later.)

Spring migration: Adult Swainson's Hawks wintering in Argentina may begin leaving winter grounds to return to breeding areas in North America in early to mid-Feb. Adults retrace the route taken in fall and primarily migrate separately from subadults and juveniles. Adults peak in s. Texas from mid- to late Mar. Spring adult migration is more expedient than fall migration, but flock sizes are much smaller. By the time adults have reached the cen. Great Plains, flock sizes are very small.

Subadults and juveniles leave the winter grounds in Argentina in Mar. Peak migration periods are unknown. Juveniles are in s. Texas in mid-Apr., but seem to trickle northward as singles and small flocks into Jun. The first 1-year-old juveniles are seen in Colorado in early to mid-May. Younger birds also retrace the same routes taken the previous autumn; however, unlike most raptors, they may not return to natal regions and spend the summer roaming around.

Extralimital movements in the East.—Sightings have been documented in the following eastern states; most are in Apr.–May and Sep.–Nov. Rare summer records occur for Maine and Massachusetts. *Connecticut:* Nine accepted records spanning early Sep. to mid-Nov. *Maine:* An adult light morph near Deblois, Washington Co., in mid-Jul. 1986. *Massachusetts:* Accepted records by the Massachusetts Audubon Records Committee at five locations since 1995, in spring, summer, and fall. (1) Plymouth Co.: Adult light morph near Middleboro from late Oct. to mid-Nov. 1995. (2) West Newbury: Adult light morph seen in early May 1997. (3) Provincetown: (3a) Juvenile light morph seen for 2 days in early Sep. 1994. (3b) Sightings of an adult light morph that spent from late Jun. to mid-Sep. 1997 at this location. A light morph seen in mid-Oct. 1997 may have been the same bird. (3c) Two immatures seen in early Oct. 1998. (4) Mt. Wachusett, Worcester Co.: Single bird seen in mid-Oct. 1997. (5) Mt. Watatic, Middlesex Co.: Single bird seen in mid-Oct. 1999. *Michigan:* Annual at Whitefish Point, Chippewa Co. in spring and at Lake Erie Metro Park, Wayne Co., in fall. *Newfoundland and Labrador:* First record for Newfoundland was at Cape Race in early Oct. 1998. One was seen in the spring of 1999 near Wabush in southeastern Labrador. *New Jersey:* Over 70 records spanning early Sep. to late Nov., most from Cape May Point S.P. in the fall hawk-watch season. There are a few spring records. Swainson's Hawks have occurred annually in the state since 1980. *New York:* Numerous records, especially from spring hawkwatch sites along the s. Great Lakes. *Nova Scotia:* First accepted record was an adult light morph in Sep. 1964 on Brier Island. Five individuals were seen in the fall of 1998 near Donkin. A juvenile dark morph banded in Cape May, N.J., in fall 1998 was found dead in Nova Scotia the following spring. This no doubt represents a bird that was off the typical migration course. *Ohio:* A few records. *Ontario:* Eighteen records from 1881 to 1985. An additional 24 records from 1988 to 1999. *Pennsylvania:* Annual sightings from hawkwatches in the eastern part of the state. Sightings have been documented in 13 counties. The first record was a specimen from Westmoreland Co. in early Sep. 1901. The species was not recorded again until 1961. *Québec:* A few records from the southern part of the province and at least one record from the Gaspe Peninsula. *Rhode Island:* A few sightings. *South Carolina:* A few records from coastal areas. *Tennessee-North Carolina:* At least one record from the border area. *Vermont:* A few sightings. *Virginia:* Regular if not annual at Kiptopeke S.P., Northhampton Co. Eight individuals were seen in fall 1998. *West Virginia:* At least one record in the east-central part of the state.

NESTING: Begins in Apr. or May and ends in Jul. or Aug. Swainson's Hawks typically do not breed until 3 years old.

Courtship (flight).—*Sky-dancing* by males and *high-circling* by both members (*see* chapter 5).

Nesting pairs are susceptible to nest desertion if disturbed during incubation, especially in areas where they are not acclimated to humans. However, a pair has been documented building new nests higher up in the same tree to escape disturbance. This occurred twice in the same pair, and each time they built the nest higher than the previous nest.

Males pick nest locations, but both sexes build new nests or refurbish old nests. In Illinois, nests are typically in the top portion of

mature trees. Live or dead trees are used as nest sites. Nest trees in Illinois are deciduous. Single, isolated trees or trees on the periphery of small tracts adjacent to fields are primary sites. Nesting has occurred within 100 ft. (30 m) of occupied farm houses.

Nests average 24 in. (60 cm) in diameter and 13 in. (32 cm) in depth. However, new nests or nests that are compressed by nestlings or are the product of poor workmanship may be flattened. Some nests, especially ones reused for several years, may become quite large. The often rather flimsy and shabbily made structures are built with thin or medium thick sticks or thistles and lined with finer material and usually greenery. Prey remains are typically on the edge of nests, particularly when nestlings are younger.

One to 4 eggs, but 2–3 is the typical clutch size (a 5-egg clutch was documented in Idaho, and in Saskatchewan a nest with 5 successfully fledged). Most of the 28-day incubation is performed by females; however, males incubate when females are off the nest feeding. Youngsters may branch in 27–33 days and fledge in 38–46 days. Family groups generally remain intact until fall migration begins.

European House Sparrows regularly build nests at the base of Swainson's Hawk nests or in the same tree, without harm to the sparrows or bother to the hawks.

CONSERVATION: No measures taken other than preventing harmful pesticide use (*see below*). In the extensively agricultural Kane and McHenry Cos. in Illinois, retaining ample foraging and nesting habitat is essential. Kane Co., in particular, is undergoing growth expansion that could be detrimental to nesting areas.

Mortality.—Pesticide contamination can be a major problem. Severe mortality was discovered in the winter of 1994–1995 in n. Argentina when 4,000 Swainson's Hawks were found dead from pesticide poisoning in one small area. In the winter of 1995–1996, biologists found 20,000 Swainson's Hawks killed by pesticides. Fewer dead hawks were found in the next 2 years. The culprit was the highly toxic organophosphate insecticide monocrotophos, which was used to control grasshoppers. The insecticide had probably been used in Argentina since the late 1980s in major wintering areas of the hawk. Argentina banned all use of the insecticide in areas where Swainson's Hawks typically winter in 1996. In late March 2000, monocrotophos was totally banned in Argentina. There have not been reports of Swainson's Hawk mortality from monocrotophos since the winter of 1998–1999. The ban was a tribute to the concerted efforts of biologists, the Argentine government, and the manufacturer of the pesticide. Since virtually the entire population of Swainson's Hawks winters in a restricted area in Argentina, continued exposure to the deadly chemical could have devastated the population. Monocrotophos was not used in the U.S. or Canada.

Organophosphate insecticides are used in North America, but it is not known if they have affected Swainson's Hawks. The hawk also faces possible contamination from the well-known organochlorine pesticide DDT south of the U.S. The deadly pesticide is still used in parts of Central America. Mexico ceased most use in 2002.

As in most large raptors, illegal shooting is still a problem. The fall Swainson's Hawk migration through portions of the West coincides with various hunting seasons of small game mammals and birds (particularly Mourning Doves). Errant hunters take their toll on the tame raptor during the fall. Natural predators include Great Horned Owl, Coyote, and foxes.

SIMILAR SPECIES: COMPARED TO ADULT LIGHT MORPH.—(1) **Short-tailed Hawk, light morph adults.**—Overlap in Florida only from late fall to early spring. PERCHED.— Similar head pattern with the mask. Has small rufous patch along the sides of the breast. Tail pattern often indistinct. FLIGHT.—Underside of remiges paler gray with larger whitish area on the outer four primaries. Tail pattern indistinct or only a few dark narrow inner bands. Does not hover or kite. (2) **Rough-legged Hawk, light morph lightly marked type adults.**—PERCHED.—Head pattern similar but has distinct dark malar mark and white throat is not sharply defined. Bib on the neck and breast can be similar to Swainson's: use caution. Flanks are spotted or thickly barred. Tarsi are feathered (not visible if belly feathers are fluffed over them). Dark tail banding is wide on inner tail. Wingtip-to-tail-tip ratio similar. FLIGHT.—Underside of remiges white.

Tail pattern as noted above. COMPARED TO JUVENILE LIGHT MORPH.—(3) **Red-tailed Hawk, "Western" (*B. j. calurus*) light morph and "Eastern" (*B. j. borealis*) juveniles.**— Overlap during migration only. PERCHED.— Iris color is pale yellow or gray. Cere typically more greenish. Lacks dark eyeline and single dark streak down the middle of the throat. Pale scapular patches are similar to Swainson's. Wingtips are distinctly shorter than the tail tip. Dark tail banding is fairly wide. FLIGHT.— Dark patagial mark on leading edge of underwing. Has pale brown upperside of the primaries. Underside of remiges white. Tail pattern as noted above. (3A) **Red-tailed Hawk, "Krider's" (*B. j. borealis*) juveniles.**—Overlap during migration only. Very similar to pale-headed 1-year old Swainson's: use caution. PERCHED.— Head rarely has a dark eyeline. White scapular patches are similar. Tail is whitish and crossed by narrow dark banding on distal two-thirds. Wingtips much shorter than the tail tip. COMPARED TO ADULT INTERMEDIATE/DARK INTERMEDIATE MORPH.—(3B) **Red-tailed Hawk, intermediate morph "Western" (*B. j. calurus*) adults.**—Overlap during migration only. PERCHED.—Forehead is dark and all of lores are white; dark throat. Rufous breast and dark belly similar to dark-bellied type of adult dark intermediate morph Swainson's. Rufous tail. FLIGHT.—Dark patagial mark on underside of leading edge of the wings. White or pale gray remiges. Dark undertail coverts. Rufous tail. COMPARED TO ADULT DARK MORPH.—(4) **Broad-winged Hawk, dark morph adults/juveniles.**—Rare overlap during migration only. PERCHED.—All pale lores. Wingtips are shorter than the tail tip. Wide pale band across mid-tail (adult) or moderately wide dark bands (juvenile). FLIGHT.—White underside of the remiges. Dark undertail coverts. Tail patterns as noted above. Does not hover or kite. (5) **Red-tailed Hawk, dark morph "Western" (*B. j. calurus*) adults.**— Overlap during migration only. PERCHED.— All of lores are pale. Rufous tail. FLIGHT.— Pale gray underside of remiges. Rufous tail. (5A) **Red-tailed Hawk, dark morph "Western" (*B. j. calurus*) juveniles.**—Overlap during migration only. PERCHED.—Pale lores. Pale yellow or gray iris. Wingtips are shorter than the tail tip. Prominent fairly wide dark tail banding. FLIGHT.—White underside of the remiges. Pale brown panel on dorsal side of primaries. Dark undertail coverts. COMPARED TO JUVENILE AND SUBADULT DARK INTERMEDIATE/DARK MORPH.— **(6) Northern Harrier, adult females.**—Rare overlap in summer; common overlap in migration. PERCHED.—Older birds have pale irises; younger similar brownish. Lacks dark eyeline. Wingtips much shorter than the tail tip. FLIGHT.—Dorsal view similar but white on uppertail coverts more extensive and forms a larger white patch. Dihedral wing attitude is similar. Pale underside of the remiges. Tail banding is very wide. **(7) Red-tailed Hawk, intermediate/dark morph "Western"** (*B. j. calurus*) **and "Harlan's"** (*B. j. harlani*) **juveniles.**—Overlap during migration only. PERCHED.—Pale yellow or gray iris. Dark throat on *calurus*, pale on *harlani* but lacks dark center streak. Lacks dark eyeline. Wingtips are distinctly shorter than the tail tip. Dark tail

banding is fairly wide. Intermediate morph of the two species very similar with the dark streaking on the ventral areas: use caution. FLIGHT.—White underside of the remiges. Pale brown panel on upper surface of the primaries. Undertail coverts are the same darker color as rest of the underparts. Tail banding is fairly wide.

OTHER NAMES: None regularly used. *Spanish:* Aguililla de Swainson, Aquililla Cuaresmera. *French:* Buse de Swainson.

REFERENCES: Anderson 2001; Bohlen 1989; Dodge 1988–1997; Duncan 1986; England et al. 1997; Hoffman and Darrow 1992; Houston 1998; Kellogg 2000; Line 1996; Lott 1999; Martell et al. 1998; McKinley and Mattox 2001; McWilliams and Brauning 2000; Paxton et al. 2000; Raptor Center 1999b; Rodriquez 1997; Stevenson and Anderson 1994; Tucker 1999; Tufts 1986; Veit and Petersen 1993; Walsh et al. 1999; Woodbridge 1997.

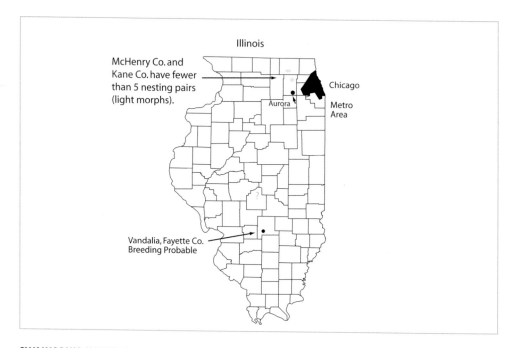

SWAINSON'S HAWK, *Buteo swainsoni.*

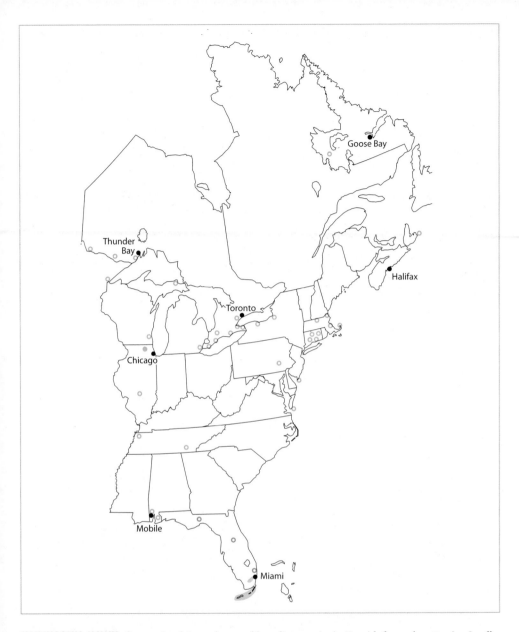

SWAINSON'S HAWK, *Buteo swainsoni:* An endangered breeding species in IL, with fewer than 5 pairs. Small numbers of w. North American population disperse into East in fall and spring. Small numbers winter in s. FL.

Plate 253. Swainson's Hawk, adult male light morph [Sep.] ▪ Gray head with a rufous nape; white forehead, outer lores, and throat. ▪ Rufous bib; white belly, flanks, and leg feathers. Upperparts often edged with tawny.

Plate 254. Swainson's Hawk, adult female light morph [Apr.] ▪ Brown head; white forehead, outer lores, and throat. ▪ Rufous-brown bib. White belly, flanks, and leg feathers unmarked, or partial barring on flanks and leg feathers. ▪ Wingtips extend past tail tip. ▪ *Note:* Palest brown bib color for females. Both sexes may have faint supercilium and pale auricular areas.

Plate 255. Swainson's Hawk, adult female light morph [Jul.] ▪ Brown head; white forehead, outer lores, and throat. ▪ Dark brown bib and white belly, flanks, and leg feathers; flanks usually lightly barred, leg feathers sometimes lightly barred. ▪ Wingtips extend past tail tip. ▪ *Note:* This is heaviest amount of ventral barring for light morph.

Plate 256. Swainson's Hawk, adult male light intermediate morph [Jul.] ▪ Gray head; white throat, forehead, and outer lores. ▪ Rufous bib. White underparts vary from lightly to heavily barred with rufous on belly, flanks, and leg feathers. White undertail coverts. ▪ *Note:* This is least amount of ventral barring for this color morph.

Plate 257. Swainson's Hawk, adult male light intermediate morph [Jun.] ▪ Gray head; white outer lores and throat (forehead typically white). ▪ Dark brown bib. White underparts lightly to heavily barred with dark brown or rufous on belly, flanks, and leg feathers. Flank feathers may have rufous wash. ▪ *Note:* Palest morph for a male to have dark brown bib.

Plate 258. Swainson's Hawk, adult female light intermediate morph [Aug.] ▪ Brown head; white outer lores and throat (forehead typically white). ▪ Dark brown bib. White or tawny underparts vary from lightly to heavily barred on flanks, belly, and leg feathers. Unmarked undertail coverts. ▪ *Note:* Heaviest amount of markings for this morph. Very worn plumage.

Plate 259. Swainson's Hawk, adult male intermediate (rufous) morph (all-rufous type) [Sep.] ▪ Gray head; white forehead, outer lores, and throat. ▪ Uniformly rufous underparts; somewhat barred on leg feathers and lower belly. White undertail coverts. ▪ *Note:* Only males have all-rufous underparts.

Plate 260. Swainson's Hawk, adult female intermediate (rufous) morph [Sep.] ▪ Brown head; white forehead, outer lores, and throat. ▪ Dark brown bib contrasts with rufous belly, flanks, and leg feathers. Brown barring often superimposed on rufous feathers. White undertail coverts. ▪ *Note:* Either sex can have contrasting rufous-brown or dark brown bib; male typically has gray head.

Plate 261. Swainson's Hawk, adult male dark intermediate (dark rufous) morph [Sep.] ▪ Gray head; white forehead, outer lores, and throat. ▪ Dark brown underparts, including leg feathers; rufous tinge on lower belly; white undertail coverts. ▪ *Note:* Quite pale-headed for a fairly dark bird. Similar to dark morph, but head as on light or intermediate (rufous) morph.

Plate 262. Swainson's Hawk, adult female dark intermediate (dark rufous) morph [Jul.] ▪ Dark brown head with white outer lores and throat; forehead dark. ▪ Breast, belly, and flanks dark brown; parts of belly and all lower belly and leg feathers rufous. White undertail coverts. ▪ *Note:* Similar to dark morph except for pale throat and rufous on portions of ventral areas.

Plate 263. Swainson's Hawk, adult (sex unknown) dark morph [Sep.] ▪ Dark brown head with white lores (typically white only on outer lores). ▪ Uniformly dark brown body; leg feathers often have slight rufous tinge. Undertail coverts pale tawny, often barred. ▪ Wingtips extend to tail tip. ▪ *Note:* Probably a female by brown head.

Plate 264. Swainson's Hawk, adult male light morph [Sep.] ▪ Gray head, white throat. ▪ Rufous bib; white belly, flanks, and leg feathers. ▪ Dark gray remiges contrast with white coverts. Long pointed wings. ▪ Wide black subterminal tail band, narrow inner bands.

Plate 265. Swainson's Hawk, adult female light morph [**Aug.**] ▪ White throat. ▪ Dark brown bib. Type with tawny underparts. ▪ Dark gray remiges contrast with tawny coverts. Long pointed wings. ▪ Wide black subterminal tail band, narrow inner bands. ▪ *Note:* Tawny underparts fairly common on light morphs.

Plate 266. Swainson's Hawk, adult female light morph [**Jul.**] ▪ White throat. ▪ Split bib type with incomplete brown bib; white underparts. ▪ Dark gray remiges contrast with tawny coverts. Long pointed wings. ▪ Wide black subterminal tail band, narrow inner bands. ▪ *Note:* Uncommon for either sex to have split bib.

Plate 267. Swainson's Hawk, adult male light intermediate morph [**Sep.**] ▪ Gray head, white throat. ▪ Breast, upper flanks, and belly rufous. Lower flanks and much of belly white, barred with rufous. White undertail coverts. ▪ Dark gray remiges contrast with white coverts. Axillaries barred with rufous. ▪ Wide dark subterminal tail band, narrow inner bands.

Plate 268. Swainson's Hawk, adult female light intermediate morph [**Sep.**] ▪ Brown head; white forehead, outer lores, and throat. ▪ Dark brown bib. Tawny belly, flanks, and leg feathers barred with dark brown. ▪ Dark gray remiges contrast with tawny coverts. Axillaries barred. Long pointed wings. ▪ *Note:* Male may be similar, including dark brown bib, but typically has gray head.

Plate 269. Swainson's Hawk, adult male intermediate (rufous) morph (all-rufous type) [Sep.] ▪ Gray head, white throat. ▪ Uniformly rufous underparts except white undertail coverts. ▪ Dark gray remiges contrast with tawny-rufous coverts. Axillaries rufous. ▪ Wide black subterminal tail band, narrow inner bands.

Plate 270. Swainson's Hawk, adult female intermediate (rufous) morph [Sep.] ▪ Dark brown bib; rufous belly, flanks, and leg feathers (often with darker brown barring). Pale tawny undertail coverts. ▪ Dark gray remiges contrast with pale tawny coverts. Axillaries barred. ▪ Wide black subterminal tail band, narrow inner bands.

Plate 271. Swainson's Hawk, adult (sex unknown) dark intermediate (dark rufous) morph (dark-bellied type) [Sep.] ▪ Dark head with some whitish streaking on throat. ▪ Rufous breast, dark brown belly and flanks (creates belly band), rufous leg feathers and lower belly. White undertail coverts. ▪ Dark gray remiges contrast with tawny-rufous coverts. Brown axillaries.

Plate 272. Swainson's Hawk, adult female dark intermediate morph (dark type) [Sep.] ▪ Brown head with whitish throat. ▪ Dark brown breast, belly, and flanks. Lower belly and leg feathers rufous. White undertail coverts. ▪ Dark gray remiges contrast with rufous coverts. Axillaries barred. ▪ Wide black subterminal tail band, narrow inner bands.

246   *Swainson's Hawk*

Plate 273. Swainson's Hawk, adult (unknown sex) dark morph [Sep.] ▪ Dark brown head. ▪ Dark brown underparts, including leg feathers. White undertail coverts partially barred. ▪ Dark gray remiges contrast with tawny-rufous coverts, which have dark diagonal bar. Brown axillaries. ▪ Wide black subterminal tail band, narrow inner bands. ▪ *Note:* A few have all-dark underwing coverts.

Plate 274. Swainson's Hawk, subadult (2-year-old) light morph [May] ▪ Dark patch on neck and streaked breast. ▪ Remiges full adultlike dark gray but just replacing outermost primary (p10) for first time (1/3 grown). Dark gray remiges contrast with pale coverts. ▪ Tail adultlike with wide black subterminal band. ▪ *Note:* Bird is completing molt that began previous spring.

Plate 275. Swainson's Hawk, subadult light morph (juvenile-like) [Aug.] ▪ Yellow cere. Medium brown iris. Pale head with thin dark eyeline, dark malar mark. ▪ Dark patch on sides of neck that merges with dark malar mark; rest of underparts lightly streaked. ▪ A few retained juvenile feathers on wings. Wingtips slightly shorter than tail tip.

Plate 276. Swainson's Hawk, subadult light morph (adultlike) [Sep.] ▪ Yellow cere, nearly all-black bill. Medium brown iris. Dark head with pale supercilium, thin dark eyeline. ▪ Dark brown upperparts have thin pale edgings. ▪ Retains a few juvenile secondaries (paler, frayed feathers). Wingtips nearly reach tail tip. ▪ Wide black subterminal tail band, narrow inner bands.

Plate 277. Swainson's Hawk, subadult dark morph (dark-bellied type) [Sep.] ▪ Medium or dark brown iris. Yellow cere. Thin dark eyeline; dark malar. ▪ Tawny streaked or mottled breast paler than solid dark brown belly and flanks; heavily barred leg feathers. White undertail coverts lightly barred. ▪ Wingtips nearly reach tail tip. ▪ Wide black subterminal tail band, narrow inner bands.

Plate 278. Swainson's Hawk, subadult dark morph (all-dark type) [Sep.] ▪ Yellow cere. Dark brown iris. Thin dark eyeline; dark malar. ▪ Dark underparts have a few tawny spots. White undertail coverts lightly barred. ▪ Wide black subterminal tail band, narrow inner bands.

Plate 279. Swainson's Hawk, subadult light morph (juvenile-like) [Sep.] ▪ Pale tawny underparts unmarked except for dark patch on sides of neck. ▪ Dark gray remiges contrast with white patch on outer 3 primaries (retained juvenile feathers) and coverts. A few retained juvenile secondaries (shorter, lack wide black band). ▪ New rectrices have wide black subterminal band.

Plate 280. Swainson's Hawk, subadult light intermediate morph (juvenile-like) [Sep.] ▪ Tawny underparts moderately marked, including barred leg feathers. ▪ Dark gray remiges contrast with white patch on outer 3 primaries (retained juvenile feathers) and coverts. Several retained juvenile secondaries (shorter, lack wide black band). ▪ Wide black subterminal tail band.

248   *Swainson's Hawk*

Plate 281. Swainson's Hawk, subadult intermediate morph (adultlike) [Sep.] ▪ Rufous-tawny underparts have dark patch on neck and barring on belly, flanks, and leg feathers. ▪ Dark gray remiges contrast with white patch on outer 3 primaries (retained juvenile feathers) and coverts. A few retained juvenile secondaries (shorter, lack wide black band). ▪ Tail has wide black subterminal band.

Plate 282. Swainson's Hawk, subadult dark morph (streaked type) [Sep.] ▪ Heavily streaked underparts. White undertail coverts. ▪ Dark gray remiges contrast with white patch on outer 4 primaries (old juvenile feathers) but blend with coverts. Several retained juvenile secondaries (shorter, lack wide black band). ▪ Wide black subterminal tail band on new rectrices.

Plate 283. Swainson's Hawk, juvenile light intermediate morph (1-year-old) [Jul.] ▪ White head. Thin dark eyeline; dark inner lores. Dark malar mark merges with dark neck patch. Pale brown iris; yellow cere. ▪ White underparts have some dark markings; barred leg feathers. ▪ Wingtips reach tail tip. ▪ *Note:* Bleached, worn plumage. Other morphs may also have pale heads.

Plate 284. Swainson's Hawk, juvenile light morph (1-year-old) [May] ▪ White head. Thin dark eyeline; dark malar mark merges with dark neck patch. ▪ Lightly marked white underparts. ▪ Pale gray remiges contrast with white coverts. Molt on inner 2 primaries (p1 and 2 are dropped). ▪ Narrow, equal-width tail bands. ▪ *Note:* First stage of molt takes a year for many birds to complete.

Plate 285. Swainson's Hawk, juvenile light morph
[Sep.] ▪ Thin dark eyeline, dark malar mark. All-black bill. Yellow cere. Pale head. ▪ Pale patch on mid-scapulars. Dark patch on side of breast merges with malar mark. Lightly spotted flanks; rest of underparts unmarked, including leg feathers. ▪ Wingtips reach tail tip. ▪ *Note:* Palest type of light morph.

Plate 286. Swainson's Hawk, juvenile light intermediate morph [Sep.] ▪ Thin dark eyeline, dark malar mark. Medium brown iris. All-black bill, yellow cere. ▪ Dark upperparts broadly fringed with tawny. Large dark patch on sides of neck and breast merges with dark malar mark. Moderately streaked underparts; lightly barred leg feathers. Unmarked undertail coverts. ▪ Wingtips reach tail tip.

Plate 287. Swainson's Hawk, juvenile intermediate (rufous) morph [Sep.] ▪ Thin dark eyeline; dark inner lores. Dark malar. Medium brown iris. All-black bill. Yellow cere. Pale forehead, supercilium, and auriculars. Wide dark center-throat streak. ▪ Dark neck patch merges with malar mark. Moderately streaked breast and belly, moderately barred flanks and leg feathers. Lightly barred undertail coverts.

Plate 288. Swainson's Hawk, juvenile dark intermediate (dark rufous) morph [Sep.] ▪ Thin dark eyeline; dark inner lores. Dark malar. Medium brown iris. All-black bill. Yellow cere. Pale forehead, supercilium, and auriculars. ▪ Dark neck patch merges with dark malar mark. Heavily streaked breast and belly, heavily barred flanks and leg feathers. Narrowly edged upperparts.

Plate 289. Swainson's Hawk, juvenile dark intermediate (dark rufous) morph (dark-bellied type) [Sep.] ▪ Thin dark eyeline; dark inner lores. Pale forehead, supercilium, and auriculars. Yellow cere. ▪ Moderately streaked breast and lower belly are paler than heavily streaked belly and barred flanks and form dark band across belly and flanks.

Plate 290. Swainson's Hawk, juvenile dark morph [Sep.] ▪ Thin dark eyeline; dark inner lores. Pale forehead, supercilium, and auriculars. Yellow cere. Dark malar mark merges with dark sides of breast. ▪ Tawny mottling on center of breast and upper belly. Heavily barred leg feathers. Barred, white undertail coverts. Upperparts have little pale edging. ▪ Wingtips somewhat shorter than tail tip.

Plate 291. Swainson's Hawk, juvenile intermediate (rufous) morph [Sep.] ▪ Thin dark eyeline; dark inner lores. Dark malar. Medium brown iris. Black bill. Yellow cere. Pale forehead, supercilium, and auriculars. ▪ Pale patch on mid-scapulars. ▪ Wingtips nearly reach tail tip. ▪ Narrow dark tail bands. ▪ *Note:* Lighter morphs similar; darker morphs virtually lack pale dorsal edging.

Plate 292. Swainson's Hawk, juvenile light morph [Sep.] ▪ Underparts lightly spotted or unmarked. Large dark patch on sides of breast merges with dark malar mark. ▪ Pointed wingtips. Medium gray remiges contrast with pale tawny, unmarked underwing coverts; unmarked axillaries. Whitish area on outer 3 primaries. ▪ Equal-width dark tail bands.

Plate 293. Swainson's Hawk, juvenile light intermediate morph [Sep.] ▪ Rich tawny underparts lightly spotted or streaked, including leg feathers. Large dark patch on sides of breast merges with dark malar mark. ▪ Pointed wingtips. Medium gray remiges contrast with underwing coverts; lightly marked axillaries. Whitish area on outer 3 or 4 primaries. ▪ Equal-width dark tail bands.

Plate 294. Swainson's Hawk, juvenile intermediate (rufous) morph [Sep.] ▪ Dark malar merges with dark neck patch. Tawny underparts moderately streaked; barred leg feathers. ▪ Pointed wingtips. Medium gray remiges contrast with tawny coverts; barred axillaries. Narrow dark rear edge of remiges. ▪ Subterminal tail band slightly wider than inner bands. ▪ *Note:* Same bird as on plates 287 and 291.

Plate 295. Swainson's Hawk, juvenile dark morph [Sep.] ▪ Pale throat. ▪ Heavily streaked underparts. White undertail coverts. ▪ Pointed wingtips. Medium gray remiges do not contrast with heavily marked underwing coverts; heavily barred or dark axillaries. Narrow dark rear edge of remiges. ▪ Dark subterminal tail band slightly wider than inner bands.

Plate 296. Swainson's Hawk, migrant flock (kettle) [Sep.] ▪ Migrants gather in flocks comprising a few hawks or hundreds or thousands.

RED-TAILED HAWK
(Buteo jamaicensis)

AGES: Adult, basic I (subadult I), and juvenile. Sexes are similar for all ages, but males tend to be less heavily marked. Adult plumage is attained when 2 years old. Iris color gradually darkens with age. Birds in full adult plumage when 2 years old may still have rather pale irises (*see* Mindell 1985). Subadult plumage is attained when 1 year old and is similar to adult plumage, but birds have pale irises, retain some juvenile remiges, and regularly retain a few juvenile rectrices. Juvenile plumage is held for much of the first year. Juveniles have shorter remiges, which create narrower wings and longer tail than in older ages.

MOLT: Accipitridae wing and tail molt pattern (*see* chapter 4). The first prebasic molt begins when about 11 months old. Southern races may begin molting in Jan., northern races in Apr. or May. Molt first appears on the innermost primary (p1) and shortly thereafter on the central two rectrices (r1). It then extends to the back, scapulars, secondaries, and underparts. The molt is incomplete, and all birds retain some juvenile remiges, upperwing coverts, and regularly a few rectrices. The outer three primaries (p8–10) and middle secondaries (s4 and 8, or also s7) are typically retained juvenile feathers. On slow-molting individuals, the outer five primaries (p6–10), several secondaries (s2–4 and 6–8), and two or three sets of rectrices (r3–5) are retained juvenile feathers. Juvenile feathering is retained until the second prebasic molt which begins the next spring or summer.

Subsequent annual prebasic molts begin later than the first prebasic molt. Females begin before males. Southern races begin molting in spring, northern races in late spring and early summer. Body and wing molt is incomplete each year, with adults having a mixture of worn and fresh feathering. Wing molt, particularly on the primaries, is serially descendant with at least two molt waves occurring at the same time. The upperwing coverts, in particular, retain a large number of the previous year's feathers. Tail molt is often but not always complete each year.

SUBSPECIES: Polytypic with 13 races in North and Central America. Two of these races breed in the e. U.S. and e. Canada: "Eastern" *B. j. borealis* and "Florida" *B. j. umbrinus*, which is also found on some of the larger islands of the Bahamas. Two additional subspecies winter in small numbers east of the Mississippi River: "Western" *B. j. calurus* and "Harlan's" *B. j. harlani.* Two other subspecies are only in the West: "Alaskan" *B. j. alascensis* of islands and coastal areas of se. Alaska and British Columbia and "Fuertes" *B. j. fuertesi* of the sw. U.S. and n.-cen. Mexico.

The population of the ne. U.S. and e. and cen. Canada was proposed to be a separate subspecies, *B. j. abieticola*, by Todd (1950) and supported by Dickerman and Parkes (1987). Proposed *abieticola* individuals are darker and more heavily marked than more southern *B. j. borealis* and have some or several *B. j. calurus*-like traits. Heavily marked individuals, as described by Todd, breed in the boreal forest from Québec to the Northwest Territories. However, birds that fit this description occur infrequently and do not support a recognizable separate population (R. Dickerman pers. comm.). An adult photographed in the northeastern part of Red-tailed Hawk range in Goose Bay, Labrador, had features similar to most southern *borealis* (photo by B. Mactavish). A few adults seen in New Brunswick, Nova Scotia, and Churchill, Man., also resemble southern *borealis* (J. Harrison pers. comm.). Also, adults with traits seen mainly in northern *borealis* or intergrades (e.g., dark throat) occasionally occur in the heart of typical *borealis* range in New Jersey (Liguori 2001 and pers. comm.).

I find many of these northern birds to be similar to many *borealis* x *calurus* intergrades that breed along the eastern edge of the Rocky Mts. from New Mexico to Alberta. Similar-looking birds can regularly be found in all of *calurus* winter range. The thousands of migrant Redtails I have observed and photographed at Duluth, Minn., over the past decade seemed to be pure *borealis* or *calurus* or had a variable number of intergrade characters. Until further evidence is provided, I do not recognize *abieticola.* Some individuals of the moist boreal forest, per Gloger's Rule, are heavily marked/northern variations of *borealis* or are *borealis* x *calurus* intergrades.

Note on North American subspecies: There is a considerable individual variation within each subspecies. Adjacent races intergrade, often over broad areas. *B. j. borealis*-looking birds occasionally occur within *calurus* breeding range (Liguori 2001). Intergrade features are more apparent in adults and subadults than in juveniles.

Additional subspecies: Following del Hoyo et al. (1994), Ferguson-Lees and Christi (2001), Palmer (1998), and Preston and Beane (1993), there are an additional seven accepted subspecies. South of the U.S., Red-tailed Hawks are resident on the Caribbean islands, in Central America, and in Mexico. Subspecies are based on minor or moderate differences in plumage, size, and geography. (1) *B. j. socorroensis* comprises a small population on isolated Socorro Island, Mexico, in the Revillagigedo group of islands south of Baja California. Similar to *calurus* but has heavier, more powerful feet and legs. (2) *B. j. fumosus* is on the isolated Islas Tres Marias off the coast of Nayarit, Mexico. Similar to *calurus* but more rusty brown on ventral areas. (3) *B. j. hadropus*, of the highlands from Jalisco south to Oaxaca, Mexico, similar to *fuertesi* but smaller and has rufous barring on belly, flanks, and legs. (4) *B. j. kemsiesi* inhabits the isolated highlands from Chiapas, Mexico, and s. Belize to n. Nicaragua. Similar to *hadropus* but has rufous barring only on the leg feathers. (5) *B. j. costaricensis* is in the isolated highlands of Costa Rica and n. Panama. A richly colored race. (6) *B. j. solitudinis* is found on Cuba and Isla de la Juventud. Similar to *umbrinus* but smaller. (7) Nominate *B. j. jamaicensis* is found on Hispaniola, Jamaica, Puerto Rico, and smaller Caribbean islands east to St. Kitts. Similar to *umbrinus* but has a more rufous wash on the ventral areas, darker and less mottled dorsal areas, and leg feathers always barred with rufous. Smaller than *solitudinis*.

Additionally, there is one proposed race, *B. j. suttoni* (Dickerman 1994), which is similar to *calurus* but smaller and more *rusty brown* on the underparts.

COLOR MORPHS: *B. j. calurus* and *B. j. harlani* are polymorphic with a continuum of plumage

trends from light to dark morph: light, light intermediate, intermediate (rufous colored in *calurus*), dark intermediate, and dark. *B. j. borealis* is polymorphic with a pale morph called "Krider's" Hawk (Clark and Wheeler 2001; Wheeler and Clark 1995). *B. j. hadropus* of cen. Mexico is polymorphic with a rare dark morph (one specimen; Palmer 1988); however, not known if there is a plumage continuum.

SIZE: A large raptor. Males average smaller than females but overlap. Subspecies subtly vary in size, particularly in wing chord and wingspan. Wing-chord measurements listed here are averages given by Preston and Beane (1993).—*B. j. borealis* 370 mm for males and 390 mm for females; "Krider's" morph of *borealis* 379 mm for males and 412 mm for females; *B. j. umbrinus* 399 mm for males and 409 mm for females; *B. j. calurus* 387 mm for males and 412 mm for females; *B. j. harlani* 381 mm for males and 408 mm for females. Wingspan varies subtly according to wing chord: the larger the wing chord, the longer the wingspan. Basic wingspan and total length measurements mainly include *borealis* and *calurus*. Lengths for *borealis* are on the smaller end of the spectrum, for "Krider's" and *harlani* in the middle, and for *calurus* on the larger end. Length: 17–22 in. (43–56 cm); wingspan: 43–56 in. (109–142 cm).

SPECIES TRAITS: HEAD.—Distal three-fourths of bill is blackish, basal one-fourth is pale blue. Lores are white or pale gray on all races and color morphs. Narrow white swath under the eyes. WINGS.—**In flight, rounded wingtips with p6–8 being nearly the same length and the secondaries bowing outward.**

ADULT TRAITS: HEAD.—Greenish or yellow cere. Irises vary from pale orangish or yellowish brown to dark brown with age. WINGS.—Trailing edge of the remiges has a wide black band.

ADULT LIGHT MORPH TRAITS: BODY.—White, pale tawny, or rufous underparts. WINGS.—**Black, dark brown, or rufous mark on the patagial region on the leading edge of the underside of the wings.**

ADULTS OF "EASTERN" (*B. j. borealis*): HEAD.—Medium or dark brown crown and nape, pale tawny or white supercilium, pale or medium-tawny or tawny-rufous auriculars, and dark brown or black malar mark. Throat is white and typically unmarked; rarely streaked or with a dark mark on the central area. The white throat typically merges with the front of the neck and breast but may have a narrow brown collar that separates it from the neck. BODY (dorsal).—Dark brown back. Forward and rear scapulars are dark brown, and each scapular has a large pale white, tawny, or pale gray patch on the mid-section. On perched birds, the patches form a pale V when viewed from the rear; on flying birds, they show as two pale patches when viewed from above. BODY (ventral).—Often pale tawny in fresh autumn plumage but may fade to white by winter. There is a rufous-brown patch on the sides of the neck and breast. Breast is unmarked. Flanks are always narrowly barred with rufous or dark brown and often have a small or large dark central-feather streak or diamond-shaped mark on each feather. The amount of markings on the mid-belly is highly variable (males of all areas are typically less heavily marked than females): (1) *Lightly marked type.*—Belly lacks dark markings, but flanks are always narrowly barred with brown or rufous-brown. *Note:* Fairly common variation throughout all of *borealis* range; mainly on males. These types can be as lightly marked on the ventral areas as a classic *fuertesi* of the Southwest. (2) *Moderately marked type.*—Belly has a moderate amount of dark streaking and forms a fairly distinct belly band. *Note:* Common variation. (3) *Heavily marked type.*—Belly has a large amount of dark streaking and forms a distinct belly band that can appear as a nearly solid black band. *Note:* Fairly common to common variation, particularly on females. The lower belly is pale tawny or white and unmarked. Leg feathers on all types are pale tawny or white and unmarked. Undertail coverts are immaculate pale tawny or white. WINGS (dorsal).—Dark brown upperwing coverts with pale tawny spotting on median and first row of lesser upperwing coverts. WINGS (ventral).—**Pale tawny or white underwing coverts with a dark brown patagial mark.** Axillaries are unmarked or have small dark spots on the tip of each feather. Underside of the secondaries and inner four or five primaries are narrowly barred; outer primaries are barred or solid black. *Note:* On perched birds, the wingtips fall somewhat short of the tail (on or just above the black subterminal band).

TAIL.—**Dorsal tail is medium or dark rufous but fades to pale or medium rufous or rufous-tawny by spring. There is a narrow or moderately wide black subterminal band and a white terminal band.** Occasionally, the black subterminal band is absent. The uppertail coverts are white. Undertail is pinkish or pale gray. In translucent lighting, it shows as rufous.

ADULTS OF "KRIDER'S" (pale morph of *B. j. borealis*):

HEAD.—In the purest form, the head is all white except for some dark streaking on the nape. Many birds have a small brown patch on the crown and a partial dark malar mark (these may be *borealis/calurus* intergrades). Throat is always white and unmarked and never has a dark collar. BODY (dorsal).—Dark brown back and forward and rear scapulars are edged with tawny-rufous. A large white mottled area covers the middle two-thirds of the scapulars. When perched, the white scapular areas form a large white V. When seen from above, two large white patches show on the scapulars. BODY (ventral).—Sides of the neck and breast have a pale rufous patch. Breast, flanks, belly, lower belly, leg feathers, and undertail coverts are pure white and unmarked. *Note:* Pure "Krider's" do not have markings on the belly or flanks. WINGS (dorsal).—Dark brown upperwing coverts are extensively mottled with white on the median and distal lesser upperwing coverts. Basal lesser upperwing coverts are often edged with tawny-rufous and may appear to form a rufous shoulder patch. Adults occasionally exhibit a large pale brown panel on the inner primaries that is similar to the panel of juveniles. WINGS (ventral).—**White underwing coverts are unmarked except for a small or moderate-sized brown or rufous patagial mark.** The secondaries and inner primaries are narrowly barred; the "fingers" on the outer primaries are broadly barred. *Note:* On perched birds, the wingtips fall somewhat short of the tail tip (on or just above the thin black subterminal band). TAIL.—**Distal third is pale rufous or pale tawny-rufous, inner two-thirds white. A narrow brown subterminal band is always present.** Uppertail coverts are white.

ADULTS OF "FLORIDA" (*B. j. umbrinus*):

HEAD.—Dark brown crown and nape, medium-tawny or tawny-rufous supercilium, medium-tawny or dark tawny-rufous auriculars, and a dark brown or black malar mark. Throat markings are highly variable: all white, white and streaked with dark brown, dark brown with white strip on the outer edges, or solid dark brown. Overall, head is quite dark (darker than *borealis* and similar to *calurus*). BODY (dorsal).—Dark brown back. Scapulars are dark brown with a small amount of tawny or gray blotching on each mid-scapular area (fewer markings than *borealis* and many *calurus*). BODY (ventral).—White underparts have a moderately or heavily marked band of black blobs or spots on the belly and flanks. Breast is unmarked. Flanks tend to lack dark inner feather barring of most other races. In spring, the breast may be quite tawny with new and fresh feathering. Lower belly is white and unmarked. Leg feathers are white and either unmarked or barred with dark brown. The undertail coverts are white and unmarked. WINGS (dorsal).—Upperwing coverts are solid brown and lack pale markings (pale markings on *borealis* and *calurus*). WINGS (ventral).—Prominent black patagial marks on the white underwing coverts. Some birds have tawny smudges on some underwing coverts. *Note:* On perched birds, the wingtips nearly equal or are somewhat shorter than the tail tip. TAIL.—Dark rufous on the dorsal surface and may have only a narrow or wide black subterminal band or partial or full dark inner tail banding.

ADULTS OF LIGHT MORPH "WESTERN" (*B. j. calurus*): HEAD.—Dark brown crown and nape, medium-tawny or tawny-rufous supercilium, medium or dark tawny-rufous auriculars, and dark brown or black malar mark. Throat is typically dark brown or black. However, it may be white and streaked with brown or black and have a dark collar or a large dark area on the central part of the throat with a white strip on the outer edges. Throat is sometimes white and unmarked except for a dark collar. BODY (dorsal).—Dark brown back. Scapulars are dark brown on the forward and rear areas and have a moderate-sized or small tawny or grayish patch on the central area. On perched birds, the two pale patches may form a V when viewed from the rear; when seen from above, two pale patches show. BODY (ventral).—(1) Rufous type, which has been considered type specimen for this subspecies, has a

uniform pale rufous wash on the underparts, including the leg feathers and undertail coverts. (2) White type has whitish underparts, including leg feathers and undertail coverts. The sides of the neck and breast have a rufous brown patch. Breast is sometimes narrowly streaked with brown or rufous. Flanks are always barred with dark rufous or brown. Belly is variably marked. Variations of belly and flank markings: (1) *Lightly marked type.*—Small amount of dark brown streaks or diamond-shaped marks that form an indistinct belly band. *Note:* A fairly common variation. (2) *Moderately marked type.*—Moderate amount of dark brown streaks or diamond-shaped marks, often with narrow rufous barring that forms a fairly distinct belly band (**no other subspecies exhibits barring on the belly**). *Note:* A common variation. (3) *Heavily marked type.*—Extensive dark markings that may form a virtually solid black band across the belly and flanks. *Note:* A common variation. The lower belly is pale rufous and often barred with dark rufous. Leg feathers on all *calurus* have moderate or extensive rufous or dark brown barring or are solid rufous and darker than the rest of the underparts. The undertail coverts are often barred with rufous or dark brown. WINGS (dorsal).—Dark brown upperwing coverts have a small amount of tawny spotting on the median and first row of lesser upperwing coverts. WINGS (ventral).— **Pale rufous or white, depending on color type, with a large dark brown patagial mark.** Axillaries are barred with dark brown. The secondaries and inner four or five primaries are covered with narrow or moderately wide barring. The outer primaries are solid black or barred. *Note:* On perched birds, the wingtips reach or are barely shorter than the tail tip. TAIL.—Dorsal tail is medium or dark rufous in fresh plumage but fades to pale or medium rufous or rufous-tawny by spring. Tail variations: (1) *Unbanded type.*—Lacks a black subterminal band. *Note:* A very uncommon variation. (2) *Single-banded type.*—Has only a black subterminal band that varies from being narrow to wide (up to 1 in. [25 mm]). *Note:* A fairly common type. (3) *Partially banded type.*—Moderate-width or wide black subterminal band and a few incomplete narrow black inner bands. Partial banding is typically on the central and outer rectrices. *Note:* A common type. (4) *Banded type.*—Moderate-width or wide black subterminal band with narrow, complete black bands on all of the inner tail. *Note:* A common type. Variations 3 and 4 account for 50% of tail variations. The uppertail coverts are typically rufous, occasionally partially white, and often barred. The undertail is pinkish or pale gray but rufous when seen in translucent light. Tail banding does not show well on the undertail unless seen in translucent light.

ADULTS OF LIGHT MORPH "HARLAN'S" (*B. j. harlani*): HEAD.—Brownish black crown and nape, stark white supercilium and auriculars, and black malar mark. Throat is sometimes white and streaked with a dark collar. BODY (dorsal).—Brownish black (not a warm brown as on most races). Small or moderate-sized white patches on the mid-scapulars. Dark markings in the white scapular areas are typically more streaked and not as barred or diamond-shaped as on other races. BODY (ventral).—Stark white underparts. Flanks always marked with blackish streaks or blobs but sometimes narrowly barred. Belly is moderately or heavily streaked or blobbed; very rarely is the belly unmarked (only one [specimen] has been seen that lacked belly markings). Leg feathers are immaculate white but may be partially barred with brown on more heavily marked birds. Undertail coverts are immaculate white. WINGS (dorsal).—Uniformly blackish brown upperwing coverts. WINGS (ventral).—**White underwing coverts have a distinct black patagial mark.** Patterns of the underside of the white or pale gray remiges are highly variable and apply to all morphs of *harlani*: (1) *Barred type.*—All remiges are neatly or irregularly barred; outer primary "fingers" are broadly barred or solid black. (2) *Mottled type.*—All remiges are mottled and speckled with black and gray; outer primary "fingers" are usually solid black but may have some barring. (3) *Unmarked type.*—Remiges lack dark markings; outer primary "fingers" are solid black. (4) *Barred and mottled type.*—Remiges are a mixture of barring and mottling; outer primary "fingers" are solid black or broadly barred. (5) *Partially marked type.*—Remiges have a mixture of barred and/or mottled and unmarked feathers; outer primary "fingers" are

generally solid black. Pattern may vary in having a few or several feathers marked. *Note:* Contrary to previously published data, the "fingers" on the outer five primaries of adult *harlani* are just as likely to be solid black as barred. *Additional Note:* On perched birds, the wingtips are typically somewhat shorter than the tail tip; however, the wingtips nearly reach the tail tip on some birds. TAIL.—There is an incredible array of dorsal tail patterns for *harlani*. When seen at close range, most *harlani* have some tinge of rufous on the dorsal surface of the distal portion of the rectrices. It is also common for very *harlani*-looking adults to have rufous on the distal half of the rectrices. If more than half of the tail is rufous, then the bird is likely an intergrade with *calurus* or *alascensis*. Variations are less apparent on the ventral surface: most are white or pale gray. When seen in translucent light, the dorsal color shows on the ventral surface. Dorsal tail variations (for all color morphs): (1) *White type.*—(1a) White and lack dark markings or (1b) have some dark marbling and mottling. The black subterminal or terminal band is moderately wide or wide and irregularly marbled. *Note:* A common type (possibly slightly more common than other types). (2) *White-rufous type.*—The basal half is white and the distal half is rufous. Tail may be marbled or mottled with dark markings or unmarked. *Note:* A fairly common type. (3) *Pale gray type.*—(3a) Nearly plain pale gray or (3b) pale gray with moderate or extensive dark marbling and mottling. The black subterminal or terminal band is moderately wide or wide and irregularly marbled or mottled. *Note:* A common type. (4) *Pale gray-rufous type.*—The basal half is pale gray and the distal half is rufous. The tail may be marbled and mottled with black or be unmarked. *Note:* A fairly common type. (5) *Medium/dark gray type.*—(5a) Nearly plain medium or dark gray or (5b) medium or dark gray and covered with black marbling and mottling. The black subterminal or terminal band is moderately wide or wide. *Note:* A common type. (6) *Medium/dark gray-rufous type.*—The distal half of the tail is rufous; however, the rufous is often mixed with the darker gray and a brownish cast is created. The tail may be marbled or mottled with black or unmarked. *Note:* A common type. (7) *White banded type.*—Rectrices are white with a fairly neat, moderately wide black subterminal band and several narrow, complete black bands on the inner tail. There is often a tinge of rufous along the edges of some black bands. *Note:* A fairly common type. (8) *Pale gray banded type.*—As in #7 but with a pale gray base color. *Note:* An uncommon type. (9) *Medium/dark gray banded type.*—As in #7 and 8 but with a medium or dark gray base color. *Note:* An uncommon type. (10) *Mottled-barred type.*—A mixture of dark marbling and barring on white and gray base, often with a rufous wash on the distal part of the tail. Dark patterns may be irregularly distributed on a few rectrices: some being marbled or mottled, some barred, or some fairly regularly patterned on most or all feathers. In many cases, the barred pattern on a feather becomes diffused and is an irregular mottled or spotted design. Uppertail coverts are white, gray, or rufous.

ADULT LIGHT MORPH INTERGRADE TRAITS: Below are some basic plumage traits that appear to be shared features between adjacent races. The degree of intergrading, however, is infinite.

Heavily marked/Northern type *borealis*: Head is dark as on most *calurus*; throat is white, white and streaked with a dark collar, or all dark. Breast and underparts are white, or the breast is often tawny-rufous or quite rufous and streaked. (The darker tawny or rufous breast on some individuals separates them from *calurus*, which typically have uniformly colored breasts and underparts.) Belly band, consisting of the flanks and belly, is moderately or heavily marked with black. Belly is not barred with rufous as on many *calurus*. Leg feathers vary from unmarked to heavily barred with rufous or brown (similar to *calurus*). Rufous tail often has a moderately wide or wide black subterminal band and may have partial or complete narrow black inner bands.

Intergrade of *borealis* x *calurus*: Faint or partial leg barring signifies acquisition of *calurus* traits. Many have a *calurus*-like streaked or dark throat. The ventral regions may remain whitish and lightly marked as on many *borealis* (even those with some leg barring); some may obtain *calurus*-like faint rufous barring on the belly. Tail often shows some partial dark inner banding, particularly on the deck and outer rectrices.

Intergrade of "Krider's" x typical *borealis*: Intergrade characters generally affect the head or tail. Some may have moderately dark heads as on typical *borealis* but have a whitish tail like typical "Krider's," or vice versa. As a rule, the dark crown and malar mark are present on darker headed birds. The supercilium may be a more pronounced white on birds with darker heads.

Intergrade of "Krider's" x *calurus*: Variations as described for *borealis* but often with partial dark bands on those with a whitish tail.

Intergrade of *calurus* x *harlani*: Head is typically similar to *harlani*: stark white and dark brown. Sides of the neck and breast are also *harlani*-like in that they lack rufous tones. Scapular are often barred and have diamond-shaped markings as on *calurus* and not streaked as on *harlani*. Tail is more than 50% rufous with white or gray mottling on the basal region next to the uppertail coverts and rufous on the distal region. In flight, the underside of the remiges may show *harlani* features of mottling or lack of markings. Dark patagial mark may have *calurus*-like rufous tones (*see* Mindell 1985).

ADULT LIGHT INTERMEDIATE MORPH TRAITS: Pertains to "Western" *B. j. calurus* and "Harlan's" *B. j. harlani*. These morphs are more heavily marked than their respective light morphs in each race and form links in the continuum from light to dark morph.

ADULTS OF LIGHT INTERMEDIATE (LIGHT RUFOUS) MORPH "WESTERN" (*B. j. calurus*): HEAD.—Dark headed as on most light morph *calurus*, including the throat. BODY (dorsal).—As on light morph *calurus* with small or moderate-sized pale tawny or gray scapular patches. BODY (ventral).—All of the underparts are washed with medium rufous (darker than light morph but paler than intermediate morph). The underparts may be uniformly medium rufous or the breast may be somewhat darker than the leg feathers, lower belly, and undertail coverts. Breast is sometimes partially streaked with dark brown. Variations of belly and flank markings: (1) *Lightly marked type.*—Small amount of dark brown streaks or diamond-shaped marks form an indistinct belly band, and underparts appear virtually solid medium rufous. *Note:* A common variation. (2) *Moderately marked type.*—Moderate amount of dark brown streaking or diamond-shaped marks, often with narrow dark rufous or dark brown barring that forms a fairly distinct belly band. *Note:* A common variation. (3) *Heavily marked type.*—Extensive amount of markings form a virtually solid blackish band. *Note:* A common variation. Leg feathers are always barred with dark rufous or brown. WINGS (dorsal).—As on light morph *calurus* with little if any pale markings on the medium upperwing coverts. WINGS (ventral).—**Underwing coverts are medium rufous with prominent, large black patagial marks.** Remiges are barred except on the outer four or five primaries; primary tips are solid black or broadly barred. *Note:* On perched birds, the wingtips reach the tip of the tail. TAIL.—Same variations as described for Adults of Light Morph "Western" except the unbanded type is rare. Uppertail coverts are medium rufous and often barred.

ADULTS OF LIGHT INTERMEDIATE MORPH "HARLAN'S" (*B. j. harlani*): HEAD.—As on light morph *harlani* with a broad white supercilium, white auricular region, dark malar, and white throat. Supercilium and auricular regions typically form a large white area and, except for the dark crown, make all of the head appear white. BODY (dorsal).—Brownish black with a moderate amount of white on the two mid-scapular patches. BODY (ventral).—The white breast is narrowly streaked with brownish black. The dark streaking covers less than 50% of the breast area. Flanks and belly are heavily mottled and blotched with brownish black and form a distinct belly band. The leg feathers are thickly barred with black and white. The undertail coverts are white with some dark barring and accentuate the dark belly band of the darker flanks and belly. WINGS (dorsal).—Brownish black without pale markings on the upperwing coverts. WINGS (ventral).—Remiges are marked in any of the five variations described for Adults of Light Morph "Harlan's." Underwing coverts are heavily mottled with black and white and exhibit a fairly distinct dark patagial mark. Axillaries are black with white barring. *Note:* On perched birds, the wingtips are somewhat shorter than the tail tip. TAIL.—Any of the variations described for Adults of Light Morph "Harlan's." The uppertail coverts are white, gray, or rufous.

ADULT LIGHT INTERMEDIATE INTERGRADE TRAITS: No data.

ADULT INTERMEDIATE MORPH TRAITS: Pertains to "Western" *B. j. calurus* and "Harlan's" *B. j. harlani.* These morphs are more heavily marked than their respective light intermediate morphs and form links in the continuum of plumages from light to dark morph.

ADULTS OF INTERMEDIATE (RUFOUS) MORPH "WESTERN" (*B. j. calurus*): HEAD.—Dark brown crown, nape, and throat. The supercilium and auricular regions are dark rufous-brown. Overall, the head appears dark rufous-brown. BODY (dorsal).—Dark brown with at most only a small tawny mottled patch on each mid-scapular region. BODY (ventral).—Breast is dark rufous but may have some dark streaking. Belly and flanks are variably marked: (1) *Lightly marked type.*—Small amount of dark brown streaks or diamond-shaped marks form an indistinct belly band, and underparts appear virtually solid dark rufous. *Note:* An uncommon variation. (2) *Moderately marked type.*—Moderate amount of dark brown streaks or diamond-shaped marks, often with narrow dark rufous or dark brown barring that forms a fairly distinct belly band. *Note:* A common variation. (3) *Heavily marked type.*—Extensive dark markings form a virtually solid blackish band. Leg feathers are always barred with dark rufous or dark brown. *Note:* A common variation. The lower belly is dark rufous and may have some darker rufous or dark brown barring. The undertail coverts are dark rufous and barred with darker rufous or dark brown. WINGS (dorsal).—Dark brown upperwing coverts lack pale markings on the median and lesser coverts. WINGS (ventral).—Dark rufous underwing coverts with a large, distinct black patagial mark. Axillaries are often barred with white. Remiges are barred except on the outer four or five primaries; primary tips are solid black or broadly barred. *Note:* On perched birds, the wingtips reach the tail tip. TAIL.—Same variations as described for Adults of Light Morph "Western" except the unbanded type is very rare. Uppertail coverts are dark rufous and often barred.

ADULTS OF INTERMEDIATE MORPH "HARLAN'S" (*B. j. harlani*): HEAD.—Uniformly brownish black, or the supercilium and auricular region may have white streaking or mottling on them.

The throat is white or white with black streaking. The white swath under the eyes is often prominent. Auriculars may also have a variable amount of white on them. Forehead is often white. BODY (dorsal).—Brownish black with somewhat pale brownish oblong streaks on the outer edges of the lower scapular. BODY (ventral).—*See* types below. The undertail coverts are brownish black with white markings. WINGS (dorsal).—Mainly uniformly brownish black on all coverts. WINGS (ventral).— Brownish black coverts are speckled with white. The axillaries may be solid black or barred or speckled with white. *Note:* There is no dark patagial distinction as seen on paler *harlani* morphs. Remiges may be any of the five variations described for Adults of Light Morph "Harlan's." *Additional Note:* On perched birds, the wingtips typically are somewhat shorter than the tail tip. TAIL.—Same patterns described for Adults of Light Morph "Harlan's." Uppertail coverts may be white, gray, or rufous.

ADULT INTERMEDIATE MORPH "HARLAN'S" (STREAK-BREASTED TYPE): BODY (ventral).— The breast has an equal amount of white and black streaking or mottling. The belly, lower belly, and flanks are abruptly darker brownish black and either solid dark or speckled with white. Leg feathers are either solid brownish black or black or have white speckling or narrow barring. *Note:* A common type.

ADULT INTERMEDIATE MORPH "HARLAN'S" (STREAKED TYPE): BODY (ventral).—The breast, belly, and flanks are uniformly marked with nearly an equal amount of white and brownish black streaking (*see* Wood 1932). *Note:* An uncommon to very uncommon type. Not depicted.

ADULT INTERMEDIATE MORPH INTERGRADE TRAITS: Shared traits between *calurus* and *harlani*. Intergrade of *calurus* x *harlani*: (1) Dark brown head and throat as on *calurus* but with small white supercilium. Breast is dark rufous with a moderate amount of white *harlani* mottling or streaking. Rest of body and wings as on *calurus*. Tail may be any of the previously described *harlani* or *calurus* types or a mixture of both subspecies. (2) Body as on intermediate (rufous) morph *calurus*, but tail is any of the *harlani* variations. *Note:* If there is a mix of *harlani* traits on the tail, it occurs on the basal

half or two-thirds, with *calurus* traits on the distal half or third.

ADULT DARK INTERMEDIATE MORPH TRAITS: Pertains to "Western" *B. j. calurus* and "Harlan's" *B. j. harlani*. These morphs are more heavily marked than their respective intermediate morphs and form links in the continuum of plumages from light to dark morph.

ADULTS OF DARK INTERMEDIATE (DARK RUFOUS) MORPH "WESTERN" (*B. j. calurus*): HEAD.—Dark brown with a hint of dark rufous on supercilium and auricular regions. Throat is always dark brown. The forehead may have some white on it. BODY (dorsal).— Uniformly dark brown. BODY (ventral).— Dark brown with dark rufous outer edges on most feathers and slightly paler and more rufous than the belly and flanks. Belly and flanks are uniformly dark brown. Leg feathers are dark brown with narrow rufous edges on most feathers. The undertail coverts are dark brown with rufous tips or barring on most feathers. WINGS (dorsal).—Uniformly dark brown coverts. WINGS (ventral).—Underwing coverts are mainly dark brown but may have a rufous tinge; however, there is not a dark patagial distinction. Axillaries may be barred with white or gray. Remiges are barred except on the outer four or five primaries; primary tips are solid black or broadly barred. *Note:* On perched birds, the wingtips reach the tail tip. TAIL.—Same patterns as described for Adults of Light Morph "Western" except the unbanded type does not occur in this morph. Uppertail coverts are dark or may have some rufous tinge.

ADULTS OF DARK INTERMEDIATE MORPH "HARLAN'S" (*B. j. harlani*): HEAD.—Uniformly brownish black but may have a white patch on the supercilium. The throat is white or white with black streaking. Forehead may have some white on it. BODY (dorsal).—Uniformly brownish black or with slightly paler oblong grayish areas on the outer edges of the lower scapular. BODY (ventral).—*See* types below. WINGS (dorsal).—Mainly solid brownish black. WINGS (ventral).—Underwing coverts are solid brownish black or have a small amount of white speckling. Axillaries are solid dark or barred with white. Pattern on the remiges as described for Adults of Light Morph "Harlan's." *Note:* On perched birds, the wingtips typically are somewhat shorter than the tail tip. TAIL.—Patterns as described for Adults of Light Morph "Harlan's." Uppertail coverts are dark but may have a rufous tinge.

ADULT DARK INTERMEDIATE MORPH "HARLAN'S" (STREAK-BREASTED TYPE): BODY (ventral).—Brownish black with a small amount of white streaking or mottling on the breast. The white markings cover less than 50% of the breast surface. Rest of the underparts uniformly brownish black or may have a small amount of white speckling. *Note:* A common type.

ADULT DARK INTERMEDIATE MORPH "HARLAN'S" (SPOT-BELLIED TYPE): BODY (ventral).—Breast is solid brownish black and belly and flanks are moderately spotted or blotched with white. The leg feathers may have a small amount of white barring. WINGS (ventral).—Underwing coverts tend to have some white speckling and white barring on the axillaries. *Note:* An uncommon type.

ADULT DARK INTERMEDIATE MORPH INTERGRADE TRAITS: Shared traits between *calurus* and *harlani*. Intergrade of *calurus* x *harlani*: Dark brown head and throat as on *calurus* but may have a small white supercilium. Breast is dark rufous or dark rufous with a small amount of white mottling or streaking. Rest of body and wings as on *calurus*. Tail may be any of the previously described *harlani* or *calurus* types or a mixture of both subspecies. If there is a mix of *harlani* traits, it occurs on the basal half or two-thirds, with *calurus* traits on the distal half or third.

ADULT DARK MORPH TRAITS: Pertains to "Western" *B. j. calurus* and "Harlan's" *B. j. harlani*. These morphs are more heavily marked than their respective dark intermediate morphs and form the final links in the continuum of plumages from light to dark morph.

ADULTS OF DARK MORPH "WESTERN" (*B. j. calurus*): HEAD and BODY.—Typically a uniformly warm dark brown but occasionally more blackish brown (perhaps having *harlani* genes). The undertail coverts have rufous tips on most feathers. WINGS (dorsal).—Uniformly warm dark brown. WINGS (ventral).—Dark brown underwing coverts; axillaries sometimes faintly barred with paler brown or gray. Remiges are barred except on the outer four or five primaries; primary tips are solid

black or broadly barred. *Note:* On perched birds, the wingtips reach the tail tip. TAIL.—Same patterns as described for Adults of Light Morph "Western" except the unbanded type does not occur in this morph. Uppertail coverts are dark brown.

ADULTS OF DARK MORPH "HARLAN'S" (*B. j. harlani*): HEAD.—Uniformly brownish black, including the throat. The forehead is dark. BODY.—Uniformly brownish black or sometimes a warm dark brown. WINGS (dorsal).—Uniformly brownish black. WINGS (ventral).—The underwing coverts are solid brownish black. Axillaries are solid dark or have faint grayish barring. Remiges have the same patterns described for Adults of Light Morph "Harlan's." *Note:* On perched birds, the wingtips are typically somewhat shorter than the tail tip. TAIL.—Same patterns described for Adults of Light Morph "Harlan's." The banded types appear to be more common in this morph than any other. Medium/dark gray type is the most common non-banded variation.

ADULT DARK MORPH INTERGRADE TRAITS: Shared traits between *calurus* and *harlani*. Intergrade *calurus* x *harlani*: Dark brown or brownish black head, body, and underwing coverts. Tail may be any of the previously described *harlani* or *calurus* types or a mixture of both subspecies. If there is a mix of *harlani* traits, it occurs on the basal half or two-thirds, with *calurus* traits on the distal part.

BASIC (SUBADULT) TRAITS (ALL SUBSPECIES AND COLOR MORPHS): Superficially similar to adults of respective race and morph. At close and moderate distances, subadults can easily be separated from adults by head and wing features. HEAD.—Iris is pale: yellowish brown, orangish brown, or brown. However, younger adults may also have pale irises. WINGS.—Retain some faded brown juvenile upperwing coverts, but these are not separable from old, faded adult feathers that are from partial prebasic molts. In flight, retained juvenile remiges are quite visible on the dorsal and ventral sides. On the dorsal side, retained juvenile remiges are paler brown than most adult remiges. The outer three to five primaries (typically p8–10, rarely p6–10) are worn, frayed, and pale juvenile feathers. If these outer primaries are barred, the juvenile barring is narrower than on most adjacent adult primaries. On the secondaries, the retained feathers are typically s4 and 8, but also s7 and sometimes more. The juvenile feathers have a narrow grayish subterminal band versus the wide black band of adults and are shorter than adjacent adult feathers. TAIL.—Some birds retain scattered juvenile rectrices.

JUVENILE TRAITS: HEAD.—Iris is pale: yellow, gray, or brown; rarely medium brown. **Cere is pale bluish green or pale green.** WINGS (dorsal).—**In flight, the primaries and respective greater coverts are paler than the secondaries and their respective coverts and create a large pale panel on the outer half of the wing. All subspecies and morphs have distinct black barring on the secondaries: narrow on light morphs, fairly wide on darker morphs.** WINGS (ventral).—In flight in translucent light, a pale rectangular window is created by the pale panel of the dorsal surface of the primaries. The subterminal band on the remiges is narrow and medium gray. *Note:* On all races, the wingtips of perched birds are moderately shorter or much shorter than the tail tip. TAIL.—Two main patterns: (1) **Numerous narrow to moderately wide equal-width black bands, which are narrower than the pale bands,** or (2) **numerous narrow or moderately wide equal-width black bands with a wider black subterminal band.** Dorsal base color of the pale bands is variable (*see* description for each subspecies/morph). Ventral color on all types is pale grayish.

JUVENILE LIGHT MORPH TRAITS: BODY (dorsal).—White markings on the mid-scapular region. BODY (ventral).—All have some sort of dark belly and flank markings. WINGS (ventral).—**All have a lightly to heavily marked dark area on the patagial region.** TAIL.—Uppertail coverts are white with dark marks on the central region.

JUVENILES OF "EASTERN" (*B. j. borealis*): HEAD.—Dark brown crown, nape, and malar mark with a broad white supercilium and brownish or tawny auricular region. White throat. On more heavily marked birds, the white throat is narrowly streaked with dark brown or has a narrow dark brown collar that separates it from the breast. BODY (dorsal).—Warm dark brown back and scapulars with a large white patch on the middle area of each scapular. The dark mark on the central part of each scapular is diamond-shaped. BODY (ventral).—White underparts are variably marked on the belly, flanks, and leg feathers. The breast is white and unmarked on older juveniles. Recently fledged birds have a tawny wash that quickly fades after fledging (this tawny color may be evident on late-fledged birds until Dec.). Belly and flanks are marked with dark brown markings: (1) *Lightly marked type.*—Dark arrowhead or diamond-shaped markings with a broad dark inner-feather bar on each flank feather and small dark streaks or diamond-shaped marks on the belly that create a poorly formed belly band. *Note:* A common variation. (2) *Moderately marked type.*—Flanks as described for #1 but belly has moderately large streaks or diamond-shaped marks that form a fairly distinct dark belly band. *Note:* A common variation. (3) *Heavily marked type.*—Flanks are more broadly marked than #1 and belly has large dark streaks or diamond-shaped marks that form a distinct, nearly solid belly band. *Note:* A fairly common variation (typical on many individuals from the northern part of their range). Lower belly is white and unmarked. White leg feathers are unmarked, lightly spotted or barred, or fairly heavily barred. *Note:* Amount of leg markings corresponds to amount of belly markings. Undertail coverts are white and unmarked. WINGS (dorsal).—**Pale panel on the primaries and respective greater upperwing coverts are pale brown.** Prominent white markings on the median and on the first one or two rows of lesser upperwing coverts. WINGS (ventral).—**Moderately large dark brown patagial marks.** There are a few scattered dark marks on other underwing coverts; axillaries have a few dark marks on them. The "fingers" on the outer five primaries are either solid dark gray or barred. TAIL.—Both banded patterns as described under Juvenile Traits are common: dark bands are the narrow pattern. Dorsal tail colors: (1) *Medium brown type.*—*Note:* A common variation. (2) *Rufous-brown type.*—A small or moderate amount of rufous or orangish rufous mixed with the brown. *Note:* A fairly common variation. (3) *Rufous type.*—Tail is totally orangish rufous or rufous and nearly rivals the color of adult tail. *Note:* Uncommon variation, but more common in *borealis* than in other subspecies.

JUVENILES OF "KRIDER'S" (pale morph of *B. j. borealis*): HEAD.—In the purest form, the head is immaculate white and lacks any dark markings except for a small amount of dark streaking on the nape. Birds that still appear quite pure may also have a white head but with a small dark area on the crown, a partial dark malar mark, and the streaked nape. BODY (dorsal).—Medium warm brown back and scapulars with a large white mottled area on the mid- and lower region of each scapular. The dark mark on the central part of each scapular is diamond-shaped. The uppertail coverts are white with a small amount of dark spotting or barring. BODY (ventral).—White underparts with small dark spots on the flanks and belly. *Note:* Juveniles always have some dark markings on the belly and flanks. Leg feathers and undertail coverts are white and unmarked. WINGS (dorsal).—**Pale panel on the primaries and respective greater upperwing coverts is pale brown or white.** Medium warm brown with large white markings on the median and the first two or more rows of lesser upperwing coverts. The greater upperwing coverts may have some white on them. WINGS (ventral).—The medium brown secondaries are distinctly barred with dark brown. The white underwing coverts are virtually white and unmarked except for a small dark strip on the tips of the primary greater coverts and the ill-defined dark streaking on the patagium. The remiges are narrowly barred, including the outer five "fingers" of the primaries. TAIL.—The distal half to two-thirds is pale brown, the basal half to third white. The brownish region is marked with numerous narrow dark brown bands; the white region either is unbanded or partially banded.

JUVENILES OF "FLORIDA" (*B. j. umbrinus*): Identical to juvenile *borealis* in all aspects.

JUVENILES OF LIGHT MORPH "WESTERN" (*B. j. calurus*): HEAD.—Dark brown crown, nape, and malar mark with a tawny supercilium and dark tawny auricular region. Throat is all dark, dark with a pale edge on each side, or white and streaked with dark; occasionally it is white. Head appears to be overall dark and darker than on juvenile *borealis*. BODY (dorsal).—Warm dark brown with small or moderate-sized white or grayish patches on the mid-scapular region. The dark marks on the central

part of each scapular feather are diamond-shaped. BODY (ventral).—Breast is white on older juveniles but tawny on recently fledged birds; it is mainly unmarked except for streaking on each side. The belly and flanks are either the moderately marked or heavily marked type as described for Juveniles of Eastern. Lower belly feathers are lightly or moderately spotted or partially barred with dark brown. Leg feathers are moderately or heavily barred with dark brown. Undertail coverts are white and lightly or moderately barred. WINGS (dorsal).—**The pale panel on the primaries and respective coverts is pale brown.** Warm dark brown with a small amount of pale grayish or tawny marks on the median and first row of lesser upperwing coverts. WINGS (ventral).—**Large dark brown patagial mark.** The underwing coverts are moderately marked and the axillaries are barred. The "fingers" on the outer five primaries may be solid dark gray or barred. TAIL.—The two banded patterns described for Juvenile Traits: pattern is narrow to moderately wide. Dorsal base color as described for Juveniles of Eastern, but rufous type is very uncommon in *calurus*. Uppertail coverts are dark with some pale markings.

JUVENILES OF LIGHT MORPH "HARLAN'S" (*B. j. harlani*): HEAD.—Crown and nape are streaked with brownish black and the dark malar mark is pronounced. The supercilium and auricular region blend as a large white unit. The throat is white and unmarked. Overall, the head appears quite white. BODY (dorsal).—Brownish black back and scapulars. The scapulars have moderate-sized white patches, and the dark mark on the central part of each feather is either a diamond shape or a streak. BODY (ventral).—White with moderately marked or heavily marked type brownish black streaking on the belly and flanks (markings are arrowhead, diamond-shaped, or barred on most other races). Leg feathers are white and unmarked. WINGS (dorsal).—**The pale panel on the primaries and respective greater coverts is pale brown or white.** Brownish black with white markings on the median and some lesser coverts. WINGS (ventral).—Large dark patagial mark on the white underwing coverts. The "fingers" on the outer five primaries are always barred. TAIL.—Three main colors of pale banding: (1) medium brown, (2) pale brown, or (3) white on part of the central rectrices and sometimes other rectrices. Some rectrices may have a rufous wash on them. *See* Mindell 1985 for additional variations. As in other races, the dark banding may be equal width or the subterminal band wider. Dark tail bands vary from narrow to fairly wide but are usually narrower than the pale bands, and are often a wavy or chevron-shaped pattern. A dark "spike" often shows along the distal feather shaft, but light morphs are less likely to have black rectrix tips as seen on darker morphs of juvenile *harlani*. Uppertail coverts are white with dark markings. Undertail coverts are white and unmarked.

JUVENILE LIGHT MORPH INTERGRADE TRAITS: Intergrade features between subspecies and color morphs of most juveniles are difficult to see.

Intergrade of typical *borealis* x "Krider's": Subspecies features are mainly seen on the head and tail. (1) Birds may have a darker head as on typical *borealis* but a white tail as on "Krider's"; (2) the head may be quite white but with a dark crown and partial or full malar marks, and the tail brown as on typical *borealis*; or (3) crown may be white but with dark malar and white or brown tails.

Intergrade of *calurus* x "Krider's": As on any of the three variations described for *borealis* x "Krider's," but the leg feathers may be quite barred and tail more widely banded.

Intergrade of *borealis* x *calurus*: Difficult to separate from the respective races because there is so much variation. Streaked throat, heavy belly band, distinctly barred leg feathers, and partial barring on the undertail coverts.

JUVENILE LIGHT INTERMEDIATE MORPH TRAITS: Pertains to "Western" *B. j. calurus*. Field-observed and museum specimens of *B. j. harlani* have not been seen for this color morph; however, it undoubtedly exists since this plumage is documented for adults. The morph of *B. j. calurus* is more heavily marked than the light morph and forms a link in the continuum of plumages.

JUVENILES OF LIGHT INTERMEDIATE (LIGHT RUFOUS) MORPH "WESTERN" (*B. j. calurus*): HEAD.—As in juvenile light morph, but throat almost always dark. BODY (dorsal).—As in juvenile light morph. BODY (ventral).—The white or pale tawny breast is narrowly streaked with dark brown with the streaking covering less than 50% of the surface. The belly and flanks are heavily marked and form a distinct dark mottled band. White or pale tawny leg feathers are heavily barred. The undertail coverts are white or pale tawny and partially barred. WINGS (dorsal).—**The pale panel on the primaries and respective coverts is pale brown.** There is a small amount of pale spotting on the median and first rows of lesser upperwing coverts. WINGS (ventral).—**Large dark brown patagial mark, but it is somewhat masked by the heavily marked underwing coverts.** Axillaries are barred. The "fingers" on the outer five primaries are dark gray. TAIL.— As described for Juvenile Traits; black banded pattern is narrow to moderately wide. Rarely has rufous type tail. Broad white terminal tail band. Uppertail coverts are dark with narrow pale tips.

JUVENILES OF LIGHT INTERMEDIATE MORPH "HARLAN'S" (*B. j. harlani*): Probably similar to respective color morph of *calurus* but more brownish black and with a white throat.

JUVENILE INTERMEDIATE MORPH TRAITS: Pertains to "Western" *B. j. calurus* and "Harlan's" *B. j. harlani*. These morphs are more heavily marked than their respective light intermediate morphs and form links in the continuum of plumages from light to dark morph.

JUVENILES OF INTERMEDIATE (RUFOUS) MORPH "WESTERN" (*B. j. calurus*): Dark crown, nape, and malar marks with a medium tawny-rufous supercilium and auricular region. Throat is always dark brown. The forehead is dark. BODY (dorsal).—Nearly uniformly dark warm brown back and scapulars, but scapulars may have a small amount of pale tawny markings. BODY (ventral).—Breast is pale tawny or tawny with dark brown streaking covering 50% of the surface. Belly and flanks are nearly solid dark brown with some tawny speckling. Leg feathers are heavily barred. Tawny undertail coverts are heavily barred. WINGS (dorsal).—Dark coverts with pale spots only on the median coverts. WINGS (ventral).—Underwing coverts are uniformly and heavily marked with dark brown and tawny. There is no distinction of a dark patagial mark because the coverts are so heavily marked. The "fingers" on the outer five primaries are dark gray. TAIL.—As described for Juvenile Traits; black bands are narrow to moderately wide. Rarely has rufous type dorsal color. Moderate-sized or broad white terminal tail band. Uppertail coverts are dark with a small amount of tawny edging.

JUVENILES OF INTERMEDIATE MORPH "HARLAN'S" (*B. j. harlani*): Crown, nape, and malar marks are brownish black; supercilium and auricular region are white. The white supercilium and auriculars may blend as a large white area on the side of the head. The throat is always white or white with narrow dark streaking. The forehead is often white. BODY (dorsal).— **Brownish black with white oval-shaped markings on the outer edges on the lower scapulars; the center of each scapular has a dark streak (diamond-shaped on other races).** BODY (ventral).—*See* types below. Leg feathers are brownish black and streaked with white. WINGS (dorsal).—**The pale panel on the primaries and respective greater coverts is pale brown or often quite white.** White oval-shaped markings on the median and first one or two rows of lesser coverts with a dark streak down the center of each feather. WINGS (ventral).—Brownish black with white speckling on the underwing coverts and white barring on the axillaries. There is no distinction of a dark patagial mark because the underwing coverts are dark and speckled. The "fingers" on the outer five primaries are distinctly barred. TAIL.—As described for Juveniles of Light Morph "Harlan's." However, the black bands are often wide and not equal in width. On the inner half of the tail, the pale bands may be narrower than the dark bands. A black "spike" runs along the feather shaft from the black subterminal band to the tip of most or all rectrices. On many birds, the dark spike extends to cover all of the tip of each rectrix (tail tip is white on other races). *Note:* The spike pattern is more prevalent on darker morphs than on light morphs.

JUVENILE INTERMEDIATE MORPH "HARLAN'S" (STREAK-BREASTED TYPE): BODY (ventral).— Breast is equally streaked brownish black and white. The belly and flanks are brownish black and speckled with white and are abruptly darker than the breast. *Note:* A common type.

JUVENILE INTERMEDIATE MORPH "HARLAN'S" (STREAKED TYPE): BODY (ventral).—The breast, belly, and flanks are nearly equally and uniformly streaked with brownish black and white. *Note:* An uncommon type.

JUVENILE INTERMEDIATE MORPH INTERGRADE TRAITS: Refers mainly to individuals with subtle variations between *harlani* and *calurus* that are difficult to assign to a particular race. Involves birds with dark throats as on *calurus* and barred outer primaries as on *harlani*, and different patterns on the tail tip. Plumages are generally a warm dark brown as in *calurus*.

JUVENILE DARK INTERMEDIATE MORPH TRAITS: Pertains to *B. j. calurus* and *B. j. harlani*. These morphs are more heavily marked than their respective intermediate morphs and form links in the continuum of plumages from light to dark morph.

JUVENILES OF DARK INTERMEDIATE (DARK RUFOUS) MORPH "WESTERN" (*B. j. calurus*): HEAD.—Dark brown with somewhat paler tawny-rufous supercilium and auricular areas. Throat is dark brown. Forehead is mainly dark but can be white. BODY (dorsal).—Uniformly warm dark brown but at close distance shows faint dark tawny-rufous mottling on the scapulars. BODY (ventral).—The breast feathers are narrowly edged with tawny or tawny-rufous and may appear quite rufous at moderate and long distances. The belly, flanks, and leg feathers are solid warm dark brown or may have a small amount of tawny-rufous edging on many feathers. The breast always appears somewhat paler than the rest of the underparts. WINGS (dorsal).—Nearly uniformly warm dark brown with a small amount of pale spotting on the median upperwing coverts. WINGS (ventral).—The underwing coverts are dark brown with a small amount of pale edging or mottling. TAIL.—As described for Juvenile Traits; black banded pattern is moderately wide. Moderately wide white terminal tail band.

JUVENILES OF DARK INTERMEDIATE MORPH "HARLAN'S" (*B. j. harlani*): HEAD.—Brownish black with a white throat and sometimes a white supercilium patch. The forehead is mainly black. BODY (dorsal).—Gray oval shapes on the scapulars with a black center streak on each feather. BODY (ventral).—*See* types below. WINGS (dorsal).—White oval shapes on median and some lesser upperwing coverts. WINGS (ventral).—Brownish black underwing coverts are lightly speckled with white; axillaries are barred with white. TAIL.—

As described for Juvenile Intermediate Morph "Harlan's." The black "spike" regularly extends onto the tail tip.

JUVENILE DARK INTERMEDIATE MORPH "HARLAN'S" (STREAK-BREASTED TYPE): BODY (ventral).—Brownish black breast has a small amount of white streaking or blotching. Rest of the underparts is uniformly brownish black or has a small amount of white speckling.

JUVENILE DARK INTERMEDIATE MORPH "HARLAN'S" (SPOT-BELLIED TYPE): BODY.—The breast is solid brownish black and the belly and flanks are spotted or blotched with white. The leg feathers are narrowly streaked with white.

JUVENILE DARK INTERMEDIATE MORPH INTERGRADE TRAITS: Refers mainly to individuals with subtle variations between *harlani* and *calurus* that are difficult to assign to a particular race. Involves birds with dark throats as on *calurus* and barred outer primaries as on *harlani* and vice versa, and different patterns on the tail tip. Plumages are generally a warm dark brown as in *calurus*.

JUVENILE DARK MORPH TRAITS: Pertains to *B. j. calurus* and *B. j. harlani*. These morphs are more heavily marked than their respective dark intermediate morphs and form the final links in the continuum of plumages from light to dark morph.

JUVENILES OF DARK MORPH "WESTERN" (*B. j. calurus*): HEAD.—Uniformly warm dark brown. BODY (dorsal).—Uniformly warm dark brown with slightly paler tawny-rufous blotches on the scapulars. WINGS (dorsal).—Warm dark brown with tawny spotting on the median coverts. WINGS (ventral).—Uniformly dark brown but may have faint tawny-rufous speckling on some feathers. TAIL.—As described for Juvenile Traits; black tail bands are moderately wide or fairly wide but still narrower than the pale brown bands. White terminal band is narrow.

JUVENILES OF DARK MORPH "HARLAN'S" (*B. j. harlani*): HEAD.—Uniformly brownish black, including the throat. The forehead is black. BODY (dorsal).—Brownish black with grayish oval shapes on the outer edges and a back center streak on most scapulars. BODY (ventral).—Uniformly brownish black and lacks any white speckling. WINGS (dorsal).—Brownish black and may have white spots on the median coverts. WINGS (ventral).—Uniformly black, including the axillaries. TAIL.—As described for Juvenile Intermediate Morph "Harlan's": black "spikes" regularly extend to tips of rectices.

JUVENILE DARK MORPH INTERGRADE TRAITS: There is a considerable amount of intergrading, and the differences are very subtle.

ABNORMAL PLUMAGES: Albinism of various types is more prevalent in Red-tailed Hawks than in any other raptor. H. Kendall (pers. comm.) has obtained data on over 550 cases of albinism in Red-tailed Hawks in recent years. Albinism is most commonly seen in the East in birds from New York, Pennsylvania, and Wisconsin (H. Kendall pers. comm.). All but one record of albinism has been on a light morph, and that was in the West. *Note:* Albinism types are based on Pettingill (1970); *see* chapter 2 *Total albinism:* All-white plumage with pink irises and fleshy parts. Extremely rare type of albinism and in Red-tail known from only one adult. *Incomplete albinism:* All white or nearly all white with a few dark feathers. Some fleshy areas are paler than on normal birds. On these types of Red-tails, the irises are a normal dark brown or may be bluish, and bill, cere, and feet are also normal color. The talons, however, are nearly always pink. Uncommon type of albinism. At a distance looks like total albinism. Seen on adults. *Partial albinism:* Plumage can be nearly all white with a few dark feathers or any amount of white feathering among normal feathering. If partially white, then scattered white feathers are often on the head, remiges, and upperparts. Ventral areas are often normal. The white areas of the plumage may be the total feather, or a portion of various feathers may lack pigmentation and be white. Most common type of albinism. Seen on adults. Seen on one migrant dark morph *calurus* adult at Duluth, Minn., that had a white collar and scattered white feathers on its dark body and remiges (Nicoletti et al. 1998). *Imperfect albinism* (dilute plumage): Brown and rufous colored areas of normal birds are tan colored in this type of albinism. Seen on adults and juveniles. Uncommon type of albinism.

HABITAT: *B. j. borealis.* **Summer.**—Inhabits a wide variety of semi-open and open dry upland moderately agricultural and natural areas. Occasionally found in suburban and urban areas.

B. j. borealis. Winter.—Similar areas as for summer, but also found in open and semi-open marshes and swamps. More likely to use open regions than in summer, but only if suitable elevated perches are available.

B. j. borealis. Migration.—Found in similar areas as summer and winter but also over large wooded expanses.

B. j. umbrinus. All seasons.—Semi-open dry upland of Cabbage Palms, pines, and oaks in moderately agricultural areas, grazing lands, logged areas, and natural savannahs. Many areas are drained cypress swamps. Absent from most marshes and swamps.

HABITS: B. j. borealis varies from being moderately tame to wary. B. j. umbrinus is moderately tame. Red-tailed Hawks perch on exposed, elevated natural and human-made perches, including utility wires. Hawks that are feeding often sit on the ground. When perched in trees, they may sit on the top-most branches or on mid- and lower outer branches. This is a solitary species except during winter in locations with high prey density. In these areas, large numbers, especially juveniles, may loosely assemble. In other areas, territories are established and defended, particularly by adults. Hackles and nape feathers are erected when agitated or in cool temperatures.

FEEDING: Perch and aerial hunter. A generalist feeder and hunts all types of small and medium-sized amphibians, birds, mammals, and reptiles. Large insects may also be eaten. Prey is captured on the ground or on outer branches of bushes and trees. Avian prey is occasionally captured in low-altitude flight. Red-tailed Hawks regularly feed on carrion, particularly during lean periods in winter.

FLIGHT: Wings are held at a low dihedral when soaring and on a flat plane when gliding. Long-winged subspecies, such as *calurus* and *umbrinus*, have a more distinct dihedral because the outer primaries flex upwards more than in shorter winged subspecies. Powered flight is used regularly and is interspersed with gliding sequences. At times, there is a fairly regular cadence of flapping and gliding. Wingbeats are moderately slow. Red-tailed Hawks regularly hover and kite. Aerial forging occurs when soaring, hovering, or kiting. Angled dives, sometimes from long distances, are made to capture prey. Legs are often extended down-wards—with wings nearly closed—for stability in the mid- and last part of a dive.

VOICE: All subspecies have similar calls. A fairly vocal raptor in all seasons. Mainly heard when agitated. Adults and subadults have discernibly different tones than juveniles. *Adults and subadults:* Drawn-out, hoarse, and raspy whistled *skee-ah, skeerh,* or *squeer. Juveniles:* Similar vocalization as older birds but lacks the hoarse, raspy tones and is a clear, high-pitched whistled call. Adults also emit a raspy squeal, *chee-aack* or *chee-aah,* at any time of year; mated pairs utter a low-pitched, nasal *gank* call to each other. Nestlings and fledglings repeatedly utter clear, high-pitched *klee, klee* or *kree, kree* notes when food-begging.

STATUS AND DISTRIBUTION: Overall population of Red-tailed Hawk is stable. It is one of the most common raptors with an estimated population of 1 million birds. B. j. borealis and B. j. umbrinus are both *common* breeders within their ranges in the East. Populations of *borealis* and, to an extent, *umbrinus,* have increased substantially since historical times with the clearing of forests and draining of wetlands (at the loss of habitat for other species of birds). Being highly adaptable, they are also readily using urban centers.

B. j. borealis. Summer.—Regularly distributed throughout all of mapped range except in extensive forested areas. Also found on larger islands such as Nantucket Island, Mass. Particularly numerous in areas with small wooded lots as found in the agricultural region of the Midwest. Intergrades with B. j. umbrinus in n. Florida peninsula.

B. j. borealis. Winter.—Vacates the northern third of breeding range (mainly south of 45° degrees North Latitude). Some adults from mid-latitude areas such as cen. Wisconsin and cen. Michigan do not leave breeding territories. A few birds of all ages may winter as far as Florida Keys. Winter density is greater in the southern half of the winter range. Severity of winter dictates density in the northern part of regular winter range. Red-tailed Hawks are found only in small numbers or are absent in portions of the higher elevations of the Appalachian Mts.

B. j. borealis. Migration.—Many adults of middle and southern latitudes are sedentary; northern adults are migratory. All juveniles are migratory. Migrants move short to moderate distances.

Late summer northward dispersal: Many recently fledged juvenile *borealis* engage in a northward dispersal. This is most notable along the south shore of Lake Ontario, particularly at Braddock Bay S. P. near Rochester, N.Y. Movements begin in late Jul., peak in mid-Aug., and end in early Sep. Hundreds of juveniles can be seen on peak days with strong southerly winds. Banding data show some juveniles captured in New York had been banded as nestlings earlier in the summer in Virginia. Banding data also indicate yongsters may head north into e. Ontario or the Northeast after leaving e. New York. One bird that was banded in New York in Aug. was found a few days later in Manitoba.

Fall migration: Age correlated, with juveniles moving before subadults and adults. *Juveniles.*—Begins in mid-Aug. (not all birds disperse northward in late summer). In Ontario and Michigan, peak movements are in mid-Oct. and taper off in early Nov. In New Jersey and Pennsylvania, peak movements are in late Oct. *Subadults and adults.*—Subadults may move in the earlier part of the adult segment. In Ontario and Michigan, peak movements occur in early Nov. and then taper off considerably. In New Jersey and Pennsylvania, peak movements span from mid- to late Nov. with small numbers continuing to move south through Dec. and early Jan.

Spring migration: Age correlated, with adults moving before juveniles and probably subadults. Sizable spring flights are only seen along the Great Lakes. *Adults.*—Along the south shore of Lake Ontario in New York, adults first appear in mid-Feb. and peak in late Mar., occasionally in mid-Mar. depending on weather. Movement of possibly northern birds and subadults continues into early and mid-Apr. along Lake Ontario. On Lake Superior, adults appear in late Mar. and peak in mid- to late Apr. *Juveniles.*—Along Lake Ontario, migrate mainly in Apr. and peak in mid- to late Apr., and continue moving in small numbers into mid-Jun. At Lake Superior latitude, they migrate mainly in May and into early Jun.

B. j. umbrinus. All seasons.—Sedentary. Resident in peninsular Florida but absent from intensely agricultural, heavily wooded, and wet lowland regions. Also found on larger islands of the Bahamas (Abaco, Grand Bahama, and probably Andros).

STATUS AND DISTRIBUTION OF WESTERN SUBSPECIES AND COLOR MORPHS IN THE EAST: Two subspecies and one color morph occur in migration and winter in portions of the East. **"Krider"s" (pale morph of B. j. borealis). Winter/migration.**—Uncommon. Fairly regular in counties along the Mississippi floodplain region from nw. Illinois to s. Mississippi. Irregular in mapped areas east of counties adjacent to the river. In the main wintering area, seen in Kentucky in the following counties: Ballard, Fulton, and Hickman along the Mississippi River region; Butler, Henderson, Livingston, Lyon, Meade, Muhlenberg, Ohio, and Warren in the western and central part of the state; and Boone, Grant, and Mercer in the eastern part of the state.

Extralimital winter/migration.—"Krider's" have been recorded in fall and/or winter in Georgia, s. New Jersey, Ohio, s. Ontario e. Pennsylvania, s. Québec., and s. Virginia. In winter, seen in Georgia and Florida. *Georgia:* Sumter Co. in early Dec. 2001. *Florida:* Several records; specimen from Leon Co. in Dec. 1980 and a sighting in nw. Palm Beach Co. in late Nov. 1996. *Ohio:* (1) Hamilton Co. in late Dec. 1953, (2) Ashtabula Co. in late Dec. 1963, (3) Muskingum Co. in late Dec. 1967, (4) Ottawa Co. in late Apr. 1979.

"Krider's" range in the West.—Breeds on the n. Great Plains with typical *borealis* and intergrades with *calurus* in western and northern parts of range.

B. j. calurus. Winter/migration.—*Common* in counties near the Mississippi River from Illinois to Mississippi. *Uncommon* to *very uncommon* in most other areas of regular winter range. Records listed for each state are based mainly on intermediate to dark morph birds. Light morph *calurus* can be similar to heavily marked *borealis*, which makes records difficult to substantiate. *Alabama:* Probably fairly regular in small numbers in winter in the northern and very western part of the state. Two banded birds from Saskatchewan were recovered in e.-cen. Alabama. *Illinois:* Adult light to dark morphs throughout the state in winter, particularly in the southern half of the state. *Indiana:* Rare but fairly regular statewide. Becomes less common in the eastern part of the state. *Kentucky:* Recorded in several counties. Most commonly seen in the western half of the state. Seen in winter in the following counties: Boone, Boyd, Calloway, Christian, Fulton, Gallatin, Henderson, Hickman, Lincoln, Livingston, Logan, Marshall, Mercer, Muhlenberg, Ohio, Oldham, Shelby, Trigg, Union, and Warren. *Michigan:* Verified winter range by adult intermediate and dark morphs wintering for several years at Shiawassee NWR, Saginaw Co., and near Mayville, Tuscola Co. Juvenile intermediate morphs are seen each winter in small numbers in the southern part of the state from Allegan Co. to Monroe Co. Darker birds are regular in fall at the hawkwatch at Lake Erie Metro Park, Wayne Co. (Southeastern Michigan Raptor Research Station), and in spring in Chippewa Co. (Whitefish Point Bird Observatory). *Mississippi:* Sporadically seen throughout the state. *Ohio:* Rare but regular during migration and winter in the state; nearly annual since 1990. Records are for 1 day unless noted otherwise: (1) Auglaize Co. in mid-Nov. 1911, (2) Hamilton Co. during winter of 1964–1965 (several birds), (3) Lake Co. for 5 days from late Mar. to early Apr. 1980, (4) Trumbull Co. in mid Dec. 1983, (5) Lake Co. in late Mar. 1991, (6) Lucas Co. in early Nov. 1991, (7) Lucas Co. in early Apr. 1992, (8) Lucas Co. in mid-Apr. 1992 (2 birds), (9) Seneca Co. in late Nov. 1992, (10) Hancock Co. in late Nov. 1993, (11) Lorain Co. in late Jan. 1995, (12) Coshocton Co. in late Mar. 1998, (13) Lucas Co. in early Apr. 1999, (14) Wayne Co. in late May 1999, (15) Lucas Co. in early Nov. 1999, (16) Lucas Co. in late Nov. 1999, and (17) Preble Co. in early Jan. 2001. *Tennessee:* Regular from late fall to early spring west of the Tennessee River, irregular in central and eastern parts of the state. A juvenile intermediate morph seen as late as early Apr. in Weakley Co. Seen in the following counties: Caroll, Henry, Obion, Stewart, and Weakley. *Wisconsin:* Farthest north record is an adult dark rufous morph in St. Croix Co.

Accidental and/or casual beyond typical wintering areas.—*Florida:* Accidental. In the early 1990s, seen in Dixie Co. and s. Monroe Co. (Everglades N. P.). A juvenile dark morph near Zellwood, Lake Co., in early 2000 (with Rough-legged Hawks). *Georgia:* Accidental. At least three records in the last 10 years of single dark birds from Baker, Clarke, and Crawford Cos. *New Jersey:* A few records at Cape Point S. P. *New York:* Casual. Up to five are seen each spring at Braddock Bay Hawkwatch near Rochester and at Derby Hill Hawkwatch near the town of Mexico. An intermediate morph has wintered near Rochester for several years. *Ontario:* Casual. Regular in the fall in very small numbers along the n. shore of Lake Ontario at Holiday Beach and Hawk Cliff Hawkwatches. *Pennsylvania:* Casual. As of the winter of 2001, an adult dark morph wintered at the same location in Northampton Co. for 10 years. Very rarely seen at hawkwatches in the eastern part of the state. *South Carolina:* Accidental. Huntington Beach S. P., Georgetown Co., in late Oct. 1999. *Québec:* Casual. One or two seen each fall in the southern part of the province, particularly at the hawkwatch near Tadoussac. *Virginia:* Casual. Rare records in Northampton Co. in fall and winter; one in winter of 1999. A juvenile dark rufous morph was seen from early Jan. to early Apr. 1999 in n. Prince William Co. and returned the following Nov. to the same location (and tree), and for the winters of 2000 and 2001.

***B. j. calurus* range in the West.**—Breeds from n. Canada to n. Mexico east of the Great Plains; also in the boreal forest to cen. Manitoba. Winters in the southern half of breeding range and eastward across the Great Plains to ne. Mexico. Large numbers winter in Arkansas, California, Louisiana, Missouri, and e. Texas.

***B. j. harlani.* Winter/migration.**—*Uncommon.* Regular in winter in counties along the Mississippi River from n. Illinois to s. Mississippi. *Illinois:* East from the Mississippi River, nearly annual or annual with one or two birds wintering in Champaign, Clinton, Madison, Sangamon, Pulaski, and Union Cos. Alexander, Cook, Franklin, Lake (Oct. migrant), Marion, Mason, Monroe, Ogle, and Randolph Cos. have irregular winter occurrences. *Kentucky:* Recorded in winter in Ballard, Bullitt, Carlisle, Fulton, Hickman, Livingston, Muhlenberg, Nelson, Ohio, Oldham, and Warren Cos. *Mississippi:* Mainly seen along the Mississippi River basin and inland in the northern fourth of the state. Records exist for the following counties: Adams, Alcorn, Calhoun, Genada, Lafayette, Monroe, Tate, Tunica, and Washington. Very irregular south to Hancock Co. *Tennessee:* Irregular in counties west of the Tennessee River. Seen in the following counties: Benton, Carroll, Fayette, Gibson, Hardeman, Hardin, Henry, Lauderdale, Lake, Madison, Shelby, and Weakely. Highly irregular east to Blount (Great Smokey Mts. N. P. in 1997) and Putnam Cos.

Accidental *harlani* records.—*Florida:* (1) Gulf Co. in mid-Nov. 1991 and (2) an adult light morph near Fort Pierce in Jan. 1988 and again from mid-Jan. to mid-Mar. 1999. *Indiana:* An early 1900s specimen from Boone Co. *Wisconsin:* Late Oct. 2000 in Ozaukee Co. Annual in the western part of the state in the fall as several are seen each autumn in Duluth, Minn. *New Jersey:* Possible records for Cape May Point S. P. but none verified with photographs. *Ontario:* Juvenile dark morph near Toronto from early Jan. to mid-Mar. 1997. *Virginia:* One well-documented adult intermediate morph in late Nov. 1998 at the Kiptopeke S.P. Hawkwatch.

B. j. harlani **range in the West.**—Breeds from cen. Alaska and w. Yukon Territory south to n. British Columbia. Winters widely in the w. U.S., with highest density from e. Colorado east to s. Iowa and south to e. Texas.

Color morph status for *B. j. calurus* **and** *B. j. harlani.*—All morphs breed throughout each respective subspecies' range. Color morph ratios locally and regionally may be higher or lower than listed.

B. j. calurus: The darker the color morph, the less common it is. Light morph.—Common. Far outnumbers darker morphs and may comprise at least 70% of the population. Light intermediate morph.—Uncommon. Intermediate morph.—Uncommon. In winter, more common west of the Rocky Mts. and outnumbered by darker morphs east of the Rockies. Dark intermediate morph.—Uncommon. In winter, found in equal numbers in all areas. Dark morph.—Uncommon. In winter, more common east of the Rocky Mts. Comprises 5–10% of the population.

B. j. harlani: The light and dark extremes are the least common. Light morph.—Very uncommon and may account for about 4% of the total population. Light intermediate morph.—Uncommon, and only slightly more numerous than light morph. Intermediate morph.—Common. The most common morph and may comprise 50% of the population. Dark intermediate morph.—Fairly common. Somewhat less common than intermediate morph. Dark morph.—Uncommon and may comprise about 5% of the population.

NESTING: *B. j. borealis.*—Some pairs begin courtship and nest construction in early Jan., even as far north as cen. Michigan and Wisconsin. Nesting mainly begins in Feb. and Mar. in most areas of the e. U.S. and in Apr. in n. Canada. Nesting ends from Jun. to Aug. depending on latitude. Mid- and southern-latitude adults may remain paired and on or near territory year-round. A few northern-latitude pairs may also remain together year-round. *B. j. umbrinus.*—Nesting begins in Jan. with egg-laying in Feb. Nesting ends in Jun.

Courtship (flight).—*High-circling* by one or both sexes, *leg-dangling* by one or both sexes, *talon-grappling* by both sexes, and *sky-dancing* by males.

Courtship (perched).—*High-perching.* See chapter 5 for courtship descriptions.

Large stick nests are built by both sexes. A new nest may be built or a pair may reuse a previous year's nest. Nests may be built in a week or less, constructed mainly in the morning. Old nests may be used for several years and become quite deep. Nests are 28–30 in. (71–76 cm) in diameter. New nests may be 4–6 in. (10–15 cm) deep; old nests may be much deeper. Finer material and greenery are added to the nest throughout the nesting season.

Nests are located where there is an expansive view of the landscape and are placed 35–90 ft. (11–27 m) high. Most nests of *B. j. borealis* and all nests of *B. j. umbrinus* are placed in trees that are the dominant live or dead species of the area. In deciduous trees, nests are placed in fairly major forks; in conifers, they are located next to the trunk. Nests of *umbrinus* are often in mature Longleaf and Slash pines. *B. j. borealis* occasionally nests on cliffs, building ledges, or other artificial structures. Two to 3 eggs, rarely 1 to 5, are incubated by both sexes for 28–35 days. Youngsters branch before fledging in 42–46 days. Being smaller, males fledge before females. Fledglings depend on parents another 30–70 days.

CONSERVATION: Since this is a highly adaptable species, no measures are needed.

Mortality.—Illegal shooting, electrocution from utility lines, and collisions with vehicles are major factors. There are some local problems with organophosphate poisoning. Great Horned Owls prey on all ages of Red-tailed Hawks. Coyotes and foxes prey on fledglings perched on the ground. Migrant Golden Eagles occasionally kill Red-tailed Hawks that harass them.

SIMILAR SPECIES: COMPARED TO JUVE-NILE LIGHT MORPH (including *harlani*).—**(1) Red-shouldered Hawk, juveniles.**—Irises darker brownish. Bright yellow cere. Ventral areas are uniformly streaked or barred. Pale tail bands are narrower than dark bands. FIGHT.—Pale tawny panels and windows on the base of the primaries. Lacks dark patagial marks on the underwing. **(2) Broad-wing Hawk, juveniles.**—PERCHED.—Irises are darker brownish. Bright yellow cere. Often have similarly marked belly band. Dorsal surface of secondaries is dark brown and unbarred. Scapulars are dark brown and lack white patches. FLIGHT.—Similar pale windows on the ventral wing; pale only on primaries on the upperwing. Does not hover or kite. **(3) Swainson's Hawk, light morph juveniles.**—PERCHED.—Irises usually darker medium brown. Inner half of lores dark. Similar white mottling on the scapulars. Large dark brown patch on the sides of the neck and breast. Wingtips equal or nearly equal to tail tip. FLIGHT.—Medium gray remiges on the ventral wing. Lacks dark patagial marks. **(4) Rough-legged Hawk, light morphs.**—PERCHED.—Yellow cere. Inner half of the lores dark. Belly markings often quite similar, especially mottled pattern of many adults. Tarsi are feathered to the toes. Wingtips equal to or extend beyond tail tip. FLIGHT.—Pale window on underside of primaries similar, but when viewed from above it is only on primaries and not primary greater coverts. White uppertail coverts similar to those of Red-tails but usually more extensive white on the basal region. COMPARED TO ADULT/JUVENILE "KRIDER'S".—**(5) Swainson's Hawk, one-year-olds.**—PERCHED.—Thin dark eye line. Medium brown irises. Dark patch on the sides of the neck and breast. Wingtips nearly equal or equal to tail tip. FLIGHT.—Medium gray remiges. Lacks dark patagial mark on the un-

derwing. Tail is uniformly medium brown on the dorsal surface. **(6) Ferruginous Hawk, light morph juveniles.**—Accidental in the East. PERCHED.—Yellow cere. Thick dark eyeline. Feathered tarsi. Dorsal surface of the secondaries is plain dark brown and unbanded. Dark dorsal tail bands are fairly wide, and rarely more than three or four dark bands. Scapulars are mainly dark brown with little if any white mottling. FLIGHT.—Small dark tips on the outer primaries (barred wingtips on all juvenile "Krider's"). COMPARED TO JUVENILE IN-TERMEDIATE MORPH (including *harlani*).—**(7) Rough-legged Hawk, light/intermediate morphs.**—Breast is similarly streaked. PERCHED.—Yellow cere. Dark inner half of lores. Thin dark eyeline. Dorsal surface of secondaries is plain brown and unbarred. Wingtips extend to tail tip. FLIGHT.—Large dark carpal patch on wrist of underwing. COMPARED TO JUVENILE DARK MORPH (including *harlani*).—**(8) Swainson's Hawk, dark morph adults.**—PERCHED.—Yellow cere. White spot on outer half of lores. Wingtips equal to tail tip. FLIGHT.—Rufous underwing coverts. Dark gray underside of the remiges. Undertail coverts are distinctly paler than the body. **(9) Rough-legged Hawk, all ages.**—PERCHED.—As described for #4. COMPARED TO ADULT INTERMEDIATE TO DARK MORPH "HARLAN'S."—**(10) Rough-legged Hawk, adult female intermediate and dark morph.**—PERCHED.—Dark inner half of lores. Thin dark eyeline. Tarsi are feathered to the toes. Wingtips equal to tail tip. Breast pattern deceptively similar: both *harlani* and Rough-leg can have whitish mottling (intermediate morph) or lack mottling on the breast (dark morph). Tail pattern of *harlani* with medium/dark gray type dorsal tail pattern can be identical to that of Rough-leg (dark mottling is not always present on *harlani* tail). Rough-legs typically have a neat, broad black subterminal tail band; however, this is also present on a few *harlani* with gray tails. FLIGHT.—Underwing coverts and axillaries may be white spotted or barred and identical to some *harlani*: use caution. Most darker morphs of Rough-legs have some rufous on the underwing coverts with a black carpal patch on the wrist area; lacking on *harlani*.

OTHER NAMES: Redtail, Tail, Black Warrior ("Harlan's"). *Spanish:* Aguililla Colirroja, Aguililla Cola Roja, Aguililla Parda. *French:* Buse à Queue Rousse.

REFERENCES: Andrle and Carroll 1988; Baicich and Harrison 1997; Bohlen 1989; Brauning 1992; Brewer et al. 1991; Buckelew and Hall 1994; Bylan 1998, 1999; Cadman et al. 1987; Castrale et al. 1998; Clark and Wheeler 2001; del Hoyo et al. 1994; Dickerman 1994; Dickerman and Parkes 1987; Dobos 1995; Dodge 1988–1997; Erskine 1992; Ferguson-Lees and Christi 2001; Godfrey 1986; Houston 1967; Howell and Webb 1995; Iliff 2001; Kale et al. 1992; Kellogg 2000; Liguori 2001; McWilliams and Brauning 2000; Mindell 1985; Nicholson 1997; Nicoletti et al. 1998; Palmer 1988; Palmer-Ball 1996; Peterjohn and Rice 1991; Pittaway 1993; Pettingill 1970; Pranty 2000; Preston and Beane 1993; Robbins 1996; Stevenson and Anderson 1994; Todd 1950, 1963; Veit and Petersen 1993; Walsh et al. 1999; Wheeler and Clark 1995; Wood 1932.

"EASTERN" RED-TAILED HAWK, *Buteo jamaicensis borealis:* Common. Many Red-tailed Hawks of the boreal forest are more heavily marked.

"KRIDER'S" RED-TAILED HAWK, *Buteo jamaicensis borealis* (Pale Morph): Breeds on n. Great Plains. Uncommon in winter in East. Found mainly along Mississippi River basin; irregular to Mid-Atlantic coast and s. FL.

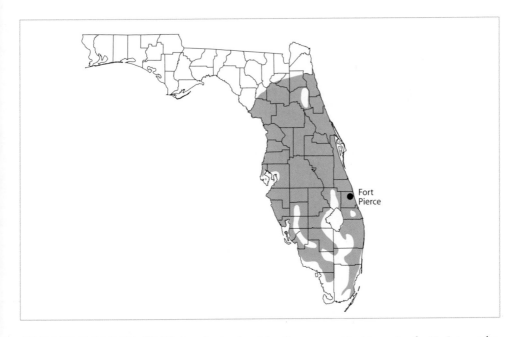

"FLORIDA" RED-TAILED HAWK, *Buteo jamaicensis umbrinus:* Common resident in peninsular FL. Intergrades with "Eastern" at n. edge of range. Also inhabits larger islands of Bahamas.

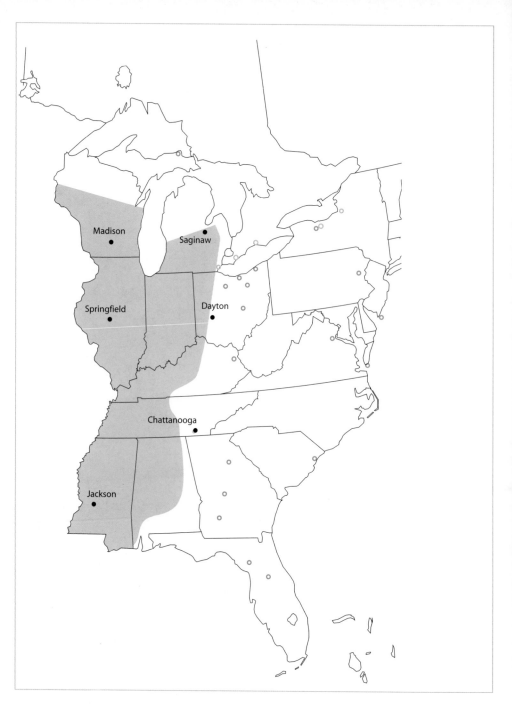

"WESTERN" RED-TAILED HAWK, *Buteo jamaicensis calurus:* Breeds west of Great Plains and east to cen. MB in Canada. Common in winter along Mississippi River basin. Uncommon to very uncommon farther east; rare in isolated locales east of major winter area.

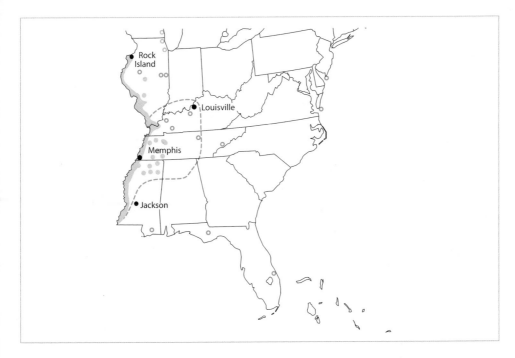

"HARLAN'S" HAWK, *Buteo jamaicensis harlani:* Uncommon. Mainly winters along Mississippi River basin. Very uncommon to rare within dashed line. Sporadic elsewhere.

Plate 297. Red-tailed Hawk, adult "Eastern" (*B. j. borealis*) [Dec.] ▪ White throat. Young adults have pale irises. ▪ Lightly marked type has white underparts with barred flanks, unmarked belly. Unmarked leg feathers. ▪ Wingtips shorter than tail tip. ▪ Rufous tail with black subterminal band. ▪ *Note:* Pale-bellied types found throughout breeding range.

Plate 298. Red-tailed Hawk, adult "Eastern" (*B. j. borealis*) [Dec.] ▪ Tawny-brown head with dark crown and malar. Streaked throat with dark collar. Old adults have dark irises. ▪ Large blotchy white patch on scapulars. Unmarked leg feathers. ▪ Pale mottling on brown wing coverts. Wingtips shorter than tail tip. ▪ Rufous tail with black subterminal band.

Plate 299. Red-tailed Hawk, adult "Eastern" (*B. j. borealis*) [Feb.] ▪ Tawny-brown head with dark crown and malar. White throat with dark collar. Old adults have dark irises. ▪ White underparts are moderately marked type with black streaking on belly, black barring on flanks. Lower belly, leg feathers, and undertail coverts are unmarked.

Plate 300. Red-tailed Hawk, adult "Krider's" (pale morph of *B. j. borealis*) [Feb.] ▪ White head with dark malar. Old adults have dark irises. ▪ Large blotchy white patch on scapulars. White blotches on coverts. Wingtips shorter than tail tip. ▪ Tail pinkish on distal 1/3, white on basal 2/3; thin subterminal band. ▪ *Note:* Purest types have all-white head.

Plate 301. Red-tailed Hawk, adult "Florida" (*B. j. umbrinus*) [Mar.] ▪ Dark tawny-brown head. Dark throat. Old adults have dark irises. ▪ Moderate-sized blotchy gray patch on scapulars. Mainly uniformly dark wing coverts. ▪ Wingtips extend to near tail tip. ▪ Tail (not shown) may be plain rufous or variably banded.

Plate 302. Red-tailed Hawk, adult "Florida" (*B. j. umbrinus*) [Mar.] ▪ Dark tawny-brown head. Dark throat. Old adults have dark irises. ▪ White underparts covered with black blobs on belly, black barring on flanks. Breast may be tawny in spring and summer. Leg feathers unmarked (but may be barred). ▪ *Note:* Darker on head and dorsal areas and more distinct blobs on belly than *borealis*.

Plate 303. Red-tailed Hawk, adult "Western" (*B. j. calurus*) **ligth morph** [Nov.] ▪ Dark tawny-brown head. Dark throat. Young adults have pale irises. ▪ Small to moderate-sized blotchy tawny patch on scapulars. ▪ Minimal pale mottling on wing coverts. Wingtips reach near tail tip. ▪ Rufous tail is banded type with full, narrow bands; wide black subterminal band.

Plate 304. Red-tailed Hawk, adult "Western" (*B. j. calurus*) **light morph** [Feb.] ▪ Dark tawny-brown head. Dark throat. Old adults have dark irises. ▪ Small to moderate-sized blotchy tawny patch on scapulars. ▪ Wingtips reach tail tip. ▪ Rufous tail is partially banded type with narrow bands on portion of rectrices; narrow black subterminal band. Orangish rufous uppertail coverts on most *calurus*.

Plate 305. Red-tailed Hawk, adult "Western" (*B. j. calurus*) **light morph** [Nov.] ▪ Dark tawny-brown head. Dark throat. Young adults have pale irises. ▪ Pale tawny underparts are heavily marked type. Barring on belly and lower belly is classic *calurus* trait. Tawny leg feathers barred. ▪ *Note:* Heaviest marked type of light morph.

Plate 306. Red-tailed Hawk, adult "Western" (*B. j. calurus*) **light intermediate morph** [Nov.] ▪ Dark tawny-brown head. Dark throat. Old adults have dark irises. ▪ Pale rufous underparts are typically heavily marked type. Barred, pale rufous lower belly and leg feathers.

Plate 307. Red-tailed Hawk, adult "Western" (*B. j. calurus*) **intermediate (rufous) morph [Oct.]** ▪ Dark tawny-brown head. Dark throat. Old adults have dark irises. ▪ Rufous breast (rufous leg feathers, lower belly, and undertail coverts hidden by perch). Belly and flanks vary from mottled with dark brown to solid dark brown.

Plate 308. Red-tailed Hawk, adult "Western" (*B. j. calurus*) **dark intermediate (dark rufous) morph [Nov.]** ▪ Dark brown head and throat. Old adults have dark irises. ▪ Rufous tinge on breast; belly, flanks, and leg feathers dark brown. Undertail coverts may be rufous. ▪ Upperparts dark brown.

Plate 309. Red-tailed Hawk, adult "Western" (*B. j. calurus*) **dark morph [Feb.]** ▪ Uniformly dark brown head. Old adults have dark irises. ▪ Uniformly dark brown body. ▪ Rufous tail is banded type but can be partially banded.

Plate 310. Red-tailed Hawk, adult "Harlan's" (*B. j. harlani*) **light morph [Mar.]** ▪ Blackish head with white supercilium and spectacles. Throat appears dark (from shadow) but is white with dark streaking. ▪ Stark white underparts lack rufous tinge on sides of neck on light morphs of other races. Large black blobs on belly, partial bars on flanks.

Plate 311. Red-tailed Hawk, adult "Harlan's" ▪
(*B. j. harlani*) **light morph [Feb.]** ▪ Brownish
black head with white supercilium and auricular
forms white spectacle look. White throat. ▪ White
blotches on scapulars form V. ▪ Wingtips shorter
than tail tip. ▪ Tail mainly gray *harlani*; possible
calurus intergrade with partly rufous tail and neat
subterminal band.

Plate 312. Red-tailed Hawk, adult "Harlan's" (*B. j.*
harlani) **light intermediate morph [Feb.]** ▪
Mainly white head, including throat; dark crown
and malar. Old adults have dark irises. ▪ White
breast sparsely streaked. Belly and flanks blackish
with white speckling. Undertail coverts white.

Plate 313. Red-tailed Hawk, adult "Harlan's" (*B. j.*
harlani) **intermediate morph [Nov.]** ▪ Dark head
with white forehead and partial supercilium; white
throat. Old adults have dark irises. ▪ White breast
broadly streaked. Belly and flanks blackish with
white speckling. Undertail coverts black with white
barring.

Plate 314. Red-tailed Hawk, adult "Harlan's" (*B. j.*
harlani) **intermediate morph [Nov.]** ▪ Dark head
with white forehead and throat. Old adults have
dark irises. ▪ White streaking on hindneck. Back
and scapulars dark. ▪ Wingtips shorter than tail
tip. ▪ White type tail. Irregular black terminal
band.

Plate 315. Red-tailed Hawk, adult "Harlan's" (*B. j. harlani*) dark intermediate morph [Nov.] ▪ Black head with white streaking on throat. Old adults have dark irises. ▪ Black breast sparsely streaked/mottled with white. Rest of body black. ▪ Wingtips shorter than tail tip. ▪ Medium/dark gray type tail.

Plate 316. Red-tailed Hawk, adult "Harlan's" (*B. j. harlani*) dark morph [Dec.] ▪ Old adults have dark irises. ▪ Black body. ▪ Wingtips shorter than tail tip. ▪ Medium/dark gray banded type tail. Gray with several dark bands and neat, wide, black subterminal band. ▪ *Note:* Uncommon *harlani* tail pattern.

Plate 317. Red-tailed Hawk, adult "Eastern" x "Western" (*B. j. borealis* x *B. j. calurus*) light morph [Nov.] ▪ Tawny-brown head and white throat as on *borealis*. ▪ Large white blotchy scapulars form a V as on *borealis*. ▪ Extensive pale mottling on wing coverts as on *borealis*. ▪ Rufous tail is partially banded type as on *calurus*.

Plate 318. Red-tailed Hawk, adult "Harlan's" x "Western" (*B. j. harlani* X *B. j. calurus*) [Dec.] ▪ Dark rufous-brown head and throat as on *calurus* with white *harlani* supercilium. ▪ Rufous breast as on intermediate morph *calurus* with small amount of white mottling as on dark intermediate morph *harlani*. Dark brown belly and flanks. ▪ Dorsal tail (not shown) pale gray as on *harlani*.

Plate 319. Red-tailed Hawk, adult "Eastern" (*B. j. borealis*) [Oct.] ▪ White throat with dark collar. ▪ Pale tawny underparts with moderately marked type belly and flanks. Unmarked leg feathers. ▪ Black patagial mark on wing. ▪ Rufous tail with dark subterminal band.

Plate 320. Red-tailed Hawk, adult "Eastern" (*B. j. borealis*) [Oct.] ▪ Dark throat. ▪ Pale tawny underparts with heavily marked type belly and flanks. Unmarked leg feathers. ▪ Black patagial mark on wing. ▪ Rufous tail with dark subterminal band. ▪ *Note:* Adults occasionally have dark throats. Photographed Kempton, Penn.

Plate 321. Red-tailed Hawk, adult "Eastern" (*B. j. borealis*) [Oct.] ▪ Large white patch on each scapular. ▪ White uppertail coverts; rufous tail with dark subterminal band.

Plate 322. Red-tailed Hawk, adult "Krider's" (pale morph of *B. j. borealis*) [Nov.] ▪ White throat. Partial dark collar. ▪ Immaculate white underparts. ▪ Rufous-brown patagial mark. Barred remiges, including "fingers" on outer primaries; wide black band on rear edge. ▪ Mainly white tail with neat, thin, dark subterminal band.

Red-tailed Hawk 281

Plate 323. Red-tailed Hawk, adult "Western" (*B. j. calurus*) **light morph** [Dec.] ▪ White streaking on dark throat. ▪ Lightly marked type underparts with minimal belly and flank markings. Narrow rufous barring on all areas but breast, including leg feathers. ▪ Black patagial marks; wide black band on trailing edge of wings. ▪ Partially banded type rufous tail is faintly banded.

Plate 324. Red-tailed Hawk, adult "Western" (*B. j. calurus*) **light morph** [Dec.] ▪ Dark throat. ▪ Heavily marked type underparts with heavy belly and flank markings. Narrow rufous barring on belly, lower belly, leg feathers, and undertail coverts. ▪ Black patagial marks; wide black band on trailing edge of wings. ▪ Banded type rufous tail.

Plate 325. Red-tailed Hawk, adult "Western" (*B. j. calurus*) **light morph** [Jan.] ▪ Dark throat. ▪ Heavily marked type underparts. Narrow rufous barring on belly, lower belly, and undertail coverts; leg feathers distinctly rufous-barred. ▪ Black patagial marks. ▪ Tail grayish or pinkish when closed.

Plate 326. Red-tailed Hawk, adult "Western" (*B. j. calurus*) **light morph** [Dec.] ▪ Dark throat. ▪ Heavily marked white type underparts white with heavy belly and flank markings. Faint rufous barring on leg feathers. ▪ Black patagial marks; wide black band on trailing edge of wings. ▪ Tail grayish or pinkish at certain angles.

Plate 327. Red-tailed Hawk, adult "Western" (*B. j. calurus*) intermediate (rufous) morph [Nov.] ▪ Dark throat. ▪ Rufous breast and leg feathers; mottled black belly and flanks. ▪ Rufous underwing coverts with black patagial mark. ▪ Partially banded type rufous tail.

Plate 328. Red-tailed Hawk, adult "Western" (*B. j. calurus*) dark intermediate (dark rufous) morph [Mar.] ▪ Dark rufous-brown head, including throat. ▪ Dark rufous-brown breast, black belly, flanks, leg feathers. ▪ Blackish underwing coverts. Wide black rear edge of remiges. ▪ Banded type rufous tail.

Plate 329. Red-tailed Hawk, adult "Western" (*B. j. calurus*) dark morph [Nov.] ▪ Head and all of body dark brown, occasionally black. ▪ Wide black band on rear edge of remiges. Outer remiges may be barred. ▪ Banded type rufous tail.

Plate 330. Red-tailed Hawk, adult "Harlan's" (*B. j. harlani*) light morph [Dec.] ▪ Pale spectacles, white throat. ▪ Stark white underparts with lightly marked type black blobs on belly and flanks. ▪ Black patagial mark. Barred type remiges, including outer primaries. ▪ Pale grayish tail with irregular black subterminal band.

Plate 331. Red-tailed Hawk, adult "Harlan's" (*B. j. harlani*) light morph [Jan.] ▪ Dark head, white throat. ▪ Stark white underparts with heavily marked type black blobs on belly and barred flanks. Barred leg feathers. ▪ Black patagial mark. Barred type remiges, including outer primaries. ▪ White tail with irregular black subterminal band.

Plate 332. Red-tailed Hawk, adult "Harlan's" (*B. j. harlani*) light morph [Mar.] ▪ White spectacles. ▪ White underparts with moderately marked type black barring on flanks and blobs on belly. ▪ Black patagial mark. Unmarked type remiges lack barring or mottling; black outer primaries. Wide black band on rear edge of remiges. ▪ Pale gray type tail; irregular black subterminal band.

Plate 333. Red-tailed Hawk, adult "Harlan's" (*B. j. harlani*) light morph [Mar.] ▪ White spectacles. ▪ Classic types lack dark barring on white part of scapulars. ▪ Pale gray-rufous type tail with gray mottling on inner half, rufous on outer half; irregular black subterminal band. ▪ *Note:* Even though rufous in tail, still classic *harlani*.

Plate 334. Red-tailed Hawk, adult "Harlan's" (*B. j. harlani*) light intermediate morph [Jan.] ▪ White head with dark neck and malar. ▪ Sparsely streaked white breast. Black belly and flanks speckled with white. White leg feathers heavily barred with black. White undertail coverts. ▪ Barred type remiges, including outer primaries. Black patagial marks. ▪ White type tail.

Plate 335. Red-tailed Hawk, adult "Harlan's" (*B. j. harlani*) intermediate morph [Jan.] ▪ Whitish throat. ▪ Breast mottled white and black. Rest of underparts, including undertail coverts, black with some white speckling. ▪ Barred and mottled type remiges; black outer primaries. ▪ Medium/dark gray type tail.

Plate 336. Red-tailed Hawk, adult "Harlan's" (*B. j. harlani*) intermediate morph [Dec.] ▪ Whitish throat. ▪ Breast mottled white and black. Rest of underparts black with white spotting. ▪ Mottled type remiges have fine gray mottling visible only at close range; black outer primaries. ▪ Mottled-barred type tail with rufous tinge on some rectrices.

Plate 337. Red-tailed Hawk, adult "Harlan's" (*B. j. harlani*) dark intermediate morph [Dec.] ▪ Black head with white speckling. ▪ Black underparts, including undertail coverts; small amount of white mottling on breast. ▪ Barred type remiges; black outer remiges. ▪ Dark gray type tail. ▪ *Note:* Same bird as on plate 315.

Plate 338. Red-tailed Hawk, subadult "Harlan's" (*B. j. harlani*) dark intermediate morph [Nov.] ▪ Black head. ▪ Black body with some white mottling on breast. ▪ Barred type remiges. Outer 3 primaries and 2 or 3 secondaries are juvenile. Juvenile primaries brown and narrowly barred; secondaries lack wide black band. ▪ Pale gray-rufous type adult tail.

Plate 339. Red-tailed Hawk, adult "Harlan's" (*B. j. harlani*) dark intermediate morph [Nov.] ▪ White throat. ▪ Spot-bellied type has black breast with white spotting on black belly, flanks, leg feathers, and undertail coverts. ▪ Barred type remiges; barred outer remiges. ▪ Pale gray banded type tail appears white in translucent light; neat black subterminal band. ▪ *Note:* Same bird as on plate 343.

Plate 340. Red-tailed Hawk, adult "Harlan's" (*B. j. harlani*) dark morph [Mar.] ▪ Head and body black or brownish black. ▪ Barred type remiges; black outer primaries. Black wing coverts. ▪ Mottled-barred type medium/dark gray tail (most dark morphs have darker gray tails). Irregular wide black terminal band (some rectrices broken).

Plate 341. Red-tailed Hawk, adult "Harlan's" (*B. j. harlani*) intermediate morph [Dec.] ▪ Dark upperparts. Whitish uppertail coverts. ▪ White or pale gray type tail with irregular black areas on several rectrices. Irregular wide black terminal band. ▪ *Note:* Same bird as on plate 313.

Plate 342. Red-tailed Hawk, adult "Harlan's" (*B. j. harlani*) dark intermediate morph [Jan.] ▪ Dark head with some white speckling; whitish throat. ▪ Mainly dark upperparts. ▪ Medium/dark gray type tail with irregular black terminal band.

Plate 343. Red-tailed Hawk, adult "Harlan's" (*B. j. harlani*) dark intermediate morph [Nov.] ▪ Pale gray banded type tail with fairly neat wide black subterminal band.

Plate 344. Red-tailed Hawk, adult "Eastern" x "Western" (*B. j. borealis* x *B. j. calurus*) [Nov.] ▪ White throat as on *borealis*. ▪ Tawny underparts with moderately marked type belly and flanks; unmarked leg feathers as on *borealis*. ▪ Black patagial mark. ▪ Banded type rufous tail as on *calurus*. ▪ *Note:* Intergrades may also have dark throats and partially barred leg feathers.

Plate 345. Red-tailed Hawk, adult "Western" x "Harlan's" (*B. j. calurus* X *B. j. harlani*) [Feb.] ▪ Pale throat. ▪ Rufous breast of intermediate morph *calurus* with white *harlani* streaking. ▪ Black patagial mark. Barred remiges, including outer primaries. ▪ Mottled-barred type *harlani* tail is white on underside, brownish on upperside; neat subterminal band.

Plate 346. Red-tailed Hawk, adult "Western" (*B. j. calurus*) light morph (partial albino) [Nov.] ▪ Body normal for this morph. ▪ Partially white or all-white feathers on some remiges. ▪ Tail normal. ▪ *Note:* Partial albinism affects remiges and dorsal areas more than other areas.

Plate 347. Red-tailed Hawk, adult "Eastern" (***B. j. borealis***) **(partial albino) [Nov.]** ▪ Head and body white with a few scattered dark feathers. ▪ Remiges white with a few partially marked normal feathers. ▪ Tail a mixture of rufous and white.

Plate 348. Red-tailed Hawk, juvenile "Eastern" (***B. j. borealis***) **[Nov.]** ▪ Broad white supercilium, white throat, pale iris. Greenish yellow cere. ▪ Large white patch on each scapular may form V. ▪ Extensive white mottling on wing coverts. Wingtips much shorter than tail tip. ▪ Pale brown tail has numerous thin, equal-width dark bands.

Plate 349. Red-tailed Hawk, juvenile "Krider's" (**pale morph of** *B. j. borealis*) **[Feb.]** ▪ White head with brown streaking on nape and hindneck, pale iris, greenish yellow cere. ▪ Belly streaked, flanks barred. Unmarked leg feathers. ▪ Distinct dark barring on secondaries. Wingtips much shorter than tail tip. ▪ *Note:* Palest type.

Plate 350. Red-tailed Hawk, juvenile "Krider's" (**pale morph of** *B. j. borealis*) **[Nov.]** ▪ Head white with brownish sides. ▪ White underparts with typical streaked belly, and barred flanks. ▪ Distinct, thin dark barring on secondaries. Extensive white mottling on wing coverts. ▪ White tail has thin, equal-width bands.

Plate 351. Red-tailed Hawk, juvenile "Western" (*B. j. calurus*) light morph [Sep.] ▪ Narrow white supercilium, dark tawny auricular region, dark throat, pale iris. Greenish yellow cere. ▪ Small white patch on each scapular may form partial V. ▪ Minimal white mottling on wing coverts. Wingtips shorter than tail tip. ▪ Pale brown tail has numerous moderately thin, equal-width dark bands.

Plate 352. Red-tailed Hawk, juvenile "Western" (*B. j. calurus*) light intermediate (light rufous) morph [Nov.] ▪ Partial tawny supercilium, dark tawny auricular region, dark throat, pale iris. Greenish yellow cere. ▪ White breast with narrow brown streaking; less on center region. Nearly solid brown band on belly and flanks. Barred leg feathers and undertail coverts.

Plate 353. Red-tailed Hawk, juvenile "Western" (*B. j. calurus*) intermediate (rufous) morph [Nov.] ▪ Dark tawny supercilium and auricular regions, dark throat, pale iris. Greenish cere. ▪ Tawny breast with wide brown streaking. Nearly solid brown band on belly and flanks. Heavily barred leg feathers and undertail coverts. ▪ Moderately thin dark tail bands.

Plate 354. Red-tailed Hawk, juvenile "Western" (*B. j. calurus*) intermediate (rufous) morph [Dec.] ▪ Dark tawny supercilium and auricular regions, dark throat, pale iris. Greenish cere. ▪ Small white blotches on scapulars. ▪ Wingtips shorter than tail tip. ▪ Numerous thin, equal-width dark bands on pale brown tail (white terminal band worn off).

Plate 355. Red-tailed Hawk, juvenile "Western" (*B. j. calurus*) **dark intermediate (dark rufous) morph** [Dec.] ▪ Dark tawny supercilium and auricular regions, dark throat, pale iris. Greenish cere. ▪ Dark brown body with tawny-rufous edges on breast feathers. ▪ Wingtips shorter than tail tip. ▪ Moderately thin tail bands, but subterminal band sometimes a bit wider (on all morphs).

Plate 356. Red-tailed Hawk, juvenile "Western" (*B. j. calurus*) **dark morph** [Nov.] ▪ Dark brown head and throat. Pale iris. Greenish yellow cere. ▪ Uniformly dark brown body. ▪ Moderately wide equal-width tail bands; narrow white terminal band.

Plate 357. Red-tailed Hawk, juvenile "Western" (*B. j. calurus*) **dark morph** [Nov.] ▪ Dark brown head and throat. Pale iris. Greenish yellow cere. ▪ Uniformly dark brown body. ▪ Moderately wide equal-width tail bands; white terminal band is absent.

Plate 358. Red-tailed Hawk, juvenile "Harlan's" (*B. j. harlani*) **light morph** [Dec.] ▪ White head, including throat, with brownish crown and malar. Pale iris. Greenish yellow cere. ▪ Brownish black upperparts. ▪ Pale brown tail has wide or narrow, often irregular, dark bands. May have dark "spike" along shafts.

Plate 359. Red-tailed Hawk, juvenile "Harlan's" (*B. j. harlani*) intermediate morph (streak-breasted type) [Jan.] ▪ Black head with white throat, supercilium, and forehead. Pale iris. ▪ White breast streaked with black. Rest of underparts black and speckled with white. ▪ Dark "spike" along feather shaft below dark subterminal band may extend onto tail tip.

Plate 360. Red-tailed Hawk, juvenile "Harlan's" (*B. j. harlani*) intermediate morph (streaked type) [Dec.] ▪ Black head with white speckling and throat streaking. Pale iris, greenish yellow cere. ▪ Underparts, including leg feathers, streaked with black and white. ▪ Dark "spike" visible on outermost rectrix and extends onto tail tip. Equal-width dark tail bands, or subterminal band wider.

Plate 361. Red-tailed Hawk, juvenile "Harlan's" (*B. j. harlani*) intermediate morph (any type) [Jan.] ▪ Black head (dark throat possible intergrade with *calurus*). Pale iris. Greenish cere. ▪ Scapular markings are classic white ovals with dark T shaped. ▪ Dark shaft streaks on feather tips on wing coverts and secondaries. ▪ Wavy or V-shaped equal-width tail bands.

Plate 362. Red-tailed Hawk, juvenile "Harlan's" (*B. j. harlani*) dark intermediate morph (streak-breasted type) [Dec.] ▪ Black head with short supercilium. Pale iris, greenish yellow cere. ▪ Black body with small amount of white streaking on breast. ▪ Equal-width dark tail bands.

Plate 363. Red-tailed Hawk, juvenile "Harlan's" (*B. j. harlani*) dark intermediate morph (spot-bellied type) [Dec.] ▪ Black head. Pale iris, greenish yellow cere. ▪ Black breast; white spotting on black belly, flanks, and leg feathers.

Plate 364. Red-tailed Hawk, juvenile "Harlan's" (*B. j. harlani*) dark morph [Jan.] ▪ Black head. Pale iris, greenish yellow cere. ▪ Black body. ▪ Wingtips much shorter than tail tip. ▪ Dark "spikes" below dark subterminal band extend onto tail tip. ▪ *Note:* Not readily separable from dark morph *calurus* except by tail tip.

Plate 365. Red-tailed Hawk, juvenile "Eastern" (*B. j. borealis*) [Sep.] ▪ Large pale panel on upperwing with pale primaries and primary coverts contrasting with darker secondaries and secondary coverts. *Note:* All juveniles have pale panel on upperwing.

Plate 366. Red-tailed Hawk, juvenile "Eastern" (*B. j. borealis*) [Oct.] ▪ Many juveniles have rufous tail with numerous narrow, equal-width dark bands; subterminal band sometimes wider. White uppertail coverts barred.

Plate 367. Red-tailed Hawk, juvenile "Eastern" (*B. j. borealis*) [Oct.] ▪ White throat. ▪ Breast white but is tawny when recently fledged. Moderately marked type belly and flanks. Leg feathers may be spotted, barred, or unmarked. ▪ Dark patagial mark. Lightly barred axillaries. White, rectangular panel. ▪ Thin tail bands; subterminal band wider. ▪ *Note: B. j. umbrinus* similar.

Plate 368. Red-tailed Hawk, juvenile "Krider's" (**pale morph of** *B. j. borealis*) [Jan.] ▪ White head. ▪ White underparts have small amount of spotting or streaking on belly and arrowhead markings or barring on flanks. Unmarked leg feathers. ▪ Faint dark patagial mark. Outer primaries finely barred. ▪ Thin, equal-width dark bands on distal half of white tail.

Plate 369. Red-tailed Hawk, juvenile "Krider's" (**pale morph of** *B. j. borealis*) [Jan.] ▪ White head. ▪ White underparts have few markings. Unmarked leg feathers. ▪ White underwing has faint dark patagial mark. Outer primaries finely barred. White panel on dorsal surface of inner primaries. ▪ Thin, equal-width dark bands on distal half of white tail. ▪ *Note:* Same bird as on plate 368.

Plate 370. Red-tailed Hawk, juvenile "Krider's" X "Eastern" intergrade (Pale morph *B. j. borealis* X typical *B. j. borealis*) [Oct.] ▪ White head with a dark crown patch and thin malar mark. ▪ Large white patch on each scapular. ▪ Large whitish panel on primaries and primary coverts. ▪ Small white area on outer base of pale brown tail. Thin, equal-width dark tail bands.

Plate 371. Red-tailed Hawk, juvenile "Western" (*B. j. calurus*) light morph [Nov.] ▪ Streaked or dark throat. ▪ White underparts are heavily marked type on belly and flanks. Heavily barred leg feathers. Lightly barred undertail coverts. ▪ Large, dark patagial mark; heavily marked wing coverts, including barred axillaries.

Plate 372. Red-tailed Hawk, juvenile "Western" (*B. j. calurus*) light intermediate (light rufous) morph [Nov.] ▪ Heavily marked type on belly and flanks. Breast partially streaked. Heavily barred leg feathers. Moderately barred undertail coverts. ▪ Dark patagial mark partially obscured by heavily marked wing coverts; heavily barred axillaries.

Plate 373. Red-tailed Hawk, juvenile "Western" (*B. j. calurus*) intermediate (rufous) morph [Nov.] ▪ Heavily marked type on belly and flanks. Breast streaked. Heavily barred leg feathers and undertail coverts. ▪ Dark patagial mark nearly obscured by heavily marked wing coverts; heavily barred axillaries. Thin tail bands with wider subterminal band.

Plate 374. Red-tailed Hawk, juvenile "Harlan's" (*B. j. harlani*) intermediate morph [Dec.] ▪ Large whitish panel on primaries and primary coverts cuts wing in half. ▪ Moderately wide dark tail bands; subterminal band wider. ▪ *Note:* Dorsal wing panel of similar looking darker morphs of *calurus* is pale brown.

Plate 375. Red-tailed Hawk, juvenile "Harlan's" (*B. j. harlani*) **intermediate morph (streak-breasted type) [Dec.]** ▪ White throat. ▪ Black and white streaked breast; rest of underparts black with small amount of white speckling, including on undertail coverts. ▪ Barred outer primaries. White speckling on black wing coverts. ▪ Moderately wide dark tail bands; subterminal band wider.

Plate 376. Red-tailed Hawk, juvenile "Harlan's" (*B. j. harlani*) **dark intermediate morph (spot-bellied type) [Dec.]** ▪ White throat with center streak. ▪ Black underparts spotted with white on belly, flanks, and leg feathers. ▪ Barred outer primaries. Dark "spikes" on tips of secondaries. ▪ Equal-width dark tail bands; dark "spikes" on tips of rectrices.

Plate 377. Red-tailed Hawk, juvenile "Harlan's" (*B. j. harlani*) **dark intermediate morph (streak-breasted type) [Nov.]** ▪ White throat. ▪ Black underparts lightly streaked with white on breast. ▪ Barred outer primaries. Dark "spikes" on tips of secondaries. ▪ Equal-width dark tail bands; dark "spikes" on tips of rectrices.

Plate 378. Red-tailed Hawk, juvenile "Harlan's" (*B. j. harlani*) **dark morph [Nov.]** ▪ Head and body uniformly dark brown or black. ▪ Barred outer primaries. ▪ Equal-width dark tail bands. ▪ *Note:* Dark morph *calurus* similar but has solid dark outer primaries. Much intergrading between *harlani* and *calurus*.

FERRUGINOUS HAWK
(Buteo regalis)

AGES: Adult and juvenile. Unlike other large buteos, Ferruginous Hawk does not have a subadult plumage with retained juvenile feathering. Juvenile plumage is held for most of the first year. Juveniles have somewhat longer tails than adults.

MOLT: Acciptridae wing and tail molt pattern (*see* chapter 4). The first prebasic molt begins on the innermost primary (p1) as early as mid-Apr. on some birds but may not occur until late Apr. or early May in very northern populations. By mid-May, many have replaced p1 and 2 and have dropped old p3 and 4. Body molt on the back, scapulars, underparts, and leg feathers begins in Jun. but is not really apparent until Jul. Molt is rapid in Jul. and Aug. and is completed, with total replacement of all juvenile feathering, in Oct. or Nov.

Subsequent prebasic molts begin on breeding birds in May or Jun. for females and in Jun. or Jul. for males. Females may replace at least half their primaries by the time nesting duties are completed, but males rarely begin molting until nesting is over. Adults are in the final stage of molt and replacing the outer one or two primaries (p9 and 10) in late Oct. Molt is generally completed in Nov. Annual molt is fairly complete but may retain a few of the previous year's feathers on the body and wing coverts. Remiges appear to completely molt each year, which is unusual for such a large raptor.

SUBSPECIES: Monotypic.

COLOR MORPHS: Polytypic. Adults have four color morphs: light, intermediate (rufous), dark intermediate (dark rufous), and dark. Light morphs have major plumage variations. Intermediate and dark intermediate morphs have minor plumage variations. Dark morphs have virtually none. There is no clinal variation between light and intermediate morphs. There is a clinal variation between intermediate and dark intermediate morphs and between dark intermediate and dark morphs.

Juveniles have three color morphs: light, intermediate (rufous), and dark. The dark morph is only subtly different than the intermediate, and they are not separable at moderate and long distances. *Note:* Previous literature considered the intermediate (rufous) morph as a dark morph. The true dark morph plumage was not recognized. However, the plumage differences between intermediate and true dark morphs are as obvious for Ferruginous Hawk as for Swainson's and Red-tailed hawks.

SIZE: A large raptor. Length: 20–26 in. (51–66 cm); wingspan: 53–60 in. (135–168 cm). Juveniles may appear longer because of their longer tail. Some males can appear deceptively small.

SPECIES TRAITS: HEAD.—**Black bill with a small pale blue area on the distal lower region of the upper mandible and on the base of the lower mandible. Large yellow cere and gape. The long gape extends to the halfway point under the eyes.** BODY.—Feathered tarsi. Thick toes. WINGS.—**When perched, the pale gray outer webs on the primaries form a distinct pale gray border on the outer edge on the folded wings. In flight, the underside of the outer five primaries (the "fingers") has small black tips. When perched, the wingtips are somewhat shorter than the tail tip. In flight, wings are moderately wide with parallel front and rear edges that taper to fairly pointed wingtips.**

ADULT TRAITS: HEAD.—Iris color varies from pale orangish brown to dark brown and may darken with increasing age. WINGS (ventral).—**The outer five primaries have moderately small, sharply defined black tips. Trailing edge of the inner primaries and secondaries has a moderately wide gray band, and often a narrow black band superimposed on the gray band (most adult buteos have a wide black band).** The primaries do not have narrow barring on the inner portion of the feathers, and the secondaries may have only minimal narrow dark barring. WINGS (dorsal).—**Medium gray secondaries are crossed with narrow black bars. Primaries have a pale gray outer web and a white inner web and in flight create a whitish panel on the dorsal surface and a pale window on the ventral surface.** TAIL (ventral).—**Uniformly white.** A few birds have a partial, irregular dark subterminal band.

ADULT LIGHT MORPH TRAITS: HEAD.—**Short, broad dark eyeline may connect to rear of the**

gape. The throat is always white. There are three main variations of head color: (1) *Pale gray type.*—Pale gray with narrow dark streaking. *Note:* Mainly on males (J. Watson pers. comm.; BKW pers. obs.). (2) *Pale brown type.*—Pale brown with narrow or moderate-width dark streaking. (3) *Medium brown type.*—Moderate brown with moderate-width or wide dark streaking. Dark eyeline still apparent. None of the variations exhibit a dark malar mark. BODY (ventral).—White, but may have a tawny wash on the breast during any time of the year and appear similar to most recently fledged juveniles. Breast, belly, and flanks can be: (1) *Lightly marked type.*—Unmarked or have a tawny wash on the breast. (2) *Moderately marked type.*—Breast may be white or tawny and either unmarked or has some narrow rufous or brown streaking. Belly is moderately spotted or barred with rufous or brown. Flanks are white and barred with rufous or brown, or rear half of flanks are rufous with dark brown barring. (3) *Heavily marked type.*—White or tawny breast is moderately or heavily streaked with rufous or brown; rarely is unmarked. Belly is heavily barred with rufous or brown. Flanks are rufous and barred with dark brown barring. Leg feathers, including tarsi, are: (1) *All-white type.*—White and unmarked. *Note:* Rare type. (2) *White type.*—White with sparse brown spotting or barring. *Note:* Fairly common type. (3) *Rufous type.*—Rufous with dark brown barring. *Note:* Common type. Undertail coverts are white and unmarked on all birds. BODY (dorsal).—Back is dark brown. **Scapulars are mainly rufous but may fade to tawny-rufous by spring.** There is a moderately wide or wide dark brown streak on the central part of each scapular. WINGS (ventral).—The white underwing coverts are: (1) *Unmarked type.*—White and lacking dark markings or have only a small amount of rufous streaking on the lesser coverts on the patagial area. (2) *Moderately marked type.*—**Lesser coverts on the patagial region have a moderate amount of rufous streaking and spotting. The median coverts also have a moderate-sized rufous tip and possibly some barring on each feather. The wrist area and primary lesser coverts are unmarked. Axillaries are mainly white with a minimal amount of rufous markings.**

(3) *Heavily marked type.*—**The lesser coverts on the patagial region are solid rufous. The median coverts are rufous on the distal half of each feather. The underwing appears two-toned with nearly solidly rufous coverts and pale remiges. The wrist area is unmarked and the primary lesser coverts are moderately marked. Axillaries are white with a moderate amount of rufous on the tip of each feather.** The tips of the primary greater coverts on all types are white on the basal region and dark gray on the tips. WINGS (dorsal).—**Lesser and median coverts are rufous with narrow dark streaking and appear as a large rufous shoulder region.** TAIL (dorsal).—Four main color variations on the outer webs of the rectrices: (1) *White type.*—**White and unmarked.** (2) *Gray type.*—**Gray with dark brown or black mottling on the distal half or two-thirds.** (3) *Rufous type.*—**Rufous with dark brown or black mottling on the distal half or two-thirds.** (4) *Mixed type.*—**Variable mix of gray or rufous and dark brown or black mottling.** Sometimes appears brownish. All types have white uppertail coverts with a small amount of rufous or brown spotting or barring or may be rufous with dark brown markings.

ADULT LIGHT MORPH (LIGHTLY MARKED TYPE): HEAD.—Pale gray or pale brown types. BODY (ventral).—Lightly marked type. Leg feathers are white type or rarely all-white type. BODY (dorsal).—Dark markings on the scapulars are moderately narrow or moderate in width. Scapulars often appear very rufous. WINGS (ventral).—Unmarked type. TAIL (dorsal).—Mainly white or gray type patterns. Rufous pigmentation is typically reduced. Uppertail coverts are mainly white and have only minimal dark markings. *Note:* Fairly common plumage type; it has a reduced amount of rufous pigmentation.

ADULT LIGHT MORPH (MODERATELY MARKED TYPE): HEAD.—Pale gray or pale brown types. BODY (ventral).—Lightly or moderately marked types. BODY (dorsal).—Dark markings on the scapulars are moderate in width and appear quite rufous. WINGS (ventral).—Moderately marked type. TAIL (dorsal).—Any of the four types, but rarely white type. Uppertail coverts may either be white or rufous. *Note:* Common plumage type; it has a moderate amount of rufous pigmentation.

ADULT LIGHT MORPH (HEAVILY MARKED TYPE): HEAD.—Medium brown type. BODY (ventral).—Heavily marked type. BODY (dorsal).—Scapulars are rufous but the dark brown central feather streak is often wide. WINGS (ventral).—Heavily marked type. TAIL (dorsal).—Mainly rufous or mixed types. Uppertail coverts are typically quite rufous. *Note:* Uncommon plumage type; it is saturated with rufous pigmentation.

ADULT INTERMEDIATE (RUFOUS) MORPH TRAITS: HEAD.—Rufous-brown, dark brown, or dark gray. Gray-headed birds may be males (J. Watson pers. comm.; BKW pers. obs.). All of the lore region is white and the forehead is dark. **The large yellow gape is prominent.** BODY (ventral).—Variably marked on the breast, but the belly and flanks are always rufous: (1) Breast is rufous and makes all of the underparts rufous. (2) Breast may be dark brown and contrast with the rufous belly and flanks. The breast may be like a bib or create a hooded appearance along with the dark head. Both types often have dark brown or black streaking or partial barring on the belly and flanks. Both types may also have a variable amount of white streaking or mottling on the breast. BODY (dorsal).—Back is dark brown. Scapulars are dark brown and each feather is narrowly edged with rufous. WINGS (ventral).—Uniformly rufous underwing coverts. The dark band on the trailing edge of the remiges may be more distinct than on many light morphs. The white basal region and dark tips of the primary greater coverts form a white "comma" (comparison only to dark Rough-legged Hawks). WINGS (dorsal).—The dark brown lesser upperwing coverts are edged with rufous and form a distinct rufous shoulder patch. Secondaries and primaries are marked as in Adult Traits. White and unmarked. TAIL (dorsal).—**Uniformly medium gray, but sometimes has a small amount of rufous or brown intermixed. At close range, may exhibit a partial mottled pattern.** Uppertail coverts are rufous and very obvious as they contrast against the dark dorsal body and gray tail.

ADULT DARK INTERMEDIATE (DARK RUFOUS) MORPH TRAITS: This morph is a link between intermediate and dark morphs and shares traits of both. HEAD.—Same three colors as on intermediate morphs. **Yellow gape is prominent.** BODY (ventral).—Two variations: (1) *Rufous breasted type.*—Rufous breast contrasts sharply with dark head and blackish brown belly, flanks, and leg feathers. (2) *All-dark type.*—All of the underparts are uniformly dark brown with a small amount of rufous speckling. Breast may have a small amount of white streaking or mottling. BODY (dorsal).—Dark brown with narrow rufous edging on all scapular. WINGS (ventral).—All have blackish brown underwing coverts with a small amount of rufous speckling. White "comma" on the base of the primary greater coverts (comparison only to dark morph Rough-legged Hawks). WINGS (dorsal).—Narrow rufous edging on the lesser upperwing coverts; forms a moderately distinct rufous shoulder patch. TAIL (dorsal).—**Uniformly medium gray but may have a small amount of rufous or brown wash and sometimes darker mottling.** Uppertail coverts are dark brown with possibly a small amount of rufous edging or mottling. *Note:* This morph has not been previously described or depicted.

ADULT DARK MORPH TRAITS: HEAD.—Blackish brown with dark forehead and white lores. **Yellow gape is prominent.** BODY (ventral).—Uniformly blackish brown and does not exhibit white mottling on the breast. BODY (dorsal).—Uniformly blackish brown and does not have rufous edging. WINGS (Ventral).—Underwing coverts are uniformly blackish brown. The white "comma" is fairly obvious on the basal area of the primary greater coverts (comparison only to dark Rough-legged Hawks). WINGS (dorsal).—Upperwing coverts are uniformly blackish brown and do not show rufous on the shoulder region. TAIL (dorsal).—**Uniformly medium gray. May exhibit some brownish but not rufous.**

JUVENILE TRAITS: HEAD.—Iris color varies: pale gray, pale brown, or pale yellow. WINGS (ventral).—The five outer primaries are pale gray with a small dark gray tip. The underside of the remiges is white and has a grayish border on the trailing edge with little if any narrow dark barring. WINGS (dorsal).—Outer web of each primary feather is pale gray and the inner web is white; as in adults, forms a distinct whitish panel on the dorsal surface and a pale window on the ventral surface. The greater primary coverts are darker than the outer webs of the primaries but paler than the secondaries. The dorsal surface of the secondaries is medium brown with three or four rows of narrow dark bars.

JUVENILE LIGHT MORPH TRAITS: HEAD.— Dark brown crown, forehead, and nape. The supercilium is tawny or white. The cheeks and auriculars are tawny or white. **Short, thick dark eyeline often connects to rear of the gape. There is no dark malar mark.** BODY (ventral).—White undersides. Sides of the neck and breast may be sparsely streaked. The belly can be (1) unmarked, (2) moderately spotted and form a slight belly band, or (3) heavily spotted and form a distinct belly band. The flanks of all birds are moderately or heavily marked with dark spots or arrowhead shapes. **In flight, the large leg muscles condense the flank feathers and force the markings into an elongated dark patch. Tibia feathers on upper leg are either lightly or moderately spotted. Tarsi feathers are either white and spotted with brown or all brown.** The undertail coverts are white and unmarked. BODY (dorsal).—Dark brown with narrow tawny edges on the scapular. Small white spots occasionally show on the basal area of some scapular. WINGS (ventral).—White underwing coverts and axillaries are variably marked with dark brown: (1) unmarked, (2) lightly spotted, or (3) moderately spotted. WINGS (dorsal).— Upperwing coverts are dark brown and have tawny or tawny-rufous edges on most feathers. TAIL (ventral).—Basal third to fourth is white and unmarked; distal region is pale gray with a moderately wide dusky subterminal band and two to four narrow, often partial, dark inner bands. TAIL (dorsal).—Basal third to fourth is white, distal region is gray in fresh plumage and medium brown in fairly worn plumage. The distal gray or brown region has a moderately wide dark subterminal band and two to four, often partial, dark inner bands. The white uppertail coverts have a dark spot on each feather.

JUVENILE LIGHT MORPH TRAITS (WORN PLUMAGE): By spring and early summer, 1-year-olds may have rather worn and faded plumage. HEAD.—**The crown, forehead, and nape may wear and fade to white and the entire head may be white except for the wide dark brown eyeline.** BODY (dorsal).—All pale

feather edgings wear off and the upperparts become uniformly brown. TAIL.—Tip can become quite frayed and broken. Juveniles, in particular, brace themselves with tail while standing on the ground while feeding. This is noticeable by mid-winter and becomes more prevalent by spring.

JUVENILE LIGHT MORPH TRAITS (RECENTLY FLEDGED): HEAD.—Supercilium and auricular regions are dark tawny. The head can appear quite brown and the dark eyeline is not always prevalent until more fading occurs. BODY (ventral).—The front of the neck and breast is either pale tawny or tawny and forms a bib. This wears off to a great extent by Sep., but some individuals still exhibit traces of it in Oct. BODY (dorsal).—Upperparts are dark brown and edged with tawny-rufous. WINGS and TAIL.—As in Juvenile Traits.

JUVENILE INTERMEDIATE (RUFOUS) MORPH TRAITS: HEAD.—Uniformly tawny-brown, including the forehead. Lores are white. BODY (ventral).—Neck and breast are tawny-brown and along with tawny-brown head give a hooded appearance. The head and breast contrast sharply against the dark brown belly, flanks, and leg feathers. At close range, the belly, flanks, and leg feathers may show narrow tawny edging on many feathers. BODY (dorsal).—Mainly uniformly dark brown. WINGS (ventral).—Dark brown underwing coverts are often mottled with tawny or white. A white "comma" is visible on most birds (comparison only to dark morph Rough-legged Hawks). TAIL.—Two patterns that are most visible on the dorsal surface: (1) *Unbanded type.*— Medium gray or brownish gray on the entire dorsal surface. There is a moderately wide darker, dusky subterminal band. The ventral surface is white with a dusky subterminal band. (2) *Partially banded/banded types.*— Medium gray or grayish brown dorsal surface. There is a moderately wide darker, dusky subterminal band and three or four partial or complete narrow or fairly narrow dark inner bands. On the banded type, the dark inner tail banding is on all rectrices but becomes less distinct on the outer sets. On the partially banded type, only the deck rectrices (r1) have somewhat distinct dark banding. The ventral surface is white with a dusky moderately wide subterminal band and partial or fairly complete narrow dusky inner bands. By late winter and spring, the dorsal grayish sheen wears off and becomes quite brownish. The uppertail coverts are dark brown.

JUVENILE DARK MORPH TRAITS: HEAD.—Uniformly dark brown, including the forehead. Lores are white. BODY (ventral).—Uniformly dark brown. The breast feathers may have a hint of tawny edging but not enough to create the pale bib as on intermediate morphs. BODY (dorsal).—Uniformly dark brown. WINGS (ventral).—Uniformly dark brown underwing coverts. White "comma" shows on most birds (comparison only to dark morph Rough-legged Hawks). WINGS (dorsal).—Upperwing coverts are uniformly dark brown. TAIL. As on intermediate morphs. Uppertail coverts are dark brown. *Note:* Not separable from intermediate morphs unless seen at close range and in good light.

ABNORMAL PLUMAGES: None documented.

HABITAT (EAST): Fall, winter, and spring.—Semi-open and open agricultural fields, idle fields, and pastures. Habitat is often the same that Red-tailed Hawks inhabit.

Winter (West).—Inhabits similar, remote, open areas as during the summer but generally at more southern latitudes and lower elevations. Winter climate is generally arid but is moderately humid for populations wintering in the eastern winter range and humid in the southeastern winter range of coastal Texas. Unlike during the breeding season, Ferruginous Hawks are very tolerant of humans and readily acclimate to rural and suburban areas during the winter. Although avoided during the breeding season, extensive agricultural areas become important winter habitat in areas where Black-tailed Prairie Dogs are absent. Wheat and irrigated alfalfa and grass hay fields often support a large prey base.

Migration (East and West).—Found in habitats and regions described for summer and winter.

HABITS (EAST): Wary during the breeding season and tame during other seasons. Ferruginous Hawks readily perch on the ground and on most elevated natural and artificial structures. They do not perch on utility wires.

FEEDING (EAST): Perch and aerial hunter. Perch hunts are a direct method of foraging.

They are launched from elevated objects or from the ground at prairie dog and gopher colonies. Aerial hunts are an indirect method of foraging (*see* Flight). Ferruginous Hawks are opportunistic and feed on prey of all sizes and types. Primary prey species in the East are probably Eastern Cottontail Rabbits and Eastern Fox and Eastern Gray Squirrels that venture into the open. Carrion is readily eaten, and Ferruginous Hawks will pirate prey from Red-tailed Hawks (and vice versa). Except in the breeding season, Ferruginous Hawks typically eat prey at the site of capture.

FLIGHT: Wings are held in a high dihedral when soaring and in a high or modified dihedral when gliding. Powered flight consists of moderately slow wingbeats interspersed with irregular gliding sequences. The upstroke has a quick snapping movement. Hunting flights: (1) *High-altitude flight.*—Soaring or gliding at high altitudes and then making a long dive for the capture. (2) *Low-altitude flight.*—Moderate-speed, low-level powered and gliding flight and then making a short dive for the capture. (3) *Surprise-and-flush flight.*—High-speed, low-level powered and gliding flight, often undulating by nearly skimming the ground and then swooping upwards, then making a fast low-angle dive for capture.

VOICE: Unless agitated, rarely heard away from the breeding grounds. Vocalizes when prey is being pirated by eagles and Red-tailed Hawks. Has a rather soft, clear, high-pitched, and drawn-out *kreeaah* or *keeeoh.* The call is sometimes louder and more forceful.

STATUS AND DISTRIBUTION (EAST): *Accidental* in all states and provinces. *Alabama:* (1) Colbert Co. in 1988 and (2) Baldwin Co. from Dec. 1985 to Jan. 1986. *Florida:* (1) Zellwood, Orange Co., from late Dec. 1983 to early Mar. 1984; (2) St. Marks NWR, Wakulla Co., in mid-Nov. 1984; and (3) Calhoun Co. from early to mid-Mar. 1986 (since these three records are prior to 1990, they are not plotted on the range map). *Illinois:* Many records attributed to misidentification with "Krider's" type of "Eastern" Red-tailed Hawk and are not verified. Eight records from 1939 to 1984. Records since 1990: (1) Pope Co. in late Oct. 1996 (juvenile light morph, seen by BKW); (2) Illinois Beach S.P., Lake Co., in Nov. 1999; (3)

Lake Chautauqua, Mason Co., in early Nov. 2000; (4) Illinois Beach S.P. in early Nov. 2000; (5) Lake Villa, Lake Co., in Nov. 2000. *Indiana:* (1) LaGrange Co. in mid-Jan. 1992 and (2) Warrick Co. in late Feb. 1998 (adult light morph). There are three older records: (1) Porter Co. in late Sep. 1934 (captured, banded, and released), (2) Porter Co. from late Nov. 1952 to early Jan. 1953, and (30) Madison Co. in May 1976. *Michigan:* (1) Whitefish Point Bird Observatory, Chippewa Co., in late Apr. 1985 (juvenile); (2) Allegan Co. from late Dec. 1989 to late Jan. 1990; (3) Whitefish Point Bird Observatory, Chippewa Co., in mid-May 1990; (4) Allegan Co. from early Nov. 1990 to mid-Feb. 1991; (5) Lake Erie Metro Park, Wayne Co., in early Nov. 1991; and (6) Huron Co. in early May 1992. *Ontario:* (1) St. Clair NWR, Kent Co., in mid-Mar. 1990; (2) Beamer Memorial Conservation Area (hawkwatch), Niagara Co., in mid-Apr. 1992; (3) Tavistock, Oxford Co., in mid-May 1992 (juvenile); and (4) Gore Bay, Manitoulin Co., in late May 1995 (juvenile). *Wisconsin:* 14 records prior to 1990 with the first in 1893 in Jefferson Co. Since 1990: Pepin Co. in early May 1991.

STATUS AND DISTRIBUTION (WEST): Overall, an *uncommon* raptor. Population trends have concerned wildlife officials in several states and provinces. In 1980, the Committee on the Status of Endangered Wildlife in Canada listed the species as Threatened in Canada. In 1992, the USFWS was petitioned to list it as Threatened species under the Endangered Species Act but determined there was not sufficient evidence to warrant the request. In 1995, Canada downlisted the species to Vulnerable because of an increasing and stabilizing population. A few states still consider the Ferruginous Hawk as Threatened or of uncertain status. Oregon designates it as Endangered and the BLM as Sensitive. Arizona and Colorado categorize it as a Species of Special Concern.

Ferruginous Hawks, along with several other threatened or endangered species of birds and mammals, are unique adaptations to the prairie ecosystem, especially the Great Plains. Since the late 1800s, the Plains, in particular, have succumbed to agriculture, urbanization, and oil, gas, and mineral exploration and recovery. These activities have greatly re-

duced breeding areas and winter prey for the Ferruginous Hawk. In Canada, the prevention of grassland fires has allowed aspen parkland to encroach southward onto the prairies and reduced Ferruginous Hawk breeding habitat. The Ferruginous Hawk's future remains a concern at the start of the 21st century.

Summer.—Regionally and locally, populations vary from rare to common. In 1992, the USFWS estimated 5,220–6,000 pairs in the U.S. and Canada.

Winter.—Locally common where prey density is high but otherwise uncommon to rare. Areas with Black-tailed Prairie Dogs support the highest numbers of hawks. The hawks acclimate to humans and human-altered habitats. Adults predominate in the northern winter range, and juveniles are more common in eastern and southern winter range.

Most birds that breed east of the Rocky Mts. remain east of the mountains in winter. Juveniles banded in Saskatchewan winter as far south as n. Mexico. Banded individuals from Alberta winter mainly in Texas, but some winter in Arizona, Colorado, Kansas, and New Mexico. Some Alberta birds winter as far south as s. Durango and e. Nuevo León, Mexico. Banded juveniles from ne. Colorado were found in Texas, n. Mexico, and one in California. High winter densities are in the following areas: Front Range area of e. Colorado, Prowers Co., in se. Colorado (which has large Black-tailed Prairie Dog towns), w. Kansas, Texas panhandle, Oklahoma panhandle, Cochise Co. in se. Arizona, n. Los Angeles Co. in California, and near Janos in n. Chihuahua, Mexico (which supports the largest Black-tailed Prairie Dog complex in North America).

Movements.—Very few Ferruginous Hawks are seen at western hawkwatch sites. Most migration data were based on banding records. Rather astounding data are surfacing with recent telemetry studies. Migration data are also based on 15 years of observations on the Great Plains.

Post-breeding dispersal: Based on telemetry data, adults in Washington State disperse northeasterly and cross the Continental Divide after nesting. Juveniles from all regions may disperse in any direction after fledging. Most dispersing birds head to the northern Great Plains of Montana and Canada where there is a late-summer abundance of juvenile Richardson's Ground Squirrels (adult ground squirrels estivate in Jul.).

After completing nesting, four telemetry-tracked adults from s.-cen. Washington headed northeast in early to mid-Jul. to the Great Plains of n.-cen. Montana, se. Alberta, and sw. Saskatchewan. They stayed on the n. Plains until early Sep. to early Oct. when they began their southward migration.

Fall migration: The first migrants arrive from late Aug. to early Sep. along Colorado's Front Range. Migrants are seen in Sep. and Oct. on the e. Plains of Colorado. Peak movement period on the Plains appears to be from early to mid-Oct. All birds have left Alberta y late Oct. A continual influx of birds is seen in Nov. and Dec. in se. Colorado. Nov. and Dec. movements may be due to food supply.

The four telemetry-tracked Washington adults took interesting routes from dispersal areas to winter areas. Two birds headed southwest and arrived in late Oct. in the Central Valley of California. One bird also headed southwest to n. California, then went back east and in late Oct. arrived in w.-cen. Nevada. The fourth bird headed southeast and arrived in late Oct. in the e. Oklahoma panhandle. Alberta, Colorado, and Saskatchewan banded birds stayed east of the Rocky Mts. and headed south and east of breeding and natal areas.

Spring migration: Adults migrate from mid-Feb. through Mar. Some juveniles migrate in Mar., but many continue into Apr. and May. "Northward" movements are no doubt highly variable, as seen with telemetry-tracked and banded individuals making diagonal movements in the fall.

Color morph status.—Intermediate, dark intermediate, and dark morphs have not been categorized separately in previous literature or personal correspondence. Most previous data concerning "dark" morphs invariably included intermediate and dark intermediate morphs as well as pure dark morphs. The highest percentage of breeding "dark" morphs are in Alberta and Saskatchewan. "Dark" morphs are substantially less common in the breeding season in the U.S. Known percentages of dark birds from the breeding season: Alberta 9, Saskatchewan 7 (based on data by C. S. Houston: 296 adults

from 1999, 2000, and 2001), Idaho 4, and Colorado 3. Other states have fewer nesting darker birds.

Based on data from 15 winter seasons (by the author), intermediate and dark intermediate morphs comprise only 5% of the birds on the Great Plains. True dark morphs comprise only 1% of the wintering population.

During the breeding season, light-light pairs are most common; light-dark pairs are common; and dark-dark pairs are very rare, even in Canada.

NESTING (WEST): Begins in late Feb. to late Mar. and ends from mid-Jun. to late Aug., depending on latitude and elevation. Adults arrive on breeding grounds in late Feb. and early Mar. in e. Colorado and by late Mar. in s. Saskatchewan. Based on known-aged birds from Alberta, Ferruginous Hawks do not breed until 3 years old.

Courtship (flight).—*High-soaring* (mutual) and *sky-dancing* by males. Both sexes perform *leg-dangling* and *cartwheeling* (with males approaching females, then locking talons and tumbling).

Courtship (perched).—*High-perching* by males. (*See* chapter 5 for a description of displays.)

Ferruginous Hawks build their own nests or may refurbish nests of other large raptors, particularly nests of Swainson's and Red-tailed hawks. New nests may also be constructed on top of old Black-billed Magpie nests. Both sexes build nests, but refurbished structures often have only a minimal amount of work done to them. Nests vary in size. New nests may be small and old nests can be large. Old nests, which can be used for decades, can rival the size of eagle nests.

Nests are placed in trees and on rocks, spires, abandoned buildings, poles, and sometimes on the ground. Nests are built of sticks. In treeless regions, sagebrush sticks are most commonly used. In areas with trees, tree sticks are used as well. Bones are often added to the structure. Horse and cow dung (formerly Bison dung), grasses, and bark comprise the inner lining of nests. Greenery of small twigs and branches may also be added to the lining. Two to 4 eggs comprise the typical clutch, but 5 eggs are occasionally laid. Highly unusual clutches of 8 eggs have occurred. Eggs are incubated by both sexes for 32 or 33 days. Youngsters fledge in 38–50 days, with females taking longest. Most branch long before they can fly. Tree-nesting branchers perch on outer branches away from the nest or, more typically, fall, jump, or glide to the ground and stay there, often considerable distances from their nest. Ground-nesting branchers simply walk away from the nest and may also remain a considerable distance from it. Fratricide among young nestlings may occur when food is scarce.

CONSERVATION: No programs in the East.

Mortality.—Ferruginous Hawks suffer from illegal shooting, particularly during upland gamebird seasons in the fall. Vehicles may hit hawks that feed on road-killed prey. Electrocution from utility poles and wires is prevalent. Since Ferruginous Hawks readily feed on carrion, secondary poisoning meant for varmints and organophosphate poisons used to control insect infestations in cattle indirectly kill scavengers feeding on animals that have died. Golden Eagles and Great Horned Owls kill adults and youngsters.

SIMILAR SPECIES: COMPARED TO ADULT LIGHT MORPHS (mainly lightly marked type).—(1) **Red-tailed Hawk (*B. j. borealis*), "Krider's" adults.**—PERCHED.—Head lacks a dark eyeline. Upperparts are very similar, but "Krider's" has large white patches on the mid-scapulars. Tarsi are bare; leg feathers are unmarked. Dark subterminal tail band is thin and neat. Otherwise tail is very similar. FLIGHT.—Rufous patagial mark on the underwing may be similar to the rufous patagial on Ferruginous Hawks: use caution. Underside of the outer primaries is fully barred. Tail pattern as in Perched. COMPARED TO JUVENILE LIGHT MORPHS.—(2) **Red-tailed Hawk (*B. j. borealis*), "Krider's" juveniles.**—PERCHED.—Lacks dark eyeline. Cere is greenish. Large white patch on the mid-scapulars. Belly band markings are similar. Tarsi are bare. Tail is similar but dark banding is very narrow. Wingtip-to-tail-tip ratio is similar. FLIGHT.—Underside of the outer primaries is fully barred. Lacks a dark mark on the sides of the flanks.

Tail pattern as in Perched. (3) **Red-tailed Hawk (*B. j. calurus*) light morph juveniles.**—PERCHED.—Dark malar mark and lack a dark eyeline. Greenish ceres. Throat is streaked or dark. White patches on the mid-scapulars. Tail is brown and fully banded with narrow dark bands. FLIGHT.—All have distinct, dark brown patagial marks on the underwing. Tail pattern as in Perched. COMPARED TO INTERMEDIATE AND DARK INTERMEDIATE MORPH ADULTS. (4) **Red-tailed Hawk (*B. j. calurus*), intermediate morph adults.**—Rare in the East. PERCHED.—Cere is often greenish. Bare tarsi. Rufous dorsal surface of tail with a neat black subterminal band; often multiple inner dark bands. FLIGHT.—Dark brown patagial mark on the underside of the wings. All-dark or barred outer primaries. Tail as in Perched. COMPARED TO INTERMEDIATE MORPH JUVENILES AND DARK MORPH ADULTS.—(5) **Red-tailed Hawk (*B. j. calurus*), dark morph adults.**—Rare in the East. PERCHED.—Bare tarsi. Rufous dorsal tail surface with neat black subterminal band; often multiple inner dark bands. FLIGHT.—All-dark or fully barred outer primaries. Tail as in Perched. (6) **Rough-legged Hawk, dark morph juveniles.**—PERCHED.—Yellow gape can be similar. White forehead and outer lores. Feathered tarsi are similar. Wingtips equal or nearly equal to the tail tip. Dorsal and ventral tail patterns can be identical. FLIGHT.—Underside of outer primaries are extensively dark. All of primary greater underwing coverts are typically dark; some have whitish comma areas as on Ferruginous. Pale wing panels/windows are similar. Tail pattern as in Perched.

OTHER NAMES: Ferrug. *Spanish:* Aguililla Real. *French:* Buse Rouileuse.

REFERENCES: Alabama Bird Records Committee 2002; Bain 1993; Bohlen 1989; Burt and Grossenheider 1976; Curry 1991; Dobos 1995; Mumford and Keller 1984; Pittaway 1995; Robbins 1991; Stevenson and Anderson 1994; Watson 1999; Wheeler and Clark 1995.

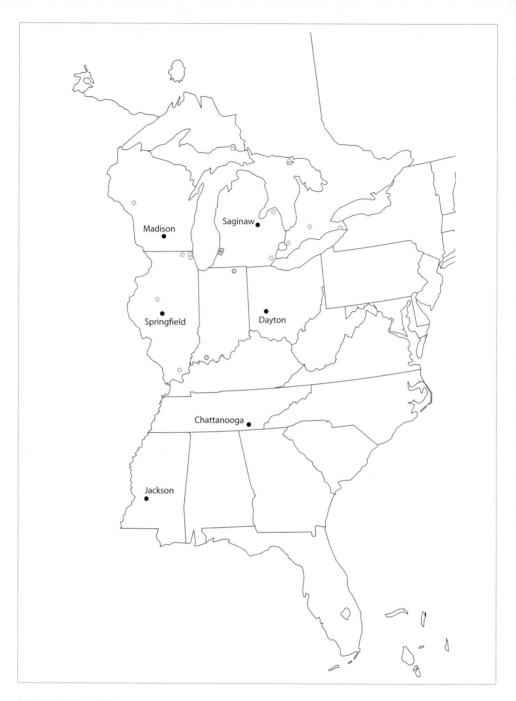

FERRUGINOUS HAWK, *Buteo regalis:* Accidental. Records are mainly in spring and fall. In 1980s, AL had 2 records and FL had 3.

Plate 379. Ferruginous Hawk, adult female light morph (moderately marked type) [Mar.] ▪ Black bill, yellow cere, and large yellow gape that extends to mid-eye. Brown head with thick dark eyeline and white throat; dark malar mark absent. ▪ Rufous upperparts. ▪ Wingtips shorter than tail tip. ▪ Dorsal surface of tail may be gray, rufous, white, or a mixture.

Plate 380. Ferruginous Hawk, adult female light morph (lightly marked type) [Dec.] ▪ Black bill, yellow cere, and large yellow gape that extends to mid-eye. Pale brown head with thick dark eyeline and white throat; dark malar mark absent. ▪ Leg feathers white with dark brown barring; rufous tarsi feathered to toes. Unmarked or lightly marked underparts.

Plate 381. Ferruginous Hawk, adult male light morph (moderately marked type) [Jan.] ▪ Black bill, yellow cere, and large yellow gape that extends to mid-eye. Pale gray head with thick dark eyeline and white throat. ▪ Rufous upperparts. Rufous leg feathers; rufous tarsi feathered to toes. White underparts lightly speckled on belly and flanks; lacks dark malar mark.

Plate 382. Ferruginous Hawk, adult female light morph (moderately marked type) [Jun.] ▪ Black bill, yellow cere, and large yellow gape that extends to mid-eye. Brown head with thick dark eyeline. ▪ Rufous upperparts. Rufous leg feathers; rufous tarsi feathered to toes. White underparts moderately marked on belly and flanks.

Plate 383. Ferruginous Hawk, adult female light morph (heavily marked type) [Jan.] ▪ Black bill, yellow cere, and large yellow gape. Brown head with thick dark eyeline and white throat. ▪ Pale tawny breast heavily streaked; belly and flanks rufous with dark barring; white lower belly lightly barred. Leg feathers hidden by lower belly feathers. ▪ *Note:* Most heavily marked type.

Plate 384. Ferruginous Hawk, adult light morph [Dec.] ▪ Rufous back and scapulars. ▪ Rufous upperwing coverts. Gray remiges with white rectangular panel on primaries formed by pale gray outer webs, white inner webs. ▪ *Note:* Typical dorsal markings on all light morph adults.

Plate 385. Ferruginous Hawk, adult light morph (lightly marked type) [Jul.] ▪ White leg feathers lightly barred. Tarsi rufous and contrast only slightly with white underparts. ▪ White remiges have small black, gray rear edge. ▪ White coverts moderately marked with rufous; may be lightly marked or unmarked. ▪ Tail white on ventral side.

Plate 386. Ferruginous Hawk, adult light morph (moderately marked type) [Jun.] ▪ Rufous leg feathers and tarsi form V that contrasts with white underparts; belly and flanks moderately barred. ▪ White remiges have small black tips, gray rear edge. Wing coverts heavily marked with rufous. ▪ Tail white on ventral side.

Plate 387. Ferruginous Hawk, adult light morph (heavily marked type) [Oct.] ▪ Rufous leg feathers and tarsi form V that contrasts with underparts; belly and flanks heavily barred and mottled; breast washed with tawny and has narrow streaking. ▪ White remiges have small black tips. Wing coverts heavily marked with rufous.

Plate 388. Ferruginous Hawk, adult male intermediate (rufous) morph (Mar.] ▪ Grayish head, including forehead and throat. Black bill and yellow cere. ▪ Small rufous markings on brown back and scapulars. ▪ Rufous upperwing covert edges. Pale gray outer edge of primaries. Wingtips shorter than tail tip. ▪ Tail mainly gray on dorsal side.

Plate 389. Ferruginous Hawk, adult female intermediate (rufous) morph [Jan.] ▪ Brown head, including forehead and throat. Black bill, yellow cere, large yellow gape. ▪ Rufous underparts. Leg feathers covered by lower belly.

Plate 390. Ferruginous Hawk, adult female intermediate (rufous) morph [Feb.] ▪ Brown head, including forehead and throat. Black bill, yellow cere, large yellow gape. ▪ Rufous underparts with white mottling on breast. Tarsi feathered to toes. ▪ Pale gray outer edges on primaries. Rufous edges on wing coverts. ▪ Tail white on ventral side.

Plate 391. Ferruginous Hawk, adult female intermediate (rufous) morph [Feb.] ▪ Rufous underparts with white mottling on breast. ▪ Rufous underwing coverts. White remiges have small black tips, gray rear edge. ▪ White ventral side of tail. ▪ *Note:* Same birds as on plate 390.

Plate 392. Ferruginous Hawk, adult dark intermediate (dark rufous) morph [Jan.] ▪ Brown head, including throat. ▪ Rufous-breasted type with rufous breast and black belly, flanks, leg feathers and tarsi. ▪ White remiges have small black tips. Black underwing coverts. ▪ White ventral side of tail.

Plate 393. Ferruginous Hawk, adult dark morph [Feb.] ▪ Uniformly dark brown head and body, including upperwing coverts and uppertail coverts. Large yellow gape. ▪ White remiges have small black tips. Dark brown wing coverts. ▪ *Note:* Rare morph consituting 1% of population.

Plate 394. Ferruginous Hawk, juvenile light morph [Dec.] ▪ Thick dark eyeline. Lacks dark malar mark. Black bill, yellow cere, large yellow gape ▪ Brown upperparts. ▪ Pale gray outer edges on primaries. Wingtips shorter than tail tip. ▪ White base on brown tail; 3 or 4 irregular dark bands with subterminal band widest.

Plate 395. Ferruginous Hawk, juvenile (one-year-old) light morph [Jul.] ▪ White head with thick dark eyeline. Black bill, yellow cere, large yellow gape. ▪ White underparts, including leg feathers and tarsi. New barred adult feather on left leg. ▪ *Note:* Full adult plumage is attained by mid-fall. Similar species lack thick dark eyeline.

Plate 396. Ferruginous Hawk, juvenile (old nestling) light morph [Jul.] ▪ Tawny-brown head with thick, dark brown eyeline. Black bill, yellow cere, large yellow gape. ▪ Tawny bib on breast fades to white by late summer. ▪ Dark brown upperparts edged with tawny. ▪ *Note:* This bird fledged a few days later.

Plate 397. Ferruginous Hawk, juvenile light morph [Dec.] ▪ Dark patch on flanks. ▪ White rectangular panel on primaries; primary coverts dark. ▪ Basal 1/3 of tail white and blends with white uppertail coverts which have dark spot on each feather. Distal 2/3 of tail brown with dark subterminal band and 2–3 narrower inner dark bands.

Plate 398. Ferruginous Hawk, juvenile light morph [Mar.] ▪ White underparts moderately spotted on belly, flanks, and leg feathers; tarsi dark. ▪ White remiges have small dark tips. White coverts moderately spotted. White rectangular window on primaries. ▪ Distal 2/3 of tail gray. Many have broken tail tips by late winter.

Plate 399. Ferruginous Hawk, juvenile light morph [Jan.] ▪ White underparts lightly spotted on flanks and leg feathers; belly unmarked. ▪ White remiges have small dark tips. Minimal dark barring on secondaries. White coverts lightly spotted. White rectangular window on primaries. ▪ Distal 2/3 of tail gray with dark subterminal band and 2–3 narrower inner dark bands.

Plate 400. Ferruginous Hawk, juvenile light morph [Nov.] ▪ White underparts heavily spotted on belly, flanks, and leg feathers; tarsi brown. ▪ White remiges have small dark tips. Minimal dark barring on secondaries. White coverts heavily spotted, especially on patagial region. White rectangular window on primaries. ▪ Distal 2/3 of tail gray with dark subterminal band.

Plate 401. Ferruginous Hawk, juvenile intermediate/dark morph [Jan.] ▪ Tawny-brown head, including forehead and throat. Black bill, yellow cere, large yellow gape. ▪ Uniformly dark brown upperparts. ▪ Pale gray outer edge on primaries (separates it from similar dark buteos). ▪ Dorsal side of tail brown with irregular dark bands.

Plate 402. Ferruginous Hawk, juvenile intermediate/dark morph [Dec.] ▪ Dark brown upperparts. ▪ White rectangular panel on primaries; primary coverts often fairly pale. ▪ Gray tail has moderately wide dark subterminal band; inner tail may be partially banded or unbanded.

Plate 403. Ferruginous Hawk, juvenile intermediate morph [Feb.] ▪ Tawny-rufous head. ▪ Tawny-rufous breast; rest of underparts dark brown. ▪ White remiges with small, dark wingtips. ▪ White ventral side of tail has gray subterminal band, often a few thin, gray inner bands.

ROUGH-LEGGED HAWK
(Buteo lagopus)

AGES: Adult, basic I (subadult I), and juvenile. There is a vast array of individual and sexual variation within each age class (*see* Color Morphs). Adults and subadults are somewhat sexually dimorphic; however, there is considerable overlap of sexual characters within each age class.

Adult characters are first attained when 2 years old. Subadult features are gained when 1 year old and retained for 1 year. Subadults have their own age distinctions (mainly iris color) but may exhibit plumage features of their own, of adults, or of juveniles. Most subadults retain a few juvenile remiges (*see* Molt). Juvenile age class is held the first year. Juveniles have shorter secondaries, which create a narrower wing and make the tail appear longer than in older ages.

MOLT: Accipitridae wing and tail molt pattern (*see* chapter 4). The first prebasic molt begins on juveniles from late Apr. through May and ends by late Nov. Molt begins with the loss of the innermost primary (p1). It then begins on the tail, then on the secondaries and body. The first prebasic molt is mostly but not totally complete on the body. Molt on the wings, including remiges and coverts, is incomplete. Primaries retain up to three old, worn, and faded juvenile feathers (p8–10). Secondaries often retain juvenile feathers at s4 (sometimes also s3), s8, and often s9. The respective greater upperwing coverts for the retained juvenile primaries and secondaries are also generally retained juvenile feathering. A few median and lesser upperwing coverts may also be retained worn and faded juvenile feathers. The tail occasionally retains one or two juvenile rectrices. *Note:* Retained juvenile feathering is held throughout the fall, winter, and spring of the second year during the subadult age period.

The second prebasic molt is fairly complete but also retains old feathering. Molt begins in Jun. or Jul., depending on sex, breeding status, and breeding success, and ends in late Oct. or Nov. This molt replaces most or all previously retained juvenile feathering but may not replace all subadult feathers. Molt begins with sequential replacement of the outer juvenile primaries, from inner to outer feathers, then many of the rest of the inner primaries are replaced, also in an inner to outer sequence. Old juvenile secondaries are also replaced prior to molt on other secondaries. Molt on the tail appears to be mainly complete.

Additional prebasic molts are also fairly complete but retain a variable amount of the previous year's feathers on the body and wings. Remiges often have serially descendent molt and replace the primaries in an irregular order. Tail molt appears to be mainly complete. Timing is the same as the second prebasic molt.

SUBSPECIES: Polytypic with three races, but only one, *B. l. sanctijohannis*, inhabits North America.

Nominate *B. l. lagopus* breeds in tundra and sometimes in the northern boreal forest from Norway east through n. Russia to the Ural Mts. Winters along eastern coastal areas of the United Kingdom and from n. France southeast to n. Italy and east to Turkey, then east to the Caspian Sea. Similar to the larger *sanctijohannis* but does not have a dark morph.

B. l. kamtschatkensis breeds in the tundra region east of the Ural Mts. of n. Siberia and east to the Bering Sea to Kamtchatka and the Kuril Islands. Winters south to the e. Caspian Sea to Turkmenistan then east through n. China, Korea, and Japan. It is the largest race and is also fairly similar to *sanctijohannis* and only marginally different than *lagopus*. A dark morph also does not exist for this subspecies.

COLOR MORPHS: Polymorphic. Light and dark morphs occur for all ages; however, adult females, subadult females, and juveniles also have an intermediate morph that forms a clinal link between light and dark morphs. For unknown reasons, adult and subadult males do not have an intermediate morph. All ages and sexes exhibit extraordinary variation within each morph.

Adult light morphs are sexually diagnostic 95% of the time based on plumage. Recent research shows that with adult dark morphs, only some males can be accurately separated from females. Adult dark morphs have exten-

sive overlapping plumage traits, particularly on tail patterns (BKW research at Bell Museum of Natural History, Minneapolis, Minn.; C. Olson unpubl. data from w. Montana; J. Bouton and D. Tetlow unpubl. data from e. New York). In the field, juvenile light and dark morphs usually can not be identified to sex.

Plumage variation and regional status of morphs adhere to Gloger's Rule (*see* Status and Distribution: Color morph status and distribution). As noted in Subspecies, dark morphs are absent in the two Eurasian subspecies.

SIZE: A large raptor. Males average smaller than females but sexes overlap. Length: 18–23 in. (46–58 cm); wingspan: 48–56 in. (122–142 cm).

SPECIES TRAITS: HEAD.—**Small bill. Cere and narrow, long gape are bright yellow. Inner half of lores dark and outer half of the lores and forehead pale and form a mask.** Gape is narrow but prominent and extends under the eyes. Large white area on the nape with a center black spot. BODY.—**Feathered tarsi. Small feet.** WINGS.—**In flight, wings are long and moderately wide with parallel front and trailing edges. The five "fingers" form a blunt wingtip. The long wings are either equal to or extend somewhat beyond the tip of the tail when perched.**

ADULT TRAITS: HEAD.—Dark brown irises. WINGS.—Moderately wide or wide black subterminal band on the trailing edge of the ventral surface. The dorsal surface of the inner and outer webs of the primaries is brownish. Dorsal surface of the secondaries is gray and barred with black. TAIL.—**Ventral surface has a neat, wide black subterminal band.**

ADULT LIGHT MORPH TRAITS: HEAD.—Thin dark eyeline. Pale supercilium and auricular regions. BODY.—Variable amount of dark markings on the neck and breast; markings are often heavier on the sides of the neck and breast and form a dark bib. Flanks are spotted, barred, or solid blackish brown. Leg feathers are spotted or barred. Uppertail coverts have a moderate-sized or large dark diamond-shaped mark on each feather with a pale tawny or white edge and appear largely as a dark area. WINGS.—Primary greater underwing coverts are dark gray or black. TAIL.—Variable-width white basal region with a broad grayish or brownish distal band and a darker subterminal band on the dorsal surface and the neat black subterminal band on the ventral surface.

Adult Male Light Morph (Lightly Marked Type): HEAD.—Varies from being quite pale tawny or whitish with a minimal or moderate amount of dark streaking on the crown and malar with minimal distinction of the white mask to being moderately heavily marked with a distinct mask. BODY (ventral).—Base color of the underparts varies from white to pale tawny. Neck and upper breast can be (1) lightly streaked and lacking a defined bib, (2) **moderately streaked and mottled and forming a fairly distinct bib,** (3) **sometimes heavily streaked and mottled,** or (4) **uniformly dark with a distinct bib.** Base color of the ventral areas is white or pale tawny. Lower breast area is unmarked and lacks a defined necklace. Belly is unmarked or lightly spotted. Flanks are white or gray and lightly spotted, moderately spotted, or barred. Moderately barred leg feathers form a V in flight. Undertail coverts are white and unmarked. BODY (dorsal).—Upperparts appear pale and speckled with dark brown. The dark mark on the central portion of each feather is small and surrounded by an extensive amount of pale gray, and often a slight tawny-rufous wash. WINGS (ventral).—The underwing coverts and axillaries are white or tawny and lightly spotted, but the patagial region is often more densely marked. The long feathers of the first row of lesser underwing coverts may exhibit a somewhat distinct pale band because of the lack of markings. The carpal region may (1) have a small dark area on the primary greater coverts with the rest of carpal area pale and sparingly marked with dark spots or (2) **be uniformly dark and form a large dark square patch.** WINGS (dorsal).—Upperwing coverts are pale grayish and mottled like the rest of the upperparts. The lesser coverts may be edged with a considerable amount of rufous. TAIL.—**Likely to have only the single wide black subterminal band or may have one or two additional narrow black bands; rarely more bands.** *Note:* As a general rule, males with pale bellies are also paler and less heavily marked on other body areas. Also called white-bellied type. Uncommon plumage type in the East.

Adult Male Light Morph (Moderately Marked Type): HEAD.—Moderately heavily marked to heavily marked and appearing moderately dark headed or dark headed. Distinct white mask. BODY (ventral).—Base color of the underparts varies from white to a rich tawny. Neck and breast are moderately or heavily marked and form a distinct bib as described above in #1 and 2 types of lightly marked type. **Lower breast has a narrow necklace consisting of an unmarked or lightly marked narrow band separating the dark breast from the moderately marked belly and flanks. Belly is moderately barred and blotched with black. Flanks are white or dark gray and distinctly barred with black.** Leg feathers are moderately or heavily barred. Undertail coverts are unmarked or some feathers may have a small dark mark. BODY (dorsal).—Upperparts are pale gray, often with a pale tawny-rufous wash, with a small dark mark on the central portion of each feather or a larger dark mark on the central area of each feather and not as grayish looking. WINGS (ventral).—The underwing coverts are white or tawny and moderately or heavily spotted, particularly the patagial area. A distinct broad, unmarked pale bar exists on the first row of lesser underwing coverts. The carpal region may (1) have a small dark area on the primary greater coverts with a heavily mottled carpal area that blends with the rest of the underwing coverts and obscurses the carpal patch or (2) **be entirely dark, forming a distinct black square shape.** WINGS (dorsal).—The upperwing coverts are lightly or moderately marked like the rest of the upperparts. TAIL.—May have at least one or two dark inner bands but likely to have the fully banded pattern of four or five dark bands. The deck set has the four or five dark bands, and there may be six or more dark bands on the outer rectrix sets. Inner dark bands may all be equal in width or get progressively narrower towards the base of the tail. On the fully banded pattern, the white basal region of the tail is less pronounced because of the additional banding. *Note:* Common plumage type in the East.

Adult Male Light Morph (Heavily Marked Type): HEAD.—As on moderately marked type. BODY (ventral).—Base color of the underparts is either a rich tawny, as in many adult females, or whitish. Neck and lower breast are extensively marked and appear as a dark bib.

An unmarked or lightly marked narrow band creates the necklace that separates the dark breast from the dark belly and flanks. Belly is heavily barred or blotched but not uniformly blackish brown. **Flanks are dark and may have faint gray barring but can also be uniformly blackish brown as on adult females.** Leg feathers are heavily barred. Undertail coverts are likely to have a dark bar on each feather. BODY (dorsal).—Upperparts have a large dark mark on the central part of each feather with grayish and often tawny-rufous wash on the outer edges and do not appear as grayish as in most lightly marked type adult males. WINGS (ventral).—The underwing coverts are extensively marked and quite dark, but there is still a pale bar on the first row of lesser underwing coverts because of a lack of markings. Carpal region is (1) heavily mottled and blends with the rest of the underwing coverts, or (2) **solid black and somewhat distinct.** WINGS (dorsal).—Marked like the rest of the upperparts. TAIL.—As in moderately marked type but more likely to be fully banded pattern. *Note:* Common plumage type in the East. Not depicted.

Adult Female Light Morph (Lightly Marked Type): HEAD.—Quite pale with little if any dark malar mark and only a light amount of streaking on the crown and hindneck. Pale mask is ill defined because the head is so pale. BODY (ventral).—Base color of the underparts is pale tawny but may fade to nearly white by spring. Lightly streaked neck and upper breast do not have a necklace demarcation. Belly is unmarked or may be sparsely marked with small dark spots and blotches. **Flanks are uniformly blackish brown or may have light tips on most feathers but are not spotted or barred as on similarly marked males.** Leg feathers are lightly covered with dark spots, bars, or diamond-shaped markings. Undertail coverts are unmarked. BODY (dorsal).—A dark brown streak is on the central part of each feather and the outer portion is edged with tawny or tawny-rufous. WINGS (ventral).—**Pale tawny underwing coverts and axillaries are lightly marked and have a distinct square black carpal patch.** Carpal area is sometimes lightly mottled with tawny. WINGS (dorsal).—Marked as on rest of the upperparts. TAIL.—Typically has a single neat black subterminal band. There

is considerable white on the base. *Note:* Uncommon plumage type in the East.

Adult Female Light Morph (Moderately Marked Type): HEAD.—Moderately streaked on the crown and hindneck and has a fairly distinct pale mask. Dark malar is moderately defined and often most distinct on the very lower portion of the lower jaw. BODY (ventral).—Base color of the underparts is a pale or rich tawny and often fades to whitish or pale tawny by spring. Neck and upper breast are lightly or moderately streaked. Birds with lightly streaked breasts do not have a bib or necklace; those with moderately marked bibs have a moderate bib and necklace demarcation. Flanks are always either solid brownish black or each feather is tipped with tawny. Two variations of belly markings: (1) *Dark bellied type.*—**Uniformly blackish brown but may have a small tawny tip on each feather** or (2) *Split-bellied type.*—**Mid-section of the dark belly is split by a narrow unmarked tawny or mottled strip.** Leg feathers are moderately barred. Undertail coverts are unmarked. BODY (dorsal).—As in lightly marked type but often darker, with narrower pale edging. WINGS (ventral).—As in lightly marked type but often with a fairly rich tawny base color. Axillaries are tawny with a few dark marks. WINGS (dorsal).—Similarly marked as rest of the upperparts. TAIL.—Often has up to three additional narrow partial or complete dark basal tail bands but not fully banded as on many males. White area on the basal region of the dorsal surface of the tail can be very reduced in width, especially on the two deck rectrices. *Note:* Common plumage type in the East.

Adult Female Light Morph (Heavily Marked Type): HEAD.—Heavily streaked with dark brown on the crown and hindneck with a distinct pale mask. Dark malar mark is well defined on all of the lower jaw. Pale supercilium and auricular areas are obvious. BODY (ventral).—Base color of the underparts is a rich tawny but fades to pale tawny or even whitish by spring. Bib is heavily marked with streaks or blotches and can be virtually solid dark. Necklace is well defined. **Flanks and belly are uniformly blackish brown but may have a small tawny tip on each feather.** Leg feathers are heavily barred. Undertail coverts may have a dark mark or bar on most feathers. BODY (dorsal).—As in previously described types. WINGS (ventral).—**Underwing coverts are a rich tawny and fairly heavily marked, but the dark carpal patch is still obvious.** Axillaries are tawny and marked with dark brown but still pale. WINGS (dorsal).—Marked similarly as rest of the upperparts. TAIL.—Regularly has up to three narrow partial or complete inner dark bands but not fully banded as on many males. White basal area of the tail is often very reduced, and white may be lacking on the deck rectrix set. *Note:* Common plumage type in the East.

ADULT INTERMEDIATE MORPH TRAITS (FEMALE ONLY): HEAD.—Fairly pale and similar to moderately and heavily marked types of light morph with a broad pale supercilium and auricular areas. White mask is fairly distinct. BODY (ventral).—All breast feathers have tawny or tawny-rufous edging and may appear streaked or mottled, with little or no necklace demarcation. Breast is paler than belly and flanks. Uniformly blackish brown belly and flanks. Leg feathers are either dark with some tawny markings or pale and heavily barred. Undertail coverts can be unmarked or have a moderate amount of dark markings. BODY (dorsal).—Dark brown with a minimal amount of pale edging on the scapulars. WINGS (ventral).—**Axillaries are dark brown (tawny colored on light morphs). The underwing coverts are tawny-rufous and more rufous than on light morphs but not as rufous as on many dark morphs. Distinct large square black carpal patch.** WINGS (dorsal).—Dark coverts with some pale edging. TAIL.—Ventral surface is marked as on many light morphs, but the white basal region is narrow. Dorsal surface is medium or dark brown with a very narrow white band at the very base of the tail. May have multiple dark bands. Uppertail coverts are tawny or dark. *Note:* Uncommon plumage type in the East. This is the interim female plumage between a heavily marked type light morph and brown type dark morph, in particular pale-headed variations of brown type dark morph (*see below*).

ADULT DARK MORPH TRAITS: HEAD.—**Very defined white mask.** Yellow gape is narrow but obvious as it contrasts against the dark head. BODY, WINGS, and TAIL.—Shared sexual traits (*see below*).

Adult Brown Type (Male/Female): HEAD.—Variable amount of pale tawny on the supercilium and auricular regions: (1) all dark without pale supercilium and auricular areas (both sexes), (2) small, pale tawny supercilium and auricular areas with a narrow dark eyeline (both sexes), and (3) large pale tawny supercilium and auricular areas with a distinct narrow dark eyeline (mainly female). White mask is obvious on all but #3. BODY.—Neck and breast have a variable amount of tawny or rufous-tawny streaking and mottling; rarely have whitish mottling. As a rule, the paler the head, the more streaked and paler the breast. There is often a rather sharp demarcation line between the more tawny-brown neck and breast and the darker, uniformly blackish brown belly and flanks. On some individuals, there is some tawny or white speckling at the junction of the breast and belly (which is the necklace area on light morphs). Leg feathers are dark brown. Undertail coverts are dark with pale tips. Dorsal region is either solid blackish brown or may have considerable pale gray mottling on the scapulars (more typical of males). Uppertail coverts are dark brown but may have a pale tip on each feather. WINGS (ventral).—Underwing coverts vary in color and pattern of markings: (1) uniformly dark brown, including the axillaries, with little or no demarcation of the carpal region; (2) **slightly or moderately rufous with a distinct black square carpal patch and dark brown axillaries; (3) very rufous with dark brown axillaries and an obvious black carpal patch (predominately females);** or (4) variably speckled with tawny or white but the carpal area is unmarked and ill defined and the axillaries are often speckled or barred with white. *Note:* In general, birds with paler heads tend to have more rufous on the underwing coverts and those with darker heads have little or no rufous on the coverts. WINGS (dorsal).—Mainly uniformly dark on the coverts. TAIL.—Four patterns. One type is only on females and only visible on the dorsal surface. The other three are shared by both sexes and are visible on both the ventral and dorsal surfaces. All have the neat, wide black subterminal band. (1) *Unbanded type* (females only).—**Ventral surface is pale gray and unmarked inside the neat, black subterminal band**; dorsal surface is uniformly medium brown. (2) *Partially banded type* (many females, some males).—Ventral surface is pale gray with partial, narrow gray bands; dorsal surface is medium brown with two or three faintly darker bands, mainly on the inner rectrix sets. (3) *Banded type* (many females, many males).—Ventral surface is pale gray with distinct, narrow dark gray bands on all the inner tail; dorsal surface is dark brown with three fairly distinct narrow pale gray bands (pattern is most pronounced on the deck and inner rectrix sets). (4) *Distinctly banded type* (many males, a few females).—**Ventral surface is gray or black with distinct, narrow white bands; dorsal surface is dark brown or black with three distinct, narrow, pale gray or white bands.** *Note:* Fairly common plumage type in the East. In-hand photographs of a large female (wing chord at the top end of the female category) banded at Point Peninsula area in Jefferson Co., N.Y., provided the first absolute documentation of an adult female with distinctly banded type tail pattern. Similar types also in Bell Museum of Natural History (also females at large size spectrum for their sex), unpublished photographs of a bird found shot by C. Olson, and several in-field photographed individuals that appeared very large and otherwise female-like.

Adult Male Black Type: HEAD.—**Pronounced white mask.** Very rarely, the white forehead may be reduced or lacking on the blackest types. Head is all black or may have a slight brownish cast. Yellow gape is quite obvious. BODY (ventral).—Black. Rarely, there is sparse white spotting at the junction of the breast and belly at the necklace region of paler birds. Leg feathers may have white spotting. Often have white spotting or barring on each undertail covert feather. BODY (dorsal).—Two main types with a clinal trend between them: (1) mainly all-black back and scapulars with minimal gray outer feather edging or mottling; (2) extensively mottled with pale gray and can nearly rival the gray dorsum of some light morphs. Uppertail coverts are black with a white tip on each feather or may have white inner bars on each feather. WINGS (ventral).—Underwing coverts are uniformly black and do not show distinction of the carpal area. Some individuals have white spotting on the coverts and barring on the axillaries. TAIL.—**Black tail is distinctly banded type.** On

the most melanin-saturated birds, the three dorsal gray or white bands may be reduced and only appear as partial bands. *Note:* Common plumage type in the East.

BASIC I (SUBADULT I) TRAITS: HEAD.—Iris is medium brown. BODY.—May possess any of the adult variations previously described. Males tend to acquire female-like traits; however, males may also molt into any of the five adult male plumage variations described above. WINGS (ventral).—Retains up to three juvenile feathers on the outermost primaries (p8–10) and two or three secondaries (s4, 8, and 9). *See* Molt. Retained feathers are frayed and pale brown. On the secondaries, the old juvenile feathers are shorter than the newly acquired adultlike feathers and lack the more distinct dark subterminal band. A few or many faded and worn juvenile feathers are retained on the upperwing coverts. WINGS (dorsal).—The inner web of the primaries is whitish or white and forms a distinct panel on the dorsal surface, and is similar to juveniles. Also, since many juveniles exhibit a white area on the outer web on the base of some of the outer primaries, and subadults typically retain these feathers, subadults may show a white patch on the base on the dorsal surface of the outer primaries. TAIL.—Generally molts into adult characters; however, a few retain one or two juvenile rectrices. Such feathers are longer than the newly acquired feathers and lack the black subterminal band.

BASIC (SUBADULT) LIGHT MORPH TRAITS: *See* male and female data below.

Basic (Subadult) Male Light Morph (All Types): May have any of the three adult male light morph plumage and tail variations described above, including lightly marked type (BKW pers. obs./photographs showing distinct molt pattern and retained juvenile feathering; unpubl. data and in-hand photos from C. Olson). The lightly marked type is very uncommon; the other two are fairly common or common. Many males also have female-like characters, including a uniformly blackish brown belly and flanks. Many males cannot be separated in the field from subadult or adult females unless seen at close range to see molt pattern or iris color. Many subadults have bib markings that extend to the front of the breast and belly and lack the unmarked necklace that adults have.

Basic (Subadult) Female Light Morph (All Types): Identical to the plumage variations of adult light morph females, including the blackish brown belly band color. Separated from adult females at close range by iris color and retained juvenile feathering.

BASIC (SUBADULT) INTERMEDIATE MORPH TRAITS (FEMALE ONLY): No data. Use iris color and retained juvenile feathering to age properly.

BASIC (SUBADULT) DARK MORPH TRAITS: Females adhere to the same variations described for adult female dark morphs. For males, several specimens and photographs substantiate brown and black types.

JUVENILE TRAITS: Sexes are similar. HEAD.—Pale yellow or brown iris. WINGS (ventral).—Gray subterminal band on the trailing edge of the wing. The "finger" primaries are generally all black or have fairly large black area on the tips. In translucent light, a pale window may show on the primaries. WINGS (dorsal).—The inner web of each primary is white and shows as a panel. On many individuals, p7, 8, and 9 may be white on the basal area of the outer web next to the greater primary coverts. TAIL.—The ventral surface has a diffused gray subterminal band. A darker smudge may occasionally be superimposed on this gray band but is never as defined as the neat black band on subadults and adults. Either sex may have partial or fairly complete bands on the dorsal surface.

JUVENILE LIGHT MORPH TRAITS: HEAD.—Thin dark eyeline. Tawny head is lightly or moderately streaked on the crown and hindneck. There is little if any demarcation of a dark malar mark on individuals with pale heads; those with darker heads may have a faint dark malar mark. BODY (ventral).—Base color of the underparts is pale or medium tawny. Neck and breast vary from sparsely to heavily streaked. Streaking extends to the top of the dark belly and flanks and is most dense on the sides of the neck and breast. **Flanks and belly are mainly uniformly warm dark brown and form a belly band (belly band is not the blackish brown of subadult and adult females).** However, many birds have a narrow tawny strip or mottling down the center of the belly. Leg feathers are tawny and may be unmarked, lightly spotted, or heavily spotted. BODY (dorsal).—Tawny or slightly grayish outer edges with a wide dark streak on the

mid-section of each dorsal feather. Some males are perhaps more grayish on the dorsal regions than are females. WINGS (ventral).—Underwing coverts and axillaries are tawny and lightly marked with dark spots. A large dark brown square patch adorns the carpal area of the underwing. WINGS (dorsal).—Pattern is similar to the dorsal areas. Middle and first row of lesser coverts have a broad pale tawny or grayish edge. TAIL (ventral).—Grayish on the distal half or two-thirds and often a darker gray on the subterminal band region. The basal half or third of the tail is white. TAIL (dorsal).—Uppertail coverts are generally white with small dark central spot or streak and much paler than on most adults. However, more heavily marked birds have tawny or white uppertail coverts with a large dark spot or diamond-shaped mark on most feathers. Dorsal surface of the tail is medium brown on the distal half or two-thirds and white on the basal half or third. On heavily marked birds, the white basal area may be limited to the basal fourth or less. Dark tail banding is often present but not well defined. As in adults, either sex can have a variable number of partial or complete narrow dark inner bands.

JUVENILE INTERMEDIATE MORPH TRAITS: HEAD.—Pale as on juvenile light morph with a thin dark eyeline. The white mask is often nondescript since the head is rather pale. BODY.—Neck and breast are extensively streaked with brown. Uniformly brown belly and flanks. Leg feathers are typically heavily marked but may be lightly marked. Undertail coverts may be unmarked or have moderate-sized dark markings. WINGS.—**Underwing coverts are rufous-tawny and more rufous than on light morphs. Axillaries are brown (tawny in light morphs). Square-shaped black carpal patch is obvious.** TAIL (ventral).—Like light morph's. TAIL (dorsal).—Uppertail coverts are tawny and may have dark markings on each feather. Basal area of the tail has a narrow white band.

JUVENILE DARK MORPH TRAITS: Two main plumage variations in either sex; see below. TAIL.—Three main variations. Patterns can be for either sex and are most noticeable on the dorsal surface. (1) *Unbanded type.*—Dorsal surface is medium brown with a slightly darker smudge on the subterminal area. Ventral surface is pale gray with a medium gray subtermi-

nal smudge. (2) *Partially banded type.*—
Medium brown dorsal surface with a darker
subterminal smudge. There are two to four
narrow or moderately wide partial dark bands
on the inner portion of the tail. The ventral
surface is pale gray with the darker subterminal
smudge and with narrow, partial gray inner
bands. (3) *Banded type.*—Dorsal surface is
dark brown with three delineated pale gray
bands. The pale gray bands may be narrower
or wider than the dark bands.

Juvenile Dark Morph Brown Type: HEAD.—
Varies from very pale and nearly rivaling those
of light morphs to moderately dark with reduced pale supercilium and auricular areas and
a fairly defined white mask. BODY (ventral).—
Neck and breast feathers are variably edged
and mottled with tawny or tawny-rufous. Belly
and flanks are uniformly warm dark brown
and contrast sharply with the paler tawny-rufous neck and breast. Leg feathers are brown.
Undertail coverts are brown with pale tips.
BODY (dorsal).—Uniformly brown. WINGS
(ventral).—**Dark brown axillaries, rufous
coverts, and a sharply defined large black
carpal patch.** WINGS (dorsal).—Dark brown
with a pale panel on the primaries. TAIL.—
Uppertail coverts are brown. *Note:* Common
plumage type in the East.

Juvenile Dark Morph Black Type: HEAD.—
Dark brown with a distinct white mask. Rarely
has a pale throat. BODY.—Uniformly dark
brown throughout, including leg feathers and
undertail coverts. TAIL.—Uppertail coverts are
dark brown. *Note:* Common plumage type for
males, but uncommon or rare for females in
the East. Numerous captured birds and specimens have been males. Probable female type
based on only one specimen from Bell Museum of National History (wing chord mea-
sured at the small end of female range and labeled as a female).

ABNORMAL PLUMAGES: Imperfect albino (dilute plumage) was photographed in Ohio in
the winter of 2000. In the West, a hybrid with
adult "Harlan's" Red-tailed Hawk (*Buteo jamaicensis harlani*) has been documented. *Note:*
Spring and early summer birds, particularly 1-
year-olds, can have very worn and faded
plumages and look somewhat albinistic.

HABITAT: Summer.—Breeds mainly in tundra
but also in semi-open spruce woodlands. Areas

with cliffs, embankments, or rocky outcrops
are preferred in most areas for nest sites. On
the island of Newfoundland, occasionally
found nesting in areas of clear-cut forests that
have nearby cliffs.

Winter.—Semi-open and open meadows; idle
fields; harvested agricultural areas; pastures;
freshwater, brackish, and saltwater marshes;
and swamps.

Migration.—All areas as described for Winter
but also found in open wooded locales for
short periods.

HABITS: Varies from wary to moderately tame.
Gregarious in spring, fall, and winter. Regularly
forms communal roosts and may roost with
other raptors. Perches on any type of elevated
perch, including utility wires. Typically seen on
small branches on treetops. Readily perches on
the ground. In very windy conditions will
perch on the ground in areas sheltered from
the wind.

FEEDING: Perch and aerial hunter. Feeds extensively on lemmings during the summer. Also
readily preys on other small rodents, young
hares, and small and medium-small birds up to
ptarmigan size. In the nonbreeding season, occasionally feeds on fish, reptiles, amphibians, and
insects. Carrion is readily eaten in all seasons.

FLIGHT: Powered by slow wingbeats interspersed with irregular glide sequences. Wings
are held in a low dihedral when soaring and in
a modified dihedral when gliding. Regularly
hovers and kites when hunting. Legs are often
lowered when hovering. Regularly crosses extensive areas of open water during migration.

VOICE: Rarely heard on the winter grounds.
May vocalize if agitated or forced to move
from a perch. Primary call is a plaintive *keeaah*.
On the breeding grounds, nesting pairs are
highly vocal towards intruders at their nests
sites.

STATUS AND DISTRIBUTION: *Fairly common.*
Population is stable but fluctuates locally and
regionally at irregular intervals because of prey
abundance and other factors.

Color morph status and distribution.—Following Gloger's Rule, dark morphs, including
the darkest types (e.g., black type adult males),
are more prevalent in the moist climate nesting
areas of n. Québec than in arctic breeding regions of the West. Likewise, dark morphs are
more common in the winter in e. Canada and

the e. U.S. than in wintering areas in the West. Interestingly, the breeding population on the island of Newfoundland has only a small percentage of dark morphs. The north-central Canadian tundra in Nunavut and the Northwest Territories is more arid than in e. Canada and the percent of dark morphs decreases substantially in this region. Dark morphs are also virtually absent at high-arctic latitudes. In Alaska, however, dark morphs again become more numerous and may exceed ratios seen in the East (in the spring of 2002, 71% were light morph and 29% dark morph).

Based on unpublished data from mainly T. Carrolan and G. Smith on 537 sightings from four winter seasons (1999–2002) in e. New York, w.-cen. Vermont, and e. Ontario: 71% light morphs, 26% dark morphs, and 3% undetermined and possible intermediate morphs. However, in local areas, dark morphs may average over 50%.

Summer.—Sizable numbers breed in Labrador, Nunavut, and Québec. Only a few pairs nest in n. Ontario. Rough-legged Hawks breed throughout all of the island of Newfoundland but are irregularly distributed and much of range is based on variable prey abundance. Juveniles may occasionally linger in the northern border states and s. Canada into early or mid-Jun.

Winter.—Locally dense in many regions in mapped winter range. There is a small wintering population in s. Newfoundland. Females of all ages winter at more northern latitudes than do males. Deep snow, which conceals prey, may force birds to vacate certain areas in winter. Irregular south of typical winter range in Tennessee, Alabama, and Georgia. Juveniles very rarely winter as far south as cen. Florida. There are over 20 sight records for Florida; however, the first photographed breeding documentation occurred in the winter of 2000 in Orange Co.

Movements.—Rough-legged Hawks engage in short or moderate-length migrations. Males of all ages migrate farther south than females. Juveniles (probably males) occasionally engage in fairly long movements south of typical winter areas. Moderate-length over-water crossings are readily undertaken.

Fall migration: First migrants are seen in s. Québec in late Sep., with a peak in late Oct., and movements continuing in small numbers throughout Nov. and possibly into early Dec.

Along the e. Great Lakes in Ontario and se. Michigan, migrants arrive in early Oct., peak from late Oct. to mid-Nov., and continue in small numbers throughout Nov. and possibly later. Migrants are rarely seen at hawkwatches in New England and the Mid-Atlantic region, even during Nov. Hawkwatch sites that do observe Rough-legged Hawks only log one or two per season. (Most autumn hawkwatches end their counts in late Nov.) In the East, most Rough-legged Hawks arrive at southern wintering areas in Dec. and later. Movements may continue on a limited basis through mid-winter in northern latitudes, depending on snow depth and food supply.

Spring migration: Migrant do not move along shoreline areas where Mid-Atlantic hawkwatch sites are located and thus are not recorded at these sites. Only the hawkwatch sites along the s. Great Lakes records migrants, and large numbers of them, in the spring. Weather is a determining factor in the timing. Adults push northward at the first hint of spring-like weather.

Along s. Lake Ontario in New York, adult migrants may be detected as early as mid-Feb.; however, in some years migrants may not be seen until early or mid-Mar. One or two peak movement periods may occur. The peak migration of adults may be as early as late Mar. or later in early or mid-Apr. Juveniles may peak in mid- to late Apr., but continue moving northward until mid-May.

On the south shore of Lake Superior in the Upper Peninsula of Michigan at White Fish Point in Paradise Co., the first adult spring arrivals are seen in late Mar. Peak flights of adults are typically in late Apr., but large numbers of adults and juveniles can be tallied until early May. Juveniles may continue moving northward in small numbers until late May. Juveniles occasionally summer in s. Canada and the n. U.S.

NESTING: Begins in May or early Jun. depending on latitude and typically ends in Jul. or Aug. but may extend into early Sep.

Courtship (flight).—*High-circling* by both sexes and *sky-dancing* by males (*see* chapter 5).

Nests are fairly large, constructed of sticks, chunks of wood, twigs, and bones and are up to 30 in. (76 cm) in diameter and 15 in. (34 cm) deep. The inner nest is lined with soft vegetation, fur, and feathers from prey. Nests are often reused and there may be alternate nests in a territory. New nests may be small, but they become larger with reuse. Males bring material and females build the nest. Nest sites are on cliffs (do not require an overhang above the site), embankments, rock outcrops, knolls, and even flat ground. Trees are occasionally used for nest sites. Tree nests are placed in the uppermost part of the tree and may be up to 30 ft. (9 m) high. Incubation of the 2–6 eggs, rarely 7, is mainly by females. Males supply food to females and nestlings. Eggs hatch in 28–31 days and youngsters fledge in 34–45 days.

CONSERVATION: A stable species, so no measures are taken. Breeding areas are not affected by human pressure. Wintering birds use vast expanses of agricultural areas.

Mortality.—Illegal shooting is prevalent, especially during small game and upland game bird and waterfowl hunting seasons. Electrocution occurs from utility wires. A few birds are hit by vehicles when feeding on roadkills.

SIMILAR SPECIES: COMPARED TO LIGHT MORPH.—**(1) Northern Harrier, all ages.**—PERCHED.—Wingtips are shorter than tail tip. FLIGHT.—Share similar white uppertail coverts with many juvenile Roughlegs but do not have white on the basal area of the tail. Dorsal surface of tail has wide dark bands. Flight mannerism similar, especially with larger-sized female harriers in that wings are held in dihedral when soaring and a modified dihedral when gliding. **(2) Swainson's Hawk, light morph adults and subadults.**—Potential range overlap only during migration periods in the East. PERCHED.—(2A) Adults similar to adult male Roughlegs, with a defined bib on the breast, including the white mask on the forehead and outer lores and wingtip-to-tail-tip ratio. Dorsal color of Swainson's is more brownish; tarsi are bare; tail banding is narrow and uniform in width (but with similar wide dark subterminal band). (2B) Subadult Swainson's are similar to adult male Roughlegs, with a partial bib consisting of streaking on the sides of the neck and breast. Use features listed above, including tail pattern, to separate. COMPARED TO DARK MORPH.—**(3) Swainson's Hawk, dark morphs of all ages.**—Range overlap as in #2. PERCHED.—(3A) Adults are similar in having pale outer lores but rarely have pale foreheads (creating a

mask). Bare tarsi. White or tawny undertail coverts. Dark banding on the tail is very narrow. (3B) Immature ages are very similar to paler headed Roughlegs, especially in head pattern (mask and thin dark eyeline), but have bare tarsi and pale undertail coverts. FLIGHT.—All ages have medium or dark gray undersides of the remiges and pale undertail coverts. **(4) "Harlan's" Red-tailed Hawk (*B. j. harlani*), dark morph or dark intermediate morph gray-type-tail adults.**—Range overlap mainly in very western portion of the East in winter and migration. PERCHED.—Lores are completely white. May have similar white nape area with the black nape spot. Bare tarsi. Wingtips are somewhat shorter than tail tip. Tail pattern nearly identical to juvenile and adult female Roughlegs with unbanded type dorsal tail pattern. Regularly perch on small treetop branches like Roughlegs. FLIGHT.—Secondaries are more broadly bowed. Subterminal/terminal black tail band is typically irregular and not as neatly formed as on Roughlegs. **(5) "Western" Red-tailed Hawk (*B. j. calurus*) and "Harlan's" Red-tailed Hawk (*B. j. harlani*), dark morph juveniles.**—Range overlap as in #4. PERCHED.—Bare tarsi. Wingtips are much shorter than tail tip. Often perch on small treetop branches. FLIGHT.—Dark "fingers" on the underside of the outer primaries on *calurus* are similar to Roughleg's; *harlani* has barred outer primaries. Both Red-tailed races have more than four dark bands on the tail. **(7) "Eastern" Red-tailed Hawk (*B. j. borealis*) and "Western" (*B. j. calurus*), light morph juveniles**—PERCHED.—May have a broad, dark band across the flanks and belly and appear similar to Roughlegs. Wingtips shorter than tail tip. Cere is greenish. FLIGHT.—Pale surface on primaries and primary coverts make all of outer wing pale. White uppertail coverts somewhat similar to Roughleg's white uppertail coverts and base of tail. Tail has multiple narrow dark bands.

OTHER NAMES: Roughleg, Roughie. *Spanish:* Aguililla Ártica. *French:* Buse Pattue.

REFERENCES: Baicich and Harrison 1997; Cadman et al. 1987; Clark 1999; Dodge 1988–1997; Forsman 1999; Godfrey 1986; Kellogg 2000; Olson and Arsenault 2000; Palmer 1988; Stevenson and Anderson 1994; Wheeler and Clark 1995.

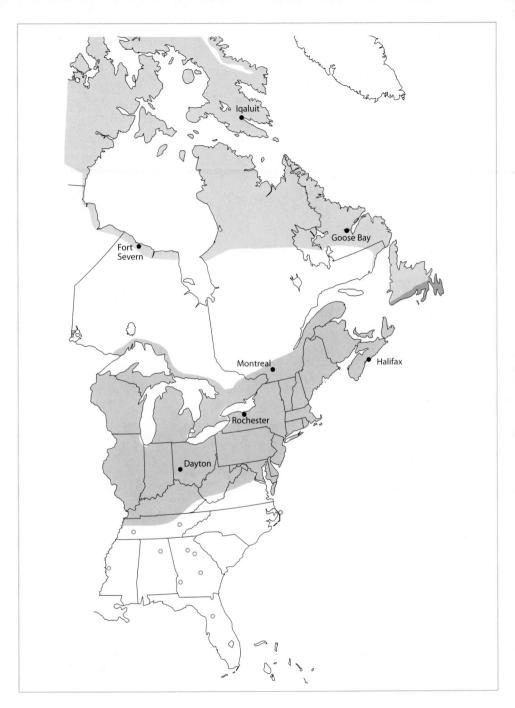

ROUGH-LEGGED HAWK, *Buteo lagopus sanctijohannis:* Fairly common. Numbers vary with fluctuations in summer prey abundance. Rare south of regular winter range. Females winter farther north than males.

Plate 404. Rough-legged Hawk, adult male light morph (lightly marked type) [Dec.] ▪ White forehead and outer lores, thin dark eyeline, dark brown iris. ▪ Underparts streaked on breast, un-marked on upper belly, unmarked or lightly spotted or barred on mid-belly, flanks, and leg feathers. Tarsi feathered to toes. ▪ *Note:* Palest type.

Plate 405. Rough-legged Hawk, adult male light morph (lightly marked type) [Jan.] ▪ White forehead and outer lores, thin dark eyeline, dark malar mark, dark brown iris. ▪ Dark mottled bib; white belly; lightly spotted or barred flanks. ▪ Wingtips extend past tail tip. ▪ Wide black subterminal tail band; narrow inner dark band.

Plate 406. Rough-legged Hawk, adult male light morph (moderately marked type) [Mar.] ▪ White forehead and outer lores, thin dark eyeline, dark brown iris. ▪ Dark mottled bib; white necklace on upper belly; mid-belly, flanks, and leg feathers are barred. Tarsi feathered to toes. ▪ Wide black subterminal tail band; narrow inner dark band.

Plate 407. Rough-legged Hawk, adult male light morph (moderately marked type) [Nov.] ▪ Dark head, whitish throat with white forehead and outer lores, thin dark eyeline, dark brown iris. ▪ Black upperparts mottled with gray. ▪ Tail has wide black subterminal band, 3 progressively narrower inner dark bands; base of tail white.

Plate 408. Rough-legged Hawk, adult male light morph (moderately marked type) [Feb.] ▪ Black upperparts mottled with gray. ▪ Gray remiges barred with black, including wide black band on rear edge. Coverts mottled with gray. ▪ Tail has wide black subterminal band, 3 progressively narrower inner dark bands; base of tail white.

Plate 409. Rough-legged Hawk, adult male light morph (lightly marked type) [Dec.] ▪ Sides of breast streaked. Flanks lightly barred, leg feathers are barred. Tarsi feathered. ▪ Lacks black carpal patch; black only on primary greater coverts. ▪ Wide black subterminal tail band; narrow dark inner band. ▪ *Note: Same bird as on plate 404.*

Plate 410. Rough-legged Hawk, adult male light morph (lightly marked type) [Dec.] ▪ Dark mottled bib; white belly unmarked, flanks lightly spotted and barred. ▪ Large black carpal patch on wrists. White remiges lightly barred. ▪ White underside of tail has wide black subterminal band, narrow partial inner black bands.

Plate 411. Rough-legged Hawk, adult male light morph (moderately marked type) [Apr.] ▪ Dark mottled bib; whitish necklace; belly, flanks, and leg feathers barred gray and black. ▪ Large black carpal patch. ▪ Tail white with wide black subterminal band, several progressively narrower inner dark bands.

Plate 412. Rough-legged Hawk, adult female light morph (lightly marked type) [Jan.] ▪ Pale head with thin dark eyeline; dark malar mark; white forehead and outer lores; dark brown iris. ▪ Lightly mottled bib, solid dark flanks, lightly mottled belly. Brown upperparts. ▪ Wingtips equal to tail tip. ▪ *Note:* Similarly marked males have spotted or barred flanks, gray upperparts.

Plate 413. Rough-legged Hawk, adult female light morph (moderately marked type) [Mar.] ▪ White forehead and outer lores blend with pale crown; dark brown iris. ▪ Mottled bib; broad white necklace on upper belly. Split-bellied type has split down center of blackish belly; solid brownish black flanks. Barred leg feathers; tarsi feathered to toes. ▪ Wingtips extend past tail tip.

Plate 414. Rough-legged Hawk, adult female light morph (moderately marked type) [Dec.] ▪ Thin dark eyeline; dark malar mark; white forehead that blends with pale crown; dark brown iris. ▪ Streaked mottled bib has minimal necklace demarcation. Dark-bellied type with brownish black band on belly and flanks. ▪ Single, wide black subterminal tail band.

Plate 415. Rough-legged Hawk, adult female light morph (heavily marked type) [Dec.] ▪ White outer lores and forehead; dark brown iris. ▪ Nearly solid dark bib; narrow, mottled tawny necklace; dark-bellied type brownish black belly and flanks. Barred leg feathers. White undertail coverts. Brown upperparts. ▪ *Note:* Heaviest marked type.

Plate 416. Rough-legged Hawk, adult female light morph (moderately marked type) [Mar.] ▪ Pale head with thin dark eyeline; dark brown iris. ▪ Dark brown upperparts have some pale mottling on scapulars. ▪ Wingtips equal to tail tip. ▪ White base on tail. Some may have narrow white base on tail or lack white base on dorsal surface. ▪ *Note:* Same bird as on plate 413.

Plate 417. Rough-legged Hawk, adult female light morph (all types) [Dec.] ▪ Brown upperparts. ▪ Uniformly brown remiges but may have slightly paler panel on primaries. ▪ Basal 1/3 of tail white. ▪ *Note:* Some moderately and heavily marked types have 3 narrow inner dark tail bands.

Plate 418. Rough-legged Hawk, adult female light morph (moderately marked type) [Nov.] ▪ Lightly streaked bib; broad necklace; split-bellied type with tawny center strip on belly, solid brownish black flanks. Barred leg feathers. ▪ Large black carpal patch. ▪ Wide black subterminal tail band with narrow partial inner band.

Plate 419. Rough-legged Hawk, adult female light morph (moderately marked type) [Nov.] ▪ Dark, mottled bib; thin tawny necklace; dark-bellied type solid belly and flanks. ▪ Large black carpal patch. ▪ Wide black subterminal tail band.

Plate 420. Rough-legged Hawk, adult male/female dark morph (brown type) [Nov.] ▪ White outer lores and forehead. Brown head. Dark brown iris. ▪ Brown breast often mottled with tawny-rufous; belly and flanks often darker brownish black. May have white or tawny speckling on breast, especially at breast-belly junction. Feathered tarsi. ▪ Wingtips extend past tail tip.

Plate 421. Rough-legged Hawk, adult male/female dark morph (brown type) [Mar.] ▪ Pale-headed type with large tawny/white supercilium and auricular areas. White outer lores and forehead. Thin dark eyeline. Dark brown iris. ▪ Brown breast mottled with tawny; belly and flanks brownish black.

Plate 422. Rough-legged Hawk, adult male dark morph (black type) [Nov.] ▪ White outer lores and forehead. Black head. Dark brown iris. ▪ Black underparts, including undertail coverts. ▪ Distinctly banded type tail with narrow black and white bands, wide black subterminal band. ▪ Wingtips extend past tail tip.

Plate 423. Rough-legged Hawk, adult male/female dark morph (brown type) [Nov.] ▪ White outer lores and forehead. Dark brown iris. ▪ Scapulars mottled with gray (females are uniformly brown). ▪ Wingtips extend to tail tip. ▪ Distinctly banded type tail has 3 or 4 narrow white or pale gray bands. ▪ *Note:* Some adult females have similarly banded tail.

Plate 424. Rough-legged Hawk, adult male/female dark morph (any type) [Jan.] ▪ Distinctly banded type tail can be found on either sex: 3 or 4 white or pale gray bands on black tail. Common trait on males, uncommon on females.

Plate 425. Rough-legged Hawk, adult male/female dark morph (brown type) [Nov.] ▪ Partially banded type tail on either sex: or 4 indistinct, narrow pale gray bands on gray tail; wide black subterminal band. Only females can have unbanded type plain gray dorsal tail surface with wide black subterminal band.

Plate 426. Rough-legged Hawk, adult male/female dark morph (brown type) [Mar.] ▪ Dark brown underparts. ▪ Large black carpal patches somewhat darker than brownish wingcoverts. Dark brown axillaries often barred. ▪ Distinctly banded type tail with wide black subterminal band and up to 5 narrow black and white bands. ▪ *Note:* Sexed as probable female by large size.

Plate 427. Rough-legged Hawk, adult male/female dark morph (brown type) [Nov.] ▪ Pale supercilium and auriculars. ▪ Dark brown underparts. ▪ Large black carpal patches somewhat darker than brownish wingcoverts. Axillaries often barred. ▪ Partially banded type tail with wide black subterminal band, thin dark inner bands. ▪ *Note:* Common tail pattern for both sexes.

Plate 428. Rough-legged Hawk, adult male/female dark morph (brown type) [Nov.] ▪ Tawny-rufous streaking on breast; brownish black belly, flanks, and leg feathers. Large black carpal patches contrast with rufous wingcoverts. ▪ Single wide black subterminal tail band. ▪ *Note:* Palest type of dark morph. Sexed as probable female by large size.

Plate 429. Rough-legged Hawk, adult male dark morph (black type) [Feb.] ▪ Uniformly black head, body, and underwing coverts. ▪ Distinctly banded type tail with 3 or 4 narrow black and white bands, wide black subterminal band. Remiges may be more heavily barred than on brown type dark morphs.

Plate 430. Rough-legged Hawk, subadult male light morph [Dec.] ▪ Medium brown iris. White outer lores and forehead. ▪ Breast streaking may extend to top of dark belly and flanks (as on juveniles). Flanks may be solid brownish black or barred. ▪ Single wide black subterminal tail band. ▪ *Note:* Males often have female-like traits.

Plate 431. Rough-legged Hawk, subadult male/female light morph [Jan.] ▪ Similar to adult but retains several faded, worn, brown juvenile upperwing coverts and remiges. Retained juvenile secondaries are shorter than new adult feathers and lack wide black rear band. (Retained juvenile outer primaries not visible at this angle.) ▪ White band on inner half of tail.

Plate 432. Rough-legged Hawk, subadult male/female light morph [Mar.] ▪ Dark-bellied type band on belly and flanks. ▪ Large black carpal patches. Retains juvenile remiges: primaries faded brownish, secondaries shorter, lack black band. Left wing has 2 retained juvenile primaries, right wing has 3 retained primaries. Secondaries s3 and 4, s7 and 8 are retained juvenile feathers.

Plate 433. Rough-legged Hawk, subadult male/female dark morph (brown type) [Nov.] ▪ Pale head. ▪ Tawny-rufous streaking on breast; brownish black belly, flanks, leg feathers. ▪ Large black carpal patches; axillaries dark brown. Outer 3 primaries faded brown juvenile; secondaries s4 and 9 are juvenile feathers. ▪ Partially banded type tail.

Plate 434. Rough-legged Hawk, juvenile light morph [Feb.] ▪ Pale brown iris; thin dark eyeline. ▪ Light to heavy breast streaking extends to belly and flanks. Belly and flanks brown, lack blackish tone of adults and subadults. ▪ Secondaries dark brown (barred on older ages). Wingtips extend to tail tip. ▪ Gray undertail.

Plate 435. Rough-legged Hawk, juvenile light morph [Feb.] ▪ Pale brown iris; thin dark eyeline; partial dark malar mark. ▪ Brown upperparts with pale edges on scapular. Dark flanks. Lightly streaked leg feathers; tarsi feathered to toes. ▪ Long wings extend to tail tip. Dark secondaries; pale edges on coverts. ▪ White base of tail.

Plate 436. Rough-legged Hawk, juvenile light morph [Jan.] ▪ Dark brown band on belly and flanks; spotted leg feathers. ▪ Large black carpal patches, often mottled. Nearly unmarked coverts, including axillaries. Rectangular window on primaries. Gray rear edge of wings. ▪ Gray band on distal half of tail, white on inner half.

Plate 437. Rough-legged Hawk, juvenile light morph [Dec.] ▪ White rectangular panel on primaries. Dark secondaries. ▪ Basal 1/3 of tail white, distal 2/3 brown. Subterminal region sometimes a bit darker.

Plate 438. Rough-legged Hawk, juvenile intermediate morph [Oct.] ▪ Heavy breast streaking extends to solid dark belly and flank band. Tawny leg feathers spotted. White undertail coverts. ▪ Large black carpal patches; rufous-tawny coverts; dark brown axillaries. ▪ Basal 1/3 of tail is white. ▪ *Note:* Similar to heavier marked light morph but axillaries dark, coverts more rufous.

Plate 439. Rough-legged Hawk, juvenile dark morph (brown type) [Jan.] ▪ Pale, tawny-streaked head with thin dark eyeline; white outer lores and forehead form white mask. Yellow cere. Pale brown iris. ▪ Tawny-rufous streaking on breast contrasts with solid brown belly and flanks. Tawny tarsi.

Plate 440. Rough-legged Hawk, juvenile dark morph (brown type) [Feb.] ▪ Pale, tawny-streaked head with thin dark eyeline; white outer lores and forehead form white mask. Yellow cere. Pale brown iris. ▪ Brown upperparts with dark secondaries. ▪ Brown dorsal surface of tail may be unmarked, partially banded, or have 3 distinct pale gray bands.

Plate 441. Rough-legged Hawk, juvenile dark morph (brown type) [Feb.] ▪ Tawny head. ▪ Tawny speckling on breast; dark brown belly, flanks, and leg feathers. White tips on dark under-tail coverts. ▪ Large black carpal patches contrast with rufous coverts; axillaries dark brown. All wingtips are dark.

Plate 442. Rough-legged Hawk, juvenile dark morph (black type) [Mar.] ▪ Uniformly brownish black head, body, and wing coverts. ▪ Banded type gray tail has 3 narrow gray bands; subterminal band slightly darker. All wingtips are dark. ▪ *Note:* Common plumage on males, very uncommon on females. Missing a primary on left wing.

GOLDEN EAGLE
(*Aquila chrysaetos*)

AGES: Adult, four interim basic/subadult ages (basic/subadult I–IV) that correspond to 1- to 4-year-old birds that are in their second to fifth years of life, and juvenile birds in their first year of life. Individual plumage variation is minimal.

Adult plumage is usually attained as a 5-year-old when in its sixth year of life. Sexes are similar, but tail patterns are sometimes marginally different.

Subadults slowly alter from juvenile to adult plumage characters through partial annual molts. Sexes are similar, but tail patterns of older subadults are sometimes marginally different based on sex. Subadult age characters are most prevalent on the remiges and rectrices, and are most visible in flight and when seen from a dorsal angle when perched. Basic/subadult III and IV are not readily separable from adults, particularly when perched. Basic/subadult II is fairly separable from other subadults and adults when in flight. Basic/subadult I is readily separable from all other ages when flying or perching.

Juvenile plumage is retained for the first year. Sexes are similar. Remiges and rectrices are longer and more pointed at tips than in older ages. Because of this, their wings are broader and tails are longer than older ages.

MOLT: Accipitridae wing and tail molt pattern. Wing and tail molt is complex and variable, and it is important to understand the various molt centers and molt waves (*see* chapter 4). Molt timing varies with latitude, diet, and other factors. Molt may be suspended when nesting or migrating. Only a portion of body, remix, and rectrix feathers are replaced each year. Young subadults have one or two molt waves in progress at the same time. Older subadults and adults may have two or three molt waves in progress with two or three ages of remiges and rectrices.

Molt data are based on Edelstam (1984); Forsman (1999); W. S. Clark unpubl. data; pers. comm.; and BKW obs. of wild birds and museum specimens.

First prebasic molt.—Molt takes place during the second year of life when a basic/subadult I. Molt generally begins in Jun. and ends in Oct. or Nov. This first molt can be very slow, and many individuals replace only a small fraction of body, remix, and rectrix feathers. Most of the head and neck feathers are replaced. On most birds, a large amount of breast, belly, and flank feathers are replaced; however, most leg feathers and undertail coverts are not molted. Unusually slow-molting birds may replace most head and neck feathers, but few, if any, feathers on the ventral regions. Many back and scapular feathers are molted. Dorsal and ventral areas appear blotchy, with new dark feathers among old and faded juvenile feathers.

Remix molt begins on the innermost primary (p1) and advances outwardly. Slow-molting birds molt only the inner three primaries (p1–3), but many molt p1–5. Slow-molting birds may molt some tertials, usually at least the innermost one (s17), but sometimes all three (s17–15: in that order). Many also molt outermost, middle, and inner secondaries (s1 or sometimes s1 and 2, s5, or sometimes s5 and 6, and s14 or sometimes s14 and 13). The respective greater upperwing coverts molt with the molting secondaries; however, lesser upperwing coverts often molt ahead of respective remiges and greater upperwing coverts. Unmolted remiges are worn and faded juvenile feathers.

At most, only a few underwing coverts are replaced. New feathers can be more adultlike or retain similar juvenile characters (e.g., white areas). Only a few upperwing coverts are replaced, and the dorsal wing appears largely worn and bleached with a few new, fresh dark feathers.

Rectrix molt is often very slow. Slow-molting birds replace only the deck set (r1). The outermost set (r6) may also be replaced. Some birds replace the r2 set, which is somewhat atypical of Accipitridae sequence. All other rectrices are retained, worn juvenile feathers. New rectrices have a mix of adult and juvenile characters.

Second prebasic molt.—Molt takes place during the third year of life when a basic/subadult II. Molt begins mainly in spring but can begin in mid-winter. A few are molting in Feb. and

Mar. and most are molting in Apr. All body feathers are fully replaced, but not all of the subdult/basic I feathers are replaced, so the body appears blotchy.

Remix molt begins where it left off in the previous molt. Molt may become irregular and not follow prescribed sequence. On the primaries, it begins with s4 or 6, then replaces p5–8 or p7–9 for the first time. P9 and 10 or only p10 are retained, very old worn and faded brown juvenile feathers. P1–3 are replaced for the second time and are newer and darker than the other primaries. *Note:* There are now three ages of feathers on the primaries. On the secondaries, s8 and 9, or s9 (which is the last secondary to molt), are often retained juvenile, but may also retain s10 and 11. All other secondaries were replaced either in the first prebasic molt or in this molt. S4 is one of the newest and darkest secondary as it was one of the last to molt and thus not subject to wearing and fading. The three tertials (s15–17) may be replaced for the second time. *Note:* There are now three ages of secondaries. Newly molted feathers are adultlike.

Most underwing and upperwing coverts are replaced. The mix of old and new upperwing coverts gives the dorsal surface of the wing a blotchy appearance.

Rectrix molt also begins where it left off in the previous molt, but r1 set may molt for the second time. Most or all rectrices are replaced by the end of the molt, with r2–5 or r3–5 being replaced for the first time. During part of the year, there are three ages of rectrices: juvenile, subadult I, and subadult II. Newly molted feathers are fairly adultlike.

Third prebasic molt.—Molt takes place during the fourth year of life when a basic/subadult III. Molt occurs from Feb. or Mar. through Nov., but can occur all winter. Some body feathers are partially replaced for a second or third time.

Remix molt continues from where it left off in the previous molt. P9 and 10 or p10 are replaced for the first time, and birds finally replaces all juvenile primaries. Inner primary molt may continue, starting at p2–4 and p1 may be replaced for the third time. All secondaries, including s9, are fully replaced. The sequence of molt waves may begin again with s1 and 5 being replaced for the second time.

However, irregular sequences of secondary molt occur, and it becomes difficult to label an exact molt sequence. Newly molted feathers are very adultlike.

Rectrix molt continues from where it left off or becomes irregular in sequence. Only a few feathers are molted, and there is a mixture of new, dark and adultlike rectrices and old, faded, and juvenile-like rectrices. R3 and 4 sets are often old subadult/basic I or II and have more juvenile-like characters.

Fourth prebasic molt.—Molt takes place during the fifth year of life, when a basic/subadult IV. Molt takes place from Feb. or Mar. through Nov., but can occur all winter. The body keeps replacing some feathers and still retains a blotchy appearance due to a mixture of feather ages.

Remix and rectrix molt often becomes highly irregular with multiple molt waves in progress. All newly molted feathers are nearly adultlike, but may still retain some juvenile-like traits on r2–5.

Subsequent prebasic molts.—Molt takes place annually from the sixth year of life; occurs from Feb. or Mar. through Nov., but can be all winter. As with previous molts, only a portion of body, wing, and tail feathers are replaced each year. With multi-ages of feathers, this plumage nearly always appears blotchy.

SUBSPECIES: Polytypic, but only one race, *A. c. canadensis,* inhabits North America. This race is also found from cen. Siberia to ne. Russia.

Four additional subspecies inhabit the Palearctic region: (1) Nominate *A. c. chrysaetos* is in Europe and east to cen. Russia. Medium-sized and palest of the races. (2) *A. c. homeyeri* is in n. Africa east to Crete, the Middle East, Saudi Arabia, and to Iran. Smaller and darker than nominate and has a darker nape. (3) *A. c. daphanea* is in e. Iran to cen. China. Averages largest of the races and intermediate in color between the two previous subspecies. (4) *A. c. japonica* inhabits Japan and Korea. This is the smallest and darkest race. Its nape feathers are quite rufous and have white on the inner webs of the rectrices.

COLOR MORPHS: None.

SIZE: A large raptor. Males average smaller but overlap with females. Juveniles are somewhat longer than older ages because of their longer tails. In flight, they may also present the illusion of being larger because of their broader secondaries. Length: 27–33 in. (69–84 cm); wingspan: 72–87 in. (183–221 cm).

SPECIES TRAITS: HEAD.—The distal half of the bill is blackish and the basal half is pale blue. Prominent yellow cere and gape. Gape extends to the rear of the eyes. Nape and hindneck are pale tawny or golden and contrast with the dark crown, auriculars, and front of the neck. BODY.—Dark brown, including the leg feathers. **Feathered tarsi are white or buff-colored.** The undertail coverts are either dark brown or tawny-rufous. The long feathers of the undertail coverts often conceal tail patterns on perched and gliding birds. WINGS (dorsal).—**Six "fingers" on the outer primaries.** Median and one or two rows of lesser upperwing coverts are paler than the rest of the coverts and remiges. WINGS (ventral).—Dark brown underwing coverts and axillaries contrast with paler grayish remiges and create a variable two-toned appearance. **There is a tawny patch on the wrist area and a tawny front edge of the inner half of the wing.**

ADULT TRAITS: HEAD.—Iris color may be yellow, yellowish brown, orangish brown, or medium brown. Iris is rarely dark brown (W. S. Clark unpubl. data). **Tawny nape has a mixture of new dark and faded old feathering but always appears quite pale.** BODY.—Since molt is not complete on all body feathers each year, dorsal and ventral areas appear blotched with a mixture of new and old, dark, and faded feathers. WINGS (dorsal).—There is a distinct pale bar on the median and first one or two rows of lesser upperwing coverts caused by excessively worn and faded feathers. The dark tertials and inner greater upperwing coverts are often marbled with pale gray designs. WINGS (ventral).—The inner four primaries and all secondaries have a wide black band on the trailing edge. These same remiges typically have a pale gray marbled or barred pattern. The underwing appears distinctly two-toned with pale remiges. *Note:* Molting birds, particularly in summer and early fall, often have white blotches on the underwing coverts caused by missing feathers. TAIL.—Three basic patterns that are somewhat sexually dimorphic and visible on dorsal and ventral surfaces: (1) *Wide-banded type* (mainly females).—Wide black or brown terminal band with two or three

wide gray bands that get progressively narrower towards the basal part of the tail. Irregularly formed moderately wide or narrow black or brown bars separate the gray bands. (2) *Narrow-banded type* (males and females).—Black or brown tail has three narrow gray bands with a wide black or brown terminal band. Gray bands are often irregularly formed. (3) *Partial-banded type* (mainly males).—Black or brown tail has narrow and incompletely formed pale gray bands. Sometimes only a single pale band shows. The pale bands may be very diffused or lack, making the tail appear solid dark.

BASIC IV (SUBADULT IV) TRAITS: HEAD—As on adults, including any of the various iris colors. BODY.—As on adults, with blotchy array of faded old feathers mixed with new dark feathers. WINGS.—Mainly as on adults. Individuals that had extensive white on the remiges as juveniles and younger subadults may still have a very small amount of white on the basal area of the inner eight primaries. The white feather area may be a narrow strip on the inside edge or a small spot. Newly molted remiges are mainly adultlike and have little if any white. Upperwing coverts are adultlike with the faded and worn tawny bar. *Note:* Due to missing feathers, molting birds may show a variable amount of white blotching on the underwing coverts. TAIL.—As on adults except may have very small white areas on some rectrices, particularly r2–5 or r3–5. White areas may be visible only when the tail is fanned.

BASIC III (SUBADULT III) TRAITS: HEAD.—As on adults, including iris color; however, irises are rarely yellow. BODY.—As on adults and subadult IV, with faded old feathers mixed with new dark ones. WINGS.—Primarily adultlike since all juvenile remiges have been replaced. Similar to subadult IV, but may have larger white areas on the underside of the inner eight primaries and possibly on some secondaries. All juvenile remiges are replaced in this age class. Outermost primaries (p9 and 10 or just p10) are new and dark. New subadult remiges may have white areas on the feathers. Upperwing coverts are adultlike with the faded and worn tawny bar. *Note:* Molting birds may show a variable amount of white blotching on the underwing coverts caused by missing feathers. TAIL.—Rectrices are a mix of two or three ages: subadult I, II, and III or subadult II and III. Feather pattern is a mix of adultlike gray barring and juvenile-like white areas, especially retained subadult I feathers (one or two feathers in r2–5 or r3–5 sets).

BASIC II (SUBADULT II) TRAITS: HEAD.—As on adults, but iris color is similar to subadult III. BODY.—As on adults and older subadults, with faded old feathers mixed with new dark ones. WINGS.—Somewhat adultlike but has a mix of very old, faded, and worn retained juvenile remiges. Outermost one or two primaries (p9 or 10, or both) are frayed and worn, pale brown juvenile; this condition is a distinctive trait of this age class. All other primaries are newer subadult feathers; the inner four have a wide black band on the trailing edge as on older subadults and adults. Most secondaries are newer subadult and appear fairly adultlike, with the broad black band on the trailing edge and inner gray marbling or barring. New subadult remiges may also have a considerable amount of white on them. Retained juvenile secondaries (p9, sometimes p4, and maybe p10 and 11) are a paler brownish and lack the black terminal band. Retained juvenile feathers are most visible when in flight. Upperwing coverts are like older subadults and adults with the worn and faded tawny bar and a mix of old and new feathers. The underwing coverts are fully molted for the first time. *Note:* Molting birds may have a variable amount of white blotches on the underwing coverts caused by missing feathers. TAIL.—Rectrices are a mix of three ages: juvenile, subadult I, and subadult II. The deck set (r1) is often quite adultlike or may have a mix of juvenile-like whitish with mottling and marbling patterns on the basal region. The outermost set (r6) is also quite adultlike. There is considerable rectrix molt in the early and mid-stages of this age class. The r3 set is replaced for the first time with adultlike feathers, and the r2 set may have already been replaced or will replaced shortly after r3. The r4 and 5 sets are retained juvenile for a while but usually molt by the end of the age class and may molt simultaneously with r3 and 2 sets. Overall appearance of the tail is a dark adultlike center and outer areas with white juvenile-like feathering isolated in two sections between the dark areas.

BASIC I (SUBADULT I) TRAITS: HEAD.—As on adults, but iris color is likely to be brownish. BODY.—As on older subadults and adults, with faded old feathers mixed with new dark feathers. The leg feathers are mainly retained juvenile and are paler than the rest of the body, which has attained many new and darker feathers. WINGS.—Pattern of old and new feathering makes this age class easy to categorize. The new inner primaries, p1–3 or p1–5, are easy to see when in flight. The secondaries may be nearly all faded brown retained juvenile feathers. Juveniles that had extensive amount of white as juveniles still show it in this age class. **Perched birds are easy to age because much of the upperwing coverts is uniformly faded and worn juvenile feathering, with only a scattering of new dark feathers. The pale tawny bar is not readily apparent because of uniform extreme wearing and fading. On some, the newly molted tertials and s14, and respective greater upperwing coverts, are darker and contrast with the paler retained juvenile secondaries.** The outer half of the first row of lesser upperwing coverts may molt ahead of the respective greater upperwing coverts and appear as a dark strip. Large white areas may appear on the basal region of the inner greater upperwing coverts and some first-row lesser upperwing coverts due to molting, missing feathers. The underwing coverts are largely juvenile. *Note:* The underwing coverts may show a variable amount of white blotches due to missing feathers. TAIL.—The deck set (r1) always molts into subadult character and is often fairly adultlike. On birds with more adultlike r1 sets, the tail is split by the two dark rectrices contrasting to the white retained juvenile outer sets. On some, the r6 set also has adultlike darker color and markings and may outline the tail. Most new subadult feathers have partial dark barring, marbling, or mottling at the junction of the basal white area and dark distal area. The dark terminal band on the retained juvenile rectrices is faded brown, and much of each pointed feather tip is worn, so tail appears more rounded than in fresh juvenile plumage.

JUVENILE TRAITS: HEAD.—By fall, exhibits the pale tawny nape and hindneck as on older ages. Because of minimal fading and wearing, the nape and hindneck are dark tawny in mid- and late summer on nestlings and recently fledged birds. Iris color is medium or dark brown.

BODY.—Since all feathers are the same age with uniform wearing and fading, the body is uniformly dark brown. WINGS.—The greater upperwing coverts, first two rows of upperwing coverts, and tertials are slightly paler than the rest of the dorsal wing surface. (This is the same region on which older ages have the pale tawny bar.) The remiges have three patterns: (1) *Extensive white type.*—A large white area on ventral surface of the inner four to eight primaries and a white strip on the basal region of most secondaries. On the dorsal surface, there is a large square white patch on the inner five or so primaries. *Note:* Uncommon type. (2) *Moderate white type.*—A medium-sized white patch on the ventral surface of the inner three to five primaries and sometimes a small white patch on the inner one to three secondaries. On the dorsal surface, there is a small white patch on the inner one to three primaries. *Note:* Common type. (3) *All-dark type.*—Ventral surface of the remiges is uniformly dark. At most, there may be a sliver of white on the innermost primary. All types may have faint, narrow barring on the inner three or four primaries. TAIL.—Somewhat wedge-shaped. Broad dark terminal band that is neatly separated from a broad inner white band. At close range, dark mottling shows on the distal white area next to the dark band. On some, grayish marbling adorns the dark band on the deck set. Two variations: (1) *Moderate white type.*—The dark and white bands are equal width. When the tail is closed, the long undertail coverts reach or extend slightly into the dark terminal band. *Note:* Common type. (2) *Extensive white type.*—The dark band is fairly narrow. When the tail is closed, a white area is always visible between the long undertail coverts and the dark band. *Note:* Uncommon type.

BARTHELEMYI VARIANT: Unusual variation that can be found on all ages and sexes (Palmer 1988).—As in typical birds but there is a small to large white epaulet on the front of the scapular tract. *Note:* Rare plumage type. Basic (subadult) I photographed by author in Duluth, Minn. in Oct. 2002.

ABNORMAL PLUMAGES: Partial albinism is rare (Clark and Wheeler 2001).

HABITAT: Summer.—On the tundra, found in remote areas with cliffs and embankments. In the boreal forest, inhabits open and semi-open areas in rugged upland and montane regions.

Winter.—Mainly found in semi-open montane regions, especially areas with open "bald" landscapes. Lesser numbers are in dry or wet semi-open lowland regions with meadows, rivers, lakes, and marshes (and often associate with Bald Eagles).

Migration.—Habitat is similar to that of winter.

HABITS: Golden Eagles are wary in the East. Long periods may be spent flying or perching. Pairs remain together year-round, even if they migrate. They often perch near each other throughout the year.

In the East, Golden Eagles are rarely seen perched on utility poles. Large, exposed branches and rock outcrops are favored perch locations; however, they readily sit on the ground.

In winter, a few Golden Eagles may feed and roost with more common and gregarious Bald Eagles.

FEEDING: Perch and aerial hunter. Pairs may cooperatively hunt but younger birds hunt singly. Eagles often capture prey much larger and heavier than themselves. Diet varies regionally and seasonally.

Arctic Hares, Snowshoe Hares, Woodchucks, muskrats, Rock Ptarmigan, Willow Ptarmigan, Canada Geese, and several duck and seabird species are typical prey for the bulk of Canadian Golden Eagles in the summer. Larger species such as Red and Arctic foxes, and possibly young Woodland Caribou are also preyed upon. In Maine, Golden Eagles feed extensively on Great Blue Herons and American Bitterns. Tennessee and Georgia populations may feed on Woodchucks, muskrats, Eastern Cottontail Rabbits, Eastern Gray Squirrels, Eastern Fox Squirrels, and various heron and waterfowl species.

Throughout the eagle's winter range, Eastern Cottontail Rabbits, Eastern Gray Squirrels, Eastern Fox Squirrels, muskrats, several duck species, Canada Geese, Snow Geese, and Great Blue Herons form the majority of prey.

Avian prey may be captured while they are airborne or on the ground.

Carrion is readily eaten in all seasons but is especially important in winter. In summer, eagles feed on dead seals and Woodland Caribou calves that are still-born or killed by Gray Wolves. During fall and winter, the increasingly large population of White-tailed Deer affords scavenging opportunities, with eagles feeding on those that die naturally and those that are wounded by hunters and die later. Dead waterfowl are also important in these seasons.

FLIGHT: Wings are held in a low dihedral when soaring and gliding. At times, wings may be raised to a high dihedral when soaring. Kiting regularly occurs in strong winds. Wings are held on a flat plane when kiting. Powered flight is used frequently. The upstroke and downstroke are an equidistant up-and-down motion. Flapping sequences may be irregularly interspersed with periods of gliding, or birds may flap for considerable lengths of time.

Perch hunting involves a direct attack on prey by diving from a high perch or launching into flight and coursing low over the ground. Aerial hunting may be initiated from high altitudes while soaring or kiting and from low altitudes while kiting or in random surprise-and-flush flights.

VOICE: Virtually silent. Rarely heard in the wild, even when approached at nest sites. Captive birds emit a moderately high-pitched yapping *yeh, yeh, yeh* when excited or agitated.

STATUS AND DISTRIBUTION: Overall *rare* to *very uncommon* in the East. The Golden Eagle population appears to be increasing in e. Canada. Consistently larger numbers have been seen in recent years at eastern hawkwatches. In e. Canada, the increase may be attributed to the 1970s ban of DDT, banning of strychnine poisoning for Coyotes and Gray Wolves, reduced use of leg-hold traps to capture furbearers, increased restrictions on guns, and greater public awareness and appreciation of raptors.

Reforestation of open areas has caused habitat loss, and pesticide contamination and human disturbance has caused nesting failures.

Summer.—CANADA: *Labrador.*—A substantial number breed in the northern part of the province and a few in the southern part. *New Brunswick.*—Summering birds may occur in highland areas of the northern part of the province, but breeding is not confirmed. *Nova Scotia.*—Summering birds and possible breeders are occasionally seen on Cape Breton Peninsula. *Ontario.*—Fewer than 10 pairs breed in the northern part of the province. *Québec.*—Data mainly by N. David and M. Gosselin: Along with Labrador, most of the breeding population

in the East is found in this province. An estimated 200 pairs and 400 juveniles and subadults inhabit Québec in the summer. Virtually all pairs are found north of a line from the southern tip of James Bay east to Sept-Iles (magenta line on range map). The largest numbers are along the east shore of Hudson Bay and on the Ungava Peninsula. A few isolated pairs breed on the Gaspé Peninsula. A few pairs may breed in montane areas north of Québec City.

UNITED STATES: Golden Eagles historically bred only in Maine, New Hampshire, and New York Nonbreeding birds are occasionally seen in montane regions of the s. Appalachian Mts. but breeding has never been confirmed. *Georgia.*—One pair bred on Pigeon Mt. in Walker Co. in the 1990s. These birds were from a large captive release program in Georgia. *Maine.*—Data by C. Todd and A. Weik: One pair, but their last nesting attempt was in 1997. This pair had nesting failures for 14 years. There have been 11 eyries in the state but only three have been used in the last 25 years, and only three eaglets have been produced during this period. The main reasons for nesting failures are organophosphate pesticides contaminating major prey species such as Great Blue Herons and encroaching forests on formerly open areas that inhibit feeding on uncontaminated prey such as Snowshoe Hare. *Michigan.*— An unusual record of a pair that nested in Kalkaska Co. in 1997. *New York.*—Few pairs were historically known to nest. From the 1940s to 1970s, there were six confirmed and five probable nest sites. The last successful nesting occurred in 1970 in Hamilton Co. In 1979, a pair attempted nesting at the same location and, until 1981, were occasionally seen there. *Tennessee.*—Golden Eagles nested near Cordell Lake in Jackson Co. in 1993, 1994, 1996, 2000, and 2001. Nesting pairs were from the Georgia release program (*See* Conservation).

Winter.—Virtually all wintering occurs in the U.S. Golden Eagles are found in low densities in all areas. The largest numbers winter from s. New England south in mainly montane regions of the cen. and s. Appalachian Mts. in North Carolina, Tennessee, Virginia, and West Virginia. A few regularly winter in isolated areas in Wisconsin, s. Michigan, w. and s. Illinois, s. Indiana. Very few winter in w. Kentucky, Louisiana, Ohio, and w. Tennessee. Juveniles irregularly occur south to the Gulf of Mexico and into Florida. Isolated wintering has occurred in ne. New Brunswick. Telemetry data of four adults from n. Québec showed their reaching wintering grounds in Michigan, Pennsylvania, Tennessee, and West Virginia. from early Nov. to early Dec. One bird continued to shift farther south into early Jan.

Movements.—Short- to moderate-distance migrant. Released birds in Tennessee and Georgia do not migrate but young birds will move out of natal territories. The majority of migrants use the Appalachian Mt. corridor in the U.S. A few birds move along the Mid-Atlantic Coast and around the Great Lakes.

Fall migration: Juveniles move first with subadults and adults moving later. At the hawkwatch near Tadoussec, Québec, juveniles may appear in early Sep., but are often not seen until early Oct. At hawkwatches along w. Lake Erie in Ontario and Michigan, the first juveniles are seen as early as mid-Sep., but typically are not seen until early or mid-Oct. Peak juvenile movement period is in late Oct. along Lake Erie. Along the Appalachian Mts. in Pennsylvania and Mid-Atlantic Coast in New Jersey, juveniles appear in early Oct. and peak in late Oct. or early Nov. Highest numbers in the East are seen along the Appalachian Mts. at the Waggoner's Gap Hawkwatch west of Carlisle, Pa.

According to telemetry of the four adults from n. Québec, they did not leave breeding areas until mid-Oct. Three of the four Québec adults passed the eastern tip of Lake Ontario between early and late Nov. Most subadults and adults pass hawkwatch sites along the Lake Erie in Nov. and probably through part of Dec. In the n. and cen. Appalachian Mts. and the Mid-Atlantic Coast, subadults and adults primarily move in Nov. and Dec. with peak movement periods varying from mid- to late Nov. Small numbers continue migrating through Dec.

Spring migration: Based on telemetry data of the Québec-nesting adults, northward movements began in early Mar., with three of four eagles retracing their southward routes. Passage of three adults along the eastern tip of Lake Ontario occurred in mid- to late Mar. and corresponds to peak adult movement period at the Derby Hill Hawkwatch on e. Lake Ontario in Oswego Co., N.Y. Adults may occur at Derby Hill in early Mar. Subadults and juveniles migrate later in Apr. and May. Juveniles peak along e. Lake Ontario in late Apr. with stragglers occurring until mid-May.

In n. Michigan at the Whitefish Point Bird Observatory in Chippewa Co., adults are seen in mid-Mar. and peak in late Mar. or early Apr. Younger birds migrate in Apr. and continue until late May.

NESTING: Canadian populations begin from early Apr. to early Jun. and end by late Aug. Those in Tennessee and Georgia may begin in Jan. or Feb.

Courtship (flight).—*Sky-dancing* by males, which may turn into *talon-grappling* by both sexes. Both sexes engage in *high-circling*.

Nests are built on low embankments, high cliffs, or trees, 10–100 ft. (3–30 m) above ground. Both sexes build the structure. Nesting materials are mainly thick branches, but thin branches, twigs, and weed stalks are also used. Materials are added onto the nest during the course of use. Greenery is often added. Nests are typically reused for many seasons and often for many decades, and may become very large. Nesting territories have several alternate nests.

Canadian pairs nest on cliffs or in trees, as did Maine breeders. Tennessee and Georgia pairs nest in trees.

New nests on embankments and cliffs may be mere shallow layer of sticks; those in trees are much deeper. Average new nests are 2.5–3 ft. (0.75–1 m) and old nests are 5–6 ft. (1.5–2 m) in diameter. Old nests are typically around 6 ft. (2 m) and occasionally up to 10 ft. (3 m) deep. Greenery is added during the nesting season.

Two eggs are generally laid, but may be only 1. Eggs are laid at 3- to 4-day intervals. Females perform most of the 43- to 45-day incubation task beginning with the laying of the first egg. Fratricide (siblicide) typically occurs. If there are two nestlings, usually only the oldest survives. Fledging takes place when they are 63–70 days old. Fledglings stay with their parents for several additional weeks, but are independent by the fall migration.

CONSERVATION: Restoration programs.—Although historical breeding has never been confirmed, Georgia, North Carolina, and Tennessee implemented hacking programs in the last two decades to create a southern breeding population. *Georgia:* From 1984 to 1992, 117 birds were hacked on Pigeon Mt. in ne. Walker

Co. Most hacked birds were nestlings taken from nests in Wyoming. Nesting attempts have occurred from birds released in the 1990s in Walker Co. *North Carolina:* From 1981 to 1984, 22 birds were hacked. Nesting has not occurred in the state as the result of the hacking program. *Tennessee:* Hacking program occurred from 1995 to 2001 at Chickamauga Lake, Hamilton Co., and Douglas Lake, Jefferson Co. There have been 40 nestlings released: 1 in 1995, 2 in 1996, 1 in 1997, 10 in 1998, 10 in 1999, 13 in 2000, and 3 in 2001. Nestlings are from eaglets born in zoos and from nests in Wyoming (1998–2000 releases). Nesting occurred in the state in 1993, 1994, 1996, 2000, and 2001 from Georgia-released birds.

Protective laws.—Golden Eagles were first protected from wanton killing in 1962, when the Bald Eagle Act of 1940 was amended to include them. In 1986, the U.S. Supreme Court held that Native Americans must abide by the slated protective eagle laws. Since the 1970s, the USFWS has collected eagle parts and feathers from zoos, rehabilitators, and state agencies; the collection is based at its National Eagle Repository in Commerce City, Colo. The US-FWS distributes the parts and feathers to Native American tribes for ceremonial uses. The repository annually receives about 900 Golden and Bald eagle carcasses for distribution.

Mortality.—Shooting and leg-hold and other traps are contributing mortality factors. However, shooting has lessened with the amended Bald and Golden Eagle Act in 1962 to cover Golden Eagles. In Maine, organochlorine pesticide residues from eating herons caused thinning and premature cracking of eggshells (as much as occurred with Bald Eagles, Ospreys, and Peregrines Falcons from the late 1940s to early 1970s). Mercury levels are also high in the Maine birds. Lead poisoning may occur when scavenging on waterfowl that are wounded or killed and not retrieved by hunters.

SIMILAR SPECIES: (1) Turkey Vulture, juveniles.—FLIGHT.—Head is small. Six "fingers" on the outer primaries. Rocks back and forth when soaring and gliding and does not kite. Tail uniformly dark gray. **(2) Bald Eagle, juveniles.**—PERCHED.—Bill and cere are black. Nape is usually dark brown, but sometimes has tawny tips on the feathers and appears similar. Throat is whitish. In fall through spring, belly is tawny. Dorsal body is paler than the head and neck. Bare yellow tarsi not always separable from whitish feathered tarsi of Golden Eagles. FLIGHT.—Extensive white on the underwing coverts and axillaries; however, be cautious of molting Golden Eagles as they may have some white mottling in similar areas. On white-tailed types, outer edge of tail (r6 rectrix set) is black and may be similar to some subadult Golden Eagles. There are six "fingers" on the outer primaries. High upstroke motion of wings when in powered flight. When soaring, wings are held on a flat plane. **(3) Bald Eagle, subadult II and III (heavily marked types).**—PERCHED.—Bills are often grayish with yellow ceres. Nape and hindneck may appear golden colored, but usually have distinctly darker auricular patches. FLIGHT.—White areas on underwing coverts and axillaries may be limited and similar to molting Golden Eagles, with white mottling caused by missing feathers. Otherwise, use flight data as described for juveniles. **(4) Red-tailed Hawk, dark-morph juveniles.**—Very uncommon to rare in much of the East. PERCHED.—Greenish cere and nondescript greenish or yellowish gape. Tail has numerous dark bars. FLIGHT.—White ventral surface of the remiges. Tail as in Perched. **(5) Rough-legged Hawk, brown type adults and juveniles.**—PERCHED.—Large females are deceptively similar in size to small male Golden Eagles. Head often appears tawny or golden, but has a thin dark eyeline. White mask on forehead. Bill and feet are small. Wingtips equal to the tail tip. FLIGHT.—Five "fingers" on the outer primaries. Underside of remiges are white or pale gray. Ventral tail is similar; dorsal tail is dark or has narrow gray or white bands.

OTHER NAMES: Golden. *Spanish:* Aquila Real. *French:* Aigle Royal.

REFERENCES: Baicich and Harrison 1997; Bohlen 1989; Brodeur et al. 1996; Burt and Grossenheider 1976; Bylan 1998; Cadman et al. 1987; Clark and Wheeler 2001; Dodge 1988–1997; Edelstam 1984; Environment Canada 2000, 2001; Ferguson-Lees and Christi 2001; Forsman 1999; Godfrey 1986; Kellogg 2000; Lee and Spofford 1990; Millar 2002; Morneau 1994; Nye and Loucks 1996; Palmer 1988; Stevenson and Anderson 1994; Todd 1963; Tufts 1986; USFWS 2000, 2001; Walsh et al. 1999.

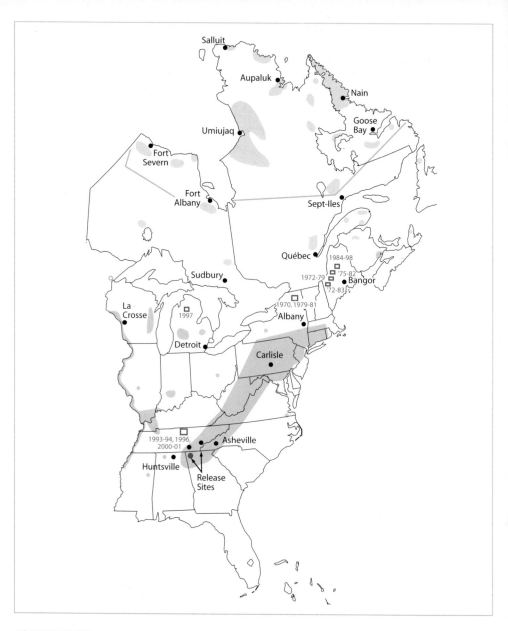

GOLDEN EAGLE, *Aquila chrysaetos canadensis:* Rare to very uncommon. Breeds mainly north of line in Canada. 200 pairs in QC, lesser numbers in LB, and a few in ON and NB. Released formerly in GA and currently in TN. Winters primarily in areas shown but also irregularly to Gulf of Mexico and to south FL. Until 1998, active eyries existed for 300 years in n.-cen. Maine.

Plate 443. Golden Eagle, adult [Dec.] ▪ Bill is black on outer half, pale blue on inner half; yellow cere, large yellow gape. Tawny nape and hindneck (nape hidden at this head angle). ▪ Dark brown body. ▪ Pale bar of bleached, worn feathers on upperwing coverts. ▪ Dark tail has 2 or 3 gray bands.

Plate 444. Golden Eagle, adult [Nov.] ▪ Tawny nape and hindneck. ▪ Dark brown upperparts. ▪ Pale bar of bleached, worn feathers on upper wing coverts.

Plate 445. Golden Eagle, adult [Oct.] ▪ Dark brown body (white mottling on breast is disarranged feathers from a distended crop). ▪ Gray barring on dark gray remiges; wide dark band on rear edge of wings. Dark coverts with tawny spot on wrists. ▪ Partial-banded type tail with indistinct, partial, pale gray bands (mainly males).

Plate 446. Golden Eagle, adult [Mar.] ▪ Tawny hindneck is visible at most angles. ▪ Dark brown body; tawny undertail coverts. ▪ Gray barring on dark gray remiges; wide dark band on rear edge of wings. Dark coverts with tawny spot on wrists. ▪ Wide-banded type tail with wide gray bands and a wide black terminal band (both sexes, but mainly females).

Plate 447. Golden Eagle, adult [Jun.] ▪ Tawny hindneck. ▪ Dark brown body. ▪ Gray barring on dark gray remiges; wide dark band on rear edge of wings. Dark coverts with tawny spot on wrists. Adults and subadults are in extensive molt in summer. Remiges are ratty; coverts may have white blotches due to molting feathers. ▪ Narrow-banded type tail with 3 distinct narrow gray bands.

Plate 448. Golden Eagle, subadult III/IV [Dec.] ▪ Bill is black on outer half, pale blue on inner half; yellow cere, large yellow gape. Tawny nape and hindneck. ▪ Dark brown upperparts. ▪ Brownish tail is mainly adultlike with gray banding, but has white areas on very basal part of some rectrices. ▪ *Note:* Older subadults are difficult to age when perched.

Plate 449. Golden Eagle, subadult I [Dec.] ▪ Bill is black on outer half, pale blue on inner half; yellow cere, large yellow gape. Tawny nape and supercilium. ▪ Wings are 90% retained juvenile feathering. Inner 3 secondaries and greater coverts are new (dark) feathers. White area on inner coverts. ▪ New, marbled mid-rectrix set; rest of tail is juvenile.

Plate 450. Golden Eagle, subadult IV [Mar.] ▪ Tawny hindneck (partly visible). ▪ Dark brown body has patches of faded old feathers. ▪ Adultlike remiges with a sliver of white on some remiges. ▪ Tail is mainly narrow-banded type with narrow gray bands. ▪ *Note:* Age based on fact that all remiges have been replaced at least once.

Plate 451. Golden Eagle, subadult IV [Nov.] ▪ Tawny nape and hindneck (partly visible). ▪ Dark brown body. ▪ Adultlike remiges with a sliver of white on some remiges. ▪ Tail is mainly narrow-banded type with narrow gray bands. ▪ *Note:* Age based on fact that all remiges have been replaced at least once.

Plate 452. Golden Eagle, subadult II [Jan.] ▪ Tawny nape and hindneck. ▪ Dark brown body with patches of faded old feathers. ▪ Outer 2 primaries and 2 middle secondaries are retained, worn, brown juvenile feathers; secondaries are longer, more pointed. Small white areas on remiges. ▪ White on basal part of rectrices.

Plate 453. Golden Eagle, subadult I [Oct.] ▪ Tawny nape, hindneck. ▪ Dark brown body has a few faded old juvenile feathers. ▪ Secondaries, except for 1–3 tertials (not visible) are retained juvenile feathers. Inner 3 primaries are new subadult; all others are retained juvenile feathers. ▪ All visible rectrices are juvenile feathers, with a white band on inner half of the tail (deck set is new).

Plate 454. Golden Eagle, subadult I [Oct.] ▪ Tawny nape and hindneck. ▪ Wing coverts are mainly faded, worn juvenile feathers with a few new (dark) subadult feathers; tawny bar on inner coverts. Secondaries are retained juvenile feathers; 3 inner primaries are new subadult feathers, all other primaries are juvenile feathers. ▪ New gray and black subadult deck rectrix set.

Plate 455. Golden Eagle, juvenile [Dec.] ▪ Black tip and pale blue base of bill; yellow cere, large yellow gape. Tawny nape, hindneck, and auriculars. ▪ Dark brown wing has a slightly paler brown bar on inner greater coverts and median coverts and first row of lesser coverts (not as pale as on older ages). Black secondaries. ▪ Tail is white on basal half and black on distal half.

Plate 456. Golden Eagle, juvenile [Dec.] ▪ Tawny hindneck. ▪ Uniformly dark brown body. ▪ Dark gray remiges have extensive white type white patch on inner primaries and basal area of most secondaries. ▪ Extensive white type tail with the inner white band extending behind long undertail coverts. Black band on the distal third of tail.

Plate 457. Golden Eagle, juvenile [Apr.] ▪ Tawny hindneck. ▪ Uniformly dark brown body. ▪ Dark gray remiges have moderate white type white patch on inner primaries. ▪ Extensive white type tail with inner white band extending behind long undertail coverts. Black band on distal third of tail.

Plate 458. Golden Eagle, juvenile [Nov.] ▪ Tawny auriculars and hindneck. ▪ Uniformly dark brown body. ▪ Dark gray remiges are the all-dark type that lack white markings. ▪ Moderate white type tail with inner white band partially covered by long undertail coverts. Black band on distal half of tail.

Plate 459. Golden Eagle, juvenile [Oct.] ▪ Tawny crown and hindneck. ▪ Upperwing coverts have a paler brown bar from inner greater coverts onto median coverts and first row of lesser coverts. Eagles with white underwing patches have white on inner primaries on upperwing. ▪ Tail is white on basal half, black on distal half. (Grayish area is an atypical pattern.)

CRESTED CARACARA
(Caracara cheriway)

AGES: Adult, basic I (subadult), and juvenile. Adult plumage is acquired when 2 years old. Basic I (subadult) is a separate plumage that does not retain juvenile feathering and is acquired when 1 year old. Juvenile plumage is worn the first year.

MOLT: Falconidae wing and tail molt pattern (*see* chapter 4). First prebasic molt from juvenile to basic I (subadult) is complete and begins when about 1 year old. As in most falcons, the first prebasic molt begins on the head. Head and body molt is virtually complete before start of wing and tail molt. Molt may begin any time of year depending when they are born.

Subsequent annual prebasic molts from subadult to adult and within adults are fairly complete each year. Molt occurs most frequently Apr.–Oct., but has been observed in all months except Dec. (Morrison 1996).

SUBSPECIES: Monotypic. At least four subspecies were formerly recognized. Recent data (Dove and Banks 1999, AOU 2000) places former subspecies at a full species level.

Former subspecies, *Caracara plancus audubonii*, of the U.S., Mexico, Central America (to w. Panama), Trinidad, and Isla de la Juventud; *C. p. cheriway* of e. Panama to n. South America (north of the Amazon Basin); and *C. p. pallidus* of Islas Tres Marias, Mexico, are now considered as one species: the Crested Caracara. Former *C. p. plancus* of South America (south of the Amazon Basin) to Tierra del Fuego and the Falkland Islands is now called the Southern Caracara (*C. plancus*). Former *C. p. lutosus,* of Guadalupe Island and s. Baja California, Mexico is now called the Guadalupe Caracara (*Polyborus lutosus*).

COLOR MORPHS: None.

SIZE: A large raptor. Males average somewhat smaller than females but sexes are not separable in the field. Length: 21–24 in. (53–61 cm); wingspan: 46–52 in. (117–132 cm).

SPECIES TRAITS: HEAD.—**Thick, pale blue bill. Bare fleshy cere, lores, orbital area, and chin.** Color intensity of fleshy areas varies with mood level: brightest during confrontations and palest when frightened; skin color alters quickly. **Dark crown and bushy crest on nape. Long, pale neck.** BODY.—**White uppertail coverts. Very long tarsi.** WINGS.—**In flight, the long, moderately narrow wings have rounded wingtips and parallel front and trailing edges. White panel on dorsal and ventral surfaces of outer six primaries (p5–10).** At close range, pale, faint, very narrow barring is visible on the secondaries. When perched, wingtips equal to tail tip. TAIL.—**Long, with a broad black and/or brown terminal band; white on distal area with numerous, very narrow dark bands.**

ADULT TRAITS: HEAD.—**Fleshy cere, lores, orbital area, and chin vary from orange to yellow.** Pale orangish or pale brown irises. **Black crown and crest. Cheeks, auriculars, and upper neck are white.** Lower neck is buff colored and finely barred with black. BODY.—**Buff-colored breast and back are finely barred with black. Belly, flanks, leg feathers, and scapulars are black. Bright yellow tarsi.** WINGS.—**Black with white panels on the primaries.** TAIL.—Wide black terminal band.

BASIC I (SUBADULT I) TRAITS: HEAD.—**Fleshy cere, lores, orbital area, and chin varies from dark pink to dull yellow.** Pale brown irises. **Dark brown crown and crest (rufous streaking is not visible in the field). Cheeks, auriculars, and front of neck are a rich tawny-buff.** BODY.—**Breast and back are a rich tawny-buff, with short bar-type markings.** Belly, flanks, leg feathers, and scapulars are dark brown. Tarsi are medium yellow or bright yellow. WINGS.—**Dark brown with white panels on the primaries.** TAIL.—Wide dark brown terminal band.

JUVENILE TRAITS: HEAD.—**Fleshy cere, lores, orbital area, and chin vary in intensity from dark pink, pale pink, or pale purple.** Pale brown irises. **Dark brown crown and crest. Cheeks, auriculars, and all of the neck are a rich tawny-buff.** BODY.—**Breast and back are a rich tawny-buff and streaked with brown.** Dark brown belly, flanks, leg feathers and scapulars. Pale grayish tarsi. WINGS.—**Dark brown with white panels on the primaries.**

Median upperwing coverts and one or two rows of lesser upperwing coverts have large white tips. TAIL.—Wide dark brown terminal band.

ABNORMAL PLUMAGES: None documented in North America.

HABITAT: Semi-open wet or dry savannas and pastures, particularly cattle rangeland with scattered medium-height and tall trees. Hot and humid climate.

HABITS: Moderately tame to tame raptor. A gregarious species, especially immatures and subadults. Adults have strong mate fidelity and remain paired throughout the year. Strong family bond. Mated pairs and offspring commonly perch side by side. An extremely aggressive raptor and dominates over Black and Turkey vultures and other scavenging raptors when communally feeding. Caracaras also pirate prey from caracaras and other raptors. Exposed branches, poles, and posts are used for perches. Concealed branches are also used for perches, especially to obtain shade. A very terrestrial species.

Head-throwback display, accompanied by vocalization, is an animated behavior. Allopreening occurs between individuals of a pair and between parents and offspring. Allopreening also takes place infrequently between Black Vultures and juvenile and subadult Crested Caracaras. Caracaras initiate the behavior by stepping closer to a nearby vulture and bowing their heads to have their napes preened and stretch out their heads to have their throats preened.

FEEDING: An aerial and terrestrial hunter and scavenger. A very opportunistic species. Caracaras fly along highways scavenging for carrion. This behavior is most apparent in the early morning before other scavengers are out feeding. Open-pit garbage dumps are also readily accessed for foraging. Caracaras also feed on small live prey: rodents, amphibians, reptiles, birds, fish, and large insects. Prey is detected while in low-altitude flight or while walking on the ground. Dislodged life forms are preyed upon at range fires and plowed fields. Caracaras use their incredibly dexterous feet to turn over chunks of dirt and cow dung in order to locate prey. Food is also pirated from other caracaras and from other raptors, even larger species. Social interactions, such as the *head-throwback display*, are prevalent when communally feeding.

FLIGHT: Powered by long series of steady, shallow, and moderately slow wingbeats interspersed with short glides. Flight is often on a straight course but caracara will sometimes bank erratically. Wings are bowed somewhat downward when gliding. Wings are held on a flat plane or bowed slightly downward when soaring. Typically unstable when soaring, and powered flight is often used for short periods in each revolution. Flight can be quite stable and bird may make numerous soaring revolutions without flapping. Leisurely soaring flights rise to high altitudes. Crested Caracaras do not hover or kite.

VOICE: Generally silent except during agonistic confrontations. *Rattle* call is a guttural, staccato, and raspy vocalization accompanying *head-throwback display*. *Cackle* note is similar, but without an animated display. *Cre-ak* note is emitted by adults when young are food-begging or when males court females. *Wuck* is a soft note emitted when an adult approaches another adult or when delivering food to nestlings.

STATUS AND DISTRIBUTION: Permanent resident.—Very restricted range in cen. Florida. Caracaras have been designated a Threatened Species since 1987 because of historical population declines and current low numbers. Loss of habitat due to urbanization and agriculture is the primary reason for current status. Current status and range appear stable. Estimated population consists of about 150 pairs and 200 immatures. Greatest concentrations are in Glades, De Soto, Highlands, Okeechobee, Osceola, and Hendry Cos. Small breeding populations in sw. Hardee, e. Polk, nw. Martin, nw. St. Lucie, and w. Brevard Cos. Probable or possible breeding in Sarasota, w. Palm Beach, e. Charlotte, and w. Indian River Cos.

Winter.—Pairs remain intact and on territory. Immatures are nomadic within typical range and congregate where there is an abundance of food.

Movements.—Localized dispersal by juveniles and subadults. Younger birds may engage in long distance dispersal northward. Adults are mainly sedentary.

Extralimital sightings.—Reported from several states and two provinces. These may be widely dispersing birds or zoo escapees. Connecticut, Massachusetts, New Brunswick, New Jersey, North Carolina, Ontario, Pennsylvania, and South Carolina.

NESTING: In Florida., Sep.–Jun. Peak nesting Jan.–Feb.

> **Courtship (flight).**—None.
> **Courtship (perched).**—*Allopreening* (*see* chapter 5).

Nests built by both adults and average 28 in. (71 cm) in diameter. Nests are placed in the top section of Cabbage Palms and are at least 8 ft. (3 m) high. Nests are not lined, but accumulate prey debris. Nests are often reused for consecutive years and become quite large. One to 4 eggs, but normally 2 or 3. Eggs are incubated by both adults for 32–33 days. Youngster fledge in about 56 days and are fed by their parents until about 116 days old. Caracaras sometime produce double clutches.

Juveniles stay with parents for another 4–7 months, often until beginning of the next breeding season. Intact family groups are common sight and are often seen perched side by side.

CONSERVATION: Population is closely monitored by scientists. Habitat loss is still affecting portions of the population; however, a majority of the habitat is currently on large private cattle ranches, offering stable, long-term protection.

Mortality.—Mainly by vehicles when feeding along highways.

SIMILAR SPECIES: (1) **Black Vulture.**—Similar white panels on outer primaries; black body, tail. (2) **Bald Eagle, immatures.**—Primarily older subadults. PERCHED.—Pale heads with similar-looking darker crowns, but with dark eyelines; dark bodies and white tails with dark terminal band are similar to caracaras. Large grayish or yellowish bills. Short yellow tarsi. FLIGHT.—Dark primaries with white only on inner two or three feathers. Very slow wingbeats with a shallow downstroke and a high upstroke.

OTHER NAMES: Caracara, Mexican Eagle. *Spanish*: Caracara Quebrantahuesos, Quelele, and Totache. *French*: Caracara Commun.

REFERENCES: AOU 2000, Clark and Wheeler 2001, Dove and Banks 1999, Howell and Webb 1995, Kale et al. 1992, Morrison 1996, Paradiso 1987, Pranty 2000, Snyder and Snyder 1991, USFWS 1987.

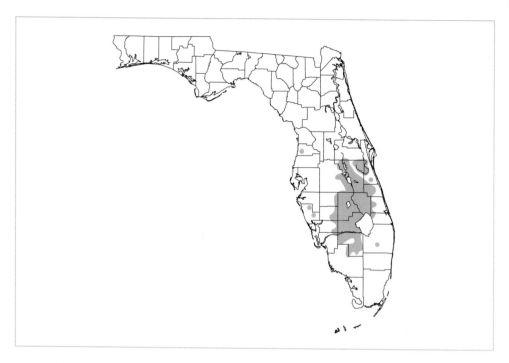

CRESTED CARACARA, *Caracara cheriway:* USFWS designates FL population as threatened. 2000 population: 150 adult pairs and 200 immatures. Breeding needs confirmation at remote sites shown by a •

Plate 460. Crested Caracara, adult [May] ▪ Pale blue bill, orange facial skin. Black crown with a bushy nape. ▪ White upper neck. White or tawny lower neck and breast and white back finely barred with black. Black belly, flanks, and scapulars. Long yellow tarsi. ▪ Black wings. Wingtips extend to tail tip.

Plate 461. Crested Caracara, adult (pair) [Oct.] ▪ Sexes alike. Some birds have dark tawny lower necks and breasts that are finely barred with black. ▪ Pairs remained together year-round and often perch side by side. ▪ *Note:* Yellowish sacks on their breasts are the skin of distended crops, visible after extensive feeding.

Plate 462. Crested Caracara, adult [Feb.] ▪ Pale blue bill, orange facial skin, and black crown. ▪ Long white neck. White lower neck and breast finely barred with black. Black belly and flanks, white undertail coverts. ▪ Large white window on outer 6 primaries. ▪ Finely banded long white tail has a wide black terminal band.

Plate 463. Crested Caracara, adult [May] ▪ Black crown, long white neck. ▪ Finely barred white back. Black scapulars and rump. ▪ Black wings except for large white panel on outer 6 primaries. ▪ Finely banded long white tail has a wide black terminal band.

Plate 464. Crested Caracara, adult (first prebasic molt) [Aug.] ▪ Pale blue bill, orange facial skin. Black crown with bushy nape. ▪ Wing coverts are mainly brown subadult with some new black adult feathers. ▪ Middle rectrices are new adult. ▪ *Note:* Head and breast as on adult. Falconidae molt head and forward body before lower body, wings, and tail.

Plate 465. Crested Caracara, subadult/basic I [Feb.] ▪ Pale blue bill, pink facial skin. Dark brown crown and bushy nape. ▪ Buff-colored upper neck. Buff-colored lower neck (and breast) with partial, fine, dark barring. Brown upperparts. Long yellow tarsi. ▪ *Note:* Some have pale yellow facial skin.

Plate 466. Crested Caracara, juvenile [Aug.] ▪ Pale blue bill, pink facial skin. Dark brown crown and bushy nape. ▪ Buff-colored lower neck, breast, and back streaked with brown. Dark brown scapulars, belly, flanks, and leg feathers. Pale gray tarsi. ▪ Median coverts and some lesser coverts have white tips. ▪ Long white tail is finely banded with brown; wide brown terminal band.

Plate 467. Crested Caracara, juvenile [Aug.] ▪ Dark brown crown, long buff-colored neck. ▪ Dark brown upperparts. ▪ Dark brown wings have a large white panel on outer 6 primaries. ▪ Long white tail finely banded, with a wide dark brown terminal band.

AMERICAN KESTREL
(Falco sparverius)

AGES: Adult and juvenile. Sexes of both ages have dimorphic plumages.

MOLT: Falconidae wing and tail molt pattern (*see* chapter 4). Juveniles go through a first prebasic body molt Aug.–Nov. However, as seen in some birds in s. Florida, some late-hatched individuals are still in full juvenile plumage in early Dec. Molt is visibly apparent at long distances only on males; plumage markings of females do not alter with this molt. As in most falcons, molt begins on the head, is nearly completed on the head, then continues down the body. Males generally attain the adult plumage by the end of the molt; however, a few may retain some juvenile feathering on the breast and other areas. Wings and tail do not molt until kestrel is 1 year old. Females of both ages have virtually identical plumages. Adult females are separated from juvenile females Jun.–Nov. by presence of wing and tail molt on adults.

Subsequent prebasic molts in adults begin in late spring or summer and are completed Oct.–Nov. Females begin earlier than males. Latitude and double brooding may affect molt timing.

Molt sequence on remiges and rectrices based on Palmer (1988). Sequence of primary molt: p4, 5, 6, 7, 2, 8, 9, 10, and 1. Secondary molt sequence: s5, 6, 7, 8, 4, 9, 3, 10, 1, and 2. Rectrix molt sequence: r1, 2, 3, 6, 4, and 5.

SUBSPECIES: Polytypic. Nominate race, *F. s. sparverius*, breeds throughout most of North America, except in the se. U.S. *F. s. sparverius* is also found in Mexico, from e. Sonora and w. Coahuila to n. Michoacán.

"Southeastern" American Kestrel, *F. s. paulus*, is resident from e. South Carolina to s. Florida; also, in s. Georgia, Alabama, and Mississippi. In the West, *paulus* extends throughout Louisiana and into e. Texas.

The "San Lucas" Kestrel, *F. s. peninsularis*, is a small and lightly marked race that is resident in the s. two-thirds of Baja California, w.

Sonora, and Sinaloa, Mexico. There are possible records, based on smaller size, for s. California and s.-cen. Arizona (Rea 1983, P. Unitt pers. comm.).

There are 14 additional races: (1) *F. s. tropicalis* is found from s. Mexico to n. Honduras; (2) *F. s. nicaraguensis* is in the lowland pine savannas of Honduras and Nicaragua; (3) *F. s. sparverioides* is on Cuba, Isle of Pines, and the Bahamas; (4) *F. s. dominicensis* is on Hispaniola; (5) *F. s. caribaearum* is on the Caribbean islands from Puerto Rico to Grenada; (6) *F. s. brevipennis* is on the islands of Aruba, Curacao, and Bonaire; (7) *F. s. isabellinus* is found from Venezuela to n. Brazil; (8) *F. s. ochraceus* is in the mountains of e. Colombia and nw. Venezuela; (9) *F. s. caucae* is in the mountains of w. Colombia; (10) *F. s. aequatorialis* is in subtropical regions of w. Ecuador; (11) *F. s. peruvianus* is in subtropical areas of sw. Ecuador, Peru, and n. Chile; (12) *F. s. fernandensis* is on Robinson Crusoe Island of the Juan Fernandez Islands, Chile; (13) *F. s. cinnamominus* is in se. Peru, Chile, south to Tierra del Fuego, Argentina; and (14) *F. s. cearae* from ne. Brazil west to e. Bolivia.

COLOR MORPHS: Polymorphic but not in any of the three North American races. *F. s. sparverioides* of Cuba and adjacent islands has a dark morph that is mainly rufous.

SIZE: A small raptor. Sexually dimorphic, but there is some overlap. Males average smaller than females. Measurements are for *F. s. sparverius*. *F. s. paulus* averages somewhat smaller than *sparverius*, but there is some overlap. However, the smaller size of *paulus* is not readily discernible in the field. MALE.—Length: 8–10 in. (20–25 cm); wingspan: 20–22 in. (51–56 cm). FEMALE.—Length: 9–11 in. (23–28 cm); wingspan: 21–24 in. (53–61 cm).

SPECIES TRAITS: HEAD.—**Two narrow black vertical facial markings on white face: one below eyes and one on the rear of auriculars. Two black spots (ocelli) on each side of the orange or white nape.** Bluish gray top of head with a rufous center crown patch; rufous patch is often reduced or lacking. Crown patch may have dark streaking. WINGS.—**In flight, wings are moderately long and fairly narrow and taper to pointed wingtips.** When perched, wingtips are distinctly shorter than the tail tip.

ADULT TRAITS: Orange nape surrounds the black ocelli spots.

Adult Male (*F. s. sparverius*): BODY.—**Lower half of the rufous back and scapulars have black cross barring. Underparts are orangish on the breast, orangish or whitish on the flanks, and whitish on the belly and lower belly.** Flanks and belly have a moderate amount of black spotting, with the largest spots on the rear of the flanks. *Note:* A few individuals, even from the northern part of their range, have reduced black spotting on the belly and flanks and can nearly rival the reduced markings of *F. s. paulus*. WINGS.—**Upper surface of secondaries and upperwing coverts are bluish gray with small black spots. Whitish undersides of wings have fine black barring and spotting. When kestrel is in flight and backlit, trailing edge of the primaries shows a row of white spots.** TAIL.—**Rufous, except on the outer rectrix set, which is white with one or two black spots or bars and a wide black subterminal band.** *Aberrant tail patterns:* (1) Deck rectrices have blue on much of feathers, but rest of the tail is the typical rufous color. (2) Deck rectrices are the typical rufous, but rectrix sets r2–4 have rufous only on the very basal area, and the distal two-thirds of r2–4 and r5 and r6 are crossed with two or three black and white bands. (3) Like example #2, but deck rectrices may have black and white bands on the distal portion. (4) Like examples #2 or 3, but deck rectrices may have blue on the distal half or blue on all portions of the deck feathers or also have blue on small portions of adjacent rectrices.

Adult Male Southeastern (*F. s. paulus*): HEAD.—**As on adult male *sparverius*, but rufous crown patch is often small or lacking and crown will be bluish gray.** BODY.—**Plain rufous back.** Rufous scapulars have a small amount of black spotting or barring only on the extreme distal portion, often having only one black bar on the most distal feather. Orange underparts have little if any black spotting on flanks and belly. WINGS.—**Upper surface of wings has little if any black spotting on the bluish gray coverts.** TAIL.—Similar to *sparverius* and probably with identical aberrant variations.

Adult Female (Races are Similar): BODY.—**Rufous back and scapulars have variable-**

width dark brown barring: (1) **equal-width dark barring or (2) narrow dark brown bars.** Underparts are white or buff-colored, with either narrow or thick rufous streaking. WINGS.—**Upperwing coverts are rufous with dark barring.** TAIL.—**Rufous with numerous, narrow dark brown or black bars; subterminal band sometimes much wider.**

FIRST ADULT MALE PLUMAGE (ALL RACES): The first prebasic molt may not be complete on some birds, and they may retain a few juvenile feathers that were not molted during the late summer and autumn. This plumage spans winter and spring. HEAD.—Some whitish feathering may be on the orange nape surrounding the black ocelli spots. BODY.—The breast is orangish as on adults but often retains a few dark juvenile spots or streaks. The flanks and belly are typically heavily spotted. Back and scapulars are typically marked as on adult males but may have a few black bars on the back and forward part of the scapulars.

JUVENILE TRAITS: Juveniles have whitish napes surrounding the black ocelli spots. Rufous crown patch and dark shaft streaking on crown region is prevalent on northern populations but decreases in southern populations (Smallwood et al. 1999).

Juvenile Male (*F. s. sparverius*) Early Stage: BODY (based on Smallwood et al. 1999).— **Rufous back and scapulars vary in the extent of black barring: (1) completely barred with black (all northern-latitude individuals) or (2) barred only on the lower one-half of the back and scapulars (some mid- and lower-latitude individuals). Whitish or orangish underparts are variably marked on breast, belly, and flanks: (1) small spots on the breast and belly with large spots on the flanks; (2) short, narrow dark streaks on the breast and belly with large flanks spots; or (3) large spots on the breast and belly and very large spots on the flanks.** WINGS.—**As on adult male.** TAIL.—**As on adult male and with identical aberrations.**

Juvenile Male (*F. s. paulus*) Early Stage: HEAD.—Rufous crown patch on blue crown is often reduced or lacking. BODY (based on Miller and Smallwood 1997).—*Upperparts:* Nearly half of the individuals studied were barred only on the distal half of the back and scapulars, the rest were either fully barred (as

in most juvenile *sparverius*) or were unmarked (similar to adult male *paulus*). *Underparts:* Vary in the amount of spotting or streaking, as seen in juvenile male *sparverius*. WINGS.— More heavily marked birds will have black spotting on upperwing coverts (as on *sparverius*); others may have little if any spotting.

Juvenile Male Late Stage: HEAD.—Nape mostly molts into the tawny color of adults. BODY.—Remnant black barring may be on the upper scapulars and back. There are a few dark streaks or spots on the breast from non-molted juvenile feathers.

Juvenile Female (Races are Similar): Plumage is identical to adult female's. Juveniles distinguished from adult females by lack of wing molt during summer and fall.

ABNORMAL PLUMAGES: Aberrant-Barred Juveniles (both sexes).—Back and scapulars are dark brown with very narrow tawny or rufous tips on each feather. All other anatomical areas are normal. Several records. Rare. **Partial albino.**—Scattered white feathers (Palmer 1988). Several records. Rare. **Incomplete/total albino.**—All-white plumage (Palmer 1988). Very rare. A few records. **Melanistic.**— Extremely rare plumage. One record for the U.S., but none for the East: Freer, Texas, in mid-Mar. 1988 (Palmer 1989, P. Palmer pers. comm.). **Gynandromorph.**— Extremely rare. At least two records of females that have partial or total male-like plumage traits (Palmer 1988). *Note:* None of the plumages is depicted. *Additional note:* There are records of oil-stained birds that appear to be melanistic!

HABITAT: *F. s. sparverius.* **Summer.**—Breeds in semi-open, undisturbed or moderately agricultural upland areas with elevated structures having cavities. *F. s. sparverius* readily adapts to urban and suburban areas that have ample foraging habitat and nesting cavities. Natural and human-made elevated structures with holes of some sort are used for nest sites, including holes and crevices in trees, buildings, nest boxes, and woodpecker holes in utility poles. Moderately humid and humid regions are inhabited.

F. s. sparverius. **Winter.**—Can be identical to breeding areas, but structures with cavities are not required, only elevated perches.

F. s. sparverius. **Migration.**—Similar to above habitats. Found in moderate numbers along mountain ridges and in large numbers along coastal areas.

F. s. paulus. **All seasons.**—Low-elevation, upland sandhill areas of semi-open, old-aged, pine woodlands interspersed with meadows. Typically found in areas of Longleaf pine, but also in Loblolly and Slash Pines. Pine woodlands have dead trees with natural cavities or large woodpecker holes. Nesting *paulus* are adapting to some semi-open areas to use nest boxes and woodpecker holes in utility poles. *F. s. paulus* are sometimes found in suburban and urban areas and nest in crevices of buildings. Found only in very humid regions. *Note:* This subspecies is an ecological adaptation to the pine woodlands of the Southeast.

HABITS: Generally fairly wary, but some become very acclimated to humans and are tame. Tail is pumped *down and up repeatedly.* Pumps tail downward then back up to the angle of the body, primarily after landing, but may do it any time while perched. Any type of exposed perch, but notably treetops and utility wires along roadways are used. *Falcons habitually elevate throat feathers.* Kestrels are gregarious after breeding season, and migrating and wintering birds may be in loosely formed groups. Very antagonistic behavior towards other raptors, especially larger species.

FEEDING: Perch and aerial hunter. Insects, small rodents and songbirds, small amphibians and reptiles, and occasionally small bats form their varied diet. Aerial prey is captured while it is on the ground, but is occasionally captured at low altitudes in the air. Very small prey, mostly insects, may be eaten while kestrel is airborne, but most prey are taken to an elevated perch to be eaten. *F. s. sparverius* feeds extensively on Green Darner dragonflies during migration. Carrion is rarely eaten.

FLIGHT: Powered by erratic, flitting sequences of lithe wingbeats interspersed with glides. Kestrels often flick their wings in a series of short bursts between glide sequences. Wings are held on a flat plane or bowed downward a bit, with primaries flexing slightly upward when gliding. Wings are held on a flat plane when soaring. Hovering regularly occurs when hunting. Kiting may occur for short periods between hovering sequences, particularly in strong winds; wings may be held in a low dihedral when kiting. Hunting dives begin at low to moderate altitudes.

VOICE: Quite vocal in all seasons. Vocalizes during antagonistic encounters and especially during courtship activities. High-pitched, rapid *klee-klee-klee-klee* is most common vocalization (also interpreted as *killy-killy-killy-killy*). During courtship, an equally high-pitched, drawnout, wavering whine, *kree, kree, kree;* a short, high-pitched guttural trill; and a short *kree* by females during pre-copulation.

STATUS AND DISTRIBUTION: *Sparverius* is overall *common* throughout its eastern North American range. Estimated population is over 2 million. As a whole, their population is stable.

F. s. sparverius. **Summer.**—Reduced numbers and poor breeding success plagues some regions of the East, especially in New England. Competition for nest sites with dominant-cavity-nesting species of birds and mammals has had a negative impact on American Kestrel reproductive success. Also, the loss of dead trees for nest sites has probably been a factor. Kestrels, however, are a highly adaptable species and readily acclimate to human-altered habitats, provided suitable nest sites and foraging habitats are available. Kestrels have undoubtedly benefited from the deforestation of much of the e. U.S., which considerably expanded semi-open habitat.

Isolated northern breeding occurs in Labrador in Churchill Falls, Goose Bay, and Red Bay area. Also in Labrador, kestrels possibly breed near Wabush, southeast of Churchill Falls, and north of Goose Bay.

F. s. sparverius. **Winter.**—Northern populations winter far south of breeding grounds. Some central-latitude and southern-latitude adults are resident on breeding territories and possibly remain paired throughout the winter. Juveniles born at similar latitudes may disperse only short distances from natal areas or remain near natal areas. In migratory populations, males winter at more northern latitudes than do females (in s. Florida: 86% females, 14% males). Generally solitary with established territories, but large groups may form in prime feeding areas. Adults have strong site fidelity and often return to the same territories each winter.

High winter densities occur in southern states and in Bermuda and the Caribbean islands of the Bahamas and Cuba (latter two islands have resident subspecies). Winter range of *sparverius* extends south to Panama. Isolated northern wintering, in very small numbers, occurs in se. Newfoundland.

F. s. sparverius. Movements.—Variable depending on latitude of breeding and natal area. Generally quite migratory; however, adults breeding in southern latitudes may not migrate (those probably nesting south of Tennessee and North Carolina). Central- and northern-latitude individuals, especially juveniles, may migrate considerable distances and "leap-frog" southern birds.

Fall migration: Begins in late Jul., with increasing numbers by mid-Aug. Numbers peak in late Sep. for juveniles and in early to mid-Oct. for adults. Migration is completed in northern regions by mid-Oct., but extends into mid-Nov. in the Mid-Atlantic areas. The largest numbers are seen at hawkwatch sites along the Mid-Atlantic Coast. The Cape May Hawkwatch at Cape May Point S.P., Cape May, N.J., holds seasonal and one-day records for the U.S. Cape May, N.J., averages over 10,000 American kestrels per year and its one-day record is 5,038 birds seen on Sep. 30, 1999. Overall numbers were higher in the early 1980s than they are now.

Spring migration: Begins in late Feb. in southern areas and in the Great Lakes region in mid-Mar. Peak numbers occur in mid-Apr. in the Mid-Atlantic region and in mid- to late Apr. along coastal New England and the Great Lakes. Flights taper off by mid-May. At Parker River NWR on Plum Island near Newburyport, Mass., which has the largest spring flights in the East, there are four distinct waves of migrants: Apr. 1 (mainly adult males), Apr. 7–10 (both adult sexes), Apr. 18–22 (both sexes and probably 1-year-olds), and Apr. 25–28 (both sexes and probably mainly 1-year-olds).

F. s. sparverius. Extralimital movements.—Documented on the Lesser Antilles, Iceland, Azores, Denmark, England, and Scotland.

"Southeastern" race, *F. s. paulus*, is a **permanent resident** and is overall *very uncommon* to *uncommon*.

Florida: Listed by the state as a Threatened Species since 1977 because of low numbers. Breeds in the following counties: Okaloosa, Madison, Walton, Leon, Suwannee, Gilchrist, Alachua, Clay, Columbia, Levy, Marion, Sumter, Putnam, Citrus, Hernando, Lake, Orange, Osceola, Pasco, Polk, Hillsborough, Highlands, Lee, Martin, and Hendry. Probably breeds in Taylor, Nassau, Volusia, Seminole, Orange, Sarasota, De Soto, Charlotte, and Palm Beach Cos. Possibly breeds in Santa Rosa and Calhoun Cos.

Formerly, locally common in open pine woodland, including from Miami to Long Pine Key. Kestrels have not bred in this region since the mid-1900s. Habitat destruction began in the early 1900s. Lumbering, the loss of large, dead pines with cavities for nest sites, and agricultural conversion appears to be primary reasons for population reductions and current low numbers in most areas. The massive conversion to citrus crops in the central sandhill counties of cen. Florida contributed to population declines in that region.

Georgia: Lists *paulus* as a Threatened Species. Population is very low. Breeding is confirmed in the following counties: Appling (Baxley: 2 pairs), Bulloch (Statesboro: 2 pairs), Evans (Bellville: 2 pairs), Tattnall (Ft. Stewart: 4 pairs; near Reidsville: 2 pairs), Emanuel (near Swainsboro: 1 pair), Toombs (near Lyons: 3 pairs), Richmond (Ft. Gordon: 20 pairs), Columbia (Grovetown: 1 pair). There are an undetermined number of pairs in these counties: Long, Bryan, Ware, Glynn, Chattahoochee, Turner, and Tift. Also, American Kestrels breed in Fulton Co. (Atlanta) and Oglethorpe Co. (Athens); however, these locations are on the northern fringe of accepted *paulus* range and are probably intergrades with *sparverius*. Habitat destruction of mature pine woodlands is possibly the main reason for low numbers in Georgia.

South Carolina: No status listing for *paulus*. Breeds in very low numbers (below the Fall Line). Mainly resident from Berkeley Co. and possibly Horry Co., to s. Kershaw Co. and south to Lexington and Barnwell Cos.

Alabama: No status listing for *paulus*. Breeding is noted only for Butler, Dale, and Coffee Cos. (Ft. Rucker in the latter two counties). Kestrels breed in Calhoun Co. at the Anniston Army Depot, Fort McClellan. However, this may be at the very northern extreme of *paulus* range. *Note:* Breeding range may be more extensive in Alabama.

Mississippi: No status listing for *paulus*. Breeding confirmed in the following counties: Chickasaw, Pearl River, Hancock, Harrison, Jackson, Hinds, Yazoo, and Holmes. *Note:* Breeding range may be more extensive in Mississippi.

F. s. paulus. Winter.—Basically sedentary and usually found near breeding areas. Some winter farther south than breeding territories and have been seen on the Florida Keys (e.g., Big Pine Key).

F. s. paulus. Movements.—This race has little in the way of noticeable movements. Some may travel short distances as described in Winter.

NESTING: *F. s. sparverius* begins nesting in a span from early Mar. to late May, depending on latitude. Many s. and cen. U.S. pairs are already laying eggs when northern birds are in peak of their migration at the same latitude. Nesting continues Jun.–Sep. Most breed when 1 year old.

Courtship (flight).—*High-circling, sky-dancing,* and *flutter-flight* (*see* chapter 5). Vocalization often accompanies courting flights, especially *flutter-flight.*

Courtship (perched).—*Food transfers.*

No nest is built. Uses cavities for nest sites: natural cavities in trees and sometimes rocks, woodpecker holes, or human-made crevices in building structures or nest boxes. Nest boxes are placed at the same height as average-height natural cavities. Very adaptable in nest sites. No material is added to nests. Nest sites are normally 10–30 ft. (3–9 m) high, but can be much higher. Four or 5 eggs, but sometimes 6. The eggs are incubated by both sexes for 29 or 30 days. Youngsters fledge in 30 days and are independent in about 51 days. After becoming independent, juveniles and some adults may form groups of up to 20 individuals derived from local nesting populations in mid- to late summer. Double clutches are common on early-nesting birds.

F. s. paulus generally begins nesting activities in mid-Apr., but may be as early as late Mar. and as late as mid-May. First broods fledge by early Jul. All other data are similar to

sparverius. Nest boxes are placed 11–20 ft. (3–6 m) high in cen. Florida.

CONSERVATION: For *sparverius,* many regions have implemented private and state-managed nest-box programs to assist breeding potential. However, in some areas, this is not helping kestrels rebuild local and regional populations. In western portions of the upper Midwest, in former prairie habitat, tree plantings and buildings have generated additional nesting habitat and assisted population growth.

For *paulus,* researchers in Florida and Georgia have created nest-box programs to help boost breeding potential in many counties. Researchers began a nest-box program in s. Georgia in 1994.

Both subspecies compete with cavity-nesting woodpeckers, Eastern Screech Owls, Eastern Bluebirds, European Starlings, and squirrels.

Mortality.—Illegal shooting occurs to a small extent in North America and south of the U.S. Accumulation of organophosphate pesticide residuals persists, especially from insect and rodent poisoning. Some kestrels collide with vehicles along highways.

SIMILAR SPECIES: None of the species listed below pumps its tail when perched. (**1**) **Sharp-shinned Hawk.**—FLIGHT.—Similar shape and size. Sharp-shinned Hawks have more rounded-tipped, broad-shaped wings; deceptively pointed, however, when gliding. Powered flight is more punctual flap-glide sequences. Juveniles may have rufous-streaked underparts. Tail has three or four wide dark bands; underside of closed tail, two to four narrow bands show. (**2**) **Merlin.**—PERCHED.—Males are same size as many female kestrels. Single, ill-defined dark vertical facial stripe below eye. Solid dark blue/brown upperparts. FLIGHT.—Powered flight with powerful, steady sequence of wingbeats (kestrels occasionally do the same). Uniformly dark underwing. Dark tail has three or four, narrow white or buff-colored bands. Voice more harsh and rapid *kee-kee-kee.* (**3**) **Peregrine.**—PERCHED.—Considerably larger. Single dark vertical facial stripe below eye. Uniformly dark brown/blue upperparts. Wingtips nearly equal or equal to tail tip. FLIGHT.—Powered flight with fairly steady, powerful wingbeats interspersed by long, stable glides. Underwing uniformly medium- or dark colored. Rarely vocalizes except at nest sites.

AMERICAN KESTREL, *Falco sparverius sparverius:* Common. Decreases are noted in e. U.S. Females winter farther south than males.

"SOUTHEASTERN" AMERICAN KESTREL, *Falco sparverius paulus:* Very uncommon to uncommon resident. Significant population decline. Classified as threatened in FL and GA.

OTHER NAMES: Kestrel, "K" bird, Little Kestrel (*paulus*); formerly called Sparrow Hawk. *Spanish*: Cernicalo, Cernicalo Americano. *French*: Crécerelle d'Amérique.

REFERENCES: Andrle and Carroll 1988; Bent 1961; Breen et al. 1995; Breen and Parrish 1996, 1997; Brewer et al. 1991; Brauning 1992; Buckelew and Hall 1994; Cadman et al. 1987; Castrale et al. 1998; del Hoyo et al. 1994; Dodge 1988–1997; Environ- ment Canada 2001; Erskine 1992; Hoffman and Col- lopy 1988; Hoffman and Darrow 1992; Howell and Webb 1995; Johnsgard 1990; Kale et al. 1992; Lane and Fischer 1997; Laughlin and Kibbe 1985; Miller and Smallwood 1997; Nicholson 1997; Nicoletti 1997; Palmer 1988; Palmer 1989; Palmer-Ball 1996; Peterjohn and Rice 1991; Post and Gauthreaux 1989; Robbins 1996; Smallwood 1990; Smallwood et al. 1999; Varland et al. 1991, 1993; Varland and Lough- lin 1992, 1993; Walsh et al. 1999.

Plate 468. American Kestrel, adult male [Mar.] ▪
Two black facial stripes; gray crown with rufous
patch; tawny nape. ▪ Unmarked tawny breast;
tawny belly and flanks are very lightly spotted
(palest type). Sparsely barred on lower half of
scapulars. ▪ Small black spots on bluish gray wing
coverts. ▪ *Note: F. s. paulus* is similar but has less
dark spotting and barring.

Plate 469. American Kestrel, adult male [Dec.] ▪
Two black facial stripes; gray crown with rufous
patch; tawny nape. ▪ Mainly unmarked pale
tawny breast; white flanks and belly are heavily
spotted. ▪ Large black spots on bluish gray wing
coverts. ▪ *Note:* First-adult with a few small dark
specks of juvenile feathers on breast.

Plate 470. American Kestrel, adult male [Feb.] ▪
Two black facial stripes; gray crown with rufous
patch; tawny nape. ▪ Tawny breast; white flanks
and belly are heavily spotted. Sparsely barred on
lower half of scapulars. ▪ Large black spots on
bluish gray wing coverts. ▪ Rufous tail with a wide
black subterminal band.

Plate 471. American Kestrel, adult male [Apr.] ▪
Tawny breast is unmarked, belly and flanks are
spotted. ▪ White band on rear edge of secondaries and a row of white spots on rear part of the
primaries. ▪ Rufous tail with a wide black subterminal band; often black bars on white outer
rectrix set.

Plate 472. American Kestrel, adult male [Nov.] ▪ Rufous back, scapulars, and rump. ▪ Bluish gray upperwing coverts; black primaries with a row of white spots on rear edge. ▪ Rufous tail with a wide black subterminal band.

Plate 473. American Kestrel, juvenile male (late stage) [Oct.] ▪ Two black facial stripes; gray crown with small rufous patch; tawny nape. ▪ Tawny breast is lightly spotted with remnant juvenile feathering; tawny belly and flanks are heavily spotted. Moderate barring on most of back and scapulars. ▪ Rufous tail.

Plate 474. American Kestrel, juvenile male (early stage) [Dec.] ▪ Two black facial stripes gray; crown lacks a rufous patch; white nape. ▪ White underparts are narrowly streaked on breast and belly and heavily streaked on flanks. Moderate barring on all back and scapular feathers. ▪ Bluish gray wing coverts are heavily spotted.

Plate 475. American Kestrel, juvenile male (early stage) [Sep.] ▪ Two black facial stripes. ▪ Streaked and spotted white underparts. ▪ Whitish underwing is moderately spotted and barred. White band on rear edge of secondaries and a row of white spots on rear part of primaries. ▪ Rufous tail has a wide black subterminal band; black bars are sometimes on a few or several rectrices.

Plate 476. American Kestrel, adult female [Apr.] ▪ Two black facial stripes; gray crown has a large rufous patch; black ocelli spot on tawny nape. ▪ Underparts streaked with rufous. Rufous brown upperparts are barred with black. ▪ Rufous brown tail is narrowly banded with black. ▪ *Note:* Juvenile females are similar in fall, but have white napes.

Plate 477. American Kestrel, juvenile female [Sep.] ▪ Two black facial stripes; white cheeks; gray crown has a small rufous patch; white nape. ▪ Whitish underparts are streaked with rufous or sometimes brown. ▪ *Note:* Nape will molt into tawny adult color by mid- to late fall.

Plate 478. American Kestrel, adult/juvenile female [Sep.] ▪ Rufous streaking on underparts. ▪ Tawny spotting on white, lightly barred remiges. Rufous markings on coverts. ▪ Rufous tail is marked with numerous thin black bands; subterminal band often wider.

Plate 479. American Kestrel, adult female [Mar.] ▪ Two black facial stripes. ▪ Rufous-streaked underparts. ▪ Narrowly banded tail is pinkish when closed. ▪ *Note:* Tawny nape color of an adult female is bleached out in this photograph.

MERLIN
(Falco columbarius)

AGES: Adult and juvenile. Adult sexes are dimorphic in color. Juveniles have minor sexually dimorphic traits on dorsal color and tail pattern. Adult plumage is gained during the second year. However, on adult females, it may take a few years to attain the "adult" rump and uppertail covert color. Juvenile plumage is held for much of the first year.

Adult and juvenile females have nearly identical plumages. Adult females are separable from juvenile females at long distances in late summer and fall by molt and retention of old, faded feathers. Adult females are difficult to separate from juvenile females after molt is completed in late fall.

MOLT: Falconidae wing and tail molt (*see* chapter 4). The first prebasic body molt varies somewhat from larger falcon species in that molt on the upper body precedes molt on the head.

Based on males, whose molt is highly visible, the first prebasic molt begins from early to late Apr.; possibly in very late Mar. on some (BKW pers. obs. of captured birds, museum specimens). One-year-old males in late Apr. and early May show definitive signs of molt. A small amount of bluish gray adult male feathering is mixed with worn and faded brown dorsal feathering on the nape, back, and forward and mid-scapulars; a few new feathers are also on the breast. Remix molt begins later in May, starting at p4, and molt occurs in both directions. Beginning at s5, the secondaries also molt in both directions. Tertial molt begins on the innermost and molts outwardly. Molt on the upperwing coverts begins after remix molt is under way. Rectrix molt, starting with r1 (deck set), also begins later, after the primaries begin to molt. All juvenile remiges and rectrices are replaced in the first prebasic molt. First-year males that begin the first prebasic molt before nesting will suspend the molt until nesting is over (M. Solensky pers. comm.). Males of *F. c. columbarius* and *F. c. richardsonii* may still have retained juvenile upperwing coverts in mid-Sep. Molt is rapid and generally completed in Oct.

Subsequent prebasic molts begin later in late May or Jun. for adult females and in late Jun. or Jul. for adult males. Molt is complete each year. Molt ends from Sep. to early Oct. for males and from Oct. to early Nov. for females. During autumn migration, females still exhibit a fair amount of old, worn upperwing coverts and dorsal feathers in early and mid-Oct. The outermost primary (p10), which is the last primary to be replaced, is typically still growing on females in mid- to late Oct. The outermost secondary (s1), which is the last secondary to be replaced, may also still be growing in mid- to late Oct. Rectrix molt is completed before remix molt is done.

SUBSPECIES: Polymorphic with three races that inhabit three major geographical regions of the U.S. and Canada. Only two subspecies are found in the East. All races are prime examples of Gloger's Rule: darkest in humid regions and palest in arid regions. The moderately dark nominate "Boreal" race, *F. c. columbarius*, breeds in the moderately humid boreal forest and taiga zone. It is the only subspecies breeding in the East. ("Boreal" means "northern" and the term typifies the range of this race, which is in more northern latitudes than the other two races; formerly used "Taiga" refers only to a very restricted habitat zone within this race's extensive habitat range.) The pale "Richardson's" race, *F. c. richardsonii*, breeds in the arid n. Great Plains and rarely shows up in very western part of the East. The dark "Black" race, *F. c. suckleyi*, breeds in the humid rain forests of the Pacific Northwest and does not occur in the East.

Six additional races breed in the n. Palearctic region of Europe and Russia and winter mainly in the s. Palearctic. Subspecies data are primarily based on Ferguson-Lees and Christi 2001: (1) *F. c. subaesalon* breeds in Iceland and winters w. Iceland and in Ireland and w. England and occasionally eastward to Norway and w. Europe. (2) *F. c. aesalon* breeds on the Faeroe Islands, and from n. Europe to w. Siberia and winters from the Mediterranean region eastward to Iran. Similar in color to *subaesalon* but smaller. (3) *F. c. pallidus* is found in w. Siberia and Kazakhstan and winters from e. Turkey to nw. India. Palest and largest of the

Eurasian subspecies. (4) *F. c. insignis* breeds in cen. and e. Siberia and winters in n. India, Korea, and Japan. Pale colored but somewhat darker than *pallidus*. (5) *F. c. pacificus* breeds in e. Siberia and winters from n. China to Japan. Darker than the previous two Siberian races. (6) *F. c. lymani* breeds in the mountains of cen. Asia and winters in China. Similar to *insignis* but has distinctly longer wings.

COLOR MORPHS: None.

SIZE: A small raptor. Sexually dimorphic with no size overlap between sexes within each subspecies. *F. c. richardsonii* average slightly larger (and heavier) than *F. c. columbarius* (and *F. c. suckleyi*). Wing-chord and tail lengths for *richardsonii* average one-half in. (12.5 mm) longer than *columbarius*; wingspan data are not available. *F. c. richardsonii* average at the high end of the respective measurements: MALE.—Length: 9–11 in. (23–28 cm); wingspan: 21–23 in. (53–58 cm). FEMALE.—Length: 11–12 in. (28–30 cm); wingspan: 24–27 in. (61–68 cm).

SPECIES TRAITS: HEAD.—Dark brown irises. Yellow cere, orbital skin, and tarsi and feet. BODY (dorsal).—Each back, scapular, and rump feather has a black shaft. BODY (ventral).—Fairly long tarsi and toes. WINGS.—**Moderately long wings. In flight, the broad secondaries taper to the pointed wingtips. When perched, wingtips are distinctly shorter than the tail tip.**

ADULT TRAITS: The sexes do not have any similarly colored plumage features.

ADULTS OF "BOREAL" (*F. c. columbarius*): HEAD.—The long, thin supercilium connects with the white forehead and extends over the eyes and auriculars. Faint dark malar mark. Pale whitish or tawny cheeks and dark auriculars. A narrow dark brown eyeline extends over the auriculars. Throat is white and unmarked. Wide black shaft streaks on crown are apparent at close range. Pale mottling on the nape. BODY (ventral).—Moderately wide dark brown streaking on the breast, belly, and forward flanks; rear flanks have a broad arrowhead-shaped mark on each feather with a wide inner bar. Leg feathers have a thin dark brown streak on each feather. Undertail coverts also have a dark feather shaft streak on each feather. WINGS (ventral).—**The dark remiges have moderate-sized pale spots that form a barred pattern. The pale spotted pattern covers 50 percent of the surface of each dark gray feather. Underwing coverts are dark brown with white spotting on the median coverts and tawny spotting on the lesser coverts. The underwings appear dark because of the moderate-sized pale spots.** TAIL (ventral).—**Three or four moderately wide pale bands are visible when the tail is widely fanned. Only one pale band shows when the tail is closed. White terminal band is moderately wide with a short dark spike extending along the shaft of the white feather tip.**

Adult male *columbarius*: HEAD.—Cere and orbital skin are medium yellow. Medium bluish gray crown and auriculars. Supercilium is white and well defined. White or tawny mottling on the dark nape. BODY (dorsal).—Medium bluish gray back, scapulars, and rump. The bluish gray on the dorsal areas graduate to a paler color from the back to the rump (M. Solensky pers. comm.). BODY (ventral).—Often has a tawny or tawny-rufous wash on the breast, lower belly, and undertail coverts. Dark barring on the distal flanks may be grayish. **Leg feathers are tawny or tawny-rufous.** Tarsi and feet are orangish yellow. WINGS (dorsal).—Medium bluish gray. The primaries are blackish and the inner primaries often have small blue spots on the outer web. WINGS (ventral).—**The pale spots on the black remiges are white.** TAIL (dorsal).—**Black with two or three sharply defined narrow bluish gray bands. Black band on the subterminal region is wider than the inner black bands.** TAIL (ventral).—**Black with three or four white bands on a fanned tail.**

Adult female *columbarius*: HEAD.—Cere and orbital skin are medium yellow. Medium brown crown and auriculars; crown is often grayish. Supercilium is pale tawny or white. Tawny mottling on the dark nape. BODY (dorsal).—Medium brown back and scapulars. In fresh plumage, each feather may have a very narrow tawny-rufous edge, otherwise, plumage is uniformly brown. Rump is grayish, but is visible only in flight from above, if the wings are drooped when perched, or if viewed in the hand. BODY (ventral).—Uniformly tawny or white, including the leg feathers, with brown streaking. WINGS (dorsal).—Medium brown. Dark brown primaries typically have small, pale tawny spots on the outer web on the inner primaries. WINGS (ventral).—**The pale spots on the brownish black remiges are tawny-rufous.** TAIL (dorsal).—**Medium brown with a wide darker blackish brown subterminal band.** There are three variations of pale banding on the dorsal surface: (1) Lacks pale dorsal bands. *Note:* Fairly common pattern. (2) **Two or three narrow tawny or slightly grayish bands on the deck rectrices and often on the inner two or three rectrix sets, but the outer three to five rectrix sets are unbanded.** *Note:* Fairly common pattern. (3) **Tail is fully banded by two or three sharply defined pale tawny or slightly grayish bands.** *Note:* Common pattern. TAIL (ventral).—**Dark brown. Three or four pale bands pale tawny-rufous show when the tail is fanned.**

Adult female (dark type) *columbarius*:
HEAD.—Cere and orbital skin are medium yellow. Dark brown crown and auriculars. Crown feathers typically have darker shaft streaking (not solid dark brown as on *F. c. suckleyi*). Cheeks may be solid dark brown or somewhat streaked with white or tawny. Dark malar mark is fairly distinct. Thin, short, pale tawny supercilium. Dark nape has a small amount of pale mottling. BODY (dorsal).—Dark brown back and scapulars. Rump is grayish. Tarsi and feet are medium yellow. BODY (ventral).—Tawny or whitish with wide dark brown streaking on the breast, belly, and lower belly; flanks are broadly barred with dark brown. Whitish or tawny leg feathers have a narrow or moderately wide dark streak on each feather. Undertail coverts have a moderately wide dark brown feather shaft streak, most pronounced on the distal feathers. WINGS (dorsal).—Dark brown and lacks pale spots on the outer webs of the inner primaries. WINGS (ventral).—**As on typical adult female *columbarius*, with moderate-sized pale tawny spots.** TAIL (dorsal).—**Same three patterns as described for typical adult female *columbarius*.** TAIL (ventral).—**As on typical adult female *columbarius*, with narrow, pale tawny-rufous bands.**

Note: Plumage is similar to *F. c. suckleyi* of the Pacific Northwest, but *suckleyi* has a darker crown, lacks discernible pale spotting on the underside of the remiges, and has larger markings on the undertail coverts.

Additional note: Data based on photographs of breeding females from Michigan (K. T. Karlson, plate 483) and Wisconsin (W. S. Clark in Clark and Wheeler 2001) and a migrant specimen from Colorado at the Denver Museum of Nature and Science.

ADULTS OF "RICHARDSON'S" (*F. c. richardsonii*):
HEAD.—The long and moderately wide white supercilium connects with the white forehead and extends over the eyes and auriculars. The dark malar mark is absent or very ill-defined. A narrow dark brown eyeline extends over the auriculars. Prominent thin dark shaft streaking on the pale crown. The cheeks are white and the auriculars are either white or have a slightly darker tinge. Throat is white and unmarked. BODY (dorsal).—The black feather shafts are very obvious because the plumage is pale. BODY (ventral).—Underparts are mainly white and covered with narrow or moderate-width dark brown or rufous-brown streaking. The distal half of the flanks are barred. Leg feathers are either thinly streaked or are unmarked. The undertail coverts are either immaculate white or have a very thin dark streak on the shaft of each feather. WINGS (dorsal).—**Large pale spots on the outer web of all primaries.** WINGS (ventral).—**Large pale spots on the dark remiges. The large pale spots cover more than 50 percent of the surface area of each dark gray feather. The underwings appear pale because of the large spots.** TAIL (ventral).—**Four or five wide pale bands show on a widely fanned tail. When the tail is closed, only one pale band shows on the mid-tail. A broad white terminal band.**

Adult Male *richardsonii*: Crown is pale bluish gray with dark shaft streaking. Nape is whitish or tawny. BODY (dorsal).—**Pale bluish gray back, scapulars and rump.** BODY (ventral).—**Leg feathers are pale tawny-rufous.** Dark markings on the rear portion of the flanks are sometimes bluish gray. WINGS (dorsal).—**Pale bluish gray secondaries and coverts. The primaries are blackish with large bluish gray spots on the outer web of all feathers.** WINGS (ventral).—**The large pale spots on the black remiges are white.** TAIL (dorsal).—**Two patterns: (1) Wide black subterminal band with three moderately wide white, very pale gray, or pale bluish gray bands. Two or three**

darker bands cross between the three pale bands. The dark band above the wide subterminal band is black; the other one or two bands may be partially black or bluish gray. If the inner dark bands are bluish gray, the inner pale bands will still show if they are white or very pale bluish gray. The pale inner tail banding will not show if the pale bands are also bluish gray. (2) Tail is black with the wide black subterminal area and three moderately wide white, very pale bluish gray, or pale bluish gray inner bands. Note: Both variations are common. TAIL (ventral).—**Black with four or five wide white bands when fanned.**

Adult female *richardsonii*: HEAD.—Crown is pale brown with thin dark shaft streaking. Nape is extensively mottled with white. BODY (dorsal).—Pale brown back and scapulars. Each back and scapular feather is neatly edged with very pale brown. Some have large white or tawny spots on the basal region of many scapular feathers and appear blotched when the feathers are fluffed. According to Warkentin et al. (1992), it may take adult females up to 4 years old to attain the grayish coloration on the rump and uppertail coverts. However, the grayish cast on the rump and uppertail coverts are difficult to see in the field. BODY (ventral).— Leg feathers are white like the rest of the underparts and may have thin brown streaking or are unmarked. WINGS (dorsal).—Upperwing coverts are pale brown and edged with very pale brown. Many coverts have small very pale tawny spots on them. Greater coverts may appear somewhat barred because of pale tawny spots. The secondaries may have pale tawny spotting, and all primaries have large pale tawny spots on the outer web of each feather. WINGS (ventral).—**Spots on the remiges are pale tawny-rufous.** TAIL (dorsal).—Two patterns: (1) Medium brown with a fairly wide blackish brown subterminal band. Three moderately wide white or very pale tawny bands neatly cross the tail above the subterminal band. Note: Common pattern. (2) Medium or brown with a fairly wide blackish brown subterminal band. The area above the subterminal band may have three faint bands on a few central rectrix sets, but the pale bands are absent on most of the rest of the rectrices. Note: Uncommon pattern. TAIL (ventral).—**Medium brown with a dark**

brown subterminal band. The medium brown area above the dark subterminal band is crossed by four or five, neat, very pale tawny-rufous bands when fanned.

JUVENILE TRAITS: HEAD.—Cere and orbital skin are medium greenish yellowish or yellow. Brown crown. Pale mottling on the dark nape. Throat is white and unmarked. BODY (dorsal).—Brown back and scapulars. The rump is also the same shade of brown as the rest of the upperparts. BODY (ventral).—Tarsi and feet are medium yellow. WINGS (dorsal).—Brown wing coverts. WINGS (ventral).—Pale tawny-rufous spotting on the dark remiges. TAIL (dorsal).—The uppertail coverts are the same brown color as the rest of the dorsal areas.

JUVENILES OF "BOREAL" (F. c. columbarius): HEAD.—Crown feathers are medium brown or tawny brown with moderately wide dark shaft streaking. BODY (dorsal).—Medium brownish back, scapulars, and rump. BODY (ventral).—Medium thick dark brown streaking on the breast, belly, and lower belly. Forward region of the flanks are streaked with dark brown and the rear portion has a broad arrowhead-shaped mark on the tip of each feather and broad inner-feather dark bars. Leg feathers have thin dark brown streaking. Undertail coverts have a thin dark brown streak along the shaft of each feather. WINGS (dorsal).—Small pale tawny spots on the outer web on the inner primaries. WINGS (ventral).— **Underside of the brownish black remiges have moderate-sized pale tawny-rufous spots that form a barred pattern. The pale spots cover 50 percent of the surface area of each dark gray feather. The underwings appear dark because of the moderate-sized pale spots.** TAIL (dorsal).—Medium brown with a wide blackish brown subterminal band. Typically have two or three fairly distinct moderately wide pale bands crossing the medium brown dorsal surface. TAIL (ventral).—**Three or four narrow pale tawny-rufous bands show on a fanned tail but only one band shows when the tail is closed.**

Juvenile male *columbarius*: HEAD, and BODY and WINGS (dorsal).—Medium brown back, scapulars, and rump have a grayish sheen. The grayish sheen on the feathers is apparent at moderate range and in good light. Upperparts often appear slightly darker than on females. TAIL (dorsal).—**Three moderately wide pale gray bands. The pale bands are sometimes diffused and tail appears partially banded.**

Note: Separable from females by their smaller size and grayish dorsal tail bands.

Juvenile female *columbarius*: HEAD, BODY, and WINGS (dorsal).—Medium brown upperparts are a warm brown and similar to an adult female. The rump is the same brown color as the rest of the upperparts. TAIL (dorsal).—**Two or three moderately wide pale tawny bands. The pale dorsal bands are typically neat and complete. The uppertail coverts are the same brown color as the rump and rest of the upperparts.**

Note: Separable from adult females only in late summer and fall by lack of molt.

JUVENILES OF "RICHARDSON'S" (*F. c. richardsonii*): Identical to adult female in nearly all aspects. BODY (dorsal).—Rump is the same pale brown color as the back and scapulars; however, this is also the case on many younger adult females (Warkentin et al. 1992). TAIL (dorsal).—Males sometimes have a slight grayish tone on the whitish tawny dorsal tail bands. *Note:* Males are separable by females by their smaller size. Females are separable from adult females only in late summer and fall by lack of molt.

ABNORMAL PLUMAGES: Incomplete albino (dilute plumage).—A few records of captured-for-banding individuals and sight records from the fall in the mid-Atlantic region (Clark and Wheeler 2001, B. Sullivan pers. comm.). One was an adult male, the others have been "brown" juveniles or adult females. What are typically medium or dark plumage features are very pale tawny-brown in this type of albino. The birds appear very pale whitish with very pale brownish dorsal areas and ventral streaking. Iris color is the typical dark brown and the cere, tarsi, and foot color is also normal yellow. **Partial albino.**—One record (Clark and Wheeler 2001).

HABITAT: *F. c. columbarius*. Summer.—Breeds in the following regions: (1) Low-elevation boreal forest zone with semi-open areas of medium-height and tall conifers and hardwoods adjacent to lakes and occasionally large meadows. Regularly nests on coniferous-wooded islands in lakes. Found throughout much of the forested regions of n. Wisconsin and n. Michigan, and Canada. Merlin may be found in human-inhabited or undisturbed areas. (2) Montane boreal forest zone with semi-open areas of tall conifers adjacent to lakes, ponds, and large meadows. Regularly nests on coniferous-wooded islands in lakes. Found in Adirondack Mts. of New York and various areas in New Hampshire, Vermont, Maine, and Canada. (3) Taiga zone with semi-open and open areas of dwarf spruce and deciduous scrub adjacent to lakes and ponds. These areas are on the very northern fringe of the boreal forest in Canada. (4) "Medium shrub" habitat of the tundra zone characterized by open expanses with scattered coniferous and deciduous shrubs, often on slopes adjacent to lakes and ponds. This ecozone is just north of the stunted trees of the taiga. (5) Suburban and urban zones with tall conifers that have American Crow nests. Merlin are increasingly using these areas in the East.

All areas are moderately humid or humid. ***F. c. columbarius*. Winter.**—A variety of habitats may be used: seashores, lakeshores, marshes, tidal flats, suburban and urban areas, and semi-open woodlands. Conifers are favored trees for roosting. The various habitats may be in temperate, subtropical, or tropical zones.

***F. c. columbarius*. Migration.**—Found in habitats similar to those listed for "winter." Small numbers are also on mountain ridges.

***F. c. richardsonii*. Summer.**—Breeds on the n. Great Plains.

***F. c. richardsonii*. Winter and Migration.**—Semi-open and open areas in Wisconsin and Illinois.

HABITS: Fairly tame to tame raptor. Perches mainly on elevated exposed branches, wires, and other suitable structures. They may also perch near or on the ground. If available, roosting birds seek coniferous trees for optimum shelter from the elements and predators. Mainly a solitary species, but a few birds may gather at night roosts.

Merlin regularly elevate forehead and throat feathers. Nape feathers are also raised.

Merlin are very antagonistic raptors and constantly harass larger raptors and birds too large to kill. They often hunt at dawn and dusk.

FEEDING: Perch and aerial hunter. Perch hunting is direct attack initiated from high, exposed perches. Aerial-hunting is mainly by high-speed, low- or moderate-altitude, surprise-and-flush forays. Merlin primarily feed on small avian species that are captured in flight. Urban nesting and wintering Merlin feed extensively on House Sparrows. Dragonflies, particularly the large Green Darners, are a major prey during fall migration. Small rodents and other vertebrates form a very small portion of their diet. Being crepuscular, Merlin often feed on small bats. Rarely pirates food from other raptors: A juvenile male was observed pirating a vole from a female American Kestrel. Rarely feeds on carrion.

Insect prey is eaten while gliding or soaring or taken to a perch or to the nest. All other types of prey are eaten at the point of capture on the ground, taken to a perch, or taken to the nest. Kill prey by breaking the neck with its notched bill. All prey are decapitated; avian prey are plucked and wings are torn off. Legs and leg bones may be swallowed whole or the meat is eaten and legs and bones are discarded.

Merlin typically forage in open areas that give them the advantage of high-speed attacks on prey that cannot seek shelter. *F. c. columbarius* regularly hunt avian prey over large bodies of water. Merlin will either force the prey into the water or the prey will dive to near or on the surface of the water to escape capture.

Attack methods: (1) *Tail-chase.*—High-speed flights following behind and trying to overtake avian prey. Flights occur at ground-skimming or treetop altitudes or sometimes higher. (2) *Ringing-flight.*—A variation of *tail-chase* in which the prey rises upward in a spiral with the Merlin following closely behind. (3) *Dive.*—Another variation of *tail-chase* in which the Merlin rises slightly above the prey, then makes short dives to capture it. (4) *Undulating-flight.*—A low-altitude, sneak-attack flight in which Merlin emulate the bouncing flight of songbirds.

FLIGHT: Powered by a long series of steady, rapid, powerful wingbeats that are interspersed with short glide sequences. Flight is very fast. Merlin are capable of quick, high-speed maneuvers. Soars infrequently. Wings are held on a flat plane when gliding and soaring. Merlin performs, undulating-flight at high speeds with quick, flicking wingbeats on the downward part of the undulation, then closes its wings into the body on the upward part of the undulation. The flight is similar to the bouncing flight of most songbirds and woodpeckers.

VOICE: Typically heard, agitated call is a rapid, high-pitched *ki-ki-ki-ki-ki-ki*. When courting, both sexes emit a *tic* call. A *chrr* note is given by males before copulating, and sometimes emitted by females. Conspecifics that come near a breeding female also emit the *chrr* call. A food-begging, whining *kree-kree-kree* is given by adult females during food transfers with mates; also given by youngsters.

STATUS AND DISTRIBUTION: Population is stable and possibly increasing. Since Merlin primarily feed on migrant birds, the organochlorine pesticide era produced thinned eggshells and affected reproduction during this period. Merlin, however, are readily adapting to human alteration of the environment as their population rebounds, particularly by nesting and wintering in urban centers, as they are drawn by large numbers of House Sparrows for food and nests of American Crows for nesting.

F. c. columbarius. **Summer.**—*Uncommon.* Distribution in Canada: Merlin are widely spread throughout the boreal forest and taiga. Lesser numbers extend somewhat north of the taiga. An increasingly common urban breeder. *Québec:* They nest in Blainville, Hull, Laval, Montreal, Québec City, Saint Hyacinthe, and Sherbrooke. *Ontario:* Nest in Ottawa. Distribution in the U.S.: *Maine.*—Breeds in much of the state. *Michigan:* Breeds in much of the Upper Peninsula. In the Lower Peninsula, breeding is confirmed for Antrim Co. and is possible or probable for Charlevoix, Presque Isle, and Alpena Cos. *New Hampshire.*—Range is extending southward in the state. Breeds in several areas in the northern part of the state in Coos Co. Breeding also occurs in urban centers in Grafton Co.: Hanover (in 2001), Plymouth, and Wentworth (in 1997). *New York:* Range is extending southward in the state. Merlin first bred in the state in 1992. A few pairs breed in Essex, Franklin, Hamilton, Herkimer, St. Lawrence, and Warren Cos. *Vermont:* Urban nests are located in Johnson and Morrisville in Lamoille Co. Nesting was first discovered in 1997. *Wisconsin:* Breeding occurs in Ashland,

Bayfield, Door, Douglas, Iron, Oneida, and Vilas Cos. May also irregularly breed throughout the northern one-third of the state.

F. c. columbarius. Winter.—Most U.S. and Canadian wintering areas are near waterways. A small number winter in s. Newfoundland. Large numbers winter along the Atlantic Seaboard, throughout Florida, and along the Gulf Coast. Lesser numbers are found along the e. Great Lakes, along the St. Lawrence River north to Québec City, Québec, and along the coastal areas of the Maritimes. A few winter along the Mississippi River. Most individuals wintering in Canada and much of the U.S. are females. Males typically winter south of the U.S. Most eastern birds winter on the Caribbean islands. Those from western areas of the East and in the West may winter as far south as n. Peru in South America.

F. c. columbarius. Movements.—As a whole, a highly migratory subspecies. Some, particularly females, short-stop their migration where food is abundant and move only short distances. Migration flights often take them over large expanses of water. Along the Atlantic Coast, daily migration flights are often offshore. Birds come in to feed and roost in late afternoon and evening. Morning flights may begin before sunrise.

Fall migration: The largest concentrations, with several hundred on peak days, occur along the Mid-Atlantic Coast. The largest numbers, often with over 2,000 birds per season, are seen at the Cape May Hawkwatch at Cape May Point S.P. (1-day record of 867 on Sep. 30, 1999), Cape May, N.J.; Fire Island, Robert Moses S.P., Long Island, N.Y.; and at Kiptopeke S.P., Northhampton Co., Va. Juveniles may begin migrating in mid-Aug. Migrants first appear at hawkwatches on the Mid-Atlantic Coast by late Aug., and may even be as far south as Kiptopeke at this time. Large numbers of juveniles are seen by mid-Sep., with peak numbers in mid- to late Sep. Adults peak in mid-Oct. Migrants taper off by late Oct., with stragglers occurring into mid-Nov.

Spring migration: Adults return north before 1-year-olds. Northward migration is also most visible along the Mid-Atlantic Coast, at Cape Henlopen S.P., Sussex Co., Del., and at Fort Smallwood S.P., Ann Arundel Co., Md. The first adults occur at these spring hawk-watches in mid- to late Mar. Peak adult movement is in mid-Apr. Lesser numbers, mainly adults and 1-year-olds, can be seen through early May. Stragglers occur into mid-May.

Few migrants are tallied along the e. Great Lakes. The first adults may show up in mid-Mar., but often not until early Apr. Peak numbers occur in late Apr. At Whitefish Point Bird Observatory near Paradise, Mich., adults make an appearance in late Mar. and peak in late Apr. One-year-olds straggle through until the end of May and possibly into early Jun.

F. c. richardsonii. Winter.—Casual in the East with sightings mainly in Wisconsin and Illinois. In the West, extends over much of the non-mountainous regions of s. Canada, the U.S., and to n. Guerrero in Mexico.

F. c. richardsonii. Movements.—Similar timing as described for *columbarius* in the fall. Spring migration is earlier for adults, with movements occurring in Feb. and Mar.

NESTING: Data concerns *F. c. columbarius*. The first adults arrive on breeding grounds in s. New Hampshire in late Mar. In the southern part of their range in Wisconsin, the first pairs reach breeding grounds in early Apr. In more northern regions, arrival on the breeding grounds is throughout Apr. and into May. Courtship occurs from early Apr. to late May. Breeding may occur when 1 year old. Pairs may be formed of adults, one adult and one yearling, or yearlings. Nesting success is highest when both pair members are adults. Pairs regularly return to the same territory but often use a different nest site.

Courtship (flight).—Both members of a pair perform *mutual high-circling* and *aerial food transfers*. Only males perform the following elaborate courting routines: *flutter-flight, power-diving, power-flight, rocking-glide,* and *slow-landing*.

Courtship (perched).—*High-perching* is used by males. *Food-begging* is performed by females. *Food transfers* and *nest displays* are performed by both sexes. Copulation often follows *food transfers. See* chapter 5 for courtship descriptions.

No nest is built. Merlin use abandoned nests built in coniferous trees by other species of birds. A majority of Merlin nests are in old American Crow nests. In n. Québec and Labrador, Merlin range extends north of the

American Crow's range, and they may use tree nests of Common Ravens and possibly Northern Goshawks. Nesting birds may occasionally use flattened leafy squirrel nests and the tops of broken tree trunks. In the taiga and tundra regions, where trees are small or nonexistent, nests are typically on the ground under dense deciduous bushes and scrub spruce. Merlins rarely nest on cliff ledges.

Tree nests are situated in the densely foliaged upper part of conifers. Tree nest heights range from 12 ft. (4 m) to 81 ft. (25 m). In Wisconsin, the lowest nests are 30 ft. (9 m) high.

The female lays 3–5 eggs, but occasionally 2–7, and females mainly perform the 30-day incubation. Youngsters fledge in 28–30 days but may remain near the nest for another 2 weeks. Most fledge by early Aug. at southern latitudes, but may extend throughout Aug. for northern regions.

CONSERVATION: As the merlin is a predator of birds and at the top of the food chain, the ban on organochlorine pesticide use, particularly DDT, no doubt assisted the recovery of its populations in the last three decades. Merlin rebounded on their own after DDT was banned in Canada and the U.S. This lethal pesticide was first used in 1946 in Canada and the U.S.

Organophosphate pesticides, although not as persistent in the environment as organochlorine pesticides, can be deadly to some species that Merlin eat. Phosphamidon was formerly used to control insect infestations in the forests of e. Canada but was found to kill songbirds. Fenitrothion, which is currently used to control insects in the forests of e. Canada, has recently been found to be harmful to songbirds.

Mortality.—Natural mortality of all ages due to depredation by large hawks and owls. Mammalian predators cause egg and nestling mortality. During migration, gulls kill over-water migrants. Carbamate pesticides may have contributed to some mortality among Merlin. Newer-generation pyrethroid pesticides are harmless to birds and mammals, but affect aquatic insects. A few Merlin may collide with wires and windows during high-speed pursuit of prey. Shooting does not appear to be a major factor in mortality.

SIMILAR SPECIES: COMPARED TO ADULT MALES.—(1) **Sharp-shinned Hawk, adults.**—Similar size. PERCHED.—Orange or red irises. Underparts are rufous barred. Long, thin tarsi. Upperparts are similar bluish gray. Tail has 3 or 4 black bands on dorsal side. FLIGHT.—Pale remiges with black barring. Rufous barred underparts. Undertail is pale with narrow black bands. COMPARED TO ADULT FEMALES/JUVENILES.—(2) **American Kestrel, females.**—Similar size. PERCHED.—Two black facial stripes. Upperparts barred with rufous and dark brown. Ventral areas rufous streaked. Tail is rufous with numerous, narrow black bands. FLIGHT.—Similar, especially when in high-speed powered flight. Wings are narrow on the secondaries; wingbeats generally lithe and wispy. Wingbeats can be deceptively powerful at times; use caution! Ventral side of remiges are pale barred. Tail is pale or bright rufous with multiple, narrow dark bands. (3) **Peregrine Falcon, juveniles.**—Much larger. Sharply defined dark malar stripe. Pale bluish orbital skin. Ventral and dorsal markings and color are similar, but pale dorsal feather edgings may be very defined (especially *F. p. tundrius*). Wingtips equal or nearly equal to tail tip. Tail may be similar with pale tawny bands on both ventral and dorsal areas. (4) **Sharp-shinned Hawk, juveniles.**—Similar size. PERCHED.—Yellow irises. Ventral and dorsal areas similar. Long, thin tarsi. Tail has 3 or 4 wide, equal-width black bands. Lacks white terminal band. FLIGHT.—Pale underside of the remiges with black barring. Pale underside of tail with narrow black barring.

OTHER NAMES: Merl, merlin (female), jack (male), blue jack (adult male), Taiga Merlin (*columbarius*), Prairie Merlin (*richardsonii*); formerly called Pigeon Hawk. *Spanish:* Esmerejon. *French:* Faucon Emerillon.

REFERENCES: Baicich and Harrison 1997; Bent 1961; Brewer et al. 1991; Bylan 1998; Cadman et al. 1987; Clark and Wheeler 2001; Dodge 1988–1997; Environment Canada 2001; Erskine 1992; Feruguson-Lees and Christi 2001; Godfrey 1986; Kellogg 2000; Palmer 1988; Paxton et al. 2000; Sodhi et al. 1993; Solensky 1997, 2001; Sullivan 1996; Todd 1963; Walsh et al. 1999; Warkentin et al. 1992.

"BOREAL" MERLIN, *Falco columbarius columbarius:* Uncommon. Sparsely distributed in all seasons. Heavily concentrated locally along Mid-Atlantic coast in fall. Winters mainly south of U.S. to n. South America. Most wintering in U.S. and Canada are females. Rare inland wintering in areas not mapped in U.S.

Plate 480. Merlin, adult male "Boreal" (*F. c. columbarius*) [Oct.] ▪ Thin dark eyeline; faint, dark malar mark; pale supercilium and cheeks; yellow orbital ring. ▪ Medium bluish gray upperparts. Streaked with brown on the breast and belly and barred on the flanks. Lightly streaked rufoustawny leg feathers. ▪ Black tail has 2 or 3 narrow bluish gray bands.

Plate 481. Merlin, adult male "Boreal" (*F. c. columbarius*) [Oct.] ▪ White or tawny underparts are moderately streaked with brown; rufous-tawny leg feathers. ▪ Moderately dark underwings: white spotting/barring covers 50% of the surface of each remix. ▪ Black tail has 3 or 4 narrow white bands.

Plate 482. Merlin, adult female "Boreal" (*F. c. columbarius*) [Feb.] ▪ Thin dark eyeline; faint dark malar mark; thin white supercilium. ▪ White underparts are moderately streaked with brown. Leg feathers and undertail coverts are white and lightly streaked. Medium brown or dark brown upperparts.

Plate 483. Merlin, adult female "Boreal" (dark type) (*F. c. columbarius*) [May] ▪ Dark head with partial white supercilium. ▪ Heavily marked underparts are streaked on breast and belly and barred on flanks. Dark brown upperparts. ▪ *Note:* Underside of remiges are spotted as on typical *columbarius*. Photographed in Paradise Co., Mich., by Kevin T. Karlson.

Plate 484. Merlin, adult/juvenile female "Boreal" (pale type) (*F. c. columbarius*) [Dec.] ▪ Faint, dark malar mark and dark auricular patch; thin dark eyeline; thin white supercilium. ▪ Moderately marked white underparts. Upperparts are paler than on typical *columbarius*. ▪ Adult females often have indistinct pale dorsal tail bands.

Plate 485. Merlin, adult female "Boreal" (*F. c. columbarius*) [Oct.] ▪ Upperparts, including upperwing coverts, are medium or dark brown and mottled with patches of old, faded brown feathers when molting from summer to mid-fall. ▪ Three narrow tawny tail bands. ▪ *Note:* Grayish rump difficult to see in the field.

Plate 486. Merlin, juvenile male "Boreal" (*F. c. columbarius*) [Oct.] ▪ Faint, dark malar mark and dark auricular patch; thin dark eyeline; thin tawny supercilium. Yellow orbital skin. ▪ Leg feathers and undertail coverts are lightly streaked. Upperparts of males are grayish brown. ▪ Dorsal tail bands are gray.

Plate 487. Merlin, juvenile female "Boreal" (*F. c. columbarius*) [Oct.] ▪ Faint, dark malar mark and dark auricular patch; thin dark eyeline; thin tawny supercilium. ▪ Moderately marked white or pale tawny underparts. Medium brown or dark brown upperparts. ▪ *Note:* Separable in summer/fall from adult females by lack of molt; from juvenile males by size and dorsal color.

Plate 488. Merlin, juvenile female "Boreal" (*F. c. columbarius*) [Sep.] ▪ Streaked underparts. ▪ Moderately dark underwings: tawny spotting/barring covers 50% of the surface of each remix. ▪ Dark tail has 3 or 4 thin tawny bands and a white terminal band.

Plate 489. Merlin, juvenile male "Boreal", (*F. c. columbarius*) [Oct.] ▪ Brown upperparts, often with a grayish sheen. ▪ Tawny spotting on primaries. ▪ Dark tail has 3 or 4 thin whitish or grayish bands (tawny on females).

Plate 490. Merlin, adult male "Richardson's" (*F. c. richardsonii*) [Feb.] ▪ Thin dark eyeline; thin white supercilium, very faint dark malar mark. Pale bluish gray crown. ▪ Lightly marked white underparts. Pale tawny-rufous leg feathers; bluish gray upperparts. ▪ Bluish spotting on primaries. ▪ *Note:* Captured a Horned Lark.

Plate 491. Merlin, adult male "Richardson's" (*F. c. richardsonii*) [Mar.] ▪ Lightly streaked white underparts. Pale tawny leg feathers. ▪ Pale underwings: white spotting/barring on dark remiges covers greater than 50% of the surface of each remix. Pointed wingtips. ▪ Black tail has 3 or 4 broad white bands.

Plate 492. Merlin, adult/juvenile female "Richardson's" (*F. c. richardsonii*) **[Nov.]** ▪ Thin dark eyeline; thin white supercilium; faint dark malar mark. ▪ Lightly marked white underparts. Pale brown upperparts are edged with pale tawny; often spotted with white or tawny. ▪ Secondaries and greater coverts are barred with tawny. ▪ Tail has broad white tail bands.

Plate 493. Merlin, adult/juvenile female "Richardson's" (*F. c. richardsonii*) **[Nov.]** ▪ Lightly streaked white underparts. White leg feathers. ▪ Pale underwings: white spotting/barring on dark remiges covers greater than 50% of the surface of each remix. Pointed wingtips. ▪ Brownish tail has 3 or 4 broad white bands and a wide black subterminal band.

Plate 494. Merlin, adult/juvenile female "Richardson's" (*F. c. richardsonii*) **[Feb.]** ▪ Pale brown upperparts are edged with pale tawny. ▪ Primaries, secondaries and greater coverts are spotted with tawny. ▪ Tail has 3 broad white/pale tawny bands and a broad white terminal band. Black subterminal band.

PEREGRINE FALCON
(Falco peregrinus)

AGES: Adult, subadult, and juvenile. Adults are somewhat sexually dimorphic in color, but juveniles are similarly marked. Juveniles have broader wings and longer tails than do adults. Subadult is an interim molt stage that retains a portion of old juvenile and new adult feathering in a distinct pattern during the first prebasic molt.

MOLT: Falconidae wing and tail molt pattern (*see* chapter 4).

The first prebasic molt begins when the birds are about 10–14 months old. An incomplete molt attains 95–98 percent of the adult plumage. On migratory birds, the molt is suspended until they have reached the winter grounds. A few juvenile feathers are often retained on the upperwing coverts, belly, scapulars, and rump until the second prebasic molt. Molt varies with the latitude and elevation at which juveniles were born. Molt typically begins in Apr. or early May in the continental U.S. and Canada; however, it may begin as early as Jan. or Feb. (N. J. Schmitt pers. comm., museum specimens) or as late as mid- to late Jun. (J. Zipp photos, BKW pers. obs.). Molt appears to begin latest on mated but nonbreeding 1-year-old females. Birds of the Northwest Pacific region often do not begin to molt until mid- to late May. Arctic birds do not begin to molt until late May or Jun. Near-adult plumage is attained from Oct. to Dec.

The first prebasic molt begins on the head, nearly completes on the head (except on the crown), then expands down the back, forward and mid-scapulars, and the breast. Molt continues down the rear portion of the body. Once molt is nearly complete on the head and partially complete on the back, scapulars, and breast, the primaries begin to molt. Primary molt begins, as on all falcons, on p4, then molts in both directions in the following order (after Palmer 1988): 5, 3, 6, 7, 2, 8, 1, 9, and 10. Secondary molt, beginning with s5 and sequentially molting in either direction, begins shortly after primary molt begins. The outermost secondaries are the last to molt, with s1 being the last. Rectrix molt begins after primary molt is well under way. Rectrix molt is in the following sequence: r1, 2, 3, 6, 4, and 5. The greater and median upperwing coverts molt in unison with the replaced remiges. The last feather tract to molt is the lesser upperwing coverts.

By mid-summer, much of the body and remiges may be adultlike, but the upperwing coverts and tail are still mainly juvenile and birds are in a distinct subadult stage.

Subsequent prebasic molts begin later than the first prebasic molt. Nonbreeding birds begin molting before breeding birds. Molt is annual and complete each year. Females begin molting when incubating and males mainly during the latter part of the nesting period or after the young have fledged. On migratory birds, molt is suspended during migration, then it is resumed and finished on the winter grounds. Molt sequence on the remiges and rectrices is the same as for the first prebasic molt; however, all areas of the body may molt in unison. Molt is completed from Oct. to early Jan., with the outermost primaries being the last anatomical area to molt. Some adults of *F. p. tundrius* and *F. p. anatum* are still growing a new outermost primary (p10) in early Jan. (based on AMNH museum specimens).

SUBSPECIES: Native subspecies in the East.— "Arctic" Peregrine Falcon, *F. p. tundrius*, inhabits the Arctic region and is the only native race of Peregrine in the East. *F. p. tundrius* was not recognized as a separate subspecies until 1968 (White 1968). It was affected by the DDT era of the late 1940s to early 1970s.

Native subspecies in the West.— "American" Peregrine Falcon, Western *F. p. anatum*, ranges widely in North America west of the Great Plains and south of the Arctic. It is subtly different from the extinct eastern *F. p. anatum* (C. M. White pers. comm.). It was greatly affected by the DDT era.

"Peale's" Peregrine Falcon, *F. p. pealei*, inhabits the Pacific region of Washington, British Columbia, and Alaska, including throughout the Aleutian Islands; also found in e. Russia on the Commander Islands and probably the Kuril Islands and coastal Kamchatka Peninsula. It was minimally affected by the DDT era.

Former subspecies in the East.—Eastern *F. p.*

anatum, the "Rock Peregrine," was extirpated east of the Great Plains and in most or all of s. Canada during the DDT era. East of the Mississippi River, the last *anatum* were seen at two historical nest sites in the U.S. in 1962 in Alabama and Maine (D. Berger pers. comm.). Ontario had nesting pairs until 1963 (Cadman et al. 1987). Eastern *F. p. anatum* was overall larger than its western counterpart. It may have ecologically evolved to hunt the also-now-extinct Passenger Pigeon.

Introduced subspecies in the e. U.S.—The current restoration-era population of Peregrine Falcons in the e. U.S. is a product of introduced, human-manipulated mix of lineages and is not a subspecies. Herein, it is called the "Eastern" Peregrine Falcon.

The subspecies used to create the population in Maine, New England, New York, and south through the Appalachian Mts. primarily came from three w. and n. North American races: *F. p. pealei* of the Queen Charlotte Islands and Aleutian Islands, *F. p. tundrius* of the North American Arctic and Greenland, and western *F. p. anatum* west of the Great Plains. The percentages of the respective subspecies that were used in the region is unknown. However, birds of *pealei* and *tundrius* lineage may have contributed to much of the lineage of the early released stock. Additionally, four foreign subspecies were used to a lesser extent (White et al. 1995; C. M. White pers. comm.): *F. p. peregrinus* of Europe (Scotland), *F. p. brookei* of the Mediterranean (Spain), *F. p. macropus* (se. Australia), and *F. p. cassini* of s. South America (Argentina).

Subspecies that were released in Illinois, Indiana, Kentucky, Michigan, Ohio, cen. Ontario, and Wisconsin were similar to the previously listed races; however, a few birds of *F. p. macropus* and *F. p. cassini* lineage were initially released but did not survive and were not used thereafter (H. Tordoff pers. comm.). The released peregrines were carefully tracked and their survival and breeding success tabulated. See Conservation for percentages of the different subspecies that were released and those surviving to breed (from Tordoff 2000).

If a true subspecies does eventually evolve, it may take hundreds of years for the conglomeration of races to sufficiently intermix to have genetic similarity among 75 percent of the population, which is required for a subspecies to be recognized. (Most subspecies are formed from one or two adjacent races.)

As described above, at least four foreign subspecies were used in building the current population of the "Eastern" Peregrine Falcon. (1) Nominate *F. p. peregrinus* is found in most of Europe south of the Arctic and north of the Pyrenees, Balkan, and Himalayan Mts. to cen. Russia. It may winter to the Mediterranean region and Iberian Peninsula. A large Peregrine. Often similar in appearance to North American *anatum*. Head is not as black and malar mark not as broad on the cheeks and auriculars as *anatum*. The ventral areas vary from whitish to medium pinkish tawny and breasts are moderately spotted on males and heavily spotted or have large teardrop-shaped markings on females. Juveniles are similar to *anatum* but have more pale edgings on the dorsum. *See* Forsman (1999) for photographs. (2) *F. p. brookei* is resident from nw. Africa and Spain and east through the Middle East and the Caspian Sea region of Iran. Dark and heavily marked race, but much smaller than *anatum*. Head is black with solid black cheeks and auriculars; nape often has rufous patches. Breast and belly are often deep pinkish rufous with heavily spotted breast and narrowly but densely barred belly and flanks. Juveniles are similar to *anatum* but are much smaller. *See* Forsman (1999) for photographs. (3) *F. p. macropus* inhabits Australia. Following Ferguson-Lees and Christi (2001), former *F. p. submelanogenys* of sw. Australia is considered as part of *F. p. macropus* since color variations of both types occur throughout the continent. A small race. The head is black with broad malar marks that cover all of the cheeks and auriculars. Ventral region varies from deep pinkish rufous on females to grayish on males, and is heavily but narrowly barred on belly and flanks; breast is usually spotted. Although small, juveniles are quite similar to *anatum* and lack distinct pale dorsal edgings on the feathers. *See* Debus (1998) and Marchant (1994), respectively, for photographs and illustrations. (4) *F. p. cassini* is resident in South America with local populations in Bolivia, Ecuador, and Peru; however, mainly found from Chile to Tierra del Fuego and the Falkland Islands. Small, dark, and heavily marked subspecies. Black malar blends with the black cheeks and auriculars. Rufous and gray ventral region with dense black barring. Juveniles are very similar to *anatum* but smaller. Also has a rare pale morph that was not used in introduction to North America. See Ferguson-Lees and Christi (2001) for illustrations.

Reintroduced/introduced subspecies in e. Canada.—Nestling western *F. p. anatum* that were taken from remnant breeding areas in 1970 in s. Alberta, nw. Northwest Territories, and the Yukon Territory were used as the original breeding stock for reintroduction in Canada; a few eastern *anatum* were from Labrador (Fyfe 1988).

A few individuals of foreign *F. p. peregrinus* and *F. p. brookei* lineage that were introduced in n. Michigan and n. Minnesota have immigrated to cen. Ontario on the north shore of Lake Superior and currently breed (Tordoff 2000). Immigration also occurs in e. Canada from the Midwest and e. U.S. In 2002, the breeding pairs in s. Ontario were comprised of the following mixture of Peregrines: 10 individuals were of U.S. origin (from Pennsylvania, Ohio, and the Midwest), seven were of Ontario or Québec origin, and seven were unknown. Likewise, Canadian-released *anatum* have immigrated south into the n. U.S. and are breeding.

See below for data on subspecies and Conservation for reintroduction details for the U.S. and Canada.

Other subspecies in the world.—There are 11 additional subspecies in Europe and Asia: (1) *F. p. calidus* inhabits the Arctic of Eurasia. Winters to throughout Africa, s. Asia, Indonesia, New Guinea, and the Philippines. Similar pale color of *tundrius* of North America and Greenland, but the breasts of most females have dash marks or spots. (2) *F. p. japonensis* of ne. Siberia and n. Japan is similar to *calidus* but somewhat darker, and smaller and even darker on the islands of the Sea of Okhotsk (possible separate race *F. p. pleskei*). (3) *F. p. minor* is resident south of the Sahara Desert in Africa. Small race with dark head and broad malar marks; may have rufous on the nape. Moderately marked buff-colored ventral region. (4) *F. p. radama* is resident on Madagascar and the Comoro Islands. Similar to *minor* but smaller, darker head, and more heavily marked on ventral areas. (5) *F. p. peregrinator* is mainly resi-

dent from Pakistan to se. China and n. North Vietnam. Very blackish dorsal and broad malar marks. Ventral is deep pinkish rufous and lightly to fairly heavily barred on flanks. (6) *F. p. ernesti* is resident on w. and peninsular Thailand, Indonesia, Philippines, New Guinea, and the Bismarck Archipelago. Small race. Darkest race. Very black head and dorsum and very grayish and heavily barred ventral region. (7) *F. p. nesiotes* is sedentary on Fiji, New Caledonia, and Vanuatu. Small and dark race like *ernesti* but more rufous on ventral region. (8) *F. p. madens* is a rare resident on the Cape Verde Islands off nw. Africa. Large and very brownish on the dorsum with much rufous on the nape. (9) *F. p. furuitii* is endangered and may be extinct on Volcano and possibly Bonin Islands, Japan. Similar to *pealei*; juvenile not as dark and heavily marked. (10) *F. p. pelegrinoides* and (11) *F. p. babylonicus* have typically been listed as subspecies of Peregrine Falcon; however, they are considered a possible separate species, the Barbary Falcon (*F. pelegrinoides*), by some recent authors. The pale western form, *pelegrinoides*, is resident in arid regions of n. Africa, Middle East, and the Arabian Peninsula. The even paler and more rufous-headed eastern form, *babylonicus*, is found in the arid regions from Iran to w. Mongolia. Color markings and patterns are similar to but paler than those of all Peregrine races; voice is identical to Peregrine's (Clark 1999). *F. p. pelegrinoides* apparently do not intergrade with the Spanish Peregrine, *F. p. brookei*, in Morocco. However, preliminary DNA samples are inconclusive in separating them from Peregrines (White et al. 1995). A falconer's escaped female *pelegrinoides* has bred with a male *anatum* Peregrine in cen. Mexico in 2001 and 2002 (R. Padilla-Borja pers. comm.). It is considered a subspecies of Peregrine by Forsman (1999), but Clark (1999) and Ferguson-Lees and Christi (2001) consider it a probable species. Museum specimens appear as pale, more rufous-headed Peregrines; however, partial rufous infusion on the head is also found on some other subspecies of Peregrine. Until taxonomic studies are more conclusive, *F. p. pelegrinoides* and *F. p. babylonicus* are considered here as a subspecies of Peregrine Falcon.

COLOR MORPHS: None in the three North American races. *F. p. cassini* of South America has a rare pale "Kleinschmidt's" morph that inhabits the Straits of Magellan in South America.

SIZE: Medium-sized raptor. Males are smaller than females, with no overlap. Juveniles are often longer than adults because many have longer rectrices. In flight, juveniles also appear bulkier than adults because of having broader remiges. Since "Eastern" Peregrines are a mix of bloodlines and encompass the spectrum of sizes from the largest race, *pealei*, to the smallest races, *brookei* and *macropus*, total lengths and wingspans are neither available nor applicable. However, wing-chord lengths for each respective race are listed below for general comparison.

F. p. *tundrius*: MALE.—Length: 14–16 in. (36–41 cm), some juveniles may be on the larger end of the spectrum because many have longer tails than adults do; wingspan: 37–39 in. (94–99 cm); wing chord: MALE.—292–330 mm. FEMALE.—Length: 16–18 in. (36–46 cm); wingspan: 40–46 in.(102–117 cm); wing chord: 331–368 mm.

Introduced races.—"Eastern" types involve a mixture of the following subspecies. F. p. *pealei*.—This large race was the basis of the lineage of a large number of released birds. Data are based on measurements by D. Varland of migrating/wintering birds in sw. Washington (unpubl. data): MALE (*n* = 4 adults, 4 juveniles; all measures similar).—Length: 16.3 in. (41.4 cm); wingspan: 36.2 in. (92.1 cm); wing chord: 320–345 mm. FEMALE (*n* = 6 adults, 7 juveniles).—Length: 19 in. (48 cm); wingspan: 44 in. (111 cm); wing chord: 356–387 mm. Additional subspecies: "Western" F. p. *anatum*.— Data are based on measurements from C. M. White (pers. comm.). Boreal forest birds are larger than southern birds, and extirpated eastern birds were larger than western birds. Male: 291–322 mm, female: 333–365 mm. F. p. *peregrinus*.—Male: 289–334 mm, female: 339–375 mm. F. p. *brookei*.—Male: 275–312 mm, female: 306–355 mm. F. p. *macropus*.—Male: 270–300 mm, female: 304–348 mm. F. p. *cassini*.—Male: 284–328 mm, female 332–358 mm.

SPECIES TRAITS: HEAD.—Dark malar mark (mustache) that extends below the eyes and onto the lower mandible. Bare orbital skin. As in all falcons, there is a baffle in the central nares region that permits breathing in high-speed flight. BODY.—Long toes. When perched, the outer toe typically bends inward and lays sideways, and the inner toes may cross over each other. WINGS.—**In flight, wings are long and taper to pointed wingtips. When perched, wingtips extend to the tail tip or are just short of the tail tip.**

ADULT TRAITS: HEAD.—Yellow cere and orbital skin, which are generally brighter on males. **Black malar mark may be one of four types:** (1) *Very wide type.*—**Malar mark covers most or all of the auriculars and creates a black helmet with all of the head being black.** (2) *Wide type.*—**A wide columnar shape and covers most of the auriculars except for a small area on the lower one-third of the auriculars.** (3) *Moderately wide type.*—**Moderately wide columnar shape with the lower one-half to two-thirds of the auriculars being white.** (4) *Narrow type.*—**Narrow black stripe, often with a break at the gape. On all types, the crown is dark gray or black and the nape is black. BODY (dorsal).—Males are bluish gray and distinctly barred and females are darker, more brownish gray or brownish black, and often have ill-defined barring and are nearly uniformly colored. When viewed from above in flight, the lower back, rump, and uppertail coverts are paler and more bluish than the rest of the upperparts and dorsal tail surface.** Males exhibit the pale lower back, rump, and uppertail coverts more than females do; females are typically more distinctly barred with black on these areas and the pale bluish is not as apparent. BODY (ventral).—Breast is unmarked or covered with black spots or dashes. Flanks are distinctly barred and the belly is partially barred or spotted. Leg feathers are covered with black barring. Yellow feet and tarsi are generally brighter on males. WINGS (dorsal).—Dorsal surface is like the back and is more bluish on males and darker and more brownish on females. WINGS (ventral).—**The dark gray underside of the remiges is equally barred throughout with white or pale tawny-rufous. The underwing coverts and axillaries are also white or pale tawny-rufous and narrowly barred with black. The underwing appears uniformly grayish at a distance.** TAIL.—**The dorsal surface of the tail is distinctly darker than the bluish back, rump,**

and uppertail coverts. It is also darker than much of the upperparts except the back and head. On the dorsal surface, the tails of males are often dark blue with equal-width blue and black bands or have narrower black bands; some males and most females have black tails with narrow blue or bluish brown bands. Both sexes have a broad white terminal band. The black bands may get progressively narrower toward the basal region of the tail. The ventral surface of the tail is darker than the rest of the underparts.

Note: At a distance, the dorsal surface of Peregrines appears black on the head, back, and tail and medium bluish or grayish on the wings and forward body; on males and many females, the pale blue lower back, rump, and uppertail coverts are obvious.

ADULTS OF "ARCTIC" (*F. p. tundrius*): HEAD.—Broad white forehead and white lores. Black malar mark is moderately wide type. The auriculars are white on the lower half and medium gray or dark gray on the upper half. The crown is medium gray or dark gray; rarely black. At close range, birds with medium and dark gray crowns have distinct black shaft streaking. Nape and hindneck are black and sometimes have a small or moderate amount of white or rufous mottling or patches on the nape. BODY (ventral).—White breast, pale pinkish tawny belly, white lower belly, and pale grayish flanks and leg feathers. WINGS.—On perched birds, wingtips equal to the tail tip. WINGS (ventral).—White barring on the remiges and white underwing coverts with narrow black barring.

Adult male (*F. p. tundrius*): HEAD.—The upper auriculars and crown are typically medium gray. Black nape and hindneck contrast with the rest of the paler bluish gray upperparts. Nape rarely has pale mottling. BODY (dorsal).—Medium bluish gray with moderately wide black cross bars on the back and front half of the scapulars. The rear half of the scapulars may be medium or pale bluish gray and have faint, partial blackish cross bars or are nearly unmarked bluish gray. The pale bluish gray lower back and rump may be unmarked or have partial, narrow blackish crossbars. The pale bluish gray uppertail coverts are faintly barred with black. Overall dorsal appearance of males is medium bluish gray. BODY (ven-

tral).—Unmarked breast. Rarely, breast is finely dashed with small dark markings on the lower half and very rarely on all of the breast. Flanks are covered with narrow black bars. Average birds have only a few small dark spots or partial bars on the belly. The palest types can be nearly unmarked. The lower belly either is thinly barred or unmarked. The leg feathers are covered with very narrow dark bars. WINGS (dorsal).—Blackish on the forward upperwing coverts, but medium bluish gray with narrow black bars on all coverts. The tertials are often pale bluish gray with faint, narrow blackish barring. The tertials may be unbarred on the palest males. The tertials blend with the pale bluish back, rump, and uppertail coverts. TAIL.—**Dorsal surface is blackish and distinctly darker than the uppertail coverts, rump, tertials, and back.**

Adult female (*F. p. tundrius*): HEAD.—Upper half of the auriculars and crown are dark gray, but are occasionally medium gray or black. Nape and hindneck are black. Females are likely to have whitish or rufous mottling or patches on the nape. BODY (dorsal).—Back and forward half of the scapulars can either be solid black or black with narrow bluish brown crossbars and outer feather edges. The rear half of the scapulars are a paler bluish black with broad medium bluish or medium bluish brown crossbars and outer feather edges. Overall appearance is more blackish and brownish than on males. The lower back, rump, and uppertail coverts are moderately paler and more bluish than the rest of the upperparts and broadly barred with black. BODY (ventral).—The breast is typically unmarked; however, heavily marked individuals have a small amount of narrow dashes or spots on the lower half of the breast and sometimes on all of the breast. Flanks are marked with narrow or moderately wide black bars. The belly is fully covered with partial black bars or spots. The lower belly is thinly barred. The leg feathers are narrowly barred with black. WINGS (dorsal).—The lesser upperwing coverts are quite black and have a minimal amount of pale bluish edgings on the feathers. Pale cross-barring becomes more evident on the median and greater secondary coverts. TAIL.—**The blackish dorsal tail surface is moderately darker than the uppertail coverts, rump, and back.**

ADULTS OF "ARCTIC" (PALE TYPE of *F. p. tundrius*): Information herein is based on photographs and data supplied on breeding birds from Rankin Inlet, Nunavut (G. Court pers. comm.). A rare plumage type or morph that exists on a very small percentage of birds inhabiting the cen. Canadian Arctic in Nunavut. It is estimated that fewer than 3 percent of females and a lesser percentage of males exhibit this pale plumage. Photographs of this type are of known-age females that are greater than 2 years old (and mated with typical adult males). This rare plumage was first noted by White (1968).

Note: Migrant and wintering birds are found in normal *tundrius* areas.

Adult male pale type (*F. p. tundrius*): As described below for females, but are decidedly bluish and not brown. *Note:* Male is not depicted in accompanying photographs.

Adult female pale type (*F. p. tundrius*): HEAD.—Forehead and central crown is white. There is a dark brown U-shape mark that starts above the eyes and loops around the rear of the crown. Lores are white. An irregularly shaped narrow type or moderately wide type black malar mark extends under the eyes (generally narrower than on typical adults). The dark malar does not connect to the narrow dark brown eyeline that runs above the all-white auriculars and extends onto the white nape as a partial dark brown "V." Fleshy areas are the typical yellow. BODY and WINGS (dorsal).—In early summer, the medium or dark brown back, scapulars, and upperwing coverts have white or pale brown crossbars and outer edges. Incoming new feathers have a slight grayish cast to them. The lower back, rump, and uppertail coverts may be bluish and barred with brown. BODY (ventral).—White. Breast is unmarked. Belly has a few dark specks, and the lower belly is unmarked. The forward flanks are lightly spotted and the rear flanks are sparsely marked with thin partial bars. The leg feathers and undertail coverts are white and unmarked. WINGS (ventral).—Similar to typical *tundrius* with barred remiges and underwing coverts. TAIL.—Uppertail coverts may be pale bluish and barred. Tail is dark brown or blackish and barred with bluish brown. Undertail is darker than rest of the ventral regions.

ADULTS OF "AMERICAN" (*F. p. anatum*): HEAD.—Forehead is solid black or has a narrow white band. Lores are typically all black even if the forehead is white. Black malar mark can be any of the three types: very wide, wide, or moderately wide (and similar to *tundrius*). *Note:* The moderately wide type malar did not occur on former eastern *anatum*. Malar marks average narrower on birds from nw. Canada and Alaska. The crown, nape, and hindneck are black. Nape is always black and lacks pale mottling. Black malar mark is sometimes a moderately wide columnar shape with white on the lower one-third of the auriculars. The crown is sometimes dark gray. BODY (ventral).—Two main types: (1) *Rufous type.*—Breast, belly, and lower belly are uniformly pale or medium tawny-rufous; flanks are pale or medium gray or are rufous on the forward half. (2) *White type.*—White breast, pale grayish flanks and leg feathers, pale tawny-rufous belly, and white lower belly. Leg feathers are sometimes pale tawny-rufous. WINGS.—On perched birds, wingtips nearly equal or equal the tail tip. WINGS (ventral).—Pale tawny-rufous or white barring on the remiges, and the coverts are either washed with pale tawny-rufous or white with black barring. Birds with pale tawny-rufous on the ventral markings are also similarly colored on the rest of the ventral areas.

Adult male (*F. p. anatum*): HEAD.—**Black malar mark is either of two types: very wide type or wide type.** Moderately wide columnar-shaped malar marks are rare on males. BODY (dorsal).—Black back and forward half of scapulars. They may have faint bluish barring and pale outer edges on some forward scapulars. Rear half of the scapulars are a paler medium bluish gray with distinct black cross bars. **The lower back, rump, and uppertail coverts are medium blue and barred with black.** BODY (ventral).—Breast, belly, and lower belly are either uniformly tawny-rufous or white. Breast is typically unmarked. Flanks are distinctly barred with black. Belly is moderately marked with small cross bars or spots, but is occasionally very lightly marked. Leg feathers are moderately marked with narrow bars. WINGS (dorsal).—Lesser upperwing coverts are black with narrow bluish gray edges. The median and greater secondary coverts have

bluish gray barring on the outer edges. The tertials are usually slightly paler than the rest of
the wing coverts and have fairly distinct black
cross bars. TAIL.—**The dark bluish or blackish
banded tail contrasts sharply with the
medium bluish gray uppertail coverts, rump,
and back.**

Adult female (*F. p. anatum*): HEAD.—Black
malar mark can be any of the three types:
very wide type, wide type, or moderately wide
type. If malar mark is a wide type or moderately wide type, then the forehead is often
white. The moderately wide type of black
malar mark occurs throughout the range, but
seems to be especially common on females inhabiting the Rocky Mts. (including precaptive-
release era). BODY (dorsal).—Back and forward half of the scapulars are black. The rear
half of the scapulars is also black and may have
grayish brown cross-barring or lack pale barring and be virtually solid blackish gray or
blackish brown. Overall appearance of the dorsal region is much darker and more brownish
than on males, and darker than on most *tundrius* females. **The lower back, rump, and uppertail coverts are somewhat more bluish
than the back and scapulars and are barred
with black.** BODY (ventral).—Those with
whitish ventral areas seem to be more prevalent in the northern part of their range or
where they intergrade with *pealei*. Breast is either unmarked, partially marked on the lower
half, or fully marked. Breast markings consist
of small dashes or small or medium-sized
spots. The flanks are moderately to heavily
barred. The lower belly is moderately barred.
Leg feathers are moderately barred. WINGS
(dorsal).—The lesser upperwing coverts are
mainly black and unmarked or, at most, have
narrow bluish brown edges. The median and
greater secondary coverts are somewhat barred
with bluish brown. The tertials are distinctly
marked with bluish brown and black bars.
TAIL.—**The black tail with pale bands is
somewhat darker than the bluish-barred uppertail coverts and rump.**

**ADULTS OF "EASTERN" (no subspecies designa-
tion):** It is difficult to describe plumages since
several subspecies were used in the captive-
breeding programs, with a vast array of intergrade characters prevailing. HEAD.—Black
malar mark varies from moderately wide type

with a large amount of white on the auriculars
as on all *tundrius* and some western *anatum*,
wide type with small or moderate white auriculars as on *pealei* and *peregrinus*, or very wide
type with all-black "helmets" and dark foreheads as on many *anatum*, *brookei*, *cassini*, and
macropus. BODY (dorsal).—Varies from being
barred with medium bluish (males) or blackish
gray or brownish with a moderate or minimal
amount of paler bluish or brownish cross-barring (females). Some females will be virtually
solid blackish on the dorsum because of the
lack of cross-barring. The lower back, rump,
and uppertail coverts will be paler bluish on all
birds since this is a distinct Peregrine trait, but
is more noticeable on males than on females.
BODY (ventral).—Variable from being white
to deep tawny-rufous as on the original eastern
anatum and on *brookei* and some *macropus*
types. Breast may vary from being unmarked
to heavily spotted as on *brookei*, *pealei*, *peregrinus*, and some western *anatum*. Flanks are
barred on all races. Belly may be lightly to
heavily spotted or barred. TAIL.—**All races
have dark dorsal and ventral tail surfaces that
contrast with the paler bluish uppertail
coverts, rump, and lower back.**

Note: The ventral-side photographs of the
two "Eastern" types illustrate different genetic
strains. The male in plate 500 is similar to
macropus of Australia. The female in plates 498
and 499 (banded known-aged bird) is nearly
identical to female *peregrinus* of Europe; however, in her fresh first-adult plumage in autumn, this bird was very rufous on the underparts and similar to *anatum*. In her juvenile
plumage, she was very heavily marked and
similar to *pealei*.

SUBADULT TRAITS (ALL SUBSPECIES): This
plumage stage may occur from mid-spring to
mid-summer. HEAD.—Fully adult with black
malar and black or gray cap and nape. A few
brown juvenile feathers may be scattered on
the crown region. Black malar area molts into
full adult feathering before other areas. Cere
and orbital skin can be fairly bright yellow on
males but nearly always pale yellow or greenish
yellow on females. BODY (dorsal).—Nearly
full or full adult bluish or grayish feathering.
Lower back and rump are often largely retained brown juvenile feathering (seen only
from above in flight). BODY (ventral).—

Largely adultlike, but all have a small amount of brown juvenile streaking retained on the mainly adultlike spotted or barred belly and forward flanks. Leg feathers are primarily barred adult type. Legs and tarsi are medium or bright yellow and usually brighter on males. WINGS (dorsal and ventral).—Ninety-five percent of the body molts before much of the wing feathers begin molting to adult feathering. A few primaries will be dark and neat adult feathers, but most will be worn and faded brown juvenile feathers. Virtually all of the upper- and underwing coverts will be retained juvenile. On the dorsal surface, the worn brown upperwing coverts contrast with the new adult bluish or grayish scapulars and back. TAIL.—Retained brown juvenile feathers until the two central deck rectrices start growing in as new adult feathers. The white tips of the worn juvenile rectrices are mostly worn off.

JUVENILE TRAITS: HEAD.—Cere and orbital skin are pale blue throughout fall. Cere and orbital skin gradually change to pale yellow by mid- to late winter and some, especially males, may be bright yellow by late winter or spring. Black malar mark is variable in width: (1) *Wide type.*—Wide black columnar shape with a small amount of tawny or white on the lower one-third of the auriculars. (2) *Moderately wide type.*—Moderately wide columnar shape, and often with a break in the dark mark at the gape region. There is a dark strip on the top one-third of the auriculars and the lower two-thirds are tawny or white. (3) *Narrow type.*—Narrow dark columnar shape, and very often with a break in the dark mark at the gape region with all of the auriculars being tawny or white. BODY.—Dorsal areas are dark brown. Tawny underparts are variably streaked with dark brown. In the fall, the pale-colored legs and tarsi are variable in color: bluish, grayish, greenish, or yellowish; however, they can be medium yellow. By mid- to late winter, legs and tarsi turn to medium or bright yellow. WINGS.—On perched birds, wingtips are somewhat shorter than (about 12 mm) or equal to the tail tip.

JUVENILES OF "ARCTIC" (*F. p. tundrius*): HEAD.—Black malar mark may be either moderately wide type or occasionally the narrow type. The black malar mark merges with the broad dark brown or black eyeline that runs along the very upper part of the auriculars and behind the eyes above the auriculars, and extends onto the nape. The lower two-thirds or one-half of the auriculars is pale tawny and unmarked. Broad pale tawny forehead. There is a large dark brown patch on the crown of the head, and the forward part extends ahead of the eyes and touches the orbital skin; most feathers are narrowly edged with pale tawny. A moderately wide pale tawny supercilium is situated between the brown crown patch and the broad dark brown or black eyeline that begins above the eyes and extends onto the nape. On the darker-headed birds, the crown is virtually all dark and the supercilium is short. Much of the nape is pale tawny and mottled with dark brown. BODY (dorsal).—The dark brown back and scapulars are moderately edged with pale tawny and create a moderately scalloped look. BODY (ventral).—Pale tawny breast, belly, and lower belly are narrowly streaked with dark brown. On the forward section, the flanks are streaked and on the distal section they are covered with large arrowhead marks with a broad bar on the basal region of each feather. The tawny leg feathers are covered with narrow dark brown streaks. The tawny undertail coverts marked with very narrow shaft streaks or are narrowly barred with dark brown. WINGS (dorsal).—Dark brown with moderately wide tawny scalloped edgings on all coverts. WINGS (ventral).—Dark gray remiges are marked with moderately wide pale tawny-rufous spots or bars. The tawny coverts are streaked and barred with dark brown. Overall appearance is a uniformly marked under wing. TAIL.—Dark brown or grayish on the dorsal surface with four or five narrow tawny-rufous bands and a broad white terminal band. The ventral surface is dark gray with several narrow tawny-rufous bands.

Note: A very common type for either sex.
JUVENILES OF "ARCTIC" (LIGHTLY MARKED/ BLONDE TYPE *F. p. tundrius*): HEAD.—The black malar mark is the narrow type. The auriculars are pale tawny and may have a narrow rufous-brown strip on the top edge. The moderately wide or narrow dark brown eyeline above the auriculars extends onto the nape. The forehead and crown are either uniformly pale tawny or there is a narrow brown region on the rear of the crown. BODY (dorsal).—

The dark brown back and scapulars are broadly edged with pale tawny, creating a scalloped appearance. BODY (ventral).—The pale tawny underparts have very narrow dark brown streaking on the breast, belly, and lower belly. The flanks are narrowly streaked on the forward part and have small brown arrowhead-shaped markings on the distal part. Leg feathers are very narrowly streaked. The undertail coverts can have a thin bar on each feather or a narrow dark streak along each feather shaft. WINGS (dorsal).—Dark brown coverts are broadly edged with pale tawny. WINGS (ventral) and TAIL.—As described for Juveniles of "Arctic."

Note: A common type for either sex. Some may be the offspring of a pale type adult; however, since they are common, they may also be paler variants that occur throughout their range.

JUVENILES OF "AMERICAN" (*F. p. anatum*): HEAD.—**Malar mark is the wide type and blends with the dark brown cap; nape may be dark or have some pale patches.** Forehead is dark or has a narrow tawny patch. The tawny auriculars are unmarked. BODY (dorsal).—Dark brown with very narrow tawny-rufous tips on some scapular feathers or can be virtually all dark brown. BODY (ventral).—Rufous-tawny (more reddish than *tundrius* juveniles) with moderately wide dark brown streaking on the breast, belly, and lower belly. The flanks are marked as on Juveniles of "Arctic." Tawny leg feathers typically have moderately wide dark streaking, but can be narrow streaking. WINGS (dorsal).—Dark brown with very narrow tawny-rufous tips on the larger coverts. WINGS (ventral).—As on Juveniles of "Arctic." TAIL.—Dorsal surface either is unmarked dark brown or grayish brown or with partial, narrow rufous-tawny pale bands.

Note: This type is found throughout this subspecies range in the West and on many released birds in the East. Brown on the dorsal surface with four or five narrow, pale rufous-tawny bands. Ventral surface is barred with narrow rufous-tawny bands.

JUVENILES OF "AMERICAN" (LIGHTLY MARKED TYPE *F. p. anatum*): HEAD.—**Wide type or moderately wide type black malar mark. Both malar types connect with a broad black eyeline that is on the top half of the auriculars and behind the eyes above the auriculars.** The

head is quite pale because the rear two-thirds or one-half of the crown is dark but the forward one-third or one-half and forehead are rufous-tawny. There is either a short pale tawny-rufous supercilium just above the eyes or the supercilium is wide and extends onto the nape. The nape is quite pale and mottled with dark brown. *Note:* Head can be as pale as on darker-headed *tundrius*. BODY (dorsal).—Dark brown with very narrow or narrow rufous-tawny edges on the lower part of the back and all scapular feathers. *Note:* Can be as lightly edged as on darker *tundrius*. BODY (ventral).—Rufous-tawny with narrow dark brown streaking on the breast, belly, and lower belly. *Note:* Similar to many *tundrius* but more reddish on the ventral base color. The forward flanks are streaked and the distal flanks are covered with large arrowhead-shaped markings and barring on the inner portion of each feather. The leg feathers are narrowly streaked. *Note:* Leg feathers are marked similarly to many *tundrius*. The undertail coverts are barred with dark brown. WINGS (dorsal).—Dark brown with narrow tawny-rufous edges on most coverts. WINGS (ventral).—Marked as described for Juvenile Traits. TAIL.—Dark brown or grayish brown on the dorsal surface with four or five narrow, pale rufous-tawny bands. Ventral surface is barred with narrow rufous-tawny bands.

Note: This type is regularly found throughout the Rocky Mts., particularly in arid regions. Some museum specimens of *anatum* from Arizona, Colorado, and Wyoming indicate that lightly marked types with pale heads existed historically long before there was any chance of possible intergrading from released stock (AMNH; C. M. White pers. comm.). This type of *anatum* has been released in e. Canada.

JUVENILES OF "EASTERN" (no subspecies designation): HEAD.—Black malar can vary from being a narrow type, wide type, or very wide type. The crown of the head may be pale as in many *tundrius* or fairly dark as in many *anatum, cassini, pealei,* and *peregrinus,* or dark as in many *anatum, brookei,* and *macropus.* BODY.—Dorsal color and pattern varies from distinctly edged with tawny as in *tundrius* or darker as in many other races. Ventral region can vary from being lightly streaked as in *tundrius* to heavily streaked as in *pealei.*

ABNORMAL PLUMAGES: A few sight records of partial albinos with a few white feathers and sight records and captured juveniles in the cream-colored imperfect albino plumage (Clark and Wheeler 2001). *Note:* Very rare plumage types are not depicted in accompanying photographs.

HABITAT: *F. p. tundrius.* **Summer.**—Low-elevation tundra of the Arctic. Breeding areas are along lakes, rivers, and sea coasts that provide embankments and cliffs for nesting sites. Absent from montane and year-round ice-pack regions, particularly interior areas of larger Arctic islands such as Baffin Island. Climate is cool or cold and damp.

F. p. tundrius. **Winter.**—In the U.S., found in mid-latitude and subtropical low-elevation areas along coastal beaches, marshes, tidal flats, and other riparian zones on coastal and southern interior locations. Urban areas and semi-open agricultural, grazed, and natural areas are also inhabited. South of the U.S., found in similar habitat but in a tropical environment. Occasionally found in montane areas, and have been seen at 14,000 ft. (4,300 m) in the Andes Mts. of South America. Cliffs are not required at this time of year, but, if present, may be used for roosting. Climate is hot and wet or dry.

F. p. tundrius. **Migration.**—Found in a wide variety of open to forested habitats from coastal lowlands to low montane areas. Largest numbers frequent coastal lowlands along the Atlantic Ocean. Favored staging areas exist on beaches, dunes, marshes, and tidal flats of coastal mainland and especially barrier islands. These areas are found from Massachusetts to Florida, and especially from New Jersey to Virginia and in Florida. Climate is variable from cool to hot and moderately wet.

F. p. anatum and "Eastern" Peregrine. **Summer/all seasons.**—Predominantly year-round in moderate-sized and large urban centers with tall buildings, bridges, and other tall structures that provide ledges or cavities for nesting sites. Tall artificial hacking and/or nesting towers with protective wooden boxes on top were installed in many coastal marshes along the Atlantic Seaboard. Forested and semi-open coastal and interior regions along lakes and rivers with cliffs are used by a small but growing number of pairs. Historical nesting cliffs used by former eastern *anatum* are being used as well as newly found cliffs. Abandoned open-pit mines with their high, steep rock walls are sometimes used for nesting. Climate is warm to hot and moderately wet.

F. p. anatum and "Eastern" Peregrine. **Winter and migration.**—Similar habitat as in summer, but some frequent same habitat as *tundrius* does.

HABITS: Fairly tame to tame species. Solitary, but a few birds may loosely assemble in areas of high prey density during migration and winter. Peregrines frequently bathe and drink, and virtually all nest sites are near water. Peregrines are active at all times of the day, including dawn and dusk, and are sometimes nocturnal. Radio-tagged migrants have been documented flying at night.

As in all falcons, Peregrines regularly fluff the throat and forehead feathers when relaxed or in cool temperatures. In strong winds, the tail is braced against the perch for added stability.

Peregrines perch on any elevated natural or artificial structure and readily stand on the ground. In coastal areas, Peregrines will stand on sandy beaches, on debris, or on dunes.

A playful species; even adults have been seen picking up and dropping and catching plastic objects. Peregrines sometimes engage in vicious, often deadly battles for nesting territories.

FEEDING: An aerial and perch hunter; rarely engages in pirating, scavenging, or terrestrial hunting. Peregrines typically prey on a few select species within regional and local areas. Particularly with migrants, diet may vary seasonally. Being crepuscular, Peregrines regularly hunt during early morning and late evening. Avian prey is mainly captured in flight, but are also captured while on the ground or over water.

Females generally hunt larger prey than do males. Peregrines mainly feed on birds ranging from small passerines to mid-size waterfowl. Unusually large avian prey such as cormorants, geese, and large herons are very rarely taken by females. Breeding pairs of Peregrine Falcons also cooperatively hunt. In mid- and lower latitudes, Peregrines feed on bats. Large flying insects, captured in flight, are mainly eaten by juveniles.

Prey of all sizes are typically grabbed and held by Peregrines. Small prey are carried to a safe eating location. Prey that is larger than a small duck (e.g., teal-size) is too heavy for even female Peregrines to carry. Large prey is latched onto and the Peregrine glides to the ground and begins to feed. Rarely, large or small prey are hit at high speeds and raked by the rear talon of a clenched foot; this attack injures or kills the prey, which drops to the ground or water. The falcon then flies down and lands on the prey or picks it off the surface of the water or ground and takes it to another location to eat it. Avian prey evading capture will often dive to the ground, into dense vegetation, or onto or into water. Peregrines may veer around and try to snatch such prey before they can gain flight.

Prey species use evasive techniques to escape capture. Some passerines and shorebirds form tight flocks, which deter Peregrines.

Peregrines immediately break the neck of captured prey. Neck-breaking occurs in flight or on the ground or perch. Prey is partially or fully plucked before eating. On large prey, often only the meat on the neck and breast is eaten. On small prey, the wings are torn off before the body is eaten; on large birds, the wings are left intact. Adults pluck and decapitate prey before bringing it back to feed nestlings. The head and wings are left intact on medium-sized and large avian prey at all times. During other seasons, large and some small prey are eaten at the point of capture; small prey may also be eaten while the Peregrine is flying or carried to another, often elevated location to be eaten. Prey that is eaten in flight is held by one foot when the falcon is gliding, kiting, or soaring. Falcons migrating over the ocean may use tall structures on ships as feeding and resting posts.

Aerial hunting.—Quarry is often targeted from long distances with the falcons engaging in moderate to long pursuits. Angled or vertical dives are initiated while gliding, kiting, or soaring at low to high altitudes. Prey is also captured by being tail-chased or intercepted on level flight from the side or front angles. Short dives are used when the previous methods fail. Peregrines will tail-chase, intercept from the side or front, or angle up underneath intended prey from low-level flight. Peregrines regularly use low-altitude, high-speed, surprise-and-flush forays.

Perch hunting.—From high perches, falcons engage in a high-speed, shallow-angled dive toward prey. From low perches, as on beaches, Peregrines will tail-chase, intercept from various angles, use short dives, or angle up underneath intended prey from low-level flight.

Pirating.—A biologist in Oregon has seen Peregrines pirate mammalian prey from Red-tailed Hawks and fish from Osprey. Peregrines have also been seen pirating prey from Merlin and Sharp-shinned Hawks and also can kill the smaller raptors.

Scavenging.—Juveniles and rarely adults eat carrion, primarily during winter, if live prey is difficult to capture. This appears to more of a trait with *F. p. pealei* on the Pacific Coast than other races.

Terrestrial hunting.—*F. p. anatum* in the West occasionally pursues prey on foot into dense vegetation, and *F. p. tundrius* walks or hops on the ground on the tundra, capturing voles, lemmings, and young birds. "Eastern" juveniles will walk into pigeon traps in order to capture pigeons.

F. p. tundrius.—The breeding season coincides with the nesting season of Arctic songbirds. In many regions, recently fledged, inexperienced and poorly flying Arctic songbirds make up an extensive part of this race's prey during the nesting season. The smaller, highly agile adult males Peregrines do all or most of the hunting during the early to mid-part of the nesting cycle, concentrating heavily on the small but common and easy-to-catch young songbirds.

At Rankin Inlet, Nunavut, Snow Buntings, Horned Larks, Lapland Longspurs, and American Pipits compose most of the Peregrine's diet. Small shorebirds, but especially Semipalmated Plovers and Semipalmated Sandpipers, form a lesser but still substantial amount of their diet. Larger birds such as Rock Ptarmigan are regionally and seasonally important. Northern species of ducks, such as adult and young Northern Pintail and Long-tailed Duck and young Common and King eiders are also preyed upon. On coastal locations, Black Guillemots are hunted. Less common avian prey are Arctic Terns and Long-tailed Jaegers. Gulls form an even lesser part of the diet.

Brown and Collared lemmings normally form a small part of the diet, but larger numbers are hunted when lemming numbers cyclically increase.

In the high Arctic and in w. Greenland, falcons also extensively feed on songbirds, which include the previously listed species, but also Northern Wheatear and Common and Hoary redpolls. Duck prey are mainly Long-tailed Duck and the two eider species. Alcids, such as Atlantic Puffin (Greenland), Dovekies, Razorbills (Greenland), and Thick-billed Murres may be important prey for coastal pairs. Gulls are also preyed upon to a lesser extent.

Shorebirds form an important dietary component during fall and spring migration. Historical migratory areas along the Atlantic Coast host large shorebird congregations in the fall. Migrant Blue Jays and Northern Flickers, which migrate extensively along the Atlantic Coast, also form a large part of the diet.

Wintering birds also feed extensively on shorebirds. However, depending on geographic region, prey may encompass a variety of tropical bird species.

Migration coincides with peak movements of prime prey species of songbirds and some shorebirds.

"Eastern" Peregrines feed on prey similar to that eaten by the former eastern *F. p. anatum*. However, the former Peregrine race probably fed extensively on Passenger Pigeons until they became rare in the late 1800s and extinct in the early 1900s. Depending on locality, urban Peregrines may rely year-round on the abundant supply of Rock Doves and, to a lesser extent, European Starlings and House Sparrows. However, even urban pairs also may feed extensively on more rural-type species. In metro Toronto, Ontario, the following species are commonly preyed upon: Mourning Doves, Northern Flickers, Blue Jays, Red-winged Blackbirds, Common Grackles, and Brown-headed Cowbirds. Smaller numbers of other passerines, ducks, gulls, and grebes are also preyed upon. In rural and remote natural areas, they may feed on the previously listed species and also on American Woodcock, Common Snipe, Eastern Meadowlarks, several swallow species, and various waterbirds that are common to a particular area. Except for bats, mammals are rarely preyed upon.

Migrant and southern wintering "Eastern" Peregrines feed extensively on shorebirds, waterfowl, and a variety of tropical species of birds.

FLIGHT: Powered flight is an irregular sequence of powerful, moderately deep wingbeats. Peregrines may flap for considerable distances before gliding or alternate short sequences of flapping and gliding. Level flight with steadily beating wings has been documented to 75 mph. (121 km/hr), but more typically at 45–60 mph (72–97 km/h) with intermittent flapping and gliding. Wings are held on a flat plane when gliding and soaring. Peregrines kite in strong winds and rarely hover.

Hunting flights: *Long-dive.*—High-altitude high-speed long, angled, or vertical descent with the wings partially or fully closed. The faster the dive, the more closed-winged and streamlined a Peregrine becomes. Vertical diving speeds of a falconry juvenile female *F. p. anatum* have been verified as exceeding 200 mph (322 km/hr) by sky-jumpers. It is believed that some Peregrines may easily achieve 250 mph (402 km/hr) and possibly 300 mph (483 km/hr), a speed that can be attained by some sky-jumpers. Long dives are initiated while perching, soaring, or kiting. If soaring, they rise up to a high altitude above the intended prey, then proceed to make a long dive. *Short-dive.*—Often used when a long dive was unsuccessful. The Peregrine swings upward above the intended prey and makes one or more short dives to intercept it. *Tail-chase.*—Direct, high-speed flight to overtake aerial prey at low or moderate altitudes. *Underside grab.*—May be initiated from a short-dive or tail-chase in which the falcon swings upward and grabs prey from underneath.

VOICE: Agitated vocalization at nest sites is a rapid, repeated, harsh *cack, cack, cack*. Vocalizations are rarely heard away from the breeding grounds. Courting birds utter several different sounds: (1) *eechip* (both sexes), (2) staccato chittering (both sexes), (3) whinning or begging *waik* (both sexes), (4) staccato chatter (males), (5) rapid *chips* (males), (6) *upchip* (females), (7) *chup-chip* (females), and (8) constant *kree, kree, kree* whine (females and young food-begging).

STATUS AND DISTRIBUTION: *F. p. tundrius.*—
Very uncommon. Their population was somewhat affected by the DDT era but not as much
as DDT affected eastern *F. p. anatum* (and
western *anatum*). This subspecies winters in
areas of Central and South America where
DDT and other organochlorine pesticides are
still used. Numbers have slowly increased and
are possibly near historical levels.

F. p. tundrius. **Summer.**—Sporadically distributed in Arctic biome of n. Labrador, w. and se.
Greenland (with an isolated population near
Thule), Nunavut, n. Québec, and on the islands
of the high Arctic, including portions of Baffin
Island. Mainly found on coastal regions except
in Nunavut. Permanent ice fields prevent them
from occupying many coastal and especially
interior regions of the high Arctic. The southernmost probable *tundrius* population in
Labrador is at 58°N, but an isolated area on
Belcher Island, Québec, is at 56°N. The northernmost nesting in North America, on Baffin
Island, is at about 73°N. On Greenland, most
of the population is south of 72°N; however, an
isolated population near Thule is at 77°N, the
highest breeding latitude for Peregrines. One of
the highest breeding densities, and nearly equal
to that of the high breeding density of *F. p.
pealei* on the Queen Charlotte Is., B.C., is
around Rankin Inlet, Nunavut.

F. p. tundrius. **Winter.**—Very expansive winter
range. In the U.S., it spans from Long Island,
N.Y., south along the Atlantic Coast to Florida
and the Gulf Coast. A rare winter record of a
juvenile banded at Rankin Inlet was found in
Simpson Co., Ky. (in Dec. 1983). Winter range
continues south throughout all of the
Caribbean, Mexico, and the northern two-
thirds of South America. Southernmost birds
are found in n. Argentina, n. Chile, and
Uruguay. Winter density is very low.

F. p. tundrius. **Movements.**—A highly migratory subspecies that engages in the longest migration of any North American subspecies of
Peregrine and any North American raptor.
Movements often entail long over-water crossings. In the fall, in particular, some birds may
be hundreds of miles from land out over the
Atlantic Ocean. These birds use ships for roosting and feeding. According to telemetry data,
some may migrate nocturnally.

Fall migration: All birds must leave the Arctic prior to severe weather when prey becomes
scarce or is not available. Adults may leave their
Arctic nesting grounds by mid- to late Aug., as
soon as their young are independent. At
Rankin Inlet, Nunavut, the last birds leave by
late Sep. The first adults can be seen in s. New
England by late Aug. and along the Mid-Atlantic Coast by early Sep. Adults form the bulk
of the early migrants and juveniles the late migrants. The overall peak movement consists of
both ages but with a high percentage of the
adult population and a moderate percentage of
the juvenile population. Recently fledged juveniles may not leave natal areas until late Aug. to
late Sep. Juveniles make up most of the late-
season migrants. In the East, the largest numbers of Peregrines are tallied along the Mid-
Atlantic Coast at Cape May Point S.P., N.J.,
and on Assateague Island, Md./Va., and in
Florida at Curry Hammocks S.P., Little Crawl
Key on the middle Keys. Other areas extensively used by migrants are: Martha's Vineyard,
Monomoy Island, Nantucket Island in Massachusetts, and Fisher's Island and Long Island in
New York. A distinct peak occurs in the Mid-
Atlantic region in late Sept. to early Oct.; on
the Keys, peak numbers are spread out from
early to mid-Oct. Numbers in all areas drop off
considerably by late Oct., with stragglers occurring at least through mid-Nov. Winter grounds
may be reached from mid-Sep. to Dec.

In the West, comparably large numbers as
seen at eastern hotspots pass through or feed
on Padre Island, Texas.

According to banding and telemetry data,
migration routes are distinctly centered along
the Atlantic Coast and through the central U.S.
(to get to Padre Island, Texas). Greenland birds
make an extensive over-water crossing to Baffin
Island or Labrador, then head down to the Mid-
Atlantic Coast or angle west across the mid-
section of the U.S. then south to Padre Island.
Banded birds from Rankin Inlet fan out and
head due south toward Padre Island or angle
farther east with band-return-points from
s. Ontario to Assateague Island. Two telemetry-
tracked adults from Ungava Peninsula, Québec,
traveled down the East Coast of the U.S. to
Florida: one crossed the Caribbean to n. South
America and the other crossed over to Central

America from Florida and continued south. Some birds make interesting diagonal transcontinental flights, with Alaskan birds being recorded on the Mid-Atlantic Coast and Florida Keys!

Spring migration: The eastern fall hotspots on the Mid-Atlantic Coast are not used during spring migration. However, in the West, similar numbers as in the autumn pass through Padre Island, Texas, in the spring. Adults arrive in the s. U.S. in early to mid-Apr. Peak number of adults are seen along Lake Ontario in New York at Braddock Bay S.P. near Greece and at Derby Hill Hawkwatch near Mexico in late Apr. At Whitefish Point, Chippewa Co., Mich., adults peak in early to mid-May. Juveniles migrate later than adults, and move from late Apr. through May and undoubtedly into Jun. in northern areas.

Adults arrive on their southernmost southern nesting grounds at Rankin Inlet, Nunavut, by May 20, but can be as early as May 10. Those breeding on high-Arctic regions will not arrive at nesting areas until early to mid-Jun. At Rankin Inlet, both sexes often arrive at nesting locations simultaneously.

Former eastern *F. p. anatum*. Summer/all seasons.—The "original" eastern *F. p. anatum*, the "Rock Peregrine," became extinct in the e. U.S. by the early 1960s due to deadly organochlorine pesticides that were extensively used for insect control on crops and forests from 1946 to the early 1970s. The Peregrine's downfall was primarily attributed to DDT and its metabolized form, DDE. DDE reduces the calcium produced by females and thins eggshells, which then break under the weight of incubating birds. However, declines were seen in some eastern states prior to pesticide use, but these are attributed to shooting, egg-collecting, and other disturbances. For example, Tennessee had nest failures and nest abandonment beginning in the 1930s; the last fully documented cliff nesting in the eastern part of the state occurred in 1944, and one pair may have produced young in 1946. The population in Georgia was extirpated by 1942, four years before DDT use. In cen. Massachusetts at the Quabbin Reservoir, nesting was going strong in the mid-1940s, probably due to a slow-down in egg-collecting. However, broken eggs attributed to DDT build-up were beginning to show in

Massachusetts eyries in 1947 and, from 1948 to 1950, nearly all eggs were breaking under the weight of incubating adults. By 1951, nesting no longer occurred in the state.

Three hundred and fifty pairs formerly nested east of the Mississippi River. In 1962, the last pairs attempted to nest in the e. U.S.: (1) Guntersville Lake on the Tennessee River in Marshall Co., Ala., and (2) Cadillac Mt. on Mt. Desert Island in Acadia N.P., Maine. The current small population of Peregrines along coastal Labrador may have been a remnant population of *F. p. anatum* from pre-DDT times. This population was not part of any reintroduction effort by Canada.

Eastern *F. p. anatum* adults were mainly sedentary, but juveniles undoubtedly dispersed, as do many juveniles, or migrated. No data are available on former movements or wintering areas of eastern birds. Some, perhaps, wintered in the Caribbean and farther south into South America, as do many western *anatum*.

"Eastern" Peregrine. Summer/all seasons.—*Very uncommon. Canada:* Restoration population of *F. p. anatum* in Canada were raised and released by the Canadian Wildlife Service and Canadian nonprofit organizations. Provincial wildlife agencies assisted in release programs. *United States:* Restoration population of mixed-lineage Peregrines in the U.S. was produced mainly by nonprofit organizations and private breeders. State wildlife agencies coordinated release programs.

Over 6,000 Peregrine Falcons have been released in Canada and the U.S. since the mid-1970s. With a viable breeding population stabilized and growing, introduction efforts slowed by the mid-1990s and nearly ceased by the early 2000s. All goals initially set for restoration projects have been exceeded. *See* Conservation for more details.

Current status of *F. p. anatum* and "Eastern."—Below is the known status of hacked, captive-released stock derived from restoration programs that have survived and are propagating on their own. The largest numbers are urban-dwelling pairs; however, an increasingly large number are expanding into rural and natural areas.

CANADA (*F. p. anatum*): Figures are for known pairs as of 2000. New Brunswick and

Nova Scotia in Bay of Fundy, including St. John, N.B.: 7 pairs. *Labrador:* 22 pairs, down from 31 pairs in 1995. Production was low in 2000 and 2001. *Ontario:* 31 pairs in the southern part of the province. In s. Ontario, resident with breeding and/or territorial pairs or hack sites in the following cities: Etobicoke, Guelph, Hamilton, Kitchener-Waterloo, London, Niagara Falls, Owen Sound, Ottawa, Richmond Hill, St. Catharines, and Toronto. There are also hack sites in Leeds Co. Peregrines are regularly seen but are not currently breeding in Barrie, Bon Echo, Mississauga, Scarborough/North York, and Windsor. *Note:* 10 individuals breeding in 2002 in s. Ontario are from U.S. origin that have immigrated into the province (from Pennsylvania, Ohio, ne. U.S., and the Midwest), seven individuals are from Ontario or Québec origins, and seven are from unknown origins. In the central part of the province, mainly found near Lake Superior. Breeding occurs at Copper Cliff, Havilland Bay, Killarney Prov. Pk., Lake Superior Prov. Pk. (Devil's Warehouse Idaho), Mink Bay region, Nipigon (Kama Bay and Kama Hills), Northwest Mollie Mt., Pie Island, Robertson Lake, Sleeping Giant Prov. Pk., Square Top Mt., Squaw Bay, Sturgeon Bay, near Sudbury (in an open pit mine), Thunder Bay area (Mt. MacRae and Mt. McKay), and an interior location at Whitefish Lake. *Note:* About 50 birds of mixed lineage were released on Isle Royale in Lake Superior, Mich., and similar numbers were released in n. Minnesota along Lake Superior and the Iron Range. Some of these birds immigrated to s.-cen. Ontario and now breed. Likewise, some Ontario birds have moved into the n.-cen. U.S. and breed. *Québec:* 23 pairs in the southern part of the province, up from 15 pairs in 1995. Resident in Montreal and Québec City, along the St. Lawrence River on the Gaspé Peninsula, along the Québec River in sw. Québec, and in the mountains north of Québec City. Over 250 Peregrines were introduced in the province.

UNITED STATES ("Eastern" type): Figures are for known pairs as of 1998. More current data, if known, are in parentheses. *Alabama:* 0. In 1962, one of the two last active eyries in the U.S. was near Guntersville Lake, Marshall Co. Historical eyries were at the mouth of the Elk River in the northwestern part of the state,

Paint Rock Valley near the mouth of the Paint Rock River, and at Fort Deposit north of Greenville. *Connecticut:* 1 pair (3 in 1999). Resident in Bridgeport, Hartford, New Haven (West Rock area), and Stamford. *Delaware:* 2 pairs. District of Columbia: 1 pair. *Florida:* 0. *Georgia:* 1 pair (Atlanta). Twenty-six birds released 1987–1994 in Atlanta, Cloudland Canyon, Mt. Yonah, Bell Mt., and Tallulah Gorge. The last original *anatum* bred in nw. Georgia in 1942. *Illinois:* 6 pairs. Resident in Chicago (8 in 2001), Evanston, Venice, and Waukegan. *Indiana:* 8 pairs (9 in 2001). Present in recent years at East Chicago (2 in 2001), Fort Wayne, Gary, Indianapolis, Kokomo, Michigan City, Muncie (6 birds hacked in 1999), Porter, South Bend, and Wheatfield. *Kentucky:* Present in Frankfort, Ghent, Lexington (10 birds hacked in 1999), Louisville, and in Trimble Co. *Maine:* 8 pairs. In 1962, one of the last two eyries in the U.S. was in Acadia N.P. Now pairs nest at three coastal sites in Acadia N.P., Mt. Kineo, and the mountain corridor from the New Hampshire border through Baxter S.P. *Maryland:* 11 pairs. Baltimore, south coastal region, and Harper's Ferry N.P. *Massachusetts:* 4 pairs (6 in 2001). Boston, Fall River, Springfield, and Worcester. *Michigan:* 8 pairs (22 in 1999). Breeding pairs or paired birds found in Detroit (3); Grand Haven; Grand Island, Alger Co.; Keweenaw Peninsula, Keweenaw Co.; Lansing; Monroe, Porcupine Mts. Wilderness S.P., Ontonagon Co.; Pictured Rocks Nat'l. Seashore, Alger Co.; Sault Ste. Marie (International Bridge); and Trap Hills, Ontonagon Co. Peregrines historically nested on Isle Royale N.P. Of about 50 birds released on Isle Royale in Lake Superior in the late 1980s and early 1990s, none has returned to nest; however, some have immigrated to Ontario and currently nest. *Mississippi:* 0. *New Hampshire:* 10 pairs (12 in 2001). Breeds at Manchester and throughout the White Mts. *New Jersey:* 15 pairs. Breeds on bridges across the Delaware River from Burlington to Cumberland Cos., coastal areas, Forsythe NWR, and urban areas near New York City. *New York:* 36 pairs. Breeds or is resident in Albany, Binghamton, Buffalo, Hudson River Valley (Dutchess, Putnam, Rock Island, Ulster, and Westchester Cos.), New York City, Niagara Falls, and Rochester. *North Carolina:* 6 pairs. Nests at Big

Lost Cove and Grandfather Mt., Avery Co.; Shortoff Mt. and Linville Gorge, Burke Co.; Jackson Co.; Whiterock Cliff, Madison Co.; Blue Rock and Hickory Nut Gorge, Rutherford Co.; Hanging Rock S.P., Stokes Co.; and Devil's Courthouse, Looking Glass, and Panthertail Mts., Transylvania Co. *Ohio:* 11 pairs. In Akron, Canton, Cincinnati, Cleveland (4 in 2001), Cleves, Columbus, Dayton, Ironton, Lakewood, Lima, and Toledo. *Pennsylvania:* 6 pairs (7 in 1999). Resident in Allentown, Harrisburg, Philadelphia, Pittsburgh, Reading, Wilkes-Barre, and Williamsport. *Rhode Island:* 0 (1 pair in 2001 in Providence). *South Carolina:* 1 pair. Table Rock S.P., Pickens Co. *Tennessee:* 2 pairs (3 in 1999). In 1947, the last tree eyrie in the U.S. prior to extirpation by DDT was at Reelfoot Lake. Now resident in Chattanooga, Unicol, and the Great Smokey Mts. Nat'l. Pk. in Sevier Co. *Vermont:* 19 pairs (25 in 2001). Breeds throughout the Green Mts. and Middlebury. *Virginia:* 13 pairs. Accomack Co. (4 pairs), Charles City Co., Lancaster Co., Madison Co., Newport News (James River Bridge), Norfolk, Northampton Co. (4 in 1999), and in Richmond. *West Virginia:* 0 (1 in 1999). Nested in Grant Co. in 1991 and 1999. *Wisconsin:* 12 pairs. Many nest on power-plant smokestacks and towers. Found in Alma, Cassville, Genoa, Green Bay, Jefferson, Kewaunee, Maiden Rock in Pierce Co. Maassen's Bluff in Buffalo Co., Manitowoc (Busch Agricultural Resources Complex), Milwaukee (5 in 2001), Oak Creek, Pleasant Prairie, Port Washington, Racine, Rothschild, Sheboygan, and Superior (on the Blatnick Bridge).

Note: Since Peregrines wander and do not adhere to international borders, there has been an emigration of Peregrines between countries (*see* Canada).

F. p. anatum and "Eastern" Peregrine.
Summer.—*Very uncommon.* Most Peregrines in Canada and the U.S. were released in urban centers. Smaller numbers were released in natural areas; however, a growing number are spreading to natural areas in some provinces and states. Some larger cities have several breeding pairs.

F. p. anatum and "Eastern" Peregrine.
Winter.—*Canada:* Released *F. p. anatum* that have attained adulthood remain in larger southern cities in Québec and Ontario, including as far north as Québec City, Québec. Recent wintering has occurred in Thunder Bay, Ontario. A few adults, presumably from Labrador, winter in se. Newfoundland. Adults in s. Maine, Michigan, and Wisconsin also remain on or near urban breeding areas. Adults in all other states typically remain near breeding areas, especially urban breeders. Many or most non-territorial adults and juveniles, particularly females, winter south of summer areas in the U.S. from coastal cen. Maine to Florida, along the Gulf states, and near the Mississippi River. "Eastern" Peregrines also winter south of the U.S. in the Caribbean, Mexico, and Central and South America.

F. p. anatum. Movements.—Telemetry data on three *F. p. anatum* juveniles released near Toronto, Ontario, in 1999 by the Canadian Peregrine Foundation shows them wintering in Panama, Central America and n. Colombia in South America. One bird was tracked for a second season as an adult in 2000 and it returned to winter in the same location in n. Colombia as it did its first winter.

Movement data described below are based on the current population of released birds from ongoing telemetry studies by the Canadian Peregrine Foundation. Based on telemetry data of released and wild *anatum* from Ontario and Québec, a few juveniles of either sex may remain near natal areas, but often wander greatly within the general region. Migrants may spend a day or a few days or even weeks in one location to feed and rest.

Fall migration: Telemetry has shown that juveniles released in Toronto depart for migration from late Sep. to late Oct. Since most youngsters fledge in early to mid-summer, they have a great deal of time to wander before actually embarking on southward journeys. Portions of their journey may be rapid or slow. Movements take place later than movements of most *F. p. tundrius.* Two juveniles that were released in the Toronto area that were tracked with telemetry in the fall and winter of 2000 stayed in the vicinity of Toronto and s. Ontario. A Québec-reared juvenile female that was raised by its parents on a cliff nest also remained in the vicinity of its natal area until late Oct. This is long after most Peregrines have left for winter grounds; however, its tracking system stopped sending data in late Oct.

Three Toronto birds that were tracked in 1999 wintered in about the same area of Panama and n. Colombia, but took different courses to reach their winter destinations. The first bird headed southeast to the Mid-Atlantic Coast, then went far out over the Atlantic Ocean and made its next landfall in Florida, then flew south over the w. Caribbean to Panama. The second bird also headed south, then out over the Atlantic Ocean, but not as far out as the first bird, then reached Nicaragua a few days later and continued to Panama. The third bird took a more southerly mainland path to Alabama and crossed over the Gulf of Mexico to the Yucatán Peninsula of Mexico, then stayed on land through Panama and onto his winter area in n. Colombia. All three birds reached their winter grounds from late Oct. to early Nov.

In 2000, one male was tracked for the second southward journey from the Toronto area, now as an adult. However, on the second trip south, he left later, in mid-Oct., then took a more southwesterly course from Ontario and stayed on land through e. Texas and Mexico rather than making a trans-Gulf of Mexico flight. He stayed on his land-based course through Central America to his winter grounds in n. Colombia.

A juvenile male that had wintered in the Dominican Republic left Ontario in late Oct. and arrived at his wintering area by mid-Nov. A female from e. Ontario went only as far as Long Island, N.Y., where she spent the winter. Another male left the Toronto area in late Oct. and arrived at his winter grounds on coastal South Carolina by late Nov.

Two juveniles that were released in the Toronto area and were tracked with telemetry in the fall and winter of 2000 stayed in the vicinity of Toronto and s. Ontario.

An adult female tracked from breeding grounds in n. Alberta in 1999 by the Canadian Fish and Wildlife Service (Environment Canada) angled southeast across the U.S. to Florida, then onto the Caribbean islands. Twice she attempted to continue south to South America via Caribbean islands. Her first attempt was thwarted by a storm and, on her second attempt, she perished in Hurricane Mitch while trying to make an overwater crossing. *Note:* Other adults tracked from Alberta headed on a more southerly course into Mexico; one passed through Mexico and Central America to winter in e. Brazil. Telemetry-tracked adults from Alberta have shown little tendency to stage: movements are swift and direct.

Spring migration: There is limited data. Of interest is the telemetry-tracked male from Toronto that wintered in Colombia. In his first northward flight as a 1-year-old juvenile, he left his winter grounds in early Apr. and was back in the Toronto area by early May. The next spring, after again wintering in Colombia, and now as an adult, left his winter quarters earlier, in early Mar., and was back in Toronto by early Apr. On both return trips, he remained on land and passed through the famed Peregrine migration area on Padre Island, Texas. After spending a few days on Padre Island, he continued north into s.-cen. Michigan, and then corrected his bearings and headed east to his natal area of Toronto.

Of special interest is the juvenile male that wintered on the Dominican Republic. Rather than taking the shortest route north back through Florida and on to Ontario, he flew west across the Gulf of Mexico to e. Mexico, then headed north toward his natal area in Ontario.

"Eastern" Peregrine. Movements.—Most southern and central latitude breeding adults are sedentary, particularly urban birds that have ample year-round food supply. Most birds from northern, severe weather regions must migrate in order to have sufficient prey. Most juvenile females have a tendency to disperse to new areas, but males are more likely to return to the vicinity of their natal area once completing migratory journeys.

Since the U.S. population comprises intergrades of multiple subspecies, including the highly migratory *tundrius* and some *anatum*, moderately migratory individuals of some *anatum*, *pealei*, and *peregrinus*, or sedentary types of *brookei*, *cassini*, *macropus*, and some *pealei* and *peregrinus*, their genetic codes dictating movements may be altered. Migrants may take similar courses as described above for released *anatum*. Peregrines with *anatum* and *tundrius* lineage may engage in long-distance movements like their ancestors and migrate into South America.

Released birds do as their name implies: wander. Falcons released in the e. U.S. have had a tendency to especially wander north into s. Canada; however, they also may wander in other directions to locate territories.

NESTING: *F. p. tundrius* begin nesting activities from late May through Jun. and end from Aug. to late Sep. Based on Rankin Inlet, Nunavut, data, either sex may be the first to arrive on the nesting grounds. Both adult sexes may arrive simultaneously, but there is no evidence that previously mated pairs arrive at the same time or have paired before arriving. Pair formation occurs quickly once breeding grounds have been reached. At Rankin Inlet, youngsters may fledge from mid-Aug. to the end of the first week of Sep. Late nesting birds of the high Arctic may not fledge young until mid- or even late Sep.

F. p. anatum in Canada may begin nesting in Mar. and Apr., and possibly in May at their northern range limits, and end nesting activities from Jun. to Aug.; occasionally later.

Depending on latitude, "Eastern" types may begin nesting from Feb. (Indiana) through Apr. and end from May to Jul.; occasionally later. Pairs may remain in the general vicinity of their territory year-round or, with dispersing and migrating birds, males often establish or re-establish territories.

Breeding typically does not occur until females are 2 years old and males are 3–5 years old. However, 1-year-old juvenile females regularly pair with older males and occasionally mate and rear young. Very rarely does juvenile male pair with an older female, and it is extremely rare for them to mate and rear young.

Courtship (perched).—As with larger falcons, Peregrines engage in perched courting displays more than other raptors do. Courting activities are often more animated and vigorous than displayed by Gyrfalcons and Prairie Falcons. Both sexes have ledge displays with *eechip* calls: *male ledge display, female ledge display,* and *mutual ledge display.* Within these ledge displays, both sexes perform *billing, food transfer, horizontal head-low bow, vertical head-low bow,* and *tip-toe-walk.* In the *head-low bows,* the head is vigorously bobbed. Copulation displays involve the *curved-neck display* by males (male silent); females utter *eechip* and *upchip* and males the *chutter* call notes prior to

copulation. Both sexes, but males, in particular, advertise territories with *high-perching display.*

Courtship (flight).—Both sexes perform aerial food transfer, aerial-kissing, flight-play, high-circling, mutual-floating display, passing-and-leading display, and talon-grappling. Males perform figure eights, flash roll, roll, and undulating roll (variation of sky-dancing), and z-flight. Females perform the flutter-flight. Vocalization occurs with all but the most intense courting flights by males.

Nest locations: *F. p. tundrius.*—Vary from gentle, open slopes to low embankments, low or high rock outcrop, or tall sheer cliffs. *F. p. anatum* and "Eastern."—Moderately high to tall sheer cliffs that are at least 40 ft. (12 m) high, bridges and tall buildings, smokestacks, and towers.

Nest sites: No nest is built. Generally nests in the same area in consecutive years but may use the same eyrie site 2 years in a row. On cliffs, alternate eyrie sites are on the same cliff. After reuse, some eyries will have a large amount of white excrement staining the area below the eyrie ledge.

F. p. tundrius.—Eyrie location is on a flat surface on a slope or on a narrow or wide ledge on a cliff. The eyrie site may be totally exposed or is sometimes protected by an overhang. The actual site is a shallow scrape in the soil, on grasses or moss, or in an abandoned sheltered or unsheltered stick nest on a ledge of a Common Raven or Rough-legged Hawk. Eyrie sites may be easily accessible to humans and predators or placed high on inaccessible cliffs.

F. p. anatum and "Eastern."—Eyrie sites are in large crevices and gutters on buildings, on ledges and gravel roofs on tall buildings, on ledges of tall smokestacks, in covered or on open wooden boxes placed on buildings and bridges, on covered wooden boxes placed on towers, on top of bridge girders, in hollow bridge girders, or on concrete bridge supports. Nests are generally placed high and are inaccessible to predators. Cliff eyries are on narrow or wide ledges, and may be exposed or protected by an overhang. Wooden boxes were sometimes placed on cliff areas for hacked birds to provide additional shelter. Some "Eastern" pairs in New Hampshire and w. Ontario use abandoned stick nests on cliffs of Common Ravens. Formerly, eastern *anatum* regularly nested high up in broken-off trunks and cavities in tall trees, especially cypress, cottonwoods, and sycamores (last tree nest in the East was in 1947 at Reelfoot Lake, Tenn.).

Three or 4 eggs are the common clutch size, 2 or 5 eggs are fairly common, and 1 or 6 are uncommon to rare. The eggs are incubated for about 33 days. Eggs are laid at 2-day intervals with incubation starting with the second or third egg. Both sexes incubate, but females perform the majority of the task, especially at night. Fledging time: males fledge in 39–46 days and females fledge in 41–49 days. With the short nesting season under the severe conditions of the Arctic, fledgling *F. p. tundrius* stay with their parents until the fall migration: a period of only 2–4 weeks, and rarely up to 6 weeks. With a longer nesting season in temperate areas, *F. p. anatum* and "Eastern" fledglings may stay with their parent for up to 8 weeks.

CONSERVATION: Peregrine Falcons needed all the assistance that was possible in order to save the existing wild birds in the West and to totally rebuild a population in the e. U.S. and s. Canada.

As previously described, the last Peregrines east of the Mississippi River attempted nesting in 1962 in Alabama and Maine. The eastern *F. p. anatum* subsequently ceased to exist east of the river and in s. Canada, with the possible exception of se. Labrador. The current population in the East, south of the Arctic, is the result of intense captive-propagation programs that hacked and released thousands of juveniles.

Pesticide bans.—The first step that was taken to benefit not only Peregrine Falcons, but all wildlife and humankind, was to ban organochlorine pesticides, particularly DDT. This lethal pesticide was first used in 1946 in Canada and the U.S. This ban, however, was established too late to help retain the original native stock of *anatum* Peregrines.

Canada took a series of steps to discontinue the sale and use of DDT that began in 1968 with a ban on spraying forests in national parks. The major Canadian ban came on Jan. 1, 1970 (announced Nov. 3, 1969), when DDT was permitted for insecticide use on only 12 of the 62 previously sprayed food crops. However, all registration for insecticide use on food crops was stopped by 1978. Canada, however,

permitted DDT use for bat control and medicinal purposes until 1985. Canadian users and distributors were also allowed to use existing supplies of DDT until Dec. 31, 1990.

The U.S. also had a series of steps to ban DDT, but halted the overall sale and use more quickly. In 1969, the USDA stopped the spraying on shade trees and tobacco crops and at aquatic locations and in homes. The USDA placed further bans on its use on crops and commercial plants and for building purposes in 1970. The EPA banned all DDT sale and use on Dec. 31, 1972; however, limited use for military and medicinal purposes were permitted until Oct. 1989. In 1974, the U.S. banned the use of Aldrin and Dieldrin, both deadly chemicals that may have affected wildlife as much as DDT did.

Mexico was expected to discontinue government-sponsored DDT use for malaria control in 2002, and has planned a total ban of DDT by 2006.

As of 2000, possibly five other Latin American countries still use DDT and other organochlorine chemicals without restrictions. Peregrine Falcons and many of their prey species regularly winter in this region and are succeptible to contamination.

There are 122 countries, including the U.S. and Canada, that have signed a United Nations-sponsored treaty banning eight deadly organochlorine pesticides: Aldrin, Chlordane, DDT, Dieldrin, Endrin, Heptachlor, Mirex, and Toxaphene. There are also two industrial chemicals, Hexachlorobenzene (also a pesticide) and PCBs, and two by-products of industrial processes, dioxins and furans, that have also been banned.

Protective laws.—Legal protection assisted Peregrines to recover after suffering from organochlorine pesticides. The USFWS designated *F. p. tundrius* as an Endangered Species from Jun. 2, 1970, to Mar. 20, 1984, and as Threatened Species from Mar. 20, 1984, to Oct. 5, 1994. In Canada, the Committee on the Status of Endangered Wildlife in Canada (COSEWIC) listed *tundrius* as a Threatened Species in Apr. 1978, but downlisted it to a Vulnerable Species in Apr. 1992. (COSEWIC has week-long assessment meetings, thus no exact "dates" are available for rulings.)

The USFWS listed the *F. p. anatum*, which

includes released "Eastern" types, as an Endangered Species from Jun. 2, 1970, to Aug. 25, 1999. COSEWIC listed *anatum* as an Endangered Species in Apr. 1978 and downlisted it to a Threatened Species in Apr. 1999. Mexico redesignated *anatum* from an Endangered to Threatened Species in 1999. From the 1999 delisting, a 5-year period took effect in the U.S. and Canada to study the effects of being delisted as an Endangered Species under the Endangered Species Act of 1973.

In the U.S., both subspecies were first protected under the Endangered Species Conservation Act of 1969, then under the Endangered Species Act of 1973. All subspecies of Peregrine Falcons were basically covered under the act by a "similarity of appearance" clause that was passed in Mar. 1984. *Note:* Provisions were also made in the act to accommodate the foreign races that were being used to boost the propagation programs in the U.S.

Population restoration (introduction) programs.—Released juveniles in Canada were produced from mated captive pairs of *F. p. anatum*. In the U.S., offspring were from mated pairs and artificially inseminated adult females of numerous races. With human manipulation, pairs would lay more eggs than are typical in the wild, thus increasing the number of eggs and young that were produced for eventual release. When a few weeks old, nestlings were placed in sheltered boxes on bridges, buildings, cliff ledges, smoke stacks, and towers. They were supplied food by human caretakers until they could fend for themselves. It was imperative during the hacking process that nestlings and fledglings did not bond with their human caretakers so they would be truly wild when fledged.

To produce enough Peregrines for the massive release programs to fill the void of the former eastern *F. p. anatum* range, as has been discussed, introduced North American and foreign subspecies were used for captive-breeding and releases.

Canada.—A government-sponsored captive breeding facility at Wainwright, Alberta, was established in 1972, and they produced 1,752 Peregrines for release in Canada from 1974 to 1996. As previously noted in Subspecies, all stock released in Canada came from native Canadian *F. p. anatum*. At least four other Canadian nonprofit, private organizations also produced Peregrines. Some nonprofit organizations, such as the Canadian Peregrine Foundation, still raise and release Peregrines, especially after Wainwright closed its facilities.

E. Ontario began captive releases in the 1977 in Algonquin Prov. Pk. Releases began in 1981 in the Toronto area, where breeding first occurred in 1983. New Brunswick and Nova Scotia began releasing birds in 1982, with the first recent-era breeding in 1989. Intense release programs ceased after 1996 because the population of formerly released birds was increasing, breeding, and expanding their range on their own. However, private nonprofit organizations, especially the Canadian Peregrine Foundation, continued sporadic captive releases in Canada through 2000 to augment the wild population.

United States.—In its desire to get large numbers of Peregrines released into the wild as quickly as possible, the U.S. relied extensively on non-native North American races and foreign races (*see* the seven races listed in Subspecies). Virtually all breeding stock came from falconry birds, injured birds that could not be released back into the wild, and illegally possessed birds confiscated by authorities that also could not be released back into the wild because they were imprinted on humans. Some *F. p. brookei* were also imported from Spain to help increase breeding stock.

Experimental captive breeding began in 1971 with *F. p. pealei* (from the Queen Charlotte Islands, B.C.) that were raised by Dr. Heinz Meng of New Paltz, N.Y. In 1970, once it was proven that captive breeding would succeed, a large captive breeding facility was constructed at Cornell University, Ithaca, N.Y., under the newly formed nonprofit organization, The Peregrine Fund, founded by Dr. Tom Cade. In 1973, 20 Peregrines were raised at Cornell; in 1974, 28 more were produced. Thereafter, production grew significantly. In Colorado in 1973, James Enderson had captive breeding success with *F. p. anatum* falconry birds. In 1974, a captive-breeding facility was also created in Fort Collins, Colo. in association with the Colorado Division of Wildlife to assist propagation. In 1984, the BLM supplied land for The Peregrine Fund to create a large breeding facility for Peregrines and other endangered raptors and birds near Boise, Idaho. Subsequently, the captive breeding facilities at Cornell and Fort Collins were closed.

The Midwest Peregrine Restoration Group formed by Dr. Patrick Redig and Dr. Harrison Tordoff of the University of Minnesota was started in 1982 and worked independently from The Peregrine Fund. They supplied most of the released stock in the Midwest and w. Ontario.

Other small nonprofit groups and private breeders have also provided birds for releases. All release programs were assisted or directed by respective state wildlife agencies. The generous donations by corporations and the public also greatly helped, especially since all release programs were conducted by nonprofit organizations.

The percentages of released subspecies and their breeding status have been carefully tracked by The Midwest Peregrine Restoration Group for Illinois, Indiana, Kentucky, Michigan, Ohio, and Wisconsin (also includes birds that have immigrated to cen. Ontario). Percentages of released/currently breeding subspecies: *anatum*, 57/54; *pealei*, 27/22; *peregrinus*, 6/9; *brookei*, 6/10; and *tundrius*, 4/5. Interestingly, in the very early stages of genetic ecological adaptation, the two foreign races, *peregrinus* of Europe and *brookei* of the Mediterranean region, have showed adaptability and have increased their status as breeders compared to the percentage that were released.

The first two restoration-era Peregrines were released in 1974 in New Paltz, N.Y. Large-scale releases began in 1975 and continued in most areas into the early to mid-1990s. Small-scale releases occurred into the late 1990s and early 2000s.

In 1979, the first release-era bird in the East, an adult female named Scarlet, laid eggs in Baltimore, Md. However, Scarlet was not mated, and her eggs were infertile. Also in 1979, a pair laid eggs at a hack-tower site in marshes of e. New Jersey, but the eggs failed to hatch. In 1980, the first restoration-era hatching occurred with two pairs of formerly hacked birds in e. New Jersey. The first cliff nesting also occurred in 1980. The first restoration-era nesting in the Midwest was in 1986. The first restoration-era nesting occurred in the follow-

ing states: New York in 1980, New Hampshire in 1981, Maryland in 1984, North Carolina and Pennsylvania in 1987, Massachusetts and Michigan in 1989, Georgia in 1996, and Connecticut in 1997.

The first release-era bird in North America to mate and raise young occurred in n. Alberta in 1977.

The original eastern *anatum* began nesting in urban environments in the 1940s in Montreal, New York, and Philadelphia. However, they succumbed to organochlorine pesticides before they had the chance to expand into additional cities.

Peregrine Falcon banding protocol for North America.—To obtain scientific data on Peregrine movements and survival, wild-captured and captive-released falcons a numbered aluminum USFWS band is fitted on each bird's right leg. A colored band with large alpha-numeric designations is put on the left leg. On perched birds, the colored band can be read with a spotting scope from several hundred feet away. The colored bands reflect the subspecies and origin of a falcon and have a two- or three-digit alpha-numeric designation. COLOR DESIGNATIONS OF BANDS: Red, captive-bred birds that are released in the e. U.S.; bicolor black/red or black/green (replaces the black/red), *F. p. tundrius* banded on breeding grounds; blue, *F. p. tundrius* or *F. p. anatum* captured during migration; black, *F. p. anatum* banded on breeding grounds.

A few biologists are anodizing USFWS bands with various colors to assist visual tracking of individuals.

Mortality.—All subspecies and released types are subject to illegal shooting in North America and on the winter grounds. Before legal protection, Peregrines were even shot for killing pigeons in cities. Poisoning, including that from organochlorine pesticides, will be prevalent for decades to come; however, the levels found in tissues of Peregrines are becoming less as time goes on. They are electrocuted by landing on utility wires and poles, and they collide with utility wires, cars, and trains. Urban Peregrines, especially juveniles, suffer very high mortality from striking windows. Urban juveniles often get caught in chimneys.

Natural mortality occurs with terrestrial predators such as Arctic Foxes, and aerial predators such as jaegers and gulls may kill young *F. p. tundrius*. Great Horned Owls were a problem to the population restoration efforts in most areas as they killed adults and especially unprotected fledglings. Captive-release locations were often in areas that had minimal depredation by owls (e.g., in cities, on coastal areas, on barrier islands, and in open marshes). Owls still prey on current nesting birds in natural locations. Migrant Peregrines may be affected by sudden, violent storms, especially hurricanes, when migrating over extensive stretches of open water of the Atlantic Ocean, Caribbean, and Gulf of Mexico. Fierce territorial aggression between Peregrines is common during the nesting season, and this may cause the death of one or both combatants.

Human disturbance at eyries by recreational rock climbing may cause nest failure. However, most popular climbing areas are closed to recreational use if nesting falcons are present.

Peregrines historically suffered from intense egg-collecting by oologists and possibly somewhat by falconers.

Falconry.—A historically popular sport that is practiced by nearly 3,000 falconers in North America. Peregrine Falcons have been one of most favored falconry species because of their beauty and speed. Prior to listing under the Endangered Species Act of 1973, Peregrines could be captured as migrants, taken from eyries as nestlings, or purchased from licensed breeders. After receiving protection from the act, only captive-bred birds could be used for falconry. West of the 100th meridian, falconry take of wild *anatum* for falconry use was allowed in 2001. Due to legal challenges, permits were not issued in 2002. In Canada, Saskatchewan issued permits in 2001, but no falcons were taken. *Note:* Falconry birds have been legally available from licensed facilities that raised captive birds during the period when Peregrines were protected from capture in the wild.

SIMILAR SPECIES: COMPARED TO ADULTS.—(**1**) **Gyrfalcon, intermediate (gray)-morph adults.**—PERCHED.—Crown and nape are gray, and dark malar mark is irregularly defined. Dorsal body similar and often very bluish gray. Ventral body can be similar on palest types, with an unmarked white breast and barred flanks and spotted belly.

Wingtips are distinctly shorter than the tail tip. FLIGHT.—Underside of the remiges is pale and barred; secondaries often more heavily barred and darker than the rest of the remiges. From above in flight, all of upperparts, including the tail, are uniformly grayish: rump and uppertail coverts are same color as all other upperparts. (**2**) **Mississippi Kite, adults.**—FLIGHT.—Narrow wings and uniformly gray on underside with a white edge on the trailing edge of the secondaries. When soaring, the outermost primary is much shorter than the wingtip. Wingtips bend slightly upward when soaring. Dark tail is square-edged. COMPARED TO JUVENILE.—(**3**) **Gyrfalcon, intermediate (gray)-morph juveniles.**—PERCHED.—Head is similar but dark malar often not as distinct. Ventral areas are white not tawny. Wingtips much shorter than the tail tip. All pale banding on tail is white, not tawny. FLIGHT.—Underside of the remiges is not uniformly colored and marked as on Peregrine. The secondaries are more heavily barred or nearly solid gray and primaries are white and narrowly barred; coverts more heavily marked than remiges. Ventral areas as described in Perched. (**4**) **Gyrfalcon, dark-morph juveniles.**—PERCHED.—Head often appears hooded as on darker-headed Peregrines; use caution. Ventral areas nearly solid dark brown with a minimal amount of pale whitish (not tawny) edgings and similar to heavily streaked birds with *pealei* lineage. Wingtips much shorter than the tail tip. FLIGHT.—Underside of remiges is uniformly pale gray and unmarked. Dark brown underwing coverts are much darker than the remiges. (**5**) **Northern Harrier, adult females and juveniles.**—FLIGHT.—Shape is similar when gliding at high altitude. However, harriers have more distinct crook at the wrist of the wing, and the wrist area is farther out on the wing. Dark brown head and neck are hooded. Axillaries and median underwing coverts are darker than the rest of the underwing; secondaries darker than the primaries on juveniles. Wide dark tail bands. Wingbeats are loose and floppy. (**6**) **Merlin (*columbarius*) females.**—PERCHED.—Poorly defined dark malar mark. Wingtips are distinctly shorter than the tail tip. FLIGHT.—Very similar brown above and dark-streaked below. Underside of wings is

"ARCTIC" PEREGRINE FALCON, *Falco peregrinus tundrius:* Very uncommon. Winters south to s. South America. Exact winter North American range is unclear as races are often difficult to determine. Fall migrants concentrate on Mid-Atlantic coast and Florida Keys. Greenland birds migrate via North America to winter grounds.

Intergrade zone with "Arctic" Peregrine Falcon

Thunder
Bay

Québec

Ottawa

1962

Albany

Richmond

1947

1962

"EASTERN" PEREGRINE FALCON (NO ASSIGNED RACE) AND "AMERICAN" PEREGRINE FALCON,

Falco peregrinus anatum: "Eastern" and "American" are very uncommon. Current populations in s. Canada and e. U.S. are from released stock. Original "American" was extirpated in e. U.S. by 1962. Canada released only "American." The U.S. released multiple races. Winters to South America. In 1962, AL and ME had last active eyries in e. U.S. prior to extirpation by DDT. Immigration occurs between n. U.S. and s. Canada.

nearly identically marked with pale spotting and barring on the dark feathers. Wingbeats are rapid; rarely glide for long distances. (7) **Mississippi Kite, juveniles.**—PERCHED.— Lack a dark malar mark. Often have large white spots on scapulars. Toes are short. Wingtip-to-tail-tip ratio similar. FLIGHT.—Similar at higher altitudes with streaked ventral and often dark underside of the remiges. Underside of remiges lack pale tawny-rufous spotting and barring. When soaring, the short outermost primary is noticeable. Those lacking pale tail bands are similar at a distance. Primary tips bend upward when soaring.

OTHER NAMES: Peregrine. Formerly called Duck Hawk. Former eastern *F. p. anatum* was called the Rock Peregrine and Great-footed Hawk (by J. J. Audubon). Females are called "falcons" and males called "tiercels." Falconers call migrant birds "passage birds," and adults of all subspecies and types are called "haggards." *Spanish:* Halcón peregrino. *French:* Faucon pélerin.

REFERENCES: Bent 1961; Berger et al. 1968; Brewer et al. 1991; Brauning 1992; Burnham 1997; Bylan 1998, 1999; Byre 1990; Cade et al. 1988, Cadman et al. 1987; Canadian Peregrine Foundation 1999a, 2002a, 2002b; Castrale and Parker 1999b; Center for Conservation, Research, and Technology 2000; Clark 1999; Clark and Wheeler 2001; Commission for Environmental Cooperation 1997; Court et al. 1988; Debus 1998; Dekker 1980, 1987, 1988, 1999; Dodge 1995, 1988–1997; Environment Canada 1999, 2000, 2001; Erskine 1992; Ferguson-Lees and Christi 2001; Forsman 1999; Franklin 1999; Fyfe 1988; Gahbauer 1999; Gahbauer and Metzger 1999; Godfrey 1986; Gustafson and Hildenbrand 1998; Harris 1979; Howell and Webb 1995; Johnsgard 1990; Kaufman and Meng 1975; Kellogg 2000; Lott 1999; Marchant 1994; McWilliams and Brauning 2000; Nicholson 1997; Olsen 1988; Palmer 1988; Redig and Tordoff 1988; Rowell and Holroyd 2001; Russell 1991; Sweig 1998; Tordoff 2000; Tordoff et al. 1997, 2000; Tucker et al. 1998; Tufts 1986; USFWS 1984, 1998, 1999b, 2001; Veit and Petersen 1993; Walsh 1999; White 1968; White et al. 1995.

Plate 495. Peregrine Falcon, adult female "Arctic" (*F. p. tundrius*) [Jul.] ▪ Moderately wide type black malar mark. Large white forehead and lores. ▪ Brownish gray upperparts with partial pale gray barring. Moderately marked white underparts are barred on flanks and barred and spotted on belly. Belly is usually pinkish tawny. ▪ *Note:* Photographed at Rankin Inlet, Nunavut, by Gordon Court.

Plate 496. Peregrine Falcon, adult female "Arctic" (pale type *F. p. tundrius*) [Jul.] ▪ Narrow type black malar mark. Center of crown and supercilium are white. Thin dark eyeline extends onto nape. ▪ White underparts are lightly marked. Leg feathers are unmarked. Brown upperparts (not shown). ▪ *Note:* Photographed at Rankin Inlet, Nunavut, by Gordon Court.

Plate 497. Peregrine Falcon, adult male "American" (*F. p. anatum*) **[Jun.]** ▪ Very wide type black malar mark that covers entire side of head; black lores and forehead. ▪ Bluish gray upperparts are barred with pale gray. Underparts are tawny-rufous except gray flanks and leg feathers. ▪ Black tail. ▪ *Note:* Mesa Co., Colo.

Plate 498. Peregrine Falcon, adult female "Eastern" (no subspecies designation) [Apr.] ▪ Wide type black malar mark. ▪ White breast is spotted/streaked, flanks are heavily barred, and tawny belly is barred. ▪ *Note:* Captive-released stock and a mix of several races. She appears much like a European Peregrine. Photographed in New Haven Co., Conn., by Jim Zipp.

Plate 499. Peregrine Falcon, adult female "Eastern" (no subspecies) [Sep.] ▪ Wide type black malar mark. ▪ Pale tawny-rufous breast is spotted/streaked, tawny-rufous flanks and belly are heavily barred. ▪ *Note:* Same bird as on plate 498, but in newly molted first-adult plumage. Photographed in New Haven Co., Conn., by Jim Zipp.

Plate 500. Peregrine Falcon, adult male "Eastern" (no subspecies) [Apr.] ▪ Very wide type black malar mark covers entire side of head; black forehead and lores. White breast; grayish flanks are narrowly barred; pale tawny belly is spotted and barred. ▪ Dark underside of tail. ▪ *Note:* Appears similar to Australian Peregrines. Photographed in New Haven Co., Conn., by Jim Zipp.

Plate 501. Peregrine Falcon, adult female "Arctic" (*F. p. tundrius*) [Oct.] ▪ Moderately wide type black malar mark. ▪ White underparts are moderately marked. ▪ Uniformly black and white marked underwing. Pointed wingtips. ▪ Blackish distal half of tail. ▪ *Note:* Cape May, N.J.

Plate 502. Peregrine Falcon, adult female "Arctic" (pale type *F. p. tundrius*) [Jul.] ▪ Narrow type black malar mark. ▪ White underparts are very lightly barred on flanks. ▪ Blackish tail. ▪ *Note:* Rare plumage type of the central Arctic. Photographed at Rankin Inlet, Nunavut, by Gordon Court.

Plate 503. Peregrine Falcon, adult male "American" (*F. p. anatum*) [Jul.] ▪ Very wide type black malar mark covers all of the side of the head. ▪ Tawny-rufous breast and belly, gray flanks. ▪ Uniformly marked underwing. Pointed wingtips. ▪ Blackish distal half of tail. ▪ *Note:* Park Co., Colo.

Plate 504. Peregrine Falcon, adult female "American" (*F. p. anatum*) [Jun.] ▪ Moderately wide type black malar is narrower and columnar-shaped (found on some adult females of this race). ▪ Tawny-rufous breast, belly, and undertail coverts; gray flanks. ▪ Blackish distal half of tail. ▪ *Note:* Mesa Co., Colo.

Plate 505. Peregrine Falcon, adult male "American" (*F. p. anatum*) [Jun.] ▪ Black head. ▪ Bluish gray upperparts: rump and uppertail coverts are a paler bluish. ▪ Blackish tail contrasts with pale rump and uppertail coverts. ▪ *Note:* Adult females are more brownish or blackish than adult males, but still have distinctly paler rumps and uppertail coverts; tail is blackish. Mesa Co., Colo.

Plate 506. Peregrine Falcon, juvenile female "Arctic" (*F. p. tundrius*) [Oct.] ▪ Moderately wide type black malar mark connects with a moderately wide black eyeline. Pale tawny supercilium; pale tawny forehead and lores. Pale blue cere and orbital skin. ▪ Tawny edges on upperparts. ▪ Wingtips equal to tail tip. ▪ *Note:* Assateague Island, Md.

Plate 507. Peregrine Falcon, juvenile female "Arctic" (blonde type *F. p. tundrius*) [Jan.] ▪ Narrow type black malar mark is broken at gape. Pale tawny crown and supercilium with dark area on sides and rear of crown. Pale greenish cere and orbital skin. ▪ Lightly streaked tawny underparts. ▪ *Note:* Cameron Parish, La.

Plate 508. Peregrine Falcon, juvenile female "American" (*F. p. anatum*) [Jul.] ▪ Wide type black malar mark. Dark crown. Pale forehead, dark lores. ▪ Lightly streaked tawny rufous underparts, including leg feathers. ▪ *Note:* Pale type of ventral markings for *anatum*. Douglas Co., Colo.

Plate 509. Peregrine Falcon, juvenile female "Arctic" (*F. p. tundrius*) [Oct.] ▪ Moderately wide type black malar mark and black eyeline. ▪ Pale tawny underparts are lightly streaked. ▪ Uniformly marked dark underwing. Pale tawny-rufous markings on remiges. ▪ Distinctly banded tail. ▪ *Note:* Cape May, N.J.

Plate 510. Peregrine Falcon, juvenile "American" (*F. p. anatum*) [Jun.] ▪ Wide type black malar mark. ▪ Tawny-rufous underparts are moderately streaked. ▪ Uniformly dark underwing. Pale tawny-rufous markings on remiges. ▪ *Note:* Photographed in Moffat Co., Colo., by Mike Lanzone.

Plate 511. Peregrine Falcon, juvenile male "American" (*F. p. anatum*) [Jul.] ▪ Wide type black malar mark. Pale headed type. ▪ Tawny-rufous underparts are lightly streaked (more rufous than other races). Arrowhead-shaped dark markings on leg feathers. ▪ *Note:* Also common type in captive-released *anatum*. Mesa Co., Colo.

Plate 512. Peregrine Falcon, juvenile (1-year-old) female "Eastern" (no subspecies) [Jun.] ▪ Wide type black malar mark. Pale yellow cere and orbital skin. ▪ Heavily streaked underparts. ▪ Dark, uniformly marked underwing. ▪ *Note:* Seen in adult plumage on plates 498 and 499. Appears much like "Peale's" Peregrine. Photographed in New Haven Co., Conn., by Jim Zipp.

GYRFALCON
(*Falco rusticolus*)

AGES: Adult, 1 or 2 years in a subadult stage (basic I, basic II), and juvenile. Full adult plumage and color of the fleshy cere, orbital skin, and feet may not be obtained until they are 2–3 years old (Clum and Cade 1994). The exact plumage transition from juvenile to adult is unknown (Clum and Cade 1994). Plumage data for adults refer to birds that have replaced all juvenile feathering.

Subadults are mainly in an adult plumage but retain some old, worn juvenile feathering. Most retained juvenile feathers are on the upperwing coverts, and a lesser amount are on other dorsal regions. During this subadult period, the cere, orbital skin, and feet also slowly change from juvenile-like to adultlike color. The amount of retained juvenile feathering and degree of color change of fleshy areas varies individually. Such color change may be based not only on advancing age, but also on diet and other factors.

Juvenile age characters are worn the first year. Juveniles have slightly longer secondaries, which creates a broader wing, and longer rectrices, which creates a longer tail than at older ages.

MOLT: Falconidae wing and tail molt pattern (*see* chapter 4). As in most falcons, the first prebasic molt begins when somewhat less than 1 year old. The molt is partially completed as 1-year-olds during their second year of life. Most probably begin molt in a span from Mar. to May. As in most raptors, molt begins on the primaries, then begins somewhat later on the rectrices. The secondaries and body feathers begin molting after the remiges and rectrices have undergone a fair amount of molt. The wing and tail molt described below is based on Clum and Cade (1994). Primary molt sequence typically starts with p4; however, it may start with p3, 5, 6, or 7. Primary molt then continues in the following sequence: p5, 6, 3, 7, 2, 8, 9, 1, and 10. Rectrix molt begins with r1 (the deck set), then continues with r2, 3, 4, 6, and 5 or an alternate sequence of r2, 6, 3, 4, and 5. The outermost juvenile primary (p10) may not be molted in the first prebasic molt, but all secondaries, rectrices, and the majority of body plumage are molted. The first prebasic molt is not complete on the upperwing coverts and sometimes other dorsal body regions. A large amount of retained juvenile feathers are visible as a faded and frayed pale brown patch on the upperwing coverts. This molt would indicate birds that are 1-year-olds in their second year of life.

The second prebasic molt are 2-year-old birds in their third year of life. This annual molt may also not be a complete molt on the upperwing coverts and possibly other dorsal areas. A small amount of juvenile plumage may still be retained as very old, frayed, and very pale brown feathers. Some may molt entirely out of any retained juvenile feathering and achieve full adult plumage at this time. The extent of the remix and rectrix molt is unknown.

Subsequent adult prebasic molts begin in Apr. or May and are completed from Sep. to Nov. (Clum and Cade 1994). Molt may not be a complete annual replacement. Females begin their annual molt during incubation and males begin toward the end of the nesting cycle. These molts would affect birds that are at least 3 years old, in their fourth year of life.

SUBSPECIES: Monotypic. Since color morphs are indicative of geographic regions, they were formerly considered subspecies.

COLOR MORPHS: Polymorphic with three primary color morphs that have a full continuum of plumage variations among them. The primary color morphs: light (white), intermediate (gray), and dark (black). There are two additional intermediate plumages that form the continuum among the three primary morphs. There is a great deal of individual variation within each color morph. Sexes are similarly marked. Color-morph distribution in the Arctic adheres to "Gloger's Rule."

SIZE: A large raptor. Males average smaller than females, but there is overlap on all anatomical features. Juveniles average longer than adults and subadults because they have longer tails. Length: 19–24 in. (48–61 cm); wingspan: 43–51 in. (109–130 cm).

SPECIES TRAITS: HEAD.—The bill is pale bluish or pinkish on white morphs and pale bluish with a dark tip on all other color morphs. The orbital region is bare flesh. BODY.—The upper body region is very broad. Talons are whitish or pale pink on white morphs and black on all other color morphs. In flight, Gyrfalcons often shows a hump on the back. WINGS.—**When soaring, the secondaries are broad and taper to moderately pointed wingtips.** When perched, wingtips are distinctly shorter than the tail tip. TAIL.— When closed, the basal area is very broad. *Note:* **The upper body is very broad and tapers to the narrower wingtip and tail area.**

ADULT TRAITS: HEAD.—Cere, orbital skin, and feet are yellow. These fleshy regions may be brighter on males, especially the cere color. BODY.—Dorsal markings consist of a barred pattern. WINGS and TAIL.—When perched, the wingtips are moderately shorter than the tail tip.

ADULT LIGHT (WHITE)-MORPH TRAITS (LIGHTLY MARKED TYPE): HEAD.—White with a few small dark specks on the nape or white and very thinly streaked with brown on the crown and nape. A very thin dark area may border the area under the eyes and in front of the orbital skin. BODY (dorsal).— Two main types of markings on the largely white upperparts: (1) a short horizontal brown bar on each back, scapular, and rump feather or (2) a few have a small, narrow arrowhead-shaped or diamond-shaped mark on all dorsal feathers. The dark brown mark covers a small area of the white feather. BODY (ventral).—Immaculate white breast, belly, leg feathers, and undertail coverts, but some birds may have a few small dark specks on the distal flanks. WINGS (dorsal).—**Two types of markings as described in dorsal body on the median and lesser coverts.** Greater secondary and primary coverts are white with narrow brown barring. The white secondaries may be unmarked, partially barred with brown, or fully barred with brown. Inner primaries are either immaculate white with a few bars on the distal area of each feather or are moderately barred. WINGS (ventral).— White underwing coverts. Underwing coverts are unmarked. The axillaries and underwing coverts may have a few small dark spots that are visible only at close range. Underside of the remiges is white except for the dark brown tips of the outer six or seven primar-

ies. The dark primary tips create a "dipped-in-ink" appearance. There is a narrow brown band on the trailing edge of the inner primaries and secondaries. On individuals that have distinct barring on the dorsal surface of the secondaries, the dark barring will also show on the inner portion of the secondaries in translucent light. TAIL.—There are three variations on the white dorsal surface of the tail: (1) is unmarked, (2) has a small amount of dark mottling on several rectrices, or (3) is partially or fully barred on only the deck rectrix set (r1). The ventral surface is white and unmarked on all types. White uppertail coverts have very small dark arrowhead-shaped marks on each feather. *Note:* **Either sex can be this lightly marked. Many are older birds. Based on museum specimens, similarly marked juveniles (lightly marked type) may molt into an adultlike plumage that is identical to these very white adults.**

ADULT LIGHT (WHITE)-MORPH TRAITS (HEAVILY MARKED TYPE): HEAD.—White with narrow brown streaking on the crown and nape, and most have fairly wide brown eyelines. There may be some faint streaking on the auriculars and even a few dark specks on the malar region. A large dark area is under the eyes and in front of the orbital skin. BODY (dorsal).—White, with one or two dark brown horizontal cross bars on each back, scapular, and rump feather. Dark brown bar on each feather covers about 50 percent of the white feather surface. BODY (ventral).—Breast, belly, forward flanks, leg feathers, and undertail coverts are immaculate white. Some may have a few small dark specks on the white distal flank and leg feathers. WINGS (dorsal).— White, but all coverts and remiges are either moderately or heavily barred with brown as on dorsal body. WINGS (ventral).—Underwing coverts are either immaculate white, including the axillaries, or are sparsely covered with small brown flecks. Remiges are either immaculate white or have partial or fully barred primaries and secondaries. With the dark tips on the outer six or seven feathers, the primaries appear as if they are dipped in ink. TAIL.—Dorsal surface is white with six to eight narrow, complete dark brown bars. However, barring may be confined mainly to the deck set (r1), with dark mottling or partial barring on the outer webs of all other rectrices. Ventral surface is immaculate white or may have brown barring on the outer web on the outermost rectrix set (r6). Uppertail coverts are white and crossed with brown bars. *Note:* Plumage type is found on either sex. Similar type of juvenile (heavily marked type) molts into this type of plumage as a subadult.

ADULT LIGHT INTERMEDIATE (LIGHT GRAY/SILVER)-MORPH TRAITS: HEAD.—White with a heavily streaked crown. The supercilium is paler but thinly streaked. The white nape is heavily streaked. There is a narrow or wide dark eyeline, which may extend downward as a dark stripe behind the auriculars. The white auriculars and cheeks may be narrowly streaked with brown. The region in front of the orbital skin and below the eyes is dark brown or blackish and typically extends onto the lower jaw as a defined dark malar mark. BODY (dorsal).—**Each back, scapular, and rump feather is dark brown with a broad white tip and a moderately wide mid-feather white bar. The dark brown area of each feather covers more than 50 percent of the feather surface.** BODY (ventral).—White with small dark spots on the sides of the neck and breast. The central area of the breast may also be covered with small spots or may be unmarked. The white flanks and belly are covered with small dark spots, the distal portion of the flanks are covered with large dark spots. Leg feathers are white with partial, narrow dark barring. Undertail coverts are white with a narrow dark bar on each feather. WINGS (dorsal).—Coverts are dark brown and narrowly or moderately barred with a white mid-feather bar on each feather as described on the dorsal body. All remiges are 50 percent light-dark barred except the dark barring is narrower on the outer half of the primaries. WINGS (ventral).—**White coverts, including axillaries, are covered with very small dark spots. The markings are most prevalent on the greater coverts and median coverts. Lesser coverts on the patagial region have very small dark markings. The primaries are white with narrow dark barring. The outer secondaries are white with moderately wide dark barring, and the inner secondaries are white with broad dark barring. Wingtips are dark brown on the outer six or seven pri-**

maries. TAIL.—**Dorsal tail surface is very pale gray with six to eight complete dark bands that are somewhat narrower than the pale bands are.** Uppertail coverts are dark with white barring. Undertail is white with dark barring. *Note:* This plumage type has not been previously described or depicted. It is found on both sexes. Depicted herein on an adult from Nome, Alaska; also, a 7-year-old female that wintered each year in Edmonton, Alberta (G. Court pers. comm. and unpubl. photographs).

ADULT INTERMEDIATE (GRAY)-MORPH TRAITS: HEAD.—*Pale type:* Pale gray or whitish with dark streaking on the crown and a white forehead. The supercilium is white and streaked with gray. There is a narrow dark eyeline above the auriculars. Auriculars are gray on the distal region but whitish on the forward area and cheeks. The dark malar stripe is either moderately distinct or ill-defined. Dark nape is mottled with white patches. *Dark type:* Dark gray crown with a white forehead and a narrow whitish supercilium that begins behind the eyes. Auriculars and cheeks are dark gray with a moderately distinct dark malar stripe. Dark nape is mottled with white. BODY (dorsal).—*Barred type* (either sex, but mainly on males): Base feather color is dark gray or brownish gray with a moderately wide or fairly wide pale gray mid-feather cross bar. The dark portion can cover 50 percent or more of the feather surface. Even on the palest birds, the pale mid-feather cross bar is gray, not white, as on light intermediate morphs. Pale cross bars are distinct on all of the scapulars and back feathers. *Partial-barred type* (either sex, but mainly on females): Dorsal color is dark gray or grayish brown with a very narrow, pale gray mid-feather cross bar. Pale cross bars are often ill-defined or nonexistent on the forward scapulars and back. Rump is grayish and barred on both types. BODY (ventral).—White with a variable amount of dark markings. *Lightly marked type* (mainly males, but may be on some females): White breast is either unmarked or very lightly marked with dark dashes. Forward flanks and belly are spotted; the rear portion of the flanks is covered with large dark spots or narrow dark bars. The white leg feathers are narrowly barred. *Heavily marked type* (both sexes): Breast is covered with moderately wide dark streaking or teardrop markings; belly, lower belly and forward flanks are covered with large dark spots; rear flanks are broadly barred. The white leg feathers are heavily barred. Both types have barred undertail coverts. WINGS (dorsal).— Marked like the two respective types of dorsal body markings as described for dorsal body. Barred types are likely to have pale gray barring on all coverts and remiges, including the inner portion of the outer primaries. Partially barred types have a reduced amount of pale barring on the coverts or many lack pale barring. Many have a reduced amount of pale barring on the remiges, including the outer primaries. **Both types, but especially barred types, have distinctly darker primaries and greater primary coverts that contrast sharply with the paler grayish secondaries and the rest of the upperwing coverts.** WINGS (ventral).—**White underwing coverts are covered with a light or moderate amount of dark markings. The median coverts may be more extensively streaked or barred and form a darker area on this feather tract. The outer primaries are white with narrow dark barring and forms a pale panel that contrasts with the more thickly barred, somewhat darker inner primaries and outer secondaries and the typically darker, solid gray inner secondaries. Note: As a rule, the underwing either appears uniformly pale with pale coverts and pale remiges or has a slightly darker band on the median coverts because of the coverts being more extensively marked.** TAIL.—**Dorsal tail is pale gray and banded and is the same color as the rest of the dorsal areas.** The dark bands may be chevron-shaped and up to 50 percent of the width of the pale area of each rectrix. There is a possible sexual difference in the width of the banding: Males may have narrow dark bands and females may have wide dark bands. Uppertail coverts are dark and crossed with pale gray bars.

ADULT DARK INTERMEDIATE (DARK GRAY)-MORPH TRAITS:

HEAD.—Similar to dark type head of intermediate morph, including the pale forehead. Head is all dark, but is often paler on the cheeks. Dark malar mark is present. Pale supercilium is generally lacking, but may have a very small amount of pale mottling on the nape. Throat is white. BODY (dor-

sal).—Dark brownish gray or brownish black with very narrow pale gray edges on most feathers. The most distal scapulars may have a faint gray bar on each feather. Rump is dark and barred with gray. BODY (ventral).—White with moderately thick dark streaking or teardrop-shaped markings on the breast and belly; the flanks are broadly barred. Dark markings cover less than 50 percent of the surface of the underparts. White leg feathers are heavily barred. Undertail coverts are covered with fairly thick barring. WINGS (dorsal).— Upperwing coverts lack pale barring like the rest of the upperparts. Tertials and secondaries may have faint gray barring. Primaries are dark. WINGS (ventral).—**Underwing coverts are quite dark and extensively spotted and barred and contrast against the paler gray remiges. There is some pale barring on the outer primaries that blends into the solid gray inner primaries and secondaries. Note: Overall, the underwing will appear slightly two-toned with fairly dark coverts and pale gray remiges.** TAIL.—Uppertail coverts are barred with gray and blend as a uniform color unit with the grayish rump. Dorsal surface is dark with pale gray barring.

ADULT DARK (BLACK)-MORPH TRAITS:

HEAD.—All of the head, including forehead and nape, is uniformly blackish brown. The throat is white. The area under and in front of the eyes and malar area are often more blackish. BODY (dorsal).—Uniformly dark blackish brown or with a very narrow partial gray cross bar on many feathers, particularly on the distal scapulars. Blackish-brown rump and uppertail coverts are barred with gray and somewhat paler than the rest of the dorsal body but similar to the tail. BODY (ventral).—**Breast is densely streaked and the belly is broadly streaked or has large dark arrowhead-shaped markings or spotting. The flanks are broadly barred. Dark markings cover 50–90 percent of the surface area of the underparts. Leg feathers are dark with narrow white barring. Undertail coverts are heavily barred.** WINGS (dorsal).—Virtually uniformly blackish brown. Occasionally, a few coverts may have a faint, partial gray bar or spot. Primaries are uniformly dark. WINGS (ventral).—**Underwing coverts are blackish brown and covered with a small amount of white spotting, particu-**

larly on the median coverts. The dark coverts contrast sharply with the nearly uniformly pale gray remiges. The outer one to three primaries may have numerous, faint, narrow pale bars. *Note:* The underwing appears two-toned with the nearly solid dark coverts and pale gray remiges. TAIL.—Dorsal surface is dark with numerous pale gray bands that are equal to or narrower than the dark bands. Ventral tail surface is medium gray and covered with narrow pale gray bands.

SUBADULT TRAITS: HEAD.—As on the respective color morph of adult except the cere and orbital skin are pale bluish in Gyrfalcon's first subadult year as a 1-year-old. Older subadults, which are subadult II or older, have pale yellow cere and orbital skin. BODY.—As on the respective color morph of adult. Molt is incomplete and may retain a small amount of juvenile feathering on the dorsal regions, particularly on the rump. On white morphs, feet may be somewhat pinkish gray until changing to the yellow adult color. On all other color morphs, feet are grayish or grayish blue on younger subadults, then gradually change to pale yellow as they get older. WINGS.—Molt is incomplete, and 1-year-olds may retain a highly visible, large patch of juvenile feathers on the lesser upperwing coverts and sometimes a few feathers on the median covert tract. Retained feathers are faded brown in all color morphs, including white morphs. Older subadults molt into a full adult feathering or may retain a few very faded scattered juvenile feathers—now 3 years old—particularly on the upperwing coverts. These individuals may exhibit three ages of upperwing coverts. TAIL.—As on respective color morph of adult. All juvenile rectrices are fully replaced in the first prebasic molt.

JUVENILE TRAITS: HEAD.—Bluish or grayish cere and orbital skin. BODY.—Feet are pale pink on white morphs and grayish on all other color morphs. TAIL.—Long tail. Wingtips extend two-thirds of way down the tail when perched.

JUVENILE LIGHT (WHITE)-MORPH TRAITS (LIGHTLY MARKED TYPE): HEAD.—Immaculate white with a few small dark specks on the nape or may have some dark streaking on the eyeline and nape. BODY (dorsal).—Scapular and back feathers are white with a narrow or moderately wide brown or dark brown vertical streak along the shaft region of each feather. Lower back and rump are white with very narrow dark brown streaking. BODY (ventral).—White with a few dark specks on the sides of the breast and flanks or all of the breast, belly, and flanks may have small dark dashes. The white leg feathers are generally unmarked, and the white undertail coverts are always unmarked. WINGS (dorsal).—**All lesser and median coverts have a narrow or moderately wide brown or dark brown streak along the shaft area of each feather. Greater coverts have partial brown barring. Secondaries may have partial brown barring or may be unmarked. Primaries have partial dark barring on the distal area of each primary and have a dark tip on all feathers.** WINGS (ventral).—**Immaculate white with dark brown "dipped-in-ink" tips on the outer six or seven primaries. There is a narrow brown subterminal band on the trailing edge of the remiges. In translucent light, partial barring is evident on the underside of the remiges.** TAIL.—Dorsal surface is white and is either unmarked or may have a very small amount of dark mottling or partial barring next to the dark shaft on the deck rectrix set.

JUVENILE LIGHT (WHITE)-MORPH TRAITS (HEAVILY MARKED TYPE): HEAD.—White with thin brown streaking on the crown, auriculars, and nape. BODY (dorsal).—**Back and scapulars are medium brown or dark brown with a medium wide white edge on each feather. The distal one-third of the scapulars may have a broad barred pattern. Lower back and rump also have brown feathering with broad white edges.** Uppertail coverts are white with a dark streak or partial narrow barring on each feather. BODY (ventral).—White with short medium brown or dark brown dashes on the breast, belly, and flanks. Lower belly, leg feathers, and undertail coverts are typically white and unmarked. WINGS (dorsal).—**All lesser and median coverts are medium brown or dark brown with broad white edges. Greater coverts and the secondaries are white with brown barring. The dark barring covers less than 50 percent of the feather surface. Greater primary coverts and most of the upper surface of the primaries are white with brown barring. The tips of the outer six primaries are dark**

brown and forms a large, dark "dipped-in-ink" brown patch on the wingtips that is highly visible when perched or in flight. WINGS (ventral).—White underwing coverts are either unmarked or have small brown dashes. Underside of the remiges may have partial brown barring. The outer six or seven primaries have the "dipped-in-ink" dark brown wingtips. TAIL.—Dorsal tail surface is white with several narrow dark brown bars. The ventral tail surface is white and unmarked, but in translucent light will show barring from the dorsal surface.

JUVENILE LIGHT INTERMEDIATE (LIGHT GRAY)-MORPH TRAITS: HEAD.—White with fairly narrow dark brown streaking on the crown, auriculars, and nape. The dark streaking may create an ill-defined malar mark. Head is similar to a pale-headed type of juvenile gray morph. Throat is white and unmarked. BODY (dorsal).—Dark brown with a moderately wide white edge on all back, scapular, and rump feathers. Additional white markings on the basal two-thirds of the scapular tract form a partially barred pattern and is similar to adult light intermediate morphs. The overall pattern of white edgings and other markings creates a darker dorsal surface than seen on a heavily marked type of white morph but paler than any gray morph. BODY (ventral).—White with narrow dark brown streaking on the breast, belly, and flanks. The white leg feathers are very narrowly streaked. The white undertail coverts have a thin dark streak along each feather shaft. WINGS (dorsal).—Lesser and median coverts are dark brown with moderately wide white edges and partial white barring on the median coverts. Greater coverts and secondaries are dark brown with white edges and two or three distinct narrow white bars on each feather. Upper surface of the primaries is also brown and barred throughout with white. WINGS (ventral).—White underwing coverts are narrowly streaked on the lesser coverts and have a somewhat darker band on the median coverts and axillaries created by moderately wide broad dark barring. Remiges are whitish with narrow gray barring on all primaries, wide gray barring on the outer secondaries, and very wide gray barring on the darker inner secondaries. The primaries appear paler than the secondaries.

Note: Overall appearance of the underwing is very pale with a somewhat darker barred area on the axillaries and median coverts. The wingtips are dark brown. TAIL.—Dorsal surface is marked with equal-width white and dark brown bands. Uppertail coverts are dark brown with white edges and a white cross bar on each feather. *Note:* This plumage has not been previously described. It is darker than heavily marked juvenile light morphs but paler than juvenile intermediate morphs. Type specimens are in the Denver Museum of Nature and Science and the AMNH.

JUVENILE INTERMEDIATE (GRAY)-MORPH TRAITS: HEAD.—Forehead is white and the crown is white with narrow dark brown streaking, and the nape is very mottled with white. There is generally a broad dark eyeline and often a dark brown area on the distal region of the auriculars. Cheeks and forward part of the auriculars are white and streaked with dark brown. There is a moderately distinct or distinct dark malar mark. White nape is streaked with brown. BODY (dorsal).—Dark brown (not gray as in adults) with narrow white edgings on all feathers. By late winter, the pale edgings often wear off and the upperparts become uniformly dark brown. Very distal region of the scapulars may have a partial or narrow white mid-feather cross bar. BODY (ventral).—White with moderately wide dark brown streaking on the breast, belly, and flanks. Dark streaking covers 50 percent of each feather surface. White leg feathers are moderately streaked with dark brown. White undertail coverts have a thin dark brown streak along the feather shaft of some or all feathers. WINGS (dorsal).—Dark brown throughout with narrow white edgings on all lesser and median coverts. The greater coverts and secondaries have narrow white edges and two or three faint partial bars. Primaries are dark brown with small white spots on all feathers. WINGS (ventral).—The secondaries are uniformly pale gray and are darker than the primaries, which are white and barred with gray. The axillaries and greater coverts are heavily barred and the lesser coverts are heavily streaked. *Note:* The underwing appears two-toned with darker streaked/barred coverts and pale grayish remiges. A few have underwings that are as pale as on light intermediate morphs. TAIL.—Dorsal tail surface is dark brown with seven or eight narrow white bands. The white bands may be offset or chevron-shaped. Ventral surface is also narrowly banded. Uppertail coverts are dark brown with white edges and sometimes a partial white bar or white spot on each feather.

JUVENILE DARK INTERMEDIATE (DARK GRAY)-MORPH TRAITS:

HEAD.—Forehead is white and crown is dark brown. There is a partial whitish supercilium and a small amount of white mottling on the nape. The cheeks and auriculars are dark brown, the dark malar mark is distinct. The throat is white. Very rarely, head is pale and streaked on intermediate morphs. BODY (dorsal).—Uniformly dark brown. BODY (ventral).—Dark brown streaking with narrow white edges on all of the breast, belly, flanks, and leg feathers. The dark area of each feather covers 50–75 percent of the feather surface. Undertail coverts are white with moderately wide dark streaks on the shaft area. WINGS (dorsal).—Uniformly dark brown on all coverts, secondaries, and primaries. WINGS (ventral).—**Dark brown with narrow white streaking on the lesser coverts and white spotting on the median coverts and axillaries. Primaries are whitish with narrow gray barring and are paler than the uniformly gray secondaries. Wingtips are dark.** *Note:* **The underwing appears two-toned with dark coverts and pale gray remiges.** TAIL.—Dorsal surface is uniformly dark brown or may have a few pale, partial bands. Ventral surface may be partially banded with narrow whitish bands or is fully banded with narrow bands. Uppertail coverts are either uniformly dark or have small white tips on each feather.

JUVENILE DARK (BLACK)-MORPH TRAITS:

HEAD.—Head is uniformly dark brown except the pale forehead and whitish streaked throat. Very rarely, head is whitish and streaked as on intermediate morph. BODY (dorsal).—Uniformly dark brown. BODY (ventral).—Dark brown with very narrow white edges on the breast, belly, leg feathers, and forward portion of the flanks; rear flanks have a small white spot on each side of the feather shaft. Lower belly is dark. On the darkest individuals, the breast and belly are all dark, but there are very thin white edges on the upper belly, leg feathers, and forward flanks; rear flanks have small

white spotting. Undertail coverts are white with broad dark barring. WINGS (dorsal).—Uniformly dark brown on all coverts and remiges. WINGS (ventral).—**Dark brown underwing coverts and axillaries have very narrow white edges on the lesser coverts and small white spots on the median coverts and axillaries. Remiges are uniformly pale gray with narrow white barring on the outer primaries.** *Note:* **Underwing appears two-toned with dark coverts and pale gray remiges.** TAIL.—Dorsal surface is uniformly dark brown. Ventral surface is dark with narrow partial white bands on the most distal part of each feather. Uppertail coverts are uniformly dark brown.

ABNORMAL PLUMAGES: None.

HABITAT: Summer.—Open, moist, and dry barren arctic and alpine tundra and fairly open areas along northern edge of the boreal forest. Breeding occurs from sea level to 5,350 ft. (1,630 m). Breeding pairs are found in areas with rocky outcrops, hard- or soft-substrate embankments and cliffs, and occasionally in small White Spruce groves. Most embankments and cliff areas are along seashores (adjacent to seabird colonies), rivers, lakes, and mountain ridges. Nonbreeding individuals may be found in open areas lacking cliffs and trees and include open tundra expanses, seashores, riverbeds, and lakeshores.

Winter.—Identical to breeding habitat for most adults and some subadults and juveniles. Many subadults and juveniles winter in entirely different habitats at more southern latitudes. Open and semi-open areas include: fields, marshes, rocky and sandy seashores and lake shores, reservoirs, barrier islands, airports, and harbors. Towns and cities are also frequented.

Migration.—As in the above locations.

HABITS: Fairly tame to tame raptor. Gyrfalcons prefer to perch on elevated natural and human-made objects, but also readily perch on the ground. All types of artificial structures, including grain elevators, bridges, on and in abandoned buildings, on occupied buildings, waterfowl hunting blinds, utility poles, fence posts, and hay bales.

As in all falcons, the throat and forehead feathers are often erected. In windy conditions, the long tail is pressed against a perch and used as a brace.

FEEDING: Perch and aerial hunter. Gyrfalcons primarily feed on birds up to the size of a goose, and, to a lesser extent, on mammals up to the size of a hare. Rock and Willow ptarmigan are the Gyrfalcon's major prey in most areas and seasons. Seasonally, Gyrfalcons feed on different ages, sexes, and species of ptarmigan. Displaying male ptarmigan are main prey in the early summer, young ptarmigan in late summer and fall; Gyrfalcon's diet often switches more toward Willow Ptarmigan in winter. Ptarmigan numbers fluctuate widely in possible cyclic patterns and often determine the breeding success of local falcon populations. Gyrfalcons nesting at seashore locations feed mainly on colonial nesting seabirds and waterfowl. Mammals are major prey at higher elevations and more northern altitudes. Arctic Ground Squirrels make up a large part of their summer diet in some of these areas. Even small prey like lemmings are extensively fed upon when they are at their peak cycles.

Avian prey are killed on or near the ground or may be pursued and subdued at fairly high altitudes. Avian species are typically hit by the hunting falcon, then fall to the ground; less frequently, may overtake and grab an avian prey in flight. To escape capture, prey species may land on the ground and form a tight group or seek dense vegetation.

During the nesting season, avian prey is generally decapitated, plucked, and the outer portion of the wing is broken off prior to being transported back to the nest. Larger mammals like Arctic Hare are cut into smaller segments before being taken back to the nest. During other seasons, prey is typically eaten at or near the point of capture. Juveniles and subadults may pirate food from conspecifics and other raptors.

FLIGHT: Powered flight is with moderately slow, stiff wingbeats interspersed with irregular glide sequences. Wings are held on a flat plane when soaring and gliding. Gyrfalcons kite on strong winds and may hover when searching for concealed prey.

Hunting methods include: (1) random, low-altitude flapping and gliding forays back and forth over an area, (2) moderate-altitude soaring and gliding stints, and (3) direct attack from a perch or while in flight.

Attack methods: (1) *Surprise-and-flush flight.*—Ground-hugging flight to surprise, panic, and capture prey. Gyrfalcons wintering in urban areas use buildings as cover to surprise prey. (2) *Pursuit flight.*—Prey that is in the open is (2A) tail-chased in level flight, often in erractic maneuvers; (2B) pursued to a higher altitude in a powerful, direct tail-chasing course, often in erratic maneuvers; or (2C) forced to the ground. (3) *Hover flight.*—Prey that is hidden in vegetation is flushed by hovering at a low altitude above the vegetation and making short dives toward the concealed prey. (4) *Diving.*—The Gyrfalcon rises above the intended prey by a rapid, direct-flapping ascent flight, then makes a short dive to capture it. (5) *Pendulum swoops.*—Shallow dives assisted by wing flapping that begins above prey that is typically in flocks, then swings upwards in a series of undulating angles from underneath into the flock to try to capture a bird.

Although Gyrfalcons typically do not engage in long vertical dives, a trained falconry bird attained the incredible speed of 353 mph (568 km/hr)! This is the fastest speed ever recorded for a bird.

VOICE: Alarm call during the breeding season is a repetitive, harsh *cack, cack, cack.* Also emitted by males during some aerial courting activities. A loud, punctuated *chup, chup, chup* is emitted by both sexes during perched courting displays, given by males during the perched food-transfer courting display, and as a feeding call note by both sexes. A rapid *chi-chi-chi-chi* is given by females when males approach for copulation. Rarely vocalizes outside of the breeding season. The *waiiiik* call is a soft, protracted crescendo whine given by copulating females. The *waiiiik* call can also be loud and vigorous and emitted by unmated males in some perched and aerial displays and by mated males when approaching the eyrie with prey. The high-pitched and harsh *scree, scree, scree* is a food-begging call given by females.

STATUS AND DISTRIBUTION: Uncommon. Population is stable. Regional population fluctuations occur due to cyclic ptarmigan numbers; however, Gyrfalcon numbers remain fairly stable. The organochlorine pesticide era of the late 1940s to early 1970s had little effect on Gyrfalcons. Most of their prey do not migrate to pesticide contaminated southern latitudes.

Summer.—*Labrador* and *Québec:* About 500 pairs. Major breeding areas are on the George and Koksoak Rivers in the Ungava region in n. Québec. *Greenland:* 500–1,000 pairs. *Iceland:* 300–400 pairs. *Northwest Territories* and *Nunavut* (which became a territory in 1999): estimated 1,300 pairs, with 5,000 individuals. The estimated world population is 15,000–17,000 pairs.

Winter.—Virtually all adult males, most adult females, and most subadult and juvenile males remain in the harsh Arctic in the winter. Many subadult and juvenile females and a few adult females winter south of the Arctic. Most wintering birds in s. Canada and the n. U.S. are females. Gyrfalcons are fairly regular in much of the mapped winter range in se. Ontario, s. Québec, and from Nova Scotia south along the Atlantic Coast to Long Island, N.Y. Most states that have irregular wintering have fewer than 20 records; New Jersey has 14 accepted records. Winter territories may be established by adults and subadults. Juveniles are prone to wanderlust in the winter and rarely establish territories. In rare cases, a mated pair may winter together south of the breeding grounds.

Movements.—Southward movements from Arctic breeding areas are mainly by females.

Fall migration: Southward journeys out of the Arctic may begin in late Aug. Regular movements occur in n. Canada, but are irregular in s. Canada and the n. U.S. Individuals may be seen in s. Canada as early as late Sep. and in the n. U.S. in late Oct. Southward movements may continue throughout mid-winter, especially by nomadic juveniles. Gyrfalcons breeding north of 70°N in Greenland migrate southward. Some Greenland birds migrate to Iceland. It is unknown if similar-latitude breeding birds of the high-Arctic latitude of Nunavut move south of breeding areas during winter.

Spring migration: Adult females may begin heading north in late winter. There are numerous Gyrfalcon records in Mar. and Apr. for the U.S. There are May records for s. Canada.

NESTING: Breeding season depends on latitude and geography. Pairs may remain together year-round in some areas. New pair formation may begin in Feb. Pairs may not breed every year: Breeding is dependent on food supply. Eggs are laid from late Mar. to late May. Most

young fledge between Jun. and late Aug. Breeding first occurs when birds are 2–4 years old.

Courtship (perched).—Either sex performs the following displays on the nest ledge: *vertical head-low bow, horizontal head-low bow, mutual ledge display,* and *billing.* Individual courtship behavior includes *male ledge display* and *female ledge display* (emitting *chup* and *waiiiik* calls), *wail-pluck display* by the male (emitting *waiiiik* call). Copulation display by male is the *curved-neck display.*

Courtship (flight).—Male displays: *roll, undulating roll, flash roll,* and *eyrie-flyby.* Female displays: *flutter-flight* (emitting *scree* call). Mutual displays: *aerial food transfer* (with *chup* and *waiiiik* calls), *high-circling, mutual-floating,* and *passing-and-leading display.*

See chapter 5 for descriptions of perched and flying displays.

Nest sites are on cliff ledges and usually in a location with an overhang to protect the incubating and brooding female and nestlings from the harsh weather. Nests may be shallow scrapes in the soil on a ledge or old stick nests on ledges of Golden Eagles, Common Ravens, or Rough-legged Hawks. Gyrfalcons occasionally use old stick nests of Common Ravens and Rough-legged Hawks that are placed in White Spruce. Nests on ledges are scraped out by both sexes by laying on their bellies and kicking dirt out behind them. Nest sites may be occupied by a pair or several pairs for many years. Nests that are reused often accumulate a buildup of excrement below the eyrie. Stick nests on ledges are typically destroyed by active nestlings.

One to 5 eggs are laid. Females do most of the incubating. Eggs can be left unattended for long periods in freezing temperatures without suffering ill effects. The eggs hatch in about 35 days. Nestlings fledge in 46–50 days.

CONSERVATION: In 2000, the USFWS proposed to transfer the Gyrfalcon from Appendix I to Appendix II of the Convention on International Trade of Endangered Species of Wild Fauna and Flora (CITES). CITES rejected the proposal, and the falcon was retained on Appendix I, the optimum protection typically granted for an endangered species. Gyrfalcons, particularly white morphs, have been popular for falconry for centuries. Canada allows the take of Gyrfalcons for private falconry use but not for commercial use. Very few nestlings are taken from nest sites for falconry. Most falconry birds are purchased from licensed breeders of falcons raised in captivity. Licensed breeders produce about 150 birds a year.

Mortality.—Birds die of natural causes in the Arctic. Those wintering south of the Arctic may become victims of illegal shooting, electrocution from power lines, and collisions with fence and power lines.

SIMILAR SPECIES: COMPARED TO ADULT INTERMEDIATE (GRAY) MORPH.—(1) **Peregrine Falcon, adults.**—PERCHED.—Head is black with more sharply defined malar. *F. p. tundrius* is most similar because head is often grayish and is mottled on supercilium and nape. Wingtips equal the tail tip. FLIGHT.— On the ventral surface, remiges are uniformly spotted or barred. Tail is dark. On the dorsal surface, the lower back and rump are paler than the rest of the upper body and the tail is very dark. (2) **Northern Goshawk, adults.**— PERCHED.—Orange or red irises. Black and white head pattern is distinct; never has a hint of dark malar mark. Blue-gray dorsal is plumage unbarred. Tail is unbanded or has 3 or 4 wide black bands. FLIGHT.—Body and wing shape are similar, especially when gliding. Distinct black barring on the underside of outer primaries. Underparts are uniformly barred. On the dorsal surface, the remiges are darker than the coverts, including the greater primary coverts. COMPARED TO JUVENILE INTERMEDIATE (GRAY) AND DARK MORPHS.—(3) **Northern Goshawk, juveniles.**—Very similar overall appearance; use caution! PERCHED.—Yellow irises. Ventral streaking and wingtip-to-tail-tip ratio are similar. Tail is distinctly banded with 3 or 4 dark bands. FLIGHT.—Underside of the remiges is very barred. Tail is prominently banded. (4) **Peregrine Falcon, juveniles.**—*F. p. tundrius* is most similar to intermediate morph; reintroduced types may be similar to either morph. PERCHED.—Head is similarly marked. Underparts quite tawny. Pale dorsal feather edgings are tawny. Wingtips equal to tail tip or barely shorter. FLIGHT.—Underwing is uniformly dark with pale tawny spotting or barring on all remiges.

OTHER NAMES: Gyr (female), jerkin (male). *Spanish:* Halcón Gerifalte. *French:* Faucon Gerfaut.

REFERENCES: Bohlen 1989; Burt and Grossenheider 1976; Clum and Cade 1994; Dekker and Lange 2001; Ferguson-Lees and Christi 2001; Forsman 1999; Godfrey 1986; Harris 1979; Johnsgard 1990; McWilliams and Brauning 2000; Mumford and Keller 1984; Palmer 1988; Perkins 1998; Sanchez 1993, 1994; Terres 1980; Todd 1963; Tucker et al. 1998; USFWS 2000; Veit and Petersen 1993; Walsh et al. 1999.

GYRFALCON, *Falco rusticolus:* Estimated pairs in 2000: Iceland: 300–400; Greenland: 500–1,000; Ungava and Labrador: 500. Wintering birds in s. Canada and U.S. are mainly female gray morphs. Very irregular to dashed line.

Plate 513. Gyrfalcon, adult white morph (unknown sex) [May] ▪ White head. Yellow cere and orbital skin. ▪ White back and scapulars are sparsely marked with arrowhead shapes and bars. ▪ Sparsely barred white wing coverts. Black wingtips. ▪ Tail is barred on central rectrices. ▪ *Note:* Photograph by Richard Fyfe.

Plate 514. Gyrfalcon, adult (unknown sex) light intermediate morph [Jun.] ▪ Whitish head with a blackish malar mark. Yellow cere and orbital skin. ▪ Upperparts are distinctly barred with white. Underparts are lightly spotted; leg feathers are lightly barred. ▪ Wingtips are shorter than tail tip. ▪ *Note:* Photographed in Nome, Alaska, by Brian Small.

Plate 515. Gyrfalcon, adult female intermediate (gray) morph [Jun.] ▪ Dark type head. Yellow cere and orbital skin. ▪ Dark gray upperparts are the partial-barred type that lack distinct pale cross bars. White underparts are lightly spotted/streaked; leg feathers are heavily barred. ▪ *Note:* Photographed in Nome, Alaska, by Jim Zipp.

Plate 516. Gyrfalcon, adult female intermediate (gray) morph [Feb.] ▪ Dark type head. Yellow cere and orbital skin. ▪ Dark gray upperparts are the partial-barred type that lack distinct pale cross bars and are nearly uniformly dark. White underparts are moderately spotted/streaked with thick barring on flanks. ▪ Wingtips are distinctly shorter than tail tip. ▪ *Note:* Boulder Co., Colo.

Plate 517. Gyrfalcon, subadult female dark morph [Feb.] ▪ Blackish-brown head. Pale yellow cere and orbital skin. ▪ Blackish-brown underparts are speckled with white on breast and belly and barred on flanks. ▪ A few faded, pale brown juvenile feathers on the upperwing coverts. Wingtips are distinctly shorter than tail tip. ▪ *Note:* Photographed in Ottawa, Ont., by Tony Beck.

Plate 518. Gyrfalcon, adult (unknown sex) white morph ▪ White underparts. ▪ White underwing with small black wingtips. ▪ White tail may be unmarked or variably banded. ▪ *Note:* Photographed in Thule Greenland, by Jack Stephens.

Plate 519. Gyrfalcon, adult (unknown sex) light intermediate morph [Jun.] ▪ Lightly spotted white underparts. ▪ Pale underwings: gray and white barred secondaries are darker than lightly barred white primaries. Lightly marked white coverts. ▪ Tail is distinctly banded. ▪ *Note:* Photographed in Nome, Alaska, by Brian Small.

Plate 520. Gyrfalcon, subadult female intermediate (gray) morph [Feb.] ▪ Heavily barred/spotted white underparts; barred flanks. ▪ Gray secondaries are darker than white barred primaries. ▪ *Note:* Subadult features on upperwing coverts, with a few faded brown juvenile feathers. ▪ Photographed in Duluth, Minn., by Frank Nicoletti.

Plate 521. Gyrfalcon, subadult female dark morph [Feb.] ▪ Blackish-brown head. ▪ Underparts are speckled with white on the breast and belly and barred on flanks. ▪ Gray remiges are paler than dark, spotted coverts. ▪ *Note:* Same bird as on plate 517. Photographed in Ottawa, Ont., by Tony Beck.

Plate 522. Gyrfalcon, juvenile (sex unknown) white morph (lightly marked type) [Jul.] ▪ Pale blue bill, cere, and orbital skin. Mainly white head. ▪ White upperparts and wing coverts are streaked. ▪ Black wingtips. ▪ White tail. ▪ *Note:* Recently fledged. Photographed on Ellesmere Island, Nunavut, by Wayne Lynch.

Plate 523. Gyrfalcon, juvenile female white morph (heavily marked type) [Feb.] ▪ Pale blue cere and orbital skin. ▪ Brown upperparts are edged and spotted with white. ▪ Dark brown wing coverts are edged and spotted with white; black wingtips. ▪ White tail is banded. ▪ *Note:* Photographed in Newfoundland by Bruce Mactavish.

Plate 524. Gyrfalcon, juvenile female intermediate (gray) morph [Dec.] ▪ Pale blue cere and orbital skin. Brown head with a pale supercilium and indistinct dark malar mark. ▪ White underparts, including leg feathers, are moderately streaked with dark brown. ▪ *Note:* Weld Co., Colo.

Plate 525. Gyrfalcon, juvenile (unknown sex) dark intermediate (dark gray) morph [Jul.] ▪ Pale blue cere and orbital skin. Dark brown head with a faint, pale supercilium. ▪ Dark brown upperparts. Heavily streaked white underparts, including leg feathers. ▪ *Note:* Recently fledged. Denali N.P., Alaska.

Plate 526. Gyrfalcon, juvenile female dark morph [Feb.] ▪ Blackish-brown head. Pale blue cere and orbital skin. ▪ Blackish-brown underparts with a few thin white streaks and spots. Uniformly blackish-brown upperparts. ▪ *Note:* A very heavily marked bird. Photographed in Ottawa, Ont., by Tony Beck.

Plate 528. Gyrfalcon, juvenile female intermediate (gray) morph [Jul.] ▪ White underparts are moderately streaked with brown. ▪ Heavily barred axillaries and greater coverts and streaked lesser coverts are darker than gray remiges. ▪ *Note:* Typical gray morph. Photographed at Rankin Inlet, Nunavut, by Gordon Court.

Plate 527. Gyrfalcon, juvenile female intermediate (gray) morph [Feb.] ▪ White underparts are thinly streaked. ▪ Secondaries are barred gray and are darker than white primaries. Heavily barred axillaries and greater coverts and streaked lesser coverts are darker than remiges. ▪ *Note:* Pale extreme of gray morph. Photographed in Ottawa, Ont., by Tony Beck.

PRAIRIE FALCON
(Falco mexicanus)

AGES: Adult and juvenile. Adult plumage is acquired when 1 year old. Adult plumage is somewhat sexually dimorphic, but not readily separable at long field distances. Juvenile plumage worn the first year. Juveniles have somewhat broader wings (longer secondaries) and longer tails than adults do.

MOLT: Falconidae wing and tail molt pattern (*see* chapter 4). First prebasic molt from juvenile to adult occurs Apr.–Nov. Molt begins on the head, then expands onto the breast, back, and forward scapulars, and then proceeds to rear of the body. Remiges and rectrices molt after most contour plumage is acquired.

Subsequent annual adult prebasic molts begin Apr. to early May at lower elevations and southern latitudes (K. Steenhof pers. comm.); birds inhabiting high elevations and northern latitudes begin from late May through Jun. Females begin molt prior to males. Body, wings, and tail molt in unison. Remix molt, based on Palmer (1988), begins on the mid-primaries (p4) then in sequence of p5, 6, 3, 7, 2, 1, 9, and 10. There is a variance in p8: it could be before p2 or after p9. Shortly after remix molt is initiated, rectrix molt begins on the deck set (r1), then in sequence of r2, 6, 3, 4, and 5. Annual molt is fairly complete.

SUBSPECIES: Monotypic.

COLOR MORPHS: None.

SIZE: A medium-sized raptor. Sexually dimorphic with little or no overlap, but sexes are not always readily separable in the field. Males average smaller than females. Juveniles are longer than adults because of having longer rectrices and may be on the larger end of the size spectrum for each respective sex. MALE.—Length: 14–16 in. (35–41 cm); wingspan: 36–38 in. (91–96 cm). FEMALE.—Length: 16–18 in. (35–46 cm); wingspan: 41–44 in. (104–112 cm).

SPECIES TRAITS: HEAD.—Large eyes with dark brown irises. Whitish supercilium either connects with the white forehead or begins over the eyes and may connect on the nape as a "V" shape. **Sharply defined white cheek area behind each eye is bordered by a brown auricu-**lar patch. Narrow dark "mustache." Falcons have bare, fleshy orbital skin. WINGS.—**Solid dark brown axillaries with moderately dark or solid dark median underwing coverts.** When perched, wingtips are moderately shorter than the tail tip. **In flight, long wings taper to pointed wingtips.**

ADULT TRAITS: HEAD.—Yellow cere, orbital skin, and feet are brighter on males, but may be the same color for both sexes (K. Steenhof pers. comm.). Partially barred flanks and leg feathers. **Brown upperparts have a variably distinct pale tawny or gray cross bar on the mid-section of most feathers.** TAIL.—Dorsal surface is brown and may have numerous, very narrow pale bands. **Dorsal surface of tail is generally much paler than the rest of the upperparts.**

Adult male: HEAD.—White supercilium is very distinct and often extends onto the nape. BODY (dorsal).—**Back, scapulars, rump, and upperwing coverts are medium brown or pale brown and always has a distinct, wide, very pale tawny or gray outer edge and a mid-feather cross bar on each feather.** BODY (ventral).—Dark markings may be small and sparse or absent on the breast. Belly is marked with small or medium-sized spots or dash marks and may overlap with markings of some adult females. WINGS.—**Dark median underwing coverts are extensively spotted or barred with white and appear only slightly darker than rest of the underwing (but accentuates the solid dark brown axillaries). Upperwing coverts are distinctly barred with a tawny or grayish bar on each feather.** TAIL.—Deck rectrices are pale brown and are either unmarked or possess very pale, narrow banding; all other rectrices are covered with very pale, narrow bands. Moderately wide white terminal band.

Adult female: HEAD.—White supercilium may be pronounced and extend onto the nape or is only a partial white stripe above the eyes. BODY (dorsal).—*Unbarred type:* **Pale feather edges and cross bars are indistinct or absent and upperparts appear almost uniformly brown.** *Note:* Majority of females are this type. *Barred type:* **Medium brown upperparts have a distinct pale outer edge and a mid-feather cross bar on each feather (male-like).** *Note:*

Only a small number of females are this type. BODY (ventral).—Breast and belly are moderately or heavily marked with large or very large dark spots. Some appear to be almost streaked because the spotting is clumped together. WINGS.—**Median underwing coverts either (1) are solid dark brown or (2) have a small amount of white spotting (but have a lesser amount of spotting than on most males; rare overlap with males). Combined with solid dark axillaries, the very dark brown underwing coverts form a broad dark band on the underwing and are much darker than on males.** Upperwing coverts are nearly solid brown on the unbarred type or have pale cross-barring on the barred type. TAIL.—**Dorsal surface is consistently paler than rest of the upperparts and exhibits little if any pale banding.**

JUVENILE TRAITS: HEAD.—Orbital skin and cere are pale yellow, but gradually turn a brighter yellow by spring. BODY (dorsal).— Medium brown upperparts have very narrow pale edges on all feathers, but lack the pale cross-barring of most adults. By late winter, pale edgings wear off and the upperparts become uniformly medium brown. By late winter and spring, upperparts also fade and wear to pale brown. BODY (ventral).—Underparts, including leg feathers and forward half of the flanks, are white with very narrow to moderately wide dark brown streaking; rear half of the flanks are mostly a solid brown patch. Males tend to have very narrow or narrow streaking, females have narrow or moderate streaking. Feet are pale yellow, but gradually turn a brighter yellow by spring. WINGS.— **Solid dark brown axillaries are distinct.** Somewhat sexually dimorphic on the underwing pattern, but is not a consistent sexual trait as seen in adults. *Male:* (1) An extensive amount of white spotting on the dark coverts as on virtually all adult males, (2) a minimal amount of white spotting on the dark coverts, or (3) uniformly dark brown coverts as on many females. *Female:* (1) Uniformly dark brown coverts that blend with the uniformly dark axillaries or (2) a minimal or moderate amount of white spotting on the dark coverts. TAIL.—Uniformly brown on the dorsal surface in fresh plumage, but fades and becomes paler than the rest of the upperparts by mid-winter,

particularly on the deck rectrices. Moderately wide terminal tail band.

JUVENILE (RECENTLY FLEDGED): HEAD.—Pale bluish cere, orbital skin, and feet. *Note:* Pale cheek area is sometimes ill-defined on a few individuals soon after fledging, but becomes more apparent after having been fledged for a few weeks and becomes a diagnostic field mark. BODY.—Dark brown upperparts with all feathers being edged with tawny-rufous; on some, the edgings are very distinctly marked with broad tawny-rufous edgings. Rich tawny-colored underparts are marked with dark brown streaking as described above. WINGS.—Pale spotting on dark median underwing coverts, if present, is either pale tawny or white. TAIL.—Uppertail is uniformly dark brown and the same color as the rest of the dorsal areas. White terminal band is very wide. (Juveniles can be separated from adults, which have narrow white terminal bands at this time of year, by width of white tail tip.) *Note:* This fresh and new plumage occurs from fledging (early Jun. to mid-Jul.) and spans to at least Sep. Thereafter, plumage gradually fades and wears to a medium brown color as noted in Juvenile Traits.

ABNORMAL PLUMAGES: Partial albino.—Several records (Clark and Wheeler 1987, Steenhof 1998). **Imperfect albino (dilute plumage).**— Several records (Clark and Wheeler 1987, Steenhof 1998). Specimens with pale "frosting" on most contour feathers (C. M. White pers. comm.). *Note:* These rare plumages are not depicted in accompanying photographs.

HABITAT (EAST): Fall, winter, and spring.— Found in open and semi-open rural locations in harvested and fallow agricultural fields, airports, idle fields, meadows, pastures, and reclaimed surface strip mines.

HABITAT (WEST): Summer.—Arid, open regions of short grass or scrub vegetation with cliffs. Nest cliffs are on buttes, hillside escarpments, or canyons and may be formed of soft or hard substrate. Nesting cliffs are occasionally amidst dense conifer woodlands and often several miles from open foraging habitat. Most areas are in undisturbed regions, but the falcons may inhabit areas interspersed with light agriculture or grazing lands. Pairs may also successfully breed in the proximity of human activity if they are not disturbed. Pairs primarily breed below timberline elevation, but are known to breed up to 12,000 ft. (3,700 m) in n. Rocky Mts. of Colorado. Semi-open woodlands, subalpine meadows, and alpine meadows up to 14,000 ft. (4,300 m) are inhabited in mid- to late summer in most montane regions of western states.

Fall, winter, and spring.—Habitat is often the same as breeding areas but without a requirement for cliffs. Winter months are generally spent at much lower elevations than in summer. Prairie Falcons inhabit open or semi-open mountain valleys; open arid prairies and deserts; open or semi-open agricultural and rural areas; open and semi-open moderately humid areas; and, occasionally, semi-open humid coastal meadows, pastures, and salt flats.

HABITS: Generally solitary. In the West, two to four juveniles (possibly siblings) may be together during the postfledging and fall migration periods and sometimes in winter. Juveniles often play games with each other, including talon-grappling. Several falcons may loosely accompany large passerine flocks during the nonbreeding season.

Falcons often erect throat and forehead feathers. Typical of large falcons, the tail may be braced against a perch for added stability in windy conditions. Quite wary in nonbreeding season, but tame individuals are sometimes encountered.

Exposed, elevated structures of any type are used for perches; Prairie Falcons also perch on the ground. Ground-perching birds often seek slightly elevated dirt chunks to sit on. Utility poles and fence posts are commonly used perches in the nonbreeding season. When perching in trees, outermost and uppermost exposed branches are preferred. Prairie Falcons are highly tolerant of climate extremes.

FEEDING: Perch and aerial hunter. Perch hunting is a direct, low-altitude attack at intended prey. Aerial hunting consists of random surprise-and-flush forays. The falcons generally hunt singly, but possible cooperative hunting has been observed, with one bird flushing prey and the other chasing it.

In the Eastern Cottontail Rabbits, mice, voles, and particularly small and medium-sized birds are probable prey. (Avian species become major prey in the nonbreeding season in the West.) Eastern Fox and Eastern Gray Squirrels

that venture out in the open may also be preyed upon.

Hunting styles: (1) *Dive-chasing.*—Short, acrobatic, shallow-angled dives that begin at moderate or low altitudes, with the falcon swinging sharply upward and grabbing the prey from underneath. (2) *Tail-chasing.*—Direct, low-level aerial pursuit of many avian and all mammalian prey. (3) *Hover flight.*—Intermittent hovering and slow flight performed by inexperienced juveniles. (4) *Passive hunting.*—Mainly a perch-hunting method in which a Prairie Falcon of any age sits and waits for a foraging Northern Harrier to flush avian prey. (5) *Pirating.*—Used against raptors such as Northern Harriers or species as large as Red-tailed Hawks. (6) *Scavenging.*—Very rarely practiced form of obtaining food.

The Prairie Falcon's notched bill is used to break the prey's neck; then, with avian prey it plucks the feathers and with mammalian prey it plucks fur, prior to eating.

FLIGHT: Powered flight is rapid and direct with moderately fast, shallow, stiff wingbeats. In powered flight, Prairie Falcons may flap for long distances or intersperse flapping with irregular gliding sequences. High-speed ground-skimming altitude often is used when hunting in direct pursuit and in random surprise-and-flush flights. High-altitude flights may occur at other times. Wings held on a flat plane when soaring and gliding. If wind velocity is sufficient, Prairie Falcons will kite for short periods along cliff faces. Juveniles may briefly hover at low altitudes when searching for hidden prey and may fly at slow speeds at low altitude between hovering stints (*see* Feeding).

VOICE: Silent away from breeding grounds. Highly vocal in the breeding season during courtship activities or when disturbed. A repetitive, harsh, and rapid *caack-caack-caack-caack* is the most typically heard vocalization. This call is often nasal in quality, especially in females. Males have a discernibly higher-pitched call.

STATUS AND DISTRIBUTION (EAST): Casual but regularly seen in Illinois, casual but irregularly seen in Kentucky, Tennessee, and Wisconsin, and accidental elsewhere. Sightings are mainly of juveniles and occur from mid-Aug. to early May. Records are from 1990 to 2002 and are 1-day sightings unless noted.

Alabama: (1) Marshall Co. from winter of 1985 to Jan. 1990, and (2) Marshall Co. in Dec. 1996. *Florida:* Three sightings but are not confirmed records for the state: (1) Okeechobee Co. in early Mar. 1977; (2) Dry Tortugas, Monroe Co., in early May 1978 (date and location seem highly unlikely for this species); (3) Sarasota Co. in early Oct. 1986 (published description fits this species). *Illinois:* Appears to be a natural eastern winter extension into historical prairie regions. (1) Urbana, Champaign Co., in early Nov. 1991; (2) DeWitt Co. from early to mid-Nov. for 2 days; (3) Forsyth, Macon Co., in mid-Nov. 1991; (4) Union Co. for 2 days in mid- and late Jan. 1992; (5) Sangamon Co. in early Mar. 1992; (6) Union Co. in mid-Mar. 1992; (7) Urbana, Champaign Co., in late Nov. 1992; (8) LaSalle Co. for 2 days in mid- to late Dec.; (9) McClean Co. in early Jan. 1993; (10) Shelby Co. in early Feb. 1993; (11) LaSalle Co. in late Feb. 1993 (adult); (12) Glenview Naval Air Station, Cook Co., from late Oct. to late Nov. 1993; (13) Rantoul, Champaign Co., in late Mar. 1994; (14) Macon Co. in early Nov. 1994; (15) Urbana, Champaign Co., for 3 days in early and mid-Nov.; (16) Clinton Co. in late Jan. 1995, (17) Monticello, Piatt Co., in early Nov. 1995; (18) Illinois Beach S.P., Lake Co., in late Apr. 1996; (19) Champaign Co. in late Apr. 1996; (20) Philo, Champaign Co., in early Dec. 1996; (21) Arcola, Douglas Co., in early Mar. 1997; (22) DeWitt Co. in mid-Nov. 1997; (23) Morgan Co. in mid-Nov. 1997; (24) Clinton Lake, DeWitt Co., in mid-Dec. 1997; and Deland, DeWitt Co., in mid-Jan. 1998. No Prairie Falcons were sighted from 1999 to 2001. There are numerous records in the state from 1930 to 1987. *Indiana:* (1) w. Gibson Co. in late Feb. 1989 and (2) Sullivan Co. (reclaimed strip mine) in early Mar. 1991. *Kentucky:* (1) Cool Springs, Ohio Co., for fall–winter (mid-Nov. to late Mar.) of 1988–1989 (strip mine); (2) Munfordville, Hart Co., in mid-Dec. 1989 (one or two birds); (3) Burgin, Boyle Co., in early Jan. 1990; (4) Reelfoot NWR, Fulton Co., in mid-Dec. 1997; (5) w. Muhlenberg Co. in early Feb. 2001; and (6) w. Fulton Co. in late Dec. 2001 (juvenile). *Michigan:* Both records are pre-1990. (1) Whitefish Point Bird Observatory, Chippewa Co., in early May 1982; and (2) Calhoun Co. for 4 days in mid-Aug. 1987. *Mississippi:* One female returned to same location at

Enid Lake, Yalobusha Co., for 8 years in the 1990s: early Dec. 1991–late Feb. 1992, mid-Nov. 1992–early Jan. 1993, mid-Nov. 1993 through winter, early Nov. 1994–early Mar. 1995, mid-Nov. 1995 through winter, not recorded in 1996, mid-Feb. 1997 for 4 days, mid-Jan. 1998, mid-Dec. 1998–early Jan. 1999; also early Jan. 2000. *Ontario:* Beamer Memorial Conservation Area (hawkwatch) in mid-Apr. 1995. *Tennessee:* Mainly observed in two counties near the Mississippi River. Sightings are single-day records unless otherwise noted: (1) Shelby Co. in early Oct. 1958, (2) Shelby Co. in mid-Oct. 1980, (3) Lake Co. for 2 days in mid-Oct. 1984, (3) Shelby Co. in early Sep. 1986, (4) Shelby Co. in mid-Mar. 1989, (5) Shelby Co. in mid-Sep. 1992, (6) Shelby Co. in early Dec. 1992, (7) Lake Co. in mid-Sep. 1987; (8) Williamson Co. in early Nov. 1997, (9) Lake Co. for 2 days in mid-Dec. 1997, (10) Shelby Co. for 2 days in early and late Apr. 2000, and (11) Lake Co. in Dec. 2001. *Wisconsin:* (1) Racine Co. in mid-Oct. 1990; (2) Eagle Valley Nature Preserve, Grant Co. in mid-Oct. 1996, and (3) Douglas Co. in late Apr. 1998. Additional records: Cedar Grove Ornithological Station in late Sep. 1957 and Oct. 1982 and in Genoa, Vernon Co., in late Oct. 1976. *South Carolina:* Two records, but falconry birds escaped from n. Georgia during this period, and thus records are suspect. (1) Pendleton, Anderson Co., in late Nov. 1977; and (2) Clemson, Oconee Co., in mid Nov. 1978. Both locations are near each other.

STATUS AND DISTRIBUTION (WEST):

Summer.—*Uncommon.* There are 4,300–6,000 pairs in the U.S., Canada, and Mexico. The largest numbers are in Nevada (1,200 pairs) and Wyoming (820 pairs). Population has always been historically low but seemingly stable. In Canada, listed as a Species at Risk in British Columbia and as a Sensitive Species in Alberta and Saskatchewan.

Except along western portions of the Snake River in sw. Idaho at the Snake River Birds of Prey Natural Conservation Area, where nesting density is extremely high with about 200 pairs, Prairie Falcons are distributed in very low density. In many regions, cyclic ground squirrel populations periodically affect regional nesting success and status.

In Mexico, sparsely distributed breeder in

arid highlands to cen. Baja California and Chihuahua, south to s.-cen. Durango and s. Coahuila, and an isolated area in ne. Zacatecas.

Winter.—Mainly winters south and east of breeding and natal areas. Individuals nesting in Wyoming and sw. Idaho have wintered northeast of breeding areas in s. Manitoba and Montana, respectively. Solitary except in areas of abundant prey. A few individuals may loosely assemble in areas where prey is abundant. Some pairs may remain together or mate on the winter grounds: a pair of adults were present in Tarrant Co. in n.-cen. Texas for two consecutive years. Generally a highly nomadic species. Many Prairie Falcons follow large flocks of prairie-dwelling passerines, particularly Horned Larks and Eastern and Western meadowlarks. Horned Larks, in particular, often mass in extraordinarily large numbers in agricultural areas, particularly wheat fields. Cattle feedlots and urban areas, especially near grain elevators, are also popular wintering locales because of large densities of European Starlings, House Sparrows, Rock Doves, Brown-headed Cowbirds, Common Grackles, or Great-tailed Grackles. However, territories may be established and the falcons may remain sedentary if prey base is ample and stable. Some winter territories may be used for consecutive years.

Major winter areas are in e. Colorado, w. Kansas, Texas Panhandle, s. Arizona, and cen. and s. California Regular in small numbers in cen. Iowa and w. and e.-cen. Missouri (mainly along the Missouri River). Irregular farther east to Scott Co., Iowa. Casual in w. Minnesota (one female wintered in St. Paul for several years). Regular but uncommon on coastal areas of Skagit Co., Wash. Rare in winter west of the Cascade Mts. in Oregon. Uncommon west of the Coast Range Mts. in California.

In Mexico, some winter to s. Baja California and as far south as the state of México. In Toluca, Mexico, they have been seen at 9,500 ft. (2,900 m).

Movements.—Mid- to late summer dispersal occurs from mid-Jun. through Aug. Juveniles disperse immediately after becoming independent, typically from mid-Jun. through mid-Jul., depending on elevation and latitude. Banding data indicates most head north, east, or southeast of natal areas. Juveniles disperse to the Great Plains, mountain valleys, or subalpine and alpine meadows. Juveniles from California have dispersed to regions east of the Continental Divide. Adult females nesting in sw. Idaho may leave breeding areas in July, often several weeks after nesting is completed, and head northeast to prairie regions in e. Montana, se. Alberta, and sw. Saskatchewan.

Mid- to late-summer dispersal allows the falcons to hunt easy-to-catch juvenile ground squirrels, which remain active later in the summer at higher elevations and northern latitudes. Falcons moving onto the Great Plains also feed on the late-summer abundance of meadowlarks, Horned Larks, and Lark Buntings. Falcons that disperse onto the Great Plains may remain in favored areas for varying lengths of time, and a few may remain all winter. Juveniles may disperse eastward to e. North Dakota by late Jul. and into w. Minnesota by early to mid-Aug. They are regularly found in cen. Iowa by mid- to late fall and, rarely, as far east as e.-cen. Iowa. There is little information on dispersal movements by adult males.

Fall migration: Actual migration is often an extension of the mid- to late-summer dispersal. Movements may continue to at least early Nov. for adult males. However, late-season sightings may also include nomadic movements by adult females and juveniles. Migration is short to moderate in distance. Movements are generally in a southeasterly direction but can be lateral or even northeasterly. Falcons that have dispersal in a northeasterly direction, especially those that headed for northern prairies, often take a more southerly direction Aug.–Oct. Juveniles and adult females move simultaneously. Peak numbers of adult females and juveniles on the cen. and s. Great Plains occur from mid-Sep. to early Oct. Adult males are generally not seen on cen. Great Plains until Oct. Migrants passing through w. Minnesota generally peak in early Oct.

Spring migration: Mid-Jan. to May. Adults are very early migrants. A notable movement of adult males occurs on the cen. Great Plains from mid-Jan. to early Feb. Adult females follow shortly thereafter. Most adults are on breeding territories by mid-Feb. to mid-Mar. Juveniles generally peak in Mar., and with some moving until May.

Falconry.—Prairie Falcons are a favored falconry species. Escaped individuals may be encountered anywhere and may sport jesses or telemetry antenna attachments on their backs or tails. Escaped individuals may also be artificial hybrids with Gyrfalcons or Peregrine Falcons. Natural hybridization rarely occurs with Peregrines.

NESTING (West): Feb.–Jul., depending on latitude and elevation. Birds in southern latitudes may be on territories by Dec., but pairs in northern latitudes and high elevations usually do not occupy territories until Feb. to mid-Mar. Males are generally the first to arrive on breeding grounds. Pairs may rarely remain together or unite on the winter grounds. Prairie Falcons normally breed when 2 years old. One-year-old females, in juvenile plumage, may occasionally breed with adult males.

No nest is built. Nest sites are scraped depressions in cavities on cliffs with protective overhangs, which gives protection against inclement late-winter and early-spring weather.

CONSERVATION: No measures taken in the East.

Mortality.—Illegal shooting, electrocution from utility wires, and collisions with fence lines and sometimes vehicles. Unlike the Peregrine Falcon, Prairie Falcons suffered only a minimal amount from the organochlorine pesticide era. Prairie Falcons do not feed as extensively on avian prey as do Peregrines and thus did not accumulate large doses of deadly chemicals. Organophosphate poisoning has occurred in local farming areas in the West.

SIMILAR SPECIES: (1) **Merlin, adult females/juveniles.**—PERCHED.—Yellow cere, orbital skin, and legs in all seasons. Nondescript pattern behind eyes. Tail same color as upperparts with three or four narrow pale bands; except some *Falco columbarius columbarius*, which may lack bands on dorsal surface of tail. *F. c. columbarius* have fairly distinct dark "mustaches." *F. c. richardsonii* lack a "mustache." FLIGHT.—Uniformly dark underwings on *columbarius* and uniformly pale on *richardsonii*. Tail patterns as in Perched. *Note:* Large female *richardsonii* are deceptively similar in size and coloration to male Prairie Falcons. (2) **Peregrine Falcon, juveniles.**—PERCHED.— *F. p. peregrinus tundrius* may have very narrow "mustache"; crown area usually pale. *F. p. anatum* have wide dark "mustaches." *F. p. tundrius* have very narrow streaking on underparts; upperparts pale, tawny edging on all feathers. Wingtips nearly reach or are equal to the tail tip. FLIGHT.—Underwings on all races are uniformly dark and have pale tawny spotting and barring. Uppertail surface is the same color as upperparts in all seasons. *Note:* Use caution in fall with *tundrius*; similar to recently fledged Prairie Falcons with the pale feather edgings. (3) **Gyrfalcon, gray morphs.**— PERCHED.—Nondescript head pattern: all dark or all pale behind eyes; some "mustache" definition. Similar wingtip-to-tail-tip ratio. FLIGHT.—Caution on underwing pattern: Many gray morphs have darker, mottled median coverts, identical to male Prairie Falcons; however, axillaries are mottled white and *are not* solid dark brown, as in Prairie Falcons. (3A) **Adult gray morphs.**—Upperparts very grayish barred. Uppertail distinctly barred with gray. The spotted or barred median underwings coverts are sometimes fairly dark, but the axillaries are also spotted or barred. (3B) **Juvenile gray morphs.**—Brown upperparts as on juvenile/adult female Prairie Falcons. Median underwing coverts and axillaries may be particularly dark but auxiliaries are always spotted or barred. Uppertail is same color as rest of upperparts in all seasons and has numerous, narrow whitish bands.

OTHER NAMES: None regularly used. Males are called "tiercels," females are called "falcons." *Spanish:* Halcón Mexicano, Halcón Pradeno, or Halcón Cafe. *French:* Faucon des Prairies.

REFERENCES: Bohlen 1989, Burt and Grossenheider 1976, Clark and Wheeler 1987, Dobos 1995, Howell and Webb 1995, Layne 1987, Millard 1993, Palmer 1988, Post and Gauthreaux 1989, Robbins and Easterla 1992, Robbins 1991, Robinson 1990, Steenhof 1998, Steenhof et al. 1984, Stevenson and Anderson 1994.

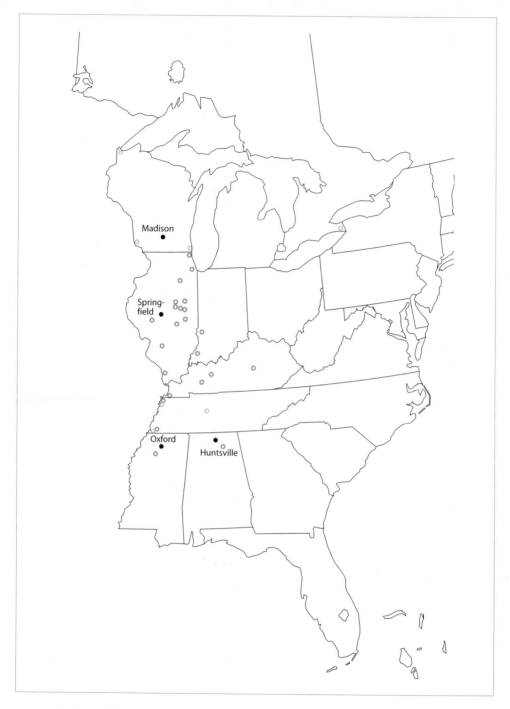

PRAIRIE FALCON, *Falco mexicanus:* Regular in Illinois, casual in Kentucky, Tennessee, and Wisconsin, and accidental elsewhere in the fall, winter, and spring. Multiple sightings for many posted locations.

Plate 529. Prairie Falcon, adult male [Jun.] ▪ White cheek extends up behind the eye; brown auricular patch; narrow dark malar mark; thin dark eyeline; full white supercilium. ▪ Medium brown upperparts are always distinctly barred with pale brown or gray. ▪ Wingtips are shorter than tail tip. ▪ Pale brown, faintly banded tail.

Plate 530. Prairie Falcon, adult female [Jun.] ▪ White cheek extends up behind the eye; brown auricular patch; narrow dark malar mark; thin dark eyeline; short, white supercilium. ▪ Medium brown upperparts are often partially barred or unbarred. ▪ Wingtips are shorter than tail tip. ▪ Pale brown, often unbanded tail.

Plate 531. Prairie Falcon, adult pair (male on left) [Jun.] ▪ Size difference between sexes that is typical of larger falcons. Males are much smaller than females.

Plate 532. Prairie Falcon, adult male [Jun.] ▪ Lightly to moderately spotted white underparts. ▪ Black axillaries. Black median underwing coverts are spotted with white and lesser coverts are lightly streaked with black. Remiges are white and uniformly barred with gray. ▪ Pale tail is banded on the underside.

Plate 533. Prairie Falcon, adult female [Jun.] ▪ Moderately to heavily spotted white underparts. ▪ Black axillaries. All-black median underwing coverts blend with the axillaries; lesser coverts are heavily streaked with black. Median coverts are sometimes lightly spotted with white. Remiges are white and uniformly barred with gray. ▪ Pale tail is banded on the underside.

Plate 534. Prairie Falcon, adult male [Jun.] ▪ Medium brown upperparts are barred with pale brown or gray. ▪ Pale brown tail contrasts to the darker upperparts. Narrow white terminal band. ▪ *Note:* Wing molt begins on primaries: p4 is newly molted, p5 is dropped and not yet regrown.

Plate 535. Prairie Falcon, adult female [Jun.] ▪ Nearly uniformly medium brown upperparts. ▪ Pale brown tail contrasts to darker upperparts. White terminal band is worn off. ▪ *Note:* Molting remiges. Primary molt with new p4 and 5 (darker, grayish feathers) and dropped p3 and 6; new middle secondaries s5 and 6.

Plate 536. Prairie Falcon, juvenile female (recently fledged) [Jul.] ▪ White cheek extends up behind the eye; brown auricular patch; thin dark malar mark. Pale blue cere and orbital skin. ▪ Dark brown upperpart feathers are broadly edged with pale brown. ▪ Wingtips are shorter than tail tip. ▪ Tail is same color as upperparts.

Plate 537. Prairie Falcon, juvenile female (worn plumage) [Jan.] ▪ White cheek extends behind eye; brown auricular patch; thin dark malar mark. Pale yellow cere and orbital skin. ▪ Brown upperparts are narrowly edged with pale brown. Underparts fade to white by mid-fall. ▪ Wingtips are shorter than tail tip. ▪ Tail has faded to pale brown.

Plate 538. Prairie Falcon, juvenile male (recently fledged) [Jul.] ▪ Tawny underparts are thinly streaked with dark brown. ▪ Black axillaries. Black median coverts are spotted with white; lesser coverts are moderately streaked with black. Remiges are white and uniformly barred with gray. ▪ *Note:* Juvenile females may also have similar white spotting on median coverts.

Plate 539. Prairie Falcon, juvenile female (recently fledged) [Jul.] ▪ Tawny underparts are moderately streaked with dark brown. ▪ Black axillaries blend with all-black median coverts and heavily streaked lesser coverts. ▪ *Note:* Juvenile males may have similar all-black underwing markings.

Plate 540. Prairie Falcon, juvenile female (recently fledged) [Jul.] ▪ Uniformly dark brown upperparts. ▪ Dark brown tail is same color as upperparts. Broad white terminal band is wider than adult's in summer.

BIBLIOGRAPHY

Alabama Birds Records Committee. 2002. Records 1988–1989 and 1990–1991. Alabama Ornithol. Soc. World Wide Web Home Page <http://www.bham.net/aos/abrc/> [Mar. 17, 2002].

American Ornithologists' Union. 1997. Forty-first Supplement to the American Ornithologists' Union *Check-list of North American Birds. Auk* 114 (3): 542–552.

American Ornithologists' Union. 1998. *Check-list of North American Birds.* 7th ed. Am. Ornithol. Union, Washington, D.C.

American Ornithologists' Union. 2000. Forty-second Supplement to the American Ornithologists' Union *Check-list of North American Birds. Auk* 117 (3): 847–858.

Anderson, B. H. 2001. Florida Report (Hawks through Shorebirds). *N. Am. Birds* 55 (2): 164.

Andrle, R. F., and J. R. Carroll. 1988. *The Atlas of Breeding Birds in New York State.* Cornell Univ. Press, Ithaca, NY.

Arnold, K. A. 2001. Red-shouldered Hawk. The Texas Breeding Bird Atlas. Version 1.10. Texas A&M Univ. System, College Station and Corpus Christi, TX <http://tbba.cbi.tamuc.edu> [Jan. 26, 2002].

Baicich, P. J., and C.J.O. Harrison. 1997. *A Guide to Nests, Eggs, and Nestlings of North American Birds.* 2nd ed. Academic Press, San Diego, CA.

Bain, M. 1993. Ontario Field Ornithologists Accepted Records. *Ont. Birds* 11 (2): 46–63.

Barclay, J. H. 1988. Peregrine Restoration in the Eastern United States. Pp. 549–558 *in Peregrine Falcon Populations* (T. J. Cade, J. H. Enderson, C. G. Thelander, and C. M. White, eds.). The Peregrine Fund, Boise, ID.

Benson, K.L.P., and K. A. Arnold. 2001. The Texas Breeding Bird Atlas. Version 1.10. Texas A & M Univ. System, College Station and Corpus Christi, TX <http://tbba.cbi.tamucc.edu> [Jan. 26, 2002].

Bent, A. C. 1961. *Life Histories of North American Birds of Prey.* Pts. 1 and 2. Dover Publ., New York, NY.

Berger, D. D., C. R. Sindelar, Jr., and K. E. Gamble. 1968. The Status of Breeding Peregrines in the Eastern United States. Pp. 165–173 *in Peregrine Falcon Populations: Their Biology and Decline* (J. J. Hickey, ed.). Univ. of Wisconsin Press, Madison.

Bildstein, K. L., and M. W. Collopy. 1985. Escorting Flight and Agonistic Interactions in Wintering Northern Harriers. *Condor* 87: 398–401.

Block, W. M., M. L. Morrison, and M. Hildegard Reiser (eds.). 1994. The Northern Goshawk: Ecology and Management. *Stud. Avian Biol.,* No. 6.

Bohlen, D. H. 1989. *The Birds of Illinois.* Indiana Univ. Press, Bloomington.

Bolen, E. G., and D. Flores. 1993. *The Mississippi Kite.* Univ. of Texas Press, Austin, TX.

Brauning, D. W. (ed.). 1992. *Atlas of Breeding Birds in Pennsylvania.* Univ. of Pittsburgh Press, Pittsburgh, PA.

Breen, T. F., and J. W. Parrish. 1996. First Evidence for Double-brooding in Southeastern Kestrels in Georgia. *Oriole* 60: 81–83.

Breen, T. F., and J. W. Parrish. 1997. Distribution and Use of Nest Boxes by American Kestrels in the Coastal Plains of Georgia. *Fla. Field Nat.* 25: 129–138.

Breen, T. F., J. W. Parrish, B. Winn, and K. Boyd. 1995. Southeastern American Kestrel Nests in Bulloch, Evans, and Columbia Counties. *Oriole* 60: 33–36.

Breining, G. 1994. *Return of the Eagle: How America Saved Its National Symbol.* Falcon Press, Helena, MT.

Brewer, R, G. A. McPeek, and R. J. Adams, Jr. 1991. *The Atlas of Breeding Birds of Michigan.* Michigan State Univ. Press, East Lansing.

Brockman, F. C. 1968. *Trees of North America.* Golden Press, New York, NY.

Brodeur, S., R. Décarie, D. M. Bird, and M. Fuller. 1996. Complete Migration Cycle of Golden Eagles Breeding in Northern Quebec. Condor 98: 293–299.

Brown, R. E., J. H. Williamson, and D. B. Boone. 1997. Swallow-tailed Kite Nesting in Texas: Past and Present. *Southwest. Nat.* 42 (1): 103–105.

Buckelew, A. R., Jr., and G. A. Hall. 1994. *The West Virginia Breeding Bird Atlas.* Univ. of Pittsburgh Press, Pittsburgh, PA.

Burgiel, J. C., R. O. Paxton, and D. A. Cutler. 2000. Hundson-Delaware (Hawks Through Cranes). *N. Am. Birds* 54 (3): 265.

Burnham, B. 1997. *A Fascination With Falcons.* Hancock House, Surrey, BC, and Blaine, WA.

Burt, W. H., and R. P. Grossenheider. 1976. *A*

Field Guide to the Mammals. Houghton Mifflin, Boston, MA.

Bylan, S. (ed.). 1998. *Hawk Migr. Stud.* 24, No. 1.

Bylan, S. (ed.). 1999. *Hawk Migr. Stud.* 25, No. 1.

Byre, V. 1990. A Group of Young Peregrine Falcons Prey on Migrating Bats. *Wilson Bull.* 102: (4): 728–730.

Cade, T. J., J. H. Enderson, C. G. Thelander, and C. M. White (eds.). 1988. *Peregrine Falcon Populations.* The Peregrine Fund, Boise, ID.

Cadman, M. D., P.F.J. Eagles, and F. M. Helleiner. 1987. *Atlas of the Breeding Birds of Ontario.* Univ. of Waterloo Press, Waterloo, ON.

Canadian Peregrine Foundation. 1999a. Richmond Hill Home Page. World Wide Web Site <http://www.peregrine-foundation.ca/tops/rh.html> [Aug. 24, 2000].

Canadian Peregrine Foundation. 1999b. Guelph Home Page. World Wide Web Site <http://www.peregrine-foundation.ca/tops/gutop.html> [Sep. 9, 2000].

Canadian Peregrine Foundation. 2002a. Project Track' em. World Wide Web Site <http://www.peregrine-foundation.ca/programs/tracem/track2000.html> [May 16, 2002].

Canadian Peregrine Foundation. 2002b. Southern Ontario Peregrine Nest Sites. World Wide Web Site <http://www.peregrine-foundation.ca/nestingsites.html> [Aug. 10, 2002].

Castrale, J. S., and A. Ferchak. 2000. Midwinter Bald Eagle Survey in Indiana—2000. Wildl. Manage. Res. Notes. Indiana Div. Fish Wildl., Feb.

Castrale, J. S., E. M. Hopkins, and C. E. Keller. 1998. *Atlas of Breeding Birds of Indiana.* Indiana Dep. Nat. Resour., Indianapolis.

Castrale, J. S., and A. Parker. 1999a. Bald Eagle Nesting in Indiana—1999 Update. Wildl. Manage. Res. Notes. Indiana Div. Fish Wildlife, Aug. 1999.

Castrale, J. S., and A. Parker. 1999b. Peregrine Falcon Nesting in Indiana—1999. Indiana Div. Fish Wildl., Aug. 1999.

Center for Conservation, Research, and Technology. 2000. Current Projects: Broad-winged Hawk. World Wide Web Home Page <http://www.ccrt.org> Version Dec. 8, 2000, for the Center for Conservation, Research, and Technology, Univ. of Maryland, Baltimore, and Boise State Univ., Boise, ID.

Clark, W. S. 1998. First North American Record of a Melanistic Osprey. *Wilson Bull.* 110: 289–290.

Clark, W. S. 1999. *A Field Guide to the Raptors of Europe, the Middle East, and North Africa.* Oxford Univ. Press, Oxford, U.K.

Clark, W. S. 2001. Aging Bald Eagles. *Birding* 33 (1): 18–28.

Clark, W. S., and R. C. Banks. 1992. The Taxonomic Status of the White-tailed Kite. *Wilson Bull.* 104: 571–579.

Clark, W. S., and B. K. Wheeler. 2001. *A Field Guide to Hawks of North America.* 2nd ed. Houghton Mifflin, Boston, MA.

Clum, N. J., and T. J. Cade. 1994. Gyrfalcon (*Falco rusticolus*). *In* The Birds of North America, No. 114 (A. Poole and F. Gill, eds.). Acad. Nat. Sci., Philadelphia, PA, and Am. Ornithol. Union, Washington, D.C.

Commission for Environmental Cooperation. 1997. North American Regional Action Plan on DDT: North American Working Group for the Sound Management of Chemicals Task Force on DDT and Chlordane. World Wide Web Site <http://www.cec.org/programs_projects/pollutants_health/smoc/ddt.cfm?varlan=english>.

Court, G. S., C. C. Gates, and D. A. Boag. 1988. Natural History of the Peregrine Falcon in the Keewatin District of the Northwest Territories. *Arctic* 41 (1): 17–30.

Craig, T. H., E. H. Craig, and J. S. Marks. 1982. Aerial Talon-grappling in Northern Harriers. *Condor* 84: 239.

Crocoll, S. T. 1994. Red-shouldered Hawk (*Buteo lineatus*). *In* The Birds of North America, No. 107 (A. Poole and F. Gill, eds.). Acad. Nat. Sci., Philadelphia, PA, and Am. Ornithol. Union, Washington, D.C.

Curry, R. 1991. Ontario Field Ornithologists Accepted Records. *Ont. Birds* 9 (2): 18–44.

Davis, R. 1999. Southern Atlantic Coast Region (Waterfowl Through Sandhill Crane). *N. Am. Birds* 53 (3): 269.

Debus, S. 1998. *The Birds of Prey of Australia.* Oxford Univ. Press, Melbourne, Australia.

Dekker, D. 1980. Hunting Success Rates, Foraging Habitats, and Prey Selection of Peregrine Falcons Migrating Through Central Alberta. *Can. Field-Nat.* 94 (4): 371–382.

Dekker, D. 1987. Peregrine Falcon Predation on Ducks in Alberta and British Columbia. *J. Wildl. Manage.* 51 (1): 156–159.

Dekker, D., 1988. Peregrine Falcon and Merlin Predation on Small Shorebirds and Passerines in Alberta. *Can. J. Zool.* 66: 925–928.

Dekker, D. 1999. *Bolt From the Blue: Wild Peregrines on the Hunt.* Hancock House, Surrey, BC, and Blaine, WA.

Dekker, D., and J. Lange. 2001. Hunting Methods and Success Rates for Gyrfalcon, *Falco rustico-*

lus, and Prairie Falcon, *Falco mexicanus*, Preying on Feral Pigeons (Rock Doves), *Columba livia*, in Edmonton, Alberta. *Can. Field-Nat.* 15 (3): 395–401.

del Hoyo, J. A. Elliott, and J. Sargatal (eds.). 1994. *Handbook of the Birds of the World.* Vol. 2. New World Vultures to Guineafowl. Lynx Edicions, Barcelona, Spain.

DeLorme Publishers. 1991a. *Illinois Atlas and Gazetteer.* DeLorme Publ., Freeport, ME.

DeLorme Publishers. 1991b. *Ohio Atlas and Gazetteer.* DeLorme Publ., Freeport, ME.

DeLorme Publishers. 1995. *Wisconsin Atlas and Gazetteer.* DeLorme Publ., Freeport, ME.

Dickerman, R. W. 1994. Undescribed Subspecies of Red-tailed Hawk From Baja California. *Southwest. Nat.* 39 (4): 375–395.

Dickerman, R. W., and F. C. Parkes. 1987. Subspecies of the Red-tailed Hawk in the Northeast. *Kingbird* 37: 57–64.

Dobos, R. Z. 1995. Ontario Field Ornithologists Accepted Records. *Ont. Birds* 13 (2): 46–55.

Dodge, J. (ed.). 1988–1997. *Hawk Migr. Stud.* Vols. 14–23.

Dodge, J. (ed.). 1995. Peregrine Falcons Tracked by Satellite. Hawk Flights. *Newsl. Hawk Migr. Assoc. N. Am.* 1:21.

Dove, C. J., and R. C. Banks. 1999. A Taxonomic Study of Crested Caracaras (Falconidae). *Wilson Bull.* 111 (3): 330–339.

Dreitz, V. 2000. The Influence of Environmental Variation on the Snail Kite Population in Florida. Ph.D. diss., Univ. of Miami, Miami, FL.

Duncan, B. 1986. The Occurrence and Identification of Swainson's Hawks in Ontario. *Ont. Birds* 4 (2): 43–61.

Dunk, J. R. 1995. White-tailed Kite (*Elanus leucurus*). *In* The Birds of North America, No. 178 (A. Poole and F. Gill, eds.). Acad. Nat. Sci., Philadelphia, PA, and Am. Ornithol. Union, Washington, D.C.

Dunn, J. L., and K. L. Garrett. 1997. A Field Guide to Warblers of North America. Houghton Mifflin Co., Boston, MA.

Dunne, P., D. Sibley, and C. Sutton. 1998. *Hawks in Flight: The Flight Identification of North American Migrant Raptors.* Houghton Mifflin, Boston, MA.

Eberly, C. 1999. Conservation From Outer Space: Boldly Tracking Migration Patterns. *Hawk Migr. Stud.* Aug.: 17–19.

Edelstam, C. 1984. Patterns of Molt in Large Birds of Prey. *Ann. Zool. Fenn.* 21: 271–276.

Ellison, W. G., and N. L. Martin. 2000. New England Region (Loons Through Vultures). *N. Am. Birds* 54 (1): 27.

England, A. S., M. J. Bechard, and C. S. Houston. 1997. Swainson's Hawk (*Buteo swainsoni*). *In* The Birds of North America, No. 265 (A. Poole and F. Gill, eds.). Acad. Nat. Sci., Philadelphia, PA, and Am. Ornithol. Union, Washington, D.C.

Environment Canada. 1999. Species at Risk: Peregrine Falcon. World Wide Web Site for the Green Lane, <http://www.nais.ccrs.nrcan. gc.ca/schoolnet/issues/risk/birds/ebirds/ prgfalcon/html> [Aug. 9, 2000].

Environment Canada. 2000. Species at Risk: American Peregrine Falcon. World Wide Web Site for the Green Lane, <http://www. speciesatrisk.gc.ca/Species/English/ SearchDetail.cfm?SpeciesID=29> [Jun. 13, 2002].

Environment Canada. 2001. Waiting for the Fiddler: Pesticides and the Environment in the Atlantic Region. World Wide Web Site for the Green Lane, <http://www.ns.ec.gc.ca/epb/ fiddle/insectic.html> [Apr. 11, 2002].

Erskine, A. J. 1992. *Atlas of Breeding Birds of the Maritime Provinces.* Nimbus Publ., Nova Scotia Mus. and Dep. Nat. Resour., Halifax, NS.

Evans, D. L., and R. N. Rosenfield. 1985. Migration and Mortality of Sharp-shinned Hawks Ringed at Duluth, MN. ICBP Tech. Publ. No. 5.

Ewins, P. J. 1995. Recovery of Osprey Populations in Canada. Pp. 14–16 *in* Bird Trends, Vol. 4 (C. Hyslope, ed.). Can. Wildl. Serv., Ontario.

Ferguson-Lees, J., and D. A. Christie. 2001. *Raptors of the World.* Christopher Helm, A & C Black, London, U.K.

Flemming, J. H. 1907. Birds of Toronto, Ontario. Pt. 2, Land Birds. *Auk* 24: 71–89.

Forsman, D. 1999. *The Raptors of Europe and the Middle East.* T. & A. D. Poyser, London, U.K.

Foushee, R. 1998. Bald Eagle on the Comeback Trail. *Wildl. in North Carolina* 62: 4–9.

Franklin, K. 1999. Vertical Flight. *N. Am. Falconers Assoc. J.* 38: 68–72.

Fuller, M. R., W. S. Seegar, and L. S. Schveck. 1998. Routes and Travel Rates of Migrating Peregrine Falcons, *Falco peregrinus*, and Swainson's Hawks, *Buteo swainsoni*, in the Western Hemisphere. *J. Avian Biol.* 29: 433–440.

Fyfe, R. W. 1988. The Canadian Peregrine Falcon Recovery Program, 1967–1985. Pp. 599–610 *in* Peregrine Falcon Populations (T. J. Cade, J. H. Enderson, C. G. Thelander, and C. M. White, eds.). The Peregrine Fund, Boise, ID.

Gahbauer, M. (ed.). 1999. Project Track 'em. *Talon Tales* 2 (4): 6–7.

Gahbauer, M., and S. Metzger. 1999. Canadian

Peregrine Foundation Project Release 1999: Final Report Analysis. Can. Peregrine Found., Toronto, ON.

Georgia Ornithological Society. 2002. "Krider's" Red-tailed Hawk. World Wide Web Site <http://www.gos.org/sightings/rtha.html>.

Gloger, C. W. L. 1833. *The Variation of Birds Under the Influence of Climate.* August Schulz, Breslau, Germany.

Godfrey, E. W. 1986. *The Birds of Canada.* Natl. Mus. Nat. Sci., Ottawa, ON.

Goodrich, L. J., S. C. Crocoll, and S. E. Senner. 1996. Broad-winged Hawk (*Buteo platypterus*). *In* The Birds of North America, No. 218 (A. Poole and F. Gill, eds.). Acad. Nat. Sci., Philadelphia, PA, and Am. Ornithol. Union, Washington, D.C.

Granlund, J. 1999. Western Great Lakes Region (Raptors Through Shorebirds). *N. Am. Birds* 53 (3): 282.

Granlund, J. 2001. Western Great Lakes (Hawks Through Gulls). *N. Am. Birds* 55 (2): 173.

Griffiths, C. S. 1994. Monophyly of the Falconiformes Based on Syringeal Morphology. *Auk* 111 (4): 787–805.

Gross, H. 1999. Hawkwatch International Band Encounters and Recaptures, 1997–1999. *Raptor Watch* 13 (3): 8–9.

Gustafson, M. E., and J. Hildenbrand. 1998. Banding Protocol for Peregrine Falcons. World Wide Web Home Page for the Bird Banding Laboratory <http://www.pwrc.usgs.gov/bbl/homepage/pefaprot.htm>.

Hall, G. A. 1983. West Virginia Birds: Distribution and Ecology. Carnegie Mus. Nat. Hist. Spec. Publ. No. 7.

Hamerstrom, F. 1968. Aging and Sexing Harriers. *Inland Bird Banding News* 40: 43–46.

Harris, J. T. 1979. *The Peregrine Falcon in Greenland: Observing an Endangered Species.* Univ. of Missouri Press, Columbia.

Herron, G. 1999. Status of the Northern Goshawk in the Great Basin. *Great Basin Birds* 2: 9–12.

Hoffman, M. L., and M. W. Collopy. 1988. Historical Status of the American Kestrel (*Falco sparverius paulus*) in Florida. *Wilson Bull.* 100: 91–107.

Hoffman, W., and H. Darrow. 1992. Migration of Diurnal Raptors From the Florida Keys Into the West Indies. *Hawk Migr. Stud.* 17 (3): 7–14.

Hope, C. D. 1949. First Occurrence of the Black Vulture in Ontario. *Auk* 66: 81–82.

Houghton, L. M., and L. M. Rymon. 1997. Nesting, Distribution, and Population Status of U.S. Osprey in 1994. *J. Raptor Res.* 31 (1): 44–53.

Houston, C. S., 1967. Recoveries of Red-tailed Hawks Banded in Saskatchewan. *Blue Jay* Sep.: 109–111.

Houston, C. S. 1998. Swainson's Hawk Productivity and Five-Young Nest. *Blue Jay* 56 (3): 151–155.

Houston, C. S., and K. I. Fung. 1999. Saskatchewan's First Swainson's Hawk With Satellite Radio. *Blue Jay* (2): 69–72.

Howell, S.N.G., and S. Webb. 1995. *A Guide to the Birds of Mexico and Northern Central America.* Oxford Univ. Press, New York, NY.

Howell, S.N.G., S. Webb, D. A. Sibley, and L. J. Prairie. 1992. First Record of a Melanistic Northern Harrier in North America. *West. Birds* 23: 79–80.

Humphrey, P. S., and K. C. Parkes. 1959. An Approach to the Study of Molts and Plumages. *Auk* 76: 1–31.

Hunt, W. G., R. R. Rogers, and D. J. Slowe. 1975. Migratory and Foraging Behavior of Peregrine Falcons on the Texas Coast. *Can. Field-Nat.* 89 (2): 111–123.

Iliff, M. J. 1998. Middle Atlantic Coast Region (Hawks to Cranes). *Field Notes* 52 (3): 312.

Iliff, M. J. 2001. Middle Atlantic Coast (Raptors to Cranes). *N. Am. Birds* 55 (2): 155–157.

Ingle, D. 1999. Hare Decline: Extraterrestrial? World Wide Web Home Page <Alloutdoors.comHome> .

Jeffers, R. D. 2000. The Mystery of the Dying Eagles. *Endangered Species Bull.*, U.S. Fish Wildl. Serv. 25 (5): 4–5.

Johnsgard, P. A. 1973. *Grouse and Quails of North America.* Univ. of Nebraska Press, Lincoln.

Johnsgard, P. A. 1990. *Hawks, Eagles, and Falcons of North America.* Smithson. Inst. Press, Washington, D.C.

Justus, K. 1997. Mississippi Kite: Purple Martins Being Included in the Aerial Hunter's Diet. *Purple Martin Update* 7 (3): 8–9.

Kale, H. W., II, B. Pranty, B. M. Stith, and C. W. Biggs. 1992. *The Atlas of the Breeding Birds of Florida.* Final Rep. Nongame Wildl. Prog. Fla. Game Freshwater Fish Comm., Tallahassee.

Kalla, P. I., and F. J. Alsop, III. 1983. The Distribution, Habitat Preference, and Status of the Mississippi Kite in Tennessee. *Am. Birds* 37 (2): 146–149.

Kaufman, J., and H. Meng. 1975. *Falcons Return: Restoring an Endangered Species.* William Morrow, New York, NY.

Kaufman, K. 1996. *Lives of North American Birds.* Houghton Mifflin, Boston, MA.

Kellogg, S. (ed.). 2000. Fall 1999 Flyway Reports. *Hawk Migr. Stud.* 26 (1).

Kerlinger, P., and S. A. Gauthreaux, Jr. 1985. Seasonal Timing, Geographic Distribution, and Flight Behavior of Broad-winged Hawks During Spring Migration in South Texas: A Radar and Visual Study. *Auk* 102: 735–743.

Kessel, B. 1989. *Birds of the Seward Peninsula, Alaska: Their Biogeography, Seasonality, and Natural History.* Univ. of Alaska Press, Fairbanks.

Kirk, D. A., and M. J. Mossman. 1998. Turkey Vulture (*Cathartes aura*). *In* The Birds of North America, No. 339 (A. Poole and F. Gill, eds.). Acad. Nat. Sci., Philadelphia, PA, and Am. Ornithol. Union, Washington, D.C.

Krebs, C. J., S. Boutin, and R. Boonstra. 2001. *Ecosystem Dynamics of the Boreal Forest: the Kluane Project.* Oxford Univ. Press, Oxford, U.K.

Lane, J. J., and R. A. Fischer. 1997. Species Profile: Southeastern American Kestrel (*Falco sparverius paulus*) on Military Installations in the Southeastern United States. Tech. Rep. SERDP-97-4. U.S. Army Engineer Waterways Exp. Sta., Vicksburg, MS.

Laughlin, S. B., and D. P. Kibbe. 1985. *The Atlas of Breeding Birds of Vermont.* Univ. Press of New England, Hanover, NH.

Layne, J. N. 1987. Prairie Falcon Sighting in Florida. *Fla. Field Nat.* 15: 77–79.

Leberman, R. C. 2000. Appalachia Regional Report (Waterfowl Through Cranes). *N. Am. Birds* 54 (4): 382.

Lee, D. S., and E. W. Irvin. 1988. Breeding Status of the Northern Harrier in North Carolina. *Chat* 52: 7–9.

Lee, D. S., and W. R. Spofford. 1990. Nesting of Golden Eagles in the Central and Southern Appalachians. *Wilson Bull.* 102: 693–698.

Levine, E. (ed.). 1998. *Bull's Birds of New York State.* Cornell Univ. Press, Ithaca, NY.

Liguori, J. 2001. Pitfalls of Classifying Light Morph Red-tailed Hawks to Subspecies. *Birding* 53 (5): 436–446.

Line, L. 1996. Accord Is Reached to Recall Pesticide Devastating Hawk. *New York Times*, Science, Oct. 15, 1996.

Lott, C. 1999. Florida Keys Autumn Raptor Migration Census. Hawkwatch Int. unpubl. rep. Project No. NG98-103.

MacWhirter, R. B., and K. L. Bildstein. 1996. Northern Harrier (*Circus cyaneus*). *In* The Birds of North America, No. 210 (A. Poole and F. Gill, eds.). Acad. Nat. Sci., Philadelphia, PA, and Am. Ornithol. Union, Washington, D.C.

Marchant, S. (ed.). 1994. *Handbook of Australian,* New Zealand, and Antarctica Birds. Vol. 2. Oxford Univ. Press, Oxford, U.K.

Martell, M., S. Willey, and J. Schladweiler. 1998. Nesting and Migration of Swainson's Hawks in Minnesota. *Loon* 70: 72–81.

Martin, R. 2000. Northern Great Plains (Kites Through Shorebirds). *N. Am. Birds* 54 (4): 396–397.

Maybank, B. 1997. Atlantic Provinces (Diurnal Raptors to Shorebirds). *Field Notes* 51 (4): 839.

McCollough, M. A. 1989. Molting Sequence and Aging of Bald Eagles. *Wilson Bull.* 101 (1): 1–10.

McKinley, J. O., and W. G. Mattox. 2001. A Brood of Five Swainson's Hawks in Southwestern Idaho. *J. Raptor Res.* 35 (2): 169.

McMillian, M. A., and B. Pranty. 1997. Recent Nesting of the White-tailed Kite in Central Florida. *Fla. Field Nat.* 25: 142–145.

McWilliams, G. M., and D. W. Brauning. 2000. *The Birds of Pennsylvania.* Cornell Univ. Press, Ithaca, NY.

Meehan, T. D., P. Ginrod, and S. Hoffman. 1997. Foreign Encountered Raptors Banded in the Goshute Mts., Nev. 1980–1996: Breeding and Winter Ranges, Mortality, and Migration Routes. Paper read at the Hawk Migration Assoc. N. Am. Conference VIII, Snowbird, UT, Jun. 12–15, 1997.

Meyer, K. D. 1994. Species Profile: American Swallow-tailed Kite. *Wildbird* Jan.: 44-49.

Meyer, K. D. 1995. Swallow-tailed Kite (*Elanoides forficatus*). *In* The Birds of North America, No. 138 (A. Poole and F. Gill, eds.). Acad. Nat. Sci., Philadelphia, PA, and Am. Ornithol. Union, Washington, D.C.

Meyer, K. D. 1996. Communal Roosts of the American Swallow-tailed Kite in Florida: Habitat Associations, Critical Sites, and Technique for Monitoring Population Status. Final rep. Fla. Game Fresh Water Fish Comm., Tallahassee.

Meyer, K. D., J. D. Arnett, and A. Washburn. 1997. Abstract: Migration Routes and Winter Range of the Swallow-tailed Kite (*Elanoides forficatus*) Based on Satellite and VHF Telemetry. Paper presented at the Raptor Res. Found. 1997 Annual Meeting. Savannah, GA, Oct. 30–Nov. 1.

Meyer, K. D., and M. W. Collopy. 1995. Status, Distribution, and Habitat Requirements of the American Swallow-tailed Kite (*Elanoides forficatus*) in Florida. Fla. Game Fresh Water Fish Comm., Non-game Wildl. Prog. Proj. Rep. Tallahassee.

Meyer, K. D., and M. W. Collopy. 1996. American Swallow-tailed Kite. Pp. 188–196 *in Endangered*

Biota of Florida, Vol. 5, Birds (J. Rodgers, H. Kale, II, and H. Smith, eds.). Univ. Press of Florida, Gainesville, FL.

Millar, J. G. 2002. The Protection of Eagles and the Bald and Golden Eagle Protection Act. *J. Raptor Res.* 36 (1): 29–31.

Millard, S. 1993. Prairie Falcon Movements Into Western Minnesota. *Hawk Migr. Stud.* 19 (1): 16.

Miller, E. K., and J. A. Smallwood. 1997. Juvenal Plumage Characteristics of Male Southeastern American Kestrels. *J. Raptor Res.* 31 (3): 273–274.

Mindell, D. P. 1985. Plumage Variation and Winter Range of Harlan's Hawk (*Buteo jamaicensis harlani*). *Am. Birds* 39: 127–133.

Moore, K. R., and C. J. Henny. 1983. Nestsite Characteristics of Three Coexisting Accipiter Hawks in Northeastern Oregon. *J. Raptor Res.* 17 (3): 65–76.

Morneau, F. 1994. Abundance and Distribution of Nesting Golden Eagles in Hudson Bay, Québec. *J. Raptor Res.* 28 (4): 220–225.

Morrison, J. L. 1996. Crested Caracara (*Caracara plancus*). *In* The Birds of North America, No. 249 (A. Poole and F. Gill, eds.). Acad. Nat. Sci., Philadelphia, PA, and Am. Ornithol. Union, Washington, D.C.

Mumford, R. E., and C. E. Keller. 1984. *The Birds of Indiana*. Indiana Univ. Press, Bloomington.

Nature Conservancy, The. 2001. Rhode Island: Places We Protect—Head Waters of the Queens River. World Wide Web Site <http://nature.org/wherewework/northamerica/status/rhodeisland/preserves/arts351.html>.

Nicholson, C. P. 1997. *Atlas of the Breeding Birds of Tennessee*. Univ. of Tennessee Press, Knoxville.

Nicoletti, F. J. 1997. American Kestrel Migration Correlated With Green Darner Movements at Hawk Ridge in Duluth, MN. Paper read at the Hawk Migr. Assoc. N. Am. Conference VIII, Snowbird, UT, Jun. 12–15, 1997.

Nicoletti, F. J., S. Millard, and B. Yokel. 1998. First Description of Albinism in a Dark-morph Red-tailed Hawk in North America. *Loon* 70: 117–118.

Nye, P. E. 1982. Restoring the Bald Eagle in New York. *Conservationist*, Jul.–Aug.: 9–13, 48.

Nye, P. E., 1988. A Review of Bald Eagle Hacking Projects and Early Results in North America. Pp. 95–112 *in* Proc. Int. Symp. Raptor Reintroduction (D. K. Garcelon and G. W. Roemer, eds.), 1985. Inst. Wildl. Stud., Arcata, CA.

Nye, P. E. 1990. A Review of the Natural History of a Reestablished Population of Breeding Bald Eagles in New York. Paper read at the New York Nat. Hist. Conference, Albany, Jul. 21, 1990.

Nye, P. E. 1992. Wintering Bald Eagles in New York State. Paper presented at the New York Nat. Hist. Conference II, Albany, Apr. 30, 1992.

Nye, P. E. 1997. Use of Satellites to Track Wintering Bald Eagles to and From New York State. Paper presented at the annual meeting of The Wilderness Soc., Snowmass, CO, Sep. 25, 1997.

Nye, P. E., and B. A. Loucks. 1996. Historic and Current Status of the Golden Eagle in New York State and the Eastern United States. Paper read at the New York Nat. Hist. Conference IV, Albany, NY, Apr. 25, 1996.

Olivo, C. 2001. Bolivia: Studying Migrating Raptors at Four Hawkwatch Sites. *Hawk Migr. Stud.* 26 (2): 32–38.

Olivo, C. 2002. First Full-Season Autumn Raptor Migration Count in Concepcion, Bolivia. *Raptor Watch* 16 (3): 12–13.

Olsen, P. 1988. Australia's Raptors: Diurnal Birds of Prey and Owls. Birds of Australia Conserv. Statement No. 2, 8 (3): 8–9.

Palmer, P. 1989. A Melanistic American Kestrel. *Hawk Migr. Stud.* 14 (2): 41.

Palmer, R. S. (ed.). 1988. Diurnal Raptors. *In* Handbook of North American Birds. Vols. 4 and 5. Yale Univ. Press, New Haven, CT.

Palmer-Ball, B., Jr. 1996. *The Kentucky Breeding Bird Atlas*. University Press of Kentucky, Lexington.

Parker, J. W. 1999. Mississippi Kite. *In* The Birds of North America, No. 402 (A. Poole and F. Gill, eds.). Acad. Nat. Sci., Philadelphia, PA, and Am. Ornithol. Union, Washington, D.C.

Paxton, R. O., J. C. Burgiel, and D. A. Cutler. 2000. Hudson-Delaware Region (Waterfowl Through Raptors). *N. Am. Birds* 54 (1): 33.

Perkins, S. 1997. New England Region (Vultures to Skimmer). *Field Notes* 51 (4): 845.

Perkins, S. 1998. New England Region (Kites Through Sandpipers). *Field Notes* 52 (3): 305.

Peterjohn, B. G., and D. L. Rice. 1991. *The Ohio Breeding Bird Atlas*. Ohio Dep. Nat. Resour., Columbus.

Pettingill, O. S., Jr. 1970. *Ornithology in Laboratory and Field*. 4th ed. Burgess Publ., Minneapolis, MN.

Pierce, A. 1998. Winter Months Organophosphate Poisoning in Raptors, Case Report and Overview. Colorado State Univ. Unpubl. rep.

Pittaway, R. 1993. Subspecies and Color Morphs of the Red-tailed Hawk. *Ont. Birds* 2: 23–29.

Pittaway, R. 1995. Ontario Field Ornithologists Accepted Records. *Ont. Birds* 13 (2): 46–55.

Poole, K. G. 1994. Lynx-Snowshoe Hare Cycle in Canada. *Cat News* 20 (Spring 1994).

Post, W., and S. A. Gauthreaux, Jr. 1989. *Status and Distribution of South Carolina Birds.* Charleston Mus., Charleston, SC.

Pranty, B. 2000. Florida Region (Raptors Through Skimmers). *N. Am. Birds* 54 (1): 44.

Pranty, B., and M. A. McMillian. 1997. Status of the White-tailed Kite in Northern and Central Florida. *Fla. Field Nat.* 25: 117–160.

Preston, C. R., and R. D. Beane. 1993. Red-tailed Hawk (*Buteo jamaicensis*). *In* The Birds of North America, No. 52 (A. Poole and F. Gill, eds.). Acad. Nat. Sci., Philadelphia, PA, and Am. Ornithol. Union, Washington, D.C.

Purrington, R. D. 2000. Central Southern Region (Raptors Through Rails). *N. Am. Birds* 54 (4): 392.

Quezon, A. J. 1997. First Confirmed Breeding Record for Mississippi Kite for Virginia. *Raptor,* Winter 1997: 1–3.

Quinn, M. S. 1991. Nest Site and Prey of a Pair of Sharp-shinned Hawks in Alberta. *J. Raptor Res.* 25 (1): 18.

Raptor Center, The. 1999a. Highway to the Tropics/Prairie Partners: Osprey (Tracking Osprey Via Satellite on the Internet). World Wide Web Site Home Page <http://www.raptor.cvm. umn.edu> [Jan. 12, 2001].

Raptor Center, The. 1999b. Highway to the Tropics/Prairie Partners: The Raptor Center Tracks Swainson's Hawks by Satellite. World Wide Web Site Home Page <http://www.raptor. cvm.umn.edu> [Jan. 12, 2001].

Rea, A. M. 1998. Turkey Vulture. Pp. 27–31 *in The Raptors of Arizona* (R. L. Glinski, ed.). Univ. of Arizona Press, Tucson, and Arizona Game Fish Dep., Phoenix.

Redig, P. T., and H. B. Tordoff. 1988. Peregrine Falcon Reintroduction in the Upper Mississippi Valley and Western Great Lakes Region. Pp. 559–563 *in Peregrine Falcon Populations* (T. J. Cade, J. H. Enderson, C. G. Thelander, and C. M. White, eds.). The Peregrine Fund, Boise, ID.

Reynolds, R. T. 1983. Management of Western Coniferous Forest Habitat for Nesting Accipiter Hawks. Gen. Tech. Rep. RM-102. U.S. Dep. Agric., Fort Collins, CO.

Reynolds, R. T., and E. C. Meslow. 1984. Partitioning of Food and Niche Characteristics of Coexisting Accipiters During Breeding. *Auk* 101: 76–79.

Reynolds, R. T., and H. M. Wight. 1978. Distribution, Density, and Productivity of Accipiter Hawks Breeding in Oregon. *Wilson Bull.* 90 (2): 182–196.

Ridout, R. 1998. Ontario Region (Vultures to Gulls). *Field Notes* 52 (3): 324.

Ripple, J. 2000. Kites of Fancy. *Birders World* 14 (3): 63–66.

Robbins, C. S. (ed.) 1996. *Atlas of the Breeding Birds of Maryland and the District of Columbia.* Univ. of Pittsburgh Press, Pittsburgh, PA.

Robbins, S. D., Jr. 1991. *Wisconsin Birdlife.* Univ. of Wisconsin Press, Madison.

Robinson, J. C. 1990. *An Annotated Checklist of the Birds of Tennessee.* Univ. of Tennessee Press, Knoxville.

Rodgers, J. A., Jr., S. T. Schwikert, and A. S. Wenner. 1988. Status of the Snail Kite in Florida: 1981–1985. *Am. Birds* 42 (1): 30–35.

Rosenfield, R. N., and J. Bielefeldt. 1993. Cooper's Hawk (*Accipiter cooperii*). *In* The Birds of North America, No. 75 (A. Poole and F. Gill, eds.). Acad. Nat. Sci., Philadelphia, PA, and Am. Ornithol. Union, Washington, D.C.

Rosenfield, R. N., and J. Bielefeldt. 1997. Reanalysis of Relationships Among Eye Color, Age and Sex in Cooper's Hawk. *J. Raptor Res.* 31 (4): 313–316.

Rosenfield, R. N., and D. L. Evans. 1980. Migration Incidence and Sequence of Age and Sex Classes of the Sharp-shinned Hawk. *Loon* 52: 66–69.

Rowell, P., and G. L. Holroyd. 2001. *Results of the 2000 Canadian Peregrine Falcon* (Falco peregrinus*) Survey.* Can. Wildl. Serv., Environ. Canada, Edmonton, AB.

Russell, R. W. 1991. Nocturnal Flight by Migrant "Diurnal" Raptors. *J. Field Ornithol.* 62 (4): 505–508.

Sanchez, G. 1993. Ecology of Wintering Gyrfalcons in Central South Dakota. M.S. thesis. Boise State Univ., Boise, ID.

Sanchez, G. 1994. Arctic Visitor. *S. Dakota Conserv. Digest* 61: 6–9.

Schmutz, J. K. 1996. Southward Migration of Swainson's Hawks: Over 10,000 Km in 54 Days. *Blue Jay* 54: 70–76.

Seibold, I., and A. J. Helbig. 1995. Evolutionary History of New and Old World Vultures Inferred From Nucleotide Sequences of the Mitochondrial Cytochrome *b* Gene. *Phil. Trans. R. Soc. London* 350: 163–178.

Shackelford, C. E., D. Saenz, and R. R. Schaefer. 1996. Sharp-shinned Hawks Nesting in the Pineywoods of Eastern Texas and Western Louisiana. *Bull. Texas Ornithol. Soc.* 29: 23–25.

Sharp, C. S. 1902. Nesting of Swainson's Hawk. *Condor* 4: 116–118.

Shefferly, N. 1996. *Lepus americanus.* World Wide Web Site for the Univ. of Michigan Mus. Zool., <animaldiversity.ummz.umich.edu/accounts/lepus/1._americansnarrative.html> [Jan. 18, 1996].

Smallwood, J. A. 1990. American Kestrel and Merlin. Pp. 29–37 *in Proc. Southeast Raptor Manage. Symp. Workshop*, Natl. Wildl. Fed., Washington, D.C. (B. G. Pendleton et al., eds.). World Wide Web Site <http://www.tnc.org/wings/wingresource.SMAInd.htm> [Dec. 12, 2000].

Smallwood, J. A., C. Natale, K. Steenhof, M. Meetz, C. D. Marti, et al. 1999. Clinal Variation in the Juvenal Plumage of American Kestrels. *J. Field Ornithol.* 70: 425–435.

Snyder, N.F.R., and H. A. Snyder. 1991. *Birds of Prey: Natural History and Conservation of North American Raptors.* Voyageur Press, Stillwater, MN.

Sodhi, N. S., L. W. Oliphant, P. C. James, and I. G. Warkentin. 1993. Merlin (*Falco columbarius*). *In* The Birds of North America, No. 44 (A. Poole and F. Gill, eds.). Acad. Nat. Sci., Philadelphia, PA, and Am. Ornithol. Union, Washington, D.C.

Solensky, M. J. 1997. Distribution, Productivity, and Nest-site Habitat of Taiga Merlin (*Falco columbarius columbarius*) in North-central Wisconsin. M.S. thesis, Univ. of Wisconsin, Eau Claire.

Solensky, M. J. 2001. Merlin Nestsite Reoccupancy in the Twin Cities and North-central Wisconsin, 2001 Report. The Raptor Center, Univ. of Minnesota, St. Paul, MN.

Stalmaster, M. V. 1987. *The Bald Eagle.* Universe Books, New York, NY.

Steenhof, K. 1998. Prairie Falcon (*Falco mexicanus*). *In* The Birds of North America, No. 346 (A. Poole and F. Gill, eds.). Acad. Nat. Sci., Philadelphia, PA, and Am. Ornithol. Union, Washington, D.C.

Steenhof, K., M. N. Kochert, and M. Q. Moritsch. 1984. Dispersal and Migration of Southwestern Idaho Raptors. *J. Field Ornithol.* 55 (3): 357–368.

Stevenson, H. M., and B. H. Anderson. 1994. *The Birdlife of Florida.* Univ. Press of Florida, Gainesville.

Sullivan, B. 1996. Summary Report of the 1995–96 Autumn Hawkwatch at Kiptopeke State Park, Va. Kiptopeke Environ. Sta. Res. Edu. Lab., Frank Town, VA.

Sweig, D. M. 1998. Shenandoah's Peregrines: Flying High Again. *Audubon Naturalist News* May: 4–5.

Sykes, P. W., Jr., J. A. Rodgers, Jr., and R. E. Bennetts. 1995. Snail Kite (*Rostrhamus sociabilis*). *In* The Birds of North America, No. 171 (A. Poole and F. Gill, eds.). Acad. Nat. Sci., Philadelphia, PA, and Am. Ornithol. Union, Washington, D.C.

Tennessee Ornithological Society. 2001. Birds Records Committee Photo Site: White-tailed Kite. World Wide Web Site <http://www.tnbirds.org/TRBC/White-tailed-Kite.htm> [Mar. 21, 2002].

Terres, J. K. 1980. *The Audubon Society Encyclopedia of North American Birds.* Alfred A. Knopf, New York, NY.

Todd, W.E.C. 1950. A Northern Race of Redtailed Hawk. *Ann. Carnegie Mus.* 31: 289–297.

Todd, W.E.C. 1963. *Birds of the Labrador Peninsula and Adjacent Areas.* Univ. of Toronto Press, Toronto, ON.

Tordoff, H. B. 2000. Percentage of Subspecies of Peregrines Released in the Midwest and Their Success Surviving to Breeding. *Conserv. Biol.* 15: 528–532.

Tordoff, H. B., M. S. Martell, and P. T. Redig. 1997. *Midwest Peregrine Restoration, 1997 Report.* The Raptor Center, Univ. of Minnesota, St. Paul.

Tordoff, H. B., M. S. Martell, P. T. Redig, and M. J. Solensky. 2000. *Midwest Peregrine Falcon Restoration, 1999 Report.* The Raptor Center, Univ. of Minnesota, St. Paul.

Toups, J. A., J. A. Jackson, and E. Johnson. 1985. Black-shouldered Kite: Range Expansion Into Mississippi. *Am. Birds* 39: 865–867.

Tucker, K. R. 1999. Good News for Swainson's Hawks. *Bird Calls* 3 (2): 9.

Tucker, V. A., T. J. Cade, and A. E. Tucker. 1998. Diving Speeds and Angles of a Gyrfalcon (*Falco rusticolus*). *J. Exp. Biol.* 201: 2061–2070.

Tufts, R. W. 1986. *Birds of Nova Scotia.* Nimbus Publ. and Nova Scotia Mus., Halifax, NS.

U.S. Fish and Wildlife Service. 1984. Reclassification of the Arctic Peregrine Falcon and Clarification of Its Status in Washington and Elsewhere in the Coterminous United States. Final Rule. *Fed. Reg.* 49 (55): 10520–10526.

U.S. Fish and Wildlife Service. 1987. Endangered and Threatened Wildlife and Plants; Threatened Status for the Florida Population of Audubon's Crested Caracara. *Fed. Reg.* 52: 25229–25231.

U.S. Fish and Wildlife Service. 1994. Final Rule.

Endangered Status for Puerto Rican Sharp-shinned Hawk. *Fed. Reg.* 59: 46710.

U.S. Fish and Wildlife Service. 1995. Final Rule to Reclassify the Bald Eagle From Endangered to Threatened in All of the Lower 48 States. *Fed. Reg.* 60: 35999 [Jul. 12, 1995].

U.S. Fish and Wildlife Service. 1998. Proposed Rule to Remove the Peregrine Falcon in North America From the List of Endangered and Threatened Wildlife. *Fed. Reg.* 63 [Aug. 26, 1998].

U.S. Fish and Wildlife Service. 1999a. Proposed Rule to Remove Bald Eagle in the Lower 48 States From the List of Endangered and Threatened Wildlife. *Fed. Reg.* 64: 36453 [Jul. 6, 1999].

U.S. Fish and Wildlife Service. 1999b. Final Rule to Remove the American Peregrine Falcon From the Federal List of Endangered and Threatened Wildlife. *Fed. Reg.* 64: 46541–46558 (Aug. 25, 1999).

U.S. Fish and Wildlife Service. 2000. Proposal to Transfer the North American Population of *Falco rusticolus* (Gyrfalcon) From Appendix I to Appendix II of the Convention on International Trade in Endangered Species of Wild Fauna and Flora (CITES), submitted Nov. 12, 1999, for consideration at the eleventh meeting of the conference of the parties to CITES.

U.S. Fish and Wildlife Service. 2001. Availability of Final Environmental Assessment of Take of Nestling American Peregrine Falcons in the Contiguous United States and Alaska for Falconry. *Fed. Reg.* 64 (92): 24149–24150 [May 11, 2001].

Varland, D. E., R. D. Andrews, and B. L. Ehresman. 1992. Establishing a Nest Box Program for American Kestrels Along an Interstate Highway. Iowa Dep. Trans., Ames.

Varland, D. E., E. E. Klaas, and T. M. Loughin. 1991. Development of Foraging Behavior in the American Kestrel. *J. Raptor Res.* (1): 9–17.

Varland, D. E., E. E. Klaas, and T. M. Loughin. 1993. Use of Habitat and Perches, Causes of Mortality, and Time Until Dispersal in Post-fledging American Kestrels. *J. Field Ornithol.* 64 (2): 169–178.

Varland, D. E., and T. M. Loughin. 1992. Social Hunting in Broods of Two and Five American Kestrels After Fledging. *J. Raptor Res.* 26 (2): 74–80.

Varland, D. E., and T. M. Loughin. 1993. Reproductive Success of American Kestrels Nesting Along an Interstate Highway in Central Iowa. *Wilson Bull.* 105 (3): 465–474.

Veit, R. R., and W. R. Petersen. 1993. *Birds of Massachusetts*. Mass. Audubon Soc., Lincoln.

Walsh, J., V. Elia, R. Kane, and T. Halliwell. 1999. *Birds of New Jersey*. New Jersey Audubon Soc., Bernardsville.

Warkentin, I. G., P. C. James, and L. W. Oliphant. 1992. Use of a Plumage Criterion for Aging Female Merlins. *J. Field Ornithol.* 63 (4): 473–475.

Watson, J. W. 1999. Telemetry Tracking of Four Adult Ferruginous Hawks (*Buteo regalis*) Banded in South-central Washington in 1999. Unpubl. rep. Washington Dep. Fish Wildl.

Whaley, W. H., and C. M. White. 1994. Trends in Geographic Variation of Cooper's Hawk and Northern Goshawk in North America: A Multivariate Analysis. West. Found. Vertebr. Zool. 5 (3): 161–209.

Wheeler, B. K., and W. S. Clark. 1995. *A Photographic Guide to North American Raptors*. Academic Press, San Diego, CA.

White, C. M. 1968. Diagnosis and Relationships of the North American Tundra-Inhabiting Peregrine Falcons. *Auk* 85: 179–191.

White, C. M., R. E. Ambrose, and J. L. Longmire. 1995. Remarks on Systematics and the Sources of Variation in *Falco peregrinus*: The Reference to the Reintroduction of Falcons in Poland. *Acta Ornithol.* 30 (1): 31–41.

Wood, N. A. 1932. Harlan's Hawk. *Wilson Bull.* Jun.: 78–87.

Woodbridge, B. 1997. Tracking the Migration of Swainson's Hawks: Conservation Lessons in a Global Classroom. Paper read at the Hawk Migr. Assoc. N. Am. Conference VIII, Snowbird, UT, Jun. 12–15, 1997.

Yates, M. A., K. E. Riddle, and F. P. Ward. 1988. Recoveries of Peregrine Falcons Migrating Through the Eastern and Central United States, 1955–1985. *In Peregrine Falcon Populations* (T. J. Cade, J. H. Enderson, C. G. Thelander, and C. M. White, eds.). The Peregrine Fund, Boise, ID.

Yukon Department of Renewable Resources. 1990. Yukon Mammal Series: Snowshoe Hare. World Wide Web Site <http://www.renres.gov.yk.ca/wildlife/snhare.html>.

INDEX

English names are printed in roman type; scientific names are in italic. An (m) before a number indicates a map.